Environmental Law

Environmental Law

Third edition

David Hughes   LLB (Liverpool), LLM (Cantab), FRSA

Professor of Housing and Planning Law,
The Environmental Law Institute,
De Montfort University, Leicester;
Editor of 'Environmental Law and Management'

Chapter 8 by
Tim Jewell   LLB, MPhil (Leicester)
Lecturer in Law and Director of the
Centre for Environmental Law,
University of Southampton;
Managing Editor of 'Environmental Law and Management'

Chapter 12 by
Neil Parpworth   LLB (Leicester), MA (London)
Lecturer in Law,
The Environmental Law Institute,
De Montfort University, Leicester;
Associate Editor of 'Environmental Law and Management'

Butterworths
London, Dublin, Edinburgh
1996

United Kingdom	Butterworths, a Division of Reed Elsevier (UK) Ltd, Halsbury House, 35 Chancery Lane, LONDON WC2A 1EL and 4 Hill Street, EDINBURGH EH2 3JZ
Australia	Butterworths, SYDNEY, MELBOURNE, BRISBANE, ADELAIDE, PERTH, CANBERRA and HOBART
Canada	Butterworths Canada Ltd, TORONTO and VANCOUVER
Ireland	Butterworth (Ireland) Ltd, DUBLIN
Malaysia	Malayan Law Journal Sdn Bhd, KUALA LUMPUR
New Zealand	Butterworths of New Zealand Ltd, WELLINGTON and AUCKLAND
Singapore	Reed Elsevier (Singapore) Pte Ltd, SINGAPORE
South Africa	Butterworths Publishers (Pty) Ltd, DURBAN
USA	Michie, CHARLOTTESVILLE, Virginia

A CIP Catalogue record for this book is available from the British Library.

First edition 1986
Second edition 1992

ISBN 0 406 08179 4

Typeset by Phoenix Photosetting, Chatham, Kent
Printed and bound by Mackays of Chatham PLC, Chatham, Kent

Preface

This book, a further successor to the first edition of 1986, examines the current state of environmental law, primarily with regard to England and Wales. Where appropriate — and it is now generally appropriate — national law is set in the context of relevant international and European Union laws, though constraints of space forbid as full a coverage of international law as could have been desired.

The same constraints also restrict the coverage of the book to consideration of those laws which relate to the three 'environmental media' — land, air and water. This entails the *general* omission of discussion of protection for plant and animal life and individual historic buildings or areas of architectural interest.

The book is intended, as before, primarily as a textbook for students in universities and colleges reading for law degrees at the undergraduate, and (increasingly popular) postgraduate levels, and for those who read for qualifications in planning and environmental health. However, previous editions proved themselves of additional use by practitioners in commerce, industry and government: it is hoped this edition will be no less useful to them.

I wish to express my gratitude to: my colleagues at De Montfort University, and particularly Professor Neil Hawke and Professor Brian Jones for their comradely friendship — it is a joy to work in a supportive atmosphere; my publishers for granting me the opportunity to write the book; numerous public servants in central and local government who courteously answered my inquiries; the staff of the Kimberlin Library at De Montfort University and the Library of the University of Leicester for help in tracking down sources and verifying references; Sheila Bramall and Lisa Evans of the Law School Office at De Montfort University for prompt and efficient help and unfailing persistence in unravelling the byzantine mysteries of my manuscript; friends and acquaintances working in the extractive and fertiliser industries who patiently answered my questions with candour and aided my researches; my colleagues on 'Environmental Law and Management', especially Malcolm Forster, friends and associates in the United Kingdom Environmental Law Association for their help, encouragement and support. A very special debt is owed to Tim Jewell for his chapter on mineral extraction and to Neil Parpworth for his work on chapter 12. Both are former students who have become highly valued colleagues.

Finally, I must mention three names: the late F J Odgers who inspired me to be an academic, Sir David Williams QC who showed me how to be an academic, and my wife, Christl, who has sustained me in that calling.

Readers of this edition who are familiar with its predecessors will note a number of changes in its style and format. First, there is the division of the chapter on extraction and infill into two — a change justified by the vast increase in the amount of law relating to waste disposal, and also because that law is now part of a more general body of land pollution law which also includes the law relating to contaminated land. Secondly, the text is, I hope, much more accessible, being broken up into smaller paragraphs with many more sub-headings. It was a justly made criticism of the last edition that the text had become slab like — rather akin in appearance on the page to those monolithic, curtain walled, monstrous offices and blocks of flats which have done so much to disfigure our towns and cities. Thirdly, case references are given in footnotes. My publishers assure me the reader wants footnotes, and finds references in the text distracting, and I shall not disagree.

I fear the text has also grown again in length. The modest volume of 1986 had to be considerably expanded for the second edition, and further expansion has had to take place for this edition. The reason is quite simple: there is a lot more law at the international, EU and national levels. There is more legislation, and there is more case law. Furthermore there has been quite a considerable development of environmental policy. Since the departure of Baroness Thatcher in 1991 the government of John Major has brought forward a number of important policy initiatives under the umbrella of the sustainable development policy. All of this has to be reflected in the book, for those who write about environmental law without setting it in the context of policy run the risk of either the Scylla of producing a dry-as-dust legal tome, divorced from reality, or the Charybdis of a work which fosters the belief that simply making laws 'magics away' problems.

To finish, however, on a more mundane note, the Environment Act 1995, which makes so many changes — major and minor — in the law is being brought into force by appointed day orders, though much was expected to be in force by 1 April 1996 when the Environment Agency actually commenced its work. The first five commencement orders brought into force ss 1, 2, 3(1)–(8), 4–23, 25–54, 55(1)–(10), 56, 57–59 (all in part), 78 and Schedule 10 (in part), 80, 81, 87–89, 90 (in part), 91–95, 96(1)–(6), 97–104, 105 and Schedule 15 (in part), 106–115, 116 and Schedule 21 (in part), 117, 118 (in part), 119, 120 and Schedule 22 (in part), 121–124, Schedules 13 and 14.

Regular reference should therefore be made to Halsbury's Statutes for further commencement dates, and also to that most useful work horse from the Butterworths stable *Is It In Force?* The law is *generally* stated as at the beginning of February 1996: the 'beastly month' in the words of Sir William Gilbert many of whose memorable lines embellish this work — along with a few contributions from others.

February 1996   David Hughes

NB The indulgence of my publishers has allowed much updating to the end of 'Merry May'.

Contents

Terms and abbreviations regularly encountered

ADAS	Agricultural Development and Advisory Service
AONB	Areas of Outstanding Natural Beauty
BATNEEC	Best Available Techniques Not Entailing Excessive Cost
BoD	Biological/Biochemical Oxygen Demand
BPEO	Best Practicable Environmental Option
BPM	Best Practicable Means
BS	British Standard, eg 5750 (quality systems) and 7750 (environmental management systems)
CAP	Common Agricultural Policy
CFCs	Chloroflurocarbons
COPA	Control of Pollution Act 1974
CPRE	Council for the Protection of Rural England
dBA	Decibel scale — an international scale of sound levels
DoE	Department of the Environment
EA	Environmental Assessment, NB: EIA (Environmental Impact Assessment) is *not* a term of art in UK law
EC	European Communities
ECJ	European Court of Justice
EINECS	European Inventory of Existing Commercial Chemical Substances
ELINCS	European List of Notified Chemical Substances
EMAS	Eco-management and Auditing Scheme
EMF	Electro magnetic fields
EPA	Environmental Protection Act 1990
EQS	Environmental Quality Standard
ES	Environmental Statement
ESA	Environmentally Sensitive Area
EU	European Union
GDPO	General Development Procedure Order
GMO	Genetically Modified Organism
GPDO	General Permitted Development Order
HBFCs	Hydrobromoflurocarbons
HCFCs	Hydrochloroflurocarbons
HFCs	Hydroflurocarbons
HMIP	Her Majesty's Inspectorate of Pollution
HSC	Health and Safety Commission
HSE	Health and Safety Executive

ICRCL	Inter Departmental Committee on the Redevelopment of Contaminated Land
ICRP	International Commission on Radiological Protection
IEHO	Institution of Environmental Health Officers
IMO	International Maritime Organisation
IPC	Integrated Pollution Control
LAAPC	Local Authority Air Pollution Control
LAWDC	Local Authority Waste Disposal Company
LFG	Land Fill Gas
LPA	Local Planning Authority
MAFF	Ministry of Agriculture Fisheries and Food
MARPOL	Maritime Convention for the Prevention of Pollution from Ships
MPG	Minerals Policy Guidance
NAWDC	National Association of Waste Disposal Contractors
NCC	Nature Conservancy Council
NFFO	Non Fossil Fuel Obligation
NNR	National Nature Reserve
NRA	National Rivers Authority
NRPB	National Radiological Protection Board
OECD	Organisation for Economic Co-operation and Development
OFFER	Office of the Director General of Electricity Supply
OFGAS	Office of Gas Services
OFWAT	Office of Water Services
PAH	Polycyclic Aromatic Hydrocarbons
PCB	Polychlorinated Biphynyls
PFA	Pulverised Fuel Ash
PIC	Prior Informed Consent
PPG	Planning Policy Guidance
RCEP	Royal Commission on Environmental Pollution
RSA	Radioactive Substances Act 1993
RSPB	Royal Society for the Protection of Birds
RWMAC	Radioactive Waste Management Advisory Committee
SAC	Special Area of Conservation
SPA	Special Protection Area
SSSI	Site of Special Scientific Interest
SWQO	Statutory Water Quality Objective
TCPA	Town and Country Planning Act 1990
TOVALOP	Tanker Owners Voluntary Agreement Concerning Liability for Oil Pollution
TPO	Tree Preservation Order
UCO	Use Classes Order
UKELA	United Kingdom Environmental Law Association
UNCED	United Nations Conference on Environment and Development (Rio '92)
VOCs	Volatile Organic Compounds
WAMITAB	Waste Management Industry Training Board
WCA	Waste Collection Authority
WDA	Waste Disposal Authority
WML	Waste Management Licence

WQO   Water Quality Objective
WRA   Waste Regulation Authority

See further Grant, M, and Hawkins, R, *Concise Lexicon of Environmental Terms* (1995) John Wiley and Sons Ltd.

Table of statutes

References in this Table to *Statutes* are to Halsbury's Statutes of England (Fourth Edition) showing the volume and page at which the annotated text of an Act may be found.

List of cases

Decisions of the European Court of Justice are listed both alphabetically and numerically. The numerical list follows the alphabetical.

Part I

The overall structure and development of environmental law

Chapter 1

Environmental law — past, present and future

'The past indicative, the present imperfect and the future uncertain'

Increasing environmental consciousness over the last 25 years should not blind us to the fact that there have been laws concerning the environment for centuries. What we have had is a number of *diverse laws relating to* the environment. The oldest sources of law on the topic are the law of public health, the law of town and country planning and the law of torts. From these, together with international and European Union law, it is now possible to see the emergence of a more coherent system. It is necessary to examine the history, development and current state of the law, and then to give time to an examination of the philosophy, ethics and principles of the law. But first a basic definition of environmental law for the purpose of this work must be given. It is the law relating to the use, protection and conservation of the three environmental media of earth, air and water. This law expresses itself in rules of environmental regulation (primarily the domain of public authorities) and environmental liability which are concerned with attributing responsibility to meet the costs and consequences of environmental harm, and for past environmental wrong doing, intentional or otherwise.

A THE HISTORICAL DEVELOPMENT OF THE LAW RELATING TO PUBLIC HEALTH

'Matters of Imperial interest, which we cannot with impunity neglect' (Stewart & Jenkins, *The Medical and Legal Aspects of Sanitary Reform*, 1867)

The need for public intervention by law arose largely from the public health problems of the nineteenth century. The vast expansion of towns and cities, and the eruption of acre upon acre of filthy insanitary slums and factories across the face of the land, led to the passage of the great Public Health Act 1875 which was designed to protect health and secure, inter alia, minimum standards of housing. However, the fact that the century was almost gone before this monumental legislation was put on the statute book is indicative of a considerable body of public and private resistance to state intervention in environmental matters. In 1875 the death rate was still almost as high as it had been 40 years previously, and the appallingly high level of infant mortality did not begin to reduce greatly until the end of the century. The enactment of the

3

1875 Act achieved a rationalised and codified law of sanitation and health, but it only ushered in a period when mortality could begin to fall. Some account of how that national code reached the statute book is needed.

In 1838 Edwin Chadwick sent Poor Law medical investigators into the London slums and in 1842 his 'Report on an Enquiry into the Sanitary Condition of the Labouring Population of Great Britain' was issued. In due course Parliament passed the Public Health Act 1848. But few of the Act's provisions were mandatory. Throughout the 1850s and 60s public health administration was not properly centrally directed, while the various local government bodies that littered the map reacted, often in a less than interested fashion, to the responsibilities increasingly laid upon them. Between 1848 and 1872 a multiplicity of enactments covering issues such as nuisances, sewage and sanitation, vaccination, diseases, general public health and common lodging houses were put on the statute book. The essential basics of modern public health law were created in this period, but, sadly, in a confused and tangled manner which was beyond the comprehension even of trained minds.

Furthermore the division of responsibility between urban and rural authorities made the operation of law unnecessarily unwieldy. Added to this complexity was the fact that most of the law was permissive and not mandatory. These basic defects made the law unworkable. It is easy to criticise the Victorians for their cumbersome administrative arrangements; as will become apparent from this and subsequent chapters, especially chapter 3 below, the twentieth century has also signally failed to create either a comprehensive system of environmental law or machinery to enforce it. The legacy of past divisions of responsibility lies heavy on us.

From the mid 1860s reform was clearly essential, while coherent duties needed to be imposed on local government. In 1868 the government agreed to set up a Royal Sanitary Commission to consider all sanitary laws. This body reported in 1871 and that led, ultimately, to the Public Health Act 1875. Subsequent attention has focused on amendment or codification. Various enactments relating to public health in the years after 1875 were consolidated in the Public Health Act 1936, supplemented by the Public Health Act 1961 and the Public Health (Recurring Nuisances) Act 1969. Other legislation has been passed to deal with *particular issues* affecting public health, or the health of *particular sections* of the community, for example statutes relating to refuse disposal, water, clean air, litter and health and safety at work, see, for example, the Clean Air Act 1993 consolidating earlier legislation.

The Control of Pollution Act 1974 marked a further major development in public health legislation in that it attempted to protect the public by ensuring certain basic standards of *environmental* protection. It was put on the statute book after an extensive series of reports and consultations by the concerned Departments of State on issues such as refuse collection, storage and disposal, and disposal of solid toxic waste, sewage disposal, noise, clean air and industrial emissions into the atmosphere. The initiatives of the 1974 legislation were continued by the Water Act 1989 which is now found as the Water Industry Act 1991 and the Water Resources Act 1991.

The Environmental Protection Act 1990 marked a further major step forward in this process in that it is concerned with protection of the environment and not just public health, and it introduced a generalised concept of 'the environment', which applies throughout many of its provisions, as being the media of air, land and water. Likewise pollution of the environment and harm to the environment are broad concepts embracing both harm to humankind *and* other living things supported by the environment, while 'harm' extends to harming the health of living organisms, or interference with the ecological system of which they form part, including harm to any human senses, or harm to human property; see s 1(2)–(4) of the 1990 Act and also s 29. This process continues as a result of the Environment Act 1995.

Pour encourager les autres

The prime legacy bequeathed to environment law by its public health origins is the use of penal sanctions for infringements of legal requirements — very often on the basis that it is not necessary for the enforcing body to prove any mens rea or guilty intent on the part of the wrongdoer. Both the courts and Parliament accept that there are incidents which 'are not criminal in any real sense, but are acts which in the public interest are prohibited under a penalty' per Wright J in *Sherras v De Rutzen*.[1] The purpose of the law in such cases is to *prevent* the occurrence of prohibited events by visiting them with strict consequences. The object is to prompt operators to do all in their power to avoid penalties by conducting their activities as well as they can.

However, there is a disbenefit in that to escape criminal liability for many regulatory offences — particularly those concerned with water — an operator has to undertake positive, and often expensive, burdens of a preventive nature, and even if such burdens are assumed liability may still be imposed if a polluting incident occurs. Many object to a system capable of imposing legal blame in the absence of moral fault. Others argue that the money spent on implementing legislation could be better spent on educating and advising operators. The consequence is that the law's severity is tempered by prosecution policies which tend to lead to charges only in cases where the law has been blatantly disregarded, or where the consequences of an incident are severe, and in all such cases the regulator will need to feel it has a good chance of winning before it will proceed. So, for example, environmental regulators follow in addition to their own policies (which will probably already reflect budgetary constraints on taking action) the Code for Crown Prosecutors which counsels prosecution only where the evidence reliably suggests realistic chances of conviction and also where it is in the public interest to prosecute. This will tend to rule out prosecutions in cases where: only nominal penalties are likely; the loss or harm was minor and the result of an isolated incident; the offence was the result of a genuine mistake, or where the defendant has put right what was amiss.

B THE GROWTH AND CURRENT STATE OF PLANNING LAW

Early attempts at town planning were based on private initiatives. The need for *public* involvement grew largely out of the obvious necessity for increased public health protection. But, as with the law relating to public health, planning law took a long time to emerge and develop. It differs from public

1 [1895] 1 QB 918 at 922.

health law in that the period of its emergence and development is much longer. Also, because of the differing land use policies of various governments, the law is not securely based on any one coherent, nationally agreed, politically irreproachable and generally acceptable philosophy as to why it exists and what aims and objectives it should seek to promote.

'We haven't any slummeries in England' (W S Gilbert, 'Utopia Limited', 1893)

The history of planning law can also be traced back to Edwin Chadwick. He called for the development of a new class of 'town surveyors' trained in science and engineering, able to build healthy towns with adequate protection for health. In 1873 the Association of Municipal Engineers was founded. This was an attempt to professionalise the 'town surveyor' ideal — an ideal that was subsequently to give rise to the profession of planning. Initially, under the Public Health Act 1875, all efforts were directed to secure public health and building standards. It was soon realised that this alone was not enough. In 1909 Unwin said in *Town Planning in Practice: An Introduction to the Act of Designing Cities and Suburbs*:

'We have, indeed . . . laid a good foundation and have secured many of the necessary elements for a healthy condition of life; and yet the remarkable fact remains that there are growing up around our big towns vast districts . . . which for dreariness and sheer ugliness it is difficult to match anywhere.'

Decent main drainage alone was insufficient: existing slums had to be demolished and replaced, and there was growing realisation that a poor environment flowed from a general lack of systematised co-ordination in town development: *planning was necessary*.

The expression 'town planning' seems to have emerged in a report of the City of Birmingham Housing Committee in 1906. It acquired legal recognition in the Housing, Town Planning, etc Act 1909. The 1909 Act allowed local authorities to prepare schemes to control the development of new housing, but little use was made of these powers. The making of planning schemes was made compulsory by the Housing, Town Planning, etc Act 1919 and further planning powers were conferred by the Town and Country Planning Act 1932 and the Restriction of Ribbon Development Act 1935. It soon became obvious that a system of planning control wider than local schemes was needed; something to cope with the emergence of conurbations straddling local areas and spreading along major trunk routes was essential. The 1935 Act was a stop-gap measure to impose some control while a better system could be devised. The Barlow Report of the 'Royal Commission on the Distribution of the Industrial Population',[2] the Beveridge Report on 'Social Insurance and Allied Services',[3] the Uthwatt 'Report of the Expert Committee on Compensation and Betterment'[4] and the Scott 'Report of the Committee on Land Utilisation in Rural Areas'[5] produced a new pattern of thinking and new principles on which to base the law

2 (1940 Cmd 6153).
3 (1942 Cmd 6404).
4 (1942 Cmd 6386).
5 (1942 Cmd 6378).

1   An end had to be made to the haphazard distribution of industry, population and urban sprawl.
2   Urban squalor had to be eliminated and public health improved by the creation of healthy, new, planned communities.
3   Older urban areas were to be revived.
4   National parks and forests had to be created and access to the countryside guaranteed.
5   A new national communications system based on planned roads and airports had to be created.
6   The emphasis in all this new work was to be on planning initiatives from central and local government. These would exist within the framework of a nationwide system of planning control in which land planning would be integrated with social and economic planning.

'We'll keep the red flag flying here?'

It fell to the 1945 Labour government to translate these principles into legislative practice. This they did in an impressive package which included the creation of a new system of social insurance and national assistance, the setting up of the National Health Service, and the passing of the New Towns Act 1946, the National Parks and Access to the Countryside Act 1949 and the Town and Country Planning Act 1947. The 1947 Act enshrined certain principles

1   All land is subject to the jurisdiction of planning authorities.
2   As a general rule land development may not take place without a grant of planning permission.
3   Such permission should not generally be granted unless the proposed development accords with a publicly prepared plan for the land in question. This last principle has always been the least honoured of the first three.
4   The development value of land should be nationalised for the public good. This did not long survive the return of the Conservatives to power in 1951.

It has never been easy for planners to ensure that development accords with prepared plans. The time taken in drawing up plans is one important factor in this. Another is that planners as a profession have felt constrained to base their plans on predictions of what they have thought *would* be the future pattern of land demand, an activity frequently outpaced by changes in economic circumstances. It is arguable that the only sure way to marry actual development with statutory plans would be, first, to give planning authorities vastly increased powers to direct and manipulate land development, that is, to draw up plans based on what planners believe *ought* to happen, and, second, to build up publicly owned 'land banks' to ensure an ample supply of land for controlled development. Neither of these processes has been politically or administratively workable in the UK. So far as the *law* of planning is concerned, the *general* rule is that the various statutory plans are only factors, admittedly very important factors, amongst many others in deciding whether planning permission should be granted. (The impact of s 54A, Town and Country Planning Act 1990 and PPG1, paras 3, 17 and 25–31 will be considered in chapter 5.) The result is a clear separation between the original impetus for forward planning according to plans and the *actual practice* of development control. This is a far cry from the intention of the framers of the 1947 legislation who believed that planning authorities should hold and be held closely to their plans.

It is to the credit of the system set up in 1947 that we have something of 'a green and pleasant land', yet there is widespread dissatisfaction with planning. Why should this be so? The answer is far from certain: the following may be reasons.

1   Planners as a profession have tended to fly somewhat indiscriminately after each passing architectural fashion. The result has been the construction of unlovely and unloved tower blocks of housing and offices which have altered beyond recognition a centuries-old skyline in too many places. The building of urban motorways has failed to solve the problem of how to provide a suitable traffic system for towns and has also led to the destruction of whole communities. At the same time developers have made great profits from the carrying out of such works.

   On the other hand it would be wrong to single out planners alone for criticism. Architects, builders, administrators and politicians have been equally, and maybe even more, to blame, and the planning profession has been made a convenient scape-goat for the mistakes of others.

2   Planners have often been seen as miniature 'big brothers', and there has been a feeling that a superiority of assumption amongst planners has to be resisted.

3   Despite legislative attempts to open up the planning system to public participation, the general public is not, *on the whole*, involved in planning. Those members of the public who do involve themselves tend to represent only certain narrowly defined, sectional interest groups.

4   The planning system is often accused of being cumbersome and slow moving.

5   Planning law has become a 'killing field' for lawyers who have made it one of the most highly technical and complex branches of legal regulation. This has made the job of the planning profession vastly more difficult.

6   There is a general feeling of disenchantment in that, despite public planning, we still have urban squalor, bad health conditions and unemployment. Many people believe there has been too much planning and that this has strangled initiatives that would have improved the environment.

By the early 1980s there was a general feeling that society had forgotten the reasons behind land use planning, while an increasingly strong body of opinion suggested that planning should exist as the handmaid of private sector enterprise and economic regeneration. Out of this we seem to have arrived at a situation where there is *no* generally agreed single reason for the existence of planning. Notions of 'the orderly management of change' command quite a degree of support, but onto this are grafted other ideas — not always compatible — of employment creation and protection, urban containment and rural preservation. Planning *as a system*, however, survives in that it provides a known structure within which developers, builders, authorities, neighbours, workers and financiers can operate.

Land, social and economic planning have also not gone hand in hand, while no system of planning yet devised has been able to stop the ever escalating price of land and to prevent profiteering from land speculation. The basic problems involved are whether land values should be pegged or taxed so that increases in value consequent on the granting of planning permission should be netted for the public good, and whether the initiative in providing land for development should come from the public or the private sector of the economy. The Labour and Conservative parties have been fundamentally divided over these issues, and the law since 1947 has been in a state of flux and confusion as first one party and then the other has imposed its policies via legislation.

The years of 'one of us' — planning under the Thatcher governments

After 1979 the law was greatly changed in order to enshrine the philosophy that development initiatives should come mainly from the private sector of the economy. The emphasis on privatisation of public assets and on land holding for development as a private enterprise function is a very different policy from that envisaged in 1947. Official thinking believes that over stringent public control of land use adds to other problems of dereliction and industrial decline. For a government committed to releasing the so-called 'spirit of enterprise', public controls over land use had to be relaxed as part of a general subordination of planning to economic regeneration. In the greatest injection of *laissez-faire* thinking into planning in 30 years, the Thatcher government introduced the notion that planning authorities should allow commerce and industry to go and expand in those locations where they found the best prospects for growth and prosperity. Central planning policy, as enunciated in DoE Circular 22/80, encouraged planning authorities, except in environmentally sensitive areas, to pick out for priority handling applications that would contribute most to economic regeneration. Authorities were also encouraged to give planning permission for development unless there were clear-cut reasons for refusal. They were requested to relax controls over land uses which did not conform to the various plans that have been made, to withdraw from detailed control of the external appearance of buildings except where the character of the area or of the particular building justified intervention, and to use planning enforcement procedures only where there was no alternative. Though it is true that the circular expressed concern that the conservation of agricultural land, green belts, the countryside, natural habitats, areas of architectural, natural, historical or scientific interest and listed buildings should be maintained, the message for urban authorities was clear: a general relaxation of planning control and a streamlining of control procedures is essential for national economic recovery.

The desire for unified, socio-economic planned public control of land use policy which lay behind the 1947 legislation is no longer enshrined in our planning law. Planning itself has been made subservient to economic goals. The work of planners during this century, and particularly since 1947, was set at risk by this change in emphasis.

Though DoE Circular 22/80 stated: '. . . authorities are now asked to pick out for priority handling those applications [for planning permission] which in their judgment will contribute most to national and local economic activity', it continued: 'This does not mean, of course, that health and safety standards, noise, smell or other pollution problems should be given less weight.' Other guidance, such as the original PPG1 of January 1988, added that the planning system 'is an important instrument for the protection and enhancement of the environment in town and country'. Nevertheless there must be some doubt as to whether, in its present form, planning law is as effective a system of environmental control as it might be.

The large measure of discretion enjoyed by planning authorities, coupled with the fact that environmental concerns are only relevant *not* overriding considerations, make planning law so imperfect an agent of environmental control. Planning law, however, has other defects such as the lengthy and cumbersome nature of its procedures, the principle that an authorised development or activity can only be halted following the payment of compensation, historically slow moving and somewhat ineffective enforcement systems, and a failure to rationalise the legislative overlap between planning law and other ad hoc industrial safety, environmental and public health measures that have grown up around it in recent years. This last named defect is readily visible in the division of responsibility for environmental issues between a wide variety of central and local agencies, see chapter 3 below. Frequently there is no *legal* obligation on these agencies to consult and co-operate with one another, though *informal* collaboration has become rather more common of late. The principal bequest to environmental law from its planning origins is the use of managerial discretion vested in a public body whereby various activities are licensed or permitted, usually subject to conditions, on the application of an operator, *possibly* with a degree of public consultative involvement and subject to the appellate oversight of the Secretary of State. Elements of this form of regulation are to be found, for example, in the law relating to integrated pollution control, water pollution and waste disposal.

C TO SUM UP SO FAR . . .

From its past development the current law inherits a number of characteristics, not all of which are easily compatible. Broad managerial discretion is planning's bequest, while that from public health law is the imposition of criminal 'pains and penalties' on those who fail to meet legal requirements. However, even these can reflect old legal values derived from the common law. This is very true with regard to statutory nuisances which may be conveniently considered at this point.

D THE CURRENT LAW RELATING TO STATUTORY NUISANCES

Action taken by local authorities or by aggrieved individuals can be a most effective means of local environmental control, and though the concept of 'statutory nuisance' is derived from nineteenth century common law it is still relevant today.

It is the duty under s 79 of the Environmental Protection Act 1990 as amended of local authorities (districts and London boroughs) to inspect their areas from time to time, and to investigate complaints from the inhabitants, in respect of 'statutory nuisances'. These are: premises prejudicial to health, or a nuisance, smoke from premises prejudicial to health or a nuisance, fumes or gases from premises, dust, steam, smell or other effluvia arising on industrial, trade or business premises, accumulations or deposits, animals, noise emitted from premises, or from or caused by a vehicle, machinery or equipment in a street, any other matter declared by statute to be a statutory nuisance, provided in each case the matter is prejudicial to health, ie actually injurious, or likely to cause injury, to health, or a nuisance. Note: contaminated land falling within Part IIA of the 1990 Act as inserted in 1995 is not to be dealt with as a statutory nuisance, see s 79 (1A)–(1B) of the 1990 Act.

Health seems to mean physical as opposed to mental health, see *Coventry City Council v Cartwright*,[6] while nuisance bears its common law meaning of a deleterious affectation of land or its use and enjoyment which arises outside that land and then proceeds to invade it.[7] However, a single instance of a deleterious act may be sufficient to ground a statutory nuisance action.[8] It should also be noted that 'dust' does not include dust emitted as a constituent of smoke, while fumes are 'airborne solid matter smaller than dust'. Likewise 'noise' includes vibration, 'premises' includes land and vessels, and 'smoke' includes soot, ash, grit and gritty particles, though statutory nuisance proceedings in respect of smoke are excluded where the smoke is emitted from the chimney of a private dwelling in a smoke control area, where smoke and steam is emitted from a railway locomotive steam engine (a merciful exemption for railway preservation buffs!) and where dark smoke is emitted from, inter alia, boiler furnaces or from industrial or trade premises, control here existing under other legislation. Without the consent of the Secretary of State local authorities may not take action in respect of smoke, dust, smell or effluvia nuisances arising on trade premises, or accumulation or deposit nuisances where proceedings *could* also be taken under, inter alia, s 5 of the Health and Safety at Work etc Act 1974. Likewise proceedings cannot be taken in respect of smoke or noise emitted from premises occupied by the Crown for military or defence purposes, or by visiting overseas forces. Furthermore, proceedings in respect of fumes, etc, can only be taken in respect of premises which are private dwellings. For specific details on noise nuisance see chapter 11 below.

The procedure for taking action in respect of a statutory nuisance: local authorities

Section 80 of the 1990 Act provides where an authority is satisfied a statutory nuisance *exists, is likely to occur or recur,* they must serve an abatement notice which will require the nuisance's abatement or prohibit or restrict its occurrence or recurrence, and may require the execution of works or taking of steps for such purposes, specifying the time within which compliance is required.

Notices under the 1990 Act must, as with those under the previous legislation, be clear and certain.[9] While a specific period of time for taking

6 [1975] 2 All ER 99, [1975] 1 WLR 845.
7 *National Coal Board v Neath Borough Council* [1976] 2 All ER 478.
8 *East Northamptonshire District Council v Fossett* [1994] Env LR 388.
9 *R v Secretary of State for the Environment, ex p Watney Mann (Midlands) Ltd* [1976] JPL 368.

action does not need to be stated[10] notices must tell their recipients what needs to be done.[11] Notices must, in all fairness therefore, tell recipients what is amiss and what remedial action will be needed, though over-particularity will not be required where it is clear from the notice and the surrounding circumstances what is wrong.[12] Though special circumstances may apply in the case of noise nuisances (see chapter 11 below), the overall effect of the case law is that a notice should be sufficiently particular to make it certain what is needed to remedy the clearly defined wrong in *one* 'package' of remedial measures.

Against whom is action taken?

Notice is to be served on the person responsible for the nuisance, save in cases of nuisances arising from structural defects, or where the person responsible cannot be found, in which case the owner is to be served. Failure to comply with a notice is an offence, and in respect of offences committed on industrial, trade or business premises the fine on summary conviction may be up to £20,000. However, it should be noted that authorities are not statutorily bound to prosecute offences, even though they may have taken default action themselves under s 81(3), which enables them, under s 81(4), to recover their expenses with interest, both constituting a charge on relevant premises, see s 81A and B. Section 81(5) further empowers authorities to commence High Court proceedings where they are of the opinion that statutory nuisance proceedings before the justices would provide an inadequate remedy.

A person served with an abatement notice may, under s 80(3) of the 1990 Act, appeal to the justices within a period of 21 days beginning with the date of service of the notice. Schedule 3 to the Act enables regulations to be made concerning such appeals. The Statutory Nuisance (Appeals) Regulations SI 1995/2644, provide in reg 2 as grounds of appeal that: the abatement notice was not justified; there has been an informality, defect or error in, or in connection with the notice, or with any copy of a notice served under s 80A(3); the authority has unreasonably refused compliance with alternative requirements, or the notice's requirements are otherwise unreasonable in character or extent or unnecessary; a reasonable amount of time has not been specified for compliance; the best practicable means defence applies (see further below); the notice should have been served on some other person as the person responsible for the nuisance, or, in structural defect cases, as the owner of the premises, or as the owner of premises where the person responsible cannot be found, or it might lawfully have been served on someone else as an occupier of the premises in question or as their owner and it is equitable for the notice to be so served, or on someone else in addition to the appellant as a person responsible, or as an owner or occupier of the premises, etc. Other grounds of appeal apply in respect of noise nuisances, see further chapter 11 below.

Where an appeal is made on the basis of informality, defect or error in a notice, or a copy thereof as the case may be, the court is to dismiss the appeal where satisfied that the informality is not material. Otherwise the court has a wide discretion to quash the notice, vary the notice as it thinks fit, but only in

10 *Strathclyde Regional Council v Tudhope* [1983] JPL 536.
11 *Network Housing Association v Westminster City Council* (1994) 27 HLR 189.
12 *Myatt v Teignbridge District Council* [1994] Env LR D18.

the appellant's favour, or dismiss the appeal. The court may make any order with regard to the person by whom work is to be executed or who is to contribute towards that work, or as to the proportions in which expenses recovered by an authority which has done work are to be borne by the appellant and other persons. In such cases the court is to take into account the terms of any tenancy existing between the owner and occupier of any premises, and whether, in a case where the ground of appeal is that the notice might lawfully have been served on some person other than the appellant, or in addition to the appellant, that other person has received a copy of the notice of appeal as if required under the regulations.

Where an appeal is made and compliance with the notice would involve any person in expenditure on carrying out works before the appeal is heard, the notice is suspended by the appeal until it has either been abandoned or decided. However, where the nuisance in question is one which is injurious to health, or is likely to be of limited duration so that the notice's efficacy would be rendered nugatory by suspension, or the expenditure referred to above would not be disproportionate to the public benefit to be expected pending the determination of the appeal in consequence of compliance, suspension may be avoided. The abatement notice *must* include a statement, eg that the nuisance is injurious to health. In such a case the notice has effect notwithstanding the appeal. The statement must also be specific as to the ground on which it is based.

It is a defence in respect of statutory nuisance proceedings to show that the 'best practicable means' (bpm) were used to prevent or counteract the effects of the nuisance. This defence is *not* available in respect of nuisances comprised of fumes or gases emitted from premises, nor in respect of smoke nuisances *unless* the smoke is emitted from a chimney, nor in respect of nuisances comprising premises, dust, steam, smell or effluvia, accumulations and deposits, animals or noise, *except* where the nuisance arises on industrial, trade or business premises. Following *Scholefield v Schunck*[13] it seems that 'bpm' means those means that are the best available to secure the end in view, and not merely those ordinarily accepted in the trade in question. However, in *National Smokeless Fuels v Perriman*,[14] an industrial tribunal case on similar wording under the Alkali, &c, Works Regulation Act 1906 and the Health and Safety at Work etc Act 1974, it was indicated that not only technical factors should be taken into account in deciding whether bpm has been used, but also social and economic factors such as working agreements made with trades unions, and the cost, excessive or otherwise, of introducing abating technology. However, mere lack of finance on the part of the party served is no reason for setting aside a notice,[15] as neither is increased expenditure or the resulting unprofitability of an activity,[16] and see s 79(9).

Taking of action in respect of statutory nuisances by private citizens

The majority of statutory nuisances are dealt with by local authorities but an individual wishing to proceed may rely on s 82 of the 1990 Act. This provides

13 (1855) 19 JP 84.
14 (1987) 1 Environmental Law No 2 p 5.
15 *Saddleworth Urban District Council v Aggregate and Sand Ltd* (1970) 114 Sol Jo 931.
16 *Wivenhoe Port Ltd v Colchester Borough Council* [1985] JPL 175 and 396.

that the magistrates may act on a complaint made by a 'person aggrieved', and where they are convinced the alleged nuisance *exists, or is likely to recur*, they may require the defendant to abate the nuisance, and execute any necessary works, and may further prohibit a recurrence of the nuisance. They may also fine the defendant. As with local authority proceedings it is the person responsible for the nuisance who is generally to be proceeded against, though where the nuisance is of a structural character, or where the 'person responsible' cannot be found, it is the owner of the premises who will be liable. Before complaining to the magistrates, however, the person aggrieved must give the potential defendant written notice of intention to commence proceedings, specifying the matter complained of. In the case of alleged noise nuisances three days' notice must be given, in all other cases not less than 21 days' notice is required. Where the magistrates make an order, it is an offence to contravene it, though where proceedings are commenced 'bpm' may be available as a defence in the case of premises, dust, steam, smell, effluvia, accumulations, deposits, or noise constituting a nuisance *provided* the nuisance arises on industrial, trade or business premises. It may also be available in respect of smoke nuisances where the smoke is emitted from a chimney.

Where on the hearing of proceedings in respect of an alleged nuisance it is shown that the nuisance did exist when the initial complaint was made, then, irrespective of whether it still exists or is likely to recur at the date of the hearing, the court *must* order the defendant to compensate the complainant for expenses incurred in bringing the proceedings. The court may also direct the relevant local authority to perform any requirements of an order to abate a nuisance where the defendant is in default. Orders made must be clear and precise.

Proceedings may, as has been stated, be commenced by a person aggrieved. This would include anyone whose health had been injured or threatened by the nuisance, or whose premises had been deleteriously affected.[17] Whether a trespasser could take action remains an open point, see *Coventry City Council v Cartwright*.[18] Section 82 proceedings can, however, only be taken where a nuisance *exists*, while local authorities may, under s 80, take action in respect of *threatened* nuisances. It should further be noted that the proceedings are criminal in nature, with the appropriate burden of proof.[19]

It is clear that a local authority may be proceeded against under this provision. In *Scarborough Corpn v Rural Sanitary Authority of Scarborough Poor Law Union*,[20] an order was made against the Corporation for having created a nuisance by collecting refuse, manure, cinders, etc, and depositing the same in a dump whence farmers could take the matter for their land. Also in *R v Epping (Waltham Abbey) Justices, ex p Burlinson*,[1] it was held that a private citizen can proceed against a defaulting authority.

---

17 *Sandwell Metropolitan Borough Council v Bujok* [1990] 3 All ER 385.
18 [1975] 2 All ER 99, [1975] 1 WLR 845.
19 *Botross v Hammersmith & Fulham London Borough Council* (1994) 27 HLR 179. This is so even in relation to noise nuisances it appears: *London Borough of Lewisham v Fenner* [1996] 8 ELM 11 (Knightsbridge Crown Court).
20 (1876) 1 Ex D 344.
 1 [1948] 1 KB 79, [1947] 2 All ER 537.

Offensive trades

Offensive trades, certain practices involving, for example, smells, were regulated under s 107 of the Public Health Act 1936.

Section 84 of the Environmental Protection Act 1990 made provision for the repeal of the offensive trades provisions, and for control in such cases to be exercised under provisions relating to atmospheric pollution, see chapter 10 below.

SI 1995/2054 repealed the offensive trades provisions as control under the 1990 Act is now in place.

E THE FUTURE DEVELOPMENT OF ENVIRONMENTAL LAW

Though there is a long history as to what is a recognisable body of environmental laws, much still remains to be done before there is a coherent body of *environmental law*. In particular, work is required to provide the subject with an adequate philosophical, juristic and doctrinal basis. As an essay, *though no more than that*, in that direction the following thoughts and questions are put forward.

'A many splendoured thing . . .?'

Enough has been said to show that the current body of laws are disparate, but underpinning the day to day *rules*, which are regularly changing, lies a set of principles which can be used to guide that process of change, while at an even deeper level lies the issue of the ethics of the law and the values it seeks to promote. This could lead to an initial, simplistic vision of the law as existing on three levels. The better view is that there is dynamic relationship between rules, principles and ethics both as to formulation of the law and as to its implementation and enforcement: see in this latter context the work emanating from the Centre for Socio-Legal studies in Oxford during the early 1980s which points to the conclusion in Keith Hawkins' study *Environment and Enforcement* at page 207: 'pollution control is done in a moral, not technological world'. Note also Hutter, *The Reasonable Arm of the Law?* (OUP 1988) and Richardson, Ogus and Burrows, *Policing Pollution* (OUP 1982).

The chapters of this work which follow will be largely concerned with the rules of the law, it is therefore essential here to examine first of all the underpinning principles and then the ethics of the law.

Sustainable development

The development of an idea

Humanity's numbers, styles of living and needs for adequate provision of food, shelter, employment, recreation, and that elusive concept 'quality of life', have to be considered globally, not in isolation, *and* in relation to the ability of the planet and its atmosphere to meet the demands made upon it. In this context there emerges the concept of 'sustainable development'. Many argue that while the world's population cannot continue to grow without unacceptable consequences for wildlife, urban congestion, pollution and energy and other resource demands, it is neither possible nor desirable to argue that economic growth must cease. If it did there would be disastrous consequences for the poorest nations of the world. *The World Conservation Strategy* (IUCN 1980) argued that: 'development and conservation are equally necessary for our survival' and the report of the World Commission on Environment and Development (Brundtland Commission), *Our Common Future* (1987) argued that sustainable development means global economic development sufficient to meet current needs while allowing future generations to achieve their needs: what is done now should not prevent future generations from pursuing their legitimate options. So, for example, where natural resources are used now there should be a compensating creation of some other form of asset — perhaps intellectual or technical — sufficient to enable future generations to have the same standard of living currently derived from the use of natural resources. Where an irreplaceable asset would be used up by an activity, sustainable development requires that activity's cessation.

The relationship with environmental economics

Lawyers and economists have given considerable thought to the evolution of the concept of sustainable development within the context of their own disciplines. In a book devoted to law it is not possible to do full justice to the very considerable development of economic thinking, and the interested reader must be referred to *Blueprint for a Green Economy* (Pearce, Markandya and Barbier, to whose work the author acknowledges his indebtedness). However, in the hope that for once a little knowledge will *not* be a dangerous thing, the following outline may be helpful. Economic thinking stresses the following issues

1 Sustainable development is a concept of rising real incomes coupled with increases in educational standards, the enhanced health of individuals and communities and improvements in the general quality of life.
2 It involves placing a substantial value on the environment, natural, built and cultural, and the realisation that environmental resources are not 'free', ie they are not 'there for the taking'.
3 The concept involves planning and forecasting over both the medium (5–10 years) and long term (30–60 years) timescales, while future dis-benefits will *not* be discounted as 'too remote to consider'.
4 It stresses that those who are least advantaged in society should have provision made for their needs (the 'intra-generational principle'), and that there should be fair treatment for future generations (the 'intergenerational principle').
5 In sum, the concept is based on three key ideas, namely, '*environment, futurity and equity*'. This means that 'future generations should be compensated for reductions in the endowments of resources brought about by the actions of present generations.' (*Blueprint for a Green Economy*, p 3.)
6 Sustainable development accepts that it is not possible to separate economic activity from the human environment, and argues that simply because the environment provides us with resources such as the ozone layer which have no market place in which they are traded, this does not mean that those resources are free. If those resources are used up by the

current generation then future generations will have been permanently impoverished.

7 Sustainable development embraces an anticipatory approach to environmental issues under which an attempt is made to determine the likely nature and cost of environmental problems in advance of their occurrence, so that appropriate measures can be taken to prevent the impoverishment of the future. This predicates a 'precautionary principle' (see further below) being an integral feature of all projects.

8 The concept does not pit 'growth' against 'environment', but rather accepts that in some cases environmental protection and conservation can promote growth in the economy, and also stresses that the real issue is *not* 'growth or no growth', but *how* growth is to be attained. In particular instances this may mean trading off environmental quality for growth, but only after a fully informed decision of the true environmental costs has been made; in other cases growth will be sacrificed in favour of environmental quality.

9 Sustainable development involves taking a broad view of development that values the well being of individuals, their freedom and self respect, and stresses co-operation.

10 There is room within the overall concept for debate as to how intergenerational equity may be achieved. Some argue that future generations should be left with the same amount of 'capital wealth' (eg goods and facilities created by humankind together with human intelligence) as that which the current generation holds. Others argue that they should be left an equal stock of environmental capital (eg water, land and air) as that currently enjoyed. The distinction between the two views is that, under the former, environmental quality and resources may be sacrificed provided there is a commensurate return of capital wealth, while the latter view inclines against such trade-offs. Overall it appears that the balance of the argument favours the view that 'the stock of environmental assets as a whole should not decrease' (*Blueprint for a Green Economy*, p 48), and that there is a notion of 'critical environmental capital' which should not be depleted, ie critical natural assets such as species, resources and habitats.

Further legal development

In the wake of the Brundtland Commission, the experts' group on environmental law of the World Commission on Environment and Development, in *Environmental Protection and Sustainable Development*, set down the following general principles with regard to rights and obligations relating to environmental resources and interests. In some cases these mirror the thinking of economists outlined above

1 There is a human right to have an environment adequate to support life and well being.

2 Nations should adopt principles of intergenerational equity in the use of the environment and its national resources.

3 There is a principle of conservation, ie the management of use of the environment and its resources so as to give the greatest sustainable benefit to the current generation while maintaining the ability of the resource base

to meet the needs of future generations. In this context 'conservation' subsumes notions of 'preservation', 'maintenance', 'utilisation', 'restoration' and 'enhancement'. This principle should be an integral part of planning processes.

4 The essential ecosystems and ecological processes of the biosphere should be subject to conservation, and the need to preserve biological diversity.

5 Nations should adopt adequate standards of environmental protection, and should monitor changes in the quality and use of environmental resources, publishing relevant data obtained.

6 Where an activity may result in significant impact on the environment or use of its resources, that activity should be subject to *environmental assessment* of its effects before a decision is taken as to whether it should be allowed to proceed, and *environmental impact assessment* of its subsequent effects.

7 Those likely to be affected by activities of the foregoing kind should be informed of the issue in good time and given access to any relevant administrative or judical proceedings.

8 Nations should co-operate in promoting the concept of sustainable development, and those nations which are more developed should assist those which are still developing.

9 Where natural resources traverse national boundaries (as, for example, does the atmosphere) they should be used by nations in a reasonable and equitable way, while nations should generally prevent environmental interferences from causing significant transboundary harm.

10 Where nations allow, or themselves undertake, beneficial activities which are also dangerous, they should take all reasonable *precautionary* measures to limit risks and to provide for compensation should there be substantial transboundary harm. Furthermore, compensation should be provided in respect of such harm where it arises from activities whose harmfulness was not appreciated when they took place. (Compare and contrast this with the economic notion of 'anticipatory' action above.)

11 Nations should apply standards in respect of transboundary environmental interferences and the use of environmental resources no less strict than those applied domestically.

12 There is a general obligation on nations to co-operate in respect of environmental problems, interferences and the use of natural resources which transcend national boundaries, and to pass relevant information concerning such matters to other concerned nations in a timely fashion.

13 Where there is an existing or potential transboundary environmental interference or use of environmental resources, concerned states should consult together in good faith at an early stage, and similarly they should co-operate in monitoring and researching such issues, collaborating in the setting of appropriate standards.

14 Nations should develop contingency plans to deal with situations where transboundary environmental interferences may arise, and where such an emergency eventuates they should warn other concerned states promptly and provide them with relevant information.

15 Where persons are affected by a transboundary interference, or their use of an environmental resource is affected, equal access and treatment should be afforded to them in any relevant administrative or judicial proceedings.

16 Nations should cease activities which are in breach of international environmental obligations and should provide compensation for harm caused, and should also settle environmental disputes by peaceful means.

How might sustainability as a notion further express itself?

A number of applications of sustainability *could* be developed, for example

1 Non-irreversability — as little as possible should be done that is not reversible.
2 Substitutionality — resources should be so used and developed so that substitutes can be found for them, while less or non-polluting technologies and uses of resources should be substituted for the more polluting consumptive ones.
3 Replaceability — resources should be used on the basis of their equivalent replacement.
4 Recyclability — material should be so used as to be capable of reuse over again.

In studying the pages which follow students should ask which of the laws considered there reflect these principles.

Sustainability in United Kingdom law and practice

(See also chapter 3 and chapter 5 below on the relationship between planning and sustainable development). 'Sustainable Development: The UK Strategy'[2] was developed in response to Agenda 21, one of the documents to emerge from the UN Conference on Environment and Development (UNCED — 'The Earth Summit'), Rio de Janiero 1992.

The basic principles to emerge from this document are

1 Decisions throughout society must be taken with proper regard to their environmental impact.
2 Sustainable development requires the encouragement of environmentally friendly economic activity and the discouragement of activities which damage the environment.
3 To a considerable extent environmental protection requires collective action.
4 Decisions about economic activity should take into account cost issues of pollution and waste and the value of resources consumed and conversely, the value of any environmental improvements made.

This last point indicates that in official thinking in the UK sustainable development has a cost/benefit element in it. The strategy actually states (at para 3.15) 'sometimes environmental costs have to be accepted as the price of economic development'.

These notions are further developed in guidance to the Environment Agency issued by Ministers under s 4 of the Environment Act 1995. This accepts that 'sustainable development entails reconciling the need for economic development and the needs of environmental protection'. The UK government's policy is that human wealth includes *both* man-made and natural

2 (Cm 2426).

environmental capital, and that it is the *net increase* in this that is of prime importance. Sustainable development seeks to bring about that increase, but where this results in demands on the environment there has to be a cost benefit allowance before an activity is allowed to proceed. However, it can be uncertain what the particular costs and benefits will be in any given case, and thus action should be taken on the basis of: the best scientific information; consideration of all relevant costs and benefits; risk analyses where there are uncertainties; taking into account both the precautionary and 'polluter pays' principles. These two must now be examined at greater length.

The precautionary principle

It is not always possible, and rarely easy, to know what environmental consequences may, at some unknown future date, flow from particular uses of the environment and its resources, or from particular industrial, or agricultural processes, nor the ways in which they may happen. This may be labelled the 'principle of uncertainty.' The law could require

1   cautious progress until a process/project is judged 'innocent';
2   ordinary progress until findings of 'guilt' are made; or
3   *no* progress until intensive research has been conducted into a proposed process and its innocence has been demonstrated.

It is 3 which represents the strongest formulation of the 'precautionary principle'. It is 2, however, which represents the historic British response to the problem. However, the White Paper, 'This Common Inheritance'[3] now states, at p 11:

'Where there are significant risks of damage to the environment, the Government will be prepared to take precautionary action to limit ... use of potentially dangerous pollutants, even where scientific knowledge is not conclusive ... particularly where there are good grounds for judging either that action taken promptly at comparatively low cost may avoid more costly damage later, or that irreversible effects may follow if action is delayed.'

Cm 2426 repeats this, and further adds from the Rio Declaration of 1992 'where there are threats of serious or irreversible damage, lack of full scientific certainty shall not be used as a reason for postponing cost-effective measures to prevent environmental degradation.' However, the implications of the oblique reference to cost/benefit equations should not be ignored, while Cm 2426 elsewhere states that the government 'remains committed to basing action on fact, not fantasy, using the best scientific information available; precipitate action on the basis of inadequate evidence is the wrong response' (para 3.12).

It is easy for views on the merits/demerits of policies and processes to polarise where there is apparently conflicting data as to consequences: where, for example, a proposal's proponents rely on demand forecasts to support their project. Demand forecasting has a history of unreliability. Likewise predictions as to the consequences of a particular process may have a strong element of subjectivity in them. There may be initial disagreement as to the test parameters to be used in the initial collection of data, and once it has been

3 (Cm 1200).

collected it needs evaluation, and hence a further departure from strict objectivity. If the results obtained indicate a degree of danger flowing from the process it may be felt necessary to build a further safety factor, or margin of error, into any recommendations made as to safety or other appplicable standards of regulation. This will be another evaluative step, though it may also be seen as an application of the precautionary principle. These matters were considered by the courts in *R v Secretary of State for Trade and Industry, ex p Duddridge*,[4] a case arising from allegations that the Secretary of State should take precautionary action to prevent risks of childhood leukaemia arising from exposure to electromagnetic fields generated by power cables. Smith J pointed out there is 'no comprehensive and authoritative definition of the pre-cautionary principle' but rejected arguments that precautionary action is needed where there is 'evidence of a possible risk even though the scientific evidence is presently unclear and does not prove the casual connection', ie 'where the mere possibility exists of a risk of serious harm to the environment or to human health'. On the contrary, Smith J considered that the government was perfectly entitled to formulate the much more restricted notion of precautionary action found in Cm 1200 which makes the threshold for taking action the perception of a *significant* risk of harm — though it is not clear who must have that perception, the government or some other agency. Where, however, there is a perception of a significant risk then the precautionary principle as enunciated in Cm 1200 will enter into the decision making equation as a relevant factor to be taken into account.

The 'polluter pays' principle

Where a process is found to have unwanted consequences questions arise as to who should 'pay' for them. In some cases it may not be easy to identify a responsible individual and it may be considered to be economically and administratively more efficient in such circumstances to place the responsi-bility for, and costs of 'clean up' measures, on some other body. This has been true of the water industry where water suppliers have borne the cost of purifying water affected by nitrates, applied by farmers, which have leached into ground and surface waters. It has been thought preferable to impose costs on water suppliers rather than to disrupt food production.

However, the principle usually argued for is, 'the polluter pays', which was developed by the Organisation for Economic Co-operation and Development (OECD) in 1972. This can be a vague notion. Some argue that it is satisfied when a polluter has to meet at least some of the administrative costs of the agencies who regulate polluting activities; an example of this is provided by provisions on administrative costs of regulation originally in the 1990 Act, now the Environment Act 1995. Others argue that it can only be satisfied by polluters having to pay the full reinstatement costs of their activities, while yet others appeal to the principle of legitimising taxation of particular activities to indicate that the use which those activities make of environmental resources is not 'free'. An example of this is provided by the arguments for 'carbon taxes' on the use of fossil fuels which produce atmospheric warming or 'greenhouse gases'. Cm 2426 contents itself with declaring that where 'production

4 [1995] 7 JEL 224. On 6 October 1995 the Court of Appeal in a short judgment upheld the Divisional Court's decision.

processes threaten or cause damage to the environment, the cost of necessary environmental measures should be borne by the producer, and not by society at large . . .' (para 3.16).

But is it the polluter pays or the user pays?

However, there is debate whether the 'polluter pays' principle is adequately satisfied if the polluter is allowed simply to treat pollution costs as mere overheads which are then passed on to customers as increased charges. This is a particular problem where a polluter is a large corporate organisation and the 'cost' is in the form of a fine for an offence involving breaches of environmental protection laws. This issue was examined by Professor Fisse in 'Sentencing Options Against Corporations',[5] to which the author acknowledges indebtedness. The problems, as elucidated by Fisse are: historic unwillingness on the part of courts to impose real, deterrent level fines on corporate offenders; the financial inability of some corporations to pay appropriately high fines so that the deterrence value of the fine becomes entirely notional; the fact that fines impinge only on a corporation's money making activities, as opposed to the desires for power, prestige and control, and creative urges which exist within corporations; the argument that fines convey no clear message that a corporate offence is socially intolerable, but may instead indicate that an offence is permissible provided a 'tariff' is paid, thus reducing criminal law to an accounting exercise; the fear that fining a corporation may divert attention from those individuals who are responsible for wrongful activities committed in the corporation's name; the argument that, following imposition of fines, there is no guarantee that the corporation will discipline itself, its members and employees to ensure no recurrence of the behaviour in question; the problem of 'spillover' whereby fines may simply be passed on to innocent persons such as shareholders, employees or consumers as opposed to the responsible managers. Against this, however, it may be argued that those who derive benefits from a corporation's activities, either by way of share dividends or remuneration, should bear the financial burdens of any wrongdoing by 'their' corporation.

Fisse goes on to point to alternative sanctions which may be more appropriate: enforced corporate dissolution; disqualification from ability to undertake certain types of work, for example, certain public contract activities; 'stock dilution' whereby a corporation is required to meet fines by issuing new shares equivalent in value to a deterrent level of fine, these shares being vested in some form of compensation fund; corporate probation whereby corporations which have offended are required, under supervision, to investigate and amend the ways which led to the offence — this might extend to requiring a polluter not just to introduce 'state of the art' anti-pollution techniques but also to go further by developing new non-polluting technologies; adverse publicity being given to a corporate offender by order of the court; community service under which, for example, a polluter might be required to set up a charitable or public service institution related to countering pollution, as in *United States v Allied Chemical Corpn*[6] where a company was ordered to set up

5 [1990] 1 Criminal Law Forum 211.
6 420 F Supp 122 (ED Va 1976).

a charity, the Virginia Environmental Endowment. The application of the 'polluter pays' principle is by no means a straightforward and non-contentious issue, though it does feature as part of European Union (EU) law, see chapter 4.

Best practicable environmental option

BPEO was initially developed as an idea by the Royal Commission on Environmental Pollution in their Fifth Report (Cmnd 6371). They returned to the matter in their 10th and 11th reports (Cmnd 9149 and 9675), defining it as 'the use of different sectors of the environment to minimise damage overall' and finding 'the optimum combination of available methods . . . so as to limit damage to the environment to the greatest extent achievable for a reasonable and acceptable total combined cost to industry and the public purse'. While BPEO takes account of local conditions and the current state of knowledge, it also weighs in the balance long term as well as short term issues, so as to produce, as the Royal Commission said in their 12th Report (Cm 310) 'the option that provides the best benefit or least damage to the environment as a whole, at acceptable cost, in the long term as well as in the short term.' BPEO is clearly a concept which links legal and economic thinking, and could be given wide application in environmental law. It is represented, however, only to a limited degree by certain provisions of the Environmental Protection Act 1990 relating to pollution control, see section 7(2), and see further below chapter 10. However, it deserves further application in planning law, and could serve as a further linking concept to environmental assessment (see chapter 5) to bring together planning and environmental protection legislation. This was, to some extent, officially recognised (see chapter 5 below) in PPG 23. Those seeking further thinking on this issue should refer to *Best Practicable Environmental Option – a New Jerusalem*, published by UKELA.

A miscellany of principles

1   Action should be taken on the basis of the best scientific data. The exact relationship of this principle with the precautionary principle is somewhat unclear — much depends upon the formulation given to the latter. The principle is enshrined in UK policy by Cm 1200 paras 1.16–1.17, and figures in the Treaty of Rome in Art 130r.
2   The concept of the 'cradle to grave' duty/life cycle analysis. This requires that the environmental impacts of a product from its initial inception in the gathering of raw materials right through to its final disposal should always be considered. The most obvious, though partial, application of the principle in UK law is the 'cradle to grave' duty of care with regard to waste, see below chapter 9.
3   The preventive principle/the requirement that harm should be rectified at source.

This is encountered in the Treaty of Rome in Art 130r and Cm 1200 at para 3.9. The concept of prevention of pollution at source underpins much of UK planning law which seeks to 'plan out' nuisances.

The exact relationship of all the foregoing principles one to another is as yet unclear. If any hierarchy exists in them it must surely be that sustainable development must be the first and greatest principle and that all others should serve that end.

There are, however, at a perhaps more mundane level principles which are relevant to the setting of individual environmental standards. Where the law imposes standards of environmental regulation there is debate over what the type of standard should be, and the parameters of any tests carried out thereunder to determine whether compliance is taking place. This is particularly marked in relation to vehicle emission standards where test parameters vary as between the United States and the European Community. The various types of standard include

1   *Absolute prohibition* of a particular activity.
2   *Specification standards* which attempt to prevent harm by means of specified design, construction and use matters.
3   *Emission standards* numerically laying down fixed upper limits for emissions from relevant processes — sometimes known as 'Uniform Emission Standards' where applied to *all* relevant discharges, or 'Local Emission Standards' where they may vary from place to place.
4   *Ambient standards* requiring regulatory agencies to apply controls so that the maximum permitted concentration of a pollutant at any given place and time is not exceeded by the aggregate of emissions of relevant local processes.
5   *Receptor standards* specifying control on a process when a particular level of damage in a receiving medium is perceived.
6   *Quality standards or objectives* whereunder a particular quality (the quality objective) goal is set for an environmental medium, usually to make it suitable for a defined use, and processes must be modified or eradicated so as not to ensure diminution of that standard, while a quality standard follows and fixes, numerically, the concentration of particular allowable substances in the medium, irrespective of source, which may not be transgressed if the quality objective is to be maintained.
7   *Managerial or licensing standards* whereunder whether or not to allow a particular activity, or level of activity, in a location is left to the discretion of some authorising agency, usually acting according to published guidelines or policies; planning law is a regulator of this type.
8   *Limit values* whereby a maximum permitted limit for discharge of an emission is set numerically, a term used in EU law.

Confusion arises where 'emission standards' and 'limit values' are used as interchangeable terms. In EU law a 'limit value' is a Community Maximum Standard, while states are sometimes free to fix their own stricter emission standards. Likewise 'quality objective' sometimes subsumes 'quality standard'. It is quite clear that there are 'families' of standards. Some require operators to achieve emission levels which regulators consider to be both low *and* reasonable. 'As low as reasonably achievable' (ALARA) is a standard sometimes found in UK practice. Its 'close cousin' in US practice is the requirement that operators should use 'reasonably achievable control technology' (RACT). Another 'relative' is the old standard of requiring use of 'best practicable means' (BPM). Each of these allows some debate between operators and regulators. Another 'family' of standards requires emissions to be 'as low as technically achievable' (ALATA) whose transatlantic counterpart is use of 'maximum achievable control technology' (MACT) and whose other 'relatives' include requirements to use 'best available techniques (originally technologies) not entailing excessive costs' (BATNEEC). Under these standards there is an obligation always to use 'state of the art' control technologies and to upgrade systems and performances in line with new developments.

The problem of choosing an appropriate standard is compounded where there is no consensus on the desirability of regulation. Generally speaking, to be successful an environmental measure to counter a hazard needs: agreed perception of a hazard, its nature, quality and consequences; a body of supportive scientific evidence detailing the issues; an available corrective technology, technique or substitute process or product; and a convergence of interest between 'the public' and 'the polluter' so that it makes economic and social sense to eradicate the hazard and for any enhanced costs flowing therefrom to be borne. Where these requirements are not met some element of compromise will exist in relation to the regulatory measure, very often reflected in its form. This may result in the measure being broadly managerial in character and discretionary in operation. Great use in such circumstances may be made of educative or exhortatory styles of regulation as opposed to strictly sanctioning approaches, and much will depend upon the ethical perceptions and professional codes of values of the regulators, as well as the moral perception of issues by 'polluters' and 'public' alike. This brings us to the issue of whether law and principles are underpinned by a deeper ethical or moral foundation.

F THE ETHICAL DEBATE

In an ethically and religiously plural world it is almost certainly impossible to find a single moral base for environmental law. Furthermore it is only comparatively recently that philosophers have turned in large numbers to the study of the moral status of the natural world.

The western tradition of thinking with its roots deep in the Judæo-Christian tradition can find there a tradition that humanity is a trustee or steward of the world in each generation, though there is also a further tradition in western thought which sees the world as simply a series of resources or instruments to be used simply as humanity desires (see further Sacks, *Faith in the Future*, 1995, chapter 29, and Sagoff *The Economy of the Earth*, 1988, particularly chapter 9).

Even so there is a wakening sense of the need to develop 'an ethic for the environment' in which search many world religions, along with those who maintain humanity can only look to itself to establish moral values, are now actively participating (see further Brown and Quiblier (eds), *Ethics of Agenda 21*, 1994, especially pp 97–118).

This thinking is still at a very early stage of development, but it is possible already to identify, as Professor Kerry Turner does in his contribution to *Blueprint 2* (chapter 11) four basic moral standpoints with regard to the natural world. Their importance is great for out of the creative tension that exists between them will come new laws and policies on the environment, while they already influence the application and implementation of the current laws.

A moral quadrilateral/matrix

1   The resource exploitative 'economic liberal' growth oriented, unfettered free market position, ie 'business as usual'. The basic philosophical stance here is utilitarian, ie the 'greatest happiness of the greatest number' — tending to refer only to currently living beings, and seeing this as achieved by maximising output. Restraint should only take place when positive, unacceptable harm can be shown to result from an individual's actions. This is a materialist or 'instrumental' position which sees the natural order as something to be made subject to individual human wants and needs as they are perceived in any given generation and by given persons.

2   The resource conservationist, environmental managerial 'stewardship' position. This remains primarily human centred in its concerns, ie it is anthropocentric, but it accepts the concepts of inter and intra generational equity, and so is not economically liberal or utilitarian. It regulates growth by seeking a new kind of sustainable growth. Non-human 'interests', eg animals and plants, receive protection as *a consequence* of the need to preserve the resource base for future generations, ie the natural order is still seen as 'instrumental', the need for some economic incentives for environmental protection is accepted.

3   The resource preservation position. This is less anthropocentic and more holistic, ie humanity is seen as simply *part* of the natural order, not its 'lord and master'. This position adopts a *very* restrictive attitude towards economic growth with zero the object. Animals and plants can be seen as having their own intrinsic *rights*, the notion of the whole ecosystem being one functioning entity — Gaia — is accepted, and the interests of the individual are subjugated to the interests of that collective 'whole'.

4   The extreme preservationist and extreme holistic position. This becomes ecologism, which can have overtones of mysticism and can descend into a pseudo-religion of quasi pagan veneration for the earth. 'Gaia' here becomes a personalised agent owned moral obligations. Those adhering to this position press for absolutely no growth, reducing use of natural resources and reductions of human populations. Nature is seen as having absolute intrinsic value irrespective of any human experience, and all species (biota) and even abiotic parts of the ecosystem (eg air) have moral rights.

Most thinking people would probably not claim to belong exclusively to one 'camp' or another: our moral positions tend to be eclectic, and the four positions outlined inevitably do violence to the range and subtlety of arguments. However, moral positions are particularly important with regard to the creation of individual legal standards.

The three rationalities

The creation of a legal standard depends on a creative tension between three areas of human thinking — the 'three rationalities'. These are The Scientific, The Economic and The Social. Scientific rationality tends to be precise, analytical, and observational — observing facts and coming to conclusions on those facts (hence it has an evaluative element). Scientific rationality may conclude that, for example, the introduction of a particular pollutant into an environmental medium will cause harm and may thus demand an end to the release of that substance.

Economic rationality is more evaluative and subjective than scientific rationality but still attempts to create principles by which particular activities can be measured, and their costs and benefits analysed and determined. Economic rationality may accept the 'need' for some environmental degradation because of benefits otherwise conferred which outweigh the environmental costs.

Social rationality is yet more evaluative — it is the 'politicoethical' dimension in which the various moral positions outlined above provide starting points for ethical debate.

Legal control will be an end product of the interaction between these three rationalities, and that interaction will vary from time to time. The same forces tend to govern the enforcement of the law, for it is clear that the law will only be effectively enforced and applied where those charged with its enforcement are

1   Happy with the form and content of the relevant legal rules, ie the rules are not too vague and excessively technical.
2   Ethically convinced that the law should be enforced generally and in given specific situations.

G THE CURRENT LEGAL AND POLICY POSITION OF THE UK

In the United Kingdom much of the present law concerning the environment reflects, as has been seen above, long development and the influence of historical forms of regulation. There is no reason to suppose that the influence of history will dissipate rapidly; see Cm 1200, p 272 on the likely continuance of 'flexible' administrative modes of regulation while the same document at p 10 broadly accepts the need for the law to reflect stewardship concepts examined above. UK law has traditionally stressed the need to reconcile conflicts between various users of the environment, with the environment itself being passive in the process; its approach has thus been one of conflict mediation and *environmental management*. Though a move towards a philosophy of *environmental protection* can be seen, UK law is still very far from regarding the environment as having inherent rights. The common law tradition vests rights in persons, not in things or animals, and certainly not in landscapes or water, etc. It may be, however, that notions of 'rights of the environment' will have to be developed, even if the vindication of such rights is entrusted to some person or body such as an environmental trustee, commissioner or ombudsman, or some form of environmental protection agency or service. Equally it is important to remember the 'Hawkins Principle' (so named after Richard Hawkins, a founder member of the United Kingdom Environmental Law Association and a tireless campaigner on the issue) that a legal evil occurs when there is 'over regulation and under enforcement'. This will arise in situations where enforcement agencies are under resourced or where the law is unclear, or where there are too many strands of regulation, or where an inapposite form of regulation has been chosen, or where regulators do not feel ethically justified in enforcing the law.

The law/economics/policy interface

The law must not only be ethically well founded, however. There must be harmonisation between legal and economic means of regulation.

Governmental moves in this direction are presaged in the White Paper Cm 1200 where, at p 8, it is accepted that: 'government needs to ensure that its policies fit together in every sector, that we are not undoing in one area what we are trying to do in another; and that policies are based on an harmonious set of principles rather than a clutter of expedients.'

Certainly both legal and economic or fiscal means of environmental regulation need to be harmonised to a greater extent than is currently so, and innovatory means of regulation developed. Appendix A of Cm 1200 provides examples of such forms of regulation, for example administrative charge recovery schemes; levies on particular industries or products to finance particular pollution control measures; pollution charges directly related to the burden on the environment of a particular activity or product; the use of subsidies, grants and schemes of public compensation to induce changes in particular activities. However, such 'economic instruments' may only work well where the cost imposed on a polluting activity is clearly appreciated by all concerned, and where the incentive or penalty, as the case may be, is very accurately targeted. Where an extra charge can simply be lost amongst many cost factors, the position may be otherwise. Thus in 1992 the European Commission proposed a punitive energy tax adding 14 pence to the price of a gallon of fuel by 2000 in order to drive down fuel consumption and cut CO_2 emissions, while in 1993 the UK government achieved more than that increase in a single budget, coupled with the yearly promise of rises in fuel duties by 3% pa in real terms as part of the same strategy.

Further moves in a similar policy trend have included examination of road pricing whereby vehicular use of roads is seen as a service in itself to be charged for and so limited.

While it is not appropriate here to examine the pros and cons of such policies, what is important is acceptance that legal regulation by itself is an insufficient means of environmental protection. 'Command and control' strategies of regulation must be integrated with economic instruments.

However, no system of regulation, no matter how well integrated, can be truly effective unless there exists the will on the part of the populace to have the law enforced; whether that is by means of campaigning pressure applied to enforcing agencies, or by virtue of the pursuit of individual rights. This brings us to the next fundamental issue in environmental law.

Access to environmental information

Attempts to confer environmental rights on individuals will fail unless those individuals have access to information enabling them to vindicate their rights. In the UK there is no one single statutory basis for the disclosure of information about the environment. Various registers exist under the Water Industry and Water Resources Acts 1991, for example the register of discharge consents under s 190 of the Water Resources Act. Similarly, a number of registers arose under the Environmental Protection Act 1990, see, for example, with regard to IPC processes s 20, and with regard to waste management licences s 64. Authorities having safety responsibilities such as the Health and Safety Executive and fire authorities are required to have registers of enforcement and safety notices they have issued, see s 1 of the Environment and Safety Information Act 1988.

A much more extensive obligation exists under Directive 90/313/EEC (freedom of access to information on the environment) which was transposed into national law by the Environmental Information Regulations SI 1992/3240 which grants rights in respect of information other than that on registers.

Applying within *Great Britain* the regulations apply to any information relating to the environment which is held by a 'relevant person' in an accessible form otherwise than for judicial or legislative function purposes, *and* is *not* either information required by statute to be provided on request to everyone who makes a request, or information contained in records which statute requires to be available for public inspection, ie registers.

Who are 'relevant persons'?

This is a little uncertain. It is arguable following *Griffin v South West Water*[7] that as water companies were held there to be 'emanations of the state' for the purposes of a directly effective employment directive (see further chapter 3 below) that they and other utilities should also fall within the scope of the regulations. Though they are not local or central government bodies with environmental responsibilities (these are clearly within the scope of the regulations) they are caught because they are bodies with environmental responsibilities which are regulated by agencies which are clearly public.

What is 'environmental information'?

It is that which relates to the state of *any* water, air, flora, fauna, soil, natural site or other land; any activities or measures which adversely affect, or are likely to adversely affect, any of the foregoing, and any activities or administrative or other measures designed to protect the first mentioned entities. 'Information itself includes anything kept in any records, including registers, reports, returns, and computer records.' The courts have, moreover, refused to recognise a distinction between 'primary' information (which has to be released) and 'secondary' information which enables its holder to check whether the primary information is correct.[8]

The general obligation to make information available

Relevant persons are under an obligation to make relevant information held available to every person requesting it and to make arrangements to see that such requests are responded to promptly and certainly within two months, and where a request is refused, to give reasons for the refusal. Similar procedural requirements are imposed in respect of the supply of information dealt with by other statutory provisions. A refusal may be made, inter alia, on grounds that a request for information is manifestly unreasonable or formulated too generally. Charges may be made in connection with the supply of information, and the obligation to make disclosure only applies in reasonable places and at reasonable times.

7 [1995] IRLR 15.
8 *R v British Coal Corpn, ex p Ibstock Building Products* [1995] 7 ELM 202.

There are, however, exceptions to the right to information. Thus 'confidential' information is excluded. Information is *capable* of being treated as confidential *only* if it relates to: matters subject to actual or prospective legal proceedings including disciplinary and public inquiry proceedings; the confidential deliberations of 'relevant persons' or the contents of internal communications of a body corporate, or other undertaking or organisation; information still in the course of completion; matters of commercial or industrial confidentiality or affecting any intellectual property. However, the apparent width of the exemption is cut down by requirements that information *must* be treated as confidential 'if and only if' where a request is made to a relevant person the information is:

1 capable of being treated as confidential and its disclosure would otherwise amount to a breach of the law or of some agreement; or
2 personal information contained in personal records on individuals who have not consented to its disclosure; or
3 the relevant person holds it having been supplied with the information by a person who was under no legal obligation to supply it, and who did not supply it in circumstances such that the relevant person is generally free to disclose it, and who has not consented to disclosure; or
4 is such that its disclosure would increase the likelihood of damage to the environment affecting anything to which the information relates.

'I also retail state secrets for a very moderate fee' (W S Gilbert, 'The Mikado' Act I)

Given the British penchant for secrecy a number of potential problems exist with regard to the application of the regulations. Refusals of requests for information could be made on the basis that the body requested is not a 'relevant person' or that it does not hold the information, or that the request is too general or is manifestly unreasonable, or that the information is within an exempted category. Furthermore there is no appeal mechanism to deal with a refusal, though the possibility of creating an appeals tribunal has been examined by the government. For further information see Mumma, *Environmental Law: Meeting UK and EC requirements* pp 231–235 and, generally, Bakkenist, *Environmental Information*.

Some final issues

There are two final topics both relevant to this chapter. Both depend upon a degree of voluntary, *almost* altruistic, self-regulation if they are to succeed. These are BS 7750, the Environmental Management System Standard, and EC Eco-management and Audit Scheme (EMAS). The *almost* is justified because many regulators argue that a 'clean' approach to industrial operations also makes economic sense; it certainly leads to a more efficient and economic use of natural resources. Both the issues for consideration also indicate, however, the increasing reliance which must be placed on voluntary self-regulation if there is to be a consistent and 'always-in-operation' style of supervision over the activities of companies and their impact on the environment. The keynote here is not so much regulation as 'environmental management', a concept involving commitment to constantly improving environmental performance coupled with an integrated approach linking environmental activity with finance, health and safety issues within each company. Such a concept must be adopted and operated 'top to bottom' within a company, and must operate on a preventive basis. Companies adopting such policies may, in an age of environmental consciousness, expect to gain approval for their commitment.

BS 7750

This was introduced in 1992 and it enables businesses to create a structure for measuring, managing, and improving environmental performance. Following an initial review of relevant legislation and impacts on the environment, a business (or indeed any organisation) may create and evaluate an environmental policy which must include a commitment to improving environmental performance. Policy objectives are then set and the whole policy is made publicly available. An appropriate manager must oversee the policy and staff must be given appropriate training. The business must also develop registers of its effects on the environment, and those of its suppliers. Environmental management programmes must be created and these should detail the business's management systems and its operational controls and records in the form of manuals and documents. These form an environmental management system which, ideally, should have responsible persons from board level down. Audits of performance are also required to check whether policies and objectives are being met, leading to the creation of management records while there should also be regular reviews of the environmental management system to ensure it is still suitable and effective. A further feature of the scheme is the existence of certification bodies whose task it is to check whether businesses meet the appropriate standard. The first accreditation certificates under BS 7750 were awarded in March 1995, though the cost of securing accreditation has been estimated at £70,000 for a company employing as few as 75 people.

EMAS (Regulation 1836/93)

The 'eco-audit' scheme is a voluntary market initiative to encourage continual improved environmental performance by businesses (including operators producing electricity, gas, steam, or hot water, and those in the waste management industry) with particular reference to production processes. As with BS 7750 participating businesses need to: establish and implement environmental policies, programmes and management systems for their various sites, periodically and systematically evaluate the foregoing, and give information on their environmental performance to the public.

Each participating business for each of its participating sites must

1 Adopt a policy of full compliance with all legislative regulatory requirements and commit itself to 'reasonable continuous improvement of environmental programmes'.
2 Conduct an environmental review of the participating site having regard to energy efficiency, waste management, product planning and eco-impacts.
3 In the light of that review introduce environmental programmes and management systems (either the business's own or based on BS 7750) for all activities at the site, consisting of an environmental protection programme

and an environmental statement for each site which describes site activities, an assessment of impacts, details of policies, programmes and objectives for the site in question, and evaluation of progress and a deadline for the production of the next statement.
4 Conduct a cyclical site environmental audit (which may be 'in-house') to provide information on the programme's progress.
5 Submit the foregoing procedures to *external* verification (the verifiers themselves being subject to external regulation via the National Accreditation Control for Certification bodies).
6 Submit the consequent validated statement to the relevant 'competent body' (in the UK the DoE) for its registration and public dissemination. As from 1 April 1996 the Environment Agency is consulted about applicants, and identifies those 'in breach' of requirements either because they have convictions for relevant offences or because their activities do not meet the demands of the law.

Participating companies are entitled to use as a logo one of four statements of participation listed in the regulations. The scheme came into effect in the UK from April 1995.

A parallel but equally voluntary scheme for local authorities to undergo eco-management came into force on 12 April 1995, see DoE Circular 2/95. The objects of this scheme are to

1 Promote local strategies for sustainable development.
2 Develop a systematic approach to environmental issues.
3 Help authorities identify their environmental impacts, both direct and indirect.
4 Promote local efficiency and effectiveness in environmental matters.
5 Provide the public with independently verified statements of environmental performance.

Authorities are to set their own environmental priorities and targets subject to the overall principle that there should be a continuous improvement in environmental performance with the goal of reducing environmental impacts, eg energy and paper consumption, and waste generation, to the minimum economically achievable.

Accordingly each participating authority is to develop a management framework with these features

1 A policy which identifies environmental aims and states commitment to continuous improvement.
2 A review of environmental impacts of relevant activities.
3 Programmes of action for attaining defined objectives translating overall policy aims into specific improvement goals.
4 An appropriate management system.
5 Periodic audits of performance.
6 Publication of statements of performance.
7 Impartial external verification of the foregoing.
8 Validation, if warranted, of the public performance statement.

EMAS was launched on 10 April 1995, and the first registrations under the scheme were in August 1995. The 'carrot' for the participating businesses is the promotion of corporate reputation, enhanced customer relations and improved profitability for it enables them to demonstrate a proactive approach to environmental issues and pressures. Companies which have already embraced BS 7750 have already made savings such as Northumbian Water which saved £850K over five years through reduced use of water, detergent savings and enhanced productivity.

At the same time as BS 7750 and EMAS have developed, the International Standards Organisation (ISO) has circulated documents — the 14000 series — which have been developed in the aftermath of the Rio Conference of 1992. The British Standards Institution (BSI) had participated in this work and has shadowed it within the UK. The ISO is developing an environmental management system which may fulfil EMAS requirements and replace BS 7750. The ISO is also preparing documents on life cycle assessment for, inter alia, products, and environmental aspects of product standards. ISO 14001, to be implemented in 1996, will largely be based on the EMAS management standards and will be similar to, but probably a little less detailed than BS 7750: those who satisfy the latter will satisfy the former. It will have the usual features of

1 Compliance with stated environmental policy.
2 Documented procedures.
3 Commitment to continuous improvement.
4 Need to use the best techniques economically viable.
5 Need to comply with all relevant legal provisions.

Further guidance will be given by ISO 14000, and in due course over the next two years there will appear ISO 14011/12 covering standards of environmental auditing, auditing qualifications and auditing methods. Further standards may be expected on environmental labelling of products and standards, indicators for environmental performance evaluation, and on 'life cycle analysis' of the impact of products and processes on the environment not just from 'cradle to grave' but from 'conception to resurrection', ie from the moment they are thought of until the whole process of thinking on the issue begins again. Yet further standards may be forthcoming giving agreed international industrial definitions of terms in common use, for example 'what is the environment' upon which, strangely, no current consensus exists!

It has, however, been pointed out that ISO standards share the weaknesses of all internationally agreed documents. They are, inevitably, compromises reflecting the attempt of some nations to reduce prescriptive or onerous requirements non-compliance with which is evidence of negligence.

Further undecided issues relate to the exact relationship of the varying international standards one with another, and whether compliance with a particular standard will *automatically* mean satisfaction of the requirements for all other regulatory regimes. Indeed the issue of cross compliance is a major problem for industry for it is well established in law that compliance with one code of regulation does not mean automatic compliance with any other. Where operators are subject to more than one legal regime, considerable expense can be incurred in meeting all compliance costs, particularly where the various requirements do not easily cohere one with another. However, there is general agreement on the basics of an effective environmental management system as illustrated overleaf.

A Make an initial appraisal of activity

1 Check compliance with legal requirements.
2 Consider a company's/process's significant environmental effects.
3 Set down principles for sound environmental action.
4 Create practices and procedures to implement policy.
5 Consider feedback from incidents and audits to ensure continuous improvement.

B Set up process controls covering issues such as training, supervision, equipment, dealing with abnormal occurrences, etc

1 Ensure there are means and procedures for verifying, measuring and testing the continuous operation of the company processes.
2 Take action to ensure compliance with set practice and procedure.
3 Keep records.

C Set up a regular audit of performance

1 Is policy leading to minimisation of waste, use of cleaner technology and the minimisation of environmental impact?
2 Is it leading to minimum resource demand impact?
3 Is it leading to sustainable development?

Further reading

Each chapter will end with a list of further reading. General reference, however, should be made to the periodical literature contained in:

The Journal of Planning and Environment Law; Environmental Liability (both Sweet and Maxwell); *The Journal of Environmental Law* (OUP); *Water Law* and *Environmental Law and Management* (ELM) (both John Wiley and Sons); and the *Environmental Data Services (ENDS) Reports* (Environmental Data Services Ltd).

HISTORY AND DEVELOPMENT OF PUBLIC HEALTH AND PLANNING LEGISLATION

Bell, C and R, *City Fathers: The Early History of Town Planning in Britain* (1972) Penguin Books.
Cullingworth, JB, *Town and Country Planning in Britain* (11th edn, 1994) Routledge.
Flinn, MW, (ed) *The Medical and Legal Aspects of Sanitary Reform* (Alexander P Stewart and Edward Jenkins) (1969) Leicester University Press.

FUTURE DEVELOPMENTS

Bateman, I, 'Social discounting, monetary evaluation and practical sustainability' (1991) 60 Town and Country Planning (6) 174.
Cairncross, F, *Costing the Earth* (1991) Business Books Ltd.

Fairley, R, 'Environmental Policy and Audit — What's in it for us?' [1995] 7 Environmental Law and Management 31.

Fisse, B, 'Sentencing Options against Corporations' (1990) 1 Criminal Law Forum 211.

Franklin, D, Hawke, N, and Lowe, M, *Pollution in the UK* (1995) Sweet & Maxwell, chapters 1, 2 and 8.

Kerry Turner, R, Pearce, D, and Bateman, I, *Environmental Economics* (1994) Harvester Wheatsheaf.

Kramer, L, 'The Open Society, its Lawyers and its Environment' (1989) 1 Journal of Environmental Law 1.

Lammers, JG (et al), *Environmental Protection and Sustainable Development: Legal Principles and Recommendations* (1987) Graham and Trotman.

McAuslan, P, 'The role of courts and other judicial type bodies in environmental management' (1991) 3 Journal of Environmental Law 195.

Nicholson, M, *The New Environmental Age* (1987) Cambridge University Press.

OECD, *Environmental Taxes in OECD Countries* (1995) Organisation for Economic Co-operation and Development.

OECD, *The State of the Environment* (1991) Organisation for Economic Co-operation and Development.

Pearce, D, Markandya, A, and Barbier EB, *Blueprint for a Green Economy* (1989) Earth Scan Publications Ltd.

Pearce, D, and Markandya, A, *The Benefits of Environmental Policy* (1989) OECD.

Pearce, D, and Turner, RK, *Economics of Natural Resources and the Environment* (1990) Harvester Wheatsheaf.

Pearce, D, et al, *Blueprint 2: Greening the World Economy* (1991) Earthscan Publications Ltd.

Pearce, D, and Warford, J, *World Without End* (1993) OUP.

Spedding, L, Jones, D, and Dering, C, *Eco Management & Eco-Auditing* (1993) Wiley-Chancery.

Tromans, S, (ed) *Best Practicable Environmental Option — A New Jerusalem?* (1987) United Kingdom Environmental Law Association.

Winter, G, 'Perspectives for Environmental Law — Entering the Fourth Phase' (1989) 1 Journal of Environmental Law 38.

World Commission on Environment and Development, *Our Common Future* (1987) OUP.

OFFICIAL PUBLICATIONS

'Policy Appraisal and the Environment' (1991) HMSO.

Winpenny, JT, 'Values for the environment: a guide to economic appraisal' (1991) HMSO.

ENVIRONMENTAL ETHICS AND POLICY

Aakvaag, T, 'Can the Needs of Society and the Environment be reconciled?' (1995) Vol CXLIII RSA Journal p 30.

Allison, L, *Ecology & Utility* (1991) Leicester University Press.

Attfield, R, and Belsey, A, *Philosophy and the National Environment* (1994) CUP.

Brown-Weiss, E, 'Agora: What Does Our Generation Owe to the Next? An Approach to Global Environmental Responsibility' (1990) 84 AJIL 190.

Carr, IM, 'Saving the Environment — does utilitarianism provide a justification?' (1992) 12 Legal Studies 92.

Dobson, A, *Green Political Thought* (1990) Harper Collins.

Eckersley, R, *Environmentalism and Political Theory* (1992) UCL Press.

Glasbergen, P, and Blowers, A, *Environmental Policy in an International Context: Perspectives*, chapters 1–4 and 6–7, (1995) Arnold.

Holdgate, M, 'How Can Development Be Sustainable?' (1995) Vol CXLIII, RSA Journal p 15.

Hurrell, A, and Kingsbury, B, *The International Politics of the Environment* (1992) OUP.

McCormick, J, *British Politics and the Environment* (1991) Earthscan Publications Ltd.

Wilson, EO, *The Diversity of Life*, chapter 15, (1992) Allen Lane, The Penguin Press.

Chapter 2

Civil action by the aggrieved individual

'Monster, dread our damages' (W S Gilbert, 'Trial by Jury')

Remedies have for long been available to persons whose interests are adversely affected by the activities of others. The law of torts may be of remedial assistance to, for example, a landholder whose land or premises have been damaged. The law may give a remedy by way of payment of a sum of money for loss suffered (damages) or by granting an order against the wrongdoer requiring him to do, or to refrain from doing, some act (an injunction). But actions at common law are time-consuming and expensive, fraught with complex technicalities and, in general, only available on an individual, rather than a class, basis. A person cannot be the plaintiff in an action at common law unless he has a vested interest in the subject matter of the action; so in an action in tort the plaintiff must be the person injured by the wrongdoer. It is impossible in a study such as this to do justice to the vast body of substantive law on the area; those requiring further information are referred to, initially, Jones, *Textbook on Torts* 4th edn, Blackstone Press, then, at practitioner level, Pugh & Day, *Pollution and Personal Injury*, Cameron May, and *Clerk and Lindsell on Torts*, Sweet & Maxwell.

A THE LAW OF TORTS AND THE ENVIRONMENT

The law as stated is that applicable in England and Wales, Scots law differs in material respects, and reference should be made to appropriate Scottish texts.

Nuisance

Nuisance can be divided into public and private nuisance, the first of which is a crime, though it can also be a tort in certain circumstances, while the second is always tortious.

Public nuisance

An act or omission materially affecting the reasonable comfort and convenience of a class of Her Majesty's subjects is a public nuisance and a criminal act; what constitutes such a class is not certain. Less than the entire population of the nation and more than just a handful of individuals, a class must be a definable section of the public in the area affected by the alleged nuisance. A requisite number are affected if the nuisance is so widespread in its range or so indiscriminate in its effect that it would be unreasonable to expect one person to take preventive legal measures as opposed to the community at large.[1] Activities that amount to environmentally damaging public nuisances include: holding a noisy pop festival, and owning or operating a tip, rubbish dump, cess pit or other collection of filth that affects the health or habitability of a locality.

The usual remedy is an indictment. It is also possible for the Attorney General to bring an action for an injunction to order the cessation of the nuisance. Such an action is known as a relator action, and is brought on the information of a member of the public, though only where the Attorney General has exercised his discretion to act. Under the Local Government Act 1972, s 222, a local authority may also bring an action in respect of a public nuisance if they consider it 'expedient for the promotion or protection of the interests of the inhabitants of their area'. It seems proper for a local authority to act in situations where it is under an obligation to protect the environment and where the alleged contravention constitutes an infringement of the authority's environmental responsibilities.[2] Where a public nuisance affects only a single local authority area it is preferable for the authority to use its s 222 powers rather than for the Attorney General to intervene. However, before instituting such proceedings an authority must consider the interests of *all* its inhabitants, not merely those of one section of the community.

The use of s 222 is generally regarded as exceptional, and it is not appropriate to remedy mere infringements of the criminal law. On the other hand an offender need not be deliberately and flagrantly flouting the law before s 222 can be used; it is enough if it can be shown that unlawful operations will continue until restrained by law, and that only an injunction can bring this about.[3] It is *not* the case that relief is only available in cases where the defendant would have no defence to a criminal prosecution.[4] An authority seeking an interlocutory injunction will not have to give a cross undertaking to pay damages to the injuncted party should the substantive issue be decided against the authority.[5]

A public nuisance may be a tort where a member of the public suffers damage *over and above* that suffered by others. Such damage may consist of inconvenience or delay, provided it is substantial, direct to the plaintiff and appreciably different from that suffered by the general public. It may consist of damage to the plaintiff's person,[6] or to goods and chattels,[7] or to pecuniary interests, provided he/she has been made to incur considerable loss or expense.[8] In such circumstances an individual may bring his own private suit to recover his loss. In the litigation arising out of the Camelford pollution

1 *A-G v PYA Quarries Ltd* [1957] 2 QB 169, [1957] 1 All ER 894.
2 *Shoreham-by-Sea Urban District Council v Dolphin Canadian Proteins Ltd* (1972) 71 LGR 261 — the case of the smelly factory.
3 *City of London Corpn v Bovis Construction Ltd* [1989] JPL 263.
4 *Newport Borough Council v Khan* [1990] 1 WLR 1185.
5 *Kirklees Borough Council v Wickes Building Supplies Ltd* [1993] AC 227.
6 *Castle v St Augustine's Links Ltd* (1922) 38 TLR 615.
7 *Halsey v Esso Petroleum Co Ltd* [1961] 2 All ER 145, [1961] 1 WLR 683.
8 *Rose v Miles* (1815) 4 M & S 101.

incident in 1988 when aluminium sulphate was introduced into drinking water, it was held *aggravated* and *exemplary* damages were not available for such a claim, though damages of up to £10,000 were accepted by victims in out of court settlements.[9]

Private nuisance

A private nuisance is any unlawful interference with a person's use or enjoyment of land or of some right over or in connection with it.[10] Private nuisance subdivides into

1 Interference with use and enjoyment of land, for example, as a result of an unpleasant smell arising from a neighbouring pig farm.[11]
2 Actual physical interference with land itself, for example, as a result of sewage collecting on it:[12] or where powerful vibrations from engines on neighbouring land cause damage to the structure of a house.[13]

The basic wrong is generally the same: an interference, usually for a substantial length of time, by an owner or occupier of property with the use, enjoyment or actual physical nature of a neighbour's land. The wrong can also be committed where the right to pure air and freedom from unnecessary noise is infringed. See also chapter 12 below on the rights of riparian owners. The basis is unreasonable and unnecessary inconvenience caused by the use of the defendant's land. To be a nuisance an act must satisfy certain conditions. First it must *not* arise on premises in the plaintiff's occupation. It must arise outside the plaintiff's land and then proceed to affect that land or its use. Second, it must generally be a continuing wrong. Most nuisances arise because of a regular, long-standing unreasonable use of land. A single instance of deleterious affectation may, however, be evidence of a continuing unreasonable use of land, or so serious and grave an occurrence in itself as to amount to an act of nuisance.[14] Third, the damage suffered must be real or 'sensible' in that it can be measured in some way.[15]

A REMEDY FOR PERSONAL INJURY?

It is doubtful whether private nuisance is a proper remedy for personal injuries and damage to goods and chattels. The authorities seem hopelessly divided on this issue. F H Newark pointed out in 'The Boundaries of Nuisance',[16] that much confusion with regard to this issue has arisen because an action for *public* nuisance consequent, for example, on some use of the highway may give a remedy for personal injuries. Where defective premises abutting a highway cause injury to a passer-by the remedy should lie in negligence, but has been *said* to lie in private nuisance. Thus nuisance has come to be thought of as a remedy for personal injuries or chattel damages. See *Woolfall v Knowsley*

9 *Gibbons v South West Water Services* [1993] 5 LMELR 6.
10 *Howard v Walker* [1947] KB 860, [1947] 2 All ER 197 at 199.
11 *Bone v Seale* [1975] 1 All ER 787, [1975] 1 WLR 797.
12 *Jones v Llanrwst Urban District Council* [1911] 1 Ch 393.
13 *Meux's Brewery Co v City of London Electric Lighting Co* [1895] 1 Ch 287.
14 *British Celanese Ltd v A H Hunt (Capacitors) Ltd* [1969] 2 All ER 1252, [1969] 1 WLR 959.
15 *Swindon Waterworks Co Ltd v Wilts and Berks Canal Navigation Co* (1875) LR 7 HL 697.
16 (1949) 65 LQR 480.

Borough Council[17] where damages were given for injury caused to the plaintiff by a fire in a pile of rubbish on land. The local authority should have moved the rubbish which lay by the highway. Likewise confusion has arisen because nuisance may *appear* to be a remedy for personal injury when it is a remedy for diminished enjoyment of land. If people are forced to stop sunbathing in their gardens because a neighbouring factory emits smuts, smoke and fumes, a nuisance action should remedy, not the coughing and retching of the unfortunate householders, nor the damage to clothing, but the fact that enjoyment of land has been seriously diminished. The most that should be said in such circumstances is that an *occupier* of land may be able to recover in nuisance for damage to the person and personal property where land or its enjoyment is also affected.

Damage sufficient to ground a nuisance action may consist of either an interference with the beneficial use of premises or physical injury to the premises. The burden of proof is generally higher in the former case and the issue of locality is also then relevant. See Lord Westbury in *St Helen's Smelting Co v Tipping*.[18]

THE INFLUENCE OF LOCATION

Where injury consists only of interference with the use and enjoyment of land the locality of the land is relevant in deciding whether there is an actionable nuisance. Someone living in the centre of a great conurbation is expected to put up with more noise and smell than a person living in a pleasant upper middle-class suburb. See Lord Halsbury in *Colls v Home and Colonial Stores Ltd*.[19] This rule fails to protect the physiological and psychological needs of people, which do not vary greatly from one area to another, but it is too deeply entrenched to be changed.

The effect of the rule is well illustrated by *Gillingham Borough Council v Medway (Chatham) Dock Co Ltd*.[20] Here a former naval dockyard was given planning permission to operate as a commercial port. This involved a massive increase in levels of traffic using the only two approach roads to the docks via a residential area. The local authority, who had originally consented to change under planning law, sought to obtain declaratory and injunctive relief in respect of the public nuisance they alleged arose from the presence of the traffic on its way to the docks. Buckley J considered, however, that those who live near highways must accept some increased noise and fumes for the greater public good. He further considered that a grant of planning permission is an authorisation to change the character of a neighbourhood, and that may result in an activity losing its potentially tortious character. However, in *Wheeler v JJ Saunders Ltd*[1] it was denied that planning permission always amounts to statutory authorisation of tortious activity: the real issue is has the grant of permission changed the character of the area? See further on this issue, in confirmation of the argument, *Hunter v Canary Wharf Ltd*, below.

17 [1992] 4 LMELR 124.
18 (1865) 11 HL Cas 642 at 650.
19 [1904] AC 179 at 185.
20 [1993] QB 343.
 1 [1995] 2 All ER 697.

In any case of alleged nuisance no action can be brought unless there is some real damage to the plaintiff. Purely superficial damage is not enough. However, the loss of one night's sleep may be a sufficiently substantial interference with the use of land to ground an action.[2] Such claims will always depend on the facts of each case. Where noise is caused, for example, by demolition or building work it will be actionable if it is caused by unreasonable activities or where the defendant takes no proper steps to avoid inconvenience to neighbours. In the middle of a city people might be expected to put up with more noise than their suburban cousins, but much will depend on the severity and character of the noise. See also *Rushmer v Polsue and Alfieri Ltd*,[3] where a dairyman lived over his premises in an area generally devoted to printing. A neighbouring printer installed a noisy machine which interrupted the plaintiff's sleep. An injunction was granted as the loss of sleep was thought intolerable even in such an industrial area.

There can be no action for damage due solely to the fact that the plaintiff is abnormally sensitive to deleterious influences, or damage arising solely because the plaintiff uses his land for purposes requiring exceptional freedom from damaging influences. In *Robinson v Kilvert*[4] the plaintiff claimed heat from the defendant's pipes injuriously affected his stock of brown paper. It was held that the plaintiff's trade was 'exceptionally delicate' and that he could not recover. The law offers little protection to sensitive operations. Persons carrying on activities needing special protection are usually expected to obtain this by agreement with neighbours, for example by obtaining restrictive covenants to benefit relevant land. In connection with 'sensitive' land uses an interesting question arises with regard to television broadcasting and reception. In *Bridlington Relay Ltd v Yorkshire Electricity Board*,[5] it was considered interference with a recreational activity such as television reception was not a sufficient interference with use of land to constitute an actionable nuisance, and also that the interference in question arose only because of the delicate nature of the plaintiff's operation as a transmitter of programmes. More recently in *Hunter v Canary Wharf Ltd, Hunter v London Docklands Development Corpn*[6] the Court of Appeal considered that while television reception is an important aspect of every day life, its interruption by the presence of tall buildings, which are also common features of our society, is not actionable in nuisance. The injury is analogous to the loss of a view when new buildings are erected: there is no cause of action; it is *damnum sine injuria*.

However, *once a subsantial interference is otherwise proved*, damage caused to sensitive and delicate objects on the plaintiff's land may be remedied in the general action for damages or an injunction. In *McKinnon Industries Ltd v Walker*,[7] the plaintiff grew flowers for sale including orchids, the growing of which is a difficult and delicate operation. He complained that his greenhouses, plants and shrubs generally were being harmed by the emission of sulphur dioxide from the defendant's works. A nuisance was found and an

---

2 *Andreae v Selfridge & Co Ltd* [1938] Ch 1, [1937] 3 All ER 255.
3 [1906] 1 Ch 234.
4 (1889) 41 Ch D 88.
5 [1965] Ch 436, [1965] 1 All ER 264.
6 [1996] 1 All ER 482.
7 (1951) 3 DLR 577, PC.

injunction granted to protect all the plaintiff's operations, including the growing of orchids.

Other factors can also be relevant in determining whether a nuisance exists. Everyone is expected to put up with a certain amount of inconvenience with regard to the enjoyment of property so that others may enjoy a similar degree of freedom. In any nuisance action the real issue will usually be, not whether there has been an interference, but whether the land use goes beyond acceptable bounds of mutual give and take, live and let live. Whether the balance between the rights of plaintiff and defendant has been upset will depend upon weighing many factors. These may include: the nature of the locality with regard to *both* the alleged nuisance and the damaged interest; the actual use made by the defendant of relevant land, so that a common and ordinary use of land is unlikely to give rise to a nuisance action if it is done conveniently and with reasonable care and skill; the burden and practicability of taking preventive action; the seriousness of the interference and the extent and nature of the harm suffered, and the social value of both the damaged interest and the defendant's activity, see *Kennaway v Thompson*.[8] It can be relevant to consider whether the plaintiff could have easily avoided the consequences of the nuisance. But defendants may not 'carve out' an area of operations for themselves by carrying on obnoxious activities which injure neighbours who move in; then claiming that they cannot recover because they 'came to the nuisance'. In *Bliss v Hall*,[9] a stinking candle factory interfered with the use of other buildings. It was held no defence for the defendant to claim that his factory had been there first.

The defendant's state of mind at the time of the alleged nuisance is not generally relevant to deciding whether there is any defence. Whether an occurrence amounts to an actionable nuisance may depend partly on whether the defendant behaved in a generally reasonable way, but once an actionable nuisance is *otherwise* shown to exist, the fact that reasonable care and skill were used will be no defence, see *Read v Lyons & Co Ltd*.[10] However, this is an extremely complex area of law, and it is uncertain whether a nuisance can be made out without it also being shown that the defendant was also in some way at fault. Some authorities say fault is necessary, others that nuisance is a tort of strict liability where there is no need to show more than the occurrence of the unlawful act for liability to be imposed. See Dias 'Trouble on Oiled Waters: problems of the Wagon Mound (No 2)'.[11] The better view of the law is that a nuisance is an interference with land or its use that is 'unreasonable' in the sense that the court has decided, on a balance of all the factors, that the action complained of goes beyond what normal 'give and take' allows. In some cases this cannot be shown unless the defendant acted in some wrongful way, ie intentionally or negligently. Where noxious fumes are emitted from the defendant's factory and these damage the plaintiff's land, the nuisance is made out because the fumes are noxious. It is no defence to the defendant to show use of the utmost care in building the factory.[12] But there may be situations

8 [1981] QB 88.
9 (1838) 4 Bing N C 183.
10 [1947] AC 156.
11 [1967] CLJ 62.
12 *Vanderpant v Mayfair Hotel Co Ltd* [1930] 1 Ch 138; *Graham & Graham v Rechem International* [1995] 7 ELM 175.

where the interference with the plaintiff's rights is not sufficiently serious of itself to justify a finding of nuisance *unless* it can also be shown that the defendant's acts are also intentional or negligent.

In *Hollywood Silver Fox Farm Ltd v Emmett*[13] the plaintiff bred silver foxes who are nervous in the breeding season and apt to miscarry or to kill their young if disturbed. The defendant maliciously instigated his son to fire a gun on four consecutive nights. The son was standing on his father's land, but as near as possible to the plaintiff's breeding pens. It was held that the malice was enough to turn the undoubted annoyance of the sound of gunfire into an actionable nuisance. Malice by itself is not, however, enough, there must also be some accompanying act classifiable as an invasion of the plaintiff's interests.[14]

Defences

Defendants may be able to avail themselves of certain defences. The first is prescription. This can only exist with regard to a private nuisance, and can only exist against another piece of land ('the servient tenement') which suffers from the alleged nuisance. Defendants have to show that in doing the acts complained of they have been acting openly and to the knowledge of the owner of the servient tenement. After 20 years' continuous existence the operations achieve legality and are not a nuisance with regard to the servient tenement. To establish the defence certainty and uniformity of the damaging activity must be proved by the defendant. The prescription period, moreover, begins to run once the damage is suffered, and it must *not* be unknown and unsuspected by the damaged landholder.[15] A more common defence in environmental cases is statutory authority. Where the doing of something otherwise unlawful is authorised by statute, the statute takes away any right of action in respect of the doing of the act. This indemnity extends not only to the doing of the act, but to all necessary consequences. Whether any consequence is a necessary result of the authorised action must be proved by the defendant who seeks to escape liability. Much depends on the wording of the statute in question, but, initially, it can be said that where an Act is imperative in its wording and actually directs an action to be done, there will generally be no liability if the action results in a nuisance or other injurious consequence. On the other hand where a statute is permissive it will generally be interpreted as giving authority only to do the action without causing a nuisance or other deleterious act.

In *Pride of Derby and Derbyshire Angling Association Ltd v British Celanese Ltd*[16] it was alleged, inter alia, that Derby Corpn were polluting rivers by pumping insufficiently treated sewage from their sewage works. They argued that under the Derby Corporation Act 1901 they were charged with providing a sewerage system, which they had, and which, at the time of construction, did not cause pollution. That system had only begun to cause pollution because it was inadequate to deal with the increased population of their area. It was held that the only question to be asked was whether the thing complained of as a nuisance was expressly or impliedly authorised by the statute or, alternatively,

13 [1936] 2 KB 468, [1936] 1 All ER 825.
14 *Bradford Corpn v Pickles* [1895] AC 587.
15 *Scott-Whitehead v National Coal Board* (1985) 53 P & CR 263.
16 [1953] Ch 149, [1953] 1 All ER 179.

whether the nuisance was the inevitable consequence of that which the Act both authorised and contemplated. The relevant statute was found to give no exemption from liability for nuisance. Indeed it actually said: 'this Act shall not exempt or be deemed to exempt the corporation from any liability for any nuisance arising from such sewage disposal works or from any proceedings which might but for this Act be taken against them.' The courts try to preserve common law remedies unless there are clear words in the statute taking these away. As stated above each case turns on the wording of the particular provison in question.[17] In *Allen v Gulf Oil Refining Ltd*,[18] it was held that the Gulf Oil Refining Act 1965 authorised the operation of an oil refinery even where this resulted in harm to neighbours, provided there was no negligence in the operation. But it must be remembered that the burden of proving that an inevitable and necessary nuisance arising from a permitted activity is within statutory authority lies on those claiming it, and it can only be discharged by showing that all reasonable scientific care and skill ('due diligence') has been used. However, clear words in an Act granting immunity may protect against liability in nuisance even where the statute fails to create an alternative scheme of compensation for affected landowners.

The law was reviewed in *Department of Transport v North West Water*,[19] and certain propositions can be made.[20]

1   In the absence of negligence, meaning here a want of reasonable regard and care for the interests of other persons, a body is not liable for a nuisance attributable to the exercise by it of a *duty* imposed by statute.[1]
2   Where a body is under a *duty* imposed by statute, and that statute expressly makes it liable, or not exempted from liability, for nuisance, liability is still actually dependent upon proof of negligence, ie a lack of reasonable diligence, care, and regard for others.[2]
3   In the absence of negligence, a body is *not* liable for nuisance attributable to the exercise by it of a *power* conferred by statute if, by statute, it is not expressly made liable for nuisance.[3]
4   A body *is* liable for a nuisance attributable to the exercise of its *powers*, even without negligence, if by statute it is expressly made liable.[4] Statute can also make a body liable, or not exempted from liability, for nuisances arising out of statutory *duties*, see the *Pride of Derby Angling Association* case, above.

The result is that a body acting under statutory authority will generally only be able to plead statutory authority as a defence to the *necessary* and *inevitable* consequences of what Parliament has authorised. Where a consequence is, however, not necessary or inevitable, liability for the nuisance will depend on proof of fault in the case of a statutory *duty*. There may be no need even to prove fault in the case of a statutory *power* where the statute

17 *Smeaton v Ilford Corpn* [1954] Ch 450, [1954] 1 All ER 923.
18 [1981] AC 1001, [1981] 1 All ER 353.
19 [1984] AC 336, [1983] 1 All ER 892.
20 See also [1983] 3 All ER 273 at 275.
 1 *Hammond v St Pancras Vestry* (1874) LR 9 CP 316.
 2 *Stretton's Derby Brewery Co v Derby Corpn Ltd* [1894] 1 Ch 431.
 3 *Midwood & Co v Manchester Corpn* [1905] 2 KB 597.
 4 *Charing Cross West End and City Electricity Supply Co v London Hydraulic Power Co* [1914] 3 KB 772 and *Dunne v North Western Gas Board* [1964] 2 QB 806.

in question either makes the holder of the power expressly liable or does not exempt him from liability. Thus it must always be asked, (a) is the defendant operating under a _power_ or a _duty_, (b) is there a liability for nuisance provision? 'Duty' plus 'nuisance' means liability only for negligence, as does 'power' plus _no_ 'nuisance', while 'power' plus 'nuisance' leads to liability even in the absence of negligence. The courts are unwilling to construe legislation so as to confer absolute and irrespective immunity, with the result that liability for failing to act with reasonable regard and care for the interests of others is, wherever possible, preserved. See per Lord Wilberforce in _Allen v Gulf Oil Refining Ltd_,[5] and per Lord Templeman in _Tate and Lyle Food and Distribution Ltd v Greater London Council_.[6]

The following pleas are not available as defences: the plaintiff 'came' to the nuisance; the act of a third party precipitated the nuisance where that act is the sort of occurrence that the defendant _ought to have foreseen_ when creating a situation that could give rise to a nuisance; the defendant was acting for the 'public benefit': see _Adams v Ursell_,[7] where the defendant set up a chip shop in a select residential area; the locality was suited to the defendant's actions; others in the area were doing the same act, see _Lambton v Mellish_,[8] where a group of factories in an area were all responsible for acts of pollution; and that all care and skill has been used. The emphasis in nuisance is not on the plaintiff's need to prove the defendant's fault, but on the defendant's need to exculpate himself. See _Wagon Mound (No 2)_[9] and _Radstock Co-op and Industrial Society v Norton-Radstock Urban District Council_.[10]

In _Leakey v National Trust for Places of Historic Interest or Beauty_,[11] the Court of Appeal went so far as to impose liability in nuisance for harm originating in the natural condition of the land, and said that no distinction was to be drawn between hazards arising from misfeasance and those arising from non-feasance, or between those of a mineral nature and those of a vegetable nature. But in such cases the steps required of landowners to prevent liability in nuisance arising will be determined according to their personal capabilities and circumstances: more will be required of those of substance than of persons of limited assets.

Furthermore in such circumstances liability will also depend on the fact that the landholder knew or ought to have known of the defective condition of the land leading to the nuisance. See also _Goldman v Hargrave_.[12]

The parties to a nuisance action

WHO CAN SUE?

The right to sue normally inheres in the person in possession of the affected land. This will mean that a freeholder, leaseholder, a licensee with a right to

5 [1981] AC 1001, [1981] 1 All ER 353 and 356.
6 [1983] 1 All ER 1159 at 1171–72.
7 [1913] 1 Ch 269.
8 [1894] 3 Ch 163.
9 [1963] 1 Lloyd's Rep 402 at 428.
10 [1968] Ch 605, [1968] 2 All ER 59.
11 [1980] QB 485, [1980] 1 All ER 17.
12 [1967] 1 AC 645, [1966] 2 All ER 989.

exclusive occupation or even a person with only de facto possession has the right, *provided that person has possession.*[13] Even a licence to have mains service pipes in a stratum of land is a sufficient interest.[14] Someone with only a reversionary interest in land can sue if able to show *permanent* injury to the reversion. It used to be argued that a person with no interest in the land cannot sue.[15] However in *Hunter v Canary Wharf Ltd*[16] it was considered that all that is needed is a 'substantial link' between the enjoyment of land and that land, eg to occupy it as one's home. In *Masters v Brent London Borough Council,*[17] it was held that where there is a continuing actionable nuisance the person in possession of an interest in property can recover the loss incurred in remedying damage caused whether it occurred before or after acquisition of the land.

The interest must be of a sort recognised by law, and the law gives no remedy in respect of aesthetic nuisances. Ruining a view is thus no cause of action because there is no such thing as *purely* visual pollution. Those wishing to protect views must try to do so by obtaining restrictive convenants.

It is up to plaintiffs to prove the interference with their interests, though the degree of the interference required depends on the nature of the infringed interest. A riparian owner need only show a 'sensible' alteration in the quantity or quality of water,[18] while someone who alleges damage as a result of fumes, smell or noise must show actual damage.[19]

WHO CAN BE SUED?

The person who creates the nuisance is liable for it. Occupiers of land whence nuisances come may be liable also. They will be liable for nuisances committed by servants, and may be liable for the acts of independent contractors where they lead to special dangers for neighbours such as: interferences with rights of support;[20] the making of noise and dust;[1] the creation of fire hazards;[2] or where a nuisance arises on the highway.[3] Occupiers are not generally liable for nuisances arising either from the actions of a trespasser or from the operation of nature *unless* they either adopt the nuisance or, having actual or constructive knowledge of the state of affairs, fail to take reasonably early and effective abatement action.[4] Those who take on the occupation of property which is the source of a nuisance will become liable for it if it can be shown they knew or ought to have known of the state of affairs.[5]

13 *Foster v Warblington Urban District Council* [1906] 1 KB 648.
14 *Newcastle-under-Lyme Corpn v Wolstanton Ltd* [1947] Ch 427, [1947] 1 All ER 218.
15 *Malone v Laskey* [1907] 2 KB 141.
16 [1996] 1 All ER 482.
17 [1978] 1 QB 841, [1978] 2 All ER 664.
18 *Young v Bankier Distillery* [1893] AC 691.
19 *Halsey v Esso Petroleum Co Ltd* [1961] 2 All ER 145, [1961] 1 WLR 683.
20 *Bower v Peate* (1876) 1 QBD 321.
 1 *Matania v National Provincial Bank Ltd & Elevenist Syndicate Ltd* [1936] 2 All ER 633.
 2 *Spicer v Smee* [1946] 1 All ER 489.
 3 *Holliday v National Telephone Co* [1899] 2 QB 392.
 4 *Leakey v National Trust for Places of Historic Interest or Natural Beauty* [1978] QB 849, [1978] 3 All ER 234.
 5 *St Anne's Well Brewery Co v Roberts* (1928) 140 LT 1.

CAN A LANDLORD OUT OF POSSESSION BE LIABLE?

Generally landlords who have let land are not responsible for nuisances arising there unless they have either authorised the nuisance,[6] or if they knew or ought to have known of the nuisance *before* letting the property. Though such nuisances are unlikely to give rise to environmental hazards, it should be noted that landlords may also be liable for certain nuisances arising out of the state of disrepair of buildings they have let where there is either an express or implied right to enter and do repairs, or where they are under covenants to repair. In *Page Motors Ltd v Epsom and Ewell Borough Council*[7] a local authority was held liable for nuisances caused by gypsies on its land after it had failed to find proper sites for the gypsies and had not enforced possession orders against them.

FOR WHAT DAMAGE WILL THE DEFENDANT BE LIABLE?

It is for plaintiffs to show that they have suffered damage. This can cause problems of proof for plaintiffs who have, for example, suffered damage by multiple pollution from a variety of sources, but the law will allow them to recover the totality of loss, from anyone with whom they can establish a sufficient causal link.[8] In such circumstances the existence of another tortfeasor whose acts by themselves could be sufficient to produce the harm complained of will not excuse the person sued who must recover what has been paid in damages from fellow wrongdoers. Where it is the cumulative effect of a number of acts of pollution that results in an actionable wrong, the plaintiff may be able to bring one action against all those who can be shown to be responsible for the individual acts. See also *Pride of Derby and Derbyshire Angling Association v British Celanese Ltd*[9] where Harman J said: 'I cannot believe that the law, while holding all of a number of defendants liable if none of them individually commits an actionable wrong, will relieve the rest if the wrong of one of them is big enough by itself to be actionable.' Furthermore it is no defence to prove that the act of the defendant by itself is not a nuisance and only became so when combined with the act of others.[10] Once the plaintiff proves the nuisance and damage the defendant will, since the decision in *Overseas Tankship (UK) Ltd v Miller SS Co Pty, The Wagon Mound (No 2)*,[11] be liable for the reasonably foreseeable consequences of the nuisance.

In this context it is important to note the implications of *Cambridge Water Co v Eastern Counties Leather plc*.[12] A water company found one of its wells contaminated by perchloroethene (PCE), a chemical used in tanning. It was concluded that the chemical had percolated down to the water after having been spilled over a number of years on the defendants' premises. The PCE was present in quantities rendering the well unusable because of contravention of drinking water standards under Directive 80/778/EEC, laid down *after* the

6 *Pwllbach Colliery Co v Woodman* [1915] AC 634.
7 (1981) 125 Sol Jo 590.
8 *Clark v Newsam* (1847) 1 Exch 131.
9 [1952] 1 All ER 1326 at 1333.
10 *Thorpe v Brumfitt* (1873) 8 Ch App 650.
11 [1967] 1 AC 617, [1966] 2 All ER 709.
12 [1994] 2 AC 264.

chemical's escape. To pollute water percolating through to another's land *can be* an actionable nuisance where wells are contaminated, see *Ballard v Tomlinson*;[13] but not only must a causal link be shown, there must be foreseeability of the broad type of harm that will result from the defendant's acts. In the *Cambridge Water Co* case, at first instance Kennedy J would not accept 'pollution' as a broad 'type' of harm, nor that those responsible for the spillages in past years could have foreseen the creation of an environmental hazard, or a material affectation of water supplies. More importantly one reason the well could not be used was because of the existence nowadays of stricter water quality standards. Those responsible for past spillages could not have foreseen the development of those standards, and their *past* acts could *not* be considered wrongful simply because *present* knowledge and standards show the risk involved.

In the Court of Appeal, *Ballard v Tomlinson* (above), however, was treated as completely determinative of the issue, but this was reversed by the House of Lords. The House of Lords held that foreseeability of the *type* of damage which has eventuated *is a prerequisite for liability* in nuisance as in negligence. In the present case there could be no liability because the defendants could not possibly have foreseen that damage of the type complained of — ie that the presence of the chemical would contravene subsequent European drinking water standards — might be caused by their spillages.

The House of Lords denied liability for 'historic pollution', ie historic spillages or emissions of material not at the time of loss subject to regulation and so not then likely to give rise to a foreseeable type of damage. They added, significantly, that there could be no *future* liability for damage arising from such a spillage where the material in question is still in the land, and is now known to be polluting another's property, where that material has passed out of the defendant's control by percolating down through strata.

It must now be asked what degree of foresight will impose liability on a defendant. It would appear there must be foreseeability of the type of affectation which gives rise to the damage complained of, and this implies a degree of specificity. So foresight of possible mere contamination, following an activity, would probably be insufficient to ground liability; rather there should be foresight of the particular type of pollution (ie a harmful or illegal condition) which ultimately eventuates. Much will thus depend upon the facts of individual cases. In *Paterson v Humberside County Council*[14] householders claimed for damages to a house caused by a tree drying out soil of medium shrinkability. The soil conditions in the area were well known and the subject of local authority advice. It was held the damage in the circumstances was foreseeable.

Remedies

A person injured by a nuisance will wish to obtain recompense for loss and cessation of the activity. The law can award damages and an injunction, but it must be asked whether the practice of the courts with regard to these remedies produces the best possible results. As has been shown by Ogus and Richardson

13 (1885) 29 ChD 115.
14 [1995] Times, 19 April.

in 'Economics and the Environment: A Study of Private Nuisance' [1977] CLJ 284 (to whom the author acknowledges indebtedness), the results can be criticised when considerations of economic efficiency are taken into account because they do not always bring about the most good for the least cost; that is they do not always remedy the harm by the cheapest means.

DAMAGES

Damages are the principal remedy for loss. The common law will grant damages for past losses. Equitable damages can be awarded in respect of future loss, though the courts frown on such awards as they effectively enable the defendant to pay in advance for a continuation of his unlawful activity. Equitable damages may be awarded in lieu of an injunction (the Supreme Court Act 1981, s 50) only in exceptional circumstances where the injury to the plaintiff's rights is: (a) small, (b) capable of being estimated in monetary terms, (c) one which can be adequately compensated by small monetary payments, and (d) where it would be oppressive to the defendant to grant an injunction. Such circumstances rarely arise.[15]

Damages awarded by the common law will generally reflect the diminished market value of the plaintiff's property.[16] Where transient interference with the use and enjoyment of land only is claimed, for example a nuisance arising from smell, only modest sums will be awarded.[17] More substantial sums may be awarded for long standing or more offensive interferences with the enjoyment of land.[18]

INJUNCTIONS

An injunction is an order requiring the abatement of a nuisance. The remedy is awarded at the discretion of the court. The order may be

1 'Perpetual', an order issued at the final end of proceedings.
2 'Interlocutory', an order issued pending the outcome of proceedings but not prejudging the final result.
3 'Mandatory', an order requiring the defendant to take *positive* steps to remedy the wrong he has done.

An interlocutory injunction will only be granted where the plaintiff establishes there is a serious issue for trial, as in *Laws v Florinplace Ltd*[19] where such an injunction was granted to restrain the operation of a sex shop in a predominantly residential area, even though no breach of the criminal law had occurred. Thereafter the court must decide whether the balance of convenience lies in favour of granting interlocutory relief, see *American Cynamid Co v Ethicon Ltd*.[20] A mandatory injunction will generally only be awarded where the plaintiff can show a very strong probability that grave

---

15 *Shelfer v City of London Electric Lighting Co* [1895] 1 Ch 287 and *Kennaway v Thompson* [1981] QB 88, [1980] 3 All ER 329.
16 *Moss v Christchurch Rural District Council* [1925] 2 KB 750.
17 *Bone v Seale* [1975] 1 All ER 787, [1975] 1 WLR 797.
18 *Halsey v Esso Petroleum Co Ltd* [1961] 1 WLR 683.
19 [1981] 1 All ER 659.
20 [1975] AC 396, [1975] 1 All ER 504.

damage will accrue in the future, and that damages would not be an adequate remedy. Moreover the amount to be expended by the defendant in discharge of the injunction must also be taken into account. The court will be more ready to impose positive requirements on a defendant who has acted wantonly than on one who has acted reasonably and whose actions have yet to result in harm. When a mandatory injunction is issued the court must ensure that it is clear what the defendant has to do.[1] In *Tetley v Chitty*[2] local residents were awarded both damages and an injunction against a local authority which had allowed go-karts to race on its land under, first, a licence and then a seven year lease.

An injunction may be issued before the occurrence of actual damage *provided* the plaintiff can show that the defendant's conduct, if unchecked, is almost certain imminently to result in substantial damages. In such circumstances the injunction is known as '*quia timet*'.[3] Once granted an injunction may be suspended. This may be coupled with an award of damages in respect of loss suffered pending implementation. This practice is followed when it is desired not to impose an immediate crushing burden on the defendant. Where the immediate loss to the defendant would vastly outweigh any immediate gain to the plaintiff a suspension may be granted.[4] A suspension is also granted to enable a public utility to continue the supply of essential services.[5]

The courts generally fail to take into account the full economic consequences of an injunction for either the defendant or third parties. Ogus and Richardson show that in some parts of the US the courts take a much wider view of the consequences of their orders. In *Boomer v Atlantic Cement*,[6] the New York Court of Appeals dismissed an application for an injunction because the economic hardship to the defendant would have outweighed the benefit to the plaintiff. In *Madison v Ducktown Sulphur, Copper and Iron Co*,[7] an injunction was refused on the ground that the resulting loss to the community consequent on unemployment would be unacceptable. It is unlikely that such considerations will find their way into the decision making processes of English courts. Nevertheless, as Ogus and Richardson point out, the results of a decision may have unforeseen economic consequences. If, for example, polluting activity is stopped by injunction, it may lead to an increase in land values in the vicinity, and hence to the charging of higher rents and rates on properties in that locality; or it may lead to higher production costs with regard to particular goods.

SELF HELP

Occupiers may take action to abate nuisances which deleteriously affect them. In so acting they must not commit any unnecessary damage. Furthermore it

---

1 *Redland Bricks Ltd v Morris* [1970] AC 652, [1969] 2 All ER 576.

2 [1986] 1 All ER 663.

3 *Midland Bank plc v Bardgrove Property Services Ltd* (1992) 37 EG 126.

4 *Stollmeyer v Petroleum Development Co Ltd* [1918] AC 498n; *Halsey v Esso Petroleum Co Ltd* [1961] 2 All ER 145, [1961] 1 WLR 683; and *A-G v Gastonia Coaches Ltd* [1977] RTR 219.

5 *Prices Patent Candle Co v LCC* [1908] 2 Ch 526 and *Manchester Corpn v Farnworth* [1930] AC 171.

6 257 NE 2d 870 (1970).

7 83 SW 658 (1904).

seems that notice must be given to the responsible party before action is taken, unless the abatement can be effected without entering the party's land, or there is an emergency in that the nuisance threatens to cause immediate harm. See generally *Lemmon v Webb*.[8]

An assessment of nuisance as a remedy in cases of environmental damage

The tort of nuisance is subject to a number of drawbacks as a remedy in cases of environmental damage. These were identified by Ogus and Richardson and are enumerated below.

1   Bringing a nuisance action is costly.
2   Most individuals do not have the time, inclination or energy to involve themselves in litigation. Also where damage is caused by a major industrial undertaking the private citizen will be psychologically predisposed to be overawed by the 'size' of the opposition, and by fear of confrontation.
3   Few people perceive that environmental issues may be brought to court via litigation concerning individual rights.
4   Where such actions are brought they are fraught with problems, one of the most serious being that of proof. Where, for example, the damage complained of is industrial pollution the polluter will have access to more apparently convincing technological arguments and information than the private citizen has. An individual may also have grave initial problems in tracing a particular effect back to its alleged cause.

These basic defects in the law are not of recent origin, they were in existence in the nineteenth century when the manifest inadequacy of the common law to cope with the spread of industrial pollution finally led to legislative intervention which continues today. Readers are further referred to J P S McLaren 'Nuisance Law and the Industrial Revolution — Some Lessons from Social History' Oxford Journal of Legal Studies Vol 3, No 2, p 155. As McLaren makes clear, the pace of industrial change was generally too rapid for existing institutions, judicial or administrative, to be able to restrain the growth of polluting activity. Sadly, what McLaren has shown to be true of the nineteenth century remains readily observably true of our own times.

Liability under the rule in Rylands v Fletcher

The status and origins of the so called 'rule' in *Rylands v Fletcher*[9] were examined in the *Cambridge Water* case, with, potentially, some considerable consequences for the law. The House of Lords denied that *Rylands v Fletcher* is a separate head of tortious liability. Rather it is a specialised application of general nuisance principles under which where defendants collect material likely to do mischief if it escapes from their land, and there is an escape causing damage, liability is imposed even where the escape is an isolated event, and even where all reasonable care and skill has been used to prevent escapes.

Before considering the relationship of this type of liability to general issues it is necessary to analyse its component parts.

8 [1895] AC 1.
9 (1868) LR 3 HL 330.

1   Persons must bring and collect material on their land. There must be an accumulation of matter and not merely a natural process of nature. Both 'land' and the nature of defendants' interests in it receive extended meanings, and liability has attached to accumulations within strata, or by persons having licences to use land.[10]

2   Must the accumulation be for the defendant's own purposes? It is generally considered that an occupier who allows another to accumulate matter on that occupier's own land can be liable under the rule. A local authority which is statutorily required to permit the discharge of sewage into its sewers may be responsible for the resulting accumulation.[11]

3   The matter must be something likely to do mischief if it escapes. The rule is *not* one of liability for the escape of 'dangerous' things. Anything is capable of causing mischief according to the circumstances. In *Sullivan v Creed*[12] Gibson J said at 325–26: 'The question of liability depends on the particular circumstances, including the nature of the dangerous article, the place, the persons likely to be brought in contact with it and the time.' Proof by the defendant that the matter is not likely to do harm may preclude liability.[13]

4   There must be an escape from the place of accumulation to some other place outside the defendant's control.[14] Thereafter the defendant is prima facie strictly liable for damage caused. That will include damage to land and to the occupier's chattels on land. The *balance* of judicial opinion seems to favour allowing damages for personal injury under the rule, though no settled answer can be given on this point; contrast *Read v Lyons* with *Hale v Jennings Bros*,[15] *Miles v Forest Rock Granite Co (Leicestershire) Ltd*,[16] *Perry v Kendricks Transport Ltd*,[17] and *Shiffman v Venerable Order of St John of Jerusalem*.[18] The point was expressly left open in the *Cambridge Water* case. It does not seem possible to recover for pure economic loss, that is loss of money-making opportunity, see *Weller & Co v Foot and Mouth Disease Research Institute*.[19]

5   The land from which the escape takes place must be subject, as a result of the accumulation, to a 'non-natural use'. Such a use was defined in *Rickards v Lothian*[20] as one which is a 'special use bringing with it increased danger to others, and must not merely be the ordinary use of the land or such a use as is proper for the general benefit of the community'. Thus, creating a lavatory in a flat from whose piping filth escapes into the flat below falls within the 'natural use' exception;[1] similarly the overflow of

---

10   *Charing Cross West End and City Electricity Supply Co v London Hydraulic Power Ltd* [1914] 3 KB 772.
11   *Smeaton v Ilford Corpn* [1954] Ch 450, [1954] 1 All ER 923.
12   [1904] 2 IR 317.
13   *West v Bristol Tramways Co* [1908] 2 KB 14 at 21.
14   *Read v Lyons and Co Ltd* [1947] AC 156, [1946] 2 All ER 471.
15   [1938] 1 All ER 579.
16   (1918) 34 TLR 500.
17   [1956] 1 All ER 154, [1956] 1 WLR 85.
18   [1936] 1 All ER 557.
19   [1966] 1 QB 569, [1965] 3 All ER 560.
20   [1913] AC 263 at 280.
 1   *WH Smith Ltd v Daw* (1987) 2 Environmental Law No 1 p 5.

water from a domestic basin in *Rickards v Lothian*. On the other hand the House of Lords in the *Cambridge Water* case considered the storage and use of chemicals in substantial quantities an 'almost classic case of non-natural use'.

Unfortunately the House of Lords gave no further explicit guidance on the meaning of non-natural. However, by implication, it appears the provision of services to a local community or to a business park or industrial estate, for example the installation of a district heating system, would be considered 'natural' as being 'for the general benefit of the community'. On the other hand the accumulation and use of chemicals could not fall within the classification merely on the basis that it led to job creation which is a rather less specific form of community benefit.

6   The damage suffered in consequence of the escape must be of a foreseeable type. This was a debatable point before the *Cambridge Water* case, see *British Celanese v A H Hunt Ltd*,[2] but it is now settled, even though in settling the point the House of Lords specifically acknowledged they were turning away from creating a rule of general liability for injuries arising from ultra hazardous activities.

The general relationship of liability under *Rylands v Fletcher* with other forms of nuisance liability may now be considered. *Rylands v Fletcher* is merely an instance of nuisance in which the principles of nuisance liability are extended to cover cases of isolated escapes, with the consequent imposition of strict liability in the sense that pleading 'no fault' or 'all reasonable care was taken' will not serve as defences.

As liability is strict the defendant can only raise a limited number of defences. These are

1   Consent, express or implied.
2   Contributory negligence (reducing the damages payable).
3   That the accumulation is maintained for the common benefit of both parties, and this may extend to the operations of statutory undertakers with respect to the supply of essential services to the public as a whole.[3]
4   That an act of a stranger caused the escape provided that act was of a kind which the defendant could not reasonably have contemplated and guarded against.
5   An act or default of the plaintiff led to the damage.
6   An act of God, that is an escape occurring without human intervention following natural causes in circumstances which no human foresight could provide against, and whose occurrence human prudence cannot be expected to recognise as possible.
7   Statutory authority.

Liability can also be excluded by statute. Much depends on the activity in question and on the wording of the relevant provision. The courts generally require that the statute must expressly, or by necessary implication, authorise the doing of the activity; thereafter there will usually be no liability in respect

---

2 [1969] 2 All ER 1252, [1969] 1 WLR 959.
3 *Dunne v North Western Gas Board* [1964] 2 QB 806, [1963] 3 All ER 916.

of anything done in respect of a mandatory obligation, provided it is done in a non-negligent fashion. There can be liability for what is *permissively* authorised where the statute preserves liability for nuisance. (See also above on this issue.) Where no such liability is preserved there can only be liability for negligence, see *Geddis v Proprietors of Bann Reservoir*.[4]

Statutory forms of liability

As Carol Harlow shows in *Compensation and Government Torts* at pp 168–70 there are no general principles of liability in respect of breach of statutory obligations. In some cases liability is imposed, in others it is not. In some cases liability is strict, in others it is made dependent on proof of fault. Some statutes exclude civil liability, others are silent on the point. Each statute has to be looked at on an individual basis, though so far as public authorities are concerned liability is generally made dependent on proof of fault. It is also generally presumed that a statute passed for the benefit of the general public confers no private rights, and also that where the statute provides its own civil, administrative or criminal remedies they exclude other remedies. But these are only presumptions and in each area the relevant statutory provisions have to be construed.

It can, however, be said that no liability will arise simply by non-performance of a public statutory duty — the remedy there, if any, lies in public law by way of judicial review.[5] Furthermore where a public authority or utility is concerned it will be borne in mind by the courts that there are special responsibilities, and hence liabilities have to be considered in the light of statutory functions — and that means courts will not be anxious to impose liability.[6]

WATER

Under the Reservoirs Act 1975, s 28 and Sch 2, where damage or injury is caused by the escape of water from a reservoir constructed after 1930 under powers granted *after* July 1930 the fact that the reservoir was constructed under the statutory power does not exonerate the persons managing and controlling it from any proceedings for which they would *otherwise* be liable. Section 100 of the Water Resources Act 1991 provides that except as is specifically provided nothing in Part III of the Act (power to prevent and control pollution of water) confers any right of action in civil litigation, nor derogates from any rights otherwise existing, eg in respect of common law nuisances. Section 208 of the Act as amended by the Environment Act 1995 imposes liability on the Environment Agency for loss or damage caused by the escape of water, however caused, from a pipe vested in the Agency, though there is no liability, inter alia, where the escape was wholly due to the fault of the person suffering the loss, his agents or servants. Similar liability is imposed on water undertakers by s 209 of the Water Industry Act 1991. For civil liability in respect of unwholesome water supplies see chapter 12.

---

4 (1878) 3 App Cas 430.
5 *Glossop v Heston & Isleworth Local Board* (1879) 12 Ch D 102.
6 *Dear v Thames Water* (1993) 4 Water Law 116.

SEWERS AND DRAINS

Generally where sewers and drains are constructed under statutory authority there is no liability save on proof of negligence. Where injury results from an authority's failure or omission to improve or enlarge sewers and drains it has taken over from a predecessor to cope with the demands of a growing population there is no cause of action in negligence, see *Hesketh v Birmingham Corpn*.[7] Where an authority fails to enlarge sewers it has itself built, liability for overflow is dependent on the wording of the statute in question.

GAS

British Gas as a 'public gas supplier' for the supply of gas, is generally only liable where it can be shown to have acted negligently.[8] 'Public gas suppliers' are 'absolutely liable' for loss of life, personal injury or damage to property caused as a result of the underground storage of gas, save where the damage is suffered as a result of the fault of the plaintiff, his servants or agents, see the Gas Act 1965, s 14.

ELECTRICITY

Liability in respect of electricity is generally dependent on proof of fault; see, for example, *Hartley v Mayoh & Co*,[9] and *Collingwood v Home and Colonial Stores Ltd*.[10] However, by virtue of s 10 and Sch 4 of the Electricity Act 1989 licensed public electricity suppliers must do as little damage as possible in installing and maintaining electrical lines or plant over, under, on, along, in or across any street, must pay compensation in respect of any damage done in consequence of such installations or maintenance works, and must ensure the installations do not become a source of public danger. It would be negligence not to make reasonable use of those powers.[11]

POLLUTION ARISING FROM WASTE DEPOSITS

Where a person deposits or knowingly allows the deposit of poisonous, noxious or polluting waste on land, civil liability may arise under *Rylands v Fletcher* as this is almost certainly a non-natural use of land. Liability, which is strict, also arises where the circumstances constitute an offence under ss 33(1) and 63(2) of the Environmental Protection Act 1990; see s 73(6)–(9) of that Act. Where waste is deposited on land in such circumstances that an offence is committed (see chapter 9) and damage (including the death of or injury to any person, and impairment of physical or mental condition) is caused thereby, the person depositing, or knowingly causing or permitting the deposit of the waste is liable for that damage. Defences *include* showing that the damage was the victim's fault, or that the victim voluntarily accepted the risk of damage.

---

7 [1924] 1 KB 260.
8 *Pearson v North Western Gas Board* [1968] 2 All ER 669.
9 [1954] 1 QB 383, [1954] 1 All ER 375.
10 [1936] 3 All ER 200.
11 *Howard-Flanders v Maldon Corpn* (1926) 135 LT 6.

Stricter liability for damage caused by waste *could* eventuate from the development and implementation of the proposed EU Directive on Civil Liability for Damage Caused by Waste, 8734/89: COM(89) 282. This proposed that producers of waste (other than nuclear waste) should be liable, irrespective of fault, for damage (ie death, personal injury or damage to property) or injury to the environment (ie significant and persistent interference with the environment caused by modifications of the physical, chemical or biological condition of water, soil and/or air). Remedies would be available (subject to a three year limitation period) to prohibit the deleterious activity in question, to ensure reimbursement of the costs of preventative action, to bring about restoration of the environment, and to indemnify for damage suffered. The burden of proof and of causation would lie on the plaintiff, and the defendant would be the 'producer' of the waste, ie any person whose occupation produces waste, and anyone else who pre-processes, mixes, or otherwise operates with waste so that it changes its nature or composition, including persons who import waste into the EU, and those who had actual control of the waste when the damaging incident occurred. It also proposes that 'public authorities' could take action in respect of injuries to the environment.

FURTHER, MORE GENERAL, PROPOSALS

More far reaching notions were put forward in 7099/93: COM (93) 47, a Green Paper on remedying environmental damage which was intended to provoke discussion without containing firm proposals. The basic concepts were (a) civil liability, an appropriate system of obtaining a remedy where there is an identifiable person to be sued, and a clear causal link between that person's specific acts or omissions and the damage, such a system being based on either fault or strict liability, (b) joint compensation schemes which are appropriate to deal with cases of chronic or cumulative pollution where a specific defendant or incident cannot be identified. The basic concept of such a compensation scheme is that relevant operators must make contributions to create a fund — a type of collective insurance — out of which payment is made for environmental damage to be remediated. The levies made would be variable and would be linked to the type of damage to be remediated. In the United States such a concept already exists in the Superfund which exists under the Comprehensive Environmental Response Compensation Liability Act 1980 which imposes liabilities in respect of clean up measures, and is at once retrospective, strict, joint and several, applying to current owners of affected sites, owners at the time damage occurred, those who have generated the harm causing waste or who have transported it, or dealt in it. Superfund meets the initial costs of emergency clean ups and then a Federal body, the Environment Protection Agency, is able to take specific action against liable parties, in order to recover the costs, which can be considerable as remediation is carried out to a very high standard.

The Green Paper built on the previous proposal for a directive on damage caused by waste. It must also be considered in the light of the Council of Europe's Convention on Civil Liability of 1993 for damage resulting from activities dangerous to the environment. This is a Convention under which a system of strict liability would arise in respect of those who have control of 'dangerous activities', ie activities professionally performed and involving dangerous substances, which are those having properties constituting a significant risk for humans, the environment or property. The environment in this context embraces air, water, soil, fauna, flora, property forming part of the cultural heritage and characteristic aspects of the landscape. Though there would be a number of specific defences, the basic strict liability concept would require relevant operators to maintain financial guarantees up to limits specified by the domestic law of individual signatory states. Multiple operators involved in the creation of damage would be generally jointly and severally liable for all the damage. This Convention mirrors the scheme of civil liability for environmental damage resulting from nuclear installations or oil spills under the Paris and Brussels Conventions of 1960 and 1969 respectively, which are in force in the UK, see further below.

'YOU IN YOUR SMALL CORNER AND I IN MINE?'

The response of the United Kingdom government to the various recent proposals has not been enthusiastic. Appealing to the principle of subsidiarity the government has opposed any pan-union measures by the European Union, but has not been very clear about its own proposals, save to put forward the measures now contained in the Environment Act 1995 dealing with contaminated land (see chapter 9 below). The issue was, however, expertly investigated by the House of Lords Select Committee on the European Communities Session 1993–94, 3rd Report 'Remedying Environment Damage', to which interested readers must be referred. The conclusions of this body can only be briefly summarised here. [References are made to the 'Community' because that is the word used by the Committee, elsewhere in this book references are given to the European Union (EU).]

1   It is prudent for the Community to adopt a framework directive to require programmes of remediation of past pollution paid for by polluters but supplemented where necessary, by State and Community funds. *Future* polluting activities should be subject to a system of strict liability reinforced by a system of financial security covering those who carry out potentially damaging operations (see further below). This framework would provide safeguards and remedies additional to those in domestic law, while, specifically, the law of the United Kingdom should extend to provide compensation for economic loss consequent on environmental damage. For these purposes the definitions of environment and damage adopted under the Council of Europe Convention (above) should apply. However, where no one has suffered direct and quantifiable damage and reinstatement measures will not immediately rectify the damage, compensation payments should be limited to the actual quantifiable costs of restoration rather than extending to cover loss of enjoyment and amenity.

2   Where a current site owner or process operator can be shown to be responsible for past incidents of pollution there should be strict liability where the owner/operator knew or should have known the activities were potentially dangerous.

3   New site owners, it should be presumed, take on responsibility for past damage, though this should be rebuttable where it can be shown the owner did not and could not reasonably have known environmental damage had

been or was likely to have been caused. Clearly such a proposal depends on potential owners making site history inquiries before purchase (see further chapter 9 below on contaminated land).

4 Where a site owner cannot be made liable under the foregoing principles liability should be on the taxpayer, with Community support where appropriate.

5 Programmes of remediation should take as their priority the ending of continuing harm or the likelihood of harm. The programmes should be nationally phased taking into account accurate data on contamination. The standard set for remediation should be consistent with an inheritance free of danger, and should enable as wide a range of possible land uses as achievable without excessive cost.

6 The legal basis with regard to *future* pollution should be that the environment is handed on in an unimpaired state, and thus strict (though not absolute) civil liability is certainly justified in respect of those who knowingly engage in dangerous or potentially dangerous activities. Such a new legal regime should come into operation on a set date ('D' day) announced some years in advance to enable operators to prepare to meet the new standard of liability. In respect of synergistic pollution, ie that occurring when a pollutant emitted *after* 'D' day combines with one emitted *before*, the controller of the operation giving rise to the second emission should be strictly liable.

7 There should be after 'D' day a limited number of defences available, *not* including compliance with regulatory standards. It should be a defence that pollution was caused by *force majeure*, and also that the operator complied with 'state of the art' practices, ie that at the date of the damaging incident, the operator can establish that, given the state of scientific and technical knowledge, it cannot have been expected that the activity could cause a damaging outcome. Furthermore there should be a limitation period of three years from the date the plaintiff became aware of or should have become aware of the damage, with a 'long stop' period of 30 years from the date of the first occurrence of the pollution leading to the damage.

8 Debate on, and resolution of, the issue of burdens of proof and causation is needed. If the present system where the burden of proof is on the plaintiff is retained there is a case for mandatory record keeping by appropriate operators (exactly who is as yet unclear) and an early disclosure in litigation of the scientific evidence of the parties. [This portion of the report it has to be admitted is much less conclusive and convincing than the rest of the argument.]

9 The new regime should apply to *all* incidents of *environmental damage caused by pollution* (ie the introduction of harmful or potentially harmful substances to the environment, not just those arising from dangerous or exceptionally dangerous activities) but should not extend to impose post 'D' day style liability retrospectively. Past incidents must be dealt with according to present principles, though subject to some modification, see paragraph 2 (above).

However, the prime liability under the new regime should always rest on the person controlling the damaging activity. If a number of operators whose independent acts combine to cause damage each should be separately liable on a pro rata basis. Where parties act in concert, however, to cause damage the present principles of joint and several liability should apply.

10 In respect of the 'unowned environment', eg water percolating through undefined channels, an adequately resourced public body should be under a duty to seek compensation for polluting activities under the new regime, and to carry out necessary remediation work. Where such a body came across a situation where prima facie there was a case for initiating legal action, but decided not to do so, it should be under a duty to state its reasons for that decision.

11 Special considerations would apply to the position of lenders on the security of affected land and insurers under the new regime. Lenders who take possession of affected land to enforce their security should not be liable for the acts of their borrowers provided they have acted responsibly in advancing finance: the position should be otherwise where an operator is financed without being checked as to its record of safe and responsible management. Lenders should be responsible where their lending enables a potentially harmful operation to proceed which they could prevent. Insurers, however, cannot be expected to meet *all* future environmental liabilities and financial cover *beyond* a high set limit will be needed. This points to the need for joint compensation schemes contributed to by relevant operators. However, the need for insurance and for financial security could be prerequisites (reinforced by sanctions against those attempting to evade the responsibility) for operators wishing to carry out activities capable of causing environmental damage. Financial security may be evidenced by the possession of insurance cover, or adequate 'own funds' to meet liabilities, and the report also countenances obligatory participation in joint compensation schemes, contributions to which would be based on assessments of the risks involved, and the scale of the intended operation. Even so there would have to be pre-set ceilings for liability under insurance, self insurance or joint compensation schemes, with liabilities in excess of those having to be met by more broadly based levies on broad sections of industry, or on the insurance industry, with the tax payer as the ultimate source of funding.

These recommendations await future action, for now we return to the current law.

DAMAGE FROM NUCLEAR INSTALLATIONS

The liability of the United Kingdom Atomic Energy Authority or other licensed bodies is contained in the Nuclear Installations Act 1965, which lays down a comprehensive and exclusive code of liability. Without a nuclear site licence no person may use a site for the purpose of installing or operating a nuclear installation such as a nuclear reactor or plant designed or adapted for the production or use of atomic energy or associated ancillary purposes, or for the storage, processing or disposal of nuclear fuel or other bulk quantities of radioactive matter resulting from the production or use of nuclear fuel. See s 1 of the 1965 Act. Section 7 of that Act imposes strict liability in respect of certain occurrences on or in connection with the uses of licensed nuclear sites, and s 8 imposes similar liability on the Atomic Energy Authority. There must be no occurrences involving nuclear matter (that is under s 26(1) fissile uranium or plutonium or radioactive material associated therewith) actually on site, nor elsewhere nor concerned with the carriage of such matter on behalf of the site licensee, save (in regard to carriage and occurrences *not* on the licensed site) where the matter though 'nuclear' is 'excepted' under s 26(1) of the Act (that is it consists only of industrial, commercial, agricultural, medical, educational or scientific isotopes, or is natural uranium, or any other uranium of which isotope 235 forms not more than 1%, or is matter of any other prescribed description). Furthermore there must be no ionising radiation emitted during the period of the licensee's responsibility either from anything caused or suffered by the licensee to be on the site which is not nuclear matter, or from any waste discharged in any form on or from the site. Strict liability arises when injury to a person or damage to property arises from radiation or from a combination of radiation and the toxic, explosive or other hazardous properties of nuclear matter. However, the damage must be physical, not purely economic loss, and it must relate to tangible, not incorporeal property or property rights, see *Merlin v British Nuclear Fuels plc*.[12] There is no need to prove an escape from the site and there is a statutory right to compensation which may be reduced if the injury was partly caused by the plaintiff himself doing an act with 'the intention of causing harm to any person or property or with reckless disregard for the consequences of his act', see ss 12 and 13 of the 1965 Act.

The maximum period for bringing an action under the 1965 Act is 30 years from the occurrence giving rise to the claim, or, where the occurrence was a continuing one, or one of a succession all attributable to a particular happening on site, 30 years from the last relevant date, see s 15(1) of the 1965 Act. Where injury is caused by a breach of duty imposed under ss 7–10 of the 1965 Act compensation in respect of the injury is payable wherever it occurred, but no other liability is incurred by any person in respect of it. Any injury or damage not actually caused by the breach but also not reasonably separable from injury so caused is deemed to have been caused by the breach, see s 12.

Claims arising under duties imposed by the 1965 Act to the extent to which, though duly established, they are not payable by the persons subject to the duties, *or* which are made after the expiry of the period of the first ten years after the occurrence, *or* arise in respect of injury arising from occurrences involving nuclear material stolen from, or lost, jettisoned or abandoned by persons subject to the duties where the claim is made after the expiry of 20 years from the date of loss, etc, must be made to the appropriate authority, generally the Secretary of State [ie the DTI]. During the first ten years after an occurrence claims are generally made to the licensed body or authority. Under s 16(1) of the 1965 Act as amended by the Energy Act 1983, s 27, enacted to satisfy international obligations, and to counter the effects of inflation, liability to pay compensation is limited to £140m in the aggregate in respect of any one occurrence, or £10m in the case of certain prescribed small operators, see SI 1994/909. These sums may be increased by order.

Under s 19 of the 1965 Act, as amended by the Atomic Energy Act 1989, licensees must make ministerially approved arrangements to make funds

12 [1990] 2 QB 557, [1990] 3 All ER 711.

available to satisfy claims made up to the amounts required under s 16. To meet claims over these limits there is an obligation under s 18 of the 1965 Act, as amended by s 28 of the 1983 and 1989 Acts, to make available, in the case of any relevant nuclear occurrence, out of money provided by Parliament, such necessary sums as will meet in the initial ten-year period claims *up to an aggregate* amount per incident of 300m 'special drawing rights' as defined by the International Monetary Fund under s 30 of the 1983 Act, though the value of a drawing right will vary from day to day according to agreed formulae. Thus a serious nuclear incident causing damage exceeding a licensee's insurance provision would place a burden on public funds. This contribution is in the nature of a 'top-up'; the sum of 300m special drawing rights represents an aggregation of public funds with those made available by the licensee to meet his obligations. Under s 16(3) of the 1965 Act where a claim is made to the Secretary of State's satisfaction, and to the extent that it cannot be satisfied out of sums provided under s 18, it must be satisfied out of funds provided by such means as Parliament may determine.

The Congenital Disabilities (Civil Liability) Act 1976, s 3, lays down that where a child is born disabled as the result of an injury to either of its parents caused in breach of duty imposed by any of ss 7–11 of the 1965 Act, the child's injuries are to be regarded as injuries caused on the same occasion and by the same breach of duty as was the injury to the parent. Thus where the child's disabilities are attributable to an incident under the 1965 Act compensation can be payable. However, under s 3(5) of the 1976 Act compensation is not payable in the child's case if the injury to the parent preceded the time of the child's conception, and at that time either or both of the parents knew the particular risk arising from the injury was that their child might be born disabled. The 1976 Act also declares that any occurrence under the 1965 Act which affects the ability of a man or a woman to have a normal healthy child, or which affects a pregnant woman so that her child is consequently disabled, is an injury for the purposes of compensation under the 1965 Act.

It is a defence to a claim under the Act to show an occurrence was attributable to hostile action in the course of armed conflict, but natural disasters, even if entirely exceptional, causing occurrences give no ground for a defence, see s 13(4) of the 1965 Act. Act of the Queen's enemies may be a defence, but act of God, for example an earthquake, it not. On a voluntary basis, and without concession of liability, British Nuclear Fuels Limited (BNFL) and the United Kingdom Atomic Energy Authority (UKAEA) operate a scheme to compensate dependents of current and past employees dying from leukaemia or other forms of cancer. The scheme does not extend to other persons. The Ministry of Defence announced in 1992 a similar scheme for certain service personnel and civilian employees suffering from cancer and previously exposed to radiation.

The problem lying at the heart of imposing liability for nuclear incidents is, as made clear by Christopher Miller in 'Radiological Risks and Civil Liability' (1989) 1 Journal of Environmental Law 10, that of causation. It *may* be comparatively easy to attribute effect to cause where a major nuclear incident occurs and those on site at the time display 'radiation sickness' symptoms thereafter. It is much harder to show causation where a person in the vicinity of a nuclear installation simply develops cancer over a period of years. In the circumstances there is much to commend Dr Miller's thesis that an alternative compensatory approach, based on enhanced social security and other pension benefits and funded by novel taxes on the activities of the nuclear industry, needs to be examined.

The causation issue was well illustrated by *Reay v BNFL plc* and *Hope v BNFL plc*.[13] In both cases compensation was sought for injury outside BNFL's concessionary scheme. Mrs Reay claimed damages in respect of her daughter who had died of childhood leukaemia, while Miss Hope claimed for affectation by non-Hodgkin's lymphoma. Mrs Reay's husband and Miss Hope's father had worked at Sellafield for many years. It was alleged that there had been exposure to plant radiation *outside* the plant while the children were in their mothers' wombs, and after birth, that radiation from the plant had damaged their mothers' ova pre-conception, and, novelly, that the fathers had suffered genetic damage to their sperm pre-conception and this had been passed on to the children. 90 days of hearings with evidence from 30 scientific witnesses — the most expensive civil action on record — led to a conclusion by French J that the plaintiffs had failed to prove on the balance of probabilities that BNFL had *caused* the injuries by breach of its statutory duties.

The overall problem is twofold. First, the scientific epidemiological evidence is simply inconclusive, and often contradictory, as to the link between exposure or radiation and subsequent development of cancer. Secondly, in any given population a number of people will die from cancer, and it appears impossible generally to distinguish a radiation-induced cancer from one otherwise occurring.

MARINE OIL POLLUTION

The Merchant Shipping (Oil Pollution) Act 1971 was enacted so that the UK could ratify the 1969 Convention on Civil Liability for Oil Pollution Damage, which was agreed in consequence of the *Torrey Canyon* disaster. The 1971 Act was extensively modified by the Merchant Shipping Act 1988 Sch 4 to give force to the International Convention on Civil Liability for Oil Pollution Damage 1984, and the International Convention on the Establishment of an International Fund for Compensation for Oil Pollution Damage 1984. The 1971 Act was further amended by the Merchant Shipping (Salvage & Pollution) Act 1994 which took account of 1992 revisions to the principal convention, ie that of 1969, see the International Convention on Civil Liability for Oil Pollution 1992. The 1994 Act also reflected recommendations made by the Donaldson Report 'Safer Ships Cleaner Seas' following the *Braer* disaster in the Shetlands in 1993. The 1994 Act's commencement details are to be found in SI 1994/1988, however, in 1995 the various provisions (along with many others) were consolidated in the Merchant Shipping Act 1995. The relevant provisions are now found in Part VI, chapter III of the 1995 Act. The 1995 Act came into force on 1 January 1996, see s 316.

The law provides that where as a result of any occurrence *any* persistent oil escapes or is discharged from any ship constructed or adapted for carrying oil in bulk as cargo, the ship owner will be liable for any damage caused in the UK by resulting *contamination*, for the cost of preventative and mitigatory action,

13 [1992] 4 LMELR 195, [1993] 5 ELM 178.

see s 153, and likewise for preventative or mitigatory action taken when there is a grave and imminent risk of such contamination. 'Contamination' will not cover damage by the oil catching fire, but some economic loss is recoverable if that is the direct and natural result of the pollution. 'Threat removal' costs may thus be claimed, and the law will also cover tankers in ballast where their bunkers give rise to pollution. 'Oil' is defined, by s 170 as 'hydrocarbon mineral oil'. The Convention defines 'persistent oil' as crude oil, fuel oil, heavy diesel, lubricating or whale oil, however. Damage under the Act is defined as including 'loss', and, under s 156(3) this will extend to 'any impairment of the environment' where this consists of 'any resulting loss of profits and the cost of any reasonable measures of reinstatement actually taken or to be taken.' Causation of such 'impairment loss' would have to be proved by any given plaintiff. The 1994 Act extended the 1971 strict liability regime to damage and the cost of pollution operations caused by persistent oil from *any* source from *any* ship — including vessels which are not sea going, see now s 154 of the 1995 Act.

Section 155 exempts ship owners from liability in cases of discharges/escapes resulting from wars or hostile action, exceptional, inevitable and irresistible natural phenomena, the activities of third parties intending to do damage, or the failure of navigation authorities to maintain lights or navigation aids. Under s 157, liability is limited in respect of relevant events to a sum defined by reference to 'special drawing rights' calculated according to International Monetary Fund figures. However, the limitation does *not* apply, under s 157(3), where it is proved the event resulted from acts or omissions of the ship owner intentionally or recklessly committed and in the knowledge that damage/costs would probably result. The limitation on liability may be uprated to take account of inflation, see s 157(2). Section 163 of the 1995 Act imposes requirements for compulsory insurance against pollution liabilities in respect of ships carrying in bulk cargoes of more than 2,000 tons of persistent oil, and s 165 further allows an injured party to sue the insurer directly where such compulsory cover exists.

To cover cases where there is an exemption from liability under the 1995 Act, or where owners cannot meet their obligations in full, or where the damage suffered exceeds the 1995 Act's limit, under the 1971 International Convention on the Establishment of an International Fund for Oil Pollution Damage, the Merchant Shipping Act 1974 made provision for a fund raised by levies on specified oil importers, see now Part VI, chapter IV of the 1995 Act.

Though the United Kingdom has a *regulatory* regime for the carriage of dangerous *goods* of various sorts, see eg SI 1990/2605, made under s 21 of the Merchant Shipping Act 1979, *civil* liability remains dependent on the ordinary rules of negligence, etc until such time as an international convention can be agreed.

It is clear that the role of strict liability is limited in case law and under statute.

Liability for negligence

Actions for negligence constitute the majority of civil claims, but the usefulness of such actions in environmental litigation is limited. An action for negligence may be the only remedy available to a person who cannot sue for nuisance because of technicalities. Also liability for certain types of statutorily authorised or permitted activity is dependent upon proof of negligence.

Nevertheless the usefulness of negligence remains limited. This is partly because of the existence of nuisance (though dicta in *Goldman v Hargrave*,[14] suggest that many nuisance actions could equally well be fought in negligence) and also because negligence requires proof of the defendant's fault. This, as has been stated with regard to both nuisance and strict liability, is never easy. Before this is examined at length, a *brief* description of the ingredients of negligence as a tort is necessary.

Negligence as a tort

Negligence as an independent tort dates from *Donoghue v Stevenson*:[15] development since has been great. It has a number of elements.

1   Duty of care — a legal requirement that the situation is one in which the defendant must show care towards the plaintiff. The existence of a duty of care is not conclusive of the question of liability, for it only determines that the area of activity in question is one where liability is potentially capable of existing. The recent attitude of the courts is to be wary of extending situations in which a duty of care applies. So in *Stephens v Anglian Water Authority*[16] the Court of Appeal denied the existence of a duty of care in respect of the abstraction of water flowing in undefined channels under their land by defendants, even where this led to damage to the plaintiff's land, and in *Gunn v Wallsend Slipway and Engineering Co Ltd*,[17] it was held that no duty of care existed in respect of a woman who had died of mesothelioma after inhaling asbestos dust from clothes worn by her husband while working in the defendants' shipyard. The same conclusion was reached in *Hewett v Alf Brown's Transport*,[18] but it is otherwise if there is an occupational link with asbestos, or one based on living and playing amidst asbestos dust.[19] Similar reticence can be seen in Scotland where in *Landcatch Ltd v Gilbert Gillies*[20] no duty of care was found to exist in respect of loss of profit following the death of young salmon brought about by a failure in a system to pump salt water through their tanks. Though there have been cases where supplying agencies have been held subject to a duty of care to warn, in respect of polluted material,[1] the general consensus, particularly since the generally restrictive attitude towards duty of care shown by the House of Lords in *Murphy v Brentwood District Council*,[2] is that a solely *regulatory* agency would not be liable simply because a person suffers pollution damage in consequence of activities of which a warning *could* have been given, but was not, see *Dear v Thames Water*[3] and in the context of planning, *Ryeford Homes Ltd v Sevenoaks District Council*.[4]

14 [1967] 1 AC 645, [1966] 2 All ER 989.
15 [1932] AC 562.
16 [1987] 3 All ER 379, [1987] 1 WLR 1381.
17 (1989) Times, 23 January.
18 [1992] 4 LMELR 48.
19 *Hancock v JW Roberts Ltd* (1996) Times, 17 April.
20 1990 SLT 688.
 1 *Barnes v Irwell Valley Water Board* [1939] 1 KB 21, *Scott-Whitehead v National Coal Board* (1987) 53 P & CR 263.
 2 [1991] 1 AC 398, [1990] 2 All ER 908.
 3 (1993) 4 Water Law 116.
 4 (1989) 46 BLR 34.

2   Breach of the standard of care imposed under the duty of care — this requirement is that there is a failure to act reasonably in a situation where reasonable care is required. What is reasonable care in any given situation is dependent on the facts of the case, and the activity being carried on. Much will depend on the degree of risk of harm.

3   Damage, which must have been factually caused by breach of duty, and which must be the reasonably foreseeable consequence of the breach. Again, however, as with nuisance it must be asked *what* is it that must be foreseeable?

A plaintiff may meet great difficulties in proving that a defendant has been in breach. Breach is nowadays thought of as an unreasonable failure to achieve the standard of care required by law. What is required in any given case will depend on many factors, including the magnitude of the risk (that is its probable gravity, imminence and frequency) the utility of the defendant's actions (that is the social importance of the desired objective) and the burden of taking adequate precautions to eliminate the risk. Once the appropriate standard of care has been set defendants will generally be accepted as having discharged it, and as having acted reasonably, if they can show they acted according to the general and approved practices of the particular sphere of activity in question. Conformation with generally accepted practice is the usual way to defeat allegations of negligence. Of course, to have followed a standard practice that is itself obviously risky will afford the defendant no defence, and those who wish to show that they have followed safe and reasonable standard practices must show that practice has kept abreast of new developments in knowledge, science and technology. Nevertheless to have followed usual trade or professional practices will generally afford a good defence in a negligence action, as will having acted according to received professional opinion. Once such a defence is available it will not be defeated by showing that the defendant was responsible for an error of judgment within the ambit of exercise of reasonable skill, nor by showing a failure to know of a risk beyond any reasonable scientific appreciation. Such a defence can only be defeated by superior expert testimony showing the inherently risky nature of accepted practice, or that the defendant's action fell below accepted levels of practice. So, for example, knowingly to continue a risky operation, and to pay workers 'danger money' to induce their continued attendance rather than expend money on safety measures may point towards breach of duty.[5]

Within the sphere of environmental hazards, defeating a defence of compliance with good professional practice will be virtually impossible for the ordinary citizen, though where an operator has been convicted of an offence arising from the same circumstances as the harm in question this can be used as evidence against the defendant. The problems of expense and lack of technological 'know-how' considered in relation to nuisance actions apply with even more force to allegations of negligence. This can be shown by illustrations from decided cases. In *Pearson v North Western Gas Board*,[6] the plaintiff and her husband were injured and their home was destroyed as a result of an explosion of gas which had escaped from a gas main and

5 *Hancock v JW Roberts Ltd* (1996) Times, 17 April.
6 [1968] 2 All ER 669.

accumulated under the floor boards. The gas had been able to escape because movements in the soil consequent on severe frost had fractured the main. The mains themselves had been laid 2ft 9in below the soil level in 1878 and, as the metal was in good condition, were expected to last 120 years. Expert evidence for the defendants showed that no reasonable steps were open to safeguard the public from the consequences of such fractures. It was held that such expert evidence rebutted any case of negligence against the defendants.

An example of the difficulties inherent in proving negligence in the conduct of allegedly environmentally damaging operations is *Budden v BP Oil Ltd*.[7] This was an important case, one of a number brought by persons then campaigning to eliminate lead from petrol. A number of parents in London brought an action on behalf of their children alleging damage to health consequent on the presence of lead in petrol. The case ran for over two years, during which time the litigation was held up by allegations that the parents were unfit to act on behalf of the children, and that the action was an abuse of the procedure of the court. The Court of Appeal ruled that the case must be struck out. It was found that the oil companies had complied with regulations made by the Secretary of State for the purpose of controlling pollution. It was presumed that those regulations had been made only after consideration of all relevant factors applicable throughout the country, not just matters affecting health in one locality. Where Parliament has sanctioned a general policy and associated standards after due enquiry, it is not negligent to comply with that policy and standards. It is not for the courts to make decisions which might have the effect of requiring compliance with a different and inconsistent policy.

Further major problems arise, not just in negligence but also in nuisance, when it comes to the issue of proving that the defendant's act *caused* the plaintiff loss. Thus for example in a case where it is alleged a particular plant has emitted substances toxic to animals and humans it is not necessary to prove that the defendant knew the precise physico-chemical details of the process leading to such emissions. It is enough to show knowledge that the plant can and does emit substances toxic to animals and humans. But as a factual issue it is also necessary to prove that those substances were actually emitted, that they were transported to the plaintiff's land where the plaintiff's animals ingested them and that that led to the injury complained of. With high technical modern processes this can be a very hard task indeed.[8]

B LIABILITY FOR SUBSIDENCE

As identified in the 1981 report, 'Coal and the Environment', the problems of subsidence include

1   Damage to land and buildings, not just those immediately above workings, but also those within a 'critical area' which is some 1.4 times the seam depth. So, for example, where a seam of coal is 500m deep, buildings 'will be affected by all workings within 700m of the point vertically beneath [them] . . .'.

7 (1980) 124 Sol Jo 376.
8 *Graham & Graham v Rechem International* [1995] 7 ELM 175.

2 Damage possibly continuing over a period of years as working progresses and even after it has ceased.
3 Damage effects being aggravated and made even more unpredictable where the land has geological faults.
4 Damage extending to subsurface installations such as pipes and cables.
5 Increased drainage problems in ill-drained areas.
6 Sterilisation of surface land so it cannot be developed.
7 Emotional strain and stress for affected landholders.

This problem has been an issue for centuries. *At common law* a landowner has a right of support for his land in its natural state from adjacent and subjacent land of other owners. The right of support exists even in respect of underlying beds of rock salt,[9] or of wet sand or silt[10] but *not* in respect of water;[11] nor will a claim lie in negligence in respect of subsidence caused by the abstraction of water flowing in undefined subterranean channels.[12] There is no *natural* right of support for buildings, see *Dalton v Angus*.[13] Such a right may, of course, be acquired as an easement by way of grant or prescription, etc. In the case of structures erected by statutory undertakers a right of support will generally arise under the relevant statutory provisions. Where ownership of minerals is severed from the land surface, the owner of the minerals may not let down the land unless he acts under statute or the express words of the grant of minerals — in such cases everything depends on the wording of the grant in question, see *Davies v Powell Duffryn Steam Coal Co Ltd (No 2)*.[14] The initial rights of the parties may be varied by subsequent events, though the burden of proof is on the party claiming the common law right of support has been varied.[15] This is especially so in regard to claims that the right of support has been *impliedly* granted away.[16]

Withdrawal of support becomes an actionable nuisance when subsidence occurs: each successive subsidence gives rise to a further cause of action, see *Darley Main Colliery Co v Mitchell*.[17] (An injunction *may* be sought to preserve the land from future or further subsidence.) At common law the person who made the excavation leading to the subsidence will be liable. Liability will exist where the condition of the land had been changed to a substantial extent by subsidence, even though there is no proof of pecuniary loss, see *A-G v Conduit Colliery Co*,[18] and Willes J in *Bonomi v Backhouse*,[19] who stated a landowner is entitled to have land 'remain in its natural state, unaffected by any act done in the neighbouring land.' Liability is *not* dependent, it seems, on proof of fault, see *Humphries v Brogden*.[20] The right to damages arises by the invasion of the surface owner's rights. Where no appreciable loss is suffered by reason of

9 *Lotus Ltd v British Soda Co Ltd* [1972] Ch 123, [1971] 1 All ER 265.
10 *Jordeson v Sutton, Southcoates and Drypool Gas Co* [1899] 2 Ch 217.
11 *Popplewell v Hodkinson* (1869) LR 4 Exch 248.
12 *Stephens v Anglian Water Authority* [1987] 3 All ER 379, [1987] 1 WLR 1381.
13 (1881) 6 App Cas 740.
14 (1921) 91 LJ Ch 40.
15 *Davies v Treharne* (1881) 6 App Cas 460.
16 *Butterley Co Ltd v New Hucknall Colliery Co Ltd* [1910] AC 381.
17 (1886) 11 App Cas 127.
18 [1895] 1 QB 301.
19 (1859) EB & E 646 at 657.
20 (1850) 12 QB 739.

subsidence, damages may be nominal. Where a right of support for buildings has been acquired, damages will be recovered if buildings are affected. Even where no such right exists the value of buildings may be recovered *if their weight has not contributed to the subsidence.*[1]

Public law controls

So far as the construction and maintenance of railways, waterworks and sanitary works is concerned the position is governed by the 'mining codes' of the Railways Clauses Consolidation Act 1845, as amended post 1923 by the Mines (Working Facilities and Support) Act 1923, the Waterworks Clauses Act 1847 and the Water Act 1945 as the case may be (see further 31 Halsbury's Laws (4th edn) paras 66–108).

With regard to coal mining subsidence the law has gone through a number of stages of development, the history of which may be found in the second edition of this work.

The current law originated in proposals made in the Subsidence Compensation Review Committee's 1984 Report 'The Repair and Compensation System for Coal Mining Subsidence Damage'. The government made its response to the reform proposals in 'The Repair and Compensation System for Coal Mining Subsidence Damage' (Cm 235) in 1987, promising legislation which finally appeared as the Coal Mining Subsidence Act 1991.

The 1991 Act's provisions continue in force despite the privatisation of the coal industry by the Coal Industry Act 1994. Section 1 of the Act defines relevant subsidence damage as that to land, and buildings, structures or works on, in or over land, which is caused by the removal of support consequent on lawful coal mining, though mere alterations of gradients or levels of land not otherwise damaged, which do not affect its fitness for the purposes for which it has been used, are *not* 'subsidence damage'. The prime liability of the person responsible in respect of such damage is, under s 2, to take *remedial* action, ie to undertake remedial works, see s 7, or to make payments in respect of such works, see ss 8 and 9, or to compensate for the depreciation of affected land, see ss 10 and 11. In certain cases of emergency works having to be done the person responsible may also have to make payments under s 12. A brief overview of the pattern of responsibility post privatisation is necessary, but see further chapter 3 below.

A tale of ownership, regulation and licensed extraction

The 1994 Act creates a Coal Authority which owns unworked coal, and licences its extraction by coal mining operators, see Parts I and II of the Act. So far as subsidence is concerned, s 37 provides that a licence may define its holder's geographical extent of liability, and it appears that this will normally be limited to places likely to be subject to affectation from March 1994 onwards. In general licensed operators are made subject to the 1991 Act's scheme of liability for subsidence by virtue of s 43 of the 1994 Act within their areas of responsibility. Thus responsibility for subsidence damage now rests on

1 *Brown v Robins* (1859) 4 H & N 186.

'the person responsible' within that person's area of responsibility; otherwise it is the Coal Authority. The 'person responsible's' liabilities, of course, apply to damage arising after licensing, but, under s 43(3)–(7), also extend to damage previously occurring, though in this latter case it appears a government indemnity will meet the costs where the former British Coal had admitted liability in relation to a particular 'area of responsibility' before its sale into the private sector was agreed.

The obligations of 'persons responsible' are, under s 45 of the 1994 Act, to be supplemented by regulations, inter alia, requiring them to give affected landowners/occupiers information on request. SI 1994/2565 has been made under this power and relates to *underground* coal mining. The object of the regulations is to ensure that those deleteriously affected by subsidence may know the full identity, address, telephone and facsimile number of the relevant 'person responsible'. The Secretary of State is further empowered by s 46 to appoint a 'subsidence adviser' to assist those affected by subsidence in making complaints or taking other steps in relation to matters arising under the 1991 Act. SI 1994/2563 has been made under this power and specifically provides for the adviser to provide information concerning the statutory rights of those affected by subsidence damage, and to investigate claims that 'persons responsible' have acted improperly in discharging relevant claims. The adviser is empowered to recover the costs and expenses incurred in operating the subsidence advice service, including staff remuneration costs, from 'persons responsible' by means of a yearly levy apportioned and collected by the Coal Authority.

The scheme of liability

The s 2 liability arises where, under s 3, the affected landowner gives the person responsible requisite notice in due time and has afforded them reasonable facilities to inspect the property. The requisite notice is one in writing stating that damage has occurred and particularising it. Such notice must be given within a period of six years beginning at the time any person entitled to give notice had the knowledge required to found a claim, ie that damage has occurred and the circumstances indicate it may be subsidence damage. Under s 4, as soon as reasonably practicable after receiving such notice, the person responsible must give the claimant a counter notice indicating whether they agree that they have a remedial obligation, and, if so, the kind or kinds of remedial action available and what they propose to do. It is *generally* up to the person responsible to determine what remedial action to take, see s 5, and this normally entails repair works, a schedule of which must be sent to the claimant and any other interested persons under s 6. These works will be those which the person responsible considers to be necessary to make good the damage, so far as is reasonably practicable, to the reasonable satisfaction of the claimant.

Section 8 of the Coal Mining Subsidence Act 1991, however, allows the person responsible to make payments at their discretion instead of executing works. Circumstances where such payments may be made *include* where the claimant wishes to arrange to have the necessary works done, or where it is proposed to merge the execution of other works on the damaged property with the subsidence damage works, or to redevelop the property rather than to remedy its condition. The person responsible may not unreasonably refuse a request from a claimant who wishes to arrange for works to be done himself or to merge remedial works with others on the property, and *in general* this means that they may not refuse a request made before they have begun execution of remedial works. A *mandatory* obligation to make a payment in lieu of remedial works arises under s 9 in respect of damage to property whose upkeep is the responsibility of a public authority, eg a highway maintainable at public expense.

A further power to make a discretionary payment in lieu of remedial action exists under s 10 in respect of depreciation where the aggregate costs of the scheduled remedial work exceed the depreciation in the value of the property by at least 20%, *or* where the property is not a dwelling and the parties agree such a payment should be made, *or* where the property is a dwelling likely to be subject to clearance action in consequence of subsidence.

In some cases emergency works have to be undertaken in order that a subsidence damaged property may continue to be used for its existing purpose, or to prevent further subsidence damage. Under ss 2(4) and 12 persons responsible are under an obligation to reimburse the costs of such works, though they must be given reasonable and adequate notice of the proposed works and afforded inspection facilities before the obligation arises. Indeed it is the general rule that *no* payment in lieu may be made unless the persons responsible have been given advance notice of works adequately particularised in due time, see s 13.

Schedule 1 of the 1991 Act applies to determine the amount of depreciation payments, ie to determine the exact units of property in question, the basis of valuation (basically according to market valuation of the property in its damaged condition), the amount of depreciation and liability for interest, etc. Basically liability extends to the actual damage caused to the land in question.[2]

Where further damage is likely within 18 months to a property in respect of which the person responsible has been given a damage notice, remedial action may be delayed under s 16 by the service on the claimant of a 'stop notice'. Such a notice will not, however, prevent the undertaking of emergency works nor any others specifically excepted by the stop notice, and in any case such notices have to be kept under review with a view to their revocation by the person responsible, see s 17. Section 18 applies where a damage notice has been given to the person responsible and further damage becomes evident before the completion of remedial works. The general rule is that the original and the further damage are to be treated as one — 'the combined damage' — and appropriate new schedules of remedial action given to the claimant.

Part III of the 1991 Act is concerned with additional remedies for those affected by subsidence damage. In relation to dwelling houses where subsidence renders a dwelling beyond reasonable action to make it fit for use as such, and it is not in fact used as such, there is a right to a home loss payment under s 22 and Sch 4 for owner occupiers and others such as lessees and statutory tenants etc. In cases of temporary dispossession however, under s 23 and Sch 5 the person responsible is under an obligation to make available reasonable alternative living accommodation to displaced occupiers, to make

---

2 *Hepworth Building Products v British Coal* [1994] 6 ELM 80.

payments in lieu in respect of reasonable expenditure incurred by displaced occupiers in respect of rent, heat, light etc, while s 24 imposes a further duty on that person to take reasonable steps to prevent or minimise the risk of temporarily unoccupied houses or their contents being damaged or otherwise lost. Regulations may also be made, under s 25, requiring the payment by persons responsible, of compensation for inconvenience or disturbance caused by the execution of remedial works to persons who reside in subsidence damaged dwellings. See SI 1994/2564 which provides for compensation to be paid to claimants who live in dwellings affected by subsidence while repairs exceeding six months' duration are carried out.

In respect of subsidence damage to agricultural land, s 26 and Sch 6 of the 1991 Act create a right in displaced occupiers to a 'farm loss payment' where, by reason of deterioration due to subsidence damage, the land in question cannot be used profitably for agriculture, while a 'crop loss payment' will be payable under s 27 in respect of crops lost on land affected by subsidence damage for the period of time which begins with the damage and ends with the discharge of remedial obligations. Claims for such payments must be made within the period of 12 months beginning with the end of the year, or part of the year, to which payment relates.

Regulations made under s 29 may provide for, inter alia, the purchase of property blighted in consequence of actual or possible subsidence damage. SI 1994/2564 now enables the owners of dwellings blighted by subsidence damage, or its possibility, to require those responsible for remedying the damage to purchase their dwellings at their unblighted market values.

'Crop loss payments' have been considered above, but a similar concept is applied under s 30 to the losses of 'small firms' on land they wholly or partly occupy which is affected by subsidence damage and in respect of which warning was, or should have been, given of underground working according to s 46 (see further below). A 'small firm' for present purposes is one effectively employing not more than 20 persons. The period within which liability occurs exists from the time affectation by subsidence begins until persons responsible discharge their remedial obligations, and the liability is to pay to an affected firm a payment equivalent to that which they would have received had a claim in negligence arisen. Liability, however, is dependent on notice being given by the firm at the earliest reasonably practicable moment after loss eventuates.

Compensation is also payable by persons responsible to affected owners under s 31 where damage is caused to movable property lawfully on land by subsidence. The damages are assessed on the 'negligence basis' already encountered in s 30, but are generally limited to the loss of the damaged article, consequential loss being excluded, *save* in the case of damaged property used for its purposes by a small firm on property in relation to which a s 46 notice has or should have been given.

Section 32 imposes a limited liability, in cases where no other action to recover damages is available, in respect of death or disability suffered by a person lawfully on land, caused by the happening of subsidence. Where death is caused, damages are to be assessed on the basis of the person responsible's attributed negligence according, in England and Wales, to the principles of the Fatal Accidents Act 1976 (the Damages (Scotland) Act 1976 in Scotland). Where disability results, the basis of assessment is attributed negligence.

Part V of the Coal Mining Subsidence Act 1991 contains a number of important supplemental provisions. Claimants are prevented by s 37 from proceeding simultaneously with a double claim for compensation by a notice under the Act and a claim against a person responsible for damages otherwise. Claimants must elect which claim for the time being they will pursue. However, where persons responsible do take remedial action under the statute, s 38 imposes liability on them to reimburse a claimant's reasonable expenses in connection with a damage notice or claim.

Disputes arising under the Act are generally, under s 40, to be determined by the Lands Tribunal, save that under s 42 disputes over the granting of access to a person responsible to land so that they may discharge their functions under the Act are to be determined by magistrates, while s 47 of the 1994 Act empowers the Secretary of State to make regulations establishing a scheme of arbitration, see SI 1994/2566 establishing a householders' arbitration scheme, and a general scheme for other cases. Section 42(2) of the 1991 Act also imposes a liability on persons responsible in that in any proceedings where a question arises as to whether damage to property is subsidence damage, and the circumstances indicate the damage *may* be subsidence damage, it is for the person responsible to show that it is not. There is a time limit under s 44 in relation to disputes as to whether persons responsible are in breach of remedial obligations. This is the end of whichever of the two following periods expires last: either the period of three years running from the earliest date on which persons responsible are in breach of remedial obligations, *or* the period allowed for giving a damage notice (ie six years from the date on which any person entitled to give a damage notice had the requisite knowledge to found a claim).

The right of a licensed operator to withdraw support to enable coal to be worked after the giving of three months' notice and due publicity in respect of specified land, originally arising under s 2 of the Coal Industry Act 1975, is retained under the 1991 Act but in a modified form, for the compensation provisions are replaced by those of the 1991 Act. In addition s 33 of the 1991 Act empowers persons responsible, where they consider that subsidence damage is *likely* to occur to any structure or works *and* that preventive works would obviate or mitigate such damage, to carry out such works or to pay for their execution, provided the consent of relevant property owners is given. An unreasonable failure to give such consent will excuse the person responsible — in whole or in part dependent upon the nature of the damage — from further remedial obligations should subsidence damage subsequently eventuate to the property in question.

The current form of the right to withdraw support

Section 38 of the 1994 Act provides authority for a licensed operator to withdraw support so that coal may be worked. This provision, along with ss 39 and 40, replace the provisions of the 1975 Act. Section 38 gives general authority for the withdrawal of support in connection with mining so far as this is a reasonably required move. However, public notice is required as is remedial action under the 1991 Act in respect of any subsidence damage caused. Only a licensed operator can give notice, see s 39 of the 1994 Act.

Section 46 of the 1991 Act imposes a further obligation on persons responsible to give notice of risk of subsidence damage to relevant property owners where any underground coal mining operations are proposed.

Supplementary notice must be given of any decision *not* to proceed with mining, or the discontinuance of mining which has been carried on, or anything giving the person responsible reason to believe there is no longer a risk of subsidence damage. See also SI 1994/2565 referred to supra. A similar obligation under s 47 relates to the giving of information to relevant local authorities (in England and Wales the district or non-metropolitan county) of proposed operations which may affect land by subsidence, and prescribed information must also be given about operations being carried on.

It should finally be noted that the Secretary of State has power under s 49 to direct persons responsible to make reports on the operation of the 1991 Act.

Further reading

Ball, S, 'Murphy v Brentwood DC: the Water Law Implications' (1990) 1 Water Law 102.

Dias, RWM, 'Trouble on Oiled Waters: Problems of the Wagon Mound (No 2)' [1967] CLJ 62.

Grandis-Harrison, A de, 'Environmental Pollution', Parts 1–3 [1986] Legal Action, February, 26, March, 39, April, 46.

McLaren, JPS, 'Nuisance Law and the Industrial Revolution — Some Lessons from Social History' Oxford Journal of Legal Studies vol 3, no 2, 155.

Newark, FH, 'Non-natural Use and Rylands v Fletcher' (1961) 24 MLR 557.

Ogus, AI, 'Water Rights Diluted' (1994) 6 JEL 137.

Ogus, AI, and Richardson, GM, 'Economics and the Environment: A study of Private Nuisance' [1977] CLJ 284.

Penner, JE, 'Nuisance and the Character of the Neighbourhood' (1993) 5 JEL 1.

Pugh, C, and Day, M, *Pollution and Personal Injury: Toxic Torts II* (1995) Cameron May.

Rutherford, L, 'The Environmental Costs of Opencast Coal Mining: Issues of Liability' (1990) 2 Journal of Environmental Law 161.

Shelbourn, C, 'Historic Pollution — Does the Polluter Pay?' [1994] JPL 703.

Smets, H, 'The cost of accidental pollution' [1990] 1 LMELR 193.

Steele, J, 'Private Law and the Environment: Nuisance in Context' (1995) 15 Legal Studies No 2, 236.

Waite, AJ, 'Private Civil Litigation and the Environment' [1989–1990] 1 LMELR 113.

Wilkinson, D, 'Moving the Boundaries of Compensable Environmental Damage caused by Marine Oil Spills: The Effect of two new International Protocols' (1993) 5 JEL 71.

Williams, DW, 'Non-Natural use of Land' [1973] CLJ 310.

Winfield, P, 'Nuisance as a Tort' [1930] 3 CLJ 189.

OFFICIAL REPORTS

'Coal and the Environment' (1981) HMSO.

'The Repair and Compensation System for Coal Mining Subsidence Damage' (1984 and 1987) HMSO.

'Paying for Pollution: Civil Liability for Damage Caused by Waste' (House of Lords Select Committee on the European Communities, Session 1989–90, 25th Report, HL Paper 84).

Chapter 3

The structure and general powers of bodies having environmental responsibilities and overall environmental policy

'Captain Corcoran, it is one of the happiest characteristics of this glorious country that official utterances are invariably regarded as unanswerable' (W S Gilbert 'HMS Pinafore', Act II)

Environmental control is not the preserve of any one institution or department of state. The Department of the Environment, for example, is concerned with environmental issues but also has important functions relating to housing and local government finance. Other central departments, such as the Ministry of Agriculture, Fisheries and Food, are responsible for policies having considerable environmental consequences. Additionally, responsibility for environmental control is shared between central and local government. The bulk of powers and duties of local authorities with regard to environmental issues has grown greatly since 1945, and they are generally entrusted with considerable discretion with regard to many of their environmental powers. Where an authority is granted a power to achieve some purpose it generally follows that they have a choice as to *whether and how* to act. Even where a mandatory requirement is imposed it is usually the case that the authority will retain some freedom with regard to *how* to discharge their obligation. The way in which authorities discharge environmental functions is usually determined by factors such as finance, and the availability of skilled manpower and other resources such as plant and machinery. These are frequently beyond local control. Central policy on allocation of resources is usually a major determinant in deciding how authorities behave.

Very important environmental functions are exercised by statutory bodies and regulatory agencies. There are also bodies having consultative, monitoring or investigatory powers, for example the Royal Commission on Environmental Pollution. Such bodies may exist under special statutory provisions or by virtue of the Royal prerogative.

The DoE can find its environmental policies conflict with those of other departments, such as, for example, Transport. Where such conflict arises much will depend on the stance of the Prime Minister in relation to the issues if mediation is called for. However, there now exists a Cabinet Standing Committee on environmental policies and, in each department, a minister nominated to consider the environmental implications of policies and spending. Annual departmental reports set out material on environmental initiatives. Departments also receive guidelines on policy appraisal where the policy affects the environment, and environmental action guides to aid civil service management in decisions on matters as diverse as building and land issues, photocopying and air conditioning, see 'This Common Heritage' (Cm 1200) pp 230 et seq. Yearly updating and monitoring of environmental policy by a White Paper also takes place.

This chapter will give an account of the structure and functions of agencies having environmental functions.

A CENTRAL GOVERNMENT

One theory of government is that ministers make policy for which they answer to a Parliament composed of the elected representatives of the people; civil servants implement that policy but do not make it. This theory does not present an adequate explanation of how government works. The ministry of the day is always drawn from the ranks of the largest party in the House of Commons, and, while they can maintain the internal cohesion and discipline of their party, ministers are almost assured of parliamentary approval for their policies. The theory also ignores the very important part played by civil servants in the creation of policy. The real relationship between the various parts of the executive 'arm' of government is most complex, as also is the relationship of government to powerful external interest groups, an issue of great importance with regard to energy policy.

A minister heads his/her department, is technically responsible for all decisions taken, and must be prepared to answer for them to the House of Commons. In practice it is impossible for a minister to know of all the decisions taken in his name. Routine decisions of comparatively minor civil servants cannot be known to the minister, and even some major decisions taken by senior civil servants can hardly be known in detail. The size of the civil service and the number and complexity of the issues it has to decide weaken ministerial control over permanent officials. Even where a decision is of such importance that it has to be made by a minister, he/she will have to listen most carefully to the advice of his permanent staff before making it. The reasons for this are not hard to understand. Rapid rates of change in ministerial appointments, even within the lifetime of a ministry, mean that individuals may frequently change jobs or achieve new office, while civil servants are permanent officials, able to take a long term view of individual issues. In addition ministerial time is limited and subject to the demands of the department, Parliament, the cabinet, colleagues, the party, the media, and a constituency, while ministerial knowledge in general and particular terms may also be limited. Ministers are thus forced to depend upon senior officials. Furthermore, once a policy is implemented, resources committed to it, contracts made under it and public expectation raised by it, it is very difficult to alter course. An incoming ministry may find it virtually impossible to depart radically, for some years at least, from the policies of their predecessors, even though they have denounced them in Parliament and campaigned against them in an election.

The Department of the Environment (DoE)

The DoE has, inter alia, responsibility for environmental protection and related policy issues with regard to:

1   Planning, including appeals and inquiries concerning planning matters, the national heritage of historic buildings and sites, inner urban problems, development plans and control, minerals and land reclamation.
2   Environmental protection including countryside and wildlife issues, the functioning of the Environment Agency (see further below), radioactive substances, air noise and waste policy, toxic substances policy.
3   Water, including the water directorate, drinking water control and the drinking water inspectorate, policy on water pollution and quality, sewage disposal policy, implementation of EU Directives concerning water, etc.
4   Environmental economics.

The responsibilities of other ministries and departments

The Ministry of Agriculture, Fisheries and Food (MAFF)

This ministry has, inter alia, a responsibility for land and resources policy, especially with regard to:

1   Agriculture, horticulture, fisheries and food, including many food safety issues.
2   Pesticide registration.
3   Setting public health standards in relation to food manufacture, etc.
4   Implementation of EU agricultural and fisheries policies, and national farming support schemes.
5   Countryside and marine protection issues.
6   Technical services for agriculture.
7   Designation of Environmentally Sensitive Areas, see chapter 6 below.

Note that under s 17 of the Agriculture Act 1986, however, that the Minister should seek to balance agricultural interests with the wider economic and social needs of rural areas and the needs of conservation and recreation.

The Department of Trade and Industy (DTI)

Concerned with the development of environmental technologies, particularly with regard to pollution prediction and control, fuel recovery from waste and chemical pollution at sea, the DTI has since 1992 also been responsible for the development of national policies on coal, electricity and atomic power as sources of energy. There is also responsibility with regard to energy efficiency.

The Home Office

Among other responsibilities the Home Office is concerned with *central* oversight over the organisation and operation of the Fire Service. Responsibilities here include fire prevention and precautions, emergency planning and civil defence.

The Department of Transport

This department is responsible for transport by land, sea and air, airports, domestic and international civil aviation, shipping, marine pollution issues, trunk roads and motorways and vehicle standards. It has often been alleged that this department is one of road building, and that it has turned its face against the development of less environmentally disruptive forms of transport such as railways. However, in 1991 the Secretary of State for Transport announced *some* change in policy by enhancing grants for rail connected industrial facilities so as to encourage movement of goods by rail rather than by road; greater use of urban rapid transit rail systems is also likely. However, the change in policy may not be great; doubling the volume of freight moved by rail would only take off the roads two months' growth in car traffic.

The Treasury

All central departments are subject to the overall review, scrutiny and financial control of the Treasury. Failure to implement or to pursue with vigour a particular environmental policy may well be attributable, not to departmental obstructiveness, but rather to Treasury insistence that the project cannot be supported by the national economy. Equally, once a considerable amount of the national wealth has been committed to a particular project, the Treasury may be unwilling to write off the money spent and to cease to fund the project in favour of some other, perhaps rather more environmentally attractive, one.

B OTHER CENTRAL AGENCIES AND BODIES

In addition to the above departments there are a number of central advisory bodies charged with various environmental responsibilities.

The Countryside Commission (England)

The Countryside Commission exists now under the Wildlife and Countryside Act 1981, s 47 and Sch 13. The Commission is a body corporate and not a part of either the Department of the Environment or the Ministry of Agriculture, Fisheries and Food, nor does it have the status of being a crown servant or agent, though its members are appointed by the Secretary of State. Subject to the approval of ministers the Commission appoints its own staff, and is charged by statute with responsibility for, inter alia:

1 Conservation and enhancement of natural beauty of the countryside in England and Wales.
2 Encouraging the provision or improvement of facilities for visitors to the countryside particularly with regard to opportunities for open-air recreation, s 1(2) of the Countryside Act 1968.
3 Designation of National Parks under the National Parks and Access to the Countryside Act 1949 (see further chapter 6 below).
4 Preparation and submission of proposals for long distance routes, ie routes to enable the public to make extensive journeys on foot, horseback or pedal cycle along primarily non-vehicular ways, eg the Pennine Way, under ss 51–55 of the 1949 Act.
5 Advising central and local government and any other body, person or persons on questions relating to natural beauty, especially with regard to any developments which might be prejudicial to natural beauty, see s 85 of the 1949 Act.

6   Providing information services, including a code of guidelines for the use of persons visiting the countryside under s 86 of the 1949 Act.
7   Under s 87 of the 1949 Act, designating areas of outstanding natural beauty (see further under chapter 6 below).

In the present context 'natural beauty' includes the preservation of an area's flora, fauna and geological and physiographical features, see s 114(2) of the National Parks and Access to the Countryside Act 1949, as amended, and 'conservation' also extends to protecting such features, see s 49(4) of the Countryside Act 1968.

(It should also be noted that s 11 of the 1968 Act states:

'In the exercise of their functions relating to land under any enactment every Minister, government department and public body shall have regard to the desirability of conserving the natural beauty and amenity of the countryside.')

The Commission has also issued guidelines on reviews of National Park plans. Submitting evidence to public inquiries into major development proposals in sensitive areas is a Commission function. Their views may also persuade the Secretary of State to use powers under planning legislation to 'call-in' a planning application for a central decision. The Commission, in co-operation with other national agencies, set up in 1984 a national system of landscape change monitoring. Additionally the Commission continues to comment on structure and local plans, especially by preparing guidelines for planning authorities on conservation, recreation and landscape protection. On the revision of existing structure plans the Commission will be particularly concerned with proposals affecting key areas in the countryside, and where local plans are made or revised proposals affecting Areas of Outstanding Natural Beauty and the fringes of urban areas will be examined.

The Commission consists of a chairman and such other members, who form a lay council and subsidiary committees, as are appointed by the Secretary of State for the Environment and the Secretary of State for Wales, and it must act in accordance with such ministerial directions as it is given, see the National Parks and Access to the Countryside Act 1949, s 3.

The Commission relies largely on voluntarism, eg persuasion of relevant landowners to undertake countryside works, and to allow public access to land, and working with voluntary bodies, often acting as a catalyst to further their work. It has few executive powers and must rely to a considerable extent on planning authorities to implement its initiatives. There are no plans to merge the Commission with nature conservancy bodies in England, in contrast with the position in Scotland (Cm 1200 p 233). See further below on the Nature Conservancy Councils.

The Royal Commission on Environmental Pollution

This is an advisory body with regard to matters concerning pollution of the environment, on the adequacy of research into such matters, and on the possibilities of danger to the environment. The Commission is a *permanent* body reporting to Parliament. Its membership reflects a wide range of disciplines, and likewise its terms of reference. It is an advisory body, but can take initiatives to study particular issues, and can take both oral and written evidence, as well as appointing its own expert assessors. The Commission's influence on policy has been subtle, not overt, and though not all its recommendations have been acted on, it can continue to press for action, and it is thought to do good by stealth, even though this may take some years to achieve. It is also the case that the Commission does not have a 'high' public profile, and its reports are primarily technical and not 'popular' in style or price.

The Forestry Commission

Although primarily concerned with the production of timber for industry, this body is also concerned with the provision of recreational facilities, wildlife management and the amenities of the countryside. To minimise conflicts of interests between its activities, for organisational purposes the Commission operates as Forest Enterprise which manages plantations and the Forestry Authority which is a regulating body. The Commission is also charged with the implementation of forestry legislation and exists under the Forestry Act 1967, ss 1, 2 and Sch 1. The Commission has a general duty to promote the interests of forestry, including the establishment and maintenance of adequate reserves of growing trees, the development of afforestation and the production and supply of timber and other forest products. Consisting of a chairman and not more than ten other members (see the Forestry Act 1981, s 5), the Commission is under a duty to comply with such ministerial directions as are given to it. (See further under chapter 6 below.) In England the ministry having overall departmental responsibility for forestry is Agriculture, Fisheries and Food (see above).

The Health and Safety Commission (executive arm, the Health and Safety Executive)

This body, which is subject to general ministerial direction, exists under the Health and Safety at Work etc Act 1974, s 10, and is responsible to appropriate ministers, under s 11, for the administration of that Act. Much of this body's work has environmental implications because, of course, there can be no rigid demarcation of the workplace and the wider environment.

The role of the Commission was somewhat exhortatory and advisory until the 1980s. However, in September 1982 the Secretary of State made the Notification of Installations Handling Hazardous Substances Regulations 1982, SI 1982/1357. The Regulations prohibit the undertaking of any activity in which there is, or is liable to be, at any given time a notifiable quantity of a hazardous substance at any site, or (generally) in any pipeline, *unless* written notice has been given in advance by the person undertaking the activity to the Health and Safety Executive. 'Notifiable quantities' of 'hazardous substances' are defined in Sch 1 to the Regulations, and are basically quantities of substances potentially able to cause harm both on and off site. The details to be given are laid down in Sch 2 and these include the notifier's name and address, and that of the site, etc. There must be at least three months' notification in advance unless the Health and Safety Executive otherwise allows. Any changes in notified particulars must themselves be forthwith notified to the Executive in writing, but any increase of three or more times the quantity of the hazardous substance may not occur before advance written notification to the Executive has been given just as if it were a new activity. (See further chapter 7 below).

The tasks of the Commission centre on the progressive updating of legislation relating to *health and safety at work*, both under national and EU law. However, it is accepted that there can be an overlap between this function and wider environmental responsibilities, because the Commission's responsibilities extend to setting safety standards at work for the protection of workers *and* the public. The Commission has acknowledged the need for close collaboration between itself and its dependent organisations and other inspectorates and agencies acting under wider environmental legislation.

The Commission is also subject to inputs to its functioning from the EU in the form of Directives on matters such as major accident hazards, chemicals, bio-releases and radiation, and from international agencies such as the International Atomic Energy Agency, and the United Nations. So, for example, Directives 89/677 and 89/678 affected the Commission's work in relation to the marketing and use of certain dangerous substances and preparations, in that the Health and Safety Executive (see below) is the prime mover in the UK for ensuring that national law etc, is harmonised with European obligations, though these themselves often reflect wider international obligations, and standards developed by bodies such as the Organisation for Economic Co-operation and Development (OECD).

The detailed implementation of the 1974 Act is delegated to the Health and Safety Executive appointed under s 10, the Commission's operational arm, and subject to its power of direction under s 11(4) of the 1974 Act. The Executive has an obligation under ss 18 and 19 of the Act to appoint inspectors. Many inspectorates previously existing under other legislation have now been brought under its aegis. The inspectorates are those relating to agriculture, factories, mines and quarries and nuclear installations. In addition there are specialist units in relation to issues such as hazardous installations, special hazards and hazardous substances.

The Environment Agency

History and development

The Environment Agency (hereafter 'the Agency') is the creation of the Environment Act 1995 and was fully operational as from 1 April 1996. It subsumes the work of Her Majesty's Inspectorate of Pollution (HMIP), the National Rivers Authority (NRA) and the Waste Regulation Authorities (WRA). Thus there is one agency dealing with water resources, water pollution control, land drainage and flood defence, fisheries, navigation and conservancy issues, regulation of waste and disposal, the integrated pollution control system and oversight of certain radioactive substances issues, alongside which the Agency has important functions in respect of contaminated land and abandoned mines. The Agency functions in England and Wales; for Scotland, which is outside the general framework of this book, the parallel body is the Scottish Environmental Protection Agency (SEPA).

The notion that there should be one environmental regulation agency for England and Wales to subsume the work of HMIP, the NRA and the WRA's was current for some years, in fact it was the logical corollary of the new regulatory powers introduced for the environmental media between 1989 and 1993 (though some of these were only a consolidation of earlier powers). The government's undertaking to set up such an agency was redeemed by the 1995 Act. This legislation grew greatly beyond its original conception and attracted a degree of controversy during its process of development. Understanding how the Agency will work demands, therefore, an understanding of how the Agency concept has matured, what the Agency will be, what powers it will have and then, perhaps more speculatively, how it will approach its tasks.

THE GROWTH OF THE 'AGENCY IDEA'

Somewhat unusually the government undertook a wide public consultation exercise before the Environment Agencies Bill 1994 (as it was then known) was introduced to Parliament. Draft clauses and schedules were released by the Department of the Environment in October 1994, while an Environment Agency Advisory Committee was created by the government on 18 November chaired by Lord De Ramsey (who subsequently became the first Chairman of the Agency) to work on organisation resource issues and key policy matters. It was announced then by the Secretary of State that the Agency would act as a cornerstone of the government's sustainable development policy. Lord De Ramsey himself added that he wanted the Agency to be a strong conservation body and to play an important part in promoting sustainable development, reconciling the needs of environmental protection, conservation and development.

Thus by November 1994 it was clear that, in initial concept, the Agency was not to be limited to a purely regulatory role, but was to be a single identifiable point of contact for all its *customers* on pollution control and environmental enhancement. It may, however, be asked if this was to be so, why was the opportunity to include the conservancy councils and the Countryside Commission within the Agency's umbrella not taken?[1]

Even so the Agency is the largest environmental protection body in Europe, and its first great task is to promote integration of its integrated pollution control and water basin management functions, together with improving the efficiency of waste regulation, responsibility for which will no longer be divided between 80 bodies.

THE AGENCY'S STRUCTURE

The Agency under s 1(1) of the 1995 Act is a non-departmental public body, ie a body corporate separate from government, and not a servant of the Crown, and somewhat akin in this respect to the former NRA. Under s 1(2) it consists of between 8 and 15 members, three appointed by the Minister of Agriculture, Fisheries and Food, the remainder by the Secretary of State (the Secretary of State for Wales made one appointment, all the others were made by the Secretary of State for the Environment). The initial membership represented a wide range of relevant expertise with members having experience of agriculture, water provision and water and flood management, fisheries, accountancy, local government, the EU, industry (particularly the food and power supply industries) and the national parks.

The details of the provisions as to membership of the Agency are contained

1 For further detail see Lane & Peto, *Blackstone's Guide to the Environment Act 1995*, chapter 2.

in Sch 1 of the 1995 Act and are largely modelled on the constitution of the former NRA.

The ministers responsible for appointing the members of the Agency may, under s 4(2), give it directions in the discharge of its functions, and that guidance has to be taken into account, though the power to issue guidance is only to be exercised following consultation with the Agency and other appropriate person and bodies, with drafts of guidance being laid before Parliament before it is issued so that Parliament has the opportunity of vetoing any such guidance. The principal ministerial parliamentary responsibility for the overall policy framework of the Agency, and for its general performance, lies with the Secretary of State for the Environment. Ministers will, however, agree annual priorities and targets in response to its annual corporate plan, and its financial functioning.

The issue of the structuring of the Agency 'on the ground' was a difficult one. The former HMIP followed county boundaries in its structure while the former NRA, being based on the pre-1989 areas of the old water authorities, took its local structures from the geographical actualities of the various river basins. After three structure models were considered a fourth was finally adopted. The regional structure of the Agency will be based on local authority boundaries for pollution control functions, while for internal water management purposes only the former NRA regional boundaries will be retained. It appears that by adapting the former NRA regional boundaries to the nearest county or district boundary for pollution control functions there is not a great deal of variation in fact from the water management regions while there is the great advantage that the Agency will operate according to boundaries already well known and understood by the public.

So far as senior staff responsibilities are concerned the Chief Executive's position went to the former Chief Executive of the NRA, while the NRA also supplied the Director of Environmental Strategy, the Director of Water Management and the Director of Finance. HMIP supplied the Director of Pollution Prevention and Control — the chief environmental regulator whose responsibilities will include chairing the Agency Policy Group which will deal with water management and environmental strategy as well as pollution control and prevention. The apparent bias towards the former NRA — and the equally apparent exclusion of former WRA officers from the highest echelon of posts — has been somewhat modified by having an operating structure in which certain HMIP and NRA concepts of management have been put together. Thus pollution *regulation* is to be separate from *water management operations*; while *policy making* is to be a central function, *operational work* is to take place at a regional level with regional managers delivering operational activity and being the 'bridges' between particular specialist staff.

No matter what the internal structure, the external face of the Agency is to prevent a pattern of *integration* of functions in that, while it accepts all staff will not be multi-media specialists, all must operate the same ethical standards and share a common approach to the Agency's tasks. Thus there must be consistency in the approach of the Agency to regulation and authorisation issues. The predominant notion is that the Agency should operate on a 'one stop' basis so that each of the customers of the Agency (eg each relevant industry) will be able to turn to a particular officer who will lead an Agency team covering all aspects of that customer's needs. It is clear Agency policy that industry must always know where it stands.

It is also expected that in the general conduct of its external relations the Agency will follow a 'Code of Openness' which should reflect central government's own Code of Practice on Access to Government Information, and which should comply with the Environmental Information Regulations and the Citizen's Charter. With regard to those it regulates, the Agency is expected also to issue a Code of Practice indicating how it will deal with its customers, which will include the creation of an overall constructive relationship with them, the giving of advice on how best to comply with regulatory requirements, and the application of the principles of fairness, proportionality, transparency and consistency of enforcement. The Agency is also expected to avoid duplication of regulatory effort, for example by liaison with the Health and Safety Executive.

It is accepted that the Agency will not be successful if it does not achieve public support. No matter how good the quality of the Agency's scientific knowledge, if it becomes divorced from local communities it will not achieve that support. Thus while the Agency is a national body it has a strong regional structure in which local people are represented. Section 11 of the 1995 Act requires the creation of a special Advisory Committee for Wales appointed by the Secretary of State to advise on all matters affecting the work of the Agency in Wales, while s 12 requires the creation of Environment Protection Agency Committees (EPACs) for each area regarded as a region of England and Wales, while one such region must consist, wholly or mainly of, or of most of, Wales.

These EPACs have to be consulted on any proposals from the Agency relating generally to the way in which it carries out its functions in their region, and they may further make representations to the Agency about any aspects of its functioning.

Section 13 requires the establishment of regional and local fisheries advisory committees primarily for consultation purposes with regard to the development, maintenance and improvement of salmon, trout, freshwater and eel fisheries, but also on wider issues relating to recreation, conservation and navigation. Sections 14–19 and Sch 5 of the 1995 Act further relate to the creation of regional and local flood defence committees.

The object of the committee system is not just to discharge particular statutory functions, it is to encourage participation by members of the public in the work of the Agency, and to this end further non-statutory advisory committees may be established.

THE AGENCY'S OBJECTS — THE 'PRINCIPAL AIM'

Section 4 of the 1995 Act states that it is the 'principal aim' of the Agency ('*subject to and in accordance with the provisions of this Act or any other enactment and taking into account any likely costs*') in discharging its functions so to protect or enhance the environment, *taken as a whole,* to bring about the ministerially specified objective of achieving sustainable development. Thus particular statutory duties may supersede the 'principal aim' while there will inevitably be a certain element of cost benefit analysis affecting the Agency's workings (see further below).

The concept of sustainable development has already been considered in chapter 1 and will be returned to below. Broadly, in the view of the government it is based on maintaining a balance between growth and ensuring that growth is sustainable. The needs of economic development and those of the environment have to be reconciled, and neither must be pursued at the expense of the other.

The Draft Management Statement for the Agency issued on 6 December 1995 indicates that the goal of sustainable development is 'to reconcile the dual objectives of achieving economic development and of providing effective protection and enhancement of the environment'. In playing its part in promoting such development the Agency is to adopt across all its functions an integrated approach which considers 'impacts of substances and activities on all environmental media and on natural resources', and which delivers 'environmental requirements and goals without imposing excessive costs (in relation to benefits gained) on regulated organisations or society as a whole'. To assist in this role the Agency will prepare the annual corporate plan referred to above which will indicate the areas of work which it wishes to emphasise and the resources it intends to devote to these tasks. This plan will be subject to ministerial approval. It will be part of a longer term corporate strategy which will be agreed with ministers.

Draft guidance of April 1995 issued to the Agency indicated that sustainable development does not mean less economic development, nor does it mean that each and every feature of the current environment must be preserved at all costs: rather it does mean that decisions are taken with proper regard to their environmental impact. The second draft followed in December 1995, and stressed the need to deliver environmental requirements without the imposition of *excessive* costs (in relation to benefits gained) on *either* regulated bodies or society as a whole.

Ecological criteria must be taken into account in decision making, eg the concept of 'carrying capacity' which, broadly, means the capacity of the environment to absorb pollution or waste. The environment cannot be asked to accept more than its carrying capacity, while habitats and ecosystems have to be considered in the light of their ability to sustain particular population species. These criteria may have to be taken into account on a precautionary basis where there is a risk of potential damage to the environment which is both uncertain and significant. Sustainable development further requires that natural resources are used prudently.

Thus it is officially accepted that a principal challenge for sustainable development strategy is to promote ways of encouraging environmentally friendly economic activity while discouraging or controlling damaging activities. At the same time renewable resources should not be squandered while those that are non-renewable are used at a rate which considers the needs of future generations, always bearing in mind the need to consider any irreversible environmental effects and their significance. In some cases environmental impacts can be reduced by the application of the 'polluter pays' principle which, by driving up the cost of operation to polluters, and thus the cost of their products to society, may reduce demand for their activities.

These issues will not all have equal weight in all situations. On occasions environmental disbenefits will be the inevitable price of economic development. The real issue is that the decision making process must make a proper allowance for the interests of future generations. This is hard to achieve in practice: techniques for analysing decision making and standard setting are still needed; likewise systems for considering environmental impacts and relating these to expenditure decisions and regulation compliance costs, bearing in mind that it remains controversial whether aspects of the environment can be given a notional monetary value so that they can be weighed in any cost benefit analysis. Furthermore there are situations where the outcome of particular decisions cannot be scientifically predicted, and here risk assessment techniques have to be developed and applied.

Applying the foregoing to the principal aim of the Agency, the draft guidance states the object is taking a holistic stance, to optimise benefits to the environment as a whole, so that activities are considered in terms of their cross media impacts. Functions should be exercised together where this contributes to sustainable development; thus water management and water pollution functions should be exercised in an integrated fashion. The Agency must take a long term view in discharging its functions, and should pay particular attention to issues raising questions of irreversible change, or change reversible, only at high cost over a long period. Conservation and 'carrying capacity' issues must be considered in relation to sites which have particular significance for maintaining biodiversity. The Agency must also adopt a 'particular' approach, ie a co-operative attitude, towards industry where possible, seeking to protect the environment by encouraging improved technologies and techniques which are cost effective and in line with investment programmes. Thus industry should be encouraged to adopt the BS 7750 and EMAS schemes referred to in chapter 1 above, and to seek convergence of growth with environmental protection. To do this the Agency will need to show it bases its actions on sound science, and analysis of risks and impacts with account taken of costs and benefits; to be consistent and to operate to high professional standards; to ensure that the action it requires is always proportionate to the objective to be achieved; to become a recognised centre of environmental knowledge and expertise, a body all sectors can trust. The draft revised guidance, however, accepted the Agency alone cannot deliver sustainable development, and that key areas of responsibility will remain outside its remit, eg land use planning and transport.

PARTICULAR POWERS AND THE PRINCIPAL AIM

With regard to particular powers the draft guidance indicates:

1 The integrated pollution control system (IPC) is to be operated so that there is an *appropriate* balance between society's interest in the environment and in industry in both the long and short term. The guidance states: the 'most sustainable form of development is that which achieves optimum distribution of any pollutants to the three media of air, water and land, according to the ability of those media to accept such pollutants, without, for example, exceeding critical loads' ... (see further chapter 10 below).

2 Powers over radioactive sources should be so exercised as to: minimise creation of waste from nuclear activity; ensure that handling and treatment of waste is carried out with due regard to environmental and workforce welfare considerations, and that waste is disposed of in appropriate ways at

appropriate times in appropriate places; require waste producers to develop their own waste management strategies in accordance with the 'polluter pays' principle in respect of costs of authorisation, licensing research and future contingent liabilities; recognise that there is a point at which the imposition of additional costs in respect of risk reduction exceeds the benefits arising from the improvements in safety achieved; nevertheless ensure that waste producers do not create nuclear waste management problems which cannot be resolved using current techniques or techniques which could be developed from current lines of development (see further chapter 9 below).

3   With regard to waste generally, sustainable development principles require the Agency to use its powers to achieve, first of all *reduction* of waste, secondly to work towards best use of any waste that is created, and finally to choose waste management practices which minimise both immediate and long term environmental and health risks (see chapter 9 below).

4   Powers over contaminated land should be used so as to permit it be kept in, or returned to, beneficial use wherever practicable, so that pressure on greenfield sites is reduced, and thus, where there is an unacceptable or potential health risk or risk to the environment, remedial action is justified provided there is an appropriate cost justified technique for remediation bearing in mind the intended use of the land; to keep in mind the foregoing principles within the overall context of policy that contaminated land should be remediated so that it is suitable for the use to which it is intended to put it; to prioritise remediation activity so that problems are dealt with in an orderly and controlled fashion to ensure that those which are most urgent are dealt with first; to encourage an efficient market in land which may have been contaminated by its development without the imposition of unnecessary financial and regulatory obligations (see further chapter 9 below).

5   Water powers should be used to protect and enhance the water environment, bearing in mind the sustainable uses to be made of it, considering the local and regional conditions and habitats, uses and abstraction demands, while achieving sustainability may involve making choices between competing demands. This requires an overall integrated approach from the Agency with regard to all its water *and other* functions, with (a) rivers being strategically managed and any site specific activities placed in a wider context, while (b) natural processes in rivers and on the coast are worked with, and (c) at the same time decision making integrates technical, economic and environmental factors following proper assessment of costs and benefits and consultation with all those likely to be affected by the Agency's powers, remembering that there needs to be (d) recognition that all hydrological activities ultimately impact on the sea, thus requiring that regard is had to the sustainability of marine environments and UK international marine obligations.

6   Air powers should be used so as to achieve the government's national air quality strategy (see chapter 10 below).

What should be apparent from the foregoing (a conclusion reinforced by the terms of the revision of the first draft) is that within the context of the Agency's powers sustainable development is *not* a self contained concept: rather it is an *approach* to problem solving in particular contexts. There is in official thinking an element of balancing issues. There is nothing new in that; what is new is that the environment is, at least, being taken into account in the balancing exercise. Whether it is being afforded sufficient weight in that exercise is another issue. The other clearly apparent feature of official thinking is the need for cost benefit analysis, and that is a matter with particular implications for the Agency.

COST BENEFIT AND THE PRINCIPAL AIM

Section 4 of 1995 Act requires the Agency to take into account 'any likely costs' in achieving its principal aim. Similarly s 39(1) requires the Agency in considering whether or not to exercise any of its powers, or the manner of exercise of such powers, to take into account the likely costs and benefits of the exercise/non exercise *'unless and to the extent that it is unreasonable for it to do so in view of the nature or purpose of the power or in the circumstances of the particular case'*. It should, however, be noted that s 39(2) modifies the foregoing 'costs and benefits' consideration duty by stating that it is not to affect the Agency's mandatory obligation to discharge *any* specific duties, comply with any requirements or pursue any objectives imposed or given to it by other legal provisions, eg specific requirements on water quality. The revised draft guidance indicates that the 'costs and benefits' duty is not to apply if it would be unreasonable in the circumstances of a particular case. Rather it *is* to apply where there is more than one way of achieving a particular object and the Agency has a discretion as to how to achieve it. In those cases the Agency is to take account of *all types* of costs and benefits when making its decisions, including both economic and environmental impacts — which may entail making an environmental assessment of a project. When making a choice in such discretionary situations the Agency will need to consider (a) whether or not to take action, (b) what are its options, including the appropriate level of control, for achieving a given environmental outcome.

It is accepted that in applying the 'costs and benefits' duty it will not always be possible to make a precise qualification of costs, and so straight comparison will have to give way to evaluative judgment of options. Even so, the Agency will be expected: to use established principles, procedures and techniques with regard to risk assessment, economic and policy appraisal; to consider the precautionary principle (see chapter 1 above); to rely on sound science; to consider the environment's 'carrying capacity' and the impact of pollutants on natural environment capital; to consider long term implications, including long term environmental benefits as well as immediate financial costs and any irreversible effects, or those reversible only at high cost over a long period.

What all this appears to mean was declared by the Secretary of State in Parliament on 18 April 1995: 'Costs are important ... costs [must be] proportionate to the benefits ... we gain. We can all give a list of desiderata, but we also need a list of priorities for we must ensure that we do not do the least important things first, or we will find that there are no resources left for doing the things that really matter ...'

In many ways this is a restatement of classical UK environmental policy: *prioritise* aims and objectives, and deal with the major problems first, but always act in a *proportionate* way so that massive costs are not incurred simply to achieve marginal improvements. However, in stressing the importance of cost benefit analysis of proposed actions it has to be remembered that 'cost' is defined by s 56(1) of the 1995 Act to *include* costs to any person and to the environment. Thus the environment is clearly no longer to be thought of as an issue external to decision making, something which supplies 'free' services but whose interests can otherwise be ignored. The influence here of environmental economics on law and policy is quite clear.

THE AGENCY'S OTHER GENERAL DUTIES

Under s 5 pollution control powers (eg those under the 1990 and 1991 legislation) are to be used to prevent, minimise, remedy, or mitigate the effects of environmental pollution. To achieve this the Agency is to compile information on such pollution and may, if ministerially required, carry out general or particular assessments of the effect or likely effect of existing or potential levels of environmental pollution, and may further present reports to ministers laying out the options available for preventing, minimising, etc, environmental pollution.

Section 6 then provides that it is the Agency's general duty to promote the conservation and enhancement of the natural beauty and amenity of inland and coastal waters and the land associated with them, the conservation of flora and fauna dependent on the aquatic environment and the use of the above mentioned water and land for recreational purposes. However, under s 40 the Agency is under a duty to receive and act on directions given by ministers which may be general or specific, and may relate to fulfilling EU or international legal obligations, and s 6(2) recognises therefore a specific duty on the Agency when directed to do what is necessary or expedient to conserve, redistribute or otherwise to augment water resources in England and Wales, and to secure the proper uses of those resources. Section 6 further imposes duties in respect of flood defence, and the maintenance, improvement and development of fisheries.

Under s 7(1) there is further *general conservation duty* on both ministers and the Agency in formulating or considering any proposals relating to Agency functions (*saving pollution control*) to exercise powers *so as to further* the conservation and enhancement of natural beauty and the conservation of flora, fauna, and geological and physiographical features of special interest. This general duty is subject to the requirement that all relevant bodies and persons must seek to achieve sustainable development. A *somewhat* similar duty applies with regard to the Agency's pollution control powers *but with one major difference*. In this case the Agency is simply to have *regard to the desirability* of conserving and enhancing natural beauty, flora, fauna, etc. The difference caused controversy throughout the legislation's parliamentary passage. At the end of the day the government argued that while the Agency must take account of conservation needs in discharging all its functions, an overriding duty to further conservation *in every case* would be inconsistent with the effective discharge of particular duties, especially in relation to the key role of issuing various licences and authorisations. Effectively this confirms the fears of some conservationists that these licences, etc are permissions to pollute whose issue cannot be resisted on conservation grounds provided conservation issues have been taken into account in the decision making process.

It should also be noted that *any* proposals relating to Agency functions *must* also *have regard to the desirability* of protecting *and conserving buildings*, sites and objects of archaeological, architectural, engineering or historic interest, and must further have in regard any effect which the proposals would have on the beauty, or amenity of any rural or urban area, or on flora, fauna, features, buildings, etc, *and* effects which the proposals could have on the economic and social well being of rural communities.

Further general duties under s 7(2) relate to the situation when proposals concerning Agency functions are being considered. Regard is to be had: to the desirability of preserving public freedom of access to woodlands, mountains, moors, heath, downs, cliffs, foreshores, and other places of natural beauty; and to maintaining public visiting or inspection of buildings, sites and objects of archaeological, architecture, engineering or historic interest. Section 7(1) and (2) is applied by s 7(3) so as to impose duties on the Agency in relation to any proposals relating to the functions of a water or sewerage undertaker, land management and certain land disposals by such an undertaker; in such cases the proposals are to be dealt with as if they related to the Agency's own functions *other* than its pollution control functions, ie in such cases the full conservation duty applies.

Under s 8 where a conservancy council concludes land (in England or Wales as the case may be) is of special interest by virtue of its flora, fauna or special features, etc *and* that it may *at any time* be affected by schemes, works, operations or activities *of* the Agency *or* under Agency authorisation, the council is to notify its conclusion to the Agency. Thereafter the Agency may not carry out or authorise the works, etc without first consulting the council. Similar provisions apply to allow National Park Authorities and the Broads authority (see chapter 6 below) to inform the Agency that land in their areas is land in respect of which ss 6(1) and 7 (above) are relevant (general duties with regard to water and recreational duties, etc) and thus to impose a consultative obligation on the Agency in respect of particular works, etc.

OTHER POWERS AND DUTIES OF THE AGENCY AND RELEVANT MINISTERS

Codes of practice   Ministers may approve codes of practice for issue by them or others for the purpose of giving practical guidance to the Agency in respect of its functions under ss 6–8, and promoting desirable practices by the Agency. Such codes, once issued, have to be taken into account by the Agency in discharging its functions, but they may not be issued until after consultation with the Agency, the Countryside Commission, conservancy councils, the Historic Buildings Commission, the Sports Council and other 'appropriate' persons.

Protection of water and pollution   The Agency's functions, under s 10(1)(b) and (2) include protecting against pollution any waters which belong to the Agency or any water undertaker, or from which the Agency or Water undertaker is authorised to take water. Similar provisions apply to reservoirs and underground strata.

Advice giving, etc   Section 37 enables the Agency to do anything calculated to facilitate or be conducive to or incidental to its functions, including acquiring and developing land, instituting criminal proceedings, advising ministers on request, providing training, advice and assistance to persons, carrying out research and publicising results.

Delegation of functions   Section 38 enables ministers to delegate to the Agency certain functions (not including legislative ones or fixing fees or charges). The duty of the Agency to have regard to costs and benefits in implementing its functions under s 39 and, under s 40, to receive and respond to ministerial directions should also be remembered.

Charging schemes   The Agency has, subject to the power of ministerial direction, wide powers to make charging schemes in respect of:

1   Abstraction and impounding licences under Chapter II of the Water Resources Act 1991.
2   Registration of persons as controlled waste carriers (see chapter 9).
3   IPC authorisations (see chapter 10).
4   Waste management licences (see chapter 9).
5   Licences and consents under the Water Resources Act 1991 (see chapter 12).
6   Registrations and authorisations under the Radioactive Substances Act 1993 (see chapter 9).
7   Registration of persons as controlled waste brokers (see chapter 9).
    [2–7 are known as 'environmental licences']
8   Costs incurred with regard to dangerous or intractable waste (see chapter 9).

In respect of environmental licences, charges may be prescribed in respect of their grant or variation, or in respect of applications therefor, their transfer, renewal, surrender, and during their subsistence to provide for the costs of monitoring. Different rates of charge may be levied in respect of different types of licence, and charge rates may also vary according to the description of activity in question, the scale of activity, the description or amount of the substance to which the activity in question relates, and the number of different authorised activities carried out by a person. Non-payment of charges may result in an authorisation being suspended or revoked.

   These schemes will in due course supersede those currently existing under the Environmental Protection Act 1990 and the Water Resources Act 1991, but they break no new legal ground. They will be, as their predecessors, essentially mechanisms for recovering the Agency's administrative costs. They will not be pollution taxes. *However*, the Agency is statutorily required under s 42(3) to strive to ensure that it does recover its costs in respect of environmental licences by virtue of its changing schemes. Schemes under s 42 are subject to ministerial controls. More particularly ministers may not approve schemes until the Agency has published its proposals and given those who wish to make representations/objections to the minister the opportunity to do so. Ministers must then consider such views before deciding whether or not to approve the scheme. The Agency may also charge, under s 43, for services and facilities provided in the course of its functions.

Entering into agreements/memoranda of understanding (MOUs)   Various MOUs are in place from April 1996 to determine the relationships between: the Agency and the DoE and MAFF with regard to radioactive waste disposal authorisations; the Agency and the HSE to minimise duplication and conflict in applying legislation applying to waste at licensed nuclear sites.

Providing information Ministers may require information from the Agency under s 51 inter alia in respect of the carrying out of its functions and general responsibilities, while the Agency must under s 52 also produce an annual report.

WILL THE AGENCY BE FINANCIALLY ABLE TO DISCHARGE ITS TASKS?

Fears for the financial ability of the Agency to meet its obligations have been expressed. The set up costs of the Agency will be £5m, while currently (1994/95) regulatory functions cost £528m of which only £175m is recouped through charging schemes, and £202m from flood defence levies. The short-fall may have to be made up from inevitable 'efficiency savings' for it has been claimed by the Labour Party that environmental protection programmes will lose £62m from their budgets by 1998. This raises fears that the Agency will possess a plethora of regulatory powers but not the wherewithal to implement them properly; the old bugbear of over-regulation and under-enforcement in another guise. However, speaking at the 1995 Garner Lecture in London, Lord DeRamsey, Chairman of the Agency, stated he considered its first year's budgetary allocation to be 'reasonable' while on 28 November 1995 the Secretary of State announced grant aid for the Agency of £107m per annum to enable it to support its statutory functions, with an extra £29m over two years to fund the integration of its work. £1.5m will be available over three years to boost work on sustainable development, while a separate pool of resources will be available to deal with contaminated land problems. Flood defence work spending will be subvented by MAFF and the Welsh office. The Agency's annual budget is 'expected to exceed £500m a year' according to official sources, but its functional costs already exceed that figure. The issue remains, will the Agency be financially able to discharge its tasks?

THE AGENCY AND THE DEREGULATION AND CONTRACTING OUT ACT 1994

The aim of the 1994 Act is to reduce the amount of regulation of business by government to a significant degree. To this end a number of business operations are specifically 'deregulated', though this is a word with many meanings — even in the 1994 Act itself. Thus in some cases businesses are exempted from particular controls; in others Ministers are required to consult with relevant businesses before making regulatory measures. In the case, however, of s 34(4A) of the Environmental Protection Act 1990 (see further chapter 9 below) there was an amendment to *clarify* the law so that where a transfer of waste takes place in stages it is treated as taking place when the first stage occurs and where there is a series of transfers between the same parties of waste of the same sort the series is treated as a single transfer taking place when the first transfer occurred, and in such cases a description of the waste has only to be given once and not on every instance to comply with the general requirements of s 34.

It is the general powers of ministers, however, under Chapter I of the Act which are controversial. Section 1 grants a power to make orders *amending or repealing* legislation passed before 1994 which, in the opinion of ministers, imposes unnecessary burdens on business, for example to impose a less onerous regulatory regime. Before such orders are made s 3 requires ministers to consult with organisations representative of interests substantially likely to be affected by proposals and with such other persons as are considered appropriate. Furthermore particular provision is made by s 3(3) and (4) and s 4 for parliamentary consideration of deregulation proposals, with a special period of being allowed for parliamentary scrutiny of such proposals by a specially created Deregulation Committee in the Commons and by the Delegated Powers Committee of the Lords. These committees may not veto proposals, but if an adverse report to Parliament is made the *usual* course of action would be for ministers to modify their proposals or withdraw them.

Section 5 of the 1994 Act enables ministers if of the opinion that the effect of a statutory provision is to impose, authorise or require the imposition of a restriction, requirement or condition affecting a person carrying on a trade, business or profession, *and* that it would be possible by exercising powers under the 1994 Act to *improve* the procedures for enforcing the restriction, requirement or condition, they may exercise such powers. However, the exercise must not jeopardise any 'necessary protection' and it must improve procedure in the sense of producing fairness, transparency and consistency. The object here is to ensure that business can clarify the status of, understand the reasons for, and be able to challenge regulatory decisions at as early a stage as possible, and to prevent over zealous and unreasonable uses of regulatory powers. Also it is policy that businesses should be able to challenge enforcement decisions they believe are unreasonable before any formal action is taken.

The particular powers ministers may exercise are found in Sch 1 of the Act and are as follows:

1   To require that when an enforcement officer advises that some remedial action should be taken by a business, that business is able to request that the officer must give, as soon as practicable, a written notice stating the nature of the remedial action he/she considers should be taken, why and within what period. The notice would also have to explain the nature of any enforcement action which could be taken. *Generally* enforcement action cannot then be taken until the business has been able to consider the statement.

2   To require enforcement officers when they do take immediate enforcement action against businesses (which they may exceptionally do where this is thought necessary) to provide as soon as practicable a statement of why immediate action was thought necessary.

3   To require enforcement officers who are considering taking enforcement action to notify the business in question of the proposal and give it the opportunity to make representations to the officer; these must then be taken into account.

4   Where enforcement action has been taken, and there is a right of appeal under relevant legislation, to require the enforcement officer to give details of that right of appeal to the business in question.

In the present context an 'enforcement officer' is any person authorised to take enforcement action, and 'enforcement action' includes any action taken with a view to imposing a sanction (criminal or otherwise) for failure to comply with a restriction, requirement or condition, *and* includes refusals to grant, renew or vary licences, imposing conditions on the grant or renewal of licences and any variation or revocation of a licence. 'Licence' includes any authorisations, howsoever called, to do anything which would otherwise be unlawful.

Orders under s 5 have to be made by statutory instrument subject to annulment by resolution of either House of Parliament.[2] Though it appears the overall thrust of the legislation is to restrain regulatory intervention in the affairs of businesses, until late 1995 it did not appear that there was to be much impact on environmental regulation. However, 1996 252 ENDS Report 3 indicated that the 'Deregulation Unit' which oversees implementation of the 1994 Act had insisted that the Agency's code of enforcement practice should 'reflect the principles of schedule 1' of the Act. The fear, as expressed in the ENDS report, must be that officers of the Agency will be inhibited from taking either speedy or, indeed, any, enforcement action, or even making suggestions as to remedial action. It is also particularly unfortunate that the proposal is effectively to apply the discipline of the 1994 Act to the Agency via the 'back door' of a code of practice, rather than the placing before Parliament of specific measures in the form of a statutory instrument. The Agency itself, however, as reported in (1996) Environment Business 14 February page 1, remains optimistic that the code will not prevent it from doing its job by virtue of inhibition of speedy action and red tape within the administrative process.

The National Radiological Protection Board

This board carries out research and provides information, advice and services for those persons and bodies having responsibilities for radiological protection.

The Nature Conservancy Councils

In controversial provisions Part VII of the Environmental Protection Act 1990 dismembered the Nature Conservancy Council into three; the NCCs for England (now known as English Nature) and Scotland and the Countryside Council for Wales, though they are co-ordinated by a committee drawn from their membership. The Welsh Council has responsibility for *all* countryside matters in Wales and is known as the Countryside Council for Wales (CCW), and a similar pattern exists in Scotland. The argument for an all embracing body for England along the lines of Scottish Natural Heritage (SNH) was rejected at Cm 1200 pp 233–234. Thus in England nature conservation is divided from the question of enjoyment of the natural beauty of the countryside. The councils are generally charged with establishing and maintaining nature reserves in their areas, advising central government and informing others about nature conservation, and commissioning nature conservation research, see s 132 of the 1990 Act. In some cases where a nature conservation issue relates to Great Britain as a whole the functions of the councils are to be discharged through their Joint Nature Conservation Committee (JNCC), see ss 128 and 133 of the 1990 Act. The councils are subject to ministerial direction, see s 131, and see generally DoE Circular 4/91 on English Nature.

2 See further the annotations to the 1994 Act in the Current Law Statutes Series to which indebtedness is acknowledged.

Nature conservation in the present context is defined by s 131(6) of the 1990 Act as the conservation of flora, fauna, geological or physiographical features.

There is a quite general feeling that the 1990 changes in the law, and the failure to unite English Nature with the Countryside Commission have weakened the voice of conservation interests.

Drinking Water Inspectorate (DWI)

The DWI exists within the Water Directorate of the DoE and is concerned with monitoring drinking water quality and fitness under the Water Supply (Water Quality) Regulations SI 1989/1147, and with advising ministers on quality issues. After some debate it was determined not to include the DWI within the Agency on the somewhat lame basis that its functions relate to public health rather than wider environmental issues.

Office of Water Services ('Ofwat')

'Ofwat' was created following the privatisation of the water industry in 1989 and now exists under the Water Industry Act 1991. The Director General of Water Services as head of the office primarily regulates pricing of water services, but also ensures water undertakers have regard to their general environmental and conservation duties under the 1991 legislation.

C CENTRAL ENVIRONMENTAL AGENCIES AND POLICIES: AN OVERVIEW

Though there is overlap and duplication of functions, there is no central body having *entire* responsibility for the development, oversight *and* operational implementation of a national environmental policy. This results in a weakened environmental policy. It remains too easy for environmental policies to be subordinated to other issues such as the commercial needs of industry or what is simplisticly accepted as the economic needs of the nation. The fragmentation and proliferation of environmental responsibilities makes it difficult for central government to take a co-ordinated overview of environmental issues, and the conservation and protection of natural and human resources.

Following Cm 1200, however, new arrangements to 'integrate environmental concerns more effectively into all policy areas' (p 230) were introduced. These include, as already stated, a Cabinet Committee to consider and co-ordinate policy on environmental issues and other measures, and (though Cm 1200 was averse to the creation of US style Environmental Protection Agency) subsequent policy developments led to the Agency which is the largest environmental protection body in Europe.

Perhaps the most important development, however, has been the emergence of the sustainable development strategy, to which allusion has already been made in connection with the Agency.

Sustainable development — UK policy

The government issued its policy in January 1994 as 'Sustainable Development, the UK Strategy' Cm 2426, the response to the commitments internationally made at the 'Earth Summit' in Rio, 1992. In his foreword the Prime Minister accepted that sustainable development is hard to define, but indicated it must be based on 'good science' and 'robust economics' though 'sensitive to the intangibles that cannot be reduced to scientific imperatives and the narrow range of economics'. The strategy document itself begins by stating the widely quoted definition of sustainable development as 'development that meets the needs of the present without compromising the ability of future generations to meet their own needs'. It proceeds on the basis that there will not be *less* economic development, arguing 'a healthy economy is better able to generate the resources to meet people's needs', and accepts that not 'every aspect of the present environment should be preserved at all costs', and concludes that what is required is that 'decisions throughout society are taken with proper regard to their environmental impact'. Those decisions should be based on the best possible scientific information and assessment of risks, though precautionary action may be needed where there is uncertainty and potentially serious risks exist. In particular ecological impacts must be considered, particularly with regard to non-renewable resources and irreversible effects, and the cost implications of decisions must be brought home to all those responsible for them via the application of the 'polluter pays' principle.

This represents not so much a decision or policy in itself but an approach to decision making and policy formulation. It also accepts that some environmental costs will have to be borne as the price of economic development, and that implies that the process is inevitably evaluative and judgmental and may be effectively political in that it will have to decide between competing claims and values. To this end better indicators of environmental impact have to be developed and systems of natural resource accounting so that the benefits/disbenefits of growth can be properly assessed and duly informed decisions taken.

Sustainability and the environmental media

The strategy document then goes on to examine the broad implications of sustainable development policy within particular sectors. Accepting first of all an increase in the home population from 57.6m in 1992 to some 61m in 2012, and stating the unacceptability of enforced family planning, the document concludes the UK will experience further potential pressures on land, water, energy and other resources to provide for housing, food, employment and transport. In sustainability terms this points to very careful use of land, with high development density in places, and with derelict or contaminated land having to be brought back into beneficial use, along with careful husbanding of other resources, minimising waste and recycling material wherever this is economical.

With regard to the atmosphere the strategy points to the UK's commitment to reduce CO_2 emissions to 1990 levels by 2000 and further accepts the need for reductions on these levels in the years beyond (see further chapter 10 below). It points to UK participation in cutting out the production and supply of CFCs and halons and again undertakes to recycle such materials whenever possible rather than releasing them into the atmosphere. However, it is further accepted that pollution from vehicles is now becoming a major urban air quality problem and that growth in traffic may well cancel out improvements made by reducing the emissions of individual vehicles, see further below on transport policies. So far as SO_2 emissions are concerned the strategy claims that, on present rates of reduction, emissions will have fallen by 2012 to levels approaching long term sustainability.

With regard to water the strategy points to historic rapidly rising demand and a further likely 10% increase in demand between 1992 and 2012. Demand will not, however, be evenly spread, and some areas could need extra ground and surface resources or have to 'import' water from elsewhere. To meet the criteria of sustainability it is, however, policy to defer major new water resource schemes by usage of water meters to drive down consumption by pushing up cost, and by measures to restrict leakage. The strategy points out that, overall, UK freshwater is of relatively good quality with 955 rivers and canals being classified fair or good. It will remain policy to clean up discharges from particular points, and to minimise diffuse pollution — eg contamination of water by agricultural fertilisers — by codes of practice and advice to farmers. Over the next 20 years groundwater protection will also be a major priority a task for the Agency (see further chapter 12 below). Similarly over the next two decades developments on land must be consistent with maintaining the marine environment, while only very limited categories of waste will be allowed to be dumped at sea in the future. It is, however, accepted that particular problems may arise in consequence of demand for marine dredged aggregates (see chapter 8 below), the fate of offshore oil and gas rigs as they reach the end of their lives, pressure on fish stocks, and pressures consequent on tourism and leisure activities.

Turning to the land, the strategy identifies erosion, irreversible decline in organic matter, acidification, industrial contamination and urban developments as potential threats. There may be between 100,000 and 200,000 ha of contaminated land in the UK and it is important to prevent future contamination, and to remediate the land currently contaminated as this can help in relieving pressures on greenfield sites. Urban development pressures on rural land could, if unrestrained, also lead to an increase in urban areas in some counties by 15% over 1981 levels by 2001. It is accepted that in the UK land use will continue to be a major problem for sustainable development as, though there is pressure to give protection to hedgerows, trees, forests, coastlines and other areas of beauty, population growth, household formation and transport create countervailing forces. It is also predicted that mineral extraction will be a continuing sensitive issue with demand for construction aggregates likely to rise sharply over the next 20 years, and, while recycling can meet some of the demand, new extraction sites will be needed.

Sustainability and its implications for particular policies

1   *Agriculture*: promote environmentally friendly farming; conserve wildlife habitats; protect and restore threatened landscapes; reduce pollution from agricultural imputs and waste; minimise pesticide use; conserve non-renewable resources; monitor agriculture's impact on the environment; press for further reform of the EU's Common Agricultural Policy to reduce over-intensive farming.
2   *Forestry*: protect remaining ancient and semi-natural woodlands: manage

all existing woodlands and forests sustainably; encourage a steady expansion of tree cover in harmony with the environment.

3   *Fisheries*: avoid over exploitation of fish stocks and work to rebuild them; avoid inadvertent capture of non-target species; carry out fishing so as to have no adverse effect on natural resources.

4   *Minerals*: encourage prudent stewardships of resources while providing necessary supplies; reduce the impact of extraction both during and after mining; research the environmental costs and benefits for using different sources of materials; encourage recycling of material and substitution where appropriate.

5   *Energy*: press for ever increasing energy efficiency; ensure that the framework of the energy market does not undermine attempts to improve energy efficiency by concentrating on increasing the quantity of energy available for supply; market forces should, however, decide the balance between particular energy sources, though such forces must take proper account of all different costs and benefits; radioactive waste arising from energy production must be managed so as to ensure the continued safety of this and future generations; promote new and renewable energy resources.

6   *Manufacturing and services*: industry creates wealth but depletes resources and emits waste, etc; it must therefore be encouraged to reduce its impacts through new techniques and designs; market based instruments (eg appropriate taxes) can assist, and are favoured by government in prompting industry to reduce its impacts; consumers can assist industry by demanding sustainable products; good environmental management, eg to BS7750 standard, is to be encouraged, as are eco-labelling and environmental reporting by companies; essential environmental standards will be protected or maintained by regulation; the financial sector will be encouraged to pursue environmentally friendly investment; biotechnology will be encouraged to promote the use of living organisms in manufacturing and service processes, but only subject to precautionary measures to ensure environmental safety; industry will be encouraged to develop new chemicals which are less hazardous and persistent in the environment and better managed; waste should be minimised as a first priority, thereafter it should be reused, recycled, recovered, eg for energy use, and only finally disposed of; economic instruments will be considered to tilt the balance of advantage away from landfill as the prime waste disposal option.

7   *Development and construction*: promotion of attractive urban areas where people will both want to live *and* work is essential; development must take place in locations likely to minimise energy consumption; regeneration of urban land and buildings must be promoted, and the restoration to use of derelict and contaminated land; rural economic development must be integrated with countryside protection; all those involved in development must be encouraged to think and act sustainably, for example in building design and construction so that impacts are reduced, multi use is encouraged to reduce the threat of buildings becoming redundant, waste in the construction process is minimised, etc.

8   *Transport*: policy must influence the rate of traffic growth and must allow for individuals to choose transport options in a way enabling

environmental objects to be met; transport decisions should be economically efficient; vehicle design must be improved to minimise emissions: the costs to the economy and the environment should be reflected in transport costing; land use planning and policies should assist people by enabling them to use less transport or less polluting modes of transport in their lives and activities; market measures and regulations should improve transport's environmental performance; public transport must be promoted over car use, and use of rail and water should be used for transport where they can meet need efficiently.

9 *Leisure*: leisure provision is now a major economic issue, but, paradoxically, many aspects of leisure enjoyment depend on the conservation of natural resources while at the same time putting pressure on the environment and leading to conflicts of interest; leisure activities must become aware of their environmental impact, while it is for central government to decide on the appropriate mix of voluntary self-restraint, economic incentives and regulation to control such activities.

It is clear that sustainable development cannot be brought about by legal means alone — indeed the overall impact of the law may be quite small. Cm 2426 makes it clear that, in the governments view, '[the] market is the most effective mechanism for maintaining the momentum of development . . . and for shaping its course towards sustainability [provided] . . . the costs of environmental damage or the benefits of environmental improvement are built into the prices charged for goods and services'. Much is also left to the voluntary efforts of companies, local authorities and private citizens as consumers, volunteers, workers, parents and as being generally aware of the issues so as to voice concerns in local affairs and by voting and exchanging views. The law's role is therefore largely to support environmental quality objectives where these are set, to ensure that environmental appraisal and assessment of projects and policies takes place where required and generally to underpin the work of environmental performance indicators as they are put in place.

To promote sustainable development further Cm 2426 announced the creation of a government Panel on Sustainable Development (to give authoritative and independent advice), a UK Round Table (to bring together representatives of the main sectors or groups) and a Citizens' Environment Initiative ('to carry the message' to individuals and communities).

Subsequent developments

The Panel gave its first advice in January 1995 and recommended:

1 Higher priority should be given to defining environmental objectives and targets and how they are to be met.
2 Discussions should be begun with industry to draw up proposals in key sectors for pilot projects involving economic instruments.
3 A comprehensive strategy for both formal and informal environmental education is needed, with a comprehensive database of appropriate resources being set up.
4 Particular action needs to be taken at sea, with the EU's Common Fisheries Policy being reformed in the interests of sustainability, the

creation of an intergovernmental panel on the oceans leading to a convention by 2000 on the sustainability of the marine environment.

The House of Lords Select Committee on Sustainable Development also examined the government's strategy in 1995. They also called for the setting of challenging but realistic explicit targets for sustainable development (such targets to be set by as open or 'transparent' a procedure as possible) with regular updatings comparing outcomes with expectations. Such targets are particularly appropriate for energy efficiency and transport policy and also with regard to waste and recycling. They further argued for shifting the burden of taxation away from labour and capital and on to resources and pollution to drive down, for example, unsustainable resource depletion, with pollution taxes being devoted ('hypothecated') to specific policy objectives. The Select Committee, however, noted that some departments are more willing than others to set targets.

The Select Committee called for, inter alia, an enhanced concept and definition of sustainable development which, while accepting the need to revise wealth making activities by taking into account environmental costs, also distinguishes between those major life or planet threatening concerns demanding imperative action and those issues which are more localised. They suggested that, with regard to precautionary action, and the difficulties caused by uncertainty consequent on lack of data and imperfect understanding, one approach is to ask whether any given change in policy or practice is likely to make activities more or less sustainable, and they counselled against any policy which shifts resources into directions which are difficult to reverse. In this connection wherever there is a high risk of irreversible damage and the costs of taking remedial action are low, a decisive response is justified by the precautionary principle.

On the particular issue of the balance between economic and regulatory instruments, the Select Committee pointed to the current state of affairs where regulatory instruments are used much more than economic ones because of the slowness of the Treasury in making fiscal changes to ensure that the polluter does pay. While recommending, as already stated, that the burden of tax should be shifted onto, for example, those whose activities pollute, the committee accepted that the two types of instrument are complimentary — neither can replace the other, and in any given situation the 'mix' between the two can only be determined according to the nature of the problem and the speed of response required. Regulation is appropriate to protect health, or to impose absolute constraints to protect features of the environment or elements of ecosystems, but over-regulation is expensive, and over-demanding standards should not be imposed unless real evidence of need justifies this. Certainly both legal and fiscal measures must act together in harmony in order to bring about changes in lifestyles and, patterns of consumption; people are, on the whole, not going to adopt sustainable practices simply for moral reasons.

The government's response

The government published its response to the select committee in October 1995 (Cm 3018). On the issue of the definition of sustainable development, it was accepted that there are two major schools of thought — those who insist on the need to establish and maintain a minimum environmental 'stock' or capacity, and those who accept that some trade off between social and economic preferences on the one hand and environmental resources on the other is inevitable. The government would not be too specific in its view, arguing that particular cases may need particular judgments and to reach these better information and tools of analysis are needed. It was, however, stated that: '[sometimes] environmental costs have to be accepted as the price of economic development, but on other occasions a site, or ecosystem, or some other aspect of the environment has to be regarded as so valuable that it should be protected from exploitation'.

So far as specific targets for sustainability are concerned, the 1995 Annual Report on sustainable development and the environment (Cm 2822) accepted that more could be done, and three initial areas for action are waste, air quality and biodiversity. The government has also undertaken to bear in mind that targets do not necessarily have to be firm or legally *imperative*, but that there is also room for indicative targets, for example, in relation to long term goals where there is also an allowance for reappraisal and adjustment. Work is also at hand on quantifiable indicators of sustainable development.

With particular regard to transport, the government accepts its strategy necessarily involves influencing the rate of traffic growth and reducing reliance on cars.

On the issue of the balance between regulation and economic instruments the government's view is that both economic instruments *and voluntary action* have a potentially greater role than regulation, but also considers that over-taxation may be as pernicious as over-regulation. Thus where new taxes or increased taxes are imposed the prime object is not to impose additional costs on industry but to enable other existing distortionary taxes to be reduced. Furthermore the government's response to tax hypothecation was lukewarm because hypothecation takes away one basic element of public finance, namely that decisions should be taken on the basis of always seeking the best value for money. The government accepted that regulation is needed where the issue at stake is public health or the protection of an important environmental resource, but is further awaiting the outcome of a study into environmental standard setting by the Royal Commission on Environmental Pollution.

Conclusion

Sadly the government's own 'Indicators of Sustainable Development for the United Kingdom' (12 March 1996) show a *lack* of sustainability. Since 1970 public transport has become dearer while private motoring is cheaper; manufacturing industry has saved energy, but its use in the home and on the roads has increased. Meanwhile journeys to work, to shop and to school have increased, while there is an accelerating rate of urbanisation predicted. The North Sea is overfished, though there is a slow rise in the recycling of metals, paper and glass.

As Stephen Tromans has pointed out in 'High Talk and Low Cunning' [1995] JPL 779, sustainable development is 'the most wonderfully wide principle', which is 'accepted as an article of faith'. He points out that it is easily stated, but that very ease, whereby the needs of the present are met without compromising the ability of future generations to meet their needs, conceals an inherent tension that the definition does nothing to resolve. The issue ultimately is political — it is about the organisation of society — and while a degree of consensus has emerged about controlling the release of certain emissions into the environment, as yet there is much less evidence of a real desire to cut emissions of CO_2 and other greenhouse gases.

Tromans points out that much of the problem centres on the concept of 'needs'. One of the West's current 'needs' is for environmental improvement, and it has the prosperity to address that need; other societies are not so fortunate. Furthermore it is not easy to consider what the needs of generations more than two or three removed from our own may be. They will certainly need to be able to exist, and thus sustainability certainly points to obligations not to bring about irreversible degradation of all that which is essential to the maintenance of life. Tromans argues further, however, 'future generations are not going to want simply to subsist, but also to develop — current development should not therefore certainly prejudice possible future development'. On that basis sustainability becomes much more of a balancing of the interests of one generation against those of another — as Tromans points out it is 'almost justiciable'.

However, Tromans then proceeds to the somewhat gloomy, but undoubtedly sound conclusion, that UK policy is hardly 'visionary or radical ... [the] ... sustainable development documents are perhaps best thought of as "soft policy", general in nature ... and not intended for application in any specific decision making context'. Even where advice on sustainability is given in the context of 'hard' policy reinforced by law (such as PPG 23, see chapter 5 below), Tromans finds it to be no more than a 'nodding reference' to the commitment to sustainable development.

Tromans does, however, find rather more hard evidence of a real commitment to sustainability in MPG 23 (guidance on aggregates provision), PPG 13 (transport) and PPG 6 (town centres and retail developments). He also points to the specific references to sustainable development in the Environment Act 1995 (see above). However, it is hard to disagree with his conclusion, 'we have an idea of where we want to get to: a sustainable future, taking an appropriately precautionary approach, and with the true costs of environmental damage internalised to the polluter, rather than imposed as externalities on the public. All this is very different to how industry, with society's blessing, has operated in the past. The question is how, and how quickly, these fundamental changes are to be brought about'. It is now time to turn from the consideration of 'high' policy and principle to investigate more day-to-day issues.

The office and powers of the Secretary of State

Constitutional fiction has it that there is only one Secretary of State. In reality many ministers bear the title and each is responsible for a department. Nevertheless by the Interpretation Act 1978, s 5 and Sch 1, the expression 'Secretary of State' means 'Any of Her Majesty's Prinicipal Secretaries of State'. This, theoretically, allows interchange between the relevant ministers in respect of the exercise of functions. In fact the allocation of functions is decided by Orders in Council, issued under the Ministers of the Crown Act 1975, s 1.

Planning and waste disposal powers (exercised by the Secretary of State for the Environment)

Apart from the ability to go to Parliament to ask for new powers should existing ones be found insufficient, the Secretary of State has a number of important functions under planning legislation. One controversial power from an environmental point of view is that to make Special Development Orders under the Town and Country Planning Act 1990, s 59. These apply only to particular areas or pieces of land, and are subject to the negative resolution procedure in Parliament, see s 333(4) and (5) of the 1990 Act. They 'short circuit' the normal planning system and can take decisions out of local control. They can be used in respect of certain strategic developments where local pressures might persuade the local planning authority to refuse planning permission. The making of a Special Development Order is a purely legislative act, rather than a judicial one, and so the Secretary of State has absolute discretion.[3] Thus the Secretary of State can use the procedure as an alternative to granting planning permission on appeal against its refusal. This was done in respect of the re-processing of nuclear fuels at Windscale, see Town and Country Planning (Windscale and Calder Works) Special Development Order 1978, SI 1978/523.

With regard to waste disposal the Secretary of State has, under the Environmental Protection Act 1990, extensive powers concerning, inter alia, directing the formation of waste companies by relevant authorities (s 32), exempting waste disposal from licence requirements (s 33), giving directions as to terms to be included in waste management licences (s 35), their variation, revocation and suspension (ss 37 and 38), and supervision (s 42), to hear appeals in respect of licences (s 43), to create a national waste strategy (ss 44A) to make regulations in respect of 'special waste' (s 62), and to issue a Code of Guidance on the duty of care concerning waste disposal (s 34).

Water powers

So far as general water policy is concerned, responsibility is joint between the Secretary of State for the Environment, and the Minister of Agriculture, Fisheries and Food, and in Wales the Secretary of State for Wales who is responsible for the exercise of nearly all powers within the Principality. The Secretary of State's prime duty, under s 2 of the Water Industry Act 1991, is to secure the proper functioning of water and sewerage undertakers. Both the Secretary of State and the Minister are further subject in the context of water regulation to general environmental duties under s 3 of that Act to further nature conservation and the protection of historic and archaeological sites; to have regard to the desirability of preserving public access to woodlands, mountains, moors, heaths and other places of natural beauty; to ensure that land and water are available for recreation.

Transport powers

Under the Highways Act 1980, s 1, and SI 1981/238, the Secretary of State for Transport is the highway authority in England for, inter alia, any road in

3 *Essex County Council v Minister of Housing and Local Government* (1967) 18 P & CR 531.

respect of which it is expressly provided he/she shall be the highway authority and for any other highway constructed by him/her, except where, by statute, the local highway authority is made responsible. The Secretary of State's principal responsibilities exist in respect of 'trunk roads'. The classification, designation and construction of trunk roads (which expression includes motorways) now depends on the Highways Act 1980, ss 10 and 24. The Secretary of State is empowered to designate and create new trunk roads, for which purpose there are compulsory purchase powers under the Highways Act 1980, ss 239 to 249. The Secretary of State is placed under a duty by s 10(2) of the 1980 Act to keep under review the national system of routes for through traffic, and may designate any highway in existence, or to be constructed, as a trunk road. The Secretary of State may designate as trunk roads those routes primarily used by local traffic, provided it is expedient for the national system of through traffic.[4]

Under the Civil Aviation Act 1982, s 25, the Secretary of State for Trade and Industry, who has general responsibility for civil aviation, has power to maintain and establish aerodromes and their ancillary facilities. The establishment of aerodromes will be further considered in chapter 7.

Energy powers

The Secretary of State for Trade and Industry is responsible for general supervision of electricity supply in England and Wales, see s 3 of the Electricity Act 1989. Inter alia the Secretary of State is also charged with responsibility to promote efficiency and economy in the supply and use of electricity, to foster research into new means of generating or supplying electricity, to protect the public from dangers in the generation and supply of electricity and generally to consider the effect on the environment of activities connected with electricity generation, transmission or supply. To assist in these, and other relevant functions, the Secretary of State may appoint a Director General of Electricity Supply under s 1 of the 1989 Act. Section 4 of the 1989 Act generally prohibits the generation and supply of electricity without a licence, and s 6 provides for the grant of licences, which may be made subject to conditions (which may reflect the Secretary of State's general duties) under s 7. Those licensed must, under s 9, develop and maintain an efficient, co-ordinated and economical system of electricity supply. Licensees have compulsory purchase powers regarding land by virtue of s 10 and Sch 3 of the 1989 Act. The Secretary of State is further empowered by s 29 of the Act to make regulations, inter alia, to protect the public from the dangers of electricity generation and supply (see chapter 1 above with regard to the precautionary exercise of these powers).

Further to protect the public interest, s 32 of the 1989 Act empowers the Secretary of State to require electricity suppliers to acquire specified electricity generating capacity from non-fossil fuel generating stations — the Non-Fossil Fuel Obligation. Failure to comply with such a requirement will constitute a criminal offence. 'Fossil fuel' for the purposes of this provision means coal, and its products, natural gas, crude liquid petroleum or its products. A non-fossil fuel generator, therefore, is any one which is or may be driven otherwise

4 *Walters v Secretary of State for Wales* (1978) 77 LGR 529.

than by fossil fuel, for example hydro-electric, nuclear or wind power, or gas coming from landfill waste.

The Secretary of State's consent is also generally required for the construction of electricity generating stations under s 36 and Sch 8 of the Electricity Act 1989, and, under s 37, for the installation of overhead power lines. These matters will be returned to at length in chapter 7.

In practice the Secretary of State (DTI) is generally responsible for the promotion and control of the development of atomic energy (that is the energy released from atomic nuclei as a result of any process including fission), see the Atomic Energy Act 1946, s 18(1). The legislation gives the Secretary of State powers, inter alia, to obtain information relating to certain materials, plant and processes, to authorise inspection of, and entry on, certain premises, to search and work for minerals, to acquire property compulsorily, and generally to control the production and use of atomic energy. The powers include the ability under the Atomic Energy Act 1946, s 6, to do work on land to discover the presence of substances which may be used for the production or use of atomic energy. This provision is coupled with compulsory purchase powers for the obtaining and working of relevant minerals, either by the Secretary of State or by the United Kingdom Atomic Energy Authority, see s 7 of the 1946 Act. The Secretary of State appoints the members of the United Kingdom Atomic Energy Authority and may give them such directions as are thought fit, see the Atomic Energy Authority Act 1954, ss 1(3) and 3(2). The Secretary of State's permit is also required before any person, other than the Atomic Energy Authority, or a government department, may use any site for the treatment of irradiated matter involving the extraction from it of plutonium or uranium, or the treatment of uranium so as to increase its proportion of isotope 235, see the Nuclear Installations Act 1965, s 2(1).

The Secretary of State's legal powers, however, cannot be separated from overall responsibilities for energy and fuel conservation policies. It is to these that we must now turn.

Energy conservation powers

In connection with *conservation* measures the general powers contained in the Energy Act 1976 should be noted. This Act implements obligations under European Union legislation, also those arising out of membership of the International Energy Agency, and those following on being a party to the International Energy Program signed at Paris on 18 November 1974. Section 1 of the Act gives the Secretary of State power to regulate or prohibit, by order, the production, supply, acquisition or use of, inter alia, crude liquid petroleum, natural gas, petroleum products, other fuels and electricity at any time but only where it appears desirable for the purpose of conserving energy, subject to a requirement that he/she should first consult those who will be affected by the order. However, if an Order in Council under s 3 of the 1976 Act is in force declaring that the fullest use of the power to conserve is needed, *either* to meet our obligations under European Union Law or other international obligations to take emergency measures against the reduction of fuel supplies, *or* because an actual or threatened fuel emergency in the UK necessitates exceptional energy controls, then the s 1 powers are freed of limitation, and, directions can be given under s 2 to undertakings as to their production, supply or use of the specified substances or electricity.

The 1976 Act contains other provisions for controlling energy sources and promoting economy in the use of energy. Section 12 contains a general prohibition (subject to specific exceptions) on the disposal of natural gas by flaring or by allowing its unignited release into the atmosphere without the consent of the Secretary of State. Section 15 enables the making of orders requiring the fuel consumption of passenger cars to be tested and the results to be recorded and published.

Under the Energy Conservation Act 1981 the Secretary of State may make orders prohibiting the supply or display of any new gas appliance, or a heat generator (ie an appliance designed for space heating or hot water production or both) which uses energy in any form to generate or transmit the heat required for the purpose, unless it bears a prescribed type approval mark and is accompanied by approved operating and maintenance instructions. See s 1 of the 1981 Act. Section 15 of that Act further empowers the Secretary of State to make grants for the purposes of any scheme for the provision of advice with a view to promoting energy conservation.

Energy conservation in the home

A boost for energy conservation is contained in the Home Energy Conservation Act 1995. Energy Conservation Authorities, that is local housing authorities under s 1 of the Act, are required, under s 2, to prepare energy conservation reports setting out the measures they consider practicable, cost-effective and likely to result in a significant improvement in the energy efficiency of accommodation in their areas. Such reports *must* contain, inter alia, assessments of the costs of energy conservation measures, the reduction of CO_2 emissions consequent on such measures, and *may* further include assessments of decreases in NO_x and SO_2, the number of jobs to be created by such measures, and an assessment of the fuel bill savings which would result from the measures. The Secretary of State prepares the programme for making such reports under s 3, and, if he/she approves any such report, is to give directions to authorities requiring them to give periodic statements of their progress in implementing their reports. Section 4 enables the Secretary of State to give guidance to authorities on the making of reports.

It should, however, be noted that nothing in the Act authorises the making of any grants or loans for energy conservation purposes.

The powers of the Secretary of State and overall energy policy

As was indicated above in relation to sustainable development policy, the official view is that market forces should decide the overall mix of energy generation options available to the nation. Currently the *principal* elements are gas, petroleum, coal and nuclear power. Energy policy tries to achieve the 'best of all possible worlds' by a balanced combination of these four energy sources, combined with the belief that cost differentials between energy sources will, of themselves, direct users to be economy and conservation minded. At the same time it is highly difficult to predict the future energy needs and consumption patterns of the nation. The result has been the production of over-capacity in the electricity generating industry.

In Parliament on 18 December 1979 the Secretary of State claimed that a strong and safe nuclear power industry is essential to national energy policy. Even with full use of coal and conservation measures the official view was that long term energy needs cannot be met without nuclear power. To supply that power the government reaffirmed official commitment to nuclear power, while stressing its continuing support for the overriding importance of safety considerations. See below, however, on the subsequent fate of the nuclear programme.

The Select Committee on Energy (First Report for the Session 1980–81, HC 114, 13 February 1981) were not satisfied with policy. They envisaged a modest programme of investment down to the year 2000. However, they also criticised policy for its failure to investigate with rigour the cost benefits of energy conservation so that these could be compared with the proposed costs of a nuclear plant.

The Select Committee again returned to the issue in its report 'Energy Policy Implications of the Greenhouse Effect' and stressed that energy efficiency 'is the most obvious and most effective response to the problem of global warming'. The Committee urged the use of regulatory mechanisms, coupled with penalties for the inefficient use of energy, and tax and fiscal incentives to promote efficiency as opposed to mere voluntary savings by individuals, companies and institutions acting in response to market forces. Cm 1200 promised, however, some increased spending on promoting energy efficiency, to encourage use of 'best practice' action in the efficient use of energy especially in central and local government buildings, and also the creation of a ministerial committee chaired by the Secretary of State for Industry 'to maintain the momentum of improvement'. This continued voluntarist approach had been presaged in the report by the National Audit Office in 1989 entitled 'National Energy Efficiency'.

Continued commitment to energy efficiency and its enhancement as a policy objective alongside the development of renewable sources of energy was announced in the government's energy expenditure plans for 1991–1994, Cm 1505.

In January 1991 the Fossil Fuel Levy was increased to 11%, with further Non-Fossil Fuel Obligation support for 150–200 MW of renewable energy projects in 1991 additional to 170 MW of projects already receiving support. Even so with some commentators predicting an increase in world energy consumption of 100% in the next century, renewable energy sources will be hard pressed to make up any shortfall in supply consequent on reductions in fossil fuel energy production.

UK power needs are being met increasingly by the creation of small localised plants, many of them gas turbine driven. However, it is still arguable that official energy policy is now so deeply committed to a major conventional energy policy, with a mix of energy sources driven by market forces, as to be blind to the possibility of other forms of policy, for example a major initiative on energy conservation, currently something of a 'Cinderella' in energy policy terms, despite significant and continuing benefits to be gained from increased conservation investment. However, the provisions of the Home Energy Conservation Act may mark a real change of direction in energy policy in favour of conservation.

Commitment to alternative energy sources however, seems more potential than actual on the part of central government. In 1989 it was announced that the government wished to see 600 megawatts of power derived from wind, water, waste, biomass and other renewable sources by 2000. This must be placed alongside the more efficient use of conventional power generation whereby water heated to produce steam for turbine generators can also be used to heat areas in the locality of the power station: this is known as Combined Heat and Power (CHP) or co-generation. Such schemes only appear viable, however, if local authorities are prepared to promote them for their areas, and if there is an acceptable economic return available on both the heat and power generation.

Renewable energy such as wind and wave power could, however, supply up to 18% of UK energy needs by 2030 if developed, and that figure is based on a conservative estimate of capacity; indeed offshore wind generation capacity is argued by some to have the capacity to produce 50% of current UK requirements for electricity. Whether such developments will take place depends upon the outcome of considering a mix of economic, environmental and other factors, the exact balance of which depends greatly on the policy stance of government.

Energy policy and nuclear power

The sustainable development strategy does not preclude some continuing reliance on nuclear power, but accepts that particular care will have to be taken with regard to the long term future of nuclear waste arising from power generation if future generations are not to be left with a most dangerous legacy.

Supporters of nuclear power point to its generally safe record of production over the last forty years or so, and its freedom from CO_2 and other atmospheric emissions. Despite the evidence which shows that nuclear systems as employed in the UK involve no more risk than oil or coal burning systems taking the whole fuel cycle of each into account from initial mining to final emissions (and probably involve less), the public views nuclear power with suspicion, particularly after the Chernobyl incident in 1986, partly because nuclear power is misunderstood and is thought to be a much greater everyday hazard than, say driving to work or operating DIY processes — when the opposite is true.

Even so the enthusiasm of the 1950s for nuclear power in the UK has long since evaporated. Between 1969 and 1979 the nuclear energy programme was in decline. In 1979, as has already been stated above, the incoming Conservative government declared a commitment to a strong nuclear programme as part of a diverse energy supply industry, and it was proposed to build 15GW of power stations using American style pressurised water reactors (PWR). However, before long doubts as to the economic viability of nuclear power crept in, and the PWR programme had shrunk to 4.8GW by 1987. In 1988 the UK withdrew from the fast breeder reactor programme, and in 1989 it was further decided not to include nuclear power stations in the initial phase of privatisation of the electricity industry. Thereafter the PWR programme was abandoned, save for Sizewell B and the formal, though unimplemented, approval of Hinckley Point C (see further chapter 7 below). Since 1990 some of the older nuclear power stations have been given extended operating lives into the next century while others have been closed down. The Non-Fossil Fuel Obligation referred to above ensures that electricity distribution companies will continue to purchase the output of existing stations.

In 1994 the government commenced its long awaited review of the prospects for nuclear power, published as 'The Prospects for Nuclear Power in the UK', Cm 2860 in 1995. This concluded that nuclear power which produces about 25% of UK electricity should continue to be a part of the 'mix' of the energy supply industry, provided it can maintain its current high safety and environmental protection standards — which is an expensive item. However, the government was unwilling to provide public sector support, ie finance, for a new nuclear station, while not ruling out the possibility that changing economic circumstances might make it attractive for the private sector to invest in such plant in the future.

Certainly it is *official policy* that the need to reduce national CO_2 emissions does not warrant new nuclear plant in the near future. Furthermore it is policy to privatise those parts of the current nuclear industry (as 'British Energy') which currently operate Advanced Gas Reactors (AGR) and Pressurised Water Reactors (PWR). The older Magnox reactors will be retained in public ownership and they will be transferred to British Nuclear Fuels Ltd (BNFL), whose long term privatisation is not ruled out. It is policy that both public and private nuclear operators will continue to be subject to the current rigorous safety regime.

However, in December 1995 it became clear that commercial pressures would not permit further private investment in new nuclear power stations. At up to £4 billion, over three times the cost of gas fired plant, such stations are not viable in the current state of the UK fuel economy. Hinckley Point C, for which planning permission exists, and the projected Sizewell C will not be built, and it is unlikely that further nuclear plant will be constructed in the UK for *at least* 10–15 years. The decision of British Energy not to press ahead was taken on commercial grounds. The price structure established by the privatisation legislation of 1989 effectively compels electricity suppliers to buy the cheapest form of electricity at any given point of time from its generators — nuclear energy currently is not the cheapest form of electricity production.

However, environmental concerns may still continue despite British Energy's decision:

1 Will it be able to maintain its culture of safety while its employees realise they are in an inevitably contracting business?
2 What could happen if cheap gas runs out?
3 What of the argument put forward by many that in the 21st century nuclear power will be an essential form of supply if global warming is to be combatted?

D CENTRAL ENVIRONMENTAL AGENCIES CONCLUDED

The United Kingdom Atomic Energy Authority (UKAEA)

The authority was established in 1954 under the Atomic Energy Authority Act of that year. It is a statutory corporation consisting of a chairman and between 7 and 15 other members appointed by the Secretary of State, and is a primarily civil undertaking. Today the authority is primarily concerned with research into the national nuclear power programme.

Under the Atomic Energy Authority Act 1971 the authority's trading enterprises were transferred to other organisations. The design, manufacture or supply of, or dealing in, inter alia, nuclear fuels, the carrying out of any processing or reprocessing of fissile materials and nuclear fuel, and the manufacture or supply of, or dealing in, radioactive substances are the objects of BNFL, an incorporated, state owned company. BNFL provides nuclear fuel services covering the design and development of plant, uranium processing and enrichment, fuel element fabrication, transport and reprocessing of spent fuel. It has three divisions: uranium enrichment; fuel manufacture; and reprocessing (which involves separating re-usable materials from irradiated fuel). The activities of the company have been expanded in a programme including the Thermal Oxide Reprocessing Plant (Thorp) at Sellafield. Increased facilities for storing spent nuclear fuel have been provided and also for reprocessing fuel for overseas customers, together with a plant for vitrifying highly radioactive waste. The opponents of such developments fear that they will lead to Britain becoming the world's 'nuclear dustbin' — a place where unproven methods of storage are used to cope with the world's most dangerous materials.

The Atomic Energy Authority Act 1995 now makes provision for the Secretary of State to direct all or any of the authority's property, rights and liabilities to be transferred to any person or persons, though such transfers may not relate to a nuclear site licence, nor a site benefiting from such a licence.

E LOCAL GOVERNMENT AND OTHER STATUTORY BODIES AND UTILITIES

Public utilities

Electricity

Under the Electricity Act 1989, the Secretary of State (DTI) has, as has been seen, various duties in respect of the generation, supply and efficient use of electricity. The actual *generation and supply* of the commodity is now primarily a private sector function under the 1989 Act. A licence to generate or supply electricity is required under ss 4–6 of the 1989 Act. Those licences may contain conditions under s 7 and are subject to a general duty imposed by s 9 on licensees to develop and maintain an efficient, co-ordinated, economical and *competitive* electricity supply and generation system. Licensees have powers, subject to ministerial confirmation, to acquire land compulsorily for their functions under Sch 3 of the 1989 Act; likewise ministerial consent is required, under s 36, for the construction, extension or operation of electricity generating stations of over 50 MW capacity, and for the overhead emplacement of power lines under s 37. Section 38 and Sch 9 of the Act further impose on those who generate/supply electricity an obligation to preserve amenity, and also on the Secretary of State when he is considering proposals for generating stations. At the Bill stage of the Act, however, there was unsuccessful pressure for more specific environmental duties to be imposed on power generators.

Part II of the 1989 Act provided for the 'reorganisation' of the electricity generation and supply industry. The law made provision for the separation of the generation, transmission, distribution and supply functions of the industry. Hence *anyone* may apply for a licence to generate and sell electricity via the transmission system, though the bulk producers are (in England) National Power plc, Powergen plc and Nuclear Electric plc, the first two being the initially privatised successors of the Central Electricity Generating Board (CEGB). They inherited coal, oil and gas powered generation stations and were sold as ordinary trading companies; the third retains the nuclear stations and is to be partly privatised. The generators of electricity, of course, have the prime environmental duties. Though both National Power and Powergen own hydro and wind driven plant, 90% of their production has historically come from coal fired plant which emits sulphur dioxide, nitrous oxide and carbon dioxide — all major environmental pollution gases. Measures taken to alleviate this problem will be examined in chapter 10 but it should here be noted that both companies have worked towards the introduction of gas turbine driven stations which do not have the same environmental disbenefits as coal fired ones, having no sulphur dioxide emissions and a 50% reduction in emissions of carbon dioxide per unit of electricity compared with coal firing.

In Scotland generation is in the hands of Scottish Power plc, Scottish Hydro Electric plc, and Scottish Nuclear Limited — the latter owned publicly, but again to be partly privatised.

Nuclear generation of electricity requires a site licence under s 1 of the Nuclear Installations Act 1965 from the Health and Safety Executive, while provision for planning controls over the creation of generating stations generally is provided for by s 36 and Sch 8 of the 1989 Act. These matters will be returned to in detail in chapter 7.

Gas

Part II of the Gas Act 1986 provided for the privatisation of the British Gas Corporation, and the Act generally provided a 'watchdog structure' similar to that for other de-nationalised utilities, with a Director General of Gas Supply.

Coal

The coal industry was nationalised by the Coal Industry Nationalisation Act 1946 and denationalised by the Coal Industry Act 1994. The former National Coal Board which had become the British Coal Corporation (popularly 'British Coal') was replaced by a new regulatory body, the Coal Authority, which owns unworked coal and other relevant property and issues licences to work coal. It is the authority's duty, inter alia, to maintain an economically viable British coal mining industry, but also to secure, so far as practicable, that any persons owed obligations by virtue of subsidence damage do not sustain loss by virtue of the failure of licensed operators to meet present and future liabilities in respect of such damage (for subsidence damage see chapter 2 above).

Part II of the Act provides for licensing of persons to mine coal, which may be worked by either deep mining or open cast working. The 1994 Act does not grant automatic planning permission along with a licence to mine coal, indeed under s 53 of the 1994 Act where there is a proposal to carry on any coal mining operations, restoration of land used in connection with carrying on such operations, or carrying on any other operations incidental to coal mining, the relevant planning authority is to have particular regard to the desirability of the preservation of natural beauty, of the conservation of flora, fauna, and special features of the site in question, of the protection of sites, buildings and structures of architectural, historical or archaeological interest. The influence of this provision was perhaps apparent in the refusal of Staffordshire County Council to grant Coal Investments permission to mine a new coal face at Hems Heath Colliery, Stoke-on-Trent in December 1995 when there were fears mining would damage homes in the area and a recently restored historic building. Those who formulate coal mining proposals are also required to have regard in their formulations to the foregoing issues and, further, to formulate proposals for the adoption of reasonably practicable measures for mitigating adverse effects on natural beauty, etc.

Under the provisions of the 1994 Act the majority of the English coal mining operation was purchased by RJB Mining, though some went to Coal Investments; that in Scotland was sold to Mining Scotland. They, along with the operators for the remaining Welsh open cast and deep mined sites, are now 'licensed operators'.

Water and sewerage undertakers

The water industry was privatised under the Water Act 1989. Parts III and IV of the Water Industry Act 1991 (as amended) now contain the powers and duties of water and sewerage undertakers, ie the commercial water companies. The general duties to develop and maintain efficient and economical water supply and sewerage systems, to supply water for domestic purposes, to supply only wholesome water for domestic purposes, and to provide, so far as reasonably practicable, that the quality of water supplied does not deteriorate, are matters to be returned to in chapter 12.

It should be remembered that for each of the privatised utility industries a regulatory framework headed by a Director General has been appointed, though their functions are less environmental than commercial in nature. Each Director General is supported by a staff: for water, the Office of Water Services ('Ofwat'), for gas, the Office of Gas Services ('Of gas') and for electricity, the Office of Electricity Regulation ('Offer').

Local authorities

In this work references to the functions of local authorities take place against the background of the two-tier system of local government introduced by the Local Government Act 1972 whereby responsibilities were shared between county and district authorities. The Local Government Act 1985 introduced a variation in that pattern in the metropolis and other major conurbations such as Merseyside, Greater Manchester and the West Midlands, etc, by abolishing the administrative counties introduced in 1972 and entrusting most functions, subject to liaison arrangements, to metropolitan district councils, single tier, multi-purpose authorities. The distinction between metropolitan and non-metropolitan areas must be borne in mind throughout the work.

In the areas of Greater London and the metropolitan counties the Local Government Act 1985 transfers a number of functions to London boroughs and district councils generally from 1 April 1986. Planning functions were transferred by s 3(1) as were mineral planning functions by s 3(3). In Greater

London s 5 of the 1985 Act required the boroughs to establish a joint committee to discharge certain planning functions, namely: consideration of matters of common interest relating to Greater London planning; giving appropriate advice to the Secretary of State when requested; liaising with other relevant planning authorities. The actual exercise of planning functions by the various types of authority will be considered in chapter 5.

Under the Local Government Act 1992 a Local Government Commission was created to review areas referred to by the Secretary of State and to consider what structural, boundary or electoral changes, if any, should be recommended, to which the Secretary of State may give effect with or without modification. The initial expectation, at least on the part of central government, was that there would be a general move nation-wide towards the creation of unitary, single tier *all purpose* authorities in the 'shire' areas, ie outside the metropolitan conurbations. The outcome has been rather different, and relations between the government, the Commission and other organisations concerned with local government became very bruised.

The initial aim of moving largely towards unitary authorities was not achieved. In most parts of most of the 39 shires two tiers of local government will remain: 75% of the people living in such areas will experience no change in their local authority arrangements. In some few places, however, county councils have been replaced by a number of unitary authorities — the areas affected being primarily counties which came into existence only in 1972, ie Avon, Humberside and Cleveland. In other cases certain large towns have been given unitary status independent of the counties around them, eg Leicester, Derby, and Nottingham — which, of course, marks a return to the pre-1972 County Borough system. In some cases old counties have re-emerged as unitary authorities, ie Herefordshire and Rutland.

In the following sections on individual functions it is therefore necessary to remember that in England the general rule will be for all functions to be exercised by unitary authorities where they exist. In Wales under the Local Government (Wales) Act 1994 a rather different system will apply in that the 1972 Act's eight County and 37 District Councils are to be replaced by 22 'principal' councils, 11 of which in rural areas will be counties, and 11 in urban areas, county boroughs. These will all be unitary authorities and under the 1994 Act they will have, generally, all the powers, rights and responsibilities of the two previous tiers of government.

Individual functions

HIGHWAYS

Though the Secretary of State for Transport is the highway authority for trunk roads, he/she may enter into agency arrangements with county councils to undertake work on highways. County councils are the highway authorities for all non-trunk roads, but they may make agency arrangements with district councils.

PUBLIC HEALTH MATTERS

Principal public health authorities are district and London borough councils. For waste functions see chapter 9 below.

PLANNING FUNCTIONS

Under the Town and Country Planning Act 1990, the division of responsibility is, *very broadly*, that county councils are responsible for making strategic 'structure plans' and for control of mineral developments, while district councils are responsible for tactical 'local plans', handling applications for planning permission and development control.

FIRE SERVICES

County councils save in London/metropolitan areas are fire authorities for their areas under the Fire Services Act 1947, ss 1(1) and 4, as amended by the Local Government Act 1972, Sch 30. They must provide efficient fire fighting forces, equipment, and advice on fire safety and fire fighting aspects in respect of buildings. These authorities also have responsibilities in respect of hazardous products such as petroleum and other inflammable substances, explosives and liquefied petroleum gas and other inflammable industrial agents.

F CONCLUSION

Though there is still a degree of over-fragmentation in environmental responsibilities, there has been a considerable change in the overall policy stance of government since the second edition of this work in 1992. The Thatcher government from 1979–1991 was avowedly opposed to the regulation of industry and for the freeing of the 'spirit of enterprise'. The Major government from 1991 onwards has developed a rather more environmentally conscious policy based on a 'common currency' of familiar, if somewhat vague, principles. In legislative terms this has led to the erection of a new administrative central framework for environmental regulation under the Environment Act 1995, and modification to the Thatcher government's 1990 and 1991 packages of legislation. What, however, unites both governments is a continuing degree of reluctance to take action on environmental issues without a body of strong scientific evidence, and a general failure to move, despite repeated protestations of intended action, towards a system in which the fiscal system is increasingly used as a means of environmental protection. There also remains a streak of strongly deregulatory policy under the Deregulation and Contracting Out Act 1994 under which those who regulate are subject to scrutiny and whose effects could yet be felt in relation to environmental matters.

For the future we may expect to see UK law continuing to be largely reactive to EU measures, a continuing debate on how to 'flesh out' principles such as sustainable development, and, possibly, a move away from Baroness Thatcher's version of 'the great car economy' and towards more emphasis on less travel generally and the promotion of less damaging forms of transport, with a consequent reduction in road building. Whether, however, some of these policy developments occur because of real environmental conviction on the part of government or because of a simple desire to cut public expenditure so as to pay for reductions in taxation is something which will only become clear over a period of time.

Further reading

GENERAL BACKGROUND

Bugler, J, *Polluting Britain* (1972) Penguin Books.
Churchill, R, Warren, L, and Gibson, J, *Law, Policy and the Environment* (1991) Basil Blackwell.
Hawkins, K, *Environment and Enforcement* (1984) Oxford University Press.
Johnson, SP, *The Politics of Environment: The British Experience* (1973) Tom Stacey Ltd.
Richardson, G, Ogus, A, and Burrows, P, *Policing Pollution* (1983) Oxford University Press.
Sandbach, F, *Principles of Pollution Control* (1983) Longmans Group.
Weeramantry, CG, *The Slumbering Sentinels* (1983) Penguin Books (especially chapters 1, 2, 3, 6, 10 and 11).

JOURNAL LITERATURE

Bateman, I, 'Social Discounting, Monetary Evaluation and Practical Sustainability' (1991) 60 Town and Country Planning (6) 174.
Blowers, A, 'Planning a Sustainable Future; Principles and Prospects' (1992) 61 Town and Country Planning (5) 132.
Davies, J, 'Striking the balance between economic forces and environmental constraints' [1992] JPL Occasional Papers Vol 18.
Hebbert, M, 'Planning a sustainable future: environmental foundations for a new kind of town and country planning' (1992) 61 Town and Country Planning (6) 166.
McAuslan, P, 'The Role of Courts and Other Judicial Type Bodies in Environmental Management' [1991] 3 Journal of Environmental Law 195.
Millichap, D, 'Sustainability: a long established concern of planning' [1993] JPL 1111.
Rowan, Robinson, J, & Ross, A, 'Enforcement of Environmental Regulation in Britain' [1994] JPL 200.
Tromans, S, 'High Talk and Low Cunning: Putting Environmental Principles into Legal Practice' [1995] JPL 779.
Walton, W, 'The Precautionary Principle and the UK Planning Systems' [1995] 7 ELM 35.
Winter, P, 'Planning and Sustainability' [1994] JPL 883.

OFFICIAL REPORTS

'The UK Environment', London (1992) HMSO.
'The UK Environmental Foresight Project', 3 Vols, London (1993) HMSO.
'Sustainable Development: the UK Strategy' (1994) HMSO.
'British Government Panel on Sustainable Development First Report' (1995) Department of the Environment.
'The Prospects for Nuclear Power in the UK', Cm 2860, London (1995) HMSO.
'House of Lords Select Committee on Sustainable Development', HL Paper 72, Session 1994/95 (1995) HMSO.
'Government Response to the Lords Select Committee on Sustainable Development', Cm 3018 (1995) HMSO.

Chapter 4

Environmental law: the international and European dimension

'Oh the man who can drive a theatrical team,
With wheelers and leaders in order supreme,
Can govern and rule with a wave of his fin
all Europe — with Ireland thrown in!'
(W S Gilbert, 'The Grand Duke', Act I)

Environmental problems raise supra national issues. Reasons of space preclude this work from dealing at length with the regulation of these problems under international law, but supra national aspects of law and practice cannot be ignored. Thus a *brief* introduction to international legal environmental issues follows, coupled with rather lengthier treatment of European Union (EU) obligations. Our membership of the EU has considerable implications for the future of the law, as well as bringing this country into partnerships with continental states some of whose nationals are, from the point of view of environmental problems, very *politically* advanced. There is hardly any aspect of environmental law that has no EU dimension.

A INTERNATIONAL ENVIRONMENTAL LAW

'Yours is the earth, and everything that's in it' (Kipling)

International law (by which here is meant 'public' international law as opposed to 'private' or 'conflict of laws') has been described as an 'indispensable body of rules regulating . . . the relations between states without which it would be virtually impossible for them to have steady and frequent intercourse',[1] and 'the system governing relations between States [covering] every aspect of inter-state relations such as jurisdiction, claims to territory, use of the sea and state responsibility to name but a few.'[2] From an environmental point of view it tends, sadly, to be a weak system of law lacking an effective system of sanctions. Though as Birnie and Boyle point out in *International Law and the Environment*, to which any serious student of the subject must be referred, despite problems remarkable progress has been made in developing international environmental law.

---

1 Starke, *Introduction to International Law*, 10th edn, p 15.
2 Lyster, *International Wildlife Law*, p 3.

The sources of international law are custom, general principles recognised by civilised states, decisions of international arbitral and judicial bodies, the views of international public lawyers of high renown and, most importantly, treaties, both general and particular, establishing rules accepted by states; see art 38 of the Statute of the International Court of Justice. None of these sources is fully adequate as a bedrock for international environmental law, but though treaty based law is inevitably likely to be the principal pathway for future developments, customary law cannot be ignored.

Customary international law though relevant in environmental issues has been weak in its impact for it has recognised the principle of state or territorial sovereignty, ie the right of states to carry on their activities and to use their resources for their own benefit, which, of course, includes the right to utilise territory and to exploit resources, to name but two issues. However, the principle of state sovereignty is not unlimited. In the *Trail Smelter* case[3] it was argued at p 1965 that: 'No State has the right to use or permit the use of territory in such a manner as to cause injury by fumes in or to the territory of another ... when the case is of serious consequence and the injury is established by clear and convincing evidence.' The United Nations Charter of Economic Rights and Duties of States reiterates that sovereign rights should only be used 'without causing damage to the legitimate rights of others'. The principle has received wide acceptance by most commentators on international law, and modern state practice appears to be founded on it. It has been adapted by the United Nations General Assembly in its Resolution 1629 of 1961: 'fundamental principles of international law impose a responsibility on all states concerning actions which might have harmful biological consequences ... by increasing levels of radioactive fall out' and adopted in the 1972 Stockholm Declaration on the Human Environment, Principle 21: 'States have ... the responsibility to ensure that activities within their jurisdiction or control do not cause damage to the environment of other states or of areas beyond the limits of national jurisdiction'.

As Birnie and Boyle (op cit) point out, two principles seem now to enjoy significant support: (a) to prevent, reduce and control polluting and environmental harms, (b) to co-operate in mitigating environmental emergencies and risks. Other customary principles for which arguments are put forward include concepts such as inter-generational equity, sustainable development and the 'polluter pays' principle, already examined in chapter 1, above. Furthermore many commentators now argue that concepts of sovereignty have to a considerable extent faded over the last 40 years as states have come to accept — to some extent at least — the concept of obligations to act within their jurisdictions for the benefit of humankind as a whole. This has led to recognition that states have a *common interest* in the global environment which may lead to the development of a body of international rules which apply to all states and are enforceable by all states. Similar linked emerging concepts are those of *common heritage* under which, for example, the management of natural resources may be seen to be a matter transcending state jurisdictions, and *common concern* which recognises the existence of entities such as the ozone layer and the global climate which are matters of

3 *United States v Canada* 3 RIAA p 1907 (1941).

international concern whose regulation demands that territorial jurisdictional claims must be transcended.

Both Birnie and Boyle (op cit) chapter 3, and Brown-Weiss, *Environmental Change and International Law* point to important customary developments such as the concept of *global* international environmental law, and the interplay which takes place between custom and treaty with the former's development underpinning the growth and importance of the latter as a system of international environmental regulation and protection.

'Soft' international environmental law

As in the case of the EU (see below) the difficulties of securing international agreements in a diverse and plural world have led to the emergence of 'halfway houses' known collectively as 'soft law'. This includes Codes of Practice, recommendations, guidelines, resolutions, declarations, etc of or by states. Though the term may be something of a 'shorthand' expression denoting a collection of rather vague legal norms, nevertheless, as Birnie and Boyle (op cit p 27) point out, states *expect* such soft law to be adhered to on a long term basis, and thus have a normative effect on international conduct even though it does not fit into conventional legal categories. On the other hand the degree of commitment by states to 'soft' law can vary greatly; though the fact that an obligation is 'soft' may enable a state to embrace its underlying concept and in consequence modify its activities when it would find it impossible to embrace the concept as a 'hard' rule in a treaty. 'Soft' law enables states to adopt a collective though flexible approach to an environmental problem when, for example, scientific knowledge points generally in the direction of caution but is otherwise inconclusive on an issue; see further Birnie & Boyle pp 26–30 to which indebtedness is acknowledged.

General principles of international environmental law

It is now commonly accepted that the future development of the law should reflect certain principles, particularly in the drafting of treaties; see below. These principles are: the 'Polluter Pays', Precautionary Action, Intergenerational Equity, see chapter 1 above, *and* Non-Discrimination: ie that a polluter who causes transboundary pollution should be treated no less severely than if the harm was caused in the polluter's own country, and Common but Differentiated Responsibilities, ie states should divide the cost of environmental measures according to their contribution to environmental degradation.

Treaty based law

Despite customary law's flexibility and current resurgence, its inherent problems have led to emphasis in environmental matters being placed on treaty based law. 'A treaty may be defined . . . as an agreement whereby two or more states establish or seek to establish a relationship between themselves governed by international law' and 'the treaty is the main instrument which the international community possesses for the purpose of initiating or developing international co-operation'.[4] Treaties can exist in various forms, but in

---

4 Starke, op cit pp 436 and 437.

environmental terms the most commonly encountered treaties are likely to be multilateral instruments made in formal style by many states or international institutions, such as the International Civil Aviation Organisation, and known as 'Conventions', together with 'Protocols' which are less formal agreements often subsidiary or ancillary to a Convention, other nomenclatures include 'covenant', 'pact' or 'act'. Treaties may be either 'law-making' in that they lay down generally applicable rules, or 'treaty contracts' which deal with individual issues concerning only two or a very few states. From a global point of view the first type is of greater importance, but environmental treaties have been made in a variety of forms by a variety of states for many years, dating from the 1868 Mannheim Convention on, inter alia, water supply on the Rhine (between Belgium, France, Germany, The Netherlands and the UK), to the numbers of multi-party arrangements made from the 1970s onwards. The yearly rate of treaty making now exceeds that for the century's opening decades. However, a warning note needs to be sounded: 'treaties are often weaker [than national legislation] because no state can be bound without its consent. The greater the number of participants in the formulation of a treaty, the weaker or more ambiguous its provisions are likely to be since they have to make compromises making them acceptable to every state involved.'[5] Treaties are also not rapidly made, and a five year negotiating time between states is average in relation to environmental issues, though, as Birnie and Boyle (op cit p 12) point out treaties can be made and can enter into force quite quickly as was the case with the 1985 Vienna Convention on Protection of the Ozone Layer.

Treaties may arise in a number of ways, for example because of pressure from a state, groups of states or an international organisation, and a treaty will normally be finally formulated at an international conference. State representatives at such a conference may sign such a document, though this creates *no* legal obligation to ratify or comply with the treaty's terms on the state's part, but a strong moral obligation and an expectation between signatories that none of them will frustrate treaty objectives. Ratification is the process whereby states undertake binding legal obligations under treaties. State practice as to the mode of ratification varies: in the UK, Parliamentary approval, normally in legislative form, is required for any treaty which, inter alia, affects the private rights of British subjects, or changes or modifies the law of the land, or requires a grant of new powers or financial responsibilities to the Crown, or which has been made expressly subject to Parliamentary approval. It is usually provided in treaties that they will come into force after a specified number of ratifications by states has been reached. Some treaties are restricted in that only certain specified states may be party to them, others are open to all to be original parties to them or, by accession, to become subsequent members of them; whilst others are also open to 'regional economic integration organisations' such as the EU. Treaties may also be made subject to 'reservations' whereunder a state releases itself from certain treaty obligations. Such a reservation may be made when a state becomes party to a treaty, and then to a substantive treaty provision, or, when a state declares it will not accept a particular regulation made according to a procedure existing under the treaty, though there is debate as to whether such a practice should properly be called a 'reservation'. As Lyster (op cit p 9) points out, reservations are useful in importing flexibility to treaties so that states which accept most, but not all, treaty obligations can become parties, but they 'also provide a loophole enabling a State to defend its vested interests, which conflict with the spirit of the Treaty'. In some cases making reservations is prohibited by the treaty itself, while reservations generally cannot be made which are incompatible with treaty objectives; see art 19(c) Vienna Convention on the Law of Treaties. The form and content of treaties also varies considerably. For example it is now the practice to have basic general provisions in one document — which may receive the title 'Convention' — while highly specified technical standards, say on emissions, are placed in subsidiary documents — which may be known as protocols — to allow for their amendment in the light of technical progress. This, however, has the disbenefit of allowing states to opt out of detailed control by objecting to the terms of the protocol. Other treaties are mere 'frameworks' simply creating no more than a generalised obligation on states to take some, unspecified, action — of course the obligation can be 'fleshed out' by a subsequent protocol, but the initiative to do this lies with states. A treaty can also take the form of an 'umbrella' whereunder there is a principal framework convention and a number of protocols each dealing with a specific issue. States ratifying the principal convention may also be required to ratify one or more of these accompanying protocols.

In 'dualist' states such as the UK it is generally further necessary, once a treaty has come into force, to pass national legislation giving the treaty domestic legal force. Thereafter what will be enforced within the state is the domestic legislation, though as Robin Churchill points out in *Law, Policy and the Environment* p 156: 'it is not unknown for a treaty to have been formally implemented by legislation but for it not actually to be applied in practice . . . because of defects in the implementing legislation or because the legislation is not properly given effect to.'

International organisations may also have powers under treaty to bind parties to such a treaty by their decisions, for example the International Maritime Organisation, the Oslo and Paris Commissions on countering certain pollution threats to the North Sea and North Eastern Atlantic, and the International Whaling Commission. Such organisations, as Birnie and Boyle (op cit p 29) point out may also adopt 'soft law' techniques by producing codes of practice which states observe in practice, while some may actually take such documents into their own legislative frameworks.

A convenient starting point for modern treaty based international environmental law is the Stockholm Conference of 1972 and its Declaration on the Human Environment. Sufficiently imprecise to leave much to the discretion of states wishing to advance their own interests, the Declaration has served as a basis for subsequent international developments and formulations of legal principle. So in 1982 at its 60th Annual Conference in Montreal, the International Law Association defined transboundary pollution in terms of the introduction by human action of material or energy into the environment so as to affect deleteriously health, living resources, ecosystems, property, amenity and legitimate use of the environment where pollution originates wholly or partly in one state and then invades another's territory. States, it was argued, should abate and control such pollution, and should limit new or increased pollution sources, and give warning of activities likely to cause significant transboundary pollution. Likewise in 1982 the United Nations set up the Intergovernmental Committee on the Development and Utilisation of New and Renewable Sources of Energy, and a gathering of 105 states at Nairobi reaffirmed the Stockholm principles. This was followed in 1983 by the creation of the World Commission on Environment and Development by the United Nations.

One current weakness of international environmental law is the problem of compliance. Disputes arising between states are initially submitted to negotiation, and only thereafter is recourse had to international arbitration and the International Court of Justice, and even then only in exceptional cases, for the remedy 'is seen as a politically unfriendly act . . . and . . . it is often difficult to achieve a satisfactory remedy by this means' (Lyster, op cit p 11). Recourse may also be had to the good offices of another state acting as a mediator between disputants. To ensure more effective compliance it is important to build into treaty provisions requirements that states: establish regular meetings to review treaty implementation and revise terms as and when necessary; create administrative agencies to assist with implementation; impose regular reporting obligations, or create monitoring or observer systems, or provide for financial sanctions or rewards as 'carrots and sticks'. Supervision by means of the creation of international agencies has been found a useful means of law enforcement, though it 'also entails the negotiation and elaboration of detailed rules, standards and practices' (Birnie and Boyle, op cit p 161).

This is not to say that international environmental law is without significance. Some principles are translated into national practice and as Lyster (op cit p 14) points out, 'there is another overriding factor which ensures that, by and large, States make every effort to enforce a treaty once they have become a Party to it: it is in the interests of almost every State that order, and not chaos, should be a governing principle of human life and if treaties were made and freely ignored chaos would soon result.' Moreover the future may see the development of a universal convention, consolidating existing and establishing new principles of legal environmental protection, and setting out the concomitant rights and duties of states. A UN Commission for Environmental Protection and Sustainable Development has been debated as a monitoring and investigative body, as has a High Commissioner or 'Environmental Ombudsman' to act as a 'trustee' for the environment and to take action on behalf of its protection. In 1989 a 24 nation conference at The Hague called for such a new authority to be known as 'Globe'. This would be an executive body, operating alongside the International Court of Justice at The Hague (the judicial compliance enforcing and arbitral body) and the UN Assembly as a legislative organ, able to lay down the framework of international environmental regulation. 'Globe', however, would be an unprecedented agency able to make decisions by majority vote, and possessing powers to enforce environmental standards. 'Globe' would also be able to pursue actions for damages against polluting states before the ICJ. The concept of 'Globe' necessarily involves some surrender of the concept of state sovereignty.

Trends in international environmental law

Since 1972 emphasis has shifted quite definitely from attempts to create an international system to ensure that states make reparation for environmental harm inflicted on other states towards a system based much more on the 'control and prevention of environmental harm and the conservation and sustainable development of the natural resources and ecosystems of the whole biosphere . . . [ie] a preventive or regulatory regime . . .' (Birnie and Boyle, op cit p 137). As Iwama points out in his contribution to *Environmental Change and International Law* there are now emerging principles of prevention and mitigation of harm. These are that: humanity has a common interest in protecting entities such as the climactic system, the ozone layer, rainforests and the biological diversity of the earth, and this is reflected in the development of measures such as those to phase out ozone depleting substances; to enter into co-operation in scientific research, systematic observation and to render mutual assistance in this connection, a very useful step on the way to later more specific agreements; to exchange information — often through the medium of an international institution; to give prior notice of activities which might entail a significant risk of transfrontier pollution, and to undertake prior environmental impact assessment of such activities and consult with other potentially affected states; where an environmental disaster occurs to have made available a prior risk assessment to other concerned states, and to provide emergency assistance to those affected. The development of a preventative regulatory framework internationally and its implementation nationally was one of the issues recognised by the 1992 Rio Conference on Environment and Development (UNCED). As is pointed out in Sand (ed), *The Effectiveness of International Environmental Agreements* (pp 24–27), the terms of Agenda 21, one of the documents to emerge from UNCED, make it clear that country specific laws and regulations are most important measures for environmental protection and regulation and the promotion of sustainable development, for it is by these that international obligations are translated into concrete action. These need, however, to conform to certain general principles. States thus need to develop and implement programmes of laws which are integrated, enforceable and effective, and which are based on sound social, ecological, economic and similar principles, and to ensure review of, and compliance with, those laws. Many states will, however, need technical assistance in achieving these objectives.

Flying on from Rio?

Rio produced a number of disparate documents: the Rio Declaration — an expansion of the 1972 Stockhold Declaration; the Framework Convention on Climate Change — a treaty providing for further negotiated protocols on issues such as greenhouse gas emissions and deforestation; the Convention on Biological Diversity — a rather hurriedly negotiated document which nevertheless aims to arrest the rate of species loss consequent on pollution and habitat destruction; a declaration on forests, and 'Agenda 21' an 800 page 'action plan' for the rest of the decade and the 21st century on a diversity of issues such as oceans, forests and industry. Though, as Professor Freestone points out in his 1993 inaugural lecture 'The Road from Rio', these treaties represent the lowest common denominator of consensus, ie what the 'most reluctant participant will accept', he also argues that Rio's main contribution to the development of international environmental law is 'through the crystallisation of principles', in particular with regard to enshrining the precautionary principle (see chapter 1, supra) as a guideline for future treaty making on all environmental issues thus entailing 'a shift in decision-making in favour of a bias towards safety and caution', ie 'preventive or remedial action is to be taken if scientific evidence makes it plausible that detrimental effects to the ... environment may result'.

Sustainable development in particular lies at the heart of Agenda 21, a document which builds on the earlier 1987 Brundtland Commission's finding that world poverty and environmental degradation are closely interrelated issues, so that environmental protection and providing for the development of third world countries must go hand in hand for the future. All nations must co-operate to combat existing environmental problems, to develop and apply environmentally sound technologies and also produce that level of economic growth and development in all countries necessary to combat poverty, especially in those countries already burdened with massive foreign debts. This involves the devotion of new financial resources on a vast scale to development coupled with environmental protection, while 'advanced' nations must also be prepared to afford favourable access to science and technology for the less developed states. The basis for this has to be the recognition by states of their common interests, mutual needs and common, but differentiated, responsibilities. To achieve this Agenda 21 has a number of themes: first, the revitalisation of growth with sustainability — this policy has implications for the pattern and content of treaties on world trade for reducing the debt burdens of poorer states, for lifestyle changes in wealthy nations, changes in consumer preferences and practices, for making the overall level, pattern and distribution of consumption and production compatible with the ecological capacity of the globe; secondly, the substantial reduction and ultimate eradication of world poverty; thirdly, the creation of a habitable, healthy and sustainable living environment for all the world's people — this policy has particular implications for pollution control and waste minimisation; fourthly, the reversal of the destruction of natural resources and the implementation of strategies for the sustainable use of land, water, biological and genetic resources, biotechnology and energy — a policy having vast implications for the task of sustainably raising the productivity and incomes of the poor without irreversibly degrading systems of life support, for energy production and consumption and for protecting the biodiversity of the world; fifthly, the creation of action programmes to protect on a total and global basis the world's atmospheric and oceanic resources; sixthly, the management of chemicals and waste to create a habitable 'clean world'.

Agenda 21 recognises that governments alone cannot achieve these goals, all relevant people and groups of people must be involved, which involves fundamental change in public education, awareness and training, great transparency in public decision making processes and a greater flow of relevant information to the public, not just within but between nations.

In order to ensure institutional arrangements to bring about the integration of environment and development issues Agenda 21 also brought about the creation of a Commission on Sustainable Development (COSD). This body reports to the UN General Assembly.

Other principles given special emphasis by Rio include those of 'differ-entiated responsibilities', ie a recognition that developed nations bear special responsibilities in respect of pursuing sustainable development because of the pressures their societies place on the environment and the technologies and resources at their command; ensuring the effectiveness of environmental laws, and creating adequate systems of environmental impact assessment. Freestone is thus able to hail Rio as a coming of age of international environmental law, but he also points out that the framework laid down at Rio has to be developed into a truly effective system of protection.

In some ways international environmental law since Rio has developed apace. In UNCED's immediate aftermath considerable attention was given to the problem of ozone depletion already addressed by the Vienna Convention 1985, and the Montreal Protocol 1987. In 1992 in London an enhanced schedule of phasing out ozone depleting chlorofluorocarbon (CFC) gases was agreed. In 1994 the USA unilaterally decided to bring forward its CFC phase out programme to 1996. The Copenhagen agreement of 1994 committed other nations to a similar programme, made arrangements to ensure financial help for third world nations to help them comply with new requirements, and also brought within regulation for the first time hydrochloroflurocarbons (HCFC) and methyl bromide which is used in commercial pesticides. In respect of the latter it was agreed to freeze production at 1991 levels by the end of 1995, with phasing out to be postponed for some years; in respect of the former, production curbs will come into force in 1996 with production falling to one third of that level by 2015, while a ban on production will operate from 2030. Even so these curbs disappointed environmental activists as not being sufficiently stringent.

Even more a cause for concern was the 1994 conclusion of the Inter-governmental Panel on Climate Change (IPCC) which argued that stringent cuts in emissions of the 'greenhouse' or global warming gases of 60% of current emissions are needed to stabilise the climate and achieve the Rio conference's objectives on climate change. The deliberate vagueness of the 1992 Climate Change Convention — designed to ensure US support for the treaty — was modified by a provision requiring the adequacy of the Convention to be reviewed at the first conference of parties to it. That Conference was held in Berlin in 1995. Accepting the principle of differential obligation (above) the 'Berlin Mandate' requires the creation of a new protocol by 1997 on measures to deal with reductions in greenhouse gases after 2000 with time scales of action by 2005, 2010 and 2020 in contemplation. It was further agreed that nations may begin joint pilot programmes of emission reduction on a voluntary basis. However, it is clear that some nations will not reach their obligations under the Rio Convention to *stabilise* greenhouse gas emissions by 2000, let alone be ready to take on new commitments, while further unfortunate features of the Berlin Mandate are: the refusal of some nations to participate at all on the post 1997 processes, eg Brazil; the entry of reservations by others, principally oil exporting states such as Kuwait, Saudi Arabia and Venezuela; and the non-creation of any voting mechanism: the old problems do not readily go away.

International environmental law: a summary and a vision?

A hesitant — though many would add far too slow — start has been made towards creating a discrete body of international environmental law having at its heart a precautionary and preventive approach to environmental protection. And while the speed of the world convoy is still that of its slowest ships, a number of encouraging developments have occurred:

1 The emergence of international prohibitions on the production and use of particular chemicals, eg those on ozone depleting substances.

2 The development of international regulations constraining permissible conduct on the part of nations and companies, for example requirements as to limiting emissions of SO_2.

3 The creation of international standards by which industry can regulate itself to ensure protection of the environment, see chapter 1, supra.

4 Gradual acceptance of the need for environmental impact assessment particularly at a world regional level.

5 Emerging recognition of the need to give as much public information as possible about the adverse consequences of activities on the environment via enhancing public access to relevant information, independent surveillance and observation of activities and monitoring programmes.

6 Continued adherence to such established principles such as the 'polluter pays'.

7 Gradual acceptance of the need to use economic and fiscal instruments to encourage clean technologies and low resource demand activities, while subsidies given to environmentally unfriendly activities are subject to increased scrutiny within the framework of international agreement on trade.

8 The emergence of international forums having jurisdiction to enforce a number of international agreements.

9 The possibility that some states may refuse to allow the import of goods not meeting international requirements — as can already happen with endangered species.

10 Acceptance of differentiated obligations by developed nations, together with an acceptance of the need to compensate, financially or otherwise, less developed nations when they take on board environmental obligations.

11 The continuing use of 'soft law' techniques.

Even so no-one should labour under any illusion that the way forward from Rio is or can be easy. We must move towards a principle of equal ecological security so that no state achieves its well being at the expense of others, towards requirements of foresight and prevention of harm, towards sharing knowledge and technology, towards, of course, sustainable development, towards acceptance that humans have the right to an acceptable environment. Much of the framework for achieving this currently exists, but how fast and far we can go depends on the will of nations and peoples. What that has been, and is, at a local world regional level is our next concern.

EC or EU — Community or Union?

Before addressing the 'internal aspect' of EU law it is important to state why this work refers to the EU rather than, as in previous editions, the EC. The initial entity was the European Economic Community (EEC) established by the Treaty of Rome in 1957 along with the European Coal and Steel Community (ECSC) and Euratom. The EEC was enlarged in 1972 when the

UK, Ireland and Denmark joined, and again in 1981 (Greece) and 1986 (Spain and Portugal). Austria, Sweden and Finland joined in 1995. Enlargement of institutional powers came with the Single European Act (SEA) 1987 and the Treaty of European Union (Maastricht Treaty) 1992. Under the latter the EEC changed its name to the European Community (EC) while the European Union (EU) was also created which subsumed the objects of the EC (such as the common internal market) and added other objectives of its own such as a single currency, common defence and foreign policies, etc. As the EU parallels the EC's policy objectives including those on the environment, EU will be used throughout this work, even in relation to matters predating its inception because the EU is the legal and political concept which draws together the EC, the ECSC and Euratom and creates the status of EU citizenship for every national of each member state. EU is the terminology increasingly commonly, if not always correctly, used.

B EUROPEAN UNION (EU) ENVIRONMENTAL LAW

Ideally, there should be vertical integration between international, regional and national systems of environmental law. In its international aspect the EU goes some way to realising this. Before examining this it is necessary to remind ourselves what the EU is. It grew out of the post 1945 desire to: rebuild western Europe; remove the likelihood of future Franco-German conflicts; counter perceived threats of Soviet aggression, with economic reconstruction and expansion as key policies. Hence in 1957 the six original member states declared their desire to create a 'European Economic Community' to establish a 'common market' and to approximate the economic policies of the states, their harmonious economic development, continuous and balanced expansion, increased stability, accelerated rising standards of living and closer relationships. Since then the EU has grown by the accession of new states and the development of community powers. Today the EU is a special entity not easily compared 'with other political entities: it contains some of the features of an ordinary international organisation and, less prominently but nevertheless quite distinctly some features of a federation. The latter are gradually becoming more prominent' (Hartley, *Foundations of European Community Law*, 3rd edn, p 9). The EU does, however, possess powers to enter into treaties either by itself or acting together with its member states. These exist in some cases under express provisions of the Treaty of Rome, the basic constituent of EU law which relates to co-operation with other international organisations. The EU also has under 'the doctrine of parallelism' implied treaty making powers that cover virtually all areas of activity covered by the EU legal system.[6]

Under its powers the EU is a party to a number of international environmental measures. It was furthermore argued by the EC Commission Task Force Report on the Environment and the Common Market that a global environmental role should be developed and that external and internal environmental policy should derive from the same principles.

6 *EC Commission v EC Council* [1971] ECR 263, [1971] CMLR 335; *North-East Atlantic Fisheries Convention Case* [1976] ECR 1279; *Opinion 1/76 on the Laying-Up Fund for Inland Waterway Vessels* [1977] ECR 741.

The influence of the EU on the development of international environmental law has already been marked. EU measures serve as models for other world regions and it appears that in the coming decade the importance of this aspect of EU law will continue to increase considerably; see further Sands, 'European Community Treaty Obligations in the Field of International Environmental Law — An Overview' in Vaughan (ed), *Environment and Planning Law*.

C THE INCEPTION OF THE EU'S ENVIRONMENTAL POLICY

In October 1972 the heads of government of the then enlarged EEC meeting for the first time in Paris called for proposals for an EEC environmental policy. Just over a year later on 22 November 1973 the First Action Programme for the Environment was formally adopted.

The decision of the summit meeting in 1972 reflected a growing awareness that the degradation of the environment was a problem of great urgency and international political significance. It followed shortly after the United Nations conference on the Human Environment at Stockholm (also in 1972).

D THE PLACE OF THE ENVIRONMENTAL POLICY IN THE OVERALL EU SCHEME

The aims of the original EEC were set out in the Treaty of Rome, art 2, and were concerned with approximating the economic policies of member states to promote increases in trade, rising living standards, and economic growth.

In its original proposal for a Community environmental policy (Bull, EC Supplement 5/73), the Commission revealed that this statement must now be taken to comprehend environmental issues: 'To remain balanced, economic growth must henceforth be guided and controlled to a greater degree by quality requirements. Conversely, the protection of the environment is both a guarantee of and a prerequisite for a harmonious development of economic activities'. Further, references to living standards had to be reinterpreted to take account of the *quality* of life.

A link was discerned between environmental policies and the functioning of the Common Market. Divergent national policies might distort competition by increasing production costs in some member states.

E THE ACTION PROGRAMMES

There have been a number of consecutive Action Programmes for the Environment. The first in November 1973 (OJ C112), the second in May 1977 (OJ C139), the third in February 1983 (OJ C46), the fourth in 1987 (OJ C328/1) the fifth in May 1993 (OJC 138) runs until 2000.

The first programmes laid down a number of underlying principles, still current, to which all subsequent legislation should adhere. The most important of these are that pollution should be eliminated or reduced at source and that the polluter should pay the cost of prevention, elimination or disposal measures.

In its early years, environmental policy concentrated on 'clean-up' measures: the reduction of pollution and the improvement of certain aspects of the environment. These were essentially curative measures, designed to deal with pressing problems. With the second and third programmes came a change of emphasis and an opportunity to take a longer term view. This was to lay stress on the preventive aspects of policy seeking to achieve an overall improvement in environmental quality.

Environmental policy now holds a centre stage position in EU affairs, though how this will relate to the Community's original, dominant objective of economic development, remains to be seen, even though in 1972 the Community's Heads of State declared 'economic expansion is not an end in itself'. The EU proceeds on the basis that strict environmental standards are economically justifiable for they can be associated with economic growth and job creation. Economic measures have tended historically to play little part in the implementation of the environmental policy, for the EC, as it was, tended to rely on legal controls such as licensing standards, emission limits, bans and other restrictions, these often existing on a segmented basis with individual controls for the individual environmental media; see further Alexander, 'Competition, Subsidy and Environmental Protection' in Vaughan (ed), *Environment and Planning Law*. Enhanced use of economic regulation is clearly cost effective, however, and following the interim review of the fifth Action Programme in 1994 it was accepted only slow progress had been made in broadening the range of policy instruments, and integrating environment policy into other policy areas. A further review was due in 1995, but is still awaited.

F THE LEGAL BASIS OF EU ACTION

Before the SEA came into effect in 1987, environmental measures were underpinned by no specific treaty provision. This did not prevent the former EEC from making more than 100 environmental instruments relating to protection of water and air quality, waste management and control, controls over chemicals, protection of flora, fauna and the countryside and noise. These were considered to be within the powers of art 100 which allowed the Council, acting unanimously on a proposal from the Commission, to issue directives to bring about approximations of the provisions of law, regulations or administrative actions in member states affecting the establishment or functioning of the common market. Reliance was also placed on art 235. A driving force behind the development of the law at this stage was a collective desire by member states to harmonise away distortions of trade by setting common standards for products, motor vehicles for example. This collective desire did, however, enable the former EEC to develop a competency in environmental issues — the so called 'soft law' technique.

Since 1987 a firm legal base for environmental action has existed. The SEA inserted Title VII — 'Environment' in Part 3 of the Treaty of Rome on EC policies. This was itself considerably modified by the Maastricht Treaty of 1992 largely because under the SEA provisions, article 130S of the Treaty of Rome had provided for environmental provisions to be adopted only unanimously, while at the same time providing under article 100A that measures intended to facilitate completion of the internal market could be adopted by qualified majority voting. This led to litigation as to which was the appropriate legal base for environmental action.

The position was clarified to an extent in *EC Commission v EC Council*[7] which turned on whether the correct legal base had been used for a directive which sought to reduce pollution by titanium dioxide by harmonising national programmes in that regard. The Commission had wished to use art 100A, the Council art 130S. The court stated that the legal basis for a directive cannot be left to the *wish* of a community institution; an objective decision has to be made and that involves considering the purpose and content of the measure in question. In the present case the directive was directed both to harmonising internal market rules and to environmental protection. The court considered that simply because a directive has an environmental component, it does *not* therefore *have* to rest on art 130S: art 100A *may* be an appropriate basis for a programme which seeks to harmonise national rules on an industry's production conditions so that distortions of competition are eliminated. This decision was a liberal interpretation of art 100A. However, in *EC Commission v EC Council*[8] the court considered that the primary objective of a Community measure should determine its legal base, and that points to use of art 130S, see also *Mondiet v Islais*.[9]

G THE INSTITUTIONS AND LEGAL BASE OF EU ENVIRONMENTAL ACTIVITY

Article 3(k) of the Treaty of Rome specifically declares that EU activity extends to the creation of 'a policy in the sphere of the environment'. To achieve this there are six 'institutions'.

The Council

Made up of ministerial representatives from each member state having power to bind their governments, the Council, whose presidency rotates amongst the states, is the EU's law-making body. A Committee of Permanent Representatives of Member States (COREPER) and the General Secretariat prepare the Council's Agenda. The actual composition of the Council varies according to the matters under discussion; thus environment ministers will meet to discuss environmental issues.

The so called 'European Council' is not an EU institution but a body provided for by the SEA. At the end of a period of the presidency the state holding that office holds a meeting of the political leaders of member states. Important decisions can be taken at this gathering, for example on the doctrine of subsidiarity, see below.

The Commission

The Commission is made up of members at least one of whom must come from each member state, larger nations such as France, Germany and the UK having

---

7 [1991] 3 LMELR 164.
8 [1993] ECR I-939.
9 [1993] ECR I-6133.

two. The Commission is headed by a President appointed by member states' governments, who must achieve unanimity on the issue, following consultation with the Parliament. The first duty of Commissioners is to the EU, they are not there to serve the interests of their home states. The Commission is a policy making body whose task is to put proposals before the Council. It is also the enforcer of EU law against member states in breach under art 169, by which if the Commission considers a member state has failed to fulfil an obligation under the treaty, it is to deliver a reasoned opinion on the issue, after giving the state in question the opportunity to make observations. If that state then still fails to comply within the Commission's stated period the Commission may bring the matter before the European Court of Justice.

The 'civil service' of the Commission consists of a number of 'Directorates General'; that dealing with the environment is DG XI.

The Parliament

The Parliament is not a legislature in the traditional sense of being primarily a law making body, though it has the functions of advising and supervising other institutions. Its members (MEPs) have political affiliations, and from them are drawn committees to examine legislative proposals and make recommendations on which the full body can vote, eg the Environment and Social Affairs Committee. Since the Maastricht Treaty the law making powers of the Parliament have increased.

The European Court of Justice (ECJ)

The ECJ consists of judges drawn from the member states, assisted by a number of Advocates-General whose task is to assist the decision making process of the Court by presenting an opinion on a case following legal argument before the Court: *normally* the Court follows this opinion in its judgment. The Court may sit in a number of chambers or panels. The principal function of the Court is to secure the observation of the Treaty of Rome according to law.

In addition to the ability of the Commission to take action against defaulting member states, member states can themselves take action against their fellows under art 170 in respect of purported breaches of treaty obligations.

Should the ECJ find that a member state has failed to fulfil its obligations that state is to be required to take the necessary measures to ensure compliance. Until the Maastricht Treaty that was all that could be done and the enforcement of the law then left much to be desired. However, art 171(2) now provides that where the 'necessary measures' have not been taken the Commission may go through the reasoned opinion process (see above) and specify the matters in respect of which compliance is still outstanding, and set a time limit for remedial action. If the requisite steps are not taken the matter may again be brought before the ECJ who may, if satisfied that there is non-compliance, impose a lump sum or penalty payment on the defaulting state. To date this procedure remains untested.

The Economic and Social Committee (ECOSOC)

This body's tasks are advisory and it deals with both the Council and the Commission.

The Court of Auditors

This body audits EU accounts.

The environmental provisions of the Treaty

The term 'environment' is not defined in the Treaty, but it extends to cover protection of humans, land use and town and country planning issues, waste, management and use of water and other natural resources, including flora and fauna, climate, and energy use; see Kramer, *EC Treaty & Environmental Law*, 2nd edn, p 41.

Article 130R provides that policy on the environment shall contribute to pursuit of: protecting, preserving and improving the environment; protecting human health; prudent and rational utilisation of natural resources; promoting international measures to deal with environmental problems. Policy is: to aim at a high level of protection, considering regional diversities; to be based on the precautionary and preventive principles, and on the principle that damage should be rectified at source and that the 'polluter pays'. Environmental policy *should* be integrated into other policies. In the preparation of policy account is to be taken of available scientific and technical data, regional environmental conditions, the costs/benefits of action/inaction, and the economic and social development of the EU as a whole and the balanced development of regions. Within their spheres of competence both the EU and members states are to co-operate with third countries and competent international organisations. Article 130T provides that protective measures adopted pursuant to art 130S do not prevent member states from maintaining or introducing more stringent protective measures of their own, provided they are compatible with the Treaty and are notified to the Commission.

The decision making procedure

The usual procedure on environmental issues under art 130S(i) is that the Council, under art 189C, after consulting ECOSOC may decide on action by way of a 'qualified majority' (see also art 148). Under this system individual states have different numbers of votes, with the largest having most, eg the UK has ten while Luxembourg has two. Currently the total number of votes is 88 of which a blocking minority is 27. However, under art 130S(2) certain measures may only be adopted unanimously. These are: those primarily of a fiscal nature; or measures concerning town and country planning and land use (*except* waste management and measures of a general nature) and management of water resources; or measures significantly affecting a member state's choice between different energy sources and the general structure of energy supply. The Council may further define those matters which are to be subject to unanimous voting. Under art 100 directives may be issued for the approximation of such laws, etc as directly affect the establishment or functioning of the common market, and here a unanimous decision is also required. However, by way of derogation from art 100, article 100A is available to provide for the adoption of measures having as their object the establishment and functioning of the internal market, but, in relation to environmental protection, any such measures must take as their base a high level of protection. The voting procedure under art 100A is also now that under art 189B (see below).

Thus the procedure to be adopted depends very much on the matter in hand. The normal rule is that the Council acts by qualified majority, *but* provisions of a primarily fiscal nature such as energy taxes, town and country planning and land use matters, the management of water resources and energy related issues are still subject to unanimity requirements, while general environmental action programmes setting out priority objectives to be attained are to be adopted by the article 189B process (see below), as are measures under art 100A. Thus there are three 'law making' procedures, in two of which the Parliament is involved in a decision making capacity.

Where unanimity is required

The procedure here is

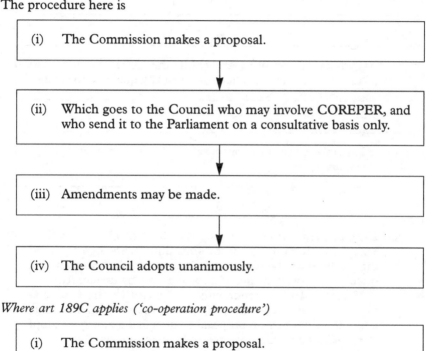

(i)   The Commission makes a proposal.

(ii)   Which goes to the Council who may involve COREPER, and who send it to the Parliament on a consultative basis only.

(iii) Amendments may be made.

(iv)   The Council adopts unanimously.

Where art 189C applies ('co-operation procedure')

(i)   The Commission makes a proposal.

(ii)   The Council receives the proposal and refers it to the Parliament for the first time.

(iii) Amendments may be made by the Commission *or* by *unanimous* decision of the Council (unusual).

> (iv) The Council by qualified majority voting adopts a 'common position' on the proposal.

> (v)   The 'common position' is sent to the Parliament — the second time the Parliament will have seen the matter — and the Parliament will also receive the Commission's opinion on the issue. Parliament may by absolute majority approve, amend or reject the proposal within three months of reception.

> (vi) If Parliament approves, or, within the three month period takes no action, the Council may *adopt* by qualified majority.

> (vii) If Parliament *rejects* the proposal the Council may only adopt it *unanimously*.

> (viii) If Parliament *amends* the proposal the amendments will be sent to the Commission. If the amendments are then accepted the proposal will be sent to the Council who may *accept* it by a qualified majority, *or amend* it further only by unanimity.
> If Parliament's amendments are *rejected* by the Commission, they must send the proposal to the Council who may adopt the Commission proposal by qualified majority *or* adopt Parliament's amendments, but only unanimously.

Where article 189B applies (joint legislative or co-decision procedure)

The stages here are as in (i)–(vii), supra, ie the point at which Parliament *rejects* or indicates an intention to amend the proposal. At this point the stages become as follows.

> (i)   A conciliation committee may be convened by the Council.

(ii) If Parliament still rejects the proposal by an absolute majority it fails.

(iii) But if Parliament only amends the 'common position' the matter will be returned to the Council and Commission.

(iv) If the Commission concurs with the Parliament's amendments the measure may be adopted by qualified majority. If the measure is not adopted within a prescribed period the matter will have to go to a further conciliation committee.

(v) If, however, the Commission is negative as to Parliament's amendments the Council may either adopt the measure (as amended) by unanimity, or if fails to adopt within a prescribed period the matter must go to a further conciliation committee.

(vi) If that committee approves a joint text, that will be returned to the Council and Parliament, who may *either* both approve by way of qualified majority, or, if one or the other fails to approve, the measure will fail.

(vii) If a joint text is not approved by the committee *and* the Council confirms the 'common position' by qualified majority *and* provided the Parliament does not reject the measure within a prescribed time, the measure will be adopted, *but* if the Council does not confirm the 'common position' in a specified time the measure will fail.

The principle of subsidiarity

Subsidiarity was introduced into EU law by the Maastricht Treaty. In danger of being an 'all things to all persons' 'get out' clause to be used by those wishing to argue for continued national sovereignty, subsidiarity has in any case a somewhat vague core of meaning. The Maastricht Treaty itself, art A, states that decisions are to be taken 'as closely as possible to the citizens'. Article 3B of the Treaty of Rome amplifies this by stating that, in areas which do not fall within its exclusive competence, the EU shall, in accordance with the principle of subsidiarity, take action 'only if and in so far as the objectives of the proposed action cannot be sufficiently achieved by the member states and can therefore, by reason of the scale or effects of the proposed action, be better achieved' by EU action. In addition the European Council has agreed that subsidiarity is to be taken into account at every stage of the legislative process.

What effect does this have on environmental policy? At the moment policy on the environment is *not* within the EU's exclusive competence, hence subsidiarity applies. In practice, however, to mount a legal challenge to, say, a Directive on the basis that it contravened the principle, it would have to be shown that each and every one of the measures and objectives of that Directive could be better achieved at member state level. It is thus likely that Professor Hartley is right in arguing that 'the effectiveness of subsidiarity will depend, to a considerable extent, on the attitude and policy of the European Court . . . it is doubtful whether the Court will want to give it any real bite' (*The Foundations of European Community Law*, 3rd edn, pp 163–164: a title to which interested readers are commended and indebtedness acknowledged). So far as UK case law is concerned, the only comment to date in an environmental context on subsidiarity was by Smith J in *R v Secretary of State for Trade and Industry, ex p Duddridge*[10] who considered that Art 3B allows member states 'to take such steps as they think right in connection with environmental and health issues until such time as [the EU] acting through its institutions produces a harmonising measure . . . to give effect to [the EU] policy on the environment which by that time will have been formulated'. This appears to state that where *a* specific EU policy on an environmental issue has been agreed and formulated and is incorporated in a measure[s] *designed to harmonise* the practice of member states, that will be sufficient to exclude the operation of subsidiarity.

H THE FORMS OF EU LEGISLATION

Article 189 lists three types of legally binding measures: regulations, directives and decisions.

Regulations are binding in their entirety and directly applicable. This means that they become law in the member states without the need for any action by national legislatures: 'they are an integral part of, and take precedence in the legal order applicable in the territory of each of the member states': *Amministrazione delle Finanze dello Stato v Simmenthal SpA*[11]. The direct applicability of regulations is secured in the UK by the European Communities Act 1972, s 2(1). Regulations are mainly employed in matters relating to the establishment of the common market and have been comparatively little used in relation to environmental issues. One regulation of particular note, however, is Council Regulation 3322/88 EEC on chlorofluorocarbons (CFCs) and halons which deplete the ozone layer. This

10 [1995] 7 JEL 224.
11 Case 106/77, [1978] ECR 629 at 643.

effectively translated into EC law the terms of the 1987 Montreal Protocol on taking precautions against ozone depletion. See further chapter 10 and Sands, 'European Community Policy on Ozone Depletion and Greenhouse Gases' in Vaughan (ed), *Environment and Planning Laws*.

Directives are binding 'as to the result to be achieved . . . but shall leave to the national authorities the choice of form and methods'. In other words, directives are *not* directly applicable and require implementation by national authorities within a given period, usually between one and two years, which is specified in the directive. The European Communities Act 1972, s 2(3), makes provision for the implementation of Community law in the UK by means of delegated legislation. However, the government does not always choose, or need, to exercise these powers. Sometimes the relevant legal provision is already in force in the UK, sometimes regulations are made under empowering legislation in other statutes and sometimes the government of the day chooses to enshrine the necessary rules in a new Act of Parliament. More controversially, the UK has in the past relied upon changes in administrative and 'managerial' practice in implementing the environmental directives. Even within the area of environmental regulation the objects of directives can vary. In some cases there will be clear procedural objectives to be achieved by member states, in others detailed substantive obligations will be stated which leave little effective discretion as to the mode of implementation by member states, in yet other cases a 'framework' will be provided to be expanded by more detailed future directives. The issue of highly detailed directives blurs the distinction between this form of legislation and regulations but this issue does not seem likely to attract judicial condemnation.[12]

Decisions are binding on those to whom they are addressed. A number of decisions (not discussed here) have been addressed to the member states in the course of the environmental programme. They deal primarily with either the establishment of information networks and advisory bodies or the entry by the Community into international agreements. There are also a number of non-legally binding 'recommendations'.

I DIRECT EFFECT

Whereas the direct applicability of regulations is laid down in the Treaty, the separate but linked notion of direct effect is a creation of the European Court of Justice. In the landmark case of Case 26/62: *Algemene Transport — en Expeditie Onderneming van Gend en Loos v Nederlandse Belastingadministratie*,[13] the Court held that:

'the Community constitutes a new legal order of international law for the benefit of which the states have limited their sovereign rights, albeit within limited fields, and the subjects of which comprise not only member states but also their nationals. Independently of the legislation of member states, Community law therefore not only imposes obligations on individuals but is also intended to confer upon them rights which become part of their legal heritage.'

12 *EC Commission v Italy* [1980] ECR 1099; *EC Commission v Italy* [1980] ECR 1115; and *EC Commission v UK* [1988] ECR 3921, [1988] 3 CMLR 437.
13 [1963] ECR 1.

Thus where a provision is directly effective, it confers rights directly upon the citizen which he can invoke before national courts. Where member states fail to translate, or translate incorrectly, a directive's requirements into their national systems such rights arise. Not all provisions of Community law give rise to direct effect — it is now clear from the judgments of the Court that in order to give rise to direct effect a measure must satisfy the following criteria:

1 It must be clear, precise and unambiguous.
2 It must be unconditional nor subject to qualifications making the obligation contingent on some other event, etc.
3 It must not be dependent on further action being taken by either the Community or member states. These requirements are met even where directives confer discretion *how* to act on member states, provided there is an inescapable minimum *obligation* which a member state owes, in the sense of having no choice as to *whether* or not to act.

These requirements apply to each relevant part of a directive; it is not enough to argue that a directive is 'clear and unambiguous' etc 'overall'.[14]

In sum, the provision must be such that the judge in the national court is able to define the right claimed with sufficient precision to enable the court to enforce it. Judges are, of course, entitled to seek the assistance of the European Court by making a preliminary reference on the interpretation of the Community measure under art 177, but if the judge cannot determine the content of the right, or of the correlative duty, it cannot be told whether or not it has been infringed and the judge will be unable to prescribe the appropriate national remedy.

For some time after the decision in *van Gend en Loos*, it was thought that although provisions of the Treaty and of regulations were susceptible to direct effect, directives were by their very nature unable to comply with the second and third conditions laid down by the Court and consequently would never give rise to direct effect. This view was finally overturned by the Court in *Van Duyn*[15].

The main reason underlying the Court's decision appears to be the principle of *'effet utile'* — the effectiveness of directives would be undermined if individuals were not allowed to rely upon them in national courts.

In *Becker v Finanzamt Münster-Innenstadt*[16], the Court returned to the topic of the direct effect of directives. Where the member state has failed to implement, or its purported implementation is defective, the member state 'may not plead ... its own failure to perform the obligations which the directive entails'. So, once the date for implementation has passed, and provided that it is unconditional and sufficiently precise, the individual may, in the absence of adequate implementing measures, rely on the directive before his/her national court.

'Direct effect', however, is only 'vertical', ie directives can give rise to rights for individuals *only* against the state or an emanation of the state, and can be

14 *Enichem Base v Comune di Cinisello Balsamo* [1989] ECR 2491, [1991] 1 CMLR 313; and *Twyford Parish Council v Secretary of State for the Environment* [1992] JEL Vol 4 No 2 p 273; and contrast *Kincardine and Deeside District Council v Forestry Commission* [1992] JEL Vol 4 No 2 p 289.
15 [1974] ECR 1337.
16 [1982] ECR 53.

relied upon by individuals even in the face of a contrary domestic legal position.[17] But what is 'the state'? Certainly state bodies charged with maintaining public order and safety are included, see *Johnston v Chief Constable of the Royal Ulster Constabulary*[18] and local authorities, see *R v Freight Transport Association Ltd v London Boroughs Transport Committee*[19]. Indeed any body or institution, no matter what its legal form, which is responsible under state measures for the provision of services under state supervision and has, for that purpose, special powers beyond those applicable between individuals *may* be an emanation of the state for this purpose, see *Foster v British Gas.*[20] Even a commercial understanding may be an 'emanation of the state' provided it carries out a public service which is under overall state control,[1] see further Howells, 'European Directives — the Emerging Dilemmas' (1991) 54 MLR 456. On the other hand it appears that a local authority may *not* rely on the doctrine of direct effect *against* an individual.[2]

Civil liability *on the part of a state* for failure to implement a directive was found capable of existing in *Francovich v Italian Republic.*[3] In a decision of major importance, the Court found that where, cumulatively:

1   A member state has failed to fulfil obligations under art 189 to take all measures necessary to achieve the end laid down by a directive.
2   The result laid down by the directive would involve individuals having rights (irrespective of direct effect) conferred on them.
3   The content of such rights may be identified from the directive's provisions.
4   There is a causal link between the state's failure to fulfil its obligations and the damage an individual has suffered, the state is responsible for making good that consequential damage. Such claims are then to be dealt with according to the normal legal order within the appropriate member state, but must be processed so that the principles relating to compensation are not less favourable than those existing ordinarily under the state's domestic laws. Thus a person injured by drinking water not supplied in conformity with the Drinking Water Directive, for example, may have a civil remedy, see Geddes [1994] JEL Vol 6 No 1 p 125.

Many of the provisions of directives concerning the environment are sufficiently precise and detailed to qualify for direct effect (although, equally, many are not, those for example which require member states to take 'appropriate measures' or state that they should 'endeavour' to achieve certain targets). Thus, it is submitted, the direct effect of *some* provisions of *some* of the environmental directives cannot be excluded. An individual could therefore,

17 *Marshall v Southampton and South West Area Health Authority (Teaching)* [1986] QB 401, [1986] 2 All ER 584; *Verbond van Nederlandse Ondernemingen v Inspecteur der Invoerrechten en Accijnzen* [1977] ECR 113, [1977] 1 CMLR 413; and *Faccini Dori v Recreb Srl* [1994] 6 ELM 149.
18 [1987] QB 129, [1986] 3 All ER 135.
19 [1991] 3 All ER 915.
20 [1991] 1 QB 405, [1990] 3 All ER 897.
1 *Griffin v South West Water Services* [1995] IRLR 15.
2 *Wychavon District Council v Secretary of State for the Environment* [1994] 6 JEL 351.
3 [1992] IRLR 84.

provided he/she could establish the necessary locus standi, bring an action in the British courts founded on such a measure. However, this is not to say that a remedy would always be forthcoming. Litigation in British courts so far has been largely concerned with the direct effect of the Environment Assessment Directive 85/337/EEC and its subsequent tardy implementation in UK law by SI 1988/1199, etc, see chapter 5. UK courts have sought to dispose of such issues on procedural grounds, such as delay in bringing an action, *R v Swale Borough Council, ex p Royal Society for the Protection of Birds*[4], or by arguing an authority has carried out the equivalent of an environmental assessment in cases where its applicability as such was not mandatory, *R v Poole Borough Council, ex p Beebee*[5], or by finding that the court should not exercise its discretion to grant a remedy by way of judicial review because the applicant could not show any substantial prejudice suffered as a result of the breach of the EU obligation, *Twyford Parish Council v Secretary of State for the Environment.*[6] It appears that a British statutory agency specifically charged in the UK with promoting a policy largely emanating from and driven by EU policy would have the necessary locus standi to seek judicial review of UK measures considered contrary to EU obligations,[7] while a large, well organised and well informed pressure group, with a long involvement in a particular environmental issue and a number of members living in the vicinity of that issue may also be accorded standing.[8] But being granted that status is no guarantee that a remedy will follow, not least because of the highly discretionary nature of judicial review proceedings, and because of the need to show harm before a remedy is granted.[9] This is an aspect of our law that has received considerable criticism, see Ward [1993] JEL Vol 5 No 2 p 221 and Geddes [1992] JEL Vol 4 No 1 p 29. However, it is now clear that a failure to comply with the 'primary' obligation of a Directive will, if it results in an adverse decision of the ECJ, result further in a 'secondary' obligation to comply with that judgment which must be achieved as soon as possible, and if it is not a party otherwise having the necessary locus standi may seek judicial review of the failure to comply with the 'secondary' obligation. Even in such a case, however, the UK courts appear to consider they retain a discretion as to whether to grant a remedy, and will order nothing in vain.[9]

It has been argued that a number of directives may well have 'direct effect':

1   Those laying down limit or maximum concentration values, eg 76/464 (protection of the aquatic environment).
2   Those prohibiting the use or discharge of certain substances, eg 78/319 on toxic and dangerous waste.
3   Those imposing clear obligations to act on member states, eg 85/337 on environmental assessment. (See further Kramer (1991) 3 Journal of Environmental Law 39, to which the author acknowledges indebtedness.) However, it is doubtful whether an individual would have locus standi to

4 [1991] JPL 39.
5 [1991] 3 LMELR 60.
6 [1991] 3 LMELR 89, 166, 196.
7 *R v Secretary of State for Employment, ex p Equal Opportunities Commission* [1995] 1 AC 1.
8 *R v HM Inspectorate of Pollution and Ministry of Agriculture, Fisheries and Food, ex p Greenpeace Ltd* [1993] 5 ELM 183.
9 *R v Secretary of State for the Environment, ex p Friends of the Earth* [1995] 7 ELM 140.

seek a remedy in relation to *all* such directives because they do not all immediately concern themselves with protection of humans, eg 76/464.

It is generally clear that member states and their emanations are under a duty to apply all directly effective provisions to the exclusion and setting aside of any provisions of national law to the contrary. Individuals may rely on this principle to ground a defence to criminal charges, or to resist demands for payments of illegal charges, or, in appropriate cases, to claim injunctive or declaratory relief. Directives may be relied on by parties to establish whether any relevant national measures accord with their provisions, and directives must be applied by national courts in cases where national provisions clash with directives. Where a directive imposes a direct obligation on the member states, the directive itself is the origin of rules of law on which, *provided the period for implementation has passed without necessary action being taken*, the individual may rely. Indeed where the relevant provisions of a directive are capable of direct effect, *and* an individual is thereunder given a right *and* has the necessary locus standi within the legal system, positive action against the defaulter can be taken in national courts.

There is increasingly an 'indirect effect' principle following statements in *Von Colson v Land Nordrhein-Westfalen*[10] that national courts should so interpret relevant national law that directive objectives are brought about, though this is subject to requirements to preserve legal certainty and avoid retroactivity, see *Officier van Justitie v Kolpinghuis Nijmegen BV*[11] and *Marleasing SA v La Comercial.*[12] In *R v Secretary of State for the Environment, ex p Greenpeace*[13] the *Marleasing* principle was adopted by Potts J who considered that, to interpret UK legislation consistently with EU law, he could read words into the UK statute *provided* he did not thereby alter its plain meaning. See also Fitzpatrick [1992] JEL Vol 4 No 1 p 121.

It must also be remembered that it is a fundamental principle of community law that any directly-effective Community provision prevails over conflicting national legislation.[14]

In the UK, the European Communities Act 1972, s 2(1), ensures the recognition and enforcement in the UK of all directly-effective Community rights. Section 2(4) provides that 'any enactment passed or to be passed ... shall be construed and have effect subject to' inter alia s 2(1). Thus the Act purports to subordinate past *and* future national legislation to Community law. English courts will give priority to Community law in accordance with s 2(4) unless and until 'Parliament deliberately passes an Act with the intention of repudiating the Treaty or any provision in it or intentionally of acting inconsistently with it and says so in express terms', per Lord Denning in *McCarthys Ltd v Smith*.[15]

---

10 [1984] ECR 1891, [1986] 2 CMLR 430.
11 [1987] ECR 3969, [1989] 2 CMLR 18.
12 [1990] ECR I-4135, [1992] 1 CMLR 305.
13 [1994] 6 ELM 82.
14 *Costa v ENEL* [1964] ECR 585.
15 [1979] 3 All ER 325 at p 329; see also *Factortame Ltd v Secretary of State for Transport* [1989] 2 All ER 692, [1990] ECR I-2433 and [1991] 1 All ER 70.

J ENFORCEMENT ISSUES

Because the Commission is a legislative initiator it is inevitably proactive, both in the formulation of proposals, and increasingly with regard to taking action against member states under art 169 in respect of failures to implement directives. The Commission can receive written complaints from individuals that Community obligations are not being satisfied, and the number of such complaints rose from eight in 1983 to 465 in 1989 and to 1185 in 1992, though these arose across every sector of the Commission's competence. This has given the Commission something of a role as an 'Environmental Ombudsman'. The Commission may also suspend regional development grants to those states who fail to implement environmental obligations, and so acted against Portugal in 1990.

The Commission's role as guardian of the treaties creating the Community is also crucial. The Commission is charged with ensuring the implementation of Community obligations, and it requires notification from member states that they have translated those obligations into national law, and further inquires whether national measures comply formally and practically with the obligations. It also has wide powers under art 155 to investigate such issues. States found to be committing infractions of obligations may, of course, be proceeded against under art 169, and see earlier comments on the revised art 171. Though most infractions appear to arise from oversight or inefficiency, the numbers of art 169 proceedings, and the consequent strain on the Commission and Court, are increasing. In 1992 there were 587 *suspected* infractions in the environmental sector — more than in any other, while the Commission remains heavily dependent on complaints from individuals/ organisations to alert it to breaches. Some commentators argue for an even stricter compliance policy by the Commission, others, however, consider that the need for such a policy could be obviated if greater thought were to be given to issues of securing *implementation* at the *formulation* stage of directives.

The role of the Court was examined at length in 'The European Court of Justice as an Environmental Tribunal' by Jacqueline Minor (in Vaughan (ed), *Environment and Planning Law* p 267 et seq) to which indebtedness is further acknowledged. The attitude of the ECJ appears to vary according to whether the EU has legislated or not, and, in the former case, whether harmonisation of national laws is full or partial. Where there should be harmonisation under EU legislation the ECJ considers the directives should be implemented in a manner fully consonant with EU obligations, so for example, the technical requirements of directives are considered exhaustive.[16] In cases of partial harmonisation, however, the ECJ has seemed to favour striking a balance between protecting the environment and promoting free trade in relation to the exercise by member states of residual powers. Where the Community has not legislated *EC Commission v Denmark*[17] (the 'Danish bottles' case) indicates environmental protection may be used as a justification for a national measure which applies *without distinction* between domestic and imported goods so as to restrict trade between member states, provided it is *proportional*, ie where

16 *EC Commission v United Kingdom* [1988] ECR 3921, [1988] 3 CMLR 437.
17 [1988] ECR 4627.

no 'measure less restrictive of trade would be as effective in protecting the environment' (Minor op cit p 275). But a measure imposing a charge equivalent to a customs duty and discriminatory internal taxation is not acceptable and cannot be justified on environmental grounds, see *EC Commission v Germany*.[18] The first case involved a national requirement that drinks containers should be reusable so as to encourage deposit and return schemes, the second concerned attempts to tax road vehicles so as to force freight from road to rail transport. Nevertheless there is a general body of opinion which views the statement in the 'Danish bottles' case that 'the protection of the environment is a mandatory requirement which may limit the application of art 30 of the Treaty' ('Quantitative restrictions on imports and all measures having equivalent effect shall ... be prohibited ...') as indicating the potential of the ECJ to emerge as a forum much concerned with environmental protection. This is largely supported by other decisions, thus domestic circumstances within a member state's legal system do not justify failure to meet environmental obligations,[19] and a merely changeable administrative practice is no fulfilment of a directive's obligations.[20]

Even so the ECJ is vigilant in maintaining a delicate balance between trade and environment issues. Article 30 of the Treaty forbids quantitative restrictions on imports and measures having equivalent effect, subject to art 36 which allows prohibitions on imports, exports, or goods in transit where these can be justified on grounds of public morality, public policy or security, protection of human life and health, protection of animal and plant life, protection of national artistic treasures, or protection of industrial or commercial property. Such prohibitions, etc, must not be arbitrary discrimination between states, nor disguised restrictions on trade. In this connection the ECJ has required that a national measure must be proportionate, ie it must not place more restrictions on trade than would have been imposed by a less restrictive measure which would still have achieved the same purpose.[1]

The Court of First Instance

Established in 1989 following amendment of the various constituent treaties by the Single European Act, the Court of First Instance was intended to deal with cases having no political or constitutional importance and to relieve the work load of the European Court of Justice. Effectively one judge sits for each member state. The Court has a particular jurisdiction in judicial review, concerning both annulment actions and actions in respect of remedies for failures to act, where action is being taken by a private individual or company against the EU itself. See further Hartley, *The Foundations of European Community Law*, 3rd edn, chapter 2, indebtedness to which is acknowledged.

However, to seek a remedy before the Court one must have a sufficient legal

---

18 [1991] 2 LMELR 210.
19 *EC Commission v Italy* [1981] ECR 3379; *EC Commission v Belgium* [1987] ECR 2415.
20 *EC Commission v Netherlands* [1982] ECR 1791 at 1819.
 1 *EC Commission v Germany* [1995] 2 CMLR 278.

interest in the matter in hand. Article 173 allows individuals (ie natural or legal persons) to challenge the legality of action taken by the Commission or other EU institution where there is '*a decision* addressed to that person' or where there is a '*decision* which, although in the form of a regulation or a *decision* addressed to another person, is of direct and individual concern' to the individual.

In effect this means that the decision must affect the individual by reason of certain attributes peculiar to him/her, or by reason of circumstances which differentiate him/her from all others. The application of this understanding makes it very hard for environmental pressure groups to challenge decisions in the Court of First Instance, for it is hard for them to demonstrate sufficient 'individual concern'. Furthermore an association which has been formed to protect the collective interests of a group of people does not have an entitlement to take action which its individual members do not have. A decision affecting a large number of people in an area may therefore not be susceptible to challenge by any one of them if all are affected in the same way and none is affected in a way distinct from others, see *Stichting Greenpeace v EC Commission*[2] and *Danielson v EC Commission*.[3]

On the other hand it must be pointed out that despite an obvious readiness to find member states in breach of environmental obligations in art 169 proceedings, the ECJ has yet to find that any of the environmental directives have direct effect which could open up many more domestic remedies for individuals and organisations in their own state courts.[4]

Clearly some more effective form of enforcement is required. That role could in future be discharged by the Environment Agency created under Regulation 1210/90, and which is located in Denmark — a state with an exceedingly 'clean' environmental record and thus, arguably, not the most appropriate place for the location of the agency which might be seen to be 'preaching to the converted'. Currently the Agency is primarily concerned to collect, process, analyse, and disseminate information on the environment, and publishes triennial reports on the state of the environment. The Agency has no enforcement role, but it could become involved in monitoring the implementation of EU law and obligations, promoting the use of 'clean' technology and processes, establishing criteria for environmental assessment purposes, etc.

K EU LAW: AN EVALUATION AND VIEW ON FUTURE PROSPECTS

Although EU policy on the environment has generated a great deal of legislation (well over 400 legislative instruments between 1967 and 1994) decision making procedures have been slow and have tended to militate

---

2 Case T-585/93 (1996) 252 ENDS Report 43.
3 Case T-219/95R (1996) 252 ENDS Report 44.
4 *Difesa Dela Cara v Regione Lombardia* [1994] 6 ELM 112; *Article 177 Reference from the Bavarian Higher Regional Administrative Court* [1995] 7 ELM 6.

against the adoption of radical proposals. There seems little doubt, however, that it has reinforced the strongly growing concern about environmental issues on the domestic political scene and has without any doubt accelerated and influenced the content of already planned domestic legislation. In some areas, notably water and air pollution, it certainly has forced a change in long established practice and approach.

The EU's attitude to environmental protection has, however, been characterised by (i) a regulatory approach, (ii) use of harmonisation of national laws, and (iii) a degree of passivity in merely upgrading environmental measures to keep pace with technology, as opposed to forcing the pace of technological change by legal requirements as is the case in the USA. As to (i) it may be commented that an over regulatory style may inhibit the use of other means of environmental protection such as fiscal or economic aid policies. Here it must be remembered that art 93 of the Treaty forbids the granting of state aids not compatible with the common market, and that art 92 forbids aids which distort competition by favouring certain undertakings or goods. This is not to say that all environmental fiscal measures fall foul of the Treaty. There is a wide, and vague, provision in art 92(3)(c) to allow aid to be given to facilitate the development of certain economic activities or certain economic areas, and aids granted to projects regarded as 'environmentally friendly' are generally acceptable, eg research into renewable energy resources, though aids are open to question where they effectively allow those aided to escape the operation of 'the polluter pays' principle, and the same is true where state aids are given to polluting industries; see further Alexander, 'Competition, Subsidy and Environmental Protection' in Vaughan (ed), *Environment and Planning Law*. Note also art 92(3)(d) which allows aid to promote culture and 'heritage conservation'. As to (ii) it can be said that harmonisation techniques were appropriate before the amendments made by the SEA and still have a significance until the completion of the internal market. As to (iii) the dominance of harmonisation appears in the past to have inhibited a pace setting approach in the creation of standards. This may be predicted to change, especially following the Maastricht agreement.

A quickening pace of change?

Despite set backs every now and again the 'curve' of EU legislative activity on the environment was definitely set upwards, with no less than 48 measures in 1994, the largest number ever. A new environment commissioner, a new director for DG XI and the formal inception of the Environment Agency in October 1994 seemed to have reinvigorated the EU in relation to environmental issues. Furthermore the enlargement of the EU on 1 January 1995 to include Austria, Sweden and Finland is expected to have repercussions as in some cases their environmental legislation is more stringent than current EU law: they are expected to argue for enhanced measures of control particularly with regard to chemicals. However, by the end of 1995 pressure had been placed on the Commission to stem the flow of environmental measures, and only two wholly new draft directives were promised for 1996. Even so there is a backlog of proposals.

By June 1995 the EU was thus in course of developing, or had set in place, the following new measures.

Air

Large combustion plants	Directive 94/66 amends 88/609 while revised emission limits expected in 12 months.
Volatile organic compounds	Directive 94/63 in place relating to VOC emissions from petrol storage and distribution, further control over refuelling releases within 12 months, while VOC emissions from solvents used in cleaning are similarly expected to be controlled.
Small combustion plants	Controls/standards expected within 1–2 years.
Non-hazardous waste incineration	More stringent controls to replace current directives expected within 1–2 years.
Air quality framework Directive	Expected within 12 months.
Hazardous waste incineration	Directive 94/67 in place.
Ozone depleting substances	Regulation 3093/94 replaces earlier regulations and tightens up the law.

Climate change

Vehicular CO_2 energy tax	Proposals still more than 2 years away.
'Least cost planning', ie energy efficiency in electricity and gas distribution sectors	Proposals still more than 2 years away.
SAVE (general efficiency programme)	Extension of current programme within 12 months.
CO_2/energy tax	Proposals still more than 2 years away.
Energy efficiency standards for fridges and freezers	Proposals within 12 months.

Hazards/chemicals

Deregulation and potential relaxation of some administrative requirements in biotechnology sector	Proposals within 12 months.
Chemical imports and exports tightened controls	Regulation 3135/94 extends notification requirements for certain chemicals. Some 1–2 years away are further proposals.
Plant protection products	Some 1–2 years away.
Marketing of biocides	Some 1–2 years away.
Revision of the Seveso Directive	Some 1–2 years away.
Worker protection against chemical agents	Proposals within 1 year.
Worker protection against physical agents (eg noise, vibration, etc)	Proposals within 1 year.
Ban on marketing and use of hexachlorethane in nonferrous metal making	Proposals within 1–2 years.
Environmental risk assessment	Regulation 1488/94 brings in general principles for assessing risks to humans and the environment from existing substances.
Evaluation of plant protection products	Directive 94/43 sets down standards for assessing new pesticides.
Restrictions on marketing use of certain chemicals	Directives 94/27, 94/48, 94/60 amend and extend ban on the use of certain substances, eg nickel in jewellery and flammables in aerosols.

Waste

Contaminated land	Proposals more than 2 years away.
Waste 'streams' (vehicles, tyres and health care waste)	Proposals within 12 months.
Waste 'streams' (electronics and demolition waste)	Proposals 1–2 years away.
Waste 'streams' (solvents)	Proposals more than 2 years away.
Land fill, ending of co-disposal	Proposals 1–2 years away.
Civil liability for damage caused by waste (see chapter 2)	Proposals more than 2 years away.
Packaging and packaging waste	Directive 94/62 in place.
List of hazardous waste	Decision 94/904 lists hazardous waste as required by Directive 91/689.

Water

Revision of Directive 76/464 on dangerous substances in water	Proposals more than 2 years away.
Revision of Directive 80/68 on groundwater	Proposals more than 2 years away.
Revision of Directive 80/778 on drinking water	Proposals 1–2 years away.
Revision of Directive 76/160 on bathing water	Proposals 1–2 years away.

Miscellaneous

To amend Directive 85/337 to harmonise EA within member states	Proposals within 1–2 years.
To extend EA to early stages of planning processes including development policies at national levels	Proposals over 2 years away.
To create a comprehensive EU requiter of polluting emissions	Proposals over 2 years away.
Integrated pollution prevention and control (IPPC)	Proposals within 1–2 years.

Protection of environmental interests under the European Convention on Human Rights (ECHR)

Some steps were made a few years ago to seek the protection of the ECHR in respect of alleged interferences with human rights arising in the environmental context.[5] The Convention does not, however, specifically mention environmental protection as a fundamental human right.[6] Thus a little creative lawyering and use of indirect means of challenge have to be employed by those seeking the Convention's assistance. However, in *Lopez Ostra v Spain*,[7] a Spanish national lived in a house near an allegedly polluting waste treatment

5 *Powell & Rayner v United Kingdom* (1990) 12 EHRR 355.
6 *X & Y v Germany*, App 7407/76, Decisions and Reports 5 p 16.
7 [1995] 7 ELM 49, Judgment of 9 December 1994, 41/1993/436/515.

plant opened in 1988, and the cause of health problems and nuisances from its beginning. Residents were evacuated at one point, the plant was ordered to cease part of its operation, and the residents were allowed to return. However, there continued to be health problems and environmental deterioration. It was alleged that this state of uncontrolled affairs constituted a breach of art 8 of the Convention — the right to respect for one's private and family life. It was held that 'severe environmental pollution may affect an individual's well being and prevent them from enjoying their homes in such a way as to affect their private and family life adversely, without, however, seriously endangering their health'. In a previous case a similar decision had been reached but without a remedy being given as it was concluded that reasonable compensation had been paid to the applicant in respect of the issue.[8]

The decision is important because under art 8 it is clear that a balance has to be struck between the competing interests of the individual and the community as a whole, while 'in any case the state enjoys a certain margin of appreciation'. However, in the instant case the state authorities had exceeded that margin. Though the plant had been built to solve a pollution problem the state authorities had failed to take steps to protect the applicant's right to respect for her home, private and family life, they had resisted judicial decisions providing remedies for those rights, and they had prolonged the applicant's affectation by appealing against a decision to close the plant by an investigating judge who considered it infringed Spanish criminal law.

It will be interesting to see whether this case, in which the applicant was awarded £19,419 in respect of her loss, will mark a major turning point in the ECHR's development. See further Garcia-Ureta 'Lopez Ostra v Spain: Environmental Protection and the European Convention on Human Rights' (1995) 3 Environmental Liability (5) p 87, to which indebtedness is acknowledged.

Further reading

EC LAW

de Búrca, G, 'Giving Effect to European Community Directives' (1992) 55 MLR 215.

Churchill, R, Warren, L, and Gibson, J, (eds) *Law, Policy and the Environment* (1991) Blackwell.

Craig, PP, 'Francovich, Remedies and the Scope of Damages Liability' (1993) 109 Law Quarterly Review 595.

Curtin, D, 'State Liability Under Community Law: A New Remedy for Private Parties' (1992) 21 Industrial Law Journal 74.

Geddes, AC, '*Foster v British Gas*: widening the field of direct effect' (1990) 140 NLJ 1611.

Glasbergen, P, and Blowers, A, *Environmental Policy in an International Context: Perspectives* chapter 5 (Kamminga) (1995) Arnold.

Hartley, TE, *Foundations of European Community Law* (3rd edn) (1994) OUP.

Howells, G, 'European Directives: The Emerging Dilemmas' (1991) 54 MLR 456.

---

8 *S v France*, decision of 17 May 1990, Decisions and Reports 65/250.

House of Lords Select Committee on the EC, Session 1994–95 5th Report, HL Paper 29, European Environment Agency (1995) HMSO.

Kramer, L, *EEC Treaty and Environmental Protection* (1995) Sweet and Maxwell.

Kramer, L, 'The Implementation of Community Environmental Directives within Member States: Some implications for the Direct Effect Doctrine' (1991) 3 Journal of Environmental Law 39.

Kye, C, 'Environmental Law and the Consumer in the European Union' (1995) 7 Journal of Environmental Law, Part I, 31.

Johnson, S, and Corcelle, G, *The Environmental Policy of the European Communities* (2nd edn 1995) Kluwer Law International.

McGrory, DP, 'Air Pollution Legislation in the United States and the Community' (1990) 15 European Law Review 298.

McRory, R, 'The Enforcement of Community Environmental Laws: Some Critical Issues' 29 Common Market Law Review 347.

Rehbinder, E, and Stewart, R, *Environmental Protection Policy* (1985) Walter de Gruyter and Co.

Rehbinder, E, and Stewart, R, 'Legal Integration in Federal Systems: European Community Environmental Law' (1985) American Journal of Comparative Law 371.

Sands, P, 'European Community Environmental Law: Legislation, the European Court of Justice and Common Interest Groups' (1990) 53 Modern Law Review 685.

Snyder, F, 'The Effectiveness of European Community Law' (1993) 56 Modern Law Review 19.

Szyszcak, E, 'European Community Law: New Remedies, New Directions?' (1992) 55 Modern Law Review 690.

Vandermeersh, D, 'The Single European Act and the Environmental Policy of the European Economic Community' (1987) 12 European Law Review 407.

Vaughan, D, (ed) *Environment and Planning Law* (1991) Butterworths.

Wils, WPJ, 'Subsidiarity and EC Environmental Policy: Taking People's Concerns Seriously' (1994) 6 Journal of Environmental Law, Part 1, 85.

INTERNATIONAL LAW

Birnie, PW, and Boyle, AE, *International Law and the Environment* (1992) OUP.

Boyle, A, 'Saving the World? Implementation and Enforcement of International Environmental Law through International Institutions' (1991) 3 Journal of Environmental Law 229.

Brown Weiss, E, *Environmental Change and International Law* (1992) UN University Press.

Churchill, R, and Freestone, D, (eds) *International Law and Global Climate Change* (1991) Graham and Trotman.

Freestone, D, 'The Road from Rio' (1993) University of Hull Press, and also (1994) 6 Journal of Environmental Law, Part 2, 193.

Lammers, JG, (ed) *Environmental Protection and Sustainable Development* (1987) Graham and Trotman.

Massey, SC, 'Global Warming and 1992 UNCED' 22 Georgia Journal of International and Comparative Law, 175.

Sand, PH, *The Effectiveness of International Environmental Agreements* (1992)
    Grotius Publications.
Sands, P, *Chernobyl: Law and Communication* (1988) Grotius Publications.
Sands, P, 'Innovation in International Environmental Governance' (1990) 32
    Environment 9.

Part II

Protection of the land

Chapter 5

The basic structure of planning control

'At last, a capital plan we've got,
we won't say how, and we won't say what
It's safe in my noddle, so off we will toddle,
and slyly develop this capital plot'
(W S Gilbert, 'Utopia Ltd', Act II)

This is *not* a book on planning law; readers must turn to standard texts such as Telling's *Planning Law and Procedure*, Heap's *Outline of Planning Law*, Moore's *A Practical Approach to Planning Law*, or, at the practitioner level, Grant's *Urban Planning Law*, or Purdue, Young and Rowan Robinson's *Planning Law and Procedure*. Nevertheless it is impossible to understand the ways in which land is used, developed, exploited and protected without having *basic* knowledge of planning law. The variations, departures, special procedures and particular controls that make up the body of land use controls can then be viewed in context. Furthermore in relation to some issues, eg protection of visual amenity, or development of wind farms (see The Times 23 April 1991) to name but two disparate matters, planning law is the principal mode of regulation. With regard to the particular issue of wind power, the UK's first commercial 'wind farm' opened in December 1991, part of a move to generate 20% or more of national electricity needs from 'renewable' sources by 2025. PPG 22 of February 1993 (Annexes of October 1994) currently gives advice on the planning implications of wind farms, and reiterates a basic planning principle that the test of whether permission should be granted is whether a proposal would have a detrimental effect on a locality generally and on amenities that ought, in the public interest, to be protected. Particular advice is given on development plan provision for likely turbine sites, safeguarding of sites with permission against other inappropriate development, siting and landscape issues, particularly within National Parks and Areas of Outstanding Natural Beauty, etc.

However, planning has limitations as a means of environmental regulation. It is basically a reactive and managerial rather than a protective system, being primarily concerned with the orderly management of change, and fundamentally political in nature, providing a framework within which various issues and values can be weighed one against the other, with economic arguments, for example, being able to outweigh environmental concerns on occasions.

Planning and sustainability

The fact that 'sustainable' is linked with 'development' in policy thinking inevitably means that the planning system which is so closely concerned with land use issues must assume greater environmental importance in future years, though sustainable development is not, nor must not, be limited solely to planning issues (see chapter 3, above). Nevertheless many planners now see a major role for planning in ensuring 'sustainability' which is often interpreted in the present context as leaving a better future for following generations. Planners may thus seek to stress the encouragement and revival of existing communities and areas rather than the establishment of new ones, the reuse and retention of existing buildings for new uses wherever possible, or the reclamation of their materials where they must be demolished, the bringing together of work and housing opportunities, and, perhaps above everything, the reduction of needs to travel either for work, shopping or leisure opportunities, with travel where necessary being encouraged by means of public transport.

However, while planning has had an environmental role for many years in relation to: elimination of nuisances by separation of residential and industrial areas; protection of 'amenity' ie the 'pleasantness' of an area; and containment of urban sprawl, there are many who argue that planning embraces change; its historic philosophy is *not* that development is bad, indeed it believes development on the whole is good. Planning is moreover a highly politicised, discretionary system of *control* over land and landbased resources which accepts a certain degree of environmental degradation and despoliation may be necessary in particular cases.

That planning and planning law remain diverse and somewhat unfocused is clear from Cm 1200 'This Common Heritage' p 17 which lists the following as features of the planning system:

1 Economic growth.
2 Provision of work opportunities.
3 Provision of housing.
4 Creating a safe environment against risks of flooding, subsidence, industrial hazards.
5 Protecting prime agricultural land for food production.
6 Ensuring there is adequate access to shops.
7 Using mineral resources to best advantage.
8 Sustaining the diversity and character of the countryside.
9 Defending greenbelts against urban encroachment.
10 Maintaining the character and vitality of existing town centres.
11 Revitalising older run down urban areas.
12 Safeguarding the amenity of existing residential areas.
13 Conserving historic and quality architecture.

Not all of the foregoing would *necessarily* qualify as 'sustainable development'. However, it must be remembered that it is in its detail and its application that planning must be adjudged.

A PLAN MAKING

Both counties and districts where they survive have planning functions as, of course, do unitary authorities. The role of counties tends to be strategic; that of districts is tactical. The functional division is laid down by the Local Government Act 1972, ss 182–84 and Sch 16, as amended by the Local Government, Planning and Land Act 1980, the Local Government Act 1992, the Local Government (Wales) Act 1994 and the Environment Act 1995. Under these Acts counties are primarily concerned with: preparation of structure plans; control of developments concerned with mineral and aggregate working and processing, and associated plants and developments; cement works, and waste disposal sites.

A note on National Parks

Sections 63 and 64 of the Environment Act 1995 grant power to the Secretary of State to replace the existing English authorities within National Parks with National Park Authorities (NPAs), with similar provisions to apply in Wales, see s 64(3). These NPAs under s 4A of the Town and Planning Act 1990 (as inserted in 1995), become the *sole* planning authority for the Park(s) in question. This, inter alia, grants mineral planning functions to the NPA. There are, however, a number of planning functions which will be exercised concurrently with NPAs by district planning authorities within Park areas, these are: tree preservation, trees in Conservation Areas, and land adversely affecting the amenity of a neighbourhood. Section 67(2) of the Environment Act 1995 further enables the Secretary of State to apply the provisions relating to Unitary Development Plans to NPAs in place of those concerned with structure and local plans.

It is intended that the NPAs should begin functioning on 1 April 1997. Unless the Secretary of State makes an order for an NPA under s 67(2) of the 1995 Act, each NPA will assume responsibility for both structure and local plans in its area.

An emerging patchwork quilt of planning authorities

In *England* recommendations may be made under s 14 of the Local Government Act 1992, and subsequently implemented under s 17, for the replacement of the existing tiers of local government with a single tier, ie either for counties to take over district functions for an area *or* for a district to take over county functions within its area.

Recommendation has to be made whether such new unitary authorities should make unitary plans for their areas under Chapter I of Part II of the Town and Country Planning Act 1990, and as to the inclusion of mineral and waste policies *or* whether the existing provisions relating to structure and local plans should continue to apply to affected areas with appropriate adjustments. *Most* of 'shire England' will not be affected by change, though some counties will find themselves denuded of their historic county towns, eg Leicestershire, while in other cases particular areas with strong local identities and economies have been given unitary status.

The Secretary of State determines whether unitary authorities should retain structure and local plans having considered whether strategic planning needs to be carried out over an area greater than that of an individual authority, eg as in Leicestershire and Leicester.

In Wales, however, the Local Government (Wales) Act 1994 provides that 22 'principal councils' shall be the local planning authorities. These bodies are 11 counties and 11 county boroughs, all of which are unitary authorities, see ss 1 and 18 of the 1994 Act. Schedule 1A of the Town and County Planning Act 1990, as inserted in 1994, distributes planning functions, while s 10A of the 1990 Act provides that the new Welsh unitary authorities shall adopt the planning system of the existing English unitary authorities, eg as to unitary plans, though s 23A provides for the Welsh authorities to make joint unitary development plans. These changes in Wales are to be brought into effect by order. DoE Circular 4/96 gives guidance on the new system.

Note also that the Broads Authority is the local plan making and development control authority for its area under s 5 of the 1990 Act, and see ss 148 and 149 of the Local Government, Planning and Land Act 1980 for the power which can be conferred on urban development corporations.

B DEVELOPMENT PLANS

Statute currently knows the following kinds of plan:

1   Unitary development plans — metropolitan areas plus the Welsh and some English unitary authorities as outlined above.
2   Structure plans — 'shire' counties and districts, and some English unitary authorities.
3   Local plans — 'shire' counties and districts, and some English unitary authorities.

No other plans have statutory force, which is not to say that they do not exist. Local authorities often have 'non statutory plans' to 'fill the gap' until a statutory plan is made, and non statutory planning is used by government. The best example of this is SERPLAN which is the DOE's regional guidance for the future development of SE England. This rests on no real statutory basis, but the important point is that such regional guidance is recognised by the courts as being a matter that local authorities have at least to take into account when exercising their statutory planning functions, particularly with regard to the revision of structure plans.

Unitary Development Plans (UDPs)

UDPs replace the two tier structure and local plans for the metropolitan districts in London, the West Midlands, Greater Manchester, Merseyside, South Yorkshire, Tyne and Wear and West Yorkshire. They exist under ss 10–28 of the TCPA 1990. UDPs were originally introduced under the Local Government Act 1985, and will, in time, cover the areas of *some* unitary authorities according to the Secretary of State's determination.

UDPs are the sole plans for their areas and supersede other plans. They provide the framework for development, development control and conservation, and cover the whole of a relevant authority's area, stating clear and concise policies on land use issues — but *not* on any matter which is not land use related, though economic and social criteria may have been had in regard in their formulation. The basic assumption is that reappraisal and replanning will take place after a ten year period. Authorities should consult with the DOE on drawing up plans, and with the Countryside Commission and the relevant nature conservancy body (in England, English Nature) where a UDP will bear upon wildlife and the countryside.

The basic scheme of the legislation is as follows:

1 The Secretary of State has issued, and in some cases has revised, strategic guidance for the areas where UDPs are to exist. This relates to land use issues going beyond individual district boundaries.
2 Commencement orders have brought the UDP provisions into force within individual MDCs and LBCs, see s 28 of the TCPA 1990.
3 Thereafter a relevant authority is required to prepare a UDP for its area, and a two year time scale was envisaged in 1985 for the first draft UDPs to be drawn up and put on public deposit, though the Secretary of State has power to direct that a particular plan must be prepared within a specific period, see s 12 of the TCPA 1990.

Further guidance may now be found in PPG 12, February 1992.

UDPs have two parts under s 12(3), (4) of the TCPA 1990. Part I is a written statement of the local authority's general development and land use policies for its area, including conservation of the natural beauty and amenity of land, improvement of the physical environment and traffic management. Part I is the framework for Part II and should contain only major policies which *should*, according to s 12(6), be drawn up having regard to:

1 The Secretary of State's strategic or regional guidance.
2 Any other current national policies (eg those in PPGs).
3 Likely available resources for realistic plan implementation.
4 Any other matters prescribed.

Part I should generally be short, illustrated by a minimum of maps and diagrams and intelligible to lay persons.

Part II must be in general conformity with Part I, see s 12(7) and must take account of centrally prescribed issues, and will be, under s 12(4), a written statement of policies and proposals to form the basis for deciding individual applications. In addition it will contain a reasoned justification of the Part I proposals, and a statement of the regard had to the matters 1–4. Part II proposals must also be shown on a 'proposals map'. Part II will give detailed guidance on those matters which are likely to form the basis of planning decisions, and on the likely conditions which will be attached. Particular locations within a plan area may be designated, under s 12(8), as 'Action Areas' for comprehensive redevelopment in accordance with plan proposals within ten years. Under s 12A the Secretary of State may direct that a UDP shall not be prepared or shall not operate in relation to the area of an Urban Development Corporation.

UDPs are to be made in a two stage process: preparation of the draft followed by its deposit, time for objections and, if necessary, a public inquiry. Consequently authorities must ensure, under s 13, that adequate local publicity is given to the proposed content of the UDP in accordance with regulations made under s 26 [see SI 1991/2794], and that any representations made in due form are considered.

Once the draft plan is drawn up, copies must, in accordance with s 26 regulations be made available and a copy sent to the Secretary of State. Any other requirements of the regulations must also be complied with. A statement of the 'prescribed period' for making objections must be made.

It is specifically provided that among the objectors to a UDP the Secretary of State is included, see s 13(5) of the TCPA 1990 as amended in 1991. A UDP may not be adopted until after any objections made have been considered in accordance with regulations, or, where there are no objections, until after the expiry of the 'prescribed period'. A UDP may be withdrawn under s 14 by the authority at any time before adoption by the authority or approval by the Secretary of State, and *must* be withdrawn if the latter so directs. Section 15 provides for the adoption of UDPs either as originally prepared or following modification to take account of objections or other material considerations. However, where the Minister of Agriculture has objected to a plan and his objections have not been acted on the authority must explain their actions to the Secretary of State and must not adopt the plan unless authorised so to do. Furthermore where objections in due form have been received a public inquiry *must* be held to consider these, while any other objections *may* be the subject of any inquiry or hearing (see s 16 of the 1990 Act as amended).

The Secretary of State has quite extensive powers concerning UDPs. Once a copy of a UDP has been sent to him/her, he/she may direct the authority to modify it as he/she directs (see s 17(1) of the TCPA 1990 as amended) and thereafter the authority may not adopt the plan unless the Secretary of State is satisfied as to modification. Alternatively he/she may 'call in' a plan for approval, see s 18, either in whole or part. Approval is then at his/her discretion under s 19, and he/she may take into account *any* matters considered relevant, though the decision on a plan must be supported by a statement of reasons. Moreover, before deciding whether or not to approve a plan the Secretary of State must consider objections made in due form. The 'call in' power is extreme, and normally will only be used where a plan raises issues of national or regional importance; where Part I is out of conformity with strategic guidance; where Part II is out of conformity with Part I; where the Ministry of Agriculture presses an objection to the plan, or where the plan is publicly controversial. The giving of a 'holding direction' freezes the entire plan (s 18(2)) and transfers the matter to the Secretary of State. Where Part I (in whole or part) alone is 'called in' the Secretary of State may hold an examination in public of relevant issues. If a whole plan or any part of Part II, however, is 'called in' a public local inquiry must, under s 20(2), be held into any objections not already considered by the local authority. If the Secretary of State decides to reject the 'called in' plan he may do so without a further inquiry. The Secretary of State's powers extend to direct modification of Part II of a 'called in' plan to make it conform to Part I (see s 19(4)). Where the Secretary of State approves such a plan he will set a date on which the plan will come into operation (see s 19(5)).

There is the usual six week period, under s 284(1) of the TCPA 1990, of challenge on a point of law after approval/adoption.

Where a UDP is drawn up, Part II *must*, according to guidance initially given in Circular DoE 3/88, incorporate any existing local plans for its area, though they may be altered and updated by the authority, and must conform to Part I. Where such an alteration is proposed it must be specified, and its extent noted in Part II, and it will be open to the right to object at the deposit stage.

No objection may be made to the incorporation of an *unaltered* local plan. It is good practice to list local plans to be incorporated in draft and deposited UDPs, and to make them available as plan documentation for public inspection. The *full* text of incorporated local plans must be published as part of an adopted UDP, and the local plans themselves labelled to show they are part of the UDP. The direction given here by DoE 3/88 is an example of a very wide power to give procedural directions, now found in s 26(4) of the TCPA 1990.

Joint UDPs may be drawn up by two or more authorities though only where they are in the same metropolitan area. The procedure is generally as outlined above (see s 23 of the TCPA 1990). [Remember that particular powers exist in Wales under the 1994 reforms, and that central planning powers there are exercised by the Secretary of State for Wales.]

As stated above UDPs are theoretically envisaged as having a ten year life cycle, whereafter they are to be replaced and they may be altered before that time at the discretion of the authority or the direction of the Secretary of State. The procedure in such cases is as for initial preparation.

Structure plans

In the shires and some unitary authorities a two fold system of plans still exists. Structure plans now cover the nation; what follows therefore relates to how such a plan is *replaced* or otherwise modified.

Before a structure plan is drawn up, s 30 of the 1990 Act requires a review of the matters which may be expected to affect the development of its area by the planning authority. Review *must* be constant, and may involve surveys. This must include a review of physical and economic characteristics of the relevant area, and those of neighbouring areas where they are likely to be of consequence; size, composition and distribution of population; communications, transport and traffic; any other matters relevant to the foregoing, or prescribed by the Secretary of State, or subject to projected change and the likely consequences for the development of the area.

Under s 31 of the 1990 Act, as amended, a structure plan contains a written statement formulating the authority's general land development policies which must include policies on conservation of the natural beauty and amenity of the land, improvement of the physical environment and traffic management, though regulations may be made under s 31(4) which prescribe those matters with which a structure plan is to concern itself, see SI 1991/2794 which requires consideration of, inter alia, social, economic and environmental issues. The plan must also contain prescribed diagrams, maps, etc, and such material as is centrally directed. Plans are to be formulated in addition taking into account regional *or* strategic planning guidance given by the Secretary of State, current national policies, resources likely to be available and other matters prescribed or directed by the Secretary of State.

In unitary areas where structure and local plans are retained it is *expected* that authorities will work together on their structure plans, and may, in effect, be required to under s 21 of the Local Government Act 1992.

Under s 32 (as substituted) an authority may at any time prepare proposals for altering its structure plan or to replace it, and must do so if directed by the Secretary of State, though they may *not* so act with regard to a plan approved by the Secretary without his/her consent. Such proposals may relate to the whole of the authority's area or a part, but must be accompanied by an explanatory memorandum explaining and justifying proposals, together with supporting information. The memorandum is not, however, part of either the structure plan nor the overall development plan for the purposes of s 54A, see below.[1] There will be public participation in the proposal making process under s 33 (as substituted), though the form and content of this will be determined by regulations made centrally under s 53, or as is otherwise centrally directed, see SI 1991/2794. Any representations then received in due form must be considered. Once the proposals are made then copies must be made publicly available and a prescribed time stated during which objections can be made. A copy must also be sent to the Secretary of State, who may also be an objector to the plan. Any objections made in due form — that form to be as prescribed under central regulations — must be considered by the authority, who may, under s 34 (as substituted) withdraw their proposals at any time before formal adoption by them or approval by the Secretary of State. Structure plan alteration/replacement proposals may be modified to take account of objections received or in the light of other material considerations and may then be adopted by the authority under s 35 (as substituted), but this is subject to the Secretary of State's power to direct them to modify their proposals before adoption, and to s 35B, see below. Section 35A further empowers the Secretary of State to 'call in' proposals before adoption. He/she then has a wide discretion as to the fate of the proposals, though he/she must consider any objections made in due form together with *any* other matters considered relevant, and in this connection a wide power of consultation is given. Reasons must, however, be given to the authority explaining the Secretary of State's decisions on proposals, though the form and content of the reasons is left to his/her decision. Section 35B further requires that before adopting proposals the authority must, unless the Secretary of State otherwise directs, cause 'an examination in public' to be held of such matters concerning the proposals as they consider should be examined, or which the Secretary of State directs are to be examined. Similarly where the Secretary of State calls in proposals he/she may hold an examination in public of any specified matter. An examination is held by persons specifically appointed by the Secretary of State, but it is not a public inquiry in the full sense, even though the Tribunals and Inquiries Act 1992 applies, for no person has a *right* to be heard, while certain bodies or persons *may* take part, for example the authority and those invited to participate by the person(s) holding the examination. Regulations may be made with respect to examinations, see SI 1991/2794, and note Annex C of PPG 12, 'Examination in public: A Guide for Local Planning Authorities', see further below.

Finally note s 35C under which an authority responsible for a structure plan must, where their alteration or replacement proposals are adopted or approved, notify local plan authorities of this and supply them with statements as to whether their local plans are or are not in conformity with the new or altered plan, and the extent of any nonconformity shall be specified.

See DoE Circular 4/96 on structure planning in unitary areas.

---

1 *Holden v Secretary of State* [1994] JPL B1.

Local plans

Section 36 of the TCPA 1990 (as substituted) provides that 'local planning authorities' (generally districts) must, within such time as the Secretary of State directs, prepare *a* local plan for their area. Such a plan must contain a written statement of detailed policies for land use and development which must include policies on the conservation of the natural beauty and amenity of the land (a phrase which must assume that there is beauty, etc, to conserve), the improvement of the physical environment (which is apt to deal with situations where there is no beauty) and traffic management. Similar requirements have, of course, already been met in relation to UDPs and structure plans. Local plans must *not* contain policies on winning and working minerals or mineral waste deposition, nor any policies on waste or refuse deposition. But plans must contain maps, illustrating policies and such other diagrams and illustrations as are prescribed, together with other material considered appropriate by authorities, and plans must also be in general conformity with structure plans. In formulating plan policies authorities must have regard to such matters as are prescribed or directed to them by the Secretary of State. Plans may designate a part of an authority's area as an 'action area' for comprehensive development, re-development or improvement within a prescribed period. Once in force a local plan may be altered or replaced at the authority's discretion, though they must *consider* alteration or replacement if supplied with a nonconformity notice under s 35C (see above) and *must* prepare proposals for alteration, etc where the Secretary of State so directs. Such alterations, etc, may relate to the whole or part of a plan area, see s 39 (as substituted).

Public participation in plan making or alteration, etc, exists under s 40 (as substituted) and is dependent on regulations made centrally, and directions given by the Secretary of State, under s 53. [See SI 1991/2794.] Representations made in due form must be considered by the authority and when their proposals are finally formulated they must make them publicly available, and send a copy to the Secretary of State. A statement of the time allowed for objecting to the proposals must also be made, and again it is specifically provided that the Secretary of State may be an objector. A plan or its alterations or replacement may not be adopted until after any duly made objections have been considered, and in any case where objections have been duly made a local inquiry or other hearing must be held for consideration purposes under s 42(1) (as substituted) while an inquiry or hearing *may* be held to consider any objections not made in due form, ie in accordance with regulations. An inquiry will be held by a person appointed by the Secretary of State. Thereafter under s 43 (as amended) the plan etc, may be adopted by resolution either as originally prepared or modified to take account of objections or any other material considerations, though proposals not in general conformity with the structure plan may not be adopted. The obligations to consult and consider, however, impose no obligation to comply with views received — even if these receive the support of the person holding a local plan inquiry into them — provided the planning authority behaves reasonably.[2]

---

2 *R v Hammersmith & Fulham London Borough Council, ex p People before Profit Ltd* [1981] JPL 869.

The Secretary of State may intervene in the local plan process at a number of points. After a copy of plan proposals has been sent to him/her, he/she may under s 43(4), as amended, direct modification before adoption, or he/she may under s 44 call in proposals, or any part of them, for consideration. If such a call is made the authority cannot take any further steps to adopt the proposals, or any of them, until the Secretary of State has given a decision, and it is for him/her to approve them or not as the case may be: if he/she does approve no further adoption by the authority is required. Section 45 then grants the Secretary of State a wide discretion to approve or reject the proposals or modify them, taking into account any matters considered relevant. However, if he/she does not determine to reject proposals he/she must consider any objections that have been made in due form and give objectors the chance to be heard, perhaps also holding a hearing or a public inquiry.

Action to ensure conformity between structure and local plans is to be taken under s 46 of the TCPA 1990 (as substituted). When preparing local plan proposals the preparing authority must notify those proposals to the structure plan authority who must within a prescribed period state whether the proposals are/are not in general conformity with the structure plan, and, if not, to what extent there is nonconformity, and any such statement is to be treated as a duly made objection to the proposals. Once the local plan is finally made/altered, etc, as the case may be and is adopted/approved its provisions will apply in any case of conflict with those of the structure plan, unless the case falls within s 35C (see above) and no remedial action has been taken to deal with the lack of conformity.

Recovery of inquiry costs

Under s 303A of the 1990 Act (introduced by the Town and Country Planning (Costs of Inquiries etc) Act 1995) the Secretary of State may make local planning authorities responsible for those costs of holding inquiries into, inter alia, local plans and examinations in public which would otherwise have fallen on him/her.

Two types of local plan remain to be mentioned, though their relevance is to mineral extraction and waste disposal, see chapters 8 and 9. Section 37 of the TCPA 1990 (as substituted) *requires* 'mineral planning authorities' (*generally* counties) for areas *other* than National Parks to prepare within such period (as any) directed by the Secretary of State a 'minerals local plan' (MLP) for their areas. This is a local plan which contains a written statement formulating detailed policies in respect of winning or working minerals or deposition of mineral waste. Within National Parks the obligation will fall on the NPA, see above. Section 38, as substituted, requires the making of 'waste local plans' (WLP) containing detailed policies in respect of refuse or waste deposition. It will *generally* be county authorities who will prepare such plans, while in Metropolitan and some other unitary areas such plans will be part of UDPs. The obligation may be discharged either by making a separate WLP or by including policies in the MLP. NPAs are under a separate but similar obligation.

In unitary areas where UDP functions are not conferred each unitary authority will make a MLP and a WLP, or will, as in Leicester, include policies in the local plan, see SI 1996/507.

Challenges to the validity of plans may be made under s 284 of the 1990 Act as amended, and s 287. Challenge is allowed on a point of law only, procedural or substantive, and may only take place within the six week period of notice of adoption or approval as the case may be as required by regulations. The challenge may be made by any 'person aggrieved' which would certainly include any person whose land is affected by the terms of a plan. For this, and an excellent example of the generally beneficent attitude of the Courts towards the powers of authorities concerning plan making, see *Westminster City Council v Great Portland Estates plc*.[3]

General considerations affecting plans and plan making

PPG 12 points out that plans exist to provide *objective* criteria against which development proposals can be adjudged, though they are not exclusive criteria in this respect. Plans nevertheless provide *guidance* to developers, *incentives* for some developments, specifically allocated preferred status in plans and *controls* to ensure that development cannot take place against the public interest. Thus while not prescriptive documents, plans must make adequate provision for development while at the same time protecting both the natural and the built environment and contributing to sustainable development.

The guidance considers the various types of plan, both statutory and non-statutory, central, regional and local, that can exist and states that where authorities use and draw up non-statutory supplementary planning guidance (SPG), though this will have *a* legal significance as a consideration to be taken into account it cannot have the same significance as the plan itself, particularly under s 54A (see below), must be issued separately from the plan, must be publicly available with its status made clear, and should *not* be used to introduce policies which are not subject to the public scrutiny which affects plans. Finally such SPG must always be consistent with plans. Informal or 'bottom drawer' plans and totally ad hoc ways of dealing with planning applications without reference to a plan are both condemned by the PPG.

PPG 12 stresses that plans should be as up to date as possible and kept under regular review, with co-operative working between neighbouring authorities welcomed. The reviews and surveys made are generally to be publicly available under the Local Government (Access to Information) Act 1985.

So far as content is concerned, plans 'must make realistic provision for the development needs of the area'. Restraint policies may be needed in Green Belts and other 'environmentally important areas' but otherwise adequate development opportunities must be provided. Furthermore plans should be succinct and easily understand eschewing over elaboration. PPG 12 points out the key features of the individual types of plan. Thus all must include policies in respect of conservation of natural beauty and amenity, improvement of the physical environment and traffic management. *Structure* plans should further indicate an overall strategic balance struck between development and conservation and how development will be served by transport and infrastructure. This plan will also contain *general* policies on housing, Green Belts, the rural and urban economies, transport, highways, mineral working and waste treatment, tourism and leisure and energy generation. *Indicative* guidance should be given on, eg the level of housing provision, and where, and

3 [1985] AC 661, [1984] 3 All ER 744.

on broad areas of environmental restraint — detailed guidance on these and other matters should be left to local plans. In the preparation of both *structure* and *Part I UDPs* authorities should pay particular heed to resources realistically likely to be available to meet plan policies, bearing in mind the influence of national policies and the need to seek the redevelopment of underused or derelict land rather than encourage the use of greenfield sites. Such plans should make provision for development over a period of at least 15 years from their inception, though a longer time scale is acceptable for restraint on development in Green Belts. At the more detailed level of local plans and Part II UPDs a planning horizon of ten years is generally counselled though different timescales should be adopted for sensitive issues such as mineral extraction or conservation projects. Plans should further take into account: infrastructure and transport provision, particularly roads and road building and the safeguarding of transport routes against inappropriate development; the infrastructure of utilities; the need to phase new development over a period of time; socio-economic issues such as urban regeneration, balancing inner city against greenfield developments, car ownership, wage levels and employment, changing bases of employment from manufacturing to service industries, agriculture and the rural economy, the impact of developments on particular groups in society; environmental implications and appraisals of plan policies and plan making (see further below) and overall development control policies.

Plans and the environment

Reference has already been made to planning and sustainability. PPG 12 makes particular comment on the need to ensure that planning plays its part in achieving the sustainable development policy.

Plans should thus ensure that *sustainable development* is a goal: 'the sum total of decisions in the planning field ... should not deny future generations the best of today's environment. This should be expressed through the policies adopted in development planning' (PPG 12, February 1992, para 1.8).

This is a major new departure in policy — how far it will go in practice remains to be seen. The 1990 Act, as amended in 1991, as already started requires plans to have policies on:

1   Conservation of natural beauty and amenity.
2   Improvement of the physical environment.
3   Traffic management.

Plans should be drawn up so that their policies interact harmoniously, and environmental considerations should be taken into account in drawing up all policies. While social and economic considerations should be taken into account in plan formulation, PPG 12, however, lays particular stress on environmental considerations. Thus provision should be made for:

1   Protecting land in its various aspects as a finite resource.
2   Sustaining the character and diversity of the countryside.
3   Defending Green Belts.
4   Aiming for energy conservation.
5   Taking full account of global warming.
6   Aiming to site new developments near public transport routes.

7 Maintaining the vitality of exisiting centres.

8 Limiting car use by siting new developments so that car use is reduced or even rendered unnecessary (this is reinforced by PPG 6 on retail developments which advises against granting planning permission for major new 'out-of-town' shopping centres such as Merryhill near Dudley or Meadow Hall near Sheffield).

9 Relating development to public transport networks.

10 Encouraging walking and cycling.

11 Where transport is needed, locating new development around existing transport nodes and corridors.

12 Limiting town centre parking.

13 Creating appropriate interchange facilities between modes of public transport.

14 Protecting groundwater against inappropriate developments.

15 Making appropriate provision for the location of hazardous installations.

16 Making appropriate provision for mineral extraction and waste disposition.

17 Making sure that policies have gone through a process of 'environmental appraisal', ie 'identifying, qualifying, weighing up and reporting on the environmental and other costs and benefits of the measures which are proposed' (including the implications of all options and trade offs between options) (see PGG 12 para 5.52). Authorities may use the DoE's guidance document 'Policy Appraisal and the Environment' for this purpose. 'Environmental appraisal' is not quite the same thing as environmental assessment (EA) (see further below) but the concepts are clearly related. The EU is likely to push for full EA of *all* policies and note that under s 71A of the 1990 Act the Secretary of State may extend EA to any *class of development*.

PPG 13 'Transport' reinforces and amplifies the foregoing by accepting the need to manage traffic demands, and by acknowledging that increasing traffic growth cannot be met in full by new road building. Acceptable alternatives to the private car have to be promoted, and planning should have as one of its aims planning for less travel and for more acceptable means of travel such as walking, cycling and public transport.

The annexes

PPG 12 contains a number of annexes giving guidance on particular aspects of plan making. Annex A is the Code of Practice on Development Plans applying *generally* to all types of plan. It deals with the stages between the deposit of a draft plan which has been prepared and the adoption of the plan. It thus begins by detailing the procedures for advertising the deposit of a draft plan and the mode by which objections can be made to it. In this latter context objectors are encouraged to be as 'specific as possible' in setting out their written objections and what they would like to see included in the plan. Those who wish to support plan proposals are further encouraged to do so in writing so that their views may be taken into account. All objections and representations must then be taken into account if received within the six week period allowed under the regulations — those received out of time are considered at the authority's discretion. Informal discussion may take place at this time to consider objections, find areas where agreement exists or could be reached or to suggest how plans can be changed to meet objections.

It is clear that in view of the increased status of plans under s 54A (see further below) that this negotiation phase can be of crucial importance in plan formulation.

The arrangements for the formal public examination of plans differ, of course, according to whether the plan is a local plan or UDP on the one hand or a structure plan on the other. There are, however, common features. In each case the prime objectives is to find out relevant facts and arguments, to report them to the planning authority with an evaluation of the evidence and recommendations as to action. This activity will be carried out by an inspector (in the case of local plans and UDPs) or a panel (in the case of structure plans) in each case appointed by the Secretary of State but paid for by the plan making authority. Assessors may be appointed where there are matters calling for special knowledge. The plan making authority will also appoint a programme officer (though not a member of their planning department) to manage the inquiry/examination process. The authority will also be responsible for providing relevant accommodation, for certain travel and subsistence expenses in the case of participants at an examination in public, and for publicising the proceedings, while the programme officer will draw up, provisionally, a timetable for the procedure: this will be subject to approval by the inspector/chairman of the panel. Objectors, etc will be informed of the timetable and the programme of the event. In the case of structure plans *only* the plan making authority should select for examination only issues where they need fuller information and discussion, and this will lead to the identification of those who should be invited to participate. It is *not* the case that all objectors to a structure plan should be invited to its examination in public, and indeed participation will not be limited solely to those who have made objections.

In some cases objections, representations and relevant points of view from a number of persons/organisations can be combined together and this should be encouraged to save time and expense.

Preliminary meetings will usually take place well before the main event conducted by the inspector/chairman to discuss the timetable and programme and deal with other procedural issues, for example, in relation to inquiries, whether sessions can be held in the evening. It is normal also to ask for those participating in the process to submit written material and 'proofs of evidence' (ie statements of their cases) before the event begins and for the plan making authority to submit its responses to those shortly afterwards. A date for doing this will be set at the preliminary meeting, and the material will thereafter be circulated and deposited for public inspection. The understanding then is that participants will have read all relevant material.

Holding the inquiry/examination in public

Where an *inquiry* is held the inspector is in charge of the proceedings but must conduct them in accordance with the principles of impartiality, openness and fairness. He/she will encourage order and discourage repetition, and normally allow questions to be put to those who give evidence as well as having power to question them him/her self. At the inquiry the plan making authority will be invited to begin and will set out the plan's overall aims and objectives, explaining how the plan reflects the structure plan at a local level. In relation to hearing objectors the normal procedure is for each objector to make a submission, for the authority to respond to this and for the objector then to have a final right of reply. It is for the inspector to decide whether to hear general objections first leaving those of a more particular nature till later. Objectors may, of course, be represented, but should not be made to feel disadvantaged if they are not.

At an *examination in public* the chairman, again, is responsible for procedure and for ensuring that contributions are constructive and not repetitious, so that the selected issues are examined in the necessary depth, especially in relation to issues where changes in the plan may be made. The form of an examination is a 'probing discussion' of the issues led by the chairman and panel between the plan making authority and the participants with the selected issues being examined in appropriate depth. There are no counsel assisting the panel, and while participants *may* be represented they should not feel disadvantaged if they are not. The chairman may involve participation from any relevant government department.

After the inquiry/examination in public

At this point the inspector/chairman will prepare a report which considers submissions made and the supporting evidence and makes reasoned recommendations, which is submitted to the plan making authority for their consideration — though, as has been already stated, the authority is not bound to accept any recommendation provided they can give a reasoned explanation for their decision. Where, however, the authority proposes to modify the plan in response to recommendation they must prepare a reasoned list of modifications and publicise this, allowing for public inspection of the issues and giving time for the making of objections. Similar notice must be given to those who made objections/representations to the original proposal. Objections to modifications (though not to the content of the original proposal) or to failures to make particular modifications as recommended by the inspector/ chairman, must be received and considered by the authority. They may decide to hold a further inquiry or reopen the examination in public.

This will only rarely happen: for example where objectors raise matters not in issue at the earlier stage such as where there is a proposal to substitute for a matter which was in the original proposed plan something that is entirely different, with the consequences that objections made to the proposed modification bring forth new evidence, *or* where following consideration of objections the plan making authority are minded to withdraw a proposed modification, and that modification was itself made to meet an initial objection so that the initial objector should be given the chance to comment on the proposed withdrawal. In any case the Secretary of State has a power to direct reopening of the examination/holding a further inquiry. Where a reopening or further inquiry is to occur it is subject to the same publicity requirements as for its predecessor, while at its conclusion there will be a further report and recommendations from the inspector/chairman to the authority who must then give a reasoned statement of decisions on the recommendations, particularly any not accepted.

The powers of the Secretary of State

The guidance makes it clear the Secretary of State will use his/her powers to issue directions that a plan should be modified before adaptation if it is considered unsatisfactory, particularly with regard to the application of national, regional or (if appropriate) structure plan policies. If a direction is given the recipient authority must decide what they must do to comply and then must follow the modification procedure accordingly, with appropriate advertisement of proposed changes. Where, however, *no* modification is proposed to secure compliance with the direction, the authority must give reasons for their decision, because, of course, the authority cannot adopt their proposed plan *unless* they either satisfy the Secretary of State they have made the necessary modifications to conform with the direction, *or* that direction is withdrawn.

The Secretary of State's 'call in' powers again are rarely used and only in limited circumstances where, for example, issues of national or regional importance are raised or where controversy over the plan extends beyond the boundaries of the plan making authority as where, for instance, the plan would seriously hinder implementation of a neighbouring authority's plan.

PPG 12 Annexes B & C give further detailed guidance on local plan inquiries and examinations in public respectively.

Proposals to speed up the local plan process were put forward by the government in 1994, but as yet no legislation to implement these changes has been enacted. The consequence is that the objective of having a system of district-wide local plans in place by December 1996 is most unlikely to be met as the current law has been productive of delay. Thus in September 1994 only 65 non-metropolitan districts had such plans in place, 44 had full coverage of part area plans under earlier legislation, 147 had part coverage under such plans while 40 had no adopted local plans at all. However, 250 districts expected to have a district-wide local plan in place by the end of 1996. At the same time only ten metropolitan districts/London boroughs had a UDP in place, though most expected to have such a plan in place by the end of 1996. However, some speeding up of the process can be achieved administratively and it was proposed in April 1995 further to revise PPG 12 to ensure (a) more effective consultation on local plans at the predeposit stage; and (b) to rework the Code of Practice on Local Plan Inquiries to produce a more effective and economical system.

What is the 'development plan'?

Section 54 of the TCPA 1990 (as amended) provides that the 'development plan', an entity to which many other provisions of the Act refer, is to be (outside Greater London and the metropolitan areas where, of course, UDPs exist) the provisions of the structure plan for the time being in operation for any area in question, alterations to such a plan, the provisions of the local plan and any MLP and WLP in force, and alterations to such plans.

C GENERAL PLANNING CONTROL

Part III of the 1990 Act promulgates the meaning of 'development' and the requirement of planning permission. 'Development' is defined by s 55, though many actions are either excluded from the definition, by the Act or orders made under it, or are given automatic planning permission by order.

The definition of development

The general rule is that development is carrying out building, engineering, mining or other operations in, on, over or under land, or making any material change in the use of land or buildings. This has two limbs, 'operational' development, and making material changes of use. With regard to operational acts the courts generally define these as matters resulting in physical alteration to land and having some degree of permanence, see *Parkes v Secretary of State for the Environment*.[4] Courts consider factors such as: the size of the operation, whether it is permanent, whether physically attached to land. These factors are not given equal weight in every case, see *Buckinghamshire County Council v Callingham*,[5] where creating a small model village was held an act of development, and *Barvis Ltd v Secretary of State for the Environment*,[6] where erection of a large tower crane running on rails, but nevertheless capable of being dismantled and moved was held to be development. (Mining developments will be dealt with in chapter 8.) Section 55(1A) of the 1990 Act, as inserted in 1991, now further provides that 'building operations' include demolition, rebuilding, structural alterations of or additions to buildings, and other operations normally undertaken by a builder. Demolition may thus (either as a 'building' or an 'engineering' operation) be an act of development requiring permission. However, s 55(2)(g), as inserted, provides that the demolition of any *description* of building specified in a direction from the Secretary of State to an authority, or authorities generally, is *not* to be an act of development. See DoE Circular 10/95 which contains the current direction, and which effectively provides that *only* the demolition of dwelling houses (and their adjoining buildings) *outside* conservation areas, and demolition of gates, walls and fences *within* conservation areas is subject to planning control. Development consisting of a 'material change of use' is more difficult to define, and is generally decided as a matter of fact and degree. It is not always necessary for a change to be one of *kind* for it to be 'material'. Indeed changes of degree made by a marked intensification of use can be *sufficient changes of character* to constitute development. This rule applies to both main and and ancillary uses of a site, see *Brooks and Burton Ltd v Secretary of State for the Environment*,[7] where production of concrete blocks rose from 300,000 to 1,200,000 per annum. The *practical* problem for planning authorities in such cases lies in detecting changes constituted by intensification, and in determining a point at which a creeping intensification reaches such a point as to be reasonably recognisable as a change of character.

Whether change is 'material' must be assessed by reference to its effect on an appropriate area of land, known as 'the planning unit'. Generally this will be the whole area in a landholder's ownership or occupation, see *Trentham v Gloucestershire County Council*;[8] a question of fact in each case. Following

---

4 [1979] 1 All ER 211, [1978] 1 WLR 1308.
5 [1952] 2 QB 515, [1952] 1 All ER 1166.
6 (1971) 22 P & CR 710. Note also *Bedfordshire County Council v Central Electricity Generating Board* [1985] JPL 43.
7 [1978] 1 All ER 733, [1977] 1 WLR 1294; note also *Hilliard v Secretary of State for the Environment* (1978) 37 P & CR 129 — intensification of one ancillary use of a farm building did not mean intensification of the use of the whole farm.
8 [1966] 1 All ER 701, [1966] 1 WLR 506.

Burdle v Secretary of State for the Environment,[9] there are three ways of dealing with the issue: (a) where an occupier has a single main purpose (with or without ancillary uses) the whole of his unit of occupation is the planning unit; (b) if there is a variety of uses, or 'composite use' where activities may vary and fluctuate, the whole unit is the planning unit; and (c) where, however, within a holding physically separate and distinct areas are occupied for different and unrelated purposes, each separate area is the planning unit. The basic test is whether physically *and* functionally there are separate uses. A unit having varying fluctuating uses may experience change without 'development', but particularly marked changes, for example major intensification of individual uses, may amount to material change of use. The main site use will generally carry with it minor and ancillary uses, minor fluctuations do not constitute changes provided they remain merely ancillary.[10] What constitutes a separate planning unit is normally a question of fact and degree. It is the factual position (not the identity of the owner) which is determinative of whether land has discrete uses, even where on a plot in single ownership there are two uses integral to the owner's overall undertaking. Two or more uses of land may be 'distantly related' by being parts of an overall business, but that does not necessarily mean that one is ancillary to the other(s).[11]

Under s 55(2)(f) of the 1990 Act the Use Classes Order 1987 SI 1987/764 (as amended), lays down that where buildings or land are used for a purpose of a specified class, their use for another purpose of that same class is deemed not to be development. Four broad 'bands' of use are identified, each subdivided, so as *to provide eleven classes*.

The basic principle of the Use Classes Order (UCO) is that a change of use of a building or land *within* a class will not be an act of development, while a change of use *across* classes *may* be, provided it is 'material,' see *Rann v Secretary of State for the Environment*.[12] Certain uses classified as 'sui generis' are excluded from the operation of the UCO and a change of use to or from such a use will, provided it is material, need planning permission. Such uses include theatres, fun fairs or scrap yards. From a broad environmental point of view the most important classes are: B1, business use, inter alia, for research or development of products and purposes or for any industrial process provided it can be carried out in *any* residential area without detriment to amenity by virtue of dust, grit, soot, smoke, smell, vibration or noise (ie, it is irrelevant to argue the area in question is noisy or dirty, etc, see *W T Lamb Properties Ltd v Secretary of State for the Environment*),[13] and B2, general industrial, processes not falling within B1. Particular provisions relating to changes of use between somewhat environmentally unfriendly uses of land previously found in the UCO have now been abandoned, as it is thought the IPC and LAAPC systems of control (see chapter 10 below) are more apt to regulate them.

It is possible to restrict these rights by conditions in a grant of planning permission, see *City of London Corpn v Secretary of State for the Environment*.[14]

---

9 [1972] 3 All ER 240, [1972] 1 WLR 1207.
10 *Wood v Secretary of State for the Environment* [1973] 2 All ER 404, [1973] 1 WLR 707.
11 *Essex Water Co v Secretary of State for the Environment* [1989] JPL 914.
12 [1980] JPL 109.
13 [1983] JPL 303.
14 (1971) 71 LGR 28, 23 P & CR 169.

D THE NEED FOR PLANNING PERMISSION

Under s 57 of the 1990 Act planning permission is generally required for acts of development. This is subject to exceptions. Lawful use of land under a grant of planning permission or a development order generally requires no further grant of permission, nor does a use continued since and commenced before 1 July 1948.

The Crown requires no permission for its developments,[15] and no enforcement notice can be issued in respect of development carried out by or on behalf of the Crown on Crown land, s 294(1) of the 1990 Act. There is a non-statutory consultation procedure under DOE Circular 18/84 whereby central departments and other Crown bodies consult local planning authorities before carrying out development. There is, of course, no need to duplicate consultations that may take place with local authorities under other legislation, for example with regard to trunk roads under the Highways Act 1980.

Departments will consult local planning authorities on proposed developments likely to be of special concern within a locality, and such consultation will be in good time, though consultation and notification procedures cannot apply in their entirety to developments involving security issues. Local authorities should give adequate publicity to proposed Crown developments generally as if permission were needed. Local authority views on proposed Crown developments should be transmitted to the relevant department, generally within eight weeks of receiving a 'Notice of Proposed Development' which is the formal notice of a firm proposal. These views should be reasoned. A proposal which departs from a development plan may be made subject to a non-statutory public inquiry, with the Secretary of State considering the issue. Strong objections to a development should be notified to relevant departments who may then refer the issue to the Secretary of State for the Environment for an inquiry and a decision. Where the local planning authority objects to a proposal, and the disagreement cannot be resolved, the Department of the Environment will also be involved, and a non-statutory inquiry may have to be held with the Secretary of State making a determination. Security considerations may, however, inhibit the use of procedures laid down in Circular 18/84, in which case the procedures have to be followed only up to the point of inhibition.[16]

Section 90 of the 1990 Act provides a procedure whereby need to apply for planning permission may be obviated. Where central authorisation is statutorily required in respect of development to be carried out by a local authority or statutory undertaker, the relevant department *may*, on granting authorisation, direct planning permission 'deemed to be' granted, subject to such conditions as may be imposed. Development is taken to be authorised where a department consents, authorises or approves a development under statute, or confirms a compulsory purchase order on land for development purposes, or otherwise appropriates land acquired by agreement to the purpose, or gives permission for borrowing money for the purpose, or

---

15 *Ministry of Agriculture, Fisheries and Food v Jenkins* [1963] 2 QB 317.
16 *R v Secretary of State for Defence, ex p Camden London Borough Council* [1994] EGCS 33.

undertakes to make a statutory grant for the purpose. Statutory undertakers are defined by s 262 as including: railway; road and water transport; docks and harbours undertakings. Likewise where consent is given under s 36 of the Electricity Act 1989 for the construction of an electricity generating station with a capacity of over 50 MG, planning consent may be deemed granted, though where the application for consent is opposed by a local planning authority a public local inquiry must be held. Similar provisions apply under s 37 of the 1989 Act to consents for the installation of above ground power lines, see further chapter 7. In practice this procedure is used only in cases where there may be a serious local environmental impact in respect of developments by the energy undertakings. Normally under s 266 of the 1990 Act statutory undertakers are expected to apply for planning permission in the usual way, though it may be that where planning permission is refused, or granted subject to unacceptable conditions, any appeal will have to be heard under s 266 by the Secretary of State and 'the appropriate minister' as defined in s 265, for example, in relation to an electricity undertaking, the Trade and Industry Secretary. Section 266 applies to the 'operational land' of statutory undertakers, as defined in ss 263 and 264, and land in which the undertakers hold, or propose to acquire, an interest with a view to using it for the purposes of carrying on their undertaking where permission, if granted, would be for development involving use of land for that purpose.

Permitted development (PD)

The Town and Country Planning (General Permitted Development) Order SI 1995/418 (GPDO) gives permission for types of development in a number of categories, thus obviating the need for an application for permission. From an environmental point of view the most important of these classes are:

Part 6, class A — carrying out on agricultural land comprised in an agricultural unit of 5 ha or more in area of works for erecting or extending a building, or excavations or engineering operations requisite for the land's use for agricultural purposes, subject to specified limitations on size, height and position. Note also classes B and C which respectively permit similar developments on agricultural units of between 0.4 and 5 ha in extent, and winning and working minerals on land held with land used for agricultural purposes of minerals for use for those purposes within the agricultural unit in question.

Part 7, class A — carrying out, subject to limits, on land used for forestry (including afforestation) of requisite building, and other operations (other than providing dwellings) and laying out private ways.

Part 8, class A — extending or altering industrial buildings or warehouses provided this is for the purposes of the undertaking concerned, and the building is not to be used for a purpose other than an industrial process or storage or distribution as the case may be. Height and volume limits must also be complied with. Note also classes B, C, and D which allow replacement or emplacement of plant, services, conveyors, etc, creation of hard standings and certain waste deposits on sites already in use for waste deposition purposes on 1 July 1948.

Part 11 — development authorised under local or private Acts, or under an order approved by Parliament, or under the Harbours Act 1964, ss 14 and 16, where the nature of the development and the designated land are specified; but where development comprises a building or an access way to a highway or erecting a bridge, aquaduct, pier or dam prior approval of detailed plans and specifications must be obtained from the relevant local planning authority, though they may not withhold approval except where satisfied that either the design of the building etc, would damage amenity and could be suitably modified, or the building ought reasonably to be placed elsewhere on the land.

Part 12 — works carried out on land by local authorities and consisting of the erection of, inter alia, lamp standards and like amenities. Note also Part 13 allowing highway authorities to undertake certain highway maintenance or improvement works.

Parts 14, 15, 16, works carried out, inter alia, by drainage bodies and sewerage undertakers in respect of certain of their functions.

Part 17 — development work by statutory undertakers, for example: development on operational railway land in connection with railway traffic, *other* than the construction of railways or railway station car parks and other specified buildings; certain development by electricity and gas undertakings.

Part 18 — certain airport developments, see chapter 7.

Parts 19, 20, 21, 22, 23 — relate to mineral works and developments, see chapter 8.

General permission is given for development of the type specified in the GPDO. Hazardous developments are generally controlled for planning purposes by the Planning (Hazardous Substances) Act 1990, see chapter 7 and SI 1995/419 art 10 (Table) (d).

Under Art 4 of the Order if either the Secretary of State or the local planning authority (*usually* the district or unitary authority council) is satisfied that development of any specified class(es) should not be carried out in a particular area, or that any particular development of any of the classes should not be carried out, unless permission is granted, they may direct accordingly. Where the direction is given by the local authority the Secretary of State's approval is required, except in matters of effectively local concern.

Simplified Planning Zones

One other means of obviating the need for planning permission, is the Simplified Planning Zone (SPZ). This follows on from the concept of the Enterprise Zone (EZ) introduced by the Local Government, Planning and Land Act 1980 which utilised a combination of tax advantages and notions of permitted development in an attempt to revive depressed areas. The SPZ was introduced in 1987 by the Housing and Planning Act 1986, see now ss 82–87 of the TCPA 1990, as amended, and for further guidance see DoE Circular 25/87 and PPG 5.

Local planning authorities (generally districts) must consider, under s 83, for which part of their areas it is desirable to have SPZ and then to keep this matter under review. Before proceeding authorities are *counselled* to consult with owners of land likely to be affected, see PPG 5. Where it is *proposed* to make a scheme certain specified bodies and persons *must* be consulted, see SI 1992/2414, reg 3. In an SPZ the designation scheme identifies the land and grants planning permission for development or classes of development specified, subject or not, as the case may be, to conditions or limitations contained in the scheme. The scheme consists of a map and written statement together with appropriate diagrams, s 82 and Sch 7 of the TCPA 1990 as amended. If it is felt that SPZ designation or alteration at any time is desirable then the local planning authority are to prepare a scheme, s 83. They must then inform the Secretary of State, and decide a date on which they will begin to prepare the scheme, see Sch 7. *Anyone* can ask an authority to make or alter an SPZ scheme, and if they refuse (except where designations or alterations were made within the previous 12 months) or do not decide to act as requested within three months, the individual or organisation involved can refer the matter to the Secretary of State, see Sch 7. If the matter is referred to the Secretary of State the local authority is notified as soon as practicable and invited to comment on the idea in writing within 28 days. Any representations made to the Secretary of State and not previously sent to the Local Planning Authority are sent to them at this point. The Secretary of State *can* consult with anyone he/she chooses and then make a direction that the authority shall make or alter an SPZ scheme. He/she must notify both the authority and the applicant and give them a statement of reasons for making or refusing to make a direction. This direction can add or exclude any area of land to or from the SPZ, it need not necessarily entirely relate to the land for which the original request was made.

Whether voluntarily or under compulsion the authority are to publicise, in a way prescribed by the Secretary of State, the fact that they are to prepare (or alter) an SPZ scheme, and any representations made in due form must be considered. The Secretary of State for Transport must also be consulted with regard to highway implications before the scheme is prepared. In a *non* metropolitan county where a *district* council decide to make an SPZ scheme, they must consult the county authority before proceeding. Where a scheme has been prepared, or where alterations to a scheme are proposed and prepared, copies of the proposals must be made publicly available and this must be advertised. Objections made in prescribed form will be received, and copies of the Scheme, etc, sent to the Secretary of State, his counterpart for Transport and the relevant county council.

If there are objections to a scheme normally an inquiry must be held with an inspector appointed by the Secretary of State, or in prescribed cases by the authority, or some other hearing may be held. After the inquiry or where no objections were received the proposals *may* be revised in the light of objections and the outcome of the inquiry. There is no obligation, however, to modify a proposal. Adoption may then take place, subject to the power of the Secretary of State to direct modifications to the proposal prior to adoption. He/she can also 'call in' an SPZ proposal and determine the form of the SPZ designation. Where this power is used he/she has wide discretionary powers, but must generally consider objections made. He/she may also hold an inquiry or some other form of hearing.

Under s 84 of the TCPA 1990 conditions and limitations which may be imposed on planning permissions, and which may be specified in an SPZ scheme may include: conditions or limitations in respect of all or some development permitted by the scheme, and conditions or limitations requiring the consent, approval or agreement of the authority in relation to particular types of development. However, nothing in an SPZ scheme may affect a person's right to do anything that is not 'development' or to carry out development for which permission is not required or for which permission has been granted otherwise than by the scheme. Where a permission containing limitations, etc, has been granted otherwise than under the scheme, those limitations are not to affect a person's right to carry out development for which the scheme gives permission.

Schemes last ten years, see s 85 of the TCPA 1990. Schemes can be modified. Modifications providing for withdrawal of permission, or to exclude land from a scheme, or to impose new conditions on development if confirmed, do not come into effect for 12 months, see s 86 of the TCPA 1990.

The Secretary of State has power by order to exclude land from, or to modify permission in, an SPZ. Furthermore, land in environmentally sensitive areas such as National Parks, conservation areas, areas of outstanding natural beauty, the Broads, green belt land, or sites of special scientific interest may *not* be included in an SPZ, see s 87 of the TCPA 1990. SPZs should *not* be set up in areas containing hazardous installations, explosive facilities and licensed nuclear sites. Central guidance stresses that SPZs will only work properly if their creation is co-ordinated with other powers relating to land assembly and disposal and grant aid and other forms of assistance. An SPZ may be of any size, and should certainly be of significant size. The form of the SPZ may also vary considerably according to the nature and location of the land and its best possible use. Schemes may be either specific, ie itemising *a* type of development permitted, or general, giving wide permission for *types* of development subject to specific exceptions which will still require grants of permission in the normal way.

SPZs in the view of central government should be flexibly used to cater for the needs of large, old, depressed urban areas, disused sites suitable for new employment, and even green field sites which have been previously targeted for development by a development plan.

SPZs, however, cannot be used to grant permission for mineral and waste disposal developments (see SI 1987/1849). SPZs should also only give permission for aerodromes, caravan sites, casinos, funfairs, scrapyards and slaughterhouses after careful thought, and should not grant permission for any other hazardous development; see PPG 5, Annex A.

SPZ schemes should, authorities have been advised, contain only the minimum number of conditions and limitations, and should not be concerned with too much detail, and they should ensure that health and safety are protected, and may need to regulate polluting emissions (except insofar as otherwise legally controlled), use of contaminated or unstable land, vehicular access and highway construction. Height and density controls for buildings may also need specification, as may floor space limited for particular developments and parking standards. Landscaping requirements may also be appropriate. Conditions should, wherever possible, be clearly expressed *in advance* of development so that only rarely should developers need to obtain specific consent to an act.

Sub zones within SPZs may be needed because of local needs — eg to exclude an area from the scheme because it is contaminated land or is to act as a buffer between the SPZ and some environmentally sensitive area, or to restore some normal planning controls, such as those over noise, within a particular part of an area.

Whether SPZs will become enduring features of the planning system remains to be seen. By December 1992 there were only three SPZs in England and a further three in Scotland.

E APPLYING FOR PLANNING PERMISSION

Applications for planning permission must, under s 62 of the 1990 Act, be in the prescribed manner. Detailed requirements are contained in the Town and Country Planning (General Development Procedure) Order SI 1995/419 (GDPO) and the Town and Country Planning (Applications) Regulations SI 1988/1812, any required details must be supplied, and the land in question must be identified. Applications may be made for outline planning permission. Where such permission is granted subsequent approval by the authority must be obtained for those 'reserved matters' (ie siting, design, external appearance, means of access and landscaping) specified by a condition in the permission. Successive applications, for the same or different development, may be made for a site.[17] Note, however, the effect of s 70A as inserted by the 1991 Act whereunder a local planning authority *may* decline to determine a planning application if in the preceding two years the Secretary of State has refused a similar application referred to him/her under s 77 (see further below) or has dismissed an appeal against the refusal of a similar application *and* the authority consider there has been no significant change since that event in the development plan or in any other material consideration. 'Significant change' is not defined by the legislation, but it would surely include a new plan or a major change in economic or demographic circumstances. 'Similar' is, however, defined by reference to the authority being of the opinion that the application in question must be the same or substantially the same. Applications are made to district councils or unitary authorities where appropriate and London borough councils. A fee is payable according to regulations made under s 303 of the TCPA 1990.

[NB By virtue of s 74(1A) of the 1990 Act and the GDPO, art 5 applications in respect of 'county matters', effectively waste and minerals applications, are to be made to the relevant county council.]

Publicity requirements

Planning law was not historically generally over-concerned with giving third parties rights at the development control stage.[18] Nevertheless there are now considerably more publicity and notification requirements under the 1990 Act.

Section 65 of the 1990 Act, as substituted, provides that a development order may make provision requiring notice to be given of any application for planning permission, and requiring any applicant for permission to issue a

17 *Pilkington v Secretary of State for the Environment* [1974] 1 All ER 283, [1973] 1 WLR 1527.
18 *Buxton v Minister of Housing and Local Government* [1961] 1 QB 278, [1960] 3 All ER 408.

certificate as to the interests in the land to which the application relates or the purpose for which it is used. Provision may also be made for publicising applications, and for 'owners' of affected land, or those who are tenants of agricultural holdings of the land, to be given notice of applications relating to the land in prescribed form. A local planning authority will not be able to entertain an application unless the requirements of the law are complied with. 'Owners' for the purposes of the provision are fee simple estate owners, those with tenancies of which not less than seven years remain unexpired, or, in prescribed cases, those entitled to mineral rights.

Under art 8 of the GDPO 1995 an obligation now lies on the Local Planning Authority to publicise applications. Basically applications are divided into three which may be denominated as: 'very major', 'major' and 'minor'.

'Very major'

Any application which is the subject of an Environmental Assessment (Sch 1 or 2 applications) and is accompanied by an environmental statement (see further below); any application not in accord with provisions of relevant development plans; any application which would affect rights of way subject to Part III Wildlife and Countryside Act 1981. Here there must be a site notice display on or near the relevant land for at least 21 days *and* local advertisement.

'Major'

Mineral working; waste disposition; provision of ten or more dwelling houses; provision of dwelling houses on a site of 0.5 ha or more where it is not known whether ten or more houses are to be built; provision of building(s) with floor space to be created of $1000m^2$ or more; development of a site of 1 ha or more. Here there must be a site notice for not less than 21 days *or* notice must be served on adjoining owners/occupiers, *and* (in either case) local advertisement. Notice served on adjoining owners, etc is appropriate where there are interested parties living in the vicinity of the proposed development and they, and only they, are likely to be interested. In addition to the legislatively specified categories, DoE Circular 15/92 lists the following as also *worthy of consideration* for local newspaper advertisement: those affecting nearby property by noise, smell or vibration; those attracting crowds, traffic and noise into quiet areas; those causing activity and noise during unusual hours; those introducing significant changes to an area; those affecting the setting of ancient monuments; those affecting trees subject to tree preservation orders.

'Minor'

In all other cases the development is classed as 'minor' in which case *either* a site notice display *or* notice to adjoining owners/occupiers is required.

Deciding the application

The basic principle with regard to deciding a planning application is enshrined in s 70(2) of the TCPA 1990: 'the authority shall have regard to the provisions of the development plan, so far as material to the application, and to any other material considerations.' A planning application is generally to be decided on the basis of all relevant considerations, even though in any given case some will be more important than others.[19] The weight to be given to each 'material' or relevant consideration is entirely a matter for the decision taker, subject to the overriding requirement that decisions must be taken fairly and reasonably. In particular cases, for instance with regard to green belts, additional tests may apply, see chapter 6, below. To this basic principle has to be added now the requirement of s 54A of the 1990 Act as introduced in 1991, that 'where in making any determination under the planning Acts, regard is to be had to the development plan, the determination shall be made in accordance with the plans unless material considerations indicate otherwise.' Clearly this section is designed to give plans an enhanced importance. Development, according to PPG 12, is a 'plan led process' in that plans provide an objective basis against which development proposals can be judged, and plans are also *guides* and *incentives* to development, setting out the main considerations on which proposals are judged. While plans are not blueprints, s 54A provides that development control decisions should accord with the development plan unless material considerations otherwise indicate, and common sense combined with the case law indicates that:

1   Where a proposed development accords with the plan the presumption is in favour of permission, though there may be isolated instances where other considerations indicate otherwise.
2   Where development clearly is in major conflict with the plan the presumption is against permission being given save where the 'march of time' has overtaken the plan or some other convincing reason can be put forward for allowing the development.
3   The plan obviously governs cases where there are *no* other material considerations and there is relevant material in the plan.
4   What of cases where there is no clear conflict, however, between the plan and the proposal, or there is only minor conflict, or the plan is silent? The decision is to be made on the basis of all relevant considerations, but *there is a presumption in favour of development.* The problem then is to distinguish major and minor conflicts.

Perhaps what is needed here is to disaggregate situations (a) where the plan is silent where the 'all relevant considerations test' applies including a presumption in favour of development; and (b) where there is, however, no clear or only minor conflict. Here the presumption in favour of the plan is only a starting point and the presumption may be quite easily rebutted.[20]

To sum up: in deciding a planning application the decision taker (usually, of course, the authority, but on appeal, for example, the Secretary of State) must first take into account *all* 'material' considerations including the general presumption in favour of developments which do not cause demonstrable harm to interests of acknowledged importance, but, secondly, must then decide the issue in accordance with the plan save where 'material' issues indicate otherwise. Thus, as PPG 1 points out (para 27), where there are other material considerations the

19   *London Residuary Body v Lambeth London Borough Council* [1990] 2 All ER 309, [1990] 1 WLR 744.
20   *St Albans District Council v Secretary of State* [1993] JPL 374; *Sainsbury plc v Secretary of State* [1993] JPL 651; *Gateshead Borough Council v Secretary of State* [1994] JPL 55; *Bylander Waddell Partnership v Secretary of State* [1994] JPL 440.

development plan should be taken as a starting point, and the other material considerations should be weighed in reaching a decision.[1] Where, however, a decision taker departs from relevant plans and policies in reaching a decision, clear and soundly reasoned arguments for that decision must be given.[2] The decision maker's duty is thus to give priority to the development plan's provisions, and where a development does not accord with them, *or* some of them, to weigh against them material considerations in favour of granting permission. Where plan provisions have been superseded by subsequent government guidance, or overtaken by other factual events they will have less weight than if they were newly or recently approved. Clearly it is still therefore necessary to identify what those other material considerations may be.

For many years the courts appeared to engage in a process of 'listing' — 'this is relevant, that is not.' Thus the following are 'relevant': development plans; consultations with affected parties (see further below); planning circulars and other publicly available ministerial guidance and policy statements, though when given in the form of after dinner speeches this is open to some doubt.[3] Clearly the physical site specific factors applying to the land in question are relevant considerations and financial considerations may be[4] (for a further exhaustive analysis of this particular issue see Purdue, Young and Rowan Robinson, *Planning Law and Procedure* pp 213–217). Other relevant considerations appear to be: amenity (a vague term but one which relates to the appearance and layout of land so as to make for a pleasant way of life); the compatibility of the proposed development with other land uses in the vicinity; safety issues, though here planning authorities must be somewhat wary of trespassing too far on the territory of other regulatory authorities and of seeking objectives attainable under other legislation; the existing use of the land and its planning history;[5] need for the development; the existence of an alternative site for the development; safeguarding land for other public developments;[6] protecting archeological sites;[7] preventing flood risks;[8] the likelihood that a development will eventuate.[9] On the other hand the following appear to be irrelevant considerations: rigid 'fetters on discretion', whereunder an authority binds itself never to allow, for example, some particular sort of development, though a 'normal policy' which may be subject to exceptions in a proper case is allowable, as is a party political leaning in favour of a particular type of development.[10] Similarly the issue of whether a development is economically worthwhile has been held irrelevant,[11] as are attempts to protect

1 *Loup v Secretary of State for the Environment and Salisbury District Council* [1996] JPL 22.
2 *EC Gransden & Co Ltd v Secretary of State for the Environment* [1986] JPL 519.
3 *Sears Blok v Secretary of State* [1987] JPL 844; *Dimsdale Developments Ltd v Secretary of State for the Environment* [1986] JPL 276; *Kent County Council v Secretary of State for the Environment* (1976) 75 LGR 452.
4 *R v Westminster City Council, ex p Monahan*, [1989] 2 All ER 74.
5 *RMC Management Services Ltd v Secretary of State for the Environment* (1972) 222 Estates Gazette 1593.
6 *Westminster Bank Ltd v Minister of Housing and Local Government* [1971] AC 508.
7 *Hoveringham Gravels Ltd v Secretary of State for the Environment* [1975] QB 754.
8 *Wimpey & Co Ltd v Secretary of State for the Environment* [1978] JPL 773.
9 *Sovmots Investments Ltd v Secretary of State for the Environment* [1979] AC 144.
10 *Stringer v Minister of Housing and Local Government* [1971] 1 All ER 65, [1970] 1 WLR 1281; *R v Exeter City Council, ex p Thomas & Co Ltd* [1991] 1 QB 471; *R v Amber Valley District Council, ex p Jackson* [1984] 3 All ER 501.
11 *Walters v Secretary of State for Wales* [1979] JPL 171.

an authority's own use of a piece of land by means of refusing permission for development,[12] and refusals based on the absence of public gain in a proposed development,[13] or purely moral objections to a development.[14]

More recently an attempt to formulate a principle whereby relevance and irrelevance can be identified has been made. In *Bolton Metropolitan Borough Council v Secretary of State for the Environment*[15] Glidewell LJ pointed out some matters have to be taken into account because statute says so. However, those are not necessarily the only matters that are 'relevant', because: 'the decision maker ought to take into account a matter which might cause him to reach a different conclusion to that which he would reach if he had not taken it into account... By the verb 'might' [is] meant where there was a real possibility that he would reach a different conclusion if he had taken that consideration into account.' This excluded matters of 'trivial or small importance'.

Some matters to be taken into account are implied from the nature of the decision and of the matter in question, and in situations of this sort 'it is for the judge to decide whether it was a matter which the decision maker should have taken into account.' Here, however, the views of Cook J in *CREEDNZ Inc v Governor-General*[16] can be prayed in aid: 'it is safe to say that the more general and the more obviously important the consideration, the readier the Court must be to hold that Parliament must have meant it to be taken into account.'

Where a judge concludes a matter is fundamental, or that it was an issue consideration of which would have made a difference to the outcome, non-consideration enables the judge to conclude the decision was invalidly made. Where a judge, however, is uncertain whether the matter would have had this effect or would have had such importance for the decision making process, he/she does not have the material necessary to conclude the decision was invalid.

Even where a decision is invalid there remains a residual discretion in the judge to refuse the reward of relief — eg in cases of no substantial prejudice to the applicant.

It may be argued on the basis of the foregoing that the following continue to be relevant considerations: representations received in respect of planning applications publicised; the effect on the land of the financial consequences of granting or not granting permission;[17] the financial implications for an area of allowing a new development elsewhere; the need to avoid creating an undesirable precedent for future development.[18] Though as stated earlier planning authorities must be wary of trespassing too far on the powers of other regulatory bodies, the desirability of 'keying in' planning controls to other forms of regulation is a relevant consideration,[19] and so are issues relating to noise, dust, smell, grit, etc, likely to emanate from a development. There is

12 *Westminster City Council v British Waterways Board* [1985] AC 676, [1984] 3 All ER 737.
13 *Westminster Renslade Ltd v Secretary of State for the Environment* [1983] JPL 454.
14 *Finlay v Secretary of State for the Environment* [1983] JPL 802; *Ladbroke (Rental) Ltd v Secretary of State for the Environment* [1981] JPL 427.
15 [1991] JPL 241.
16 [1981] 1 NZLR 172.
17 *Sovmots Investments Ltd v Secretary of State for the Environment* [1979] AC 144; *Sosmo Trust Ltd v Secretary of State for the Environment* [1983] JPL 806.
18 *Collis Radio Ltd v Secretary of State for the Environment* (1975) 73 LGR 211.
19 *Esdell Caravan Parks Ltd v Hemel Hempstead Rural District Council* [1966] 1 QB 895.

little judicial guidance as to how far an authority may go in using planning powers to control matters that could be controlled under other environmental legislation. Ministerial appeals are a little more helpful; in the *Ferro Alloys and Metals Smelter, Glossop* decision[20] the minister indicated planning controls could be used to supplement controls under air pollution controls in that the former provided reasonably easily enforced long term protection. It was accepted in Cm 1200 at para 6.39 that potential pollution dangers constitute a 'relevant consideration' and that planning permission should not be given if the result is to expose people to danger. On the specific issue of the relationship between IPC and planning controls, see also chapter 10 and p 196, below. But note that an *inflexible* adherence to the principle of furthering another body's pollution control policies is an unlawful fetter on discretion.[1]

In some circumstances the planning authority must consult with other bodies before coming to a decision. Districts must consult with counties under the terms of Sch 1 of the 1990 Act, which provides for consultation: where a proposal is made which materially conflicts with or would prejudice the policies and proposals of a structure plan or its proposed replacement; where a proposal, by reason of scale or nature, would be of major importance for the implementation of a structure plan; where the proposed development is situated in an area stated in writing by the county to the district as one where development is likely to affect or be affected by mineral working (other than coal), or where (in England) it is notified by the county that they have proposed use of the relevant land for waste disposal; where the land has been stated in writing by the county as subject to their proposed development, or where the application development would prejudice their development, or a proposed use of the land for waste disposal, and so notified to the district.

In these cases the district may not determine the application until it has received and taken into account county representations, or has been notified that the county has none to make. Districts being under a duty to seek to achieve the general objectives of the structure plan also safeguards county interests to some extent.

The GDPO 1995 imposes requirements to consult, inter alia, with other planning authorities where it appears a development will affect land in their areas; with the Secretary of State where it appears a development will increase traffic on a trunk road; with the Coal Authority where a building or pipeline is to be erected in a notified area of coal working; with the Agency where, inter alia, the development consists of storage of mineral oils and derivatives, or use of the land for waste, refuse, sewage or sludge disposal; with nature conservation authorities in areas of special interest under the Wildlife and Countryside Act 1981, Sch 17, Part I and s 28; with the Ministry of Agriculture in respect of developments of agricultural land for non-agricultural purposes and not in accordance with a development plan involving the loss of specified amounts of land, and with the Health and Safety Executive where it appears the development will involve the manufacture or use, etc, of notifiable quantities of hazardous substances. With regard to installations handling hazardous substances, the Health and Safety Executive will inform local planning authorities

---

20 [1990] 1 LMELR 175.
1 *Ynys Mon Borough Council v Secretary of State for Wales* [1993] JPL 225.

of instances notified to them, see further chapter 7. Note further the consultation paper 'Policy and Practice for Groundwater' (November 1991, issued by the former National Rivers Authority) in which it is made clear that in consultations they would resist development proposals, including highways, railways, mines and boreholes, that could adversely affect groundwater; the Agency is likely to maintain this stance, see further chapter 12, below on groundwater protection. In November 1991 it was reported that planning consent for a £20m toxic waste incinerator near Doncaster had been refused by the Secretary of State because the underlying aquifer had no impermeable clay shield.

It is presumed the Agency will continue the policy of HMIP outlined in its August 1995 document 'Planning Liaison with Local Authorities', which, inter alia, is directed towards the avoidance of duplicated controls. Thus it is policy that applications for Integrated Pollution Control (IPC) authorisation should be contemporaneously prepared with any relevant planning application, while joint working arrangements and discussions on such matters with planning authorities are welcome. During planning consultation the Agency will indicate whether a proposed development is likely to comply with statutory IPC requirements; provide relevant data on releases from the proposed development; comment on whether an authorisation is likely to be granted; provide relevant information about other relevant authorised processes in the area; give other relevant environmental information. See also below for problems consequent on overlaps between the Environmental Assessment and Integrated Pollution Control systems.

Discretionary consultation may also take place with bodies and individuals likely to be affected by a proposed development. Views received are relevant in deciding applications. In *R v Sheffield City Council, ex p Mansfield*[2] it was held that a planning authority has wide discretion as to whom to consult; ratepayers and local residents have no right to be consulted as such. It may be *wise* to consult organised bodies where these can be identified but there is no *obligation* to do so.

As stated earlier planning law has not been historically particularly concerned with granting rights generally to third parties. This may be changing for a variety of reasons, partly because of greater use of judicial review as a remedy in planning disputes and partly as a result of EU intervention.

The obligation to act fairly

The courts require authorities to conduct their planning functions fairly, and not to mislead applicants for permission or objectors to proposed developments by conduct or representations, or failing to give proper notice of the likely outcome of deliberations; though it is for those who challenge decisions to prove that they have been prejudiced, and that had they been given a chance to state their arguments this would have affected the outcome.

In *R v Great Yarmouth Borough Council, ex p Botton Bros Arcades Ltd*[3] an authority had a non-statutory plan identifying the need for commercial entertainment development on their sea front, though general policy was not

2 (1978) 37 P & CR 1
3 [1988] JPL 18.

to give permission for new amusement arcades. A developer wished to convert a hotel into an amusement arcade. At first the authority did not wish to grant permission, but after further consideration, including giving the developer's architect a hearing, the planning committee decided in favour of the application. During the course of the deliberations Botton Bros learned of the application. They did not initially object because they knew of the policy bias against permission for new arcades. On hearing rumours that permission was to be granted, they asked for the decision to be deferred so they could enter an objection. The local authority refused to defer and granted permission. Botton Bros applied for judicial review of the grant.

Otton J pointed out that there was no *duty* to give Botton Bros notice of any sort, nor did they have a right to be heard before the planning application was decided. Furthermore thay had no 'legitimate expectation' of consultation in that they had no enforceable right that would be affected by the planning decision, nor could they show that such an expectation had arisen from past practice or undertakings that their views would be taken into account. However, the council was under a duty to act fairly in administering the planning sytem. What is 'fair' is a question of fact in each case, and on the facts of this case that duty had been broken. However, there is no general rule that potential objectors must be provided with an opportunity to object on every occasion when an application falls to be decided, or even when a decision in favour of an application will depart from normal policy. The *sort* of facts that might lead a judge to find a 'breach of fairness' in any given case are:

1 Where the authority misleads objectors as to its intentions.
2 Where special treatment is given to an applicant while potential objectors are not even informed of the application.
3 Where the authority knows a leading objector would wish to press his case at any appeal, and they fail to inform him of an appeal.[4]

The courts seem to prefer basing third party rights on a general duty of authorities to act 'fairly', rather than on the basis that any given third party has a legitimate expectation that an authority will act in a particular way, and some sort of statement or action relevant to the matter in hand on the part of the authority seems requisite, though mere past practice is not enough.[5] The notion of 'legitimate expectation', was, however, taken up in *R v Swale Borough Council, ex p Royal Society for the Protection of Birds*[6] where Simon Brown J concluded that assurances that consultation would take place before development was permitted gave rise to a legitimate expectation on the part of the would be consultee and gave it locus standi to make a challenge.

F ENVIRONMENTAL ASSESSMENT

The introduction of Environmental Assessment (EA) also gives cause to believe that planning law is broadening out to encompass a wider range of issues and interests. The product of the first major incursion of EU law into the

4 Note also *R v Torfaen Borough Council, ex p Jones* [1986] JPL 686; and *Wilson v Secretary of State for the Environment* [1988] JPL 540.
5 *R v Secretary of State for the Environment, ex p Barratt (Guildford) Ltd* (1989) Times, 3 April.
6 [1991] JPL 39.

planning system in pursuance of Directive 85/337 which came into effect in July 1988, EA is a technique to ensure that a development's likely effects on the environment will be taken into consideration before the development is authorised to proceed. The technique is applicable to projects other than those needing planning permission, and there are parallel regulations applying to them, see SI 1988/1241 on trunk roads and motorways, SI 1989/167 and SI 1990/367 on power stations, overhead power lines and long distance oil and gas pipelines, SI 1988/1207 on afforestation projects, SI 1988/1217, as amended by SI 1995/2195, on land drainage improvement projects, SI 1988/1336 on port and harbour projects, SI 1988/1218 on marine salmon farming projects, SI 1990/442 and SI 1996/422 on electricity and pipeline works: for provisions relating to Scotland see SI 1988/1221, and see also SI 1995/1541 for EA in relation to developments under the Transport and Works Act 1992, see further on this Act chapter 7, below. With regard to marine dredging of minerals which is licensed by the Crown Estates Commissioners under the Royal prerogative, EA will occur where it is considered the dredging is likely to have significant environmental effects. In all cases, however, the EA requirements are comparable to those now to be discussed in relation to planning procedures.

The EU's objective in adopting EA was to prevent pollution at source by requiring environmental information to be considered as part of project authorisation procedures. The preferred method of implementing the EU requirement in the UK has been to incorporate EA requirements almost entirely into existing planning procedures, and by ensuring that where there is a dispute as to the need for EA there is a right of appeal for the developer to the Secretary of State and tight timetabling of questions about the need for EA. Detailed advice to local authorities on how to identify projects needing EA is given in the regulations which came into force on 15 July 1988 (SI 1988/1199, as amended by SI 1992/1494 and SI 1994/677). EA applies to projects having significant environmental effects, and requires a systematic analysis of such effects before a decision on whether to permit the project is taken. EA goes beyond simple land use considerations. This is done by requiring information about environmental effects to be provided by the developer for the deciding agency to consider in the decision making process, and further gives bodies with relevant environmental responsibilities an opportunity to comment before consent is given. Certain information has to be given to the public.

EA gives a chance to adopt or modify a scheme to mitigate adverse environmental consequences, and for taking the environmental dimension into account in project decisions. This is not to say that environmental considerations will override all others, but they will have to be considered. EA is, furthermore, not a document but a process, needed to reach a decision on a relevant application, involving the collection of information, the consideration thereof and the final decision, by virtue of the submission of an 'environmental statement' by the developer, and the taking into account by the authority of 'environmental information' which includes the statement and consultations thereon.

EA is mandatory in relation to certain projects (85/337 Annex I) and may be extended to others (85/337 Annex II) where member states so require. EA in the EU requires 'developers' to prepare statements. Though first proposed in the second action programme on the environment in 1977 a formal proposal was not made by the Commission until 1980, and five years of debate ensued until 85/337 appeared (see further Haigh, *EEC Environmental Policy and Britain* (2nd edn) pp 352–354). In the course of debate the proposal was much modified, largely because of British objections. Annex I was reduced in scope, and the information to be supplied by the developer is only such as the member state concerned considers relevant. The UK government's initial attitude was that EA should not generally add significantly to existing procedures and should be implemented wherever possible within existing legal procedures without undue recourse to extra subordinate legislation. In 1986 a Consultation Paper was issued by the DoE. This led to the first batch of regulations in the summer of 1988 to begin implementation of the Community obligation. Initially the government proposed that EA for Annex II projects should be at the discretion of the Secretary of State. This in the view of the Commission was less than the Directive required. Taken as a whole the Directive requires EA in relation to Annex II projects likely to have significant environmental effects by virtue, inter alia, of size, location, nature etc; discretion is therefore limited to deciding whether a particular project's characteristics are such that they are/are not likely to be 'significant'. DoE Circular 15/88 indicated the central view that EA will apply to the second class of projects where they are major and of more than local importance, or irrespective of size, they affect particularly sensitive or vulnerable locations, or where they have unusually complex and potentially adverse environmental consequences making it desirable that a detailed, expert analysis of those consequences takes place, provided that examination is relevant to the issue of deciding whether or not a development should be permitted, see further below.

In addition to the principal regulations on EA and planning, SI 1988/1199, as amended, see also SI 1995/417 on EA in relation to permitted development rights, and SI 1995/2258 on EA and unauthorised development where enforcement action is taken, see also DoE Circular 13/95.

EA has importance in the UK because of the *range* of issues to be considered in the development process. Issues of pollution control will now, in relation to certain developments, be relevant considerations, and planning authorities will not be limited to mere land use considerations.

In some cases (as stated) EA is mandatory, eg crude oil refineries, large (300 or more megawatts) thermal power stations, and nuclear stations; radioactive waste storage/disposal facilities; integrated iron and steel initial melting works; asbestos extraction and processing installations, subject to some size limits; integrated chemical installations, ie linked processes to manufacture of olefins from petroleum products or sulphuric, nitric or hydrofluoric acid, chlorine or fluorine; motorway and express roads, long distance railway and airport construction with runway lengths of 2,100m or more; trading ports and inland waterways allowing passage of vessels over 1,350 tonnes; special waste treatment, incineration or landfill installations for special wastes. In any given year, however, there will probably be no more than a few dozen of these, and not all, of course, fall within the ambit of the planning laws (see Sch 1 of SI 1988/1199).

In other cases EA will take place if the project will leave 'significant' effects on the environment. In relation to matters needing planning permission it will be the local planning authority who decide whether EA is required, though a developer may voluntarily offer one either pre-application or at the application stage. The authority will give a reasoned statement for their decision if they believe EA is required. Any disputes will be referred to the Secretary of State who may in any case require EA. There are guidelines as to what is meant by 'significant', but each case will depend, initially at least, on its merits, and it will take some time, and perhaps litigation to determine a set of working practices.

Relevant planning projects (under Sch 2 of SI 1988/1199) include: *Agriculture* — poultry rearing (DoE Circular 15/88 indicates units for 100,000 or more broilers or 50,000 layers), pig rearing (the Circular indicates units for 400 or more sows or 5,000 or more fattening pigs), water management (the Circular mentions new drainage or flood defence works), land reclamation, salmon hatching or rearing; *Extraction* — extracting peat, deep drilling, mineral extraction of sand, gravel, shale, etc, coal extraction, petroleum and natural gas extraction, extracting ores, open cast extraction, ancillary surface installations, coke ovens, cement manufacture (the Circular mentions any such activity in a national park or AONB, new deep mines, or workings over 50 ha, and extraction of 300 or more tonnes per day of oil/gas); *Energy industries* — smaller non-nuclear power stations, installations for carrying gas steam or hot water or overhead electrical cables, gas storage, fossil fuel storage, nuclear fuel enrichment or reprocessing plants, hydro-electric production installations; *Metal Processing* — foundries and rolling mills, non-ferrous metals production plant, boilermaking plant, shipyards, aircraft construction or repair plant, railway equipment manufacturers, metallic or sintering plant; *Glass making; Chemical processes* — pesticide or paint making or storage; *Food industries* — vegetable or animal fat manufacturers, dairy product making, brewing, slaughter houses, fish meal factories, sugar factories; *Textile, leather, wood and paper industries; Rubber industries*; (in relation to all the foregoing much will depend on site size — eg 20–30ha or more — whether emissions controlled under atmospheric pollution laws are made, whether discharges to water have to be consented, whether hazardous or polluting substances would be involved, whether radioactive or hazardous waste would arise, consultation with the Agency may be necessary in such cases to determine whether EA is needed); *Infrastructure projects* — industrial estate or urban development projects, dams, tramways, aquaducts, marinas (the Circular again mentions size as an indicative criterion, and the closeness of significant numbers of dwellings in the vicinity — say 1,000 or more within 200m of the site in question); *Other projects* — holiday villages and hotel complexes, vehicle race tracks, waste treatment plants, scrap iron storage, gunpowder making, knackers' yards (the Circular draws a distinction between reuse of previously developed land and use of virgin sites, in which latter case the 'land take,' proximity of dwelling and square meterage of what is to be provided are indicative criteria, and also points to sensitivity of location and the need for special consideration of out of town shopping schemes of over 20,000 sq m.) (Note also DoE Circular 24/88 on EA in SPZs and EZs.)

EA: the procedural steps

The basic rule is, with regard to planning authorities, reg 4 of SI 1988/1199: an authority (including the Secretary of State) may not grant planning permission unless they have first taken environmental information into consideration in relation to projects for which EA is required. Where EA takes place it is only a factor to take into account in the determination process; though an important factor, it will not necessarily be solely determinative. On 1 July 1988 the Under Secretary of State for the Environment stated: 'no-one is saying that environmental considerations must override all others. There will always be other factors to be taken into account . . . But environmental concerns are not going to go away' [1988] JPL 520.

In some cases it will not be initially clear whether a project will be one within either Sch 1 or 2, and reg 5 enables the developer to ask the authority to state their opinion as to which Schedule is appropriate and, if the matter falls within Sch 2, whether the project's effects are sufficient to require EA. The authority then has, generally, three weeks to give the opinion sought, and if they conclude that EA is required they must support this with reasons. If they fail to respond in time, or the project developer is unhappy with an opinion that EA is required, he/she may apply to the Secretary of State for a direction on the matter. He/she has, generally, three weeks to issue his direction, and, of course, the developer is required to inform the LPA that an application for the Secretary of State's direction has been made; see reg 6.

Developers may inform the authority in advance that they intend to make an application falling within either Sch 1 or 2 and may submit an environmental statement (ES) with the application for planning permission. In such circumstances the developer must identify the land in question, state the nature and purpose of the proposed development and indicate the main environmental consequences to which the ES will refer. Where such a notification is received or where the Secretary of State directs that EA is required, the authority *must* inform certain public bodies such as the Countryside Commission *and* in relation to certain mining manufacturing or waste disposal operations likely to give rise to certain wastes, or involving works which make emissions into the atmosphere, the Agency. Regulation 22 then further enables the authority or any of the informed agencies to assist in the preparation of the ES by consultation with the developer and helping with the provision of information, though they are not required to disclose confidential information.

Where applications are made without environmental statements, and authorities believe they are Sch 1 or 2 applications they have three weeks in which to inform applicants in writing saying clearly and fully why a statement is needed. Applicants may then, within two weeks, accept this view and undertake to provide an ES, or state that they are applying to the Secretary of State for directions. If they, however, do nothing, their applications are deemed to be refused, but *no* appeal to the Secretary of State will lie. Where the authority indicate an ES is required and one is not submitted the general rule is they may not deal otherwise with the application than to refuse it. Similar rules apply where an application without an ES is referred to the Secretary of State and to situations where an appeal is made following a refusal of planning permission and in the course of its consideration it is concluded that the matter is one falling within Sch 1 or 2. Effectively in this latter case the appeal is 'frozen', the Secretary of State will inform the parties, and the appellant may then undertake to submit an ES. Without an ES the appeal will be lost.

Regulation 13 provides for those cases where ES is required but one was not submitted with the application. In such cases where applicants wish to submit one in the course of the planning procedure, they may do so subject to giving adequate publicity to their actions.

Where developers submit an environmental statement to the authority they must submit an extra copy for the authority to transmit to the Secretary of State. The authority must register the ES along with the application under s 69 of the TCPA 1990, and further advise the statutory consultees, if not already served with notice by the developer, that the ES is to be taken into account, and elicit whether they wish to receive a copy of the ES (if they do it is for the developer to supply the necessary copies of the ES) and of their right to make representations. A similar procedure applies where it is one of those cases where the Secretary of State receives the ES. The normal course will be for the ES to be submitted along with the planning application. The consultation taking place on the ES generates environmental information (EI) which is what the authority must take into account in determining the application.

Under reg 16 the normal eight week period for consideration of a planning application is extended to 16 weeks where consideration of EI must take place, and generally that period will not begin to run until an ES is submitted. Regulations 18–20 provide for a reasonable number of copies of environmental statements to be made available for the public at reasonable cost.

The problem of the inadequate statement

Though planning permission should not be refused solely on the ground that an ES is inadequate, bodies that have to decide applications in which an ES is involved may in writing require developers to provide further information under reg 21 if such information can be forthcoming from them, having regard to current knowledge and means of assessment, and whether such information is reasonably required for the assessment process. A developer so required to give further information is under a duty to give it. Where an ES is *incomplete*, for example because of the omission of material required to be included (see further below), the authority should also require the developer to rectify the omission under reg 21. However, it must be reiterated that an authority may not refuse to register an ES simply on grounds of disagreement with the analyses or judgments it contains, or because they feel it pays insufficient attention to particular topics. If statements and conclusions are unsubstantiated the only remedy is to ask for further information or evidence. In this context checking the ES against the development plan may indicate the existence of issues on which further information is needed. Disagreements over completeness, however, may not be referred to the Secretary of State, and the developer's only remedy would be, on the expiry of the determination period to make a planning appeal (see further below).

Regulation 25A applies the EA procedures with appropriate modification to a local planning authority's own development applications.

Under reg 23 the Secretary of State must be notified of planning decisions taken by authorities involving consideration of environmental information, and also of any conditions subject to which any permission was granted.

The form of an ES

The basic form of an environmental statement is laid down in the Schedules to the various regulations, eg SI 1988/1199 Sch 3.

Thus: a statement is a document or series of documents containing specified information. That information is:

1 Descriptive of the proposed development, its site, design, size and scale.
2 Informative as to data needed to identify and assess the main effects of the development on the environment.
3 Descriptive of likely significant effects (direct or indirect) on the environment by reference to possible impacts on humans, flora, fauna, soil, water, air, climate, landscape, material assets, cultural heritage, and interactions between the physical components of the environment.
4 Descriptive of measures envisaged in order to avoid, reduce or remedy identified significant adverse effects on the environment.
5 A summary of the above in non-technical language is also required.

Further information, explaining or amplifying any specified information may be given in the statement on:

1 A development's physical characteristics, and land use requirements during construction and operation.
2 The main features of any production processes including the nature and quality of materials used.
3 Estimates of type and quantity of residues and emissions from the plant in operation.
4 An outline of main alternatives (if any) studied and an indication of the reasons for opting for the submitted proposal taking into account its environmental effects.
5 Likely environmental effects resulting from use of natural resources, emissions of pollutants, creation of nuisances, elimination of waste.
6 Forecasting methods used.
7 Difficulties encountered in compiling specified information.

The practice of EA

In practice, EA may go much further than the strict letter of the law. Some consultants in the area have recommended the use of an independent third party to audit the quality of the ES and the information required. There has been further disquiet as to the following issues.

1 Where an authority has to undergo EA, who audits its ES?
2 Should there be a requirement for post-authorisation monitoring of projects made subject to EA?
3 Is the whole EA process something of a public relations exercise?
4 Are there sufficient numbers of skilled personnel to undertake EA, and, in any case, is it not true that many EA techniques are inexact?
5 Current DoE guidance is not particularly helpful, being vague and inexact, the meaning of 'significant', particularly in discrete areas, needs clarification.
6 There is no standard formula for a statement.
7 Statements vary widely in quality.

To introduce greater order into the EA process the DoE in 1994 published a 'good practice guide': 'Evaluation of Environmental Information for Planning Projects'. This accepted that the practices of authorities had varied greatly, with those authorities having the most experience of EA being much more 'at home' with the issue. The guide counsels authorities to:

1　Determine internal procedures for evaluating an ES on receipt.
2　Decide who is to be responsible for which tasks — primarily by appointing an appropriately trained individual case work officer for each ES, or in some cases a whole team, and to ensure close liaison between all relevant departments, consultees and the public.
3　Map out a programme of work on the ES.

This last identified issue may involve creating an internal panel of appropriate officers: to review the initial sufficiency of the ES, a task in which they may be assisted by an external assessor, and to determine whether further information is needed (see above); to assist the case officer with evaluating the areas of environmental impact of the project and to help identify the key issues that will affect the ultimate decision. In reviewing the ES the tasks to undertake are to determine whether: the descriptions given of the development (eg as to size and number of buildings, manufacturing processes and raw materials to be used) and existing environmental conditions are full; likely trends in environmental conditions have been considered; potential impacts, their identification, magnitude and significance have been assessed; the scope for avoiding and/or mitigating impacts has been explored and whether unavoidable impacts have been identified; the overall findings are fairly, objectively and unambiguously presented. The guide furthermore argues that a good ES should make reference to any risks of accidents or hazards referable to the proposed development, *even though this is not a legal requirement*. When the task of review is complete a report of conclusions should be made.

The guide stresses the desirability of pre-application discussions between developers and statutory consultees, however, to ensure that environmental impacts are 'designed out' as far as possible at the earliest stage while the proposed scheme's benefits are maximised.

Once the ES is received and the consultation begins there commences an iterative process leading on from checking the validity of statements in the ES and its conclusions to the development (from the flow of EI) of a picture of the key matters which will be relevant to decision making. A good ES should not present the planning authority and the consultees with a major task of verifying the factual issues surrounding the proposal, and where such an ES has been received the next step is to examine the nature and character of individual impacts, their causes and effects, the timescale and duration of effects and their consequences. Following this the significance of individual impacts can be evaluated; their extent, scale and probability can be considered and steps to mitigate them: this is a stage where close liaison with statutory consultees is needed. Once the body of EI is complete the authority's officers must begin the task of evaluating it. The evaluative report should describe the proposal, confirm the characteristics of the land in question and its surroundings, identify each major impact, highlight relevant planning policies and whether they support or oppose the proposal, summarise the key issues and arguments for and against, review consultations and representations received, introduce any other 'material' considerations, and make a recommendation.

The decision

In coming to a decision following the work of their officers, a planning authority will, first, need to consider the relationships between environmental issues arising from the proposal and the relative weight they attach to each, and, secondly, will draw together all relevant social, economic and environmental matters. Some environmental effects will be so strong they will have the capacity to be determinant of the decision in themselves, while others may merely influence a decision, or be found to be of little importance: it is useful to categorise issues in this way.

In tandem with the 1994 guide is the 1995 DoE guide: 'Preparation of Environmental Statements for Planning Projects that Require Environmental Assessment' which is intended for developers and their advisers. The following 'best practice' recommendations are made.

1 The unique feature of EA is the 'emphasis on the systematic analysis and presentation of information about environmental effects'. Thus it is necessary first to: have baseline studies giving a thorough knowledge of the environmental character of the area likely to be affected by the development; identify natural and manmade processes affecting the site and consider their interaction with the proposed use; predict the good and bad environmental effects of the development on the environment, introduce mitigating techniques at the design stage.
2 Great care must be devoted to: defining the brief for drawing up the ES, which will involve determining the context of the ES; observing a programme and timetable for its creation, and assembling an appropriately skilled and knowledgeable 'team' to create the ES.
3 Current and future environmental trends affecting a site must be established, particularly with regard to forecasting change over the lifetime of a project, and in relation to such trends the plans and policies of local authorities and others with influence over land use and environmental quality standards should be carefully considered.

After these initial preliminary preparatory stages have been passed the next major issues are:

4 Defining the scope of the exercise, which should be wide enough to cover all relevant issues yet not so loosely defined that unnecessary material gets included. Certainly there should be included information describing the project, the site and its environment, an assessment of the effects of the proposal, mitigating measures, and risk assessment and any hazardous development proposals. Scoping should be informed by knowledge of other relevant environmental controls such as IPC. Early consultation with the local planning authority and statutory consultees should help in this respect. All 'significant' or 'key' environmental issues should be identified.
5 Developers are well advised that they should show they have considered alternative ways of going about furthering their proposals, and also the need and demand for them.
6 Good practice also points to the use of public consultation *before* the planning application is submitted as a means of identifying key environmental issues, and project features which could be modified and likely

matters of controversy. The scoping phase includes determining the most appropriate point to involve the public.

7 During the scoping phase the key topic areas will be identified, ie those in which the development has potential to cause either adverse or beneficial effects on the environment. This enables potential impacts to be identified, and also those *processes* in the development which will give rise to *effects*, and whether the links between processes and effects will be direct or indirect.

8 Care has to be taken to ensure that each identified impact is assessed in terms of whether it is direct or indirect, lies in the short, medium or long term, is reversible or irreversible, is beneficial or adverse, and whether it is cumulative — both qualitative and quantitative methods of prediction can be used in this assessment.

9 Preparing for an EA may involve dealing with uncertainty as to an event's probability, severity, consequences and its interaction with other events. In relation to such matters, and indeed to any analysis undertaken as part of the process, great care must be taken to distinguish between matters of fact, judgment and appraisals and opinions, with all sources of information identified.

10 Thus to sum up, the preparatory phases of an EA are undertaken by the developer and involve defining the scope of the EA, undertaking baseline studies, assessing environmental trends and considering policy and plan implications. There should also be some preliminary findings on the analysis of potential impacts, predicting and evaluating their magnitude and significance, and leading to proposals for mitigatory measures.

The next step is to prepare the ES itself. There can be a number of ways of doing this; each section may be prepared by a different specialist, or one author may prepare the whole document, or, individual specialist documents may form appendices to a main report written by one author. However, while there is no prescribed form for authors to follow, good practice indicates that a useful structure for an ES is: (a) the non-technical summary which is statutorily required; (b) a statement of methods used; (c) a statement of key issues; (d) the description of the project; (e) a description of environmental conditions within and around the site; (f) an assessment of environmental effects by topic; (g) technical appendices. Though a method statement is not statutorily required good practice indicates its usefulness in saying who has prepared the ES, how it was prepared and what preliminary studies were undertaken to justify its conclusions.

An ES will vary in length according to the complexity of the issues involved, but between 50 and 150 pages is the preferred target size. It should include the findings of the scoping study to show which topics were identified as 'key' issues for detailed investigation. Certain information is statutorily required, eg the project, site characteristics, physical layout of development proposals, the phasing of development, while good practice points to inclusion of material on the discussion of alternatives where such are possible. The level of description used in drawing up the ES should be such that the processes and nature of the proposed plant and equipment can be fully understood by all concerned.

Material for inclusion in the ES may have to be selected, and while certain matters have to be dealt with by law, the level of information given has to be carefully judged. Material not directly related to areas of concern or which does not indicate further likely significant environmental effects may obscure issues if included. Where material is thus included in only a short form the ES should make it clear *why* it is not being included in detail.

Material should be included on relevant policies and plans, for example national and international policies and development plans, and, where appropriate, government standards and guidelines.

Each topic selected during the initial scoping phase should be discussed in a logical sequence stating potential impacts, the existing borderline conditions, predicted impacts, their nature, extent and magnitude, scope for mitigation of adverse impacts, an evaluation of the significance of unavoidable impacts, with each impact for each phase of the development and its life being considered. Attention may be paid to impacts arising from accidental or unplanned events. Methodologies used in assessment techniques should be stated.

It should be noted that there is no provision made in SI 1988/1199 for a third party to initiate the EA process.

EA in court

Some guidance on the application of EA has been given by the courts. The first was *R v Swale Borough Council, ex p Royal Society for the Protection of Birds*.[7] In 1989 planning permission was granted for the reclamation of Medway mudflats. These were important for migrating birds, but further proposals envisaged further reclamation and development schemes in the area, and it was found that the 1989 grant was truly part of a much larger development proposal. The RSPB opposed the grant, pointing to the use of the mudflats, and their proposed designation as a Site of Special Scientific Interest (SSSI). The RSPB contended that environmental assessment should have taken place and that the local planning authority had erred in not requiring this. The RSPB argued that *either* there was a desire to provide a trading port (which would fall within Sch 1, and thus require mandatory assessment) *or* that it fell within Sch 2 on the basis that the development would have significant environmental effects. Simon Brown J disposed of the case on a procedural ground but laid down other important guidelines for the applicability of the EA regulations.

A decision as to whether a particular development falls within either of the schedules to the regulations, and if so which one, is entirely a matter for the relevant planning authority as a question of 'fact and degree not of law'. The authority's decision may then only be challenged on '*Wednesbury* grounds'. Moreover, the authority's decision in relation to EA relates to the application it receives, not the permission it gives, and so the decision as to whether EA is required must be made in relation to the development applied for, not any development contemplated beyond that. But where an application relates to Sch 2 matters the above requirement must be somewhat modified if the reality is that the application project is part of greater development: developers could otherwise defeat the regulations by making piecemeal development proposals. In such cases the authority must not consider the application in isolation. The developer's ES should thus address itself to the wider issues.

7 [1991] JPL 39.

A further issue related to locus standi. When the possibility of the development of docks had been mooted, the planning authority had assured the RSPB it would be consulted, and a reasonable bystander would have concluded the RSPB was justified in thinking it would be. Simon Brown J therefore concluded that the RSPB had a 'legitimate expectation' of consultation, and had locus standi accordingly.

The next decision was *R v Poole Borough Council, ex p Beebee*.[8] The authority applied to itself in respect of housing development on an area of heathland. The land had been previously considered suitable for housing development, but six months before the grant of permission the Nature Conservancy Council (NCC) had told the authority it intended to extend an existing SSSI to include the land. In consequence of this, NCC was consulted before permission was granted; it objected but its objections were overruled. NCC had, in fact, extended the SSSI before the council took its decision to grant permission but the council were unaware of this, and thought the matter was still only a proposal. The decision was challenged, by, inter alia, the British Herpetological Society (BHS). The case raised a number of issues including whether the proposed development should have been subject to EA.

On the EA issue, the argument was that the project in question could have fallen within Sch 2 of SI 1988/1199, as being an 'urban development project' which might have 'significant' environmental effects. The authority had not apparently even considered whether the proposal fell within Sch 2, even though the 1988 regulations make it clear that EA may apply to local authority developments.

Where EA is *mandatory*, to conclude the authorisation process without EA would be ultra vires. The position would be similar where an authority, having decided that EA was necessary, decided to ignore completely the environmental information flowing from the EA: that would be a procedurally ultra vires act. However, in the present circumstances the most that could be said was that the authority had decided EA was not necessary, and indeed they do not seem to have thought about the issue at all. Schiemann J held the failure to undertake EA did not invalidate the decision. NCC and BHS had both brought the significant environmental effects of the issue to the local planning authority's attention so that it had before it relevant environmental information prior to the decision. It cannot be said that the case indicates that the decision on whether or not to require EA (apart from mandatory cases) is *entirely* a matter for authorities. Circumstances may make it abundantly clear that a proposal will have 'significant' environmental implications while the relevant authority steadfastly refuse to require EA. Such a decision would surely be impugned as being perverse or absurd.

Note also the finding in *Twyford Parish Council v Secretary of State for the Environment*[9] that the requirements of EA do not apply to projects 'in the pipeline' at the time when the date for implementing the EU Directive arrived, and also of interest in that McCullough J argued that, though the Directive had direct effect, individuals seeking to rely on it must still show that they have suffered in consequence of any failure to implement it. He further pointed out the grant of a remedy is in any case at the discretion of the court.

8 [1991] 3 LMELR 60.
9 [1992] 1 Env LR 37.

In *Kincardine and Deeside District Council v Forestry Comrs,*[10] however, a Scottish court considered that the Directive did not possess direct effect as it is insufficiently plain and unconditional as to whether EA is required — at least in relation to 'Annex II' projects. The *Twyford* case, of course, related to an Annex I project. Subsequently in *Wychavon District Council v Secretary of State for the Environment*[11] an English court doubted whether the Directive is capable of direct effect as *some* of its provisions lack insufficient precision. It has to be said, however, that the better view of the law is that it is the individual provisions of a Directive which have to be construed to see whether they have direct effect; it is not necessarily the Directive as a whole. The *Wychavon* case further denied that 'pipeline' projects such as that in the *Twyford* case can fall within the scope of the regulations.

EA: an assessment

Confusion exists as to when EA is required, as witness the *Beebee* case supra, and some projects appear to evade EA. Developers may submit an 'environmental document' without calling it an environmental statement while authorities themselves interpret the guidance given by DoE 13/88 on Sch 2 matters in different ways. The consultation process has been found to operate unevenly, with some potential consultees not being consulted, or not being involved in presubmission consultations on statements, while voluntary groups and the public appear to be, in some cases at least, marginalised.

Research carried out for the DoE in 1991 further revealed the following major issues:

1   It is hard to assess the effect of EA because there is deficient monitoring of relevant projects.
2   Many involved in the EA process are not sufficiently trained, so procedures are not always followed, this applies to both authorities and developers.
3   It is unclear what information should go in the statement and what in the planning application.
4   DoE guidance needs clarification.
5   More pre-application consultation is needed.

In view of the inadequacy of some statements, the inability of authorities to refuse applications simply because of a deficient statement is a problem, especially as the 16 week period for making a decision continues to run while the deficiency is remedied.

Long term changes in the EA system may require the submission of the ES relating to an application in draft, with the creation of some sort of EA review body to advise authorities on the quality of the ES.

Section 15 of the Planning and Compensation Act 1991 added s 71A to the 1990 Act whereunder regulations may be made not just to implement the requirements of the Directive but for other EA purposes also. It appears the EU wishes in any case to extend the scope of EA by applying it to programmes and policies relating to farming, fisheries, forestry, energy, mineral-extraction, water supply, waste disposal and transport issues.

10 [1992] 1 Env LR 151.
11 [1994] Env LR 239.

It has also been pointed out that developers can be faced with difficulties when their projects are subject to both EA and Integrated Pollution Control (IPC) (see further chapter 10, below). Until this problem is overcome by a totally integrated pollution control and permitting system — as is proposed by the EU — separate systems of control will continue to exist for a number of projects such as certain oil refineries, power stations, iron and steel works, acid making plants, installations handling asbestos, incinerators, etc.

The consequential problems are:

1   While an IPC authorisation application is made to a politically neutral body (the Agency) and is usually highly technical, EA takes place under the aegis of a local democratically answerable and politically conscious body, and may be a very wide ranging, non-technical process.
2   There is some confusion in industry as to who is responsible for what as a result of the dual system.
3   Dual controls add to the length and expense of the 'pre-creation' phase of any given project.
4   Dual controls can lead to conflicts of requirements, eg where a small chimney stack is required for amenity reasons, while pollution control demands a tall one.

To meet these and other problems it has been suggested that rationalisation of the two system could bring benefits. Thus the ES could be expanded to fulfil the information requirements of both EA and an IPC authorisation application. Similarly the systems should not operate totally in isolation but wherever possible in parallel, thus encouraging even more dialogue between regulators and enabling the creation of solutions acceptable to all where problems are encountered. This is an appropriate method of proceeding where it is clear a development proposal will involve a process prescribed for IPC purposes, see *Overlaps in the Requirement for Environmental Assessment* (United Kingdom Environmental Law Association and the Institute of Environmental Assessment, 1993), and note earlier comments on the Agency's likely policy with regard to duplication of controls.

G CALL IN POWERS

Section 77 of the TCPA 1990 empowers the Secretary of State to give directions requiring applications for planning permission to be referred to him. Before determining such an application the Secretary of State must, however, give the parties the opportunity of a hearing before a person appointed by him. This power is only selectively used, as was originally made clear in DoE Circular 2/81 and clarified in 'Planning Appeals Call-in and Major Public Inquiries' (Cmd 43); generally only where controversial issues of more than local importance are involved, eg the airport developments of Stansted and the London STOLPORT (see chapter 7). 'Call in' may also be utilised where an issue affects a greenbelt or high grade agricultural land, or may lead to conflict with development plan policies or where there is a proposal to build 150 or more houses, or one raising novel or other important development control issues, or where mineral development is proposed or where a retail development of over 100,000 sq ft is proposed, or the proposal raises significant legal difficulties. The Secretary of State's decision on whether or not to exercise his powers is, however, subject to judicial review.[12]

Reasons do not have to be given for 'calling-in' an application, though they usually are.[13]

H THE GRANT OF PLANNING PERMISSION, PLANNING CONDITIONS AND OBLIGATIONS

The general rule is that once permission is given for development the grant enures for the benefit of the land and all those interested in it, see s 75. Section 91, however, limits this by imposing an implied condition that the development in question must be *begun* within five years of the date on which the permission is granted. This is subject to exceptions, eg where a specific time limit it laid down in the grant. In any case for development to be *begun* very little needs to be done provided it is genuinely intended to be an inception of the work.[14]

By virtue of s 78(2) and art 20 of the GDPO 1995 authorities should give notification of their decision on an application within eight weeks. As a general rule non-determination gives rise to a right of appeal to the Secretary of State. However, many developers agree to extend the decision making period knowing that authorities have consultative obligations. In any case an out of time decision is not void.[15] Section 70A of the 1990 Act, as inserted in 1991, further empowers an authority to decline to determine an application where within the two year period ending with receipt of the application the Secretary of State refused a similar application on 'call in' or refused on appeal to overturn a decision refusing a similar application provided the authority consider there has been no significant change in circumstances concerning the development plan or any other material consideration.

Section 73 of the 1990 Act permits applications to develop land without compliance with any conditions previously attached. In such cases only the conditions may be considered. Authorities may refuse such applications if they believe the original conditions should continue to apply, or the conditions may be lifted or varied. Disappointed applicants may, of course appeal. (For the power to impose conditions see below.)

Planning authorities may under s 70 impose 'such conditions as they think fit' on a grant of permission. This is supplemented by s 72 which allows the imposition of conditions for regulating the use of any land *under the applicant's control*, whether or not comprised in the application, so far as is expedient *in connection with the authorised development* (the power under s 70 only extends to land comprised in the application,[16] but is not dependent on the applicant's

---

12 *R v Secretary of State for the Environment, ex p Newprop* [1983] JPL 386; *Lakin Ltd v Secretary of State for Scotland* [1989] JPL 339.

13 *South Northamptonshire District Council v Secretary of State for the Environment* (1995) 70 P & CR 224.

14 *Hillingdon London Borough Council v Secretary of State for the Environment* [1990] JPL 575; *Malvern Hills District Council v Secretary of State for the Environment* (1982) 262 Estates Gazette 1190.

15 *James v Secretary of State for Wales* [1966] 1 WLR 135.

16 *Peak Park Joint Planning Board v Secretary of State for the Environment and Imperial Chemical Industries* (1979) 39 P & CR 361.

control of the land),[17] and for requiring the removal of works or the discontinuance of a use at the end of a specified period: a 'permission granted for a limited period'.

DoE Circular 11/95 gives general guidance on the imposition of planning conditions. It has been central policy since the issue of Cmnd 9571 that conditions may be imposed to protect the environment against appreciable risk of harm, but that onerous conditions should not be imposed where environmental problems are less certain to occur, reliance being placed, in case of future difficulties, on public health or pollution control legislation. Furthermore conditions should only be imposed where they are necessary, relevant to planning matters, relevant to the development permitted, enforceable, precise and generally reasonable. Conditions should usually only be imposed where, if they were not, permission would have to be refused, and conditions not satisfying this criterion need special and precise justification. Conditions should thus be imposed where they are needed to meet specific problems. Conditions should not duplicate controls available under other statutes,[18] nor should they import forms of control into planning issues simply because such control is considered socially desirable,[19] nor should they seek to usurp the powers of central regulatory agencies.[20] Circular 11/95 points out that planning conditions are not appropriate to control the level of emissions from proposed developments where these are subject to pollution controls, but adds they: 'may be needed to address the impact of emissions to the extent that they might have land-use implications and are not controlled by the appropriate pollution control authority'. PPG 23 paras 3.23–3.28 gives further guidance on this issue, and points out that conditions may be used to control the amenity issues arising from a development, eg its impact on the landscape, or its hours of operation. They may further be used to: secure the use of particular modes of transport to/from the site of development; ensure decontamination of soil so that a site can be suitable for particular afteruses after development has taken place; ensure relocation and after care of landfill sites; require provision, where appropriate, of recycling facilities. Conditions should not be used to require provision of information to enable the impact of the development to be monitored save insofar as this relates to some definite planning objective. Conditions may, however, be used where there are parallel systems of regulation where this enables a development to proceed acceptably and to avoid the later onerous and invasive other use of other powers, eg to secure adequate sewerage provision on a site. Conditions may also be attached to a permission granted after EA to ensure incorporation of mitigation measures proposed in the ES, provided these do not duplicate other legislative controls, and do not substitute the planning authority's views on pollution for those of the appropriate pollution control body. Planning conditions may be used for noise control purposes, see chapter 11. The use of conditions to effect general environmental improvement by requiring the tidying up of eyesores has been condemned.[1]

---

17 *Atkinson v Secretary of State for the Environment* [1983] JPL 599.
18 *Fawcett Properties Ltd v Buckingham County Council* [1961] AC 636, [1960] 3 All ER 503.
19 *Chertsey Urban District Council v Mixnam's Properties Ltd* [1965] AC 735, [1964] 2 All ER 627.
20 *British Airports Authority v Secretary of State for Scotland* [1980] JPL 260.
 1 *Newbury District Council v Secretary of State for the Environment* [1981] AC 578, [1980] 1 All ER 731.

The power to impose conditions is, as stated above, subject to requirements of reasonableness. Conditions must be imposed only for relevant reasons, and must be such as a reasonable authority would impose.[2] The decisions of the courts, coming to and applying these rules, have resulted in planning conditions being limited to somewhat narrow land use considerations. Planning conditions may thus legally, as well as in terms of policy guidance, only serve a planning purpose and must not seek to promote an ulterior object.[3] They must not derogate from an existing permission by pursuing an aim having no necessary, essential, direct or close connection with the authorised development.[4] They must not be unreasonable, in that they are so oppressive, arbitrary or partial in their operation that no reasonable authority could have imposed them. Authorities may not seek the payment of money or money's worth, nor may they destroy private rights of property, or seek to transfer a public burden to private shoulders. However, the courts will not lightly set conditions aside, interpreting them benevolently to preserve the discretion of authorities.

A bad condition dealing only with minor issues, and which does not go fundamentally to the heart of the permission, may be severed and the rest of the permission saved.[5]

Planning obligations

As an alternative to imposing a planning condition, an authority may seek to reach an agreement (now a 'planning obligation') with a developer concerning the use and development of land. Such agreements (as they were known) *have* had the character of restrictive covenants which are enforceable despite the existence of any subsequent inconsistent grants of planning permission.[6] Indeed authorities have been able to apply for injunctions to restrain breaches of agreements even where other planning enforcement procedures have not been exhausted.[7] Under the provisions of the legislation as amended in 1991 positive covenants may be imposed, and see further below.

A problem, however, relates to what it is legitimate for a planning obligation to bring about. DoE Circular 16/91 warns authorities to be generally cautious in their use of obligations, and it is clear that obtaining unreasonable returns by way of obligation could give rise to suspicion that there has been bartering of planning permission. Circular 16/91 was an attempt to make it clear that obligations are not to be used by authorities to obtain extraneous gains from developers, nor should they be used to duplicate controls imposed by condition. Obligations *should* only be utilised where necessary and relevant, and an unacceptable development should not be allowed because a developer offers some benefit. However, despite policy guidance recent decisions by the courts enable what can only be called a 'highly creative' use of obligations, so

---

2 *Pyx Granite Co Ltd v Minister of Housing and Local Government* [1958] 1 QB 554, [1958] 1 All ER 625.
3 *R v Hillingdon London Borough Council, ex p Royco Homes Ltd* [1974] QB 720, [1974] 2 All ER 643.
4 *Allnatt London Properties Ltd v Middlesex County Council* (1964) 15 P & CR 288.
5 *Kent County Council v Kingsway Investments (Kent) Ltd* [1971] AC 72, [1970] 1 All ER 70.
6 *Re Martin's Application* [1989] JPL 33; *Abbey Homesteads (Developments) Ltd v Northamptonshire County Council* (1986) 278 Estates Gazette 1244.
7 *Avon County Council v Millard* (1985) 50 P & CR 275.

that very little is required of an obligation to satisfy general public law requirements as to its *vires*. The cases appear to establish that:

1   Each situation requires careful evaluation on its own facts.
2   Much is going to depend on the 'planning background' of each obligation, ie the plans and other policy documents relevant to the development in operation which may have indicated for all to see that particular developments could not go ahead without contributions from developers towards infrastructure costs, etc, for there is nothing illegitimate in arguing that those whose proposed developments will come to fruition as a result of the provision of infrastructure by a public body should not contribute towards its cost.
3   In cases such as the former it is perfectly acceptable to use percentage formulae based on the enhanced value of land with planning permission to calculate what a developer's contribution should be, provided it is bona fide used only to transfer an appropriate percentage of costs to developers' shoulders.
4   The offer, however, of benefits by a developer where these are wholly unconnected with the development is a matter not to be taken into account by a planning authority, and its consideration technically renders an authority's decision open to challenge.
5   Conversely an authority should not seek benefits wholly unconnected with a proposed development.
6   Where there are two competing development proposals it is legitimate for a planning authority to choose that one offering the more attractive package of on site benefits, or off site benefits provided these can be seen as linked to the proposed development.

Planning obligations must be reasonable, in the general administrative law sense of that term; they must serve a planning purpose, but, provided what is offered by way of benefit or 'planning gain' is in some way *connected with* the proposed development, there is no legal requirement that a benefit has to be *necessary* to, or *proportionate* to, the development. What constitutes the necessary *connection* between an obligation and a proposed development remains to be worked out on a case by case basis. However, there would appear to be no reason why a developer should not offer to undertake a major environmental 'clean-up' or restoration of land provided that can be seen to be related to the proposed development by, for example, making the site more attractive to the developer's customers.[8]

Where a developer puts forward a series of unrelated proposals, or proposals that appear composite but are in fact unrelated, where some proposals offer the allure of public gain while others would bring about unacceptable detriment to an interest of acknowledged importance, benefits available by way of an agreement are not to be used as counterbalances to the disbenefits. Where however, proposals are related it appears proper to weigh benefits against disbenefits.[9]

8 *R v Plymouth City Council, ex p Plymouth and South Devon Co-operative Society* [1993] JPL 1099; *Good v Epping Forest District Council* [1994] 2 All ER 156; *R v South Northamptonshire District Council, ex p Crest Homes* [1995] 7 ELM 11; *Tesco Stores v Secretary of State for the Environment* [1995] 2 All ER 636.
9 *Barber v Secretary of State for the Environment* [1991] JPL 559.

Obligations: the technicalities

Section 106 of the TCPA 1990 (as substituted) allows *any* person interested *in land* in the area of a local planning authority to enter into a planning obligation (by agreement or otherwise) with the effect of:

1 Restricting the development or use of the land in a specified way.
2 Requiring specified operations/activities to be carried out in, on, under or over the land.
3 Requiring the land's use in a specified way.
4 Requiring sums to be paid to the authority on a specified date(s) — or periodically.

Such an obligation may be conditional or unconditional, it may be time limited or indefinite, and may in relation to payments require them to be of a specified amount, or fixed according to a formula. Such an obligation is also enforceable against the original obligatees and those deriving title from them, and any restrictions/requirements imposed are enforceable by injunction. Furthermore the authority with whom the obligation is struck may enter on the land, on giving 21 days' notice to the obligatee, to do any operations required by the obligation and may recover their costs.

A planning obligation will have to take the form of *a deed*, stating that a planning obligation is created thereby, and identifying the land and the obligatee's interest therein and which identifies the obligatee and the relevant authority. Such an obligation then becomes a local land charge.

Obligations may be imposed either by agreement, *or* by a unilateral undertaking on the part of the obligatee.

Section 106A allows for a prescribed period (or where none such exists a period of five years) to elapse after which the obligatee may apply to the planning authority for the obligation to be modified or discharged. Thereupon the authority must determine either to continue, modify or discharge the obligation. Section 106B enables appeals to be made against decisions to continue obligations unmodified, or in cases of non-determination. The appeal will be made to the Secretary of State, and may take the form of a hearing.

Application of planning control to land of interested planning authorities and development by them

Section 316 of the 1990 Act was replaced by the 1991 Act so that in relation to land of interested planning authorities and the development, singly or jointly with others, of land by such authorities, development control, enforcement and special controls will apply subject to regulations to be made centrally.

The Town and Country Planning General Regulations, SI 1992/1492 now provide that:

1 Where a local authority wishes to carry out development itself on land in its area it must make, and may grant, the necessary planning application.
2 Where there is a proposal to carry out development on local authority owned land by other parties, the authority must seek permission from the relevant development control authority, ie the district in most cases.
3 Authorities applying for permission are in generally the same position as all other applicants.

4   The normal publicity requirements apply to authority applications.
5   Applications must, however, be determined by persons/committees not responsible for the land in question.

I   CHALLENGING A PLANNING DECISION

Section 78 of the Act allows disappointed developers to appeal to the Secretary of State against, inter alia, refusals or conditional grants of planning permission. The Secretary of State has wide powers to allow or dismiss appeals, or to vary or reverse any part of the original decision, and may deal with the application as if it had been made to him/her in the first instance. Most appeals are heard and determined by ministry inspectors. This serves somewhat to distance appeals from the executive arm of government, but it remains in the eyes of many, a weakness of planning law that the appeals and inquiry system is not independent, nor sufficiently open to public participation, see McAuslan, *The Ideologies of Planning Law* pp 45–74. The formal, frequently legalistic, and sometimes theatrical English inquiry does not always compare well with French practice in the Enquête Publique, see Macrory and La Fontaine *Public Inquiry and Enquête Publique*. (See further chapter 7, below on particular types of inquiry.)

Where either the applicant or the authority request it the Secretary of State must hold an inquiry *or* hearing, though they may opt for the matter to be settled by way of written representations, a procedure used in the majority of all cases. Where an inquiry is held it will usually be a local inquiry under s 320 of the Act. Procedure at the inquiry is governed by Inquiries Procedure Rules, in the case of matters determined by the Secretary of State, SI 1992/2038, and for those determined by inspectors, SI 1992/2039. Procedure is similar until the post inquiry stage. (For procedure on written representations see SI 1987/701.)

The overwhelming majority of appeals are now under SI 1981/804 and SI 1995/2259 determined by inspectors, but the Secretary of State has indicated he/she will 'recover' jurisdiction in relation to issues such as: major residential development proposals, ie 150 or more houses; major developments having more than local significance, or raising novel issues; developments consisting of 100,000 sq ft or more of retail space; greenbelt developments; major mineral working proposals; proposals raising major legal issues or where a government department has raised a significant objection: in 1994/95 the Secretary of State 'recovered' 188 cases.

In 1992 procedure rules are designed to enhance the speed with which appeals are dealt, by bringing about exchanges of information between the parties and identification of the points of dispute before the inquiry begins.

Once it has been determined by the Secretary of State that an inquiry is to be held the planning authority must inform him of all those who have made representations to them in consequence of being served with notice of the application because they are owners of the land or its agricultural tenants. The rules further ensure that any views expressed by a body or institution on which the planning authority intend to rely must be made known to the appellant in advance of the inquiry. In relation to major planning issues where the matter is one for the Secretary of State a pre-inquiry meeting may be held, and the *Code of Practice on Preparing for Major Planning Inquiries* (Annex I of DoE Circular 10/88) will apply, see further chapter 7. In relation to matters to be decided by an inspector, however, provision is also made for a pre-inquiry meeting to be held and for the inspector to indicate what matters he/she believes are relevant to the consideration of the appeal. At such a meeting issues such as hours of sitting, estimates of duration of the parties' cases, order of presentation, venue facilities, identification of issues, agreements on preparing and exchanging proofs of evidence, etc, will be addressed. Both authorities and appellants have to serve statements of their cases according to a timetable fixed by the rules, and other persons who wish to appear *may* be required to provide a statement of case by the Secretary of State. Those who are required to provide statements will then have the right to appear, however. Statements give the full particulars of a party's case and list relevant documents, thus identifying what the issues in dispute are and aiding the efficiency of the inquiry. Details of supporting data and methodologies should also be given. These statements will circulate between the principal parties and those third parties who have been required to give a statement. Inquiries *may* be timetabled, and *have to be* with regard to major inquiries. Where an assessor is appointed to assist the inquiry that person's name and address will be notified to the parties, as will the date of the opening of the inquiry which has to take place within a set period, and once that date is fixed it will only be altered in exceptional cases. The set periods are, where a pre-inquiry meeting is held under rule 5 of SI 1992/2038, ie a major inquiry to be decided by the Secretary of State, not *later* than eight weeks from the last session of that meeting, in other cases 22 weeks from 'the relevant date', ie the date of notification an inquiry is to be held, or 20 weeks from that date in cases to be decided by the Secretary of State or an inspector respectively. Often an inquiry will happen before these periods are expired, though not less than 28 days notice of the inquiry may be given. Publicity concerning the inquiry is left largely to the discretion of authorities, but they are counselled to ensure that all those who are known to have an interest in the issue are informed of the date of the inquiry. In any case the Secretary of State may direct publicity requirements.

Holding the inquiry

At the inquiry the following are entitled to appear: the applicant, the local planning authority, other planning authorities in whose area the land in question is situated, eg the county council, and persons who are the owners or agricultural tenants of the land and who having been made originally aware of the planning application made representations concerning it. In addition the Secretary of State may in relation to inquiries to be determined by himself or an inspector require any other person who has notified him of a desire or intention to appear to serve a statement of case on the 'statutory parties' and such persons then have a right to appear. Other persons appear at the discretion of the inspector, though this limitation on third party rights is modified in practice by the willingness of inspectors to allow all genuinely interested persons the chance to appear.

The inquiry will be held largely at the inspector's discretion. He/she must observe the rules of natural justice, and conduct the inquiry fairly with regard to the rights of parties to be heard and present an adequate case,[10] as must the

---

10 *Performance Cars Ltd v Secretary of State* (1977) 34 P & CR 92; *Nicholson v Secretary of State for Energy* (1977) 76 LGR 693.

Secretary of State.[11] Though inspectors may have an opinion of the merits of an appeal before commencing, they must give all those appearing before them proper opportunities to state their cases.[12] Inspectors may help unrepresented parties, where appropriate, to put their cases, but are under no obligation to be advocates.[13] Parties are not permitted to be noisy and disruptive, and may lose their rights in cases of misbehaviour.[14] The inspector has discretion to proceed if a person entitled to appear fails to do so. A person permitted to appear is entitled to have his views considered.[15] Statements ('proofs') of evidence from those entitled to appear, and intending to speak or to call evidence, are to be submitted to the inspector, normally three weeks in advance of the inquiry, and provision is made for such material to be circulated to other parties by the sets of inquiries procedure rules.

Generally at an inquiry the appellant opens and has a final right of reply, other persons entitled to appear do so in the order permitted by the inspector, as do those permitted to appear. Those entitled to appear may call evidence, and the appellant, authority and owners, etc, of the land may cross-examine, otherwise the examination of evidence is at the inspector's discretion. Inspectors may refuse to permit examination or cross-examination which is irrelevant or repetitious, though inspectors must behave fairly and reasonably in the exercise of this power.[16] The rules of fairness and natural justice apply to the discretion to allow cross-examination, though an inspector must consider, before allowing cross-examination on technical issues, the nature of the evidence, the qualifications of the witness and the cross-examiner to deal with the material, and whether the cross-examination will lead to the production of a better report, or will merely unnecessarily prolong the inquiry. Government policy may not be debated at an inquiry. In *Bushell v Secretary of State for the Environment*,[17] the House of Lords commented on what may be a matter of 'government policy'. National policies, debateable in Parliament, are clearly such. At the other extreme minute details and particular issues of implementation of policy in individual cases clearly are not. In the 'grey area' between lie established departmental practices for deciding national priorities between possible implementations of policy and the 'need' for action. It seems these should not be debated at individual local inquiries. However, it appears that it can be arguable that central policy is not applicable in a given context or to a particular locality.[18] Certainly while a government representative may *not* be *required* (as is laid down in the sets of inquiries procedure rules) to answer questions relating to the merits of central policy, such a question may be *allowed* where the representative is *prepared* to answer it.

Evidence at planning inquiries must be given in public, though the Secretary of State may direct otherwise where satisfied it would result in the disclosure of information as to national security, or the security of any premises or

11 *R v Secretary of State for the Environment, ex p Field Estates (Canvey) Ltd* [1989] JPL 39.
12 *Halifax Building Society v Secretary of State for the Environment* [1983] JPL 816.
13 *Snow v Secretary of State for the Environment* (1976) 33 P & CR 81.
14 *Lovelock v Secretary of State for Transport* (1979) 39 P & CR 468.
15 *Turner v Secretary of State for the Environment* (1973) 28 P & CR 123.
16 *Nicholson v Secretary of State for Energy* (1977) 76 LGR 693.
17 [1981] AC 75.
18 *R v Secretary of State for Transport, ex p Gwent County Council* [1988] QB 429, [1987] 1 All ER 161.

property, and that this would be contrary to the public interest, see s 321 of the 1990 Act.

It must be remembered that one purpose of an inquiry is to ensure citizens closely affected by a scheme are given the opportunity to state the case for their objection to it, and thereby the minister is better informed of the facts. Inquiries should not be 'over-judicialised'. They are not like civil litigation, even though a decision is challenged. The concept of a 'burden of proof' is inappropriate, as the inquiry is into whether there are sound and clear cut reasons emerging from the facts for a refusal of permission. It is unclear how far a policy contained in a statutory plan can place a burden of proving why permission should be granted on an appellant.[19] Inspectors may make unaccompanied inspections of the site before or during inquiries without giving notice to the parties, and must inspect it if requested by the appellant or the authority, at which time the appellant, the authority and the owners, etc of the land are entitled to be present. *Accompanied* site inspections may also take place during the inquiry. Receipt of other information on this visit, for example by making inquiries of neighbours, as in *Hibernian Property Co Ltd v Secretary of State for the Environment*,[20] or coming to conclusions on observations which the parties are given no opportunity to deal with,[1] may amount to a denial of natural justice.

After the inquiry, in cases to be ministerially decided, the inspector makes his/her report to the Secretary of State, including conclusions and recommendations or reasons for not making recommendations, any assessor's report made must be appended to the inspector's report with comments thereon. The report must fairly and accurately present principal arguments; irrelevant and peripheral issues may be omitted, so that the issues are intelligible to the Secretary of State, and so that proper material is set before him/her.[2] Where the Secretary of State differs from the inspector on a matter of fact, or after the inquiry takes into account new evidence of facts (not being matters of government policy), and is consequently not disposed to agree with the inspector's recommendations, he/she must not come to a decision at variance with the recommendations without notifying the persons who were entitled to appear of his views and reasons therefor, and afford them a chance to make representations. The Secretary of State has a discretion in any case to reopen an inquiry, and *must* reopen it if either the applicant or the local planning authority request it where he/she has taken into account new evidence or new matters of fact which are not matters of government policy. (A similar provision applies to appeals to be determined by an inspector.) These rules do not apply to disagreement by the Secretary of State with the inspector's judgments, see for example *Lord Luke of Pavenham v Minister of Housing and Local Government*,[3] where there was a disagreement whether a development would harm the countryside. An *opinion* on a matter of fact, is not itself a matter of fact.[4] The Secretary of State is also free to consider matters of

---

19 *Federated Estates v Secretary of State for the Environment* [1983] JPL 812.
20 (1973) 27 P & CR 197.
1 *Fairmount Investments Ltd v Secretary of State for the Environment* [1976] 2 All ER 865, [1976] 1 WLR 1255.
2 *North Surrey Water Co v Secretary of State for the Environment* (1976) 34 P & CR 140.
3 [1968] 1 QB 172, [1967] 1 All ER 351.
4 *Portsmouth Water plc v Secretary of State for the Environment* [1994] JPL 1001.

government policy, and to consult other ministers, even without giving the parties an opportunity to comment.[5]

The decision on appeal

Decisions and supporting reasons must be notified to the statutory parties, and to any other person who appeared at the inquiry and asked to be notified. Reasons must be adequate, clearly intelligible, reasonably precise, and must set out the relevant issues.[6]

The law was recently reviewed in *Save Britain's Heritage v Secretary of State for the Environment*.[7] The question here was whether a decision letter satisfied the requirements of the Inquiries Procedure Rules that 'the Secretary of State shall notify his decision . . . and his reasons for it . . .' Lord Bridge reviewed the existing case law. In *Re Poyser and Mills' Arbitration*[8] Megaw J stated that a duty to give reasons is one to give proper and adequate reasons, reasons which are intelligible and deal with the substantive points that have been raised, ie reasons which enable a person to know on what grounds an issue has been decided, and which identify in sufficient detail the conclusions reached on the principal issues of controversy.[9] Reasons must also be understandable to those to whom they are addressed, though a decision letter's reasons are to be read as a whole, and not construed as a statute, ie not sentence by sentence or paragraph by paragraph.[10] Added to this, it appears from the '*Save*' case that decision letters may also be read with a degree of benevolence. However, can it also be said, as Woolf LJ argued in the Court of Appeal, that reasoning should be such as to enable the person receiving it to make a proper assessment as to whether a further challenge should be mounted?

Lord Bridge accepted Woolf LJ's contention — sufficient particularity is required in order to enable the recipient of a decision to make a proper assessment of whether or not to mount a further challenge. Nevertheless as a general principle Lord Bridge declined to move far from the basic tests laid down in in *Re Poyser and Mills' Arbitration*. Lord Bridge further added that even if reasons were not found to be adequate, a remedy should not be given unless it can be shown that the applicant has been substantially prejudiced by the failure to give adequate reasons. Lord Bridge did, however, deny a contention that an inadequacy of reasoning may itself give rise to a presumption of substantial prejudice which it is then the duty of the decision maker to rebut. Thus a decision letter does not have to refer to every material consideration, no matter how insignificant, nor does it have to deal with every argument, no matter how peripheral. Indeed provided reasons are *adequately* expressed they do *not* have to be *well* expressed.[11]

5 *Kent County Council v Secretary of State for the Environment and Burmah Total Refineries Trust* (1976) 33 P & CR 70.
6 *Givaudan & Co Ltd v Minister of Housing & Local Government* [1966] 3 All ER 696, [1967] 1 WLR 250.
7 [1991] 2 All ER 10.
8 [1964] 2 QB 467.
9 *Westminster City Council v Great Portland Estates plc* [1985] AC 661 at 673; *Hope v Secretary of State for the Environment* (1975) 31 P & CR 120 at 123.
10 *Ward v Secretary of State for the Environment* (1989) 59 P & CR 486 at 487.
11 *Bolton Metropolitan District Council v Secretary of State for the Environment* [1996] 1 All ER 184.

Under s 250 of the Local Government Act 1972 and s 320 of the TCPA 1990 the Secretary of State may award costs at an inquiry, and this power now extends to proceedings determined by written representations: indeed inspectors may now exercise the cost awarding power. Principles governing the exercise of the power are contained in DoE Circular 2/93. These relate to situations where an appellant has failed to follow procedural requirements, or has behaved in such a way that proceedings have been adjourned or unnecessarily prolonged, or is wilfully unco-operative, or failed to pursue the appeal or has failed to attend meetings, or has introduced new grounds of appeal at a late stage, or has pursued an appeal with no reasonable chance of success. Planning authorities may be subjected to costs where they fail to comply with procedural requirements, fail to provide planning evidence to substantiate their decisions or to show they have taken into account relevant laws and policies, or where they have behaved obstructively by refusing to discuss a planning application, or where they have introduced new grounds for refusal at a late stage in proceedings, or have imposed unreasonable conditions or pursued unreasonable demands in connection with a grant of permission. Section 322A further empowers the Secretary of State to award costs against a party in respect of any other party where arrangements have been made for an inquiry or hearing which does not then take place. This contemplates situations where either the authority or the appellant pull out of an inquiry before it has opened leaving the other side with abortive preparation costs. Note also s 79(6A) under which if at any time during the determination of an appeal it appears to the Secretary of State that the appellant is responsible for undue delay in the progress of the appeal, he/she may warn the appellant that the appeal will be dismissed unless specified steps are taken to expedite matters, and may then dismiss the appeal if those steps are not taken in due time.

Further challenge

'Persons aggrieved' by the decision on appeal have, under ss 284 and 288, a six-week right to apply to the High Court on a point of law to quash the decision. That period begins to run from the date of typing, signing and stamping of the Secretary of State's notification, not its date of reception.[12] The time limit is absolute.[13] The term 'persons aggrieved' is given an extended meaning. Mere busybodies are not included, but third parties, such as neighbours, who have been allowed to appear at the inquiry are within the formula.[14] The grounds of challenge are limited to arguments that the appeal was substantively or procedurally ultra vires. Courts will intervene where there is no evidence on which the minister could have acted, or where the evidence cannot reasonably support conclusions made. Furthermore he/she must not act perversely or misinterpret the statute, or take into account irrelevant factors, or vice versa. Ministers must comply with statutory procedures, especially with regard to the holding of inquiries and should apply the

---

12 *Griffiths v Secretary of State for the Environment* [1983] 2 AC 51, [1983] 1 All ER 439.
13 *R v Secretary of State for the Environment, ex p Ostler* [1977] QB 122, [1976] 3 All ER 90.
14 *Turner v Secretary of State for the Environment* (1973) 28 P & CR 123; *Bizony v Secretary of State for the Environment* [1976] JPL 306.

principles of natural justice which involve giving a fair hearing.[15] With regard to procedural irregularities, applicants must show consequential substantial prejudice to their interests, though generally the discretion of the court not to quash will be exercised only if a point is purely technical or where there could be no possible detriment to the applicant.[16]

Appeals may only be on points of law, not on the merits of the planning application. This is not always an easy distinction to draw, but is illustrated by *R v Haringey London Borough Council, ex p Barrs*.[17] An attempted challenge was made on the grounds of the architectural standard of the development. The Court declined to act as a forum of taste, stating it could only intervene where a development was of such a character that no one could reasonably permit it in its location. It is not enough to justify intervention for the Court merely to disagree with a decision on its facts.[18]

A non-statutory mode of questioning planning decisions for which the Act of 1990 makes no specific provision for challenge, *especially those of local planning authorities*, is application for judicial review under RSC Ord 53 and the Supreme Court Act 1981, s 31. So far as the powers of planning authorities are concerned this is the method of proceeding for the order of certiorari, the most usual remedy; mandamus or prohibition may also be sought. Injunctions and declarations are also available, but will not often be awarded.[19] Leave must be sought to make applications. This is granted at the court's discretion. The attitude of the courts is, where there is an alternative remedy by way of appeal, a remedy by way of judicial review should only be granted where the alternative is not convenient, or where there is a real question as to the way in which the authority reached its decision.[20] Applications for leave to apply for judicial review must be made promptly, and usually within three months of the date when grounds for the application arose. In considering applications the courts may frown on delay in general and be unwilling to grant relief that would be detrimental to good administration, see the Supreme Court Act 1981, s 31(6), and *R v Swansea City Council, ex p Main*.[1] The three month period for applications does not entitle a party to wait for almost three months before applying, prompt action is almost always needed.[2] The court will only grant leave where it considers the applicant has a sufficient interest in the matter; for example an association of local residents likely to be affected by a development,[3] or a ratepayer living close to a development site,[4] or a neighbour whose privacy would be invaded by a development,[5] but not, it seems, an applicant who is a user of the highway adjoining the site

15 *Seddon Properties Ltd v Secretary of State for the Environment & Macclesfield Borough Council* (1978) 248 Estates Gazette 950.
16 *Peak Park Joint Planning Board v Secretary of State for the Environment and Imperial Chemical Industries* (1979) 39 P & CR 361.
17 (1983) Times, 1 July.
18 *Asher v Secretary of State for the Environment* [1974] Ch 208, [1974] 2 All ER 156.
19 *R v Secretary of State for the Environment, ex p Ward* [1984] 2 All ER 556; *R v Secretary of State for the Environment, ex p Greater London Council* [1985] JPL 543.
20 *R v Secretary of State for the Environment, ex p Ward* [1984] 2 All ER 556.
 1 (1981) Times, 23 December.
 2 *R v Poole Borough Council, ex p Beebee* [1991] 3 LMELR 60.
 3 *Covent Garden Community Association Ltd v Greater London Council* [1981] JPL 183.
 4 *Steeples v Derbyshire County Council* [1981] JPL 582.
 5 *R v North Hertfordshire District Council, ex p Sullivan* [1981] JPL 752.

in question but who lives some miles away.[6] The courts will consider the nature of the statutory power, and the implications for the applicant of its use, in deciding what is a 'sufficient interest', likewise the applicant's history of involvement with the matter. However, the law will not recognise that a group of persons has locus standi simply because they form themselves into an interest group to campaign on the issue in question. Though a person may not need a direct interest in an issue to have locus standi in relation to it, some sort of indirect interest, such as residence in an area likely to be affected by a proposal, or a close involvement with the site in question over a number of years may be needed.[7]

The position appears to be different, however, with respect to commercial undertakings, so, for example, a company may have a 'sufficient interest' where there is a real possibility that its commercial interests may be prejudiced by a grant of permission to another, so that it is likely the first company is likely to be refused permission on its application, or its development is likely otherwise to be adversely affected.[8] Likewise a very well established and reputable environmental pressure group, with a number of its members living in an area affected by a proposed development, who raise a serious and well focused objection to that development, and who can pursue their challenge with much greater ease and efficiency than could any individual, may well be considered to have a 'sufficient interest' for judicial review purposes.[9] However, it also appears such a pressure group must also have the 'capacity' to bring an action, ie it must have legal personality, for example by way of incorporation.[10]

J FINANCIAL CONSEQUENCES OF REVOKING OR REFUSING PERMISSION

Permission granted on an application may be revoked or modified under s 97 before an operational development has been completed or a change of use has taken place. An order revoking permission requires the Secretary of State's confirmation, save where under s 99, the parties affected by the order have in writing stated they do not object. The Secretary of State must not confirm an order without affording affected persons and the authority a hearing or a local inquiry. Where planning permission is revoked or modified, compensation may be payable under s 107 to persons interested in the land who have incurred expenditure in carrying out work rendered abortive by the revocation or modification, or have otherwise sustained loss or damage directly attributable thereto (including elements in respect of depreciation in value of the claimant's interest), subsequent to the grant of permission (*or* in connection with preparatory plans or matters for the work in question).

Section 102 of the 1990 Act allows planning authorities to secure by order

6 *R v Bradford-on-Avon Urban District Council, ex p Boulton* [1964] 2 All ER 492, [1964] 1 WLR 1136.
7 *R v Secretary of State for the Environment, ex p Rose Theatre Trust Co* [1990] 1 QB 504.
8 *R v Canterbury City Council, ex p Springimage* [1994] JPL 427; *Morbaine Ltd v Secretary of State for the Environment* [1994] JPL 381.
9 *R v HM Inspectorate of Pollution and Minister of Agriculture, Fisheries and Food, ex p Greenpeace* [1993] 5 ELM 183.
10 *R v Darlington Council, ex p Association of Darlington Taxi Owners* [1994] COD 424.

the discontinuance of any *use* of land, for example, scrap sorting,[11] or the removal of the buildings and works, or imposition of conditions on a continued use, in the interests of the proper planning and amenity of their area, including the preservation of amenity in the future.[12] The power does not apply to *continuing* building or engineering developments, but may apply to buildings or works thereby produced. Orders under this section must be confirmed by the Secretary of State. Persons affected by the order, having been served with due notice by the authority, have the right to a hearing or a local inquiry, as also do the authority. Where an order requires steps to be taken for the alteration or removal of buildings and works, and no action ensues, the authority may enter the land and take action, see s 190. Section 102 orders can apply to land uses that have never needed planning permission. Where an order is made, compensation is payable under s 107 in respect of depreciation of value of a person's interest in the land suffered in consequence of the order or as a result of disturbance. Where a person carries out works in compliance with an order he/she is entitled to compensation in respect of reasonable expenses. The rules for assessing compensation are under s 117, laid down by the Land Compensation Act 1961, s 5.

In principle compensation is not payable in respect of *refusals* of permission for developments, even where this means a loss of profit to a prospective developer. More important are situations where a purchase notice can be served, particularly in relation to plots of land which the owner wishes to 'off-load'. Sections 137–148 of the 1990 Act lay down procedures whereby a purchase notice can be served by the owner of relevant land who claims, as a result of the refusal or conditional grant of permission, the land has become incapable of reasonably beneficial use in its existing state, *or* beneficial use is inconsistent with compliance with planning conditions, *and*, in either case, that the land *cannot* be beneficially used by carrying out other development for which permission is available. Purchase notices are served on district councils. They may pass a notice on to another local authority or statutory undertaker who agrees to comply with it in their place. Disputed notices are referred to the Secretary of State who has certain powers, subject to holding a hearing. Where convinced that the land is incapable of reasonably beneficial use, he/she may confirm the notice unconditionally, or may confirm it with the substitution of another local authority or statutory undertaker as the acquiring body, or may grant planning permission for the development comprised in the application, revoking or amending conditions where appropriate, or may make provision for a grant of permission for other development. A successful purchase notice operates as a type of 'reverse compulsory purchase'. The relevant authority are forced to acquire the site. Purchase notices may also be served as a result of revocation or modification of planning permission, or required discontinuations where land has in consequence become incapable of reasonably beneficial use in its existing state, see s 137.

Having to pay compensation in respect of interferences with existing land uses seems to deter authorities from taking action, or even from refusing permission in some cases. (NB Special rules apply in respect of mineral developments. These will be considered in chapter 8.)

11 *Parkes v Secretary of State for the Environment* [1979] 1 All ER 211, [1978] 1 WLR 1308.
12 *Re Lamplugh* (1967) 19 P & CR 125.

K ENFORCEMENT

No system of control is effective unless enforced, and until quite recently enforcement was the 'Cinderella' of planning, bedevilled by complex and uncertain legal provisions and not highly esteemed as a function. Officers were irritated at the cumbersome legal procedures involved and the feeling that they were 'fighting with one arm tied behind their backs' as the record of magistrates' courts in punishing those prosecuted for infringing enforcement action has not been good, with a generally low level of fines imposed. Following publication of the Carnwath Report, *Enforcing Planning Control*, in 1989 the legal provisions were amended by the 1991 Act. Unauthorised development is still not a criminal offence, but the new provisions are a clear advance in clarity on their predecessors, and enhanced penalties are provided for those who flout the law. Furthermore the most recent study of enforcement ('Evaluation of Planning Enforcement Provisions,' DoE, 1995) has concluded that the new provisions are working well.

The current law

Section 171A defines expressions; thus a *'breach of planning control'* arises where development requiring permission takes place without permission, or where any conditions in a grant or permission are not complied with; *'enforcement action'* consists of either issuing an enforcement notice, or a breach of condition notice (a *new* term).

Section 171C applies where the local planning authority suspect a breach of planning control. They may serve a *'planning contravention notice'* (PCN) on 'any person' who is the owner/occupier of the land, or who is carrying out operations on, under or over it, or using it. This will require specified information to be given as to operations, uses, any conditions, etc, imposed in any grant of permission, etc. Particular questions may be asked about when an activity began. The PCN may give notice of a time and place at which the person served with it may make representations or make an offer to apply for planning permission, or undertake to refrain from activities or carry out remedial works. The PCN must also inform the person served of the likely consequences of failure to respond, and that enforcement action may be taken. Serving a PCN does not affect any other enforcement powers. However, a PCN may only be used where there is evidence upon which a reasonable authority would conclude there is an indication of a breach of control. The procedure cannot be used for mere 'fishing trips'.[13]

Section 171D makes it an offence to fail to comply with a PCN's requirements within 21 days, though defences will exist of having a reasonable excuse for failure to comply with the requirements of the PCN. It is likewise an offence intentionally or recklessly to make false or misleading statements in response to a PCN.

These provisions go some way towards meeting the often repeated criticism that planning authorities have been in a weak position when taking enforcement action because they have frequently been in no position to know exactly what has unlawfully been going on on the land in question.

---

13 *R v Teignbridge District Council, ex p Teignmouth Quay Co* [1995] 7 ELM 55, [1995] JPL 828.

Substitute s 172 provides that an enforcement notice may be issued where it appears there has been a breach of planning control, and that it is expedient so to act, considering the provisions of the development plan and other material considerations. A copy of this notice is to be served on the owner/occupier of relevant land, and others having materially affected interests in the land, and service is to take place not more than 28 days after the date of issue and not less than 28 days before the specified date for the notice to take effect.

The notice must, under the new s 173, state the matters *appearing* to constitute a breach of control and whether in the authority's opinion they consist of *either* unauthorised development *or* a breach of condition. A notice will be taken to comply with this requirement if it enables the person on whom it is served to know what the matters constituting the alleged breach are. The notice will have to specify the steps to be taken, or the activities to be ended, in order to achieve, *in whole or part*:

1   Remedying the breach by complying with the terms of any relevant planning permission or restoring land to its original condition, or by discontinuing any use.
2   Remedying any injury to amenity.

In particular a notice may require demolition of buildings, carrying out of operations, cessation of a land use, reduction of a use/activity to a specified level, contouring of refuse or waste materials. The notice will also have to state the date on which it will take effect, and the period(s) within which steps are to be taken or activities concluded. However, a notice cannot require more than is necessary to cure the breach, for example by requiring the cessation of an otherwise lawful use of land.[14]

Where the alleged breach consists of demolition of a building, the notice may require construction of a 'replacement building' generally similar to that demolished, subject, of course, inter alia, to any relevant building controls. Certain prescribed matters must be included in the notice, including rights of appeal.

Section 173A provides for the withdrawal of an enforcement notice before it takes effect, and for the informing of all those served with copies of the notice. *Alternatively* the authority is able to waive or relax enforcement notice requirements, *and* this power is exercisable even after a notice has taken effect, though again notice of intention to vary will have to be served on every person originally served, and any representations made in consequence considered. This power is without prejudice to the authority's ability to issue a further notice.

Section 174 of the 1990 Act (as amended) provides that appeals against enforcement notices may be brought on the following grounds, namely that:

1   In respect of any breach of control covered by the notice permission ought to be granted or the condition/limitation discharged, as the case may be.
2   The matters alleged have not occurred.
3   The matters do not amount to a breach.
4   At the date when notice was issued no enforcement action could be taken (eg because of limitation, see further below).
5   Copies of the notice were not served as required.

14 *Mansi v Elstree District Council* (1964) 16 P & CR 153.

6 Steps required to be taken, etc, exceed what is necessary to remedy any breach of control in the circumstances.

7 Time periods specified for taking action are unreasonably short.

The appeal is to be made either by giving written notice to the Secretary of State, or by sending the notice to him/her by post, in the latter case before the notice would have taken effect but for delays in the post, or before it does take effect. The grounds of appeal must be specified in the notice of appeal together with such other information as is specified.

Section 175 empowers the Secretary of State to make regulations concerning appeals procedures, in particular to govern the submission of the planning authority's case and other exchanges of information (see SI 1991/ 2804). Note also Sch 6 of the 1990 Act. Enforcement appeals are generally dealt with in a manner similar to appeals against refusal of permission. The Secretary of State's discretion concerning the outcome of an appeal under s 176 as amended is wide. He/she may correct misdescriptions, defects or errors in enforcement notices or vary their terms, provided this will not cause injustice to the appellant or the authority, while s 177 permits the grant of permission for development, or part of a development, or a development on part of relevant land, or discharge conditions, or the determination of lawful land uses. However, in exercising these powers the Secretary of State must consider the development plan and any other relevant considerations.

Section 178 of the TCPA 1990 (as amended) provides that where steps required by an enforcement notice are not taken, the planning authority may enter the land and take them and may recover their reasonable expenses from the then owner of the land. Thus an authority may now take action against, for example an unauthorised *use* so that it complies with any grant of permission; the previous law only allowed the taking of action to restore land to an existing use.

Substituted s 179 provides that where at the end of a compliance period any steps required by an enforcement notice have not been taken, or where an activity has not been terminated, a breach of enforcement notice occurs. This is an offence, and a continuing one until the state of affairs constituting the breach ceases. Defences include showing that the person charged did everything in his/her power to secure compliance with the notice. Further defences include showing that the person charged has not been served with a copy of the enforcement notice, or that the notice has not been duly registered under s 188. Likewise a person who is an occupier of relevant land must not carry on or cause or permit to be carried on an activity required to end by an enforcement notice, and non-compliance after the end of the period for compliance is, again, an offence. On summary conviction a fine of up to £20,000 may be levied, on indictment the fine is unlimited, but in either case the court in calculating the fine is to take into account any financial benefit accruing to the accused from the commission of the offence. Criminal proceedings can only be defended by way of a challenge to the vires of an enforcement notice where it is defective on its face and a nullity, in all other cases where vires is in issue the proper course of action is to seek an adjournment of the trial and to apply for judicial review of the enforcement notice.[15]

15 *R v Wicks* [1995] 7 ELM 128.

Section 180, as substituted, provides that where after service of a copy of an enforcement notice or breach of condition notice (see further below) planning permission is granted for any development carried out previously the notice shall, in so far as inconsistent with the grant, cease to have effect, though this does not exculpate persons in respect of previous criminal liabilities already incurred. Section 181 then provides that compliance with an enforcement notice does not prevent it from applying to any later unauthorised act of development to which the notice applies.

With specific regard to enforcement of planning conditions, a new s 187A provides a new optional procedure so that where conditions are not complied with a 'breach of conditions notice' (BCN) may be served on the person responsible through having committed the breach of having control of the land, requiring compliance with the conditions specified in the BCN, and the steps to be taken/activities ended in order to secure compliance. A compliance period of not less than 28 days beginning with the date of service is to be allowed, though the authority may extend this. If the steps specified to be taken are still lacking, or where an activity to be ended goes on, the person responsible will be in breach of the BCN and will commit an offence, though it will be a defence to prove that all reasonable measures to secure compliance with conditions were taken.

A BCN *cannot* be appealed, though challenge is available on a point of law by way of judicial review.

Enforcement: further action

In some cases enforcement action alone will be insufficient to deal with unauthorised development. In some instances an immediate cessation of the activity in question will be desirable, and here the 'stop notice' provisions of the 1990 Act may be resorted to (see further below). In other cases stronger remedies may be needed. The persistent unauthorised developer may regard any fines imposed as 'mere overheads' and the threat of imprisonment for contempt of court may be a more potent deterrent, hence injunctive relief is available, originally under s 222 of the Local Government Act 1972. The remedy is, of course, discretionary, and will not be issued as a matter of course. Evidence of a breach of control must be clear, the breach must be deliberate and it must appear that the breach will occur or continue unless restrained.[16]

A new s 187B specifically provides that injunctive relief may be applied for in either the County or High Court where the local planning authority consider it necessary or expedient for *actual or apprehended* breaches of planning control, whether or not any other enforcement powers are to be used. It is clear, following *Croydon London Borough Council v Gladden*[17] and *Runnymede Borough Council v Harwood*[18] that the power to apply for injunctive relief is a wide and flexible one which applies *equally* to cases of apprehended breaches of planning control as well as actual ones. Furthermore it is no longer necessary for a planning authority to show that an injunction is needed

---

16 *Westminster City Council v Jones* [1981] JPL 750; *City of London Corpn v Bovis Construction Ltd* [1989] JPL 263; *Southwark London Borough Council v Frow* [1989] JPL 645n.
17 [1994] JPL 723.
18 [1994] JPL 724.

because the criminal law alone is insufficient to deter a person's unlawful development activities. The decision in *Kirklees Metropolitan Borough Council v Wickes Building Supplies Ltd*[19] that a local planning authority does not have to give a cross-undertaking in damages where an interim injunction is sought against an activity (ie where its cessation is sought while its legality is being determined) may promote the popularity of seeking injunctive relief in respect of contravention of planning control. The previous rule that an authority had to undertake to indemnify the injunctee should the final decision be there was no illegal activity in the first place, which could have led to authorities facing claims for considerable losses of profit, was from a planning authority point of view most unfortunate.

The stop notice provisions of the 1990 Act were extensively modified in 1991. Section 183 is largely substituted with new provisions which provide that where a planning authority consider it expedient that a 'relevant activity' (ie any activity the authority require to cease, and any ancillary or associated activity) should cease before the date for compliance with the enforcement notice, they may, *when* they serve a copy of that notice, or afterwards, also serve a 'stop notice' prohibiting the activity on the land in question, or on any part of it. The notice may be served on any person with an interest in the land, or engaging in the prohibited activity. However, such a notice may not be served:

1   Where the enforcement notice has taken effect.
2   Where the unauthorised activity is use of a *building* as a dwelling house.
3   Where the activity has been carried out (continuously or not) for a period of *four* years ending with service of the notice, though no account is to be taken of any period during that time when the activity was permitted by planning permission, *and* this prohibition on taking action does *not* extend to prevent service of a stop notice prohibiting activity consisting of or incidental to building, engineering, mining or other operations or depositing refuse or waste.

Section 184 provides that a stop notice must refer to the enforcement notice to which it relates and have a copy of that notice annexed to it.

Under s 184(3) a stop notice will take effect on a date specified and which must not be earlier than three days after service, *unless* the authority consider special reasons justify an earlier commencement, and a statement of those reasons is served with the stop notice. Likewise a notice must *not* commence later than 28 days after its first service on any person.

Section 187(1) and (2) as amended provides that if a person contravenes a stop notice after such a notice has been served on him/her, or a site notice (under s 184 stating stop notices have been served) has been displayed, he/she commits an offence. Contravention will include causing or permitting contravening activities.

Fines may be up to £20,000 on summary conviction or unlimited on indictment in respect of stop notice contraventions, but, as with the similar provisions relating to enforcement notices, the court is to take into account any financial benefit accruing to the accused from the breach. Stop notices may be challenged by defending on the merits of the case any criminal proceedings brought under them,[20] or by attacking their legality in an application for judicial review.[1]

Reference has been made above to time limits within which enforcement action has to be taken. Section 171B of the TCPA 1990 as inserted in 1991 provides that where there has been a breach of planning control which consists of operational development *no* enforcement action may be taken after the end of four years beginning with the date on which operations were *substantially* completed. This may introduce complexities for authorities who may find unauthorised developers arguing that the time for taking action has passed because their operations were substantially complete more than four years previously. Section 171B(2) further provides that where the breach consists of a *change of use* of any building to that of a *single* dwelling house again there is a *four* year limitation. In the case of any other breaches of control eg all other *material changes of use* the limitation period is *ten* years from the date of the breach.

Enhanced rights of entry for enforcement purposes are given by sections 196A–C. These allow any person duly authorised in writing by a local authority to enter land at any reasonable hour to ascertain whether a breach of control has taken place, and to determine how and whether enforcement powers should be used, provided reasonable grounds for entering the land exist. The Secretary of State has similar authorising powers, though only after consultation with the local planning authority. This power under s 196A exists without a warrant. Section 196B will allow application to a magistrate where an entry could be made under s 196A and where admission has been refused, or refusal is reasonably apprehended, or where the case is one of urgency. The magistrate may issue a warrant authorising entry at a reasonable hour (or at any time in urgent cases), and this entry may take place at any time up to one month from the warrant's issue. Under s 196C it will be an offence to obstruct these powers of entry.

Finally note s 289(4A), (4B) and (5A). The High Court now has power to order that, pending determination and consequential proceedings an enforcement notice shall have full or modified effect. The making of such orders is at the discretion of the Court and authorities may be required to give cross undertakings in damages in the event of the final outcome being to strike down the enforcement actions. Section 289(6) further provides that s 289 proceedings may only be brought by leave of the Court. This is designed to deter frivolous and unmeritorious appeals.[2]

L CERTIFICATES OF LAWFUL USE/DEVELOPMENT

Sections 191–194 of the TCPA 1990 as substituted, provide that where any person wishes to ascertain the lawfulness of any *existing* use of buildings or land, or any operations, or any matter which might constitute a breach of condition, an application specifying the issues may be made to the local planning authority. Under s 191 which relates to current uses, etc, uses and operations will be lawful if:

20 *R v Jenner* [1983] 2 All ER 46, [1983] 1 WLR 873.
 1 *R v Epping Forest District Council, ex p Strandmill Ltd* [1990] JPL 415.
 2 *Huggett v Secretary of State for the Environment* [1995] 7 ELM 99.

1 no enforcement action may be taken in their regard either because they never needed planning permission or because lapse of time precludes enforcement; and

2 they do not contravene any current enforcement notice. Similar requirements apply in respect of conditions.

If, on an application, the authority are provided with information satisfying them on the lawfulness of the matter in question they must certify accordingly, otherwise they must refuse to certify. The certificate, if given, must specify the land, and the matter in question, giving reasons for the determination of lawfulness and stating the date of the application. Such a certificate also has a significance for the purposes of other legislation, eg s 36(2) of the EPA 1990. Section 192 makes provision (similar to that under s 191) for applications to determine whether a *proposed* use or development would be lawful.

Applications for ss 191 and 192 certificates must be in prescribed form, see s 193, and specific provision is made in this respect by the GDPO. A certificate may be given in respect of all or some relevant land, and, where uses are multiple, in respect of one, or more, or all of them. Certificates may be revoked if the local planning authority discover statements made to them in connection with certificates were false or that material information was withheld, and s 194 provides that it is an offence knowingly or recklessly to give false information or use false or misleading documentation in this connection.

Further reading

BOOKS

Blowers, A, *The Limits of Power: The Politics of Local Planning Policy* (1980) Pergamon Press.

Bruton, M, and Nicholson, D, *Local Planning in Practice* (1987) Hutchinson.

Carnwath, R, (ed) *Blundell and Doby's Planning Appeals and Inquiries* (4th edn) (1990) Sweet and Maxwell.

Churchill, Gibson and Warren, *Law, Policy and the Environment* (1991) Blackwell.

Fortlage, CA, *Environmental Assessment* (1990) Gower.

Grant, M, *Urban Planning Law* (1982) Sweet and Maxwell.

Grove-White, R, 'Land Use, Law and the Environment' in Churchill, Gibson and Warren.

McAuslan, P, *The Ideologies of Planning Law* (1980) Pergamon Press.

Miller, C, and Wood, C, *Planning and Pollution* (1983) Clarendon Press.

Moore, V, *A Practical Approach to Planning Law* (1995) Blackstone.

Morgan, P, and Nott, S, *Development Control: Law Policy & Practice* (1995) Butterworths.

Purdue, M, *Planning Appeals: A Critique* (1991) Open University Press.

Purdue, M, Young, E, and Rowan Robinson, J, *Planning Law and Procedure* (1989) Butterworth.

JOURNALS

Alder, J, 'Environmental Impact Assessment' [1993] JEL 203.

Blowers, A, 'Planning a Sustainable Future' (1991) 60 Town & Country Planning 174.

Bruton, M, and Nicholson, D, 'A future for development plans?' [1987] JPL 687.

Carnwath, R, 'The Planning Lawyer and the Environment' [1991] 3 Journal of Environmental Law 57.

Cocks, R, 'Unreasonable Behaviour' (1988) 138 NLJ 730.

Healey, R, 'The Role of Development Plans in the British Planning System: An Empirical Assessment' (1986) 8 Urban Law and Policy 1.

Herbert-Young, 'Reflections on Section 54A' [1995] JPL 292.

Hinds, W, 'Third Party Objections to Planning Applications: An Expectation of Fairness' [1988] JPL 742.

Hough, 'Standing in Planning Appeals' [1992] JPL 319.

Lichfield, N, 'From Planning Gain to Community Benefit' [1989] JPL 68.

Millichip, D, 'Sustainability: A long established Concern of Planning' [1993] JPL 1111.

O'Keefe, J, 'Planning Law — Section 54A' [1993] 5 ELM 117.

Purdue, M, 'The Impact of s 54A' [1994] JPL 399.

Tromans, S, and Clarkson, M, 'The Environmental Protection Act 1990: Its relevance to planning controls' [1991] JPL 507.

Walton, W, Ross-Robertson, A, and Rowan-Robinson, J, 'The Precautionary Principle and the UK Planning System' [1995] 7 ELM 35.

REPORTS

'Environmental Assessment: A Guide to the Procedures' (1989) DOE.

'An Examination of the Effects of the Use Classes Order 1987 and the General Development Order 1988' (1991) HMSO.

'Costs Awards at Planning Appeals' (1990) National Housing and Town Planning Council.

'Monitoring Environmental Assessment and Planning' (1991) HMSO.

'Simplified Planning Zones: Progress and Procedures' (1991) HMSO.

'Evaluating the Effectiveness of Land Use Planning' (1992) HMSO.

'The Use of Planning Agreements' (1992) HMSO.

'Development Plans: A good practice guide' (1992) HMSO.

'Environmental Appraisal of Development Plans' (1993) HMSO.

'Gains from Planning' (1993) Rowntree Foundation.

'Evaluation of Environmental Information for Planning Projects' (1994) HMSO.

'Community Involvement in Planning and Development Processes' (1994) HMSO.

'The Efficiency & Effectiveness of Land Plan Inquiries' (1994) HMSO.

'Attitudes to Town & Country Planning' (1995) HMSO.

'British Government Panel on Sustainable Development First Report' (1995) HMSO.

Chapter 6

The use of land in rural areas and powers to deal with derelict land

'Ill fares the land, to hastening ills a prey
where wealth accumulates and men decay'
(Goldsmith, 'The Deserted Village')

Thinking of agriculture as 'natural' land use is far from correct. Patterns of non-urban land use have changed dramatically, often controversially (sometimes with the consequences of violence and misery) over the centuries, and still change. Agriculture is certainly now an industry. Its use of land puts pressure on the natural environment and calls in question the future of traditional landscape patterns with habitats for flora and fauna. That such use of land must be controlled and managed so that we produce food truly needed at prices realistically affordable, consistent with the protection of the natural environment is increasingly a major issue for central and local authorities — with sharp divisions of opinion in the debate. Calls from environmentalists and conservationists to protect the rural environment *can* represent pressure from small numbers of highly articulate persons whose views, if implemented, might prejudice the long term well being of others by opposing change and ignoring cases that can be made for changes in rural development patterns.

Pye-Smith and Rose in *Crisis and Conservation: Conflict in the British Countryside* point to: agriculture's virtual exemption from planning control, and resistance by agricultural interests to its introduction; the subsidisation of agriculture by the British government and the EU; the influence of substantial landowners in Parliament; the impact of technological farming and the disappearance of hedgerows; increasing impact of chemicals on natural cycles of flora and fauna; bringing into agricultural use of marginal lands — wetlands and moors for example — and blanket afforestation with exotic species of overseas trees as causes for concern. To these may be added: demands for land in rural areas for expensive residential development; need to use rural areas for amenity and recreation, and concern over the vulnerability of sites supporting rare flora and fauna. Debate goes on against a background of little consensus on, and increasing politicisation of, the issues involved: the debate over the countryside is not just about urban versus rural conflicts but includes debates *between* rural interests.

The skeins in the tangled web of argument are: growing demand for preservation of rural landscapes for amenity and access; the realisation, dating from the second world war, that 'home grown' food and timber are of major

217

importance to the life of the nation; the desire to contain urban development within greenbelt boundaries; beliefs that farmers should be the prime custodians of the countryside and its traditional appearance and ways of employment — a belief increasingly untenable as mechanised 'agribusiness' has superseded agriculture with consequent loss of landscapes and employment; transfers of population between town and country as agricultural workers have left the land to be replaced by middle class town dwellers seeking 'country lifestyles' or second homes; the emphasis on voluntarism (ie reliance on co-operation by farmers and landowners in countryside conservation, very often aided by grant aid) evinced by central government and bodies such as the Countryside Commission, and opposed by many voluntary and campaigning bodies, and the realisation that it is impossible to separate ownership of land from its control. This last point needs elaboration. The vast majority of land in the UK is privately owned, most of it by a comparatively small body of persons and institutions — for the detail see chapter 3 of Marion Shoard's *This Land is our Land*. As the law currently stands though the *legal* and *beneficial* ownership of land can be separated, this applies only between individuals and there is no *general* concept that land should be held in trust for all, ie that the ownership of land carries with it *obligations* to allow others access to and over it, and to keep it in good heart and more than just cosmetically attractive so that it can provide sustenance and support — not just for humans — for generations to come. This has forced governments largely to rely on the voluntarist approach outlined above; which is not to say that change cannot be perceived. Following Cm 1200 the government undertook to integrate environmental issues more fully into the economics of the countryside, and to pursue particular policies to this end (see further below).

A THE EU DIMENSION

What is also clear is the close connection between UK and EU food and agricultural subsidy policies and the current changes in the face of Britain's countryside. Subsidies take away market forces and the controls inherent in them, and at the same time cost the taxpayer dear. It is not possible in this work to go into the full complexities of the EU's Common Agricultural Policy (CAP). Suffice it to say that the Treaty of Rome enshrined principles of *increased* agricultural productivity, technical progress, optimum utilisation of all factors of production, increased agricultural earnings, stable markets, certainty of supply and reasonable consumer prices. These were further supported by community wide marketing arrangements for particular products. Great use has been made of regulations in this context, with particular emphasis being laid on the fixing of various prices for products. CAP was undoubtedly a victim of its own success. Living standards amongst farmers did increase, but so did food costs: production increased, but so did accumulation of unwanted surpluses.

CAP 'capped'

In May 1992 CAP was substantially reformed and the £23bn pa paid to farmers which led to food prices being artificially high *and* the creation of food 'mountains and lakes' was redistributed with, for example, farmers receiving a 29% cut in grain prices, while at the same time having to take 15% of cereal land out of production — for which, however, compensation is payable to relieve what could otherwise have been a jolting sudden drop in farm incomes. Grants of up to £88 per acre were agreed for British farmers taking 15% of their land out of production. By 1993 some £800m was being set aside — to rise to £1,000m in 1994 — to pay farmers to 'set aside' land by leaving it fallow. Arable farmers were paid £104 per acre to leave land uncropped. These schemes were introduced under EU Regulations 1765/92 and 2293/93. Criticism of the scheme was not, however, long delayed. Many argued the programme was primarily a food production reduction scheme, not one of positive countryside conservation whereunder farmland surplus to require-ments could be taken out of production on a long term basis and positively managed to encourage wildlife and species diversification. Under the EU scheme farmers had to rotate the 15% of the land set aside so that a different area each year was taken out of production and left to lie fallow, the object here being to prevent farmers 'mothballing' the least productive land on a long term basis. The requirement to leave land fallow also forced farmers to leave their set aside land in a semi-derelict condition and they were not allowed even to graze it because of fears that they might substitute meat production for grain. It was further pointed out that the level of compensation paid under 'set aside' was 20 times as much as farmers would be paid for adhering to conservation practices in areas of land designated as Environmentally Sensitive Areas (see below): rotational neglect brought in more money than positive conservation.

Set aside reformed

Note initially SIs 1994/1291, 1292 and 1293 (as amended by SI 1995/2871 and 2891) under which, in pursuance of regulation 2078/92, payments may be made in respect of persons who undertake in relation to particular pieces of land not to use them for 20 years for agricultural purposes and instead to pursue other land uses such as the creation of salt marshes, management of reed beds, the protection or improvement of wildlife habitats, etc. Further note the Organic Farming (Aid) Regulations SI 1994/1712 which enable ministers to make payments, in respect of up to 300 ha per holding, to applicants who satisfy certain organic farming standards (the 'UKROFS' standards).

In June 1995 the set aside rules were further changed so that, as from 1996, farmers will be able to count as land set aside areas they include within forestry schemes. The £136 per acre set aside grant in relation to such land is replaced by a £100 per acre payment plus an initial grant of £450 per acre to cover planting costs. This major improvement in set aside which can encourage long term conservation of species may, however, still be com-promised if insensitive planting of inappropriate trees takes place.

However, the consequences of taking land out of use for food production should not be forgotten. The EU is not insulated from the world's agricultural economy, and in November 1995 the 'food mountain' produced under CAP had virtually disappeared as global demand for grain soared in consequence of drought reduced harvets. EU provision was accordingly made for exports of food to be taxed and for set aside land to be reduced.

The EU has also taken action on pesticides. Beginning with Directive 76/895[1] and further by 86/362,[2] the EU has acted, *principally to protect consumers*, to set limits on food pesticide residues. Maximum limits for such residues are laid down for specified fruits and vegetables, though these limits are not subject to mandatory enforcement. Particular limits also apply to cereals, meat and meat products, eggs and dairy products. These limits were to be in force by 1988 but are subject to a derogation for member states which apply residue monitoring systems which in combination with other measures effectively achieve the limits laid down in 86/363, *and* which assess their population's total dietary exposure to pesticide residues. Further pesticide action was taken in Directive 79/117[3] and 78/631[4] which prohibit the marketing and use of specified products containing specified substances, eg DDT, aldrin, dieldrin, chlordane, hexachlorabenzene, nitrofen — the list has grown over the years — requiring those pesticides that are sold to be classified and appropriately labelled and packaged. (See further below on the Food and Environment Protection Act 1985.)

In order to protect wildlife by protecting its natural habitats Directive 79/409[5] sought to conserve wild birds by, inter alia, protecting their habitats by the creation of 'specially protected areas' (SPAs), which member states have been requested to designate and notify to the Commission which is to make an inventory of them; UK implementation is achieved under the National Parks and Access to the Countryside Act 1949, the Countryside Act 1968 and the Wildlife and Countryside Act 1981, see further below. Once an SPA is established by a member state that state has no general power to alter or reduce its area, and may only do so in exceptional cases where general public interest requires flood prevention or coastal protection and this justifies disturbance of the interests of wildlife, though the degree of disturbance must not exceed the minimum necessary to achieve the general public interest. Economic or recreational interests only will not justify disturbance of a designated SPA.[6]

Directive 92/43, aiming to promote biodiversity by establishing a 'favourable conservation status' for types of habitats and species possessing an EU 'interest', extends the techniques established under 79/409 to such habitats and species. As nature conservation is generally outside the scope of this book interested readers are referred to Nigel Haigh's treatment of the issue in his *Manual of Environmental Policy: the EC and Britain* at section 9.9. The relevant UK implementing measures are to be found in SI 1994/2716, and the effect of these on grants of planning permission will be considered below. The first UK list of what are to be known as 'Special Areas of Conservation' was sent to the Commission in 1995.

Though international law, in the form of treaties, has concerned itself with the protection of flora and fauna, for over a hundred years, it was not until the

---

1 Amended by 80/428, 82/528, 88/298, 90/642, 93/58, 94/30.
2 Amended by 90/654, 93/57 and 94/29.
3 Amended by 83/131, 85/298, 86/214, 86/235, 87/181, 87/477, 89/365, 90/335, 90/533, 91/188.
4 Amended by 79/831, 81/187, 84/291 and 92/32.
5 Amended by 81/854, 85/411, 86/122, 91/244 and 94/24.
6 *EC Commission v Germany* [1991] 3 LMELR 97.

Ramsar Convention of 1971 (protocol added 1982) that it turned specifically to the protection of habitats, more particularly wetlands of international importance as water fowl habitats. Note also the Berne Convention of 1979 on the conservation of European wildlife and natural habitats.

The UK has been a contracting party to the Ramsar Convention since 1976, and so falls within the general treaty obligation to promote conservation of relevant habitats, particularly by establishing nature reserves. There are further obligations to adapt planning policies to further the conservation of wetlands designated and listed under the treaty provisions, with each contracting state listing at least one such site. Following designation and listing sites may only be reduced on the basis of 'urgent national interests': compare and contrast the EU and ECJ approach under Directive 79/409. 'Wetlands' include marshes, fens, peatlands, and water, whether these are natural or human created, permanent or temporary, while water may be static or flowing, brackish or salt, and marine water up to six metres deep may be included. Adjacent land such as banks and islands may also be included.

Implementation in the UK of the Convention is largely by means of designating sites as of Special Scientific Interest under the Wildlife and Countryside Act 1981.

Biodiversity

The UK is a signatory of the Convention on Biological Diversity, Rio, 1992. Again the topic of nature conservation under international law is largely outside this work's coverage: interested readers are referred to Cm 2428 'Biodiversity: the UK Action Plan'. Rather more relevant is the Statement of Forest Principles also adopted at Rio, though not a legally binding Convention. The UK is, nevertheless, committed to the forest principles and has set out its policy response in Cm 2429, 'Sustainable Forestry: the UK Programme'. This will be referred to as appropriate below.

B AGRICULTURE AND PLANNING LAW

Under the Town and Country Planning Act 1990, s 55(2)(e), use of any land for the purposes of agriculture or forestry, including afforestation, and use for any of those purposes of any building occupied together with land so used does not involve an act of development. Planning permission is not required for bringing any land or building into agricultural use, nor for changing from one agricultural use to another. The provision allows a change of use *from* non-agricultural *to* agricultural use.[7] Section 336(1) of the 1990 Act defines agriculture as including horticulture, fruit and seed growing, dairy farming, livestock breeding and keeping, including fur and wool farming, market gardening, and the use of woodlands ancillary to the farming of land. Within this definition fall allotments,[8] and using land for grazing, as opposed to the

7 *McKellan v Minister of Housing and Local Government* (1966) 198 Estates Gazette 683.
8 *Crowborough Parish Council v Secretary of State for the Environment and Wealdon District Council* [1981] JPL 281.

breeding for non-farming purposes, of horses.[9] Whether land is being used for the purposes of agriculture is a question of fact for the local planning authority whose decision can be challenged if taken on the basis of insufficient evidence.[10]

Though some agricultural and forestry ancillary operations *may* require planning permission, considerable permitted development rights are given under the Town and Country Planning (General Permitted Development) Order SI 1995/418. Thus Part 6 Class A permits the carrying out on units of five hectares or more of works to erect, extend or alter a building, or to carry out excavation or engineering operations reasonably necessary for agricultural purposes within the unit. This wide power is, however, subject to conditions and limitations. Thus it does not apply to land which is a separate parcel of land, though part of the unit, less than one hectare in area, nor does it permit erection, etc, of dwellings. It does not extend to permit non-agricultural buildings and is subject to size, and location, limits. Nor does it allow the erection, etc, of a building, etc, to be used for accommodating livestock, or to store slurry or sewage, where the building, etc, would be within 400 m of the curtilage of a 'protected building' ie a permanent building occupied by people. Note also that the foregoing rights may be restricted in certain ways in relation to the erection or extension or alteration of buildings or the laying out of private ways, in that prior notification of the proposal must be given to the local planning authority.

The developer must apply to the planning authority for a determination whether their approval is needed as to siting, design and external appearance. A written description of the development and proposed materials must be submitted, and a plan. Development consisting of a 'significant' extension or alteration may only be carried out *once* by virtue of Class A. In this context a 'significant extension' is one where the original cubic content of the building would be exceeded by more than 10%. Following notification, the proposal may not proceed until a written statement is received from the authority that prior approval is not required, *or*, where notification is given within 28 days of receipt of the application that approval is required, following such approval — before which the applicant must give public site notice publicity to the proposal for not less than 21 days; where no notification is given within 28 days of receipt the proposal may proceed. Thereafter the development should, where prior approval is required, take place in accordance with the approval, otherwise in accordance with submitted details. Note that the limitations outlined above apply to agricultural permitted rights *everywhere*.

Further permitted agricultural development rights include the winning and working on land held or occupied with land used for the purposes of agriculture of any minerals reasonably necessary for agricultural purposes within the unit of which it forms part. This is subject, inter alia, to use and movement restrictions.

On units of *less* than five hectares but more than 0.4 hectares, permitted development rights extend to extending or altering agricultural buildings,

9 *Belmont Farm Ltd v Minister of Housing and Local Government* (1962) 13 P & CR 417; and *South Oxfordshire District Council v Secretary of State for the Environment* [1981] 1 All ER 954, [1981] 1 WLR 1092.
10 *R v Sevenoaks District Council, ex p Palley* [1995] JPL 915.

installing/replacing plant/machinery, providing or replacing sewers and mains, etc, providing/rearranging private ways, providing/rearranging hard surfaces, waste deposits, carrying out certain fish farming activities such as repairing ponds, provided the development is reasonably necessary for agricultural purposes. Once again there are restrictions on such development similar to those above.

The permitted development (PD) rights given to agriculture are extensive, and can extend to placing structures *on* land, no matter that they are inappropriate, providing they are for agricultural use or uses ancillary thereto, for example old caravans providing shelter during rain for agricultural workers.[11] However, to enjoy the PD rights the land itself must not only be agricultural, it must be comprised in an agricultural unit, ie agricultural land occupied as a unit for agricultural purposes. Thus land that has been appropriated for leisure is no longer 'agricultural',[12] while a grazing site in the middle of playing fields would also not qualify as the 'unit' is not agricultural.[13]

Forestry has similar PD rights including erecting, etc, buildings other than dwellings and the formation of ways for the purposes of forestry and afforestation.

Planning control, however, continues to have a limited role with regard to agriculture. Concern over generally weak controls was expressed in the House of Lords Select Committee on the European Communities 20th Report on 'Agriculture and the Environment', Session 1983–84. This criticised CAP over inflated prices of products, consequent overproduction of which was a threat to wildlife habitats and marginal land. Also noted was criticism that the Department of the Environment was ineffective in its environmental responsibilities in rural areas, and was too ready to follow the lead of the Ministry of Agriculture. The overlap of functions and responsibilities between ministries has led to confusion and uncertainty in the application and conception of policies. (See also HL Select Committee on Science and Technology 4th Report on 'Agricultural and Environmental Research', Session 1983–84 (272).) In response to public disquiet, and the views of the Royal Commission on Environmental Pollution, an 'Environmental Unit' was set up within the Ministry of Agriculture. Indeed it is possible, as Michael Winter has pointed out in 'Agriculture and Environment: The Integration of Policy?' (in Churchill, Warren and Gibson, *Law, Policy and the Environment*) to detect some 'greening' of the Ministry of Agriculture (MAFF) from 1984 onwards, and to see in the introduction of Environmentally Sensitive Areas (ESAs) from 1987 onwards some coming together of notions of landscape protection and nature conservation. These had hitherto been the largely separate provinces of the DoE and MAFF. ESAs will be returned to in detail subsequently.

Wider issues of countryside planning and policy

In 1989 the Countryside Commission put forward its principles to guide planning in *Planning for a Greener Countryside*, namely that: development

11 *Wealden District Council v Secretary of State for the Environment* [1988] JPL 268.
12 *Pittman v Secretary of State for the Environment* [1988] JPL 391.
13 Note also *Salvatore Cumbo v Secretary of State for the Environment* [1992] JPL 366; *Clarke v Secretary of State for the Environment* [1993] JPL 32; and *Brill v Secretary of State for the Environment* [1993] JPL 253.

control should be sensitive to local needs within the countryside while seeking to conserve natural beauty and landscape diversity; 'new countryside' should be created by regeneration of degraded land; greenbelts should serve not just as means of urban containment but as enhancers of beauty and providers of recreational opportunity (see further below); where development has to take place in the countryside environmental benefits should be sought as part of the development; new housing should be so designed as to add positively to the countryside; major development in rural areas should be avoided wherever possible and should be subject to very strict control; countryside agencies should co-operate more, and countryside management should cohere with planning policies.

Consider also Planning Policy Guidance Notes nos 7 and 9, 'The Countryside and the Rural Economy and Nature Conservation'.

It is not, however, easy to divorce planning issues from wider matters of overall countryside policy. Hence planning matters were inevitably mixed in with other issues in the government's 1995 White Paper: 'Rural England: a Nation Committed to a Living Countryside' Cm 3016. The proposals included there were designed to encourage voluntary effort to improve and sustain country living, and included a wide range of proposed economic and regulatory measures.

The principal objectives of countryside policy will be: to meet the needs and aspirations of those who live *and* work in rural areas, improving their access to services and giving their communities a greater involvement in issues affecting them; to assist rural businesses to be more competitive; to reverse wildlife decline and maintain the diversity of rural landscapes and the enhancement of the environment by new buildings; to increase opportunities for countryside enjoyment for all, *especially close to where they live*.

To this end, and with particular relevance to land use planning, guidance will be given on how authorities may promote the diversification of economic activity in rural areas. PPG 7 is also proposed for revision so that authorities are enabled to discriminate in favour of the re-use of rural buildings for business as opposed to residential uses. Similarly a Rural Business Use Class may be introduced under the Use Classes Order to encourage business diversification without uncontrolled expansion. PPG 1 is further proposed for revision to allow authorities even more to favour regionally and locally based designs for new buildings in their areas.

More specifically it is proposed that landowners will be encouraged to bring forward sites in villages with less than 3,000 inhabitants where affordable housing can be built by housing associations, and with any entitlement on the part of tenants to purchase those dwellings excluded, while enhanced grant aid to housing associations to fund small housing schemes in villages is also proposed. In addition, the government has proposed the establishment of a steering group to advise on the development of environmental land management schemes. Such schemes include the Countryside Stewardship Scheme, the Farm and Conservation Grants Scheme, the Habitat Scheme, Countryside Access Schemes and the Moorland Scheme. The intention is to ensure that schemes complement each other effectively with national and regional fora for regular consultation on relevant matters. A doubling of woodland cover in England over the next 50 years is also proposed.

Rural policy is to be set within the context of general sustainable development policy and hence there is also an emphasis placed on keeping facilities, such as general stores and post offices, local, and the promotion of community (as opposed to private) transport. It is furthermore intended to clarify the weight to be attached to the agricultural importance of land in grade 3a, for example where there is little land in lower grades, so that the environmental consequences of development decisions can be better appreciated. Further discussion will also take place on general housing developments which take green field sites. In addition, it is policy that renewable energy projects should be encouraged in rural areas, eg wind generated electricity and energy generated from chicken litter.

These policies will be generally promoted within the context of existing legislation and grant schemes. It is specifically declared that further classes of statutory designation of land will not be introduced. The matter of current constraints and policies on development in rural areas will be returned to below, and more particularly in the context of green belt policy.

C AGRICULTURE AND COUNTRYSIDE LEGISLATION

Few environmental controls over agriculture have had, historically, the force of law. The voluntary approach, supplemented in some cases by Codes of Practice, has been favoured by central government and farmers. Though there is some evidence of a change of policy by central government in relation to those issues, such legislation as there is tends largely to reflect the voluntary approach.

The Countryside Act 1968, s 11, imposes a vague duty on ministers, government departments and public bodies to have regard, in the exercise of their functions relating to land under statute, to the desirability of conserving the natural beauty and amenity of the countryside. Section 37 of the 1968 Act, as amended in 1981, imposes a duty on ministers, the Nature Conservancy Councils for England, Scotland and Wales and the Countryside Commission in the exercise of their functions under the 1968 Act, the Wildlife and Countryside Act 1981 and the National Parks and Access to the Countryside Act 1949 to have due regard to the needs of agriculture and forestry and the economic and social interests of rural areas. More particularly s 41 of the 1981 Act imposes an obligation on ministers to give advice to farmers on the conservation and enhancement of the natural beauty of the countryside, and on diversifying into other enterprises of benefit to the rural economy, and to other bodies concerned with such diversification. However, the former Nature Conservancy Council (NCC) admitted in *Nature Conservation in Great Britain* that the law has never been generally effective in giving adequate support to nature conservation. This is true of the principal legislation, the Wildlife and Countryside Act 1981, an Act most severely criticised by commentators, and one, moreover, not backed by sufficient resources to ensure that even its limited provisions can be effective.

A troubled Act

Part II of the Act is concerned with the conservation of nature and protection of the countryside. Section 28 lays down provisions relating to the creation of sites of special scientific interest (SSSIs). Sites were at one time notified to local planning authorities, and these remained operative on an interim basis, but must now also be notified to owners and occupiers of relevant land, see s 28(1) of the 1981 Act. (Hereafter in relation to the 1981 Act owners and occupiers will be referred to as 'landholders'.) Notification must specify the location of the site, the nature of its special interest and any operations likely to damage that. Since 1981 the former NCC (now the successor councils for England, Scotland and the Countryside Council for Wales), where of the opinion that land is of special interest by reason of any flora, fauna, or geological or physiographical features, must notify that to the local planning authority, landholders and the Secretary of State. Thus a duty to notify arises once there is an opinion the site has 'special interest', thereafter there is a *discretion* to *confirm*. It appears a notification may be withdrawn.

The legal concept of the SSSI embraces land otherwise classified as a National Nature Reserve (NNR) or subject to Nature Conservation Review (NCR) or Geological Conservation Review (GCR) or as a Special Protection Area (SPA) or as a Special Area of Conservation (SAC).

Section 28, which provides the notification procedure for SSSIs, was amended by the Wildlife and Countryside (Amendment) Act 1985 to ensure that sites would be more speedily protected against the unscrupulous who proceeded, under the previous law, with operations before the law applied to the land in question. Section 28(2) provides that the preliminary notice served by a conservancy council (in Wales the Countryside Council) under s 28(1) must specify a period of not less than three months from the date of notice within which representations about the proposal may be made, and places the council under an obligation to consider representations received. This notice must be given to the affected bodies and persons, and that given to land-holders must specify the flora, fauna, geological or physiographical features constituting 'special interest' and any operations appearing to the council to be likely to be damaging thereto. Section 28(4A) further provides that where the preliminary notice has been given the council may, within a period of nine months, which commences to run on the date notification was served *on the Secretary of State* (see above) *either* give notice of withdrawing the notification or confirming it, with or without minor modifications.

Challenges to notification

A notification may be challenged by way of judicial review, and it is reasonable for English Nature to confirm a notification so long as the special interest initially existed, unless it will soon be unavoidably eliminated.[14]

Following notification *and while it remains in force* landholders must not, without reasonable excuse on pain of committing an offence, carry out the specified operations unless, after service of the notification, written notice of proposals to carry out an operation, specifying its nature and the affected land, has been given to the relevant council by a landholder, *and one* of the following conditions is fulfilled: the operation is carried out in accordance with the

---

14 *R v Nature Conservancy Council, ex p London Brick Property Ltd* [1995] 7 ELM 95, [1996] JPL 227; see also *R v Nature Conservancy Council, ex p Bolton MBC* [1996] JPL 203.

council's written consent; it is carried out in accordance with a management agreement with the council under the National Parks and Access to the Countryside Act 1949, s 16, or the Countryside Act 1968, s 15; or that four months have expired from the giving of notice to the council. The parties may agree to waive this 'four month' rule, however. It is a 'reasonable excuse' to carry out an operation in an emergency, or where authorised by a grant of planning permission. In such circumstances the local planning authority will have consulted the relevant council before granting permission, see Art 10(1)(u) of The Town and Country Planning (General Development Procedure) Order SI 1995/419. A development potentially damaging to a SSSI may be softened in impact by the imposition of suitable conditions in a grant of planning permission. The conservancy councils welcome the opportunity to discuss development proposals before planning applications are made.

Note also SSSI designation powers under s 5 of the Norfolk and Suffolk Broads Act 1988, and s 4 of the Water Industry Act 1991.

Once a water or sewerage undertaker has received such notification from the appropriate council, the undertaker must consult with them before carrying out *any* works, etc, appearing to the undertaker to be likely to destroy or damage flora, or fauna, etc, though this does not apply in emergency situations where the duty is merely to inform. Note also that National Parks Authorities and The Broads Authority may also notify undertakers of land in their areas which is of particular importance for the purposes of undertakers' general environmental duties under s 3 of the 1991 Act and which may be affected by schemes or operations etc, of undertakers, and thereafter a similar consultative obligation arises. Similar powers exist in relation to land likely to be affected by the schemes and operations of the Environment Agency, again raising consultative obligations on the part of that body, see section 8 of the Environment Act 1995. The 'Code of Practice on Conservation, Access and Recreation' (SI 1989/1152) issued ministerially in 1989 (see now s 18 of the Water Resources Act 1991) goes further than the legislation in suggesting that every operation affecting a relevant site should be notified to the appropriate council.

The former NCC issued guiding criteria for the selection of SSSIs in *Selection of Sites of Special Scientific Interest*. The principal object is scientific: the aim is to maintain wild animal and plant diversity as opposed to the promotion of amenity or recreation. Likewise there is a desire to ensure a reasonably even geographical distribution of sites of biological interest. Geological sites clearly can only be designated where they lie, and the object here is therefore to maintain sites for earth science education and research purposes.

SSSIs should be the best examples of wildlife habitats, geological features and land forms occurring in the nation, and the designation powers can extend to rivers. 27 rivers were identified by 1995 as 'the best examples' of their types and English Nature has proposed their designation as SSSIs by 1998. This has caused concern, however, to riparian owners and other affected landholders lest there should be unnecessary regulation, and conflict, as a result of both English Nature and the Agency having powers in relation to a designated river. A protocol was agreed between English Nature and the Agency's predecessor the former NRA detailing their respective roles, and ensuring that particular activities are not subject to dual control. Concern remains amongst landholders, however, that SSSI designations may stretch out too far beyond river banks, and there is opposition to any form of automatic designation of land out to a particular width from banks.

Following notification of a site the appropriate council may receive notice from a landholder of a potentially damaging operation. The council may consent, or may indicate a desire to negotiate to modify the proposal, or they may offer a management agreement (see further below). In some cases, however, special procedures apply.

On receiving notice from a landholder of a potentially damaging proposal appropriate council's responses are set out in the 'Code of Guidance on Sites of Special Scientific Interest', prepared under s 33 of the 1981 Act by relevant ministers, and approved by Parliament. An initial response will be made within one month. This may give consent. It may explain the council's position, indicating a desire to modify the proposal or offering a management agreement (see below).

The situation of a landholder affected by a SSSI who wishes to carry out capital grant aided works

Where the intention is to seek a 'farm capital grant' under the Agriculture Act 1970, s 29, proposed operations may proceed and grant be claimed where the appropriate council gives written consent. Where the council consider the operation would damage the interest of the site, the applicant and the Agricultural and Advisory Service (ADAS) will be informed. Where it is found the proposal is, in principle, eligible for grant aid, ADAS will offer advice in reaching a solution of the issues. If agreement is reached the council will consent to the modified operation. Where no agreement is reached the council will give the Ministry of Agriculture a detailed statement of the case for conservation. ADAS will give the parties an appraisal of the agricultural proposals. Within three months of the applicant's original notice the council will advise the applicant and the Ministry whether it wishes to object to the proposal on the grounds set out in its detailed statement. At this stage either party may seek a management agreement (see below). Where objection is pressed the Minister of Agriculture, in consultation with the Secretary of State for the Environment, will, under s 32 of the 1981 Act, determine the issue and inform the parties; where grant aid is refused in consequence, the council *must* offer, under s 32(2), to enter into a management agreement which will impose restrictions on the applicant's activities, but also provide for compensation. It is open to the appropriate council to buy or lease land subject to notified potentially damaging operations. Compulsory purchase powers exist where the council is unable to conclude a satisfactory management agreement that the land will be managed as a nature reserve, *and* it is expedient *in the national interest* that it be so managed. Authorisation by the Secretary of State is required, see the National Parks and Access to the Countryside Act 1949, ss 17 and 103. Where grant aid is not refused it remains open to the council to offer a management agreement. Under s 32(1)(a) of the 1981 Act where an application for a farm capital grant is made, in respect of land notified as a SSSI, or under s 29(3) of the 1981 Act (see below), the Minister must generally exercise functions so as to further nature conservation.

'Farm capital grant' in this context means a grant under s 29 of the Agriculture Act 1970 or a grant made under regulations made under s 2(2) of the European Communities Act 1972.

The consequences of designation as a SSSI

Under s 28(7) of the 1981 Act it is an offence for the *landholder* to carry out a specified potentially damaging operation (PDO) without complying with the requirements of the Act. This offence can be committed by landholders where they cause or permit a third party to carry out the operation. However, the person proceeded against must be the occupier of the affected land, it is not enough to be the perpetrator of the act and the owner/occupier of *other* land within the same SSSI not affected by the act in question. Furthermore to be an occupier it seems a person should have an interest in land amounting at least to a tenancy or long term licence, as opposed to some merely transitory relationship with the land, such as a temporary permission to be present. See *Southern Water Authority v NCC*.[15]

SSSIs are registered as local land charges under s 28(10). PDOs are not totally prohibited but are simply 'frozen' for a period of four months under s 28(5) & (6) of the 1981 Act from the time the landholder gives notice of intention to carry out the PDO in question, unless in the meantime the relevant conservancy council gives consent or the PDO is carried out in accordance with a management agreement on the land. However, to proceed with the PDO within the four months is a criminal offence unless 'reasonable excuse' exists. Planning permission can constitute such a excuse, as can acting in an emergency.

Nature Conservation Orders

Section 29 of the 1981 Act enables the Secretary of State for the Environment to give special protection by order to land after consultation with the appropriate council. The protection, known as a Nature Conservation Order, will extend to land of particular sensitivity, which is land (a) of special interest by reason of its flora, fauna, geological or physiographical features and (b) needing protection to secure the survival in Great Britain of any kind of animal or plant or to comply with international obligations, *or* is (a) of special interest for the aforementioned reasons and (b) is of national importance and needing protection to conserve its flora, fauna, etc. Some such sites may become national nature reserves (see below). Protection applies immediately once the Secretary of State makes his order. This should be contrasted with procedure for a SSSI. Section 29 sites have been dubbed 'Super SSSIs,' and are not common. They have also been the subject of litigation. In *Sweet v Secretary of State for the Environment*[16] it was argued that *only* land of national importance by virtue of its flora or fauna, etc, could be comprised in a s 29 order, whereas land had been included in this case on the basis that it was desirable it should be managed *together* with land that was of national importance. In the High Court it was held that not every part of an area of

---

15 [1992] 1 WLR 775.
16 [1989] 2 PLR 14, [1989] JPL 927.

land subject to s 29 has to possess special features. Land closely inter-connected with the 'special' land in a linked environment may have to be included in order to protect the core area.

Procedure for making the order is laid down in Sch 11 to the 1981 Act. Notice of the order is published in the *London Gazette* and local newspapers and affected landholders are served with notice of the order. The notices set out the order or describe its effect, state its date of coming into effect, give the name of a place where the order can be inspected, and state the time, minimum period 28 days, and the method, for making representations about or objections to the order. Where an order is opposed the Secretary of State must cause a local inquiry to be held or otherwise arrange for objections to be heard. The report of the inquiry or hearing must be considered and thereafter the Secretary of State's decision on whether to amend, revoke or keep the order in force will be notified. A 'person aggrieved' may in the High Court, on a point of law, challenge an order that has taken effect, and on which the Secretary of State has given his final decision, within six weeks of the Secretary of State's notice of his decision; otherwise the validity of orders may not be challenged in legal proceedings.

Once the order is made *no* person (whether or not the landholder) may carry out any operation on the land which appears to the Secretary of State to be likely to destroy or damage the relevant flora or fauna, etc, and which has been specified in the order, unless, the operation is one carried out by a landholder *and*, the appropriate council has been given written notice of operation *and either*, they have given written consent, *or* the operation is carried out in accordance with a management agreement (see below), *or* three months have elapsed since the landholder's notice to the council, though this period can be extended, see s 29(6), (7). It is an offence to contravene these requirements without reasonable excuse. It is a reasonable excuse to proceed under a grant of planning permission, or in an emergency. Where land subject to a Nature Conservation Order is also a SSSI, as will generally be the case, powers with regard to proposed operations, grant objections, offers to purchase or lease land, etc, will apply. In particular, under s 29(6) of the 1981 Act, where, before the expiry of three months from the landholder's notice of a proposal to carry out a potentially damaging operation, the council offer, following consultation, to enter an agreement to acquire the landholder's interest, or a management agreement, providing for payments to be made to the landholder during the initial period of three months, *and* where that agreement is not concluded by the end of that initial period, the time during which prohibited operations may not be carried out is extended to up to 12 months. Where a council is satisfied it cannot conclude a reasonable management agreement, and uses its compulsory purchase powers, the period during which prohibited operations may not take place is extended until the council takes possession of the land, see s 29(7). In practice the councils do not resort to compulsory purchase.

In *Ward v Secretary of State for the Environment*[17] the question arose whether it was legitimate to make a s 29 order on land including a bridleway when that order prohibited engineering works and damage to vegetation while there was

17 [1995] 7 ELM 153.

a contemporaneous obligation under s 41 of the Highways Act 1980 to maintain the bridleway — an activity almost certainly involving such damage. It was considered it was legitimate to make the order: if work had to be carried out the 1980 Act would supply the necessary 'reasonable excuse'.

Compensation may be payable under s 30 where an order is made under s 29. In particular where it is decided under Sch 11 that an order should stay in effect, landholders may claim compensation from the council for depreciation in the value of their interests, provided they are comprised in an agricultural unit, where the depreciation is attributable to the order being made. Where the period during which proposed operations may not be carried out is extended under s 29(6) or (7) as described above, compensation may be claimed by any person having an interest in relevant land in respect of reasonably incurred expenditure rendered abortive by the extension of the prohibition period, or other loss or damage directly attributable to the effects of the extended prohibition.

It is an offence to contravene a s 29 order, see s 29(8). Under s 31 of the 1981 Act there is power for the court to require the taking of restorative action. Failure to comply with such an order is an offence. Default in this connection enables a council to enter the land to take requisite action, and recover reasonable expenses from the person in default.

Note the wide powers of entry granted to the conservancy councils by s 51 of the 1981 Act on land to ascertain whether an order under s 29 should be made in relation to it. Note also that under s 69 where a body corporate commits an offence under the 1981 Act with the consent or connivance, etc of its directors or officers, those individuals may be liable along with the body corporate.

D MANAGEMENT AGREEMENTS, GRANTS AND ENVIRONMENTALLY SENSITIVE AREAS

These agreements may be made under a number of powers.

The National Parks and Access to the Countryside Act 1949, Part III, relates to sites receiving protection as nature reserves, designated under ss 15–22 of the 1949 Act. Those reserves considered to be of national importance may be further designated by the appropriate council as 'National Nature Reserves' under s 35 of the 1981 Act. As previously stated such sites will also be classified as SSSIs. 'National' reserves will normally be owned, leased, managed or controlled directly by a conservancy council. Section 15 of the 1949 Act defines a nature reserve as land (which may include an area of foreshore, *Burnet v Barclay*)[18] managed to provide opportunities under suitable conditions and control for study and research into fauna and flora, their physical conditions and geological and physiographical features of interest in such areas, and/or for preservation of such flora and fauna, etc. Section 16 provides the principal means of providing such reserves by way of agreement with owners, lessees and occupiers of affected land which, in the national interest, should be managed as a nature reserve. Such an agreement may

18 1955 SLT 282, see also *Evans v Godber* [1974] 1 WLR 1317.

impose restrictive and positive management obligations. Agreements are supplemented by compulsory purchase powers under ss 17 and 18 of the Act where a satisfactory management agreement cannot be achieved, or where an agreement made has been breached in such a way as to prevent or impair the satisfactory management of the land as a reserve. The power of the councils to create nature reserves, and further to protect them by way of byelaws, see ss 19 and 20 of the 1949 Act, is supplemented by powers for local authorities, in consultation with conservancy councils, to establish nature reserves in their areas under s 21.

The Countryside Act 1968, s 15, enables the appropriate council to enter into management agreements in respect of land notified as a SSSI. Under s 39 of the 1981 Act management agreements may be made, for the purposes of conserving or enhancing the natural beauty or amenity of any land which is in the countryside and within their areas (or for promotion of enjoyment of such land by the public), between relevant authorities (which includes the Broads Authority in respect of land in the Broads) and persons *having interests in the land.*

Authorities exercising countryside functions, *generally*, are counties within National Parks, and elsewhere counties and districts as 'local planning authorities', while it should be remembered that the *councils* referred to are those for England (known as 'English Nature'), Scotland and the Countryside Council for Wales.

Agreements, which are not reinforced by powers of compulsion, will generally bind the land, and may provide for restrictions on cultivation or other agricultural use of the land, or on the exercise of other rights over the land. An agreement may also impose a positive obligation, and may give the authority power to carry out works in connection with functions under the Acts of 1949 and 1968. Under s 41(3) of the 1981 Act where an application is made for a capital grant under the Agriculture Act 1970, s 29, in respect of land which is in a National Park, including the Broads (see below), or an area specified by ministers, the Minister of Agriculture must, so far as is consistent with the terms of s 29, exercise his functions to further the conservation and enhancement of the beauty and amenity of the countryside and its enjoyment by the public. In such circumstances a 'relevant authority' (see above) may object to the making of a grant on grounds that the activities for which aid is sought will have adverse effects on the natural beauty or amenity of the countryside. Where such objection is made the Minister may not make a grant before considering the objection and consulting the Secretary of State. Where the grant is in consequence refused, the 'relevant authority' *must*, within three months of receiving the Minister's decision, *offer* a management agreement which will impose restrictions on the activities for which aid was sought. Offers need not be accepted.

Section 50 of the 1981 Act lays down the general rules for determining payments to be made by the councils or 'relevant authorities' who offer management agreements. Payments are of such amounts as the council or authority may determine in accordance with guidance given by ministers, see DoE Circular 4/83. Inter alia, guidelines provide for payment either on a lump sum or annual basis where an agreement affects a land *owner*; annual payments only are available to tenants. Lump sum payments should be calculated so as to be equal to the difference between the restricted and unrestricted value of the owner's interest, calculated on the basis of the rules contained in the Land Compensation Act 1961, s 5. Annual payments should reflect net profits foregone because of the agreement. The amount offered under an agreement may be referred, under s 50(3), to an independent arbitrator. The Circular contemplates agreements operating over 20 year periods. Other periods, or indeed perpetuity, are available options to the parties.

In *Thomas v Countryside Commission for Wales*[19] the High Court considered that, despite the less than clear guidance in Circular 4/83, the basis of assessing compensation should be as for ordinary cases of contractual or liability, ie compensation should be paid for all pecuniary less directly and naturally flowing from the making of the designation as a SSSI. On this basis it must be asked: (a) what would the landholder have achieved if allowed to continue previous practices; (b) what has been achieved post designation; (c) in the post designation period has the landholder done anything so unreasonable that the difference between (a) and (b) can no longer be said to follow from the designation? See also *Cameron v Nature Conservancy Council*[20] where in Scotland a not dissimilar conclusion was reached. It may well be that the consequence of these decisions may be to lift compensation levels to such heights as to discourage very considerably the making of management agreements.

The financial consequences of making a management agreement have for many years been the subject of much adverse comment, while the decisions in *Thomas* and *Cameron* serve to push up the level of compensation payable under management agreements. Even so the official view is that no landholder should suffer loss simply because he/she enters into an agreement. The consequence is that the law is only workable if considerable amounts of money are made available for implementation. The number and cost of management agreements has increased along with the number of designated sites. In 1982 there were 2,600+ sites, by 1993 3,707. At that time there were 1,700 management agreements costing some £7m. At the same time evidence has continued to mount that designation of a site as an SSSI is no guarantee by itself that it will continue undisturbed. In the year ending 31 March 1989 the former NCC reported 241 cases of loss or damage to SSSIs, while some 161 cases were reported in the previous 12 months. Some of the damage (to 39 sites) was long term, usually following grants of planning permission, eg for peat cutting, while there were 20 examples of sites being totally destroyed, again usually after a grant of permission — hence the importance of obtaining control by a management agreement. On the other hand the NCC was loath to exercise its powers to the full. It was not until 1990 that it used compulsory purchase powers — and that led to the litigation with Mr Sweet considered above. Further evidence of the weakness of the law is found in *SSSIs: A Health Check* (Wildlife Link, 1991). 40% of SSSIs have suffered some deterioration since the 1981 Act, roughly 5% per annum of sites suffering some damage, from activities as diverse as overgrazing, tree felling, building works or leisure activities, as well as from pollution. It can be argued that management agreements are part of the problem: they do not encourage landowners positively to conserve sites, rather they pay them to *refrain* from otherwise damaging activities.

The villain of the piece?

One frequently voiced criticism is that planning controls can be positively hostile to SSSIs; that permitted development rights are too extensive and that designated sites are vulnerable to grants or planning permission. Recent changes in law and practice, some of them consequent on EU obligations, may go some way to changing this, though in fact grants of planning permission pale into insignificance as causes of loss or damage to SSSIs compared with agricultural activity, insufficient management, recreational use and the operations of statutory undertakers, see 'Protecting and Managing SSSIs in England', National Audit Office, 1994.

PPG 9 (October 1994) now gives guidance on the interaction between planning controls and SSSIs.

The basic principle is that nature conservation is a *relevant consideration* in relation to all planning activities affecting rural and wasted land uses, and in those urban areas possessing important wildlife interest. Relevant plans should identify the various types of nature conservation sites and policy should reflect their relative significance. Furthermore plans should include policies on the wider issues of the conservation of natural beauty and amenity, including policies on encouraging landscape management so as to conserve landscape features important for flora and fauna. Local plans should further state the weight to be given to nature conservation issues in making planning decisions, and where an application is received for development of any type of nature conservation site it should be judged against criteria clearly set out in the local plan, bearing in mind that some sites, because of their type of designation, will rank for much more stringent degrees of protection than others.

In taking a planning decision an authority must, of course, consult the relevant conservancy council in respect of development within a SSSI. However, permission should not be refused where conditions can be imposed to prevent damage to natural features, or where there are other material considerations overriding the interests of nature conservation.

These considerations, of course, apply to any site having nature conservation significance, but where the site is also a SSSI special procedures will have to be followed. If, following consultation with the relevant conservancy council a planning authority decides, against advice, to grant permission, they should give the council good notice so a decision can be made whether or not to ask for 'call-in' of the matter.

This will normally occur where the affected site is in addition to being a SSSI is an NNR, NCR or GCR upon which development will have a significant effect, otherwise call-in will take place if issues of more than local importance are raised. This procedure applies not just to land *in* a SSSI, but to land *around* such a site, or in relation to any application *likely to affect* such a site. The conservancy councils have been asked to define the consultation areas around sites — and though the usual extent is 500m from the edge of a SSSI, it may extend for up to two kilometres particularly in relation to wetlands. Planning authorities should also consider requiring EA in relation to any Schedule 2 project (see chapter 5, above) likely to have a significant effect on a SSSI — and even more so where a special protection area or special area of conservation is concerned.

Many would argue, however, that PPG 9 does not go far enough in protecting sites of conservation value. Before its issue some planning authorities had policies in their plans which created positive presumptions against development in SSSIs Green Belts (see below) and local wildlife sites unless there was an overwhelming case for such development. Conservationists fear up to 12,000 sites of natural interest could now have *less* protection as a result of the guidance.

Particular considerations also apply where a mineral extraction permission is applied for, see MPGs 1,2,6,7,10 and 13, the last one particularly applying where the application is in respect of peat cutting — though here voluntary agreement between English Nature and Fisons plc, the principal commercial extractor, has safeguarded 3240 ha of lowland peat in Somerset, Humberside, South Yorkshire and Cumbria.

Note also that PD rights in SSSIs are limited under SI 1995/418 Sch Part 4B in that temporary use of land for clay pigeon shooting, motorsports and wargames is not allowed.

The 1995 Report of the Committee on Public Accounts 'Protecting and Managing Sites of Special Scientific Interest in England' (HC Session 94–95, 11th Report 375) further points to SSSIs being more at risk from other matters than from planning decisions. One issue particularly highlighted by the report was an apparent reluctance on the part of English Nature to prosecute offenders: 1005 instances of damage have led to nine prosecutions in seven years. English Nature, which has brought only one successful prosecution since it was set up, believes in prosecution only as a last resort and then only in cases of deliberate and malicious damage. Furthermore as only six months is allowed for bringing prosecutions it can be difficult to assemble sufficient evidence. Is this, however, yet another instance of over regulation and under enforcement?

Special Protection Areas and Special Areas of Conservation

Under EU Directives 79/409 and 92/43 the UK is bound to have particular rules for the protection of SPAs and SACs. The Conservation (Nature Habitats) Regulations SI 1994/2716 implement these requirements. The object here is (a) to take special measures to conserve the habitats of certain bird species; (b) to contribute to bio-diversity by conserving natural habitats and wild fauna and flora of EU importance; (c) to create a coherent EU wide network of SACs (to subsume existing SPAs) known as Natura 2000; (d) to take steps to avoid in SACs and SPAs *significant deterioration* of habitats; and (e) to ensure that proposed developments not directly connected with site management and likely to have an effect on a SPA or SAC should be assessed for their conservation implications and should only go ahead if it is found the proposal will not affect the integrity of the site. Under the 1981 legislation there is no obligation to prevent deterioration of a site arising because of neglect, so the new requirement to do this is a major change in the law. However, how will the obligation be fulfilled? Will land being neglected be compulsorily acquired? Until now compulsory acquisition powers have been used only once in respect of a SSSI.

Where a development proposal is received affecting a SPA or SAC, if following *assessment* of the proposal a negative effect is found, the development may only be allowed if there is no alternative solution *and* there are imperative public interest reasons which override the conservation interest. In such a case there is an obligation on member states to compensate the loss so as to preserve the overall coherence of Natura 2000. In some cases where particular habitats or species are at risk ('priority sites') a development scheme may only be considered if there are overriding reasons of human health or public safety, or there will be beneficial consequences of primary importance for the environment, or where the EU Commission considers there are other imperative overriding public interest reasons. Exactly what form the 'assessment' required for the foregoing purposes will take remains uncertain.

Not all SSSIs will be designated as SACs, but all SACs will *also* be designated as SSSIs, and under reg 22 of the Habitats Regulations the Secretary of State may then, on the advice of the appropriate conservancy council, make a Special Nature Conservation Order (SNCO) specifying operations not to be carried out *at any time* without the conservancy council's consent. If then a plan or project is put forward likely to affect the site significantly it must be made subject to an 'appropriate assessment', and if the conclusion of the conservancy council following this is adverse to the proposal, it cannot be consented, though the matter can be referred to the Secretary of State who may only permit it where 'there being no alternative solutions, the plan or project must be carried out for reasons of overriding public interest' (see above for the particular requirements where the land in question is also a 'priority site'). The loss of rights consequent on the making of a SNCO is compensatable, and the guidelines in DoE Circular 4/83 will apply.

Prior to designation of land as a SPA/SAC, ie as a 'European site', planning authorities are asked to consider unimplemented or partially implemented grants of permission affecting the area, and should indicate whether implementation would have significant effects on the ecological value of the land. The Natural Habitat Regulations (SI 1994/2716), regs 50, 51, 55–58 require a review as soon as reasonably practicable of grants of permission in relation to existing SPAs, to future SPAs as declared and SACs on the agreed designation by the government and the Commission. The appropriate conservancy council will give advice in relation to this matter. Where the integrity of the site would be adversely affected, and provided the permission in question would not satisfy the requirements which would apply to approving a new development proposal, the potential for harm must be removed unless the planning authority conclude there is no likelihood of the development being carried out or continued. The safeguarding action for the land the authority may take includes entering into planning obligations to restrict or regulate the use of the site, otherwise revocation or modification action may take place — subject to central consent — though, of course, compensation may be payable. Note that similar provisions apply to secure the review, etc of other consents/ authorisations for highway construction or improvement, electrical, and pipe line consents, Transport and Works Act 1992 consents, Environmental Protection Act 1990 authorisations and discharge consents under the Water Resources Act 1991, etc.

The 1994 regulations also make provision to ensure that PD rights under SI 1995/418 do not result in breaches of relevant EU obligations. Development which would be likely to significantly affect a SPA or SAC may not benefit from PD status unless the relevant planning authority decides, after consulting the appropriate conservancy council, that it would not affect the integrity of the site (see also chapter 5, above on EA and PD rights).

Agricultural grant aid (further types)

The Agriculture Act 1986 imposes an obligation on the Minister of Agriculture in England in discharging agricultural land functions to have regard to, and endeavour to achieve, a reasonable balance between the promotion and maintenance of stable and efficient agriculture, the economic and social interests of rural areas, the conservation and enhancement of the natural beauty and amenity of the countryside and the promotion of the enjoyment of the countryside by the public.

Thus the Farm and Conservation Grant Scheme (see SI 1989/128, as amended, and SI 1991/1630, as amended) emphasised grant aid for improved handling of farm waste, regeneration of woodland and aid for traditional types of building. This continues, with some modifications, see SI 1994/3002 and 3003. Note also the countryside stewardship campaign of 1991 whereunder payments may be made for the recreation of heathlands, and in respect of enhanced access to the countryside, see Cm 1655, pp 114–155. In this latter connection note further the Countryside Access Regulations SI 1994/2349 implementing Council Regulation 2078/92 under which payments may be made to farmers who undertake for five years to permit the public to have access to particular areas of 'set aside' land (see above) known as 'access areas' for the purposes of quiet recreation, and to manage it in accordance with the regulations. See also SI 1996/695 on payments under the Countryside Stewardship scheme.

More significant, perhaps, is s 18 of the 1986 Agriculture Act under which where it appears to the Minister that it is particularly desirable to conserve and enhance the beauty of an area, and its flora or fauna, geological or physiographical features, or to protect buildings or other archaeological, architectural or historic features, *and* that the maintenance or adoption of particular agricultural methods are likely to further such ends, he may designate relevant land as an 'environmentally sensitive area' (ESA). Such designation takes place after consultation with the Secretary of State for the Environment, the Countryside Commission and the appropriate conservancy council. Management agreements may be made with appropriate landowners in ESAs, and requirements as to agricultural practices and methods may be specified for such agreements in the order designating an ESA, together with requirements as to the length of such agreements (initially five years), remedies for breach and rates of payment under agreements. Such agreements once made in England and Wales act as restrictive covenants over the land in question.

The origins of ESAs derive from attempts to conserve areas of the Broads grazing marshes, and allowance by the EU (Regulation EC/797/85) of state aid to farmers to encourage farming practices favourable to the environment in areas of high conservation value. Since 1987 Regulation EC/1760/87 has further permitted community grant aid to go to such schemes. The criteria for designation are that the land must be of national environmental significance, its conservation must depend upon the maintenance, adoption or extension of particular farming practices, these practices must have changed so as to pose an environmental threat and each ESA must be a clearly separate and coherent area of environmental interest.

ESAs once designated have, under s 18(8) of the 1986 Act, to be reviewed and monitored and this occurs according to environmental, economic and social criteria. It is asked whether environmental enhancement or preservation has followed designation, what interest in designation has been shown by farmers, what savings and costs have eventuated, and what effect on farm business has occurred.

The ESA concept appears to represent a concerted attempt to tie together conservation and agricultural policies within a wider context of preservation of amenity, and currently some 3.4 million ha of land falls within ESA designations. Concern must still be voiced, however, at the lack of such coherence with regard to land outside such areas.

E LIMESTONE PAVEMENT ORDERS

Under s 34 of the 1981 Act where the appropriate conservancy council or the Countryside Commission are of the opinion that any land in the countryside comprising a 'limestone pavement' (ie an area of limestone lying wholly or partly exposed on the surface and fissured by natural erosion) is of special interest by reason of its flora, fauna, geological or physiographical features, it is their duty to notify that fact to the local planning authority for the area. Where the Secretary of State or the planning authority consider that the character of any land so notified would be likely to be adversely affected by the removal or disturbance of the limestone, either the Secretary of State or the authority may make a 'limestone pavement order' designating the land and prohibiting the removal of limestone on or in it.

The procedure for making orders, as with s 29, is laid down in Sch 11 to the 1981 Act, see above. Orders may be amended or revoked. It is an offence to remove or disturb limestone in designated land without a reasonable excuse. Such an excuse is provided by a grant of planning permission under the 1990 Act. There are no compensation provisions, nor any excluding agricultural operations from the control such an order imposes. The weakness of designation is that while suburban dwellers continue to desire lumps of limestone in their gardens, clandestine removal will still take place. It is not a market solution that is required here, but market dissolution.

F PESTICIDE CONTROL

The seventh report of the Royal Commission on Environmental Pollution considered pesticide control. Pesticides have played a major role in increasing agricultural production. Ending their use would dramatically reduce cereal crop yields. However, there are risks inherent in pesticide use. Interference with biochemical processes may increase food yields, but may release into the environment substances harmful to human and animal life. The process of manufacturing some pesticides may put production workers at risk. The process of discovering new biologically active chemicals is a lengthy and expensive one with a 'trial and error' element. No matter how stringent testing and development processes are, the possibility of unforeseeable and undesirable side-effects remains.

Current policy, as declared, in Cm 1200, is that: pesticide use should be limited to the minimum necessary for pest control compatible with human health and environmental protection; in taking decisions on pesticides ministers will consider health, environmental and amount efficacy issues; approvals for use will be regularly reviewed and withdrawn if new evidence indicates harmful health or environmental effects; in general information about pesticides should be publicly available, subject to commercial scrutiny, approval procedures must be independent of sectoral interests.

The relevant UK law is to be found in the Food and Environment Protection Act 1985. Part III, as amended by the Pesticides (Fees and Enforcement) Act 1989, is the relevant portion.

Part III is specifically concerned with pesticide control, specifically with a view to developing means to: protect human, animal and plant health; protect the environment; secure safe, efficient and humane methods of controlling pests; make information about pesticides publicly available. Ministers have extensive powers under s 16 to impose specified prohibitions on pesticides, though this is subject to ministerial power to exempt specific pesticides from prohibition, or approve and give consent in relation to specified pesticides to an otherwise prohibited act. The specified prohibitions include bans on import-ation, sale, supply, storage, use and advertisement. Ministers have powers to seize and dispose of pesticides where there has been a breach of a prohibition, and these powers extend to items treated with the pesticide. Other remedial actions may be directed. Overall, provisions governing pesticide authorisation must, under Directive 91/414 secure a high level of protection, while pesticides posing risks to health, groundwater and the environment should not be authorised. Regulations may provide that pesticides imported in breach of a prohibition shall be removed from the UK. They may also lay down how much pesticide or pesticide residue may be left in any crop, food or feeding stuff, and that where such limits are exceeded ministers shall have power to seize and dispose of the crop, etc. Regulations are to be made in the form of statutory instruments (see for example the Pesticides (Maximum Residue Levels etc) Regulations SI 1994/1985, as amended by SI 1995/1483), and ministers may set up an advisory committee to give advice on pest control issues and the purposes of Part III of the 1985 Act. This committee must be consulted, inter alia, on regulations contemplated by ministers. Information may be required by ministers of importers, exporters, manufacturers and users of pesticides for controlling pesticides in the UK and to fulfil international obligations. It is an offence to contravene regulations without reasonable excuse.

In this connection pest means organisms harmful to plants, wood or plant products; pesticides are substances, preparations or organisms for destroying pests, and Part III also applies to any substance, etc, used to protect plants, etc, from harmful organisms, to regulate plant growth, to give protection against harmful creatures or to render them harmless, to control organisms with unwanted effects on other systems, buildings or products or to protect animals against ectoparasites as if it were a pesticide.

Under s 17 ministers may, after appropriate consultation, issue and keep up to date codes of practice to give practical guidance on the provisions of Part III and the regulations.

Section 18 (as amended) enables ministers to charge fees to applicants seeking approval of pesticides, and payments may be required in respect of the handling and evaluation of applications, the collation of relevant information and monitoring the effect of pesticide use in the UK, and the amount to be paid may be calculated by reference to either or both of the turnover in the UK within a specified period of a pesticide to which an approval relates, *or* turnover in the UK of *all* pesticides to which approvals relate held by the person who is to make the payment. Section 19 (as amended) confers extensive powers of enforcement, and these may be exercised either by a ministerially authorised person or by a duly authorised officer of a local authority, and local authorities have jurisdiction over, inter alia, pesticide sale and use, etc, in wholesale and retail outlets from April 1992. It has also been proposed by MAFF that there should be enhanced public access to safety data about pesticides. Newer pesticides receiving approval are subject to evaluation disclosure, but MAFF considers that older approved pesticides should also be subject to such disclosure. Note also the Plant Protection Product Regulations SI 1995/887 implementing Directive 91/414, under which products for plant protection can only be marketed and used if approval by ministers, and then only in accordance with ministerially specified conditions.

Control over aerial spraying

Spraying of potentially hazardous chemicals from aircraft has been a cause for concern for many years. Use of aerial spraying has increased, offering certain technical advantages over conventional spraying techniques. Present controls are found in the Air Navigation (No 2) Order SI 1995/970, art 50.

Articles, including pesticides, may not be dropped for agricultural, horticultural or arboricultural purposes from an aircraft unless the operator holds an aerial application certificate from the CAA. The operator's staff must also be properly trained and supplied with an application manual containing relevant safety information. The CAA must grant an aerial application certificate only if satisfied that an applicant is a fit person to hold such a certificate, and is competent, having regard in particular to previous conduct and experience, equipment, organisation, staffing and other arrangements, to secure the safe operation of the aircraft specified in the certificate for aerial spraying flights. The certificate may be granted subject to such conditions as the CAA thinks fit for ensuring that neither the aircraft nor any sprays endanger persons or property. A certificate may be revoked, suspended or varied by the CAA under art 71 of the 1995 order, but otherwise remains in force for the period specified in the certificate.

G NATIONAL PARKS, ACCESS TO, AND LEISURE IN, THE COUNTRYSIDE

National Parks are defined by the National Parks and Access to the Countryside Act 1949, s 5, as amended in 1995. They are areas of extensive open countryside where particular measures are necessary to conserve and enhance natural beauty, and the wildlife and cultural heritage of those areas, and where opportunities for understanding and enjoying the special qualities of those areas by the public are to be promoted. These measures may not be the same in each park, and those responsible for parks need to consider how best to reflect their areas' particular characteristics in their policies. However, conservation is not preservation, and relevant authorities must co-operate with those who live and work in National Parks, and take into account their needs and aspirations. So far as promotion of the understanding of parks by the public is concerned, particular emphasis should be placed on enabling the public to savour open space, wildness and tranquillity, particularly in remote and less heavily visited areas — though the legislation as amended does not limit public appreciation of the parks — as some would have wished — to *quiet* activities only. Areas of Outstanding Natural Beauty (AONB) are defined by s 87(1) of the 1949 Act as areas, not in National Parks, which are of such outstanding natural beauty that they should be so designated.

The National Parks are not publicly owned, but are publicly administered. This has always raised in some minds the question of whether supervision minus ownership can lead to effective control. They were designated (and in theory other areas may be) by the National Parks Commission (*now in England* the Countryside Commission, in Wales the Countryside Council for Wales) under ss 6 and 7 and Sch 1 to the 1949 Act. Designation is subject to confirmation by the Secretary of State, and the usual procedure for publicising designation proposals, receiving objections, and holding hearings applies under Sch 1 to the 1949 Act. Powers exist to vary boundaries of National Parks, see s 7 of the 1949 Act as amended. The administrative framework for the Parks was previously laid down by the Local Government Act 1972, Sch 17.

Section 63 of the Environment Act 1995 now enables the Secretary of State in England to establish National Park Authorities (NPAs) for any existing or new National Park and for these to supersede any existing authorities: particular provision is made for the establishment of such bodies in Wales by s 64 of the 1995 Act.

NPAs supersede in the case of existing parks the 'existing authorities', ie under s 79(1) of the 1995 Act any joint or special planning boards previously existing under Sch 17 of the 1972 Act (the Peak and the Lake District authorities) *and* any National Park Committees (the remainder of the parks). The NPAs are the local planning authority for their areas and also the hazardous substances authority in place of other local authorities any part of whose area lies within a National Park, see further SI 1995/2803 which brought the new system into effect in Wales on 1 April 1996.

Under Sch 7 NPAs are corporate bodies consisting of some members appointed by relevant local authorities and some by the Secretary of State, with the former in the majority. While the Secretary of State's appointees will represent the wider national purposes of park designation, where possible they will also have local connections with 'their' park. Provision is further made for the Secretary of State's appointees to include 'Parish members', ie persons who serve on relevant Parish Councils and meetings within park areas. Each NPA must appoint a National Park Officer (NPO) who is responsible for co-ordinating the ways in which the NPA carries out its functions. Schedules 8 and 9 confer further powers on NPAs, including the power to acquire land compulsorily, and functions with regard to Nature Reserves and the establishment of Country Parks.

However, the prime functions of NPAs, under s 65 of the 1995 Act, are to conserve and enhance the natural beauty, wildlife and cultural heritage of parks and to promote opportunities for public understanding and enjoyment of the parks, including general powers to protect countryside interests and avoid pollution under ss 37 and 38 of the Countryside Act 1968, and to do anything calculated to facilitate, or conducive or incidental to, the accomplishment of these purposes. In particular under s 11A of the 1949 Act NPAs in pursuing their park objectives must *seek to foster the economic and social well being of local communities but without incurring significant expenditure* in doing so, and must, for those purposes, co-operate with other relevant public bodies and local authorities. However, in performing any functions with regard to land they must bear in mind their duty to conserve and enhance natural beauty, and if it appears there is a conflict between purposes they are to favour the conservation duty.

The object of the amended legislation is to free each park to express its character individually within a national framework. Consultation, however, will be encouraged so that the new NPAs can bear in mind the interests of those living and working in parks, those whose living is derived from park resources and those who visit the parks. The NPAs will work closely with the Countryside Commission and also with the appropriate conservancy council, the Sports Council, Tourist Boards, and the Rural Development Commission, and relevant local authorities.

Within the context of the NPA's prime conservation duty it should be noted that while *no* recreational activity is excluded in principle, it is accepted that some are inappropriate in certain areas. The task of NPAs, by careful planning and management, is to accommodate as many types of leisure interest as possible. Codes of Practice should be drawn up to ensure an amicable and effective segregation of uses. Where, however, a recreational activity would cause unacceptable damage or disturbance to natural beauty, etc, and that also affects the understanding and enjoyment of that beauty, *the conservation duty is to come first*. Mediation, negotiation and co-operation will be used to try to ensure an absence of such conflicts but where reconciliation is not possible then the duty to conserve must take precedence.

Section 66 of the 1995 Act requires the continuation of National Park Management Plans created under the Local Government Act 1972, and also that new plans shall be made following quinquennial review.

Section 4A of the Town and Country Planning Act 1990 (inserted in 1995) provides that where an NPA has been established for a park it is to be exclusively the *sole* local planning authority for the whole area of the park, including mineral planning functions. The NPA will have planning authority functions under the Wildlife and Countryside Act 1981, see s 69 of the 1995 Act, and s 68 for further amplification of planning powers enjoyed by NPAs.

Planning in the National Parks: further considerations

Development control exists in National Parks under the same laws as elsewhere, though there are detailed modifications in the law and variations in practice. Design features of a development and implications for nature conservation or the beauty of the countryside will loom large in considering a planning application. How far the previous authorities were successful in preserving the National Parks from intrusive development is likely to remain for some time a matter of some controversy. The issue is particularly controversial with regard to mineral extraction in the parks, see *Peak Park Joint Planning Board v Secretary of State for the Environment*,[1] but is otherwise a subject of debate. Note, however, the guidance of MPG 1 with regard to extraction within parks, namely that it should take place only where demonstrably in the public interest, and after strict examination of the need for the material from a national point of view, the impact of permission or refusal on the local economy, the cost and availability of alternative supplies, and detrimental environmental and landscape effects. Formal EA will normally be required in such cases. Ann and Malcolm MacEwan in *National Parks: Conservation or Cosmetics?* showed that the number of planning applications varies greatly each year between parks. However, there was no real evidence to suggest that the previous park planning authorities were more strict in rejecting planning applications than other authorities. In their *Greenprints for the Countryside* (1987) the MacEwans were rather more generally hopeful in regard to this issue. The parks have been largely successfully protected against urban developments, but, of course, the controversial operations of agriculture and forestry are largely beyond the control of planning law. Furthermore, there is only some evidence that planning controls over building designs have been in any way successful in preserving the use of local building styles and materials in the parks. Planning seems to have had little success with regard to the positive planning of parks, but has had to bow to pressures created by commerce, education, water supply, sewerage, transport and health and other service policies. This was historically particularly evident with regard to attempts to restrict house building to serve local needs only. Structure plans were modified by the Department of the Environment where they sought to promote such policies.

Note, however, that PD rights in National Parks (as also in Areas of Outstanding National Beauty and The Broads) are restricted, because on so called art 1(5) land such rights are only exercisable to a limited degree in respect of enlargement/improvement of dwelling houses, the extension of industrial buildings and warehouses, certain developments by certain statutory undertakers and by telecommunications code system operators. Further restrictions also exist on PD rights with regard to land in a park or Area of Outstanding Natural Beauty with regard to exploratory borehole drilling and the removal of material from mineral-working deposits.

The evidence in the Countryside Commission's 1991 Report 'Landscape Change in the National Parks' was that agriculture and forestry have been primarily responsible for landscape change in the parks over the last 20 years. Some 1,000 acres per annum of heath and moorland had gone, while a similar acreage of conifers had been planted. Quarrying, house and road construction have consumed only 2% of the parks' areas, but it is the loss of grass moor, rough pasture, lowland heath, bracken, upland heath and scrub that was marked, while conifer forest, improved pasture, cultivated land, and developed land all increased, the first three markedly. Rather more positively broad leaf and mixed woodland, rocky and coastal land and water and wetlands have also

1 (1979) 39 P & CR 361.

somewhat increased. The Report nevertheless argued that the worst effects of intensive farming and forestry had been avoided while expressing fears for the future of traditional upland farming.

The Wildlife and Countryside Act 1981, ss 42–44, confers extra protection on certain land in National Parks. Under s 42, replacing the Countryside Act 1968, s 14, ministers may apply an order in the form of a statutory instrument to any land consisting of or including moorland or heath in a National Park. Thereafter no person may, on pain of committing an offence, plough or otherwise convert into agricultural land any such moor or heath which has not been agricultural land at any time within the preceding 20 years, or carry out on such land other agricultural operations or forestry operations specified in the order as likely to affect its character or appearance. This protection does not cover operations carried out, or caused or permitted to be carried out, by the owner or occupier of the land, if notice of the proposed operation has been given to the planning authority *and* that authority have *given* their consent, *or* where they have *neither given nor refused* consent, three months have expired since notice was given, *or* where they have *refused* consent 12 months have expired since notice was given. Where the authority refuse consent they therefore have a period of 12 months during which they may offer a management agreement under s 39 of the 1981 Act, see above.

One other authority is relevant in connection with the parks. The Broads Authority exists under the Norfolk and Suffolk Broads Act 1988, and was established following growing disquiet over the fate of this area of some 111 square miles of land in the valleys of the Bure, Ant, Thurne, Yare and Waveney. Concern in particular focused on the division of responsibility for the area between disparate authorities, and there were calls for the Broads to be designated as a National Park. In the end a special regime was created whereby the Broads Authority is, by virtue of s 2 of the 1988 Act, to conserve and enhance the natural beauty of its area, to promote its enjoyment by the public and to protect the interests of navigation. However, the conservation of beauty includes conserving flora, fauna, geological and physiographical features, see s 25(2) of the 1988 Act. The authority thus has a definite environmental role, along with its other tasks of protecting its area's natural resources from damage, while remembering the needs of agriculture and forestry and the interests of Broads dwellers along with the importance of the area as a nationally popular place of beauty and recreation. Though the authority has no structure planning functions, it is generally otherwise the planning authority for its area and it must also prepare, under s 3, 'The Broads Plan', a strategic document, subject to quinquennial review, which sets out its policies with regard to its functions. Section 4 further requires the authority to prepare a map showing areas within the Broads whose natural beauty it is particularly important to conserve. Such a map must be kept under review, and must be prepared after consultation with English Nature and other representative bodies, while guidelines with regard to this task may be issued by the Countryside Commission. Ministers may further, under s 5 of the 1988 Act specify both certain types of land (grazing marsh, fen marsh, reed bed or broad leaved woodland) within the Broads, and operations appearing to them likely to affect the character or appearance of such an area. Thereafter the specified operations may only be carried out lawfully after the Broads Authority has been notified and has consented in writing *or* has allowed three months to pass from the notification without either giving or refusing consent, *or* has refused consent and twelve months have gone by. Management agreements may be made to ensure proposed activity does not take place. It is an offence without 'reasonable excuse' (not defined by the 1988 Act) to contravene a prohibition on designated activities. The foregoing procedure is clearly akin to, but different in material respects from, that in respect of SSSIs.

One final issue is whether there are enough parks. Marion Shoard's *This Land is our Land* after pointing out, pp 464–465, that there are limits to the protection afforded to land *within* parks, goes on to point out that many areas of great beauty are not designated, and that there has been official resistance to further designation. London has no National Park within 150 miles; other areas such as the South Downs, Somerset Levels and the coasts of Cornwall and Devon could well have been designated as parks, while in 1972 ministers refused to hold an inquiry into the designation of parts of mid-Wales as a National Park. It is true that some of Shoard's favoured areas now enjoy ESA status, but that simply adds one more piece to the confused patchwork of rural designations — evidence of a continuing failure to pursue a policy which integrates access, conservation, economic and social policies within an overall framework which maintains a vibrant countryside but one where the soil and its natural flora and fauna, etc, are maintained in good heart.

H AREAS OF OUTSTANDING NATURAL BEAUTY (AONB)

These are designated by the Countryside Commission (in Wales the Countryside Council) under s 87 of the 1949 Act. While there are 10 National Parks (excluding the Broads) covering 1.4 million ha of Great Britain, there are 39 AONB covering 2 million ha, the final designation being the Tamar Valley in August 1995.

Before designation the Commission must consult with affected local authorities and publicise their proposals in the *London Gazette* and relevant local newspapers. The publicity must state the right of the public to make representations to the Commission, who must duly consider any made. Designations must be confirmed by the Secretary of State, and when a designation order is submitted to him the Commission must forward any local authority comments and other representations received. The Secretary of State must consult with the Commission and relevant local authorities where he proposes to refuse confirmation or to confirm an order with modifications. Where designation is controversial, an inquiry may be held to test the merits of the proposal.

These areas are responsibilities of relevant local planning authorities, both counties and districts. Authorities have powers under Sections 6(4)(e), 9, 62(1), 64(5) and 65(5) and (5A) of the 1949 Act in respect of plan making and arrangements for public access. However, under s 88 of the 1949 Act, as substituted in 1995, the planning powers of authorities within an AONB are enhanced in that an authority whose area consists of or includes the whole or any part of a AONB has power to take all such action as appears to them to be expedient for accomplishing the purpose of conserving and enhancing the natural beauty of the AONB. Thus it is hoped, by the Countryside Commission, that planning authorities will be in a better position to resist inappropriate developments in AONBs such as caravan parks, golf courses, marinas and intrusive housing schemes. However, it has to be remembered that while planning powers may *prevent* harmful develoment, they cannot prevent harmful neglect: they are not powers *to manage* the countryside. Furthermore designation as an AONB does not protect against intrusive highway development.

Planning law nevertheless has an important role to play in relation to these areas, though where an AONB comprises land in a number of areas joint advisory committees of relevant authorities, amenity groups and landed interests, supported by specialist staff, are needed if planning policies are to be co-ordinated. Preparation of structure and local plans should reflect the national importance of AONBs. Planning obligations under the Town and Country Planning Act 1990, s 106, regulating the use of land, may be appropriate. Major industrial developments are inappropriate in an AONB, but blanket policies of refusing permission for such developments are not permissible. Each case must be considered on its merits. Mineral workings in an AONB may be unavoidable, but planning applications for such development must be vigorously examined. Central policy is that where new road construction has to take place in an AONB it should do so only after clear evidence of need has been adduced. Routing must cause as little environmental harm as possible. Minor industrial development in an AONB can be desirable, especially to protect local employment opportunities, but new industrial units should be in sympathy with historic landscapes and architecture. Particular planning controls include: a requirement that the Countryside Commission must be consulted on development plans, ss 9 and 88 of the 1949 Act, and the availability of Commission advice on development proposals, ss 6 and 88. Additionally, the local planning authority will have powers to make byelaws to protect their land comprised in an AONB (as also in a National Park), see s 90 of the 1949 Act. Under the Road Traffic Regulation Act 1984, s 22, roads in or adjacent to an AONB (or in a National Park, country park (see below), nature reserve (see above), long distance route (see below) or land held inalienably by the National Trust) can be made subject to traffic regulation orders. The Countryside Commission may make submissions to the Secretary of State as to the desirability of making an order. (The counterpart bodies for Wales and Scotland have similar powers.)

I COASTLINE PROTECTION

Much of the coastline is within National Parks or AONBs. Development plans may also indicate coastal sites as 'Areas of High Landscape Value' or 'Areas of Scientific Interest'. The coastline is, however, vulnerable to development, particularly where permission is sought for proposals involving the creation of major facilities handling great quantities of bulky and/or potentially harmful cargoes (see chapter 5 above on the special rules relating to EA and development). In 1992 PPG 20 replaced earlier guidance on coastal planning. This, though land based, acknowledges the need for consideration to be given to the offshore impacts of an onshore development, and thus it is a step towards integrated coastal zone management. Furthermore, a pro conservation policy is favoured in that constraints on coastal zone development will be in general supported, while recognising that some exceptions have to be made for developments needing access to the sea. Authorities are encouraged to consider policies dealing with flooding, erosion and soil instability, though the emphasis is placed on pursuing such policies as will avoid putting other development at risk and obviating need for expensive engineering coast protection works.

The overall policy stance is to maintain the natural character of undeveloped coastline where it survives, thus constraining development in such areas, especially where an area has been designated as having landscape value and there is a need to limit development, particularly anything visually intrusive. Development plans should include policies for improving and enhancing the coast in any area of natural beauty and/or possessing convervation value. Policies should also be included on regenerating run down coastal towns and for restoration of despoiled areas.

The PPG is a step forward but even so it could be criticised for not addressing such issues on the cumulative effect of small develoments, none of which may be visually intrusive individually but which despoil by incremental progression. Furthermore there remained a distinct lack of integration of coastal planning with other marine and nature conservation measures, see further Warren and Smith 'Planning for the Use of the Coast' [1994] 6 ELM 57, to which indebtedness is acknowledged.

Some attempt to remedy this has, however, been made by the DoE's 1995 'Policy Guidelines for the Coast' which tries to bring together within the overall framework of the sustainable development policy, and the functions of the DoE, all the diverse strands of policy and those activities which impact upon the coast, ie coastal planning and development, coast defence, marine aggregate dredging (see further chapter 8), ports and harbours, construction and development in the sea, shipping, fisheries, disposal at sea (see chapter 12), water quality, landscape, nature conservation, the historic environment, leisure sport and tourism. There is also now an Interdepartmental Group on Coastal Policy including representatives from all government departments having coastal interests and responsibilities, and a Coastal Forum whose membership includes representatives of a wide range of bodies with an interest in the coast. In November 1995 it was further announced that new policy guidelines on the coast would be published in 1996, and that there would be a review of byelaw making powers for the coast with special emphasis on managing leisure demand. On a *non-statutory* basis 'Heritage Coasts' may be designated, following consultation with the Countryside Commission. Some may fall within existing National Parks or AONBs. Policies with regard to Heritage Coasts should be clearly incorporated in relevant structure and local plans so the public may know what uses and activities are/are not likely to be permitted. Non-statutory plans may be used as an interim measure until statutory plans are made. In making any plans authorities should consult the Countryside Commission. Authorities should monitor development pressures on undeveloped coastlines, and significant changes that occur, to check the effectiveness of coastal policy. By 1990 there were 1,455 km of designated coastline, and Cm 1655 announced exploration of further measures to protect coastal areas.

The National Trust has also, over the last 25 years, in its 'Operation Neptune' scheme protected some 450 miles of shoreline, and hopes to extend its scheme. Note also the voluntary Coastal Forum launched in 1994 enables all interested bodies to exchange views on, promote understanding of, foster good practice on, and evaluate, coastal zone initiatives.

J ACCESS TO THE COUNTRYSIDE AND PUBLIC RIGHTS OF WAY

Part V of the 1949 Act provides the basic legal structure for public access to the countryside, based on the principle of access for recreation in the 'open country', defined by s 59(2) as areas consisting wholly or predominantly of mountain, moor, heath, down, cliff or foreshore, to which the Countryside Act 1968, s 16, adds *certain* woodlands, rivers, canals and their banks, etc. However, no *right* to wander through such countryside is given by the 1949 Act save where land is acquired compulsorily for such a purpose, or made subject to an access order or access agreement.

Under s 61 of the 1949 Act local planning authorities were put under a duty to review their areas for the purpose of considering open country and access arrangements thereto. Section 64 empowers authorities to make *access agreements* with persons who have interests in land in open country in their areas. Agreements may provide for payments to be made by authorities. In respect of land situated in a National Park before an access agreement is made the relevant authority must consult with the Countryside Commission in England, the Countryside Council in Wales. Where an access agreement (or order) is in force under s 60, the public entering and being on the land for open air recreational purposes, without doing any damage, are not to be treated as trespassing. Open air recreation does not include *organised* games, see s 114(1) of the 1949 Act. Agreements (and orders) may impose restrictions on access. The right of access does not extend to certain categories of excepted land, *including:* agricultural land, other than land which is agricultural land solely because it is used to rough graze livestock; land covered by buildings; parks, gardens and pleasure grounds; surface mines and quarries; railway land; golf courses, race courses and aerodromes and other operational land of statutory undertakers; and Nature Reserves, see s 60(5). Agreements (and orders) must also exclude from access all land expedient for the purpose of avoiding danger to the public, or to persons employed on such land, see s 80 of the 1949 Act. Section 18 of the Countryside Act further empowers authorities who make access agreements to agree restrictions in such agreements on the rights of other parties and thus provide for agreements not to convert land into excepted land under s 60(5).

Once an agreement (or order) is in force persons interested in affected land, not being excepted land, may not carry out any works thereon having the effect of substantially reducing the area to which the public have access, see s 66. Local planning authorities have power under s 68 to enforce this provision. Agreements (and orders) may, under s 67 of the 1949 Act, make provision for securing sufficient means of access to affected land. Section 69, however, allows suspension of access rights where, on the application of a person interested in affected land, the relevant authority decide that, in view of exceptional weather conditions, there is a risk of fire.

Access *orders* may be made, under s 65 of the 1949 Act, by local planning authorities, subject to ministerial confirmation, where it appears to an authority that making an access agreement to secure public access for open air recreation is impracticable. Sections 70 to 73 of the Act enshrine the right to, and lay down procedures for obtaining, compensation in respect of access orders. Where the value of a person's interest in land is depreciated in consequence of the making of an access order compensation is payable by the local planning authority in whose area the affected land is. Such compensation, however, cannot be claimed or be payable before the end of five years from the coming into force of the order so that compensation may be assessed in the light of experience gained of the effect of the order on the land. Section 72 allows payments on account during the initial five year period in a case of special hardship.

Section 76 of the Act of 1949 confers powers of compulsory purchase, subject to ministerial confirmation, on planning authorities in respect of land, other than excepted land, where the acquiring authority consider it expedient and requisite for the purpose of public access that acquisition should take place. Section 77 of the Act confers a supplementary compulsory purchase power for access purposes on the Secretary of State in respect of open country in National Parks, other than excepted land.

The powers to create access to the countryside have been attacked as ineffective, largely because of the general presumption of the law that entry upon another's land is a trespass save in narrowly defined exempted circumstances. In *This Land is Our Land,* for instance, Marion Shoard called for adoption of the system in Sweden, 'The Right of Common Access,' whereby all have the *right* to cross the land of others on foot, provided no damage is done, and subject to exceptions to ensure privacy and the safety of crops. It appears, however, that there is only a limited will on the part of government to respond to this call. Nevertheless in 1986 the Countryside Commission and the Sports Council considered in *Access to the Countryside for Recreation and Sport* that following reform of CAP public access as a land use should be a major component of future rural land policy. The Countryside Access Regulations SI 1994/2349 now go some way in meeting calls for an open access policy in that farmers may be paid grant aid for a period of five years from 15 January following the date of acceptance of their applications for aid where they permit members of the public to have free access to areas of set aside land known as 'access areas' for quiet recreational purposes. The land must be managed in accordance with centrally specified criteria relating to maintenance and mowing of suitable ground cover, the outlawing of new fences and gates, keeping the land free of litter and bulls, maintaining access ways and way marking, excluding activities such as shooting and caravanning, horse and cycle riding.

Public rights of way and long-distance routes

The National Parks and Access to the Countryside Act 1949, Part IV, laid down provisions relating to and requiring the ascertaining, surveying and definitive mapping of public footpaths, bridleways and other public highways in the countryside. Provision was made for regular reviews of 'the definitive map'. The law was unsatisfactory in practice. Earlier provisions have been generally replaced by the Wildlife and Countryside Act 1981, ss 53–58. Under s 53 'surveying authorities' (generally county councils) are required, on the happening of certain specified events, to modify the definitive map and statement of public rights of way, and to keep the map and statement continuously under review. The specified events 'triggering' modification of the map and statement are: (a) the stopping up, diversion, widening or extension of a public highway required to be shown on the map; (b) the ceasing of any highway shown on the map to be a highway of the type shown; (c) the creation of a new right of way over land in the area of the map; (d) the passage of 20 years without interruption during which the public has used a way so as to raise the presumption of dedication as a public path (even where at the time of that use the way was not included in the definitive map, it appears); and (e) the discovery of evidence showing omissions or mis-descriptions in the map. Any person may apply to the surveying authority for an order to make modifications requisite in consequence of events falling within heads (d) and (e) above. Such applications are to be made and determined in accordance with Sch 14 to the 1981 Act. There is a right of appeal to the Secretary of State in the event of a refused application. Schedule 15 also applies to modifications made to maps and statements, following reviews, and/or the occurrence of specified events, *other* than the events specified in heads (a), (b) and (c) above, in which case the order making the modification comes into effect on its being made. Schedule 15 provides for: consultation in relation to the making of orders; publicity on making orders; opportunities for making objections to orders; holding of inquiries into objections; appointment of inspectors to chair inquiries; confirmation by the Secretary of State with or without modification; and appeals, on points of law, to the court following the coming into effect of an order.

The court is precluded from entertaining an application to quash a decision to make a modification order until after it is confirmed,[2] but where a variation is sought *and refused* judicial review of that decision may be possible.[3] See further DoE Circular 2/93, Annex B and SI 1993/12.

'I'm happy when I'm hiking' (old music hall song)

Litigation has recently made it clear that the duty to maintain a 'definitive map' is a continuing one, and that the map though stated in s 56 of the 1981 Act (see further below) to be 'conclusive evidence' is actually of an interim nature because of the ongoing obligation to keep the map under review, and revision is to occur not just on the happening of particular acts, such as a stopping up order, but on the discovery of evidence that a way is shown incorrectly, or is not shown at all. Accordingly rights shown on such a map can be both down and upgraded in status where evidence comes to light that the record of the map is incorrect, see *R v Secretary of State for the Environment, ex p Simms and Burrows*[4] and *R v Devon County Council, ex p Fowler*.[5] However, a definitive map should only be altered after careful consideration of all the evidence and observance of all procedural requirements, see *R v Isle of Wight*

---

2 *R v Cornwall County Council, ex p Huntingdon* [1994] 1 All ER 694.
3 *R v Secretary of State for the Environment, ex p Bagshaw* [1994] 6 ELM 117. See also *O'Keefe v Secretary of State for the Environment and Isle of Wight County Council* [1996] JPL 42.
4 [1990] JPL 746.
5 [1991] 3 LMELR 133 and *Fowler v Secretary of State for the Environment* (1991) 64 P & CR 16.

County Council, ex p O'Keefe.[6] Note that a right of way can exist even if it is used only for recreational walking, see *Dyfed County Council v Secretary of State.*[7]

By virtue of s 56 of the 1981 Act the map and statement are conclusive evidence (until revised) of: (a) where the map shows a footpath, that the public had the right to pass on foot, without prejudice to any greater right for the public; (b) where the map shows a bridleway, that the public had the right to pass with horses, without prejudice to any greater right for the public; (c) where the map shows a byway open to all traffic (a BOAT), that the public had rights for vehicular and all other kinds of traffic; and (d) where the map shows a road used as a public path (a RUPP), that the public had a right to pass on foot or with horses, but without prejudice to any other greater right for the public. In deciding what rights the public has a crucial provision is s 31 of the Highways Act 1980 under which the presumed dedication of a way of a particular type may arise by the conduct and intention of parties. The important questions here are whether on the part of the public there has been use of the way in the manner claimed, as of right, for a full period of 20 years and whether on the part of the landowner this can be rebutted by sufficient evidence of a lack of intention to dedicate.[8] However, the procedure under the 1981 Act is not to be used for the purpose of closing the whole length of a public right of way — the procedure for doing that lies in ss 116, 118 and 119 of the Highways Act 1980. These provide that, subject to ministerial approval, a way may be stopped if it is expedient on the basis it is no longer needed for public use.[9] See also SIs 1993/10 and 11 on public path orders. The 1981 Act on the other hand is concerned with the classification of ways.

In relation to the question of whether a way has been enjoyed 'as of right', the test is to ask whether there has been an honest belief that there is a public right of passage on the part of those who use the way. Use of a way knowing that this can occur only because of the landowner's toleration is not, however, enough.[10] Section 57 requires the surveying authority to keep the map and statement and its modifications available for inspection by the public, free of charge at all reasonable hours in one or more places in each district comprised in the area to which the map and statement relate.

The form of the definitive map and statement

The definitive map and statement originally acquired under the 1949 legislation and now maintained under the 1981 Act does not have to be a particular form of document. What is required is that there should be provision of substantial information about public paths sufficient to meet the requirements of the legislation. The statement must supplement the map as appropriate and must be reasonably related to it, but need not be physically annexed to it.[11]

---

6 [1990] 1 LMELR 209.
7 [1990] 1 LMELR 209.
8 *R v Secretary of State for the Environment, ex p Cowell* [1993] JPL 851; and *Jacques v Secretary of State for the Environment* [1994] 6 ELM 117.
9 *R v Secretary of State for the Environment, ex p Cheshire County Council* [1991] 2 LMELR 206.
10 *O'Keefe v Secretary of State for the Environment and Isle of Wight County Council* [1996] JPL 42.
11 *O'Keefe v Secretary of State for the Environment and Isle of Wight County Council* [1996] JPL 42.

The National Parks and Access to the Countryside Act 1949, ss 51–55 and 57, relate to the creation of long-distance routes for walking, riding and cycling. Such routes, which must not pass for the whole or greater part of their length along roads mainly used by vehicles, are proposed in reports by the Countryside Commission (in England, but similar powers exist for the Countryside Council in Wales) and are subject to ministerial confirmation. A proposed route map must show existing rights of way over which the long-distance route will pass, and for providing and maintenance of such new public paths as may be required to enable the public to journey along the route. Proposals for providing ferries where needed, and for accommodation, meals and refreshment along the route must also be shown on the maps, together with recommendations for restriction of traffic on existing highways along which the route will pass. The proposals must also be costed out on an estimated capital and annual recurrent cost basis.

Ministerial approval of a report does not mean that the long-distance route will *immediately* be available for public use. One reason is that the *implementation* of approved proposals is in the hands of local authorities who have to use their powers under the Highways Act 1980 to create new footpaths and bridleways by agreement, or by compulsion. The Countryside Commission has no executive power to bring about implementation. Even so under Cm 1200 it remains policy that the entire network of rights of way should be in good order by 2000, and by 1995 within National Parks.

The creation of new ways and the recording of old ones is only a partial answer to the access issue: ways must be kept open and usable, something that is often not the case. The Rights of Way Act 1990 was passed in an attempt to deal with this problem. The Act amends the Highways Act 1980 to provide that, under s 131A of that Act it is an offence for anyone without lawful authority or excuse to disturb the surface of a bridleway, footpath or any other highway (other than a made up carriage way) so as to render it inconvenient to exercise the public right of way, though taking proceedings is limited to local authorities, including highway and parish councils. A substituted s 134 then provides that where a footpath or bridleway (other than a field edge path) passes over agricultural land and the occupier wishes, in accordance with principles of good husbandry, to plough, etc, the land and it is not reasonably convenient to avoid disturbing the path, the public right of way is subject to a condition that the land may be ploughed and the way disturbed. However, the surface so disturbed must be *made good* to not less than its minimum width (1 metre, for example, in the case of a footpath) and the line of the path must be indicated. This duty must be discharged within 14 days where a path has been disturbed for crop sowing, otherwise within 24 hours of disturbance, and it is an offence not to comply, though the compliance period may be extended on application to the highway authority. Further obligations are laid on occupiers under s 137A to prevent encroachment of crops on rights of way, while Sch 12A empowers highway authorities, inter alia, to take default action where a way has been disturbed, and to recover their costs from relevant occupiers. Section 135 further empowers authorities to authorise works for agricultural purposes which may disturb paths, and they may also authorise a temporary diversion, see further Circulars 17/90 and 2/93. It remains most doubtful, however, whether these provisions are effective to ensure free access to lawful rights of way, and many argue local authorities do not enforce the law as they should.

K COUNTRY PARKS

The Countryside Act 1968, ss 6 to 10, confers powers on local authorities (that is (in England) county and district councils, in and around London, London borough councils, and the National Park and Broads authorities) to provide, maintain, and manage 'country parks' on suitable country sites, to provide for public enjoyment of the countryside, having regard to the location of the area in question in relation to urban areas, and the availability and adequacy of existing facilities for public enjoyment of the countryside. Supplementary services and facilities may be provided on such sites. Local authorities may acquire land by agreement or compulsorily to create a country park, or the park may be set up on land belonging to others by agreement with them. Such parks exist for recreational and leisure purposes, and for furthering the enjoyment of the countryside by the population. For the powers of Welsh authorities the position under the Local Government (Wales) Act 1994 should be checked.

L FORESTRY

The Forestry Act 1967, s 1, continues the Forestry Commission (FC) constituted under the Forestry Acts 1919 to 1945 and charges it with the general duty of *promoting the interests of forestry, the development of afforestation, and the production and supply of timber, including the provision of adequate reserves of growing trees.* These duties are predominantly, but not exclusively, commercial, though the Commission is concerned with nature conservation and management. Its policy is to consult with the Countryside Commission over proposals for new planting, and to try to produce varied tree cover wherever consistent with its duties. Where disagreements arise between the Forestry and Countryside Commissions the issue is referred to ministers for adjudication (see further below). For administrative purposes the FC is divided into Forest Enterprise, which manages plantations and the Forestry Authority which is a regulatory body.

The Wildlife and Countryside (Amendment) Act 1985, s 4, imposed a new duty on the Forestry Commission. In the discharge of their functions, they must, so far as it is consistent with their other proper duties, endeavour to achieve a reasonable balance between afforestation, forest management and the production and supply of timber and the conservation and enhancement of natural beauty, and of flora, fauna and geological and physiographical features of special interest. To aid in achieving this duty the Commission introduced new Broadleaved Woodland Grants from October 1985, see, generally, the Forestry Act 1979, s 1.

Forestry policy

Current policy, as declared in 'Our Forests: the Way Ahead' (1994) is that forests should be sustainably managed to meet the 'social, economic, ecological, cultural and spiritual needs of present and future generations' and seeks to combine sustainability with multi-purpose management — an aim of the Rio conference. Thus timber production is stressed, as is preventing woodland loss, especially ancient woodland, alongside public access to woodlands whose environment is to be maintained and improved. While planting of conifers is to continue to meet commercial demands, broadleaf and mixed woodland will be encouraged where suitable, with planting of small woods as an alternative use of land to that of agriculture.

As has been earlier stated private afforestation is subject to few controls. It does not fall within the definition of development for planning purposes. Voluntary schemes provide, however, for private forestry proposals in the National Parks to be submitted informally to the appropriate park authorities, and, as a matter of practice, land is informally allocated as being acceptable for afforestation or subject to stronger or weaker presumptions for such use. The maps enshrining these proposals take much time, often years, to produce and negotiate; may be incomplete; are frequently compromises, and do not bind. Central policy, however, remains to encourage private afforestation, with the proportion of productive forests held by the FC falling from over 50% of woodlands to under 40% since 1980.

The impact of commercial afforestation was most felt in the National Parks. The Forestry Commission's 1983 Report 'England, Census of Woodlands and Trees; Wales, Census of Woodland and Trees' claimed that the total area of woodland in England had risen by some 14% since 1945, and in Wales by 40%. In England broad leaved woodland still accounts for 57% of the total, but much of this is in southern and eastern England, and conifer plantations in Wales have grown from 42,000 ha in 1947 to 168,000 ha. 'Our Forests: the Way Ahead' recognised the decline of natural and other broadleaf woodlands, and pointed to measures to reverse it such as the private sector's voluntary code 'The Forestry and Woodland Code' of 1985, together with other documents from the FC designed to be the basis of environmental standards for woodlands in both sectors. A policy of encouraging broadleaf planting was introduced in 1985 and by 1993/94 more than 60% of new planting was of broadleaves. Furthermore since 1988 there has been a move away from blanket planting of upland areas. Some uplands continue to be planted with native woodlands but these plantations have to be considered environmentally sensitive, and are particularly appropriate where they replace lost native woodlands. Woodland planting of course also helps to husband the invaluable natural resource of wood and to combat the greenhouse effect by mopping up CO_2 — though the amounts which can be so dealt with are small indeed compared to the capacity of the threatened equatorial forests.

Grant aid

The Forestry Act 1967, s 5, empowers the FC to enter into forestry dedication agreements to provide for the afforestation of land and its long term restriction to such use by means of restrictive covenants. Grant aid is given to agreed dedication schemes containing appropriate covenants in return for which the landowner further agrees to manage the land in accordance with an approved plan. Grant aid is given under the Forestry Act 1979, s 1, from the Forestry Fund maintained under the Forestry Act 1967, s 41, and is given on such terms as the FC thinks fit. Local planning authorities and other interested statutory bodies (eg the Countryside Commission) are invited to comment on proposals for dedication of land to forestry use. Local and national amenity groups may be informed and consulted; they have no right to be; since 1992 there has been a public register of grant applications. Furthermore the discussion of proposals is conducted confidentially, with no advertisement or publication. Disagreements over proposals which cannot be resolved locally and informally are referred, for their assistance, to Regional Advisory Committees maintained under the Forestry Act 1967, s 37, *and appointed by the FC.* These have representatives of forestry, agricultural, planning, environmental and trades union interests. Where disagreements cannot be resolved with the assistance of the appropriate committee, the FC seeks the views of the Minister of Agriculture. He will also consult the Secretary of State for the Environment, where there are 'planning or amenity' issues. The final decision rests with the FC, which was criticised, along with the Ministry of Agriculture as not being receptive to the arguments of environmental organisations, see *National Parks: Conservation or Cosmetics?* p 229. Note also s 2 of the Farm Land and Rural Development Act 1988 under which, in England, the Minister of Agriculture (in Wales and Scotland the appropriate Secretary of State) may grant aid conversion of land from agricultural to woodland use, including subventing consequential financial loss, see further the Farm Woodland Premium Scheme and SI 1992/905.

The grant schemes are primarily administrative in nature apart from the basic statutory authority to pay money, though it appears the FC's decisions on grants may be open to judicial review.[12] Grant applications are examined to see whether they are acceptable in silvicultural, landscape, nature conservation and other environmental terms, and the consultations alluded to above will assist in this process. Where initial afforestation may lead to adverse ecological changes EA may have to take place according to Directive 85/337, and the Environmental Assessment (Afforestation) Regulations SI 1988/1207 (see chapter 5 above for procedures). Not all afforestation projects are caught by this procedure, only those likely to have significant effects by virtue, inter alia, of size, nature or location. It appears that, so far, where EA has been required it has usually been because of the effect of planting on a SSSI. Where EA is required it must, of course, be taken into account by the FC in its grant aiding decision.

The present grant system was introduced in 1988 as the Woodland Grant Scheme (WGS) and was put into its current form in 1990. It takes account of both timber production and environmental issues as opposed to just the former. Hence there are requirements that there should be species diversity, watercourse protection, open spaces for wildlife, etc. Grants are paid in instalments or in arrears so the 'power of the purse' can be maintained, while grant aid is increased in respect of broadleaf planting to encourage the return of native woodlands.

The FC's environmental guidelines have to be met for an application for grant aid to be approved. Planning authorities may play an enhanced role with regard to afforestation for they may prepare Indicative Forestry Strategies which should be done in consultation with all relevant interests in their areas, even though the government remains opposed to bringing forestry within the control of planning legislation. Obviously in preparing and pursuing the

12 *Kincardine & Deeside District Council v Forestry Comrs* 1992 SLT 1180.

implementation of such strategies authorities need to collaborate most closely with the FC. (See further 'Forestry and the Environment', Cm 2259, 1993.)

Local planning authorities can also use other planning powers. Section 197 of the Town and Country Planning Act 1990 requires authorities to use their powers when granting planning permission to preserve, where appropriate, trees. Some indication of local authority thinking on woodlands may be included in structure and local plans, and, of course in Indicative Forestry Strategies. Under the 1990 Act s 198, local planning authorities, that is *generally* district councils and London borough councils, while in National Parks the appropriate NPA, have power to make tree preservation orders on trees, groups of trees or woodlands to preserve them in the interests of amenity. Such an order may, inter alia, prevent the felling, lopping or uprooting of trees without consent, which may be given subject to conditions, of the local planning authority. Where felling, etc, is permitted by an order, the order may also require replanting. What constitutes a tree for the purposes of the law is uncertain. Larger growths with a diameter of seven inches or more would seem to be contemplated, *Kent County Council v Batchelor*.[13] Smaller saplings *may* also be covered, *Bullock v Secretary of State for the Environment*,[14] but not, it seems, hedges, bushes and scrub. DoE Circular 36/78 counsels authorities only to make orders where public benefit will accrue in consequence, and where the removal of a tree or area of woodland would have significant environmental effects.

The procedure for making an order is laid down in SI 1969/17. The local planning authority on making an order must: place on deposit for inspection a copy of the order in a place convenient to the locality of the trees; send a copy to the Conservator of Forests and the District Valuer; serve on affected owners and occupiers of land a copy of the order stating their reasons for making the order, and the right to make representations or objections in connection with the order. Such representations must be in writing and must be received within 28 days of service of notice of making the order. Representations received must be fairly considered before the authority confirm the order. On confirmation affected owners and occupiers of land, the Conservator of Forests and the District Valuer must be informed as soon as practicable. Once an order is in force the protected tree or woodland may not be cut down, lopped, damaged or uprooted save in particular circumstances, see below, and consequently as the mode of challenge to a tree preservation order (TPO) is limited to a six weeks right of challenge in the High Court following confirmation, great care is needed in making orders, see *Bellcross Co Ltd v Mid Bedfordshire District Council*.[15] Under s 199 a TPO does not take effect until it is confirmed, and can be modified before confirmation, but not to the extent that a totally different type of order is substituted for that initially made.[16] A TPO will not apply to cutting down, etc, a tree that is dying, dead or dangerous, though where this defence is raised in a prosecution the burden of proof lies on the defence,[17] while 'dangerous' in the present context appears to

13　[1978] 3 All ER 980, [1979] 1 WLR 213.
14　(1980) 40 P & CR 246.
15　[1988] 1 EGLR 200.
16　*Evans v Waverley Borough Council* [1995] 7 ELM 178.
17　*R v Brightman* [1990] 1 WLR 1255.

mean dangerous by virtue of disease, damage, size or location.[18] Exemptions do exist where a tree is felled, etc, in pursuance of obligations imposed under an Act of Parliament.

'Woodman, spare that tree' (Victorian parlour ballad)

Section 203 of the 1990 Act provides that a TPO may make provision for the payment of compensation by a planning authority in respect of loss or damage caused in consequence of the refusal of any consent required under the order, or its conditional grant. However, consequent on the decision in *Bell v Canterbury City Council*[19] the model TPO issued centrally provides that *no* compensation is payable where it is certified that the refusal was in the interests of good forestry or that the trees have an outstanding or special amenity value.

Where a tree subject to a TPO is unlawfully removed, etc, s 206 of the 1990 Act provides that the landowner shall be under a duty to replace it with a tree of appropriate species and size. Where trees in a woodland are removed, however, the duty is to replace the same number of trees on or near the land where the previous trees stood or on such other land as the authority may agree, in both cases at points designated by the authority. The s 206 duty may be enforced by the local planning authority under s 207 of the 1990 Act, as amended in 1991, by a notice which specifies a period at the end of which it will come into effect, not being less than 28 days from service of the notice. An appeal against such a notice may be made under s 208, while default powers are given to authorities by s 209 as amended and it is an offence wilfully to obstruct an authority exercising this power. Section 210 as amended provides for offences in connection with non-compliance with TPOs. Thus it is an offence to cut down, uproot or wilfully destroy a relevant tree, or to wilfully damage, lop or top a tree so as to be likely to destroy it. Liability is not dependent on knowledge of the TPO,[20] but does not extend to situations where an independent contractor with knowledge of a TPO and in breach of specific instructions *not* to touch a tree nevertheless uproots it.[1] A fine of up to £20,000, on summary conviction, may be imposed, and in all cases the court is to take into account in fixing the fine any financial benefit accruing to the accused in consequence of the offence. Section 214A, as inserted in 1991, further provides that injunctive relief may be sought to prevent apprehended offences, while extensive rights of entry to relevant land are granted by ss 214B–D.

In July 1994 the government announced the outcome of the review of TPOs, promising several reforms, but giving no time scale for action — certainly the Environment Act 1995 is silent on the issue. Promised action, however, includes clarification of the position on trees causing a nuisance, a code of practice for sensitive tree management by statutory undertakers and utilities, enhanced discretion on the siting of replacement trees, clarification of compensation rights, limitations on the power to make TPOs in respect of

---

18 *Smith v Oliver* [1989] 2 PLR 1.
19 (1988) 56 P & CR 211.
20 *Maidstone Borough Council v Mortimer* [1980] 3 All ER 552.
 1 *Groveside Homes Ltd v Elmbridge Borough Council* [1988] JPL 395.

areas of trees, the creation of new offences of reckless destruction of, or damage to, trees and of failure to comply with a tree replacement notice, repeal of exemptions in respect of work on dying trees.

The relationship between the provisions of the Forestry Act 1967, controlling felling, and of the Town and Country Planning Act 1990 relating to tree preservation is somewhat complex. Control of felling by virtue of s 9 of the 1967 Act under a Forestry Commission licence is not always the best way of protecting individual trees or small groups of trees for which a tree preservation order is appropriate. Making a tree preservation order is inappropriate where the management of large areas of woodland may require regular lopping and thinning. For such woodlands felling control under the 1967 Act is a better system of regulation. Some trees will be subject to one form of control, some to the other, some to both.

Where a tree is subject to control *only under the 1967 Act* because no tree preservation orders have been made, control is in the hands of the Forestry Commission. In this connection it should be noted that, under s 200 of the 1990 Act, where land is subject to a *forestry dedication covenant* entered into under s 5 of the 1967 Act, a tree preservation order may only be made if there is no plan of operations approved under the covenant by the Forestry Commission and in force in respect of the land, *and* if the Commissioners consent to the order. Furthermore where an order is made in these circumstances, it may not have effect so as to prohibit, or require the local planning authority's consent for cutting down any tree in accordance with a Forestry Commission approved plan of operation in force under a covenant, or under a woodlands scheme of covenants and agreements made under s 5 of the 1967 Act. Thus 'dedicated' woodlands agreed by the Commission cannot be made subject to a parallel system of control by the local planning authority.

Where, however, trees are subject to both forms of control, applications to fell must be made to the Forestry Commission, and may not be entertained by the local planning authority, see ss 10 and 15 of the 1967 Act. The Commission may refuse a felling licence, refer the matter to the local planning authority for it to be dealt with under the 1990 Act, or notify the local planning authority they propose to grant the licence. Should that authority object to such a grant, they may require the application to be referred to the Secretary of State to be dealt with under the 1990 Act. Where no such objection is made, the Commission's licence is also a grant of consent to fell under the tree preservation order.

The Forestry Act 1967, s 9, *generally* requires that growing trees may only be felled under a Forestry Commission licence, which is granted, under s 10, at the discretion of the Commissioners. In the exercise of this discretion there is a general presumption against allowing the clear felling of hardwood areas where the owner intends to put the land to another use.

It is an offence under s 17 of the 1967 Act to fell relevant trees without a licence — such trees are those that are growing and meet certain size criteria, and which are *not* fruit, orchard or garden trees, or which stand in churchyards or public open spaces. (Neither does the prohibition extend to the topping or lopping of trees or laying of hedges.) Where an offence is committed under s 17, the Forestry Commission has power under s 17A(4) (as inserted in 1986) to require the restocking of the land, though this power does not extend to trees subject to TPOs.

M HEDGEROWS

A major countryside concern for many years has been the rate of hedgerow loss, which itself is a feature of overall species loss noted in particular in the government's *Countryside Survey* of 1990. Modern farm machinery functions best in large open spaces and this, coupled with the drive to bring more land under cultivation, led to large numbers of hedges being 'grubbed up' from 1945 onwards. What is not always realised, however, is that many of those hedges were themselves quite recent being the result of enclosure awards in the 18th and 19th centuries. Between 1984 and 1990 9,500 km of hedgerow disappeared each year, but this has since declined to 3,600 km, while new planting has reversed the decline of hedgerows, with some 4,400 km being planted annually. The problem now is the expense of hedgerow maintenance. Payments under the ESA and Countryside Stewardship campaign have helped here, but farmers often find it economic to let hedges go derelict by allowing them to grow into lines of bushes or trees, to the detriment of biodiversity and amenity. From 1992 the hedgerow incentive scheme has aimed to reverse this trend.

Section 97 of the Environment Act 1995 enables ministers to make regulations to protect what they determine to be 'important hedgerows', in particular by allowing for the prohibition of certain acts without permission on pain of criminal conviction. Section 98 reinforces this, and in fact goes *much* further, by making provision for the payment of grants to persons who undertake *anything* conducive to the conservation or enhancement of the natural beauty or amenity of the countryside or the promotion of its beauty by the public. These powers are additional to any other grant aiding powers by relevant ministers.

N GREEN BELTS AND DEVELOPMENT IN RURAL AREAS

There is a long-standing concern over the future of rural land control regarding loss of land to non-agricultural uses, particularly at the edge of urban areas, and where the land has only been marginally used for agriculture, perhaps in hope that it could be sold for more profitable urban uses. The issue is complicated often with disagreement as to the rate of loss of rural land. In 1992 the DoE claimed 190 square miles pa were built on, the Council for the Preservation of Rural England claimed it was 460 square miles pa. Certainly between 1984 and 1990 the area of rural land covered by buildings and roads increased by 4%. There is frequently no 'clean break' between town and country. The 'fringe' of an urban area is often a place for a patchwork of mixed uses. Land may also be under pressure for amenity or recreational use. There may be a pattern of mixed administrative responsibility. The Department of the Environment and the Ministry of Agriculture will have an interest in such areas. More than one local planning authority may be involved. Concern is particularly voiced over loss of the best qualities (Grades 1 and 2) of agricultural land to urban development, and the gradual urbanisation of pleasant villages within commuting distance of towns as urban dwellers move out to more pleasant locations. Planning strives to restrict the erosion of rural land both on the urban fringe and in the open countryside, and to create 'clean breaks' between urban and rural land uses. Its task is far from easy.

Thus containing new development in urban areas by means of planning law has the effect of producing whole areas of the country entirely dependent on an agriculture which, in its increasing mechanisation and technology, has had job opportunities for fewer and fewer people. On the other hand attempts to introduce new economic activities in previously rural areas, especially by the Council for Small Industries in Rural Areas (CoSIRA), can meet with resistance from some planners, landed interests and environmentalists. Decline in the numbers *employed* in the countryside has been matched by a decline of other rural services. Furthermore, considerable numbers of urban-employed middle-class people have in fact moved out of towns to live in commuter homes set in rural areas for planning controls have not stopped housing developments in small towns and villages. But in the continuing debate over the planning of rural areas one strand in the argument remains the view that more economic activities should be encouraged in rural areas so that there may be an increase in the numbers of those who both live *and* work there.

It is against this background that the issues of the green belts must be set. Ebenezer Howard, the pioneer of planning, formulated ideas of cities whose growth would be limited by belts of green land kept permanently open. The idea of a 'green girdle' around London was proposed in 1933 by Sir Raymond Unwin, another founder of planning. The Green Belt (London and Home Counties) Act 1938 led to some 60,000 acres of land in the area of London and the home counties being subject to special constraints on development and sale requiring the consent of the Secretary of State and appropriate local authorities. The Town and Country Planning Act gave planning authorities the power to restrict development in safeguarded rural areas without having to acquire the land compulsorily. Under this legislation the London green belt was incorporated in county development plans between 1954 and 1959. The idea of green belts for other major urban areas was canvassed by MOHLG Circular 42/55, especially to prevent the development of further conurbations. The circular counselled in general against new construction in green belt areas. Guidance was amplified by MOHLG Circular 50/57. Policy has been not so much to protect the countryside but to shape, separate and contain urban growth by green belt land used for agriculture, recreation, cemeteries and some other institutional uses. Central policy also favoured dispersal of population from over-crowded cities into new towns developed beyond the green belt.

Green belts have now been generally established under structure plans in the vicinities of, Newcastle and Sunderland, York, South East Lancashire and North East Cheshire, West and South Yorkshire, the Potteries, Nottingham and Derby, the West Midlands, Burton-on-Trent, Cheltenham, Oxford, Cambridge, Luton, Hertfordshire and Southern Bedfordshire, Greater London and its surrounding counties, Bristol and Bournemouth. The total area is 1,556,000 ha.

The various green belts have many diverse characteristics, but share the common aim of *urban containment rather than countryside protection*. To this end they impose strict constraints on development, stricter indeed than those on development in open countryside beyond. Current green belt policy is contained in PPG 2 (January 1995).

PPG 2 largely repeats the guidance of its 1988 predecessor, and previous guidance back to 1955, and begins by stating the general underlying principles of green belts, ie to prevent urban sprawl by keeping land permanently open, and reaffirms them, including encouraging the recycling of derelict and other urban land, and the protection of *all* countryside (not just the immediately surrounding countryside) from encroachment. Objectives for the use of land in green belts are set by PPG 2 which confirms that such areas must be protected as far as is foreseeable, hence their boundaries should be carefully set in accordance with central guidance while sufficient land is also safe-guarded for development needs. Thus once a green belt boundary is fixed it should only be changed in exceptional circumstances and only after all other development possibilities have been considered. Furthermore attempts should be made to ensure that green belts are some miles wide so as to create an appreciable open area around a built up core. PPG 2 continues the presumption against 'inappropriate' development in green belts and refines the categories of development considered 'appropriate', including providing for the future of major existing developed sites and revising policy on the re-use of redundant buildings. New positive uses for green belt land are listed, including: provision of access to open countryside; providing opportunities for outdoor sport and recreation near urban areas; retaining attractive landscape; enhancing landscape near residential areas; improving derelict and damaged land around towns; adding security to areas with conservation interest; retaining agricultural, forestry and related uses. Even so land is not to be included within a green belt solely because of its attractiveness. Land is to be included because it needs protection, and that is the dominant purpose of designation.

On the basis that green belt boundaries once fixed should only be exceptionally altered, the Court of Appeal in *Carpets of Worth Ltd v Wyre Forest District Council*[2] considered that an extension of a green belt should be made only where this can be justified for the purposes for which the green belt was designed, though it appears that change may also be made where as a result of supervening changes in a structure plan original green belt boundaries become meaningless or anomalous. However, the courts are otherwise generally unwilling to enter into debate on the drawing of green belt boundaries, restricting themselves to situations where it is alleged that a planning authority has failed to consider the relevant factor of central guidance in a proper fashion.[3]

Turning to development control in green belts, PPG 2 points out that general countryside development policies apply within green belts. These are concerned with development involving agricultural land generally, and reflect the move away from seeing agricultural land in terms of its food production capacity and towards a wider view comprising the need to diversify the rural economy and also to 'protect the countryside for its own sake'. Accordingly, development plans should contain appropriate policies on agricultural land, and the making of such plans should reflect consultation between planning

---

2 (1991) 89 LGR 897.
3 *Stewart v Secretary of State for the Environment* [1991] 3 LMELR 63; and *Grosvenor Developments (Avon) plc v Secretary of State for the Environment* [1991] 3 LMELR 165.

authorities and MAFF. Likewise consultation is obligatory under art 10 of SI 1995/419 in respect of development concerning the loss of more than 20 ha of land of Grades 1, 2 or 3a quality, or the loss of less than 20 ha where this is likely to lead to future losses cumulatively leading to a +20 ha loss: non-statutory consultation may also take place in relation to other developments coming to MAFF's attention. Grades 1 and 2 land account for 17% of the agricultural land in England and Wales and are the most adaptable and fertile land; such land should not be irreversibly developed unless there is no site suitable for the particular purpose proposed. Grade 3 land is subdivided into a, b and c, and together these grades account for 50% of the land in England and Wales. Grade 3a land has comparatively few agricultural limitations and may well be the best land in an area; it should normally therefore receive comparable protection to Grades 1 and 2 land. Grades 3 b, 3 c, 4 and 5 land are of poorer quality, and development of such land will not normally be resisted on agricultural grounds, though there will be exceptions in respect of upland areas. Note also the general policies and constraints laid down in PPG 9, above.

To these constraints, which it is stressed apply to *all* agricultural land, green belt guidance adds the principles that within a belt planning consent should not be given, save in very special circumstances, for construction of new buildings, or the change of use of existing ones, for purposes *other* than agriculture, forestry, outdoor sports, cemeteries, institutions standing in extensive grounds or other appropriate rural uses (including mineral extraction provided high environmental standards are maintained and good restoration takes place).

These principles have been considered in court, and again the judicial 'line' is that it is for authorities to take decisions that will affect green belts, but that legal intervention is appropriate where there is a failure to take into account relevant considerations, such as the principle that development should normally only be permitted where special circumstances justify an exception to green belt policy.[4] Furthermore the courts have laid down that the national presumption in favour of development (see chapter 5) is superseded in green belts by the notion that where a proposed development is inappropriate, in the light of central guidance, there is an assumption that there is demonstrable harm to an interest of acknowledged importance. This will *not always* be fatal where the applicant can show the proposed development carries advantages that outweigh the disbenefits of inappropriate development. Applicants may also point to any relevant plan policies in their favour *and* to any planning permissions already given for inappropriate development in the greenbelt in question, though it may be argued such past developments should be reasonably close to the proposed development site. It is then for the planning authority to weigh the issues and decide whether that special circumstance exists that justifies an exception to normal greenbelt policy.[5]

Thus the basic position appears to be that where an application to develop land in a green belt is received the first task is to determine whether it is an 'appropriate' or 'inappropriate' development. If the latter, the presumption is

4 *Grosvenor Development (Avon) plc v Secretary of State for the Environment* [1991] 3 LMELR 165.
5 *Vision Engineering v Secretary of State for the Environment* [1991] 3 LMELR 199; and *R v Secretary of State for the Environment, ex p Tesco* [1991] 3 LMELR 199.

against a grant of permission, for such development is per se 'harmful' to the green belt though the decision taker must weigh the disbenefits of allowing the development against any benefits flowing from it. The onus is on the applicant to show the balance tips in favour of the development. The courts will not interfere with this exercise unless the decision taker comes to an utterly unreasonable decision, or where the decision taker puts the wrong components into the balance.[6] PPG 3 lists the following as 'inappropriate': the construction of new building *unless* for agricultural/forestry purposes, or as essential facilities for outdoor leisure, or as limited extensions/replacement of existing buildings, or as limited infilling in existing villages, or as redevelopment of a major existing developed site. Re-use of buildings, mineral extraction, community forests, higher and further education facilities are *not* per se 'inappropriate'.

One issue that has been particularly controversial for a number of years is that of housebuilding, not just in greenbelts but in rural areas generally. The problem is complicated by the need to ensure that there is a sufficient number of houses at affordable prices in rural areas for those who traditionally live and work there, and because housebuilding proposals vary from those to build just a few units to those to build whole new settlements.

'What's the use of yearning for Elysian Fields when you know you can't get 'em, and would only let 'em out on building leases if you had 'em' (W S Gilbert, 'Patience', Act I)

PPG 3 (revised 1992) is the principal source of guidance on land for house building. So far as housing (either in small blocks or as new settlements) in rural areas is concerned this accepts that some new greenfield sites outside existing areas will be needed, but any such development must be related to existing patterns of settlement and must have 'proper regard' for other countryside protection policies. It accepts that some villages have reached their natural limit of growth, while others can only take modest additions without damage, while pointing out that new development in villages can maintain their economic and social vitality. The most recent (August 1995) figures on household formation, however, point to a rise in households from 19.2 million in 1991 to 22.7 million as in 2011 — a 900,000 increase on previous projections. Much of this increase would fall on the already over popular South West and South East of England where green belt land might have to be released to meet housing demand. Such an increase, many argue, cannot be met simply by better use of urban sites and is likely to refuel demand for the creation of entirely new urban settlements.

So far as such entirely new settlements are concerned, eg substantial 'stand alone' village and small towns, these have been generally resisted by central and local planning authorities with only a tiny minority of the 180 proposals put forward since 1980 receiving consent. They will only be acceptable where: (a) preferable to and more satisfactory than expanding existing local settlements; (b) clearly supported by local planning preferences and policies of authorities; (c) unlikely to coalesce with existing settlements; (d) such a

---

6 *Barnet Meeting Room Trust v Secretary of State for the Environment* [1993] JPL 739; and *Barnet London Borough Council v Secretary of State for the Environment, Cox, Archdean and Pointon York Trustees Ltd* [1993] JPL 767.

settlement is likely to result in positive environmental improvements, eg through reclamation of derelict land; (e) likely to protect alternative sites from development pressure; (f) *not* within green belts, National Parks, AONB, SSSIs or on the best agricultural land. In addition the pollution consequences of any new settlement insofar as it encourages travel to work have to be considered. Wherever possible it is *generally* considered a new settlement should be of a size (at least 10,000 dwellings) sufficient both to generate and supply its own demands for employment, social, and educational provision, while government guidance also stresses the need to plan for walking, cycling and the use of public transport. Private developers, however, seem to prefer developments of not more than 5,000–8,000 dwellings.

PPG 3 further addresses the need for affordable housing, arguing that in both urban and rural areas any new housing developments on a substantial scale should incorporate a range of housing types to cater for a range of housing needs, though the guidance is averse to the *imposition* of the inclusion of affordable housing in new developments. Planning law also does not generally permit authorities to restrict the tenure, price or ownership of housing. Hence the emphasis is laid on s 106 obligations and coming to partnership arrangements with builders and local housing associations.

O DERELICT LAND

Derelict land has been a problem in both urban and rural areas for many years, sometimes being compounded by problems of contamination. A further difficulty was the lack of accurate surveys of the size of the problem. However, in 1991 the DoE published 'The Survey of Derelict Land in England 1988'. This found 40,500 ha of derelict land, with 31,600 ha justifying reclamation.

The follow up 'Survey of Derelict Land in England 1993' was published in 1995. This found 39,600 ha of derelict land on 10,400 sites with 34,600 ha considered worth reclamation. Industrial dereliction and spoil heaps account for 48% of the total, most of this percentage also being in urban areas. In rural areas dereliction is often the result of past military use, or use for metaliferous spoil heaps, or the consequence of excavation and pits. Almost half the derelict land is in Northern England, with the smallest amounts being in East Anglia and London. Almost half the derelict land was in private sector ownership, local authorities owned 16% and other public sector bodies 20%. Where authorities' areas are afflicted by derelict land there tends to be quite an area of such affliction, and such authorities are usually urban.

Between 1988 and 1993 9,500 ha of derelict land was reclaimed, 55% by local authorities, nearly all of this with DoE grant aid. This led to a decrease in the stock of such land by 2%, much less than the 11% decrease between 1982 and 1988. Of the reclaimed land 8,400 ha has been put to beneficial use, 40% for 'hard' uses, eg industry and commerce, but 'soft' end uses, eg recreation, predominated in rural areas.

Land continues to become derelict, with 8,600 ha falling into this category between 1988 and 1993. Much of this, however, was a result of abandonment of military uses of land, but the DoE has recognised that the flow of land into dereliction is a problem which, though it cannot be eradicated, needs to be reduced — if only to reduce demands for grant aided restoration. Restoration conditions in mineral planning permissions have helped towards preventing dereliction and it has been argued such conditions should be included in development permissions, say, for major heavy industrial developments, though there could be debate as to the appropriate standard to which reclamation should take place. The alternative would be to grant authorities enhanced powers under s 215 of the Town and Country Planning Act 1990 to enable them to take action in respect of serious dereliction of land where landholders have failed to initiate a programme of reclamation and where the derelict land is adversely affecting the amenity of a part of their area.

At the end of 1995 in response to the report 'Derelict Land Prevention and the Planning System' ministers indicated that it is up to both developers and planners to look beyond the expected life of a proposal and to make provision for the eventual rehabilitation and re-use of the land. Appropriate guidance will be given to planning authorities, while strengthened controls over untidy sites will need new legislation. However, as part of the sustainable development policy land should not just be reclaimed from dereliction for reuse and the reduction of pressure on green field sites, it should be developed so that it does not become derelict.

Legislation dealing with derelict land has been on the statute book for many years, and was to be found in the National Parks and Access to the Countryside Act 1949, the Local Authorities (Land) Act 1963, the Local Government Act 1966, the Countryside Act 1968, the Local Employment Act 1972 and the Local Government, Planning and Land Act 1980. The various provisions are now largely contained in or substituted by the Derelict Land Act 1982. However, the basic power of local authorities to reclaim derelict land has been s 89 of the 1949 Act. This granted local planning authorities, that is county and district authorities, powers to:

1   Plant trees on land in their area to preserve or enhance natural beauty.
2   Carry out reclamation works on land in their area appearing to be either derelict, neglected or unsightly, or likely to become so by reason of the actual or apprehended collapse of the surface resulting from underground mining operations, *other* than coal-mining, which have ceased. This power extends to improving land, or bringing it into use, and enables work on the land in question and on other land. The powers may be exercised over an authority's own land, or over other persons' land with their consent. Land may be compulsorily acquired by authorities exercising the powers, subject to ministerial confirmation under s 103 of the 1949 Act.

The restoration powers are supplemented by the Mineral Workings Act 1985, ss 7 and 8. Section 7 gives local authorities certain powers of entry, and to search and bore, in relation to land which is being considered for reclamation in consequence of past underground mining operations, otherwise than for coal. Section 8 allows reclamation work to proceed *without* the consent of those who are interested in the land where in the relevant authority's opinion the surface of the land under which mining was carried out has collapsed, or is in danger of collapse, *and* the works are urgently necessary to protect persons, *and* consent to the work has been unreasonably withheld. Notice of intention to proceed under this power must be given to those interested in the land, and such persons may appeal to the Secretary of State who shall decide the issue.

Section 1 of the 1982 Act relates to grant aid in respect of derelict land. The Secretary of State, subject to Treasury comment, may make such grants in respect of appropriate expenditure.

Policy on derelict land grants was revised with effect from June 1991. Until then grant aid had been concentrated on the restoration of land for urban building purposes. The new policy is broader in encompassing both restoration for development and general environmental improvement, with encouragement for local authorities to create their own programmes for derelict land. Voluntary organisations now receive more funding for restorative and reclamation projects, particularly with a view to the promotion of nature conservation and creation of new habitats on reclaimed land.

A further change occurred in 1993 with the enactment of the Leasehold Reform, Housing and Urban Development Act, under Part III of which an Urban Regeneration Agency (URA) was created. This body's functions extend to securing the regeneration of land in England which is contaminated, derelict, neglected or unsightly or which is likely to become derelict, neglected or unsightly by reason of the collapse of its surface as a result of past underground operations, and that there is a clear parallel with the work of local authorities. However, URA (which is publicly known as 'English Partnerships') is subject to ministerial direction and is particularly concerned with securing the development and reuse of land. To this end it has wide powers under s 160 of the 1993 Act to acquire, manage and develop land. It may also give financial assistance, for example by way of grant/loan, advice, services and facilities to others to promote its statutory functions.

Derelict land grant has been integrated into a unified system of financial support *operated* by URA, though of course, funding still comes from central government. The implications of this for reclamation activity must now be considered.

Derelict land grant reclamation activity has been generally considered a success in value for money terms, at least with regard to reclamation for further development. The 1994 'Assessment of the Effectiveness of Derelict Land Grant in Reclaiming Land for Development' found that, over the years, a wide range of derelict sites had been reclaimed with a high (66%) rate of development after reclamation. Programme objectives have been largely met at a reasonable cost (on average £54,000/ha) and local authorities have carried out their tasks well.

The report recommended that URA under its unified grant scheme should continue the work of reclamation subject to improved site investigations taking place, formal assessment at the time of application of net scheme costs, *and* (NB) the need for reasoned justification to be given of proposed reclamation works and for there to be substantial evidence of demand for sites for development in the area in which relevant land is situated. See further chapter 9, below on contaminated land.

While not all derelict land is contaminated within the statutory definition, much of it is, and the current policy in relation to contaminated land is that clean up costs should not primarily fall on the public purse. Hence it is not surprising that derelict land policy should also appear to now be moving in the direction of the concentration of public resources on those areas where they are most needed, *and* where there is evidence that land once reclaimed will be put to beneficial new developed uses.

P CONCLUSION

The laws regulating land use in rural areas continue to be a microcosm of the confused state of environmental law and policy. They illustrate the fragmented nature of environmental control, with responsibility being divided, unnecessarily perhaps in many cases, between central government, local authorities and a range of statutory ad hoc agencies or 'quangos'. The number of involved bodies could be reduced: the answerability of those remaining could be increased. Rural land use policy also reflects a general lack of consensus on environmental issues. One's stand on a land use issue may be eccentricity to another, and elitist politics to a third. Debate becomes confused. It is hard to distinguish 'friends' from 'foes' in relation to particular issues: various groups use similar words with different meanings. Nevertheless there remains concern for the future of the countryside and over the need to reform CAP, where there is increasing realisation that much more sophisticated land management is required if the countryside is to continue to give us the food we need, the employment many seek, the amenities and recreation we require, and a habitat for the other species with whom we share our land.

Further reading

BOOKS

Elson, MJ, *Green Belts* (1986) Heinemann.
Howarth, W and Rodgers, C, *Agriculture, Conservation & Land Use* (1992) University of Wales Press.
Lowe, P, Cox G, MacEwen M, O'Riodan T, and Winter M, *Countryside Conflicts* (1986) Temple Smith/Gower.
MacEwen, A, and M, *National Parks: Conservation or Cosmetics* (1982) George Allen and Unwin.
MacEwen, A, and M, *Greenprints for the Countryside* (1987) George Allen and Unwin.
Moss, G, *Britain's Wasting Acres* (1981) The Architectural Press.
NHTPC, CPRE & ADC, *Planning Control Over Farmland* (no date) Association of District Councils.
Pye Smith, C, and Rose, C, *Crisis and Conservation* (1984) Penguin Books.
Reid, C, *Nature Conservation Law* (1994) W Green/Sweet & Maxwell.
Shoard, M, *This Land Is Our Land* (1987) Paladin.
Winter, M, 'Agriculture and the Environment' in Churchill, R, Warren, L, and Gibson, J, *Law, Policy and the Environment* (1991) Basil Blackwell.

JOURNALS, OCCASIONAL AND CONFERENCE PAPERS

Basden, A, 'Cramping Our Style' (1991) 60 Town and Country Planning 294.
Chesman, GR, 'Local Authorities and the Review of the Definitive Map under the Wildlife and Countryside Act 1981' [1991] JPL 611.
Corbett, B, 'Protecting the Human Resources of the Countryside — affordable housing initiatives' [1994] 6 ELM 64.
Forster, M, 'The Countryside and the Law: making the new Rights of Way Act work' [1990] 2 LMELR 126.

Hawke, N, 'Contemporary Issues in Environmental Policy Implementation' [1987] JPL 241.

Robinson, PC, 'Tree Preservation Orders: Felling a Dangerous Tree' [1990] JPL 720.

Scrase, AJ, 'Agriculture — 1980s Industry and 1947 Definition' [1988] JPL 447.

OFFICIAL REPORTS AND CONFERENCE PAPERS

House of Commons Environment Committee: '1st Report on Green Belt Land and Land for Housing', Session 1983–84, HC 275-1 and 275 i–xii.

House of Commons Agriculture Committee: '2nd Special Report on The Effects of Pesticides on Human Health', Session 1986–87, HC 379-1.

House of Lords Select Committee on the European Communities: '20th Report on Agriculture and the Environment', Session 1983–84, HL 247.

'Access to the Countryside for Recreation and Sport', CCP 217 (1986) Countryside Commission.

'New Opportunities for the Countryside', CCP 224 (1987) Countryside Commission.

'Planning for Countryside in Metropolitan Areas', CCP 244 (1987) Countryside Commission.

'Urban Wasteland Now' (1988) Civic Trust.

'Growing against the Grain' (1987) CPRE.

'The Countryside Tomorrow' (1986) Royal Society for Nature Conservation.

'Planning for a Greener Countryside' (1989) Countryside Commission.

'Environmentally Sensitive Areas' (1989) HMSO.

'A Farmer's Guide to the Planning System' (1993) HMSO.

'Housing Land Availability' (1991) HMSO.

'Permitted Development Rights for Agriculture and Forestry' (1991) HMSO.

'Survey of Derelict Land in England 1993' (1995) HMSO.

'The Effectiveness of Green Belts' (1993) HMSO.

'Our Forests: the Way Ahead' (1994) Cm 2644 HMSO.

'Protecting and Managing Sites of Special Scientific Interest in England' (1994) National Audit Office No 379, HMSO.

House of Commons Environment Committee; 3rd Special Report Session 1994–1995, 'The Environmental Impact of Leisure Activities', HC 761.

'Assessment of the Effectiveness of Derelict Land Grant in Reclaiming Land for Development' (1994) HMSO.

'Derelict Land Prevention and the Planning System' (1995) HMSO.

Land Use Consultants: 'Planning Controls Over Agricultural and Forestry Development and Rural Building Conversions' (1995) HMSO.

Elson et al: 'Planning for Rural Diversification' (1995) HMSO.

Royal Commission on Environmental Pollution, Nineteenth Report: 'Sustainable Use of Soil', Cm 3165 (1996) HMSO.

Chapter 7

Controversial operations and hazardous uses of land

'Belch forth your venom, toads' (W S Gilbert, 'The Sorcerer', Act I)

A INTERNATIONAL AND EU PROVISIONS

The previous chapter considered controls relating to land use in rural areas. This chapter considers first a number of particularly controversial land use issues such as nuclear plants. Some of these have common features: they are expensive; consume considerable quantities of land; are effectively permanent features of the landscape once constructed; are environmentally disruptive; involve a number of central departments as well as local authorities; normally require environmental assessment (see chapter 5); and involve public inquiries. Public inquiries, already dealt with at some length in chapter 5, will form the subject of much of this chapter.

NB International and EU law are somewhat less prominent in relation to these matters than with regard to other environmental issues, apart from the need for environmental assessment already touched on above. The principal relevant treaties are largely concerned with security control, such as the Paris Convention of 1957, worker protection — the Geneva Convention of 1960 — or third party liabilities — the Paris Convention of 1960 (see also Brussels 1963 and Paris Protocols (× 2) 1963). These are of course, now supplemented by the Vienna Conventions of 1986 on assistance in the case of nuclear accidents, etc and on early notification of nuclear accidents which followed the Chernobyl incident. In a work such as this primarily devoted to national law, reasons of space forbid elaborate treatment of international provisions. Interested readers are, however, referred to Cameron, Hancher and Kuhn *Nuclear Law After Chernobyl*, and to chapter 9 in Birnie and Boyle's *International Law and the Environment*.

The EU's contribution to nuclear power issues is also not extensive. There have been a number of Council *resolutions*, some of them favouring an expansion of nuclear energy so as to reduce the EU's dependence on imported oil. Furthermore the EURATOM treaty committed member states to the development of the nuclear industry so that by 1989 nuclear power accounted for one third of the EU's energy balance. Basic standards for the protection of the public and workers against ionising radiations were laid down in Directive 59/211/Euratom, and these have been updated, eg in 1962, 1966, 1976, 1979, and 1984; see now Euratom Council Directives 80/836 and 84/467. Workers are to receive protection by systems of prevention of radiation, dose limitation, and evaluation of risks, coupled with medical supervision, while public protection is generally limited to surveillance procedures though exposure levels for the public are prescribed. Prior authorisation is required for relevant activities such as producing, transporting, possessing and disposing of nuclear materials. Article 37 of Euratom further requires all radioactive waste disposal installation proposals to be communicated to the Commission. The EU has also commissioned extensive research into radioactive waste and the after care of closed nuclear power stations. The Commission has further harmonised national safety criteria for nuclear equipment by the mutual exchange of information on national laws and practices. See below on SI 1985/1333 for UK implementation.

Commission Regulation 3227/76/Euratom, made under Arts 77, 78, 79 and 81 of the Treaty establishing the European Atomic Energy Community, provides for the application of the Euratom safeguards provisions. These are particularly concerned with transfers and flows of stocks of nuclear materials, record keeping, surveillance systems over nuclear material, and notification of imports/exports of relevant materials. Euratom Regulation 1493/93, applying to intra-union shipments of sealed sources of radioactive material and certain other materials but *not* nuclear fuel requires basic information on the substances being transported to be notified to relevant 'competent authorities' in receiving states by those who are exporting the material. The object of the regulation is to ensure that national requirements concerned with notification of shipments are complied with and the making of appropriate financial arrangements.

Euratom Directive 92/3 has, since 1 January 1994, applied to shipments of nuclear *waste* within and outwith the EU, though this does not apply to spent or irradiated nuclear fuel. The pattern of control here is that for internal shipments 'competent authorities' in the country of transit and/or destination must grant their consent to the equivalent authority in the country of origin before a shipment can commence. An automatic approval system can, however, operate on the part of transit/receiving states who so inform the Commission. Where material is to be transported out of the EU the nation of destination must be contacted, and shipment may then only be authorised if that state's stipulations on receiving nuclear waste are satisfied. There is a total prohibition on exports to some non-EU states, for example those considered as lacking the capacity to deal with the waste, but some material escapes control, such as sealed sources containing only non-fissile material, and processed or reprocessed waste being returned to its nation of origin. The Directive is implemented in the UK by the Transfrontier Shipment of Radioactive Waste Regulations SI 1993/3031.

EU legislation is more prominent in relation to the control of hazardous activities involving chemicals, etc.

EU policy on dangerous substances, etc — an overview

Initially policy was directed towards the elimination of barriers to trade which were the potential outcome of differing national standards on the classification, packaging and labelling of harmful substances. This led to the first Directive on the issue, 67/548 (see below) which has since been massively revised. The basis of regulation adopted under this Directive is that manufacturers of new chemical products have to test them and submit those test results to a national competent authority for evaluation of possible harmful results. These evaluations are passed to the Commission which informs appropriate authorities in other member states. If there are no objections the product has free access to the internal market, subject to requirements on labelling and packaging which are also designed to act as protection measures.

A second technique for controlling harmful substances is encountered in the form of restrictions on the marketing and use of substances — even outright bans in some cases. Thus Directive 76/769 (amended by 89/678) is a framework Directive laying down such restrictions in general, and since then a whole series of 'daughter' directives have dealt with specific substances by applying the restrictions to them, see further below.

These techniques have been particularly applied to pesticides, some of which are restricted as to their marketing and use, while others are banned, see Directive 79/117, as amended and also Directive 91/414 which introduced a new scheme of authorising and marketing pesticides.

With regard to pesticides a further control technique is to specify what residues of such substances can be left in food after their use, and this is encountered in Directive 76/895, as amended.

The concept of 'prior informed consent' has been used as a regulatory technique with regard to restricting, or in some cases banning, the sale of certain chemicals (those on the International Register of Potentially Toxic Chemicals), especially pesticides, to non-member states. Here Regulation 2455/92, as amended by 41/94 and 3135/94, introduces a system whereby exports to and imports from non-member states are subject to a 'prior informed consent' (PIC) system following notification of the proposed trade.

Particular systems of control have been developed for dealing with individual substances, either generally, or within particular contexts. Materials dealt with in one or more of these ways include asbestos (see further below), lead, chlorofluorocarbons, and cadmium.

Health and safety requirements and general requirements for the protection of the civilian population in the vicinity of plants handling particular substances are further techniques of regulation, as in the 'Seveso' Directive, 82/501, as amended by 87/216 and 88/610, and see further below, and the Directive on Worker Protection, 80/1107, as amended by 88/642 and 91/322, with its daughter directives on the regulation of exposure to lead and asbestos, etc.

Classification, etc, of dangerous substances

The first directive on the classification, packaging and labelling of dangerous *substances* was 67/548. It defined substances as dangerous if they were 'explosive, oxidising, flammable, toxic, harmful, corrosive and irritant'. This Directive was amended on a number of occasions, and the 'package' was effectively replaced by the '7th Amendment' Directive 92/32 which replaced the original articles.

The list of relevant daughter and other Directives is now too long to be accommodated in this work, and interested readers should refer to Haigh's *Manual of Environmental Policy: the EC and Britain*, to which, as ever, considerable indebtedness is acknowledged. It should, however, be noted that the various Directives require listing of commercial chemical substances so that appropriate controls may be identified; these listings are the European Inventory of Existing Commercial Chemical Substances (EINECS), relating to substances on the market before 18 September 1981, the European List of Notified Chemical Substances (ELINCS) which is updated annually to take account of subsequently developed products and the List of Substances Classified as Dangerous (SCD), setting out a number of categories of dangerous material. The basic requirement is that 'new' substances, ie those not on the market on 18 September 1981, must, inter alia, be notified to a 'competent authority' before they can be put on the market along with a dossier of information enabling evaluation of foreseeable risks, certain required test results, a declaration of the unfavourable effects of substances in view of their likely foreseeable use, the proposed classification and labelling. Substances must then be classified on the basis of intrinsic properties according to 15 preset categories of danger, including 'danger to the environment'. Thereafter they may not be marketed unless they are packaged and labelled according to strict requirements set down in the Directives. The UK has implemented these requirements under the Health and Safety at Work etc Act 1974 and SI 1994/3247.

Classification, etc, of dangerous preparations

Similar provisions have been developed with regard to the classification packaging and labelling of dangerous *preparations*, ie materials containing at least one *substance* classified as dangerous under 67/548 etc and which are regarded as dangerous on the basis that they are explosive, oxidising, flammable, etc, following evaluation according to specified criteria. The provisions are found in Directive 88/379, adapted by 89/178, 90/492 and 93/18.

The basic scheme here is that member states must take steps to require that certain specified dangerous preparations which are marketed comply with the terms of relevant Directives, eg as to the labelling of containers and packages. Thus certain products have to be provided with child resistant fastenings, while others must have tactile danger warnings. The Directives in this group are much concerned with controls over the classification, packaging and labelling of solvents and paints. The UK's implementing measure is, in general, SI 1994/3247.

To deal with material where packaging and labelling requirements are insufficient protection from danger, Directive 76/769 amended by 89/678 lays down restrictions on marketing and use. The prime obligation is that member states may only allow marketing and use subject to specified requirements which can amount to bans. Initially the directive related only to poly-chlorinated bi and ter phenyls (PCBs and PCTs) and monomer vinylchloride (VCM), restricting their use only to certain electrical equipment and banning VCM as an aerosol propellant. This has subsequently been extended by 79/663 banning certain dangerous chemicals, eg triphosphate, in ornamental objects and certain textiles; 82/806 (benzene in toys); 83/264 (ban on the use of certain chemicals, eg polybrominated biphenyls, in textiles and others, eg aluminium sulphide, in jokes and hoaxes); 83/478 (a general ban on the marketing and use of crocidolite ('blue' asbestos) fibres and material containing such fibre); 85/467 (new applications of PCBs and PCTs banned, as also, marketing of second hand equipment containing such material and fluids containing them); 85/610 (restricting the marketing and use of products such as toys, paints and varnishes, etc, where they contain asbestos fibres other than crocidolite, most recently there have been restrictions on nickel in costume jewellery, flammable substances in aerosol generators and on, inter alia, creosote and chlorinated solvent).[1]

ASBESTOS

Further specific attention to the problem of asbestos is found in Directive 87/217. This applies to various types of asbestos (ie crocidolite (blue asbestos), actinolite, anthophyllite, crysotile (white asbestos), amosite (brown asbestos), and tremolite), and requires member states to take steps to ensure that discharges of asbestos to land, air and water are, so far as is reasonably practicable, reduced at source and prevented. With regard to asbestos use the 'best available technique not entailing excessive costs' (BATNEEC) must be used to achieve this end, and may entail the adoption of recycling or treatment. There are various exemptions for activities using less than 100 kg of raw asbestos pa for plants emitting under 5,000 m^3/hour total gaseous discharges, though the general limit for atmospheric emissions of asbestos is 0.1 mg/m^3 of air discharged. There are recycling requirements for liquid asbestos effluent in connection with asbestos cement, paper and board making, but in the case of cement where recycling is not economically feasible, liquid waste discharges must not exceed 30 g total suspended matter per m^3 of effluent discharged. Further requirements relate to ensuring that working with asbestos does not cause significant environmental pollution by asbestos fibre or dust, likewise demolition of buildings, etc, containing asbestos, eg bans on release of fibres during landfill and on spillages of liquid asbestos waste, and special landfill containment requirements. Monitoring of discharges is further required. Periodic reports on the implementation of the Directive are made by the Commission under Directive 91/692.

EU controls over biological agents

Turning from chemical hazards to those of a biological nature Directives 90/219 and 90/220 are concerned with genetically modified organisms (GMOs). The Directives (the first of which is based on art 130S and the latter on art 100A) are derived from preventative principles and the protection of human health and the environment being concerned with the contained use of GMOs (90/219) and their deliberate release into the environment (90/200).

Directive 90/219, as amended by 94/51, defines GMOs (as does 90/220) as micro-organisms whose genetic material has been altered in a way not naturally occurring but capable of replication or transferring genetic material. Such GMOs are then further sub-classified as those falling within Group 1 of Annex II of 90/219 and the rest (Group 2 – which are actually potentially more

---

1 See Directives 94/27, 94/48 and 94/60. For relevant UK legislation see Haigh, op cit, Table 7.5.2.

dangerous). Group 1 are, generally, non-pathogenic and having a proven 'safe track record', Group 2 may need containment measures. Likewise operations involving GMOs are classified as 'A' or 'B'. A is basically research and development, B is the rest which includes the industrial use of GMOs. The Directive requirements thereafter differ according to which *group* of GMOs is being used in which *type of operation*. The basic requirement is that member states must take appropriate measures to avoid adverse effects arising from the *contained* use of GMOs and such uses must be subject to prior risk assessment taking account of the requirements of the Directive as to characteristics of material, environmental and health considerations, see further Annex III.

The minimum requirements in respect of Group 1 are that principles of good microbiological practice, occupational safety and hygiene must apply. For Group 2 there must be containment measures which must be kept under periodic review. Where an installation is to be used for the first time for contained use of GMOs in *either* group a 'competent authority' must be informed according to the requirements of Annex V, this relates to specified information concerning inter alia, names of responsible persons, relevant addresses, the Annex III information; numbers of workers involved; the activity using the GMO, and equipment to be used; waste management practices; accident prevention and emergency response plans. Particular information processes are laid down for specified operations on material falling within particular groups. The requirements are stricter for Group 2 than for Group 1, and include information as to waste management, accident prevention and emergency response plans. There is a continuing obligation to update relevant information supplied. Competent authorities must ensure before operations commence that emergency plans for health and environmental protection have been drawn up as required and that information on safety measures has been made publicly available. Such information must additionally be circulated between member states, this latter requirement reinforces the duties of states to consult with others likely to be affected in the case of an accident in drawing up emergency plans. Should accidents occur reporting requirements are laid down, and mechanisms for reporting to the Commission are established, though provision is also made for the protection of confidential information and intellectual property rights. Yearly reports on Group 2 Type B operations have to be sent to the Commission by member states, who must also submit a triennial overall report on experience with the Directive.

Directive 90/220 as amended by 94/15 obligates member states to avoid adverse health or environmental effects which might arise from the deliberate release, or placing on the market, of GMOs, and again requires competent authorities to exercise supervision, though the measure is primarily a 'harmonising' one under art 100 A. Where a deliberate release for research and development purposes is proposed the competent authority must be informed and given specified information and a risk assessment, including information on the conditions for release, the state of the receiving environment, and interactions between that and the GMO. Competent authorities examine notifications to check for compliance with the Directive and pay particular attention to the risk assessment.

Consultation with interest groups or the public may take place, and summary details of the notification are sent to the Commission who will forward them to other member states, who may then make their observations. These must be taken into account by the competent authority who will then inform the notifier in writing whether the release complies with the Directive and whether it may proceed, with the Commission and other member states being informed of the decision on this point. The release may then only proceed in compliance with this written consent and may even then be stopped should the competent authority consider significant consequence of risk is involved. The notifier must inform the authority after due release of any resulting risks to health and the environment.

Where the proposal is to place a GMO on the market, there must be a notification first to the competent authority containing specified information, again with an assessment of risks to human health and the environment. The proposal must be checked for compliance with the Directive, the competent authority here also pays special attention to the risk assessment. If the conditions of the Directive for release are not met the notification must be rejected. If, however, the authority feels the proposed release complies they must forward their opinion and the dossier of relevant material to the Commission. The dossier is forwarded by the Commission to competent authorities in other member states, and if they raise no objections within a period of 60 days the relevant national competent authority will consent in writing to the release, informing the Commission and other member states. Where, however, an objection is raised and cannot be resolved the matter reverts to the Commission, who will consult the advisory committee of national experts set up for this purpose. If the Commission assents the relevant national authority will approve as above.

Consented products may be used throughout the EU, subject to any condition of the consent, though a provisional restriction/prohibition on sale/use may be imposed by a member state considering a product is a risk to the environment or human health. In such a case the Commission and other member states must be informed and the Commission will take a decision on the issue utilising the advisory committee procedure.

We now return to matters national, some of which correspond to EU obligations.

B TRUNK AND SPECIAL ROADS

'Look down, look down that lonesome road, before you travel on' (old spiritual song)

The Highways Act 1980 provides for creation, improvement and maintenance of roads, and for acquisition of land. The Act creates highway authorities. In England central government functions with regard to highways are exercised by the Secretary of State for Transport who is responsible, inter alia, for 'trunk roads', see s 1(1)(a) of the 1980 Act. Otherwise the normal highway authority outside Greater London in England is the county council or metropolitan district where appropriate, to whom the 'Secretary of State may delegate powers of maintenance, improvement and dealing with' in respect of trunk roads under s 6 of the Act (see chapter 3, above for the pattern of local government responsibilities). Agreements may also be made with county authorities for construction of trunk roads, see s 6(5). It should be noted that, under s 337 of the 1980 Act, nothing in the Act authorises carrying out of development without planning permission of operations for which permission is required. Engineering operations in connection with trunk road building would generally require planning permission from the appropriate authority, but for the rule that planning legislation does not bind the Crown,[2] see also s 294 of the Town and Country Planning Act 1990. *Non-statutory* consultation procedures in respect of Crown developments are not generally applied to trunk road proposals; it is considered that procedures under the highways and compulsory purchase legislation should not be duplicated. Maintenance and improvement work carried out by *local* highway authorities within the boundaries of a road is excluded from the definition of development under s 55(2)(b) of the 1990 Act.

Trunk roads and special roads, which expressions include motorways, are provided for under the Highways Act 1980, Part II. A 'special road' is one reserved for use by traffic of particular classes, see ss 10 and 16 of that Act. The various classes of traffic for special roads are prescribed under s 17 by reference to those set out in Sch 4 to the 1980 Act. The Minister is under a duty under s 10(2) to keep under review the national system of routes for through traffic. After considering the requirements of national or local planning, including the requirements of agriculture, the Minister may conclude it is expedient to extend, improve or reorganise that system, and may accordingly by order direct that any highway, or any highway he/she proposes to construct should be a trunk road. It should be noted that roads principally used for local traffic may still be classified as trunk roads provided that is expedient for the *through* system of traffic nationally.[3] In London Part II of the Road Traffic Act 1991 enables the Secretary of State for Transport to make 'priority route orders' on roads so as to create a network of roads to improve traffic flow. Such an order may only be made, under s 50 of the 1991 Act, after consultation with relevant authorities, eg London Boroughs, while s 51 further empowers the Secretary of State to issue traffic management guidance to authorities. Section 52 authorises the appointment of a 'Traffic Director for London' who is charged, inter alia, with overseeing the relation of traffic management action to the operating of priority routes. That person is also charged, under s 53, with the planning, designing and operation of the priority route network. Relevant authorities are under a duty to respond to the Secretary of State's guidance and the network plan by preparing, under s 54, local plans of their proposals for priority routes. These plans will, inter alia, indicate what use of Highways Act 1980 and Road Traffic Regulation Act 1984 powers the authority proposes with regard to priority routes. Such plans are subject to approval by the Director. The Director may be required by the Secretary of State under s 55 to prepare a local plan in relation to any priority route which is also a trunk road, again indicating what use of highway, etc, powers should be made; alternatively under s 56 the Secretary of State may make such a plan himself.

2 *Ministry of Agriculture, Fisheries and Food v Jenkins* [1963] 2 QB 317, [1963] 2 All ER 147.
3 *Walters v Secretary of State for the Environment* [1979] JPL 171.

The introduction of these powers came at the same time as an announcement that to relieve traffic congestion in London reliance would be placed on 300 miles of 'Red Routes'; ie roads with severe parking restrictions to ease traffic flow. The 1991 Act is designed to further this policy by utilising *existing* road space more effectively so as to enable traffic to move. Some commentators, however, view the new policy as the 'back door' creation of motorways arguing that *any* provision of road space by any means simply increases traffic demand, see further Harwood 'Motorways by Stealth' (1991) 60 Town and Country Planning 199.

Special roads are provided under the authorisation of schemes prescribing their routes, but before making or confirming such a scheme the Minister must consider the requirements of national and local planning and those of agriculture. Such roads in due course become trunk roads, see s 19. Section 18 of the 1980 Act further allows the transfer to the Minister as 'the special road authority' of existing highways comprised in the route prescribed in the scheme authorising the special road and the appropriation of existing highways already under the Minister's jurisdiction for this purpose. Section 24 of the 1980 Act actually empowers the Minister, with the approval of the Treasury, to construct new highways.

Procedure

Before a trunk or special road is constructed there is a lengthy process of preparation of which public inquiry procedures are but part. This procedure was summarised in the National Audit Office Report, Department of Transport: 'Environmental Factors in Road Planning and Design' (1994). The procedure (see further below) should take some 10 years, but there are some commentators who argue this ten year scenario is wrong, and that reality is closer to 15 years — a period many consider unduly protracted. However, equally the 'procedure' provides little opportunity for public involvement while the Department of Transport will have become committed to promoting roads proposed, partly because of the historic commitment of the Department to extensive road building programmes, see 'National Road Traffic Forecasts (Great Britain)' 1989 and 'Roads for Prosperity' Cm 693, and partly because of 'administrative momentum' which builds up behind proposals as they are processed. Frequent criticism of governmental claims to be 'environmentally conscious' are made by those who point to major spending on road building programmes, with the majority of the transport department's allocation of public finance being earmarked for road building.

Traditionally Department of Transport road building plans have been based on a cost benefit analysis (COBA) whereby the cost of building the road, which includes land acquisition and engineering costs, has been balanced against 'benefits' to be derived from its construction, for example shortened journey times and accident prevention.

COBA has taken into account shortened journey times, reduced accident rates and lower operating costs and has extrapolated them over a 30 year period, comparing such costs against the schemes' construction costs. A value was placed on shortened journey times by considering how much people would pay to have reduced journey to work times. COBA has been supplemented by QUADRO which estimated traffic costs caused by lane maintenance closures. COBA *did not* 'monetise' environmental considerations, however, though environmental factors did lead to *modifications* of some schemes, even where this led to their having *negative* cost benefit assessments. As from March 1992, however, monetisation techniques were introduced to set a notional 'price' on countryside features at the start of the road planning process for COBA evaluation.

This was the first step in changes in road planning policy and procedure whose exact outcome remains uncertain. Much of this stemmed from public opposition to, and official concern over, the cost of widening the M25 around London. In June 1992 it was announced that sections of the M25 were to be widened to 14 lanes, at a cost of £144m. By July the proposal was for two 14 lane sections at a cost of £250m. In 1993 a leaked report from the Department of the Environment indicated that the roads programme in general was costed at £236m over 15 years, that 243 road projects were potentially controversial, with 103 likely to engender high controversy with 118 in all also likely to have a particularly damaging effect on the environment as they would affect SSSIs and other land of high conservation interest, etc. At this time direct protest against road building became regular, with, for example, those opposed to the building of the M11 link road setting up tree houses in the path of the development. At the same time the total cost of widening existing motorways was found to be 78% above initial estimates; this led in March 1994 to the scrapping of 49 road projects, one third of the 1989 programme, some of them on environmental grounds. Even so concern over the rest of the programme continued especially as some proposals were only 'postponed'.

Even by that date certain changes had occurred in road planning policy. The National Audit Office's report on road planning revealed that as from July 1993 the Department of Transport had introduced environmental assessment techniques into the road planning programme at a number of points. The stages in road planning thus are:

---

1 Identification for the need for a scheme and its entry into the road programme — subject to an assessment of environmental constraints and, where possible, costed proposals to mitigate undesirable effects.

---

2 Broad assessment of the environmental impact of a scheme (which is *not* necessarily, nor even usually, an examination of a *whole* road) takes place.

---

3 Consultation with the public on the initial options for road schemes, followed by an analysis of the results of this exercise.

---

4 The preferred route is announced.

5 There is then a detailed environmental appraisal of the preferred route. This will follow the pattern required by Directive 85/337, but will certainly draw together material on the effects of the scheme on air quality, cultural heritage disruption, nature conservation, the landscape, existing communities, agriculture, traffic noise and vibration, road users, views, water, underlying soils and geology, other policies and plans for roads — *where possible* combined and cumulative assessments will be undertaken where schemes are linked.

6 The draft statutory orders and environmental statement are published and views and objections sought.

7 A broad analysis of the views and alternative proposals put forward by any objectors will be undertaken.

8 A public inquiry will be held according to statute and the environmental impacts will be considered in the inspector's report.

9 The Secretary of State gives his/her decision.

10 Measures to mitigate the impact of the road will be incorporated into the design.

11 The contract will be prepared.

12 The mitigation measures will be incorporated in the road's construction.

```
13 The road is built.
```

```
14 The road is opened.
```

It should be noted, however, as the National Audit Office pointed out, that this procedure does not deal with the global and cumulative effect of schemes, though this short coming had been pointed out and the Department had agreed to examine the possibility of extending the overall procedure.

The road to hell is paved with good intentions

In September 1994 came two major policy critiques. The Standing Committee on Trunk Road Assessment (SACTRA) delivered its report 'Trunk Roads and the Generation of Traffic' which concluded that: extra traffic (known as 'induced traffic') does occur simply because of improvements in the road system; the amount and significance of this traffic will vary considerably from place to place, but is likely to be most significant on roads in and around urban areas, on estuary crossings and on 'strategic capacity-enhancing interurban schemes', including motorway widening; that the current COBA system fails to take adequate account of induced traffic and so may overestimate the benefits of road schemes. SACTRA concluded: 'scheme appraisal must be carried out within the context of economic and environmental appraisals at the strategic area-wide level which take account of induced traffic . . . Much more emphasis needs to be placed on the strategic assessment of trunk routes . . .' Then in its 18th Report, 'Transport and the Environment' Cm 2674 the Royal Commission on Environmental Pollution recommended, inter alia, that a sustainable transport system needs to ensure that traffic is moved from roads to less damaging modes of transport, and accordingly 'a fundamental review of the definition and purpose of a separate system of trunk roads' was recommended, *together with* the subjugation of the road development programme to the development control system, and changes in highways inquiry procedures so that government representatives should be capable of being required to answer questions on the merits of roads policy, and so that an inspector at such an inquiry (see further below) should be able 'to take account of the interactions of the proposal with other government policies in his recommendation'. The Royal Commission went on to argue that insofar as a central government road programme survives, the construction or widening of trunk and special roads should only be undertaken where that is the *best practicable environmental option* for meeting access needs. Furthermore road schemes not yet subject to contractual arrangements should be reassessed in the light of changes in policy and road assessment methodology, and planned motorway expenditure reduced by a half. By April 1996, however, ministers had declined to set specific targets for decreasing car journeys and increasing journeys by cycle and public transport.

At a time (mid-1994) when responsibility for the roads programme was being transferred from the Department of Transport to a 'nextsteps' body — the Highways Agency — it thus appeared that cost considerations, expert external advice, and public opposition might combine with Treasury doubts as to the veracity of the argument that road schemes stimulate economic growth to bring about a major change in transport policy. Ministers were certainly changing road building funding policy in favour of privately built toll motorways and the introduction of charge metering schemes for other major public roads, while at the same time reducing road spending by £400m over the years 1994–96. By December 1994 ministers had agreed to implement the SACTRA recommendation that all future road schemes should be assessed on the basis of gauging their 'induced traffic' impact, though this would not apply to schemes which had already gone through a public inquiry process.

By March 1995 even the policies of favouring private sector road building via 'Design, Build, Finance and Operate' (DBFO) schemes and charge metering for road use were subject to doubt. Road building using private funds was found to be more expensive than public development, and it was realised that those who build roads for gain are likely to do everything to *increase* unsustainable road traffic in order to earn a reward from their investment. Furthermore the House of Commons Transport Committee in its 3rd Report for 1994–95 'Urban Road Pricing' recommended, inter alia, that 'physical measures [traffic restrictions, etc] have a significant potential to reduce traffic in towns, and have the advantage that they have been, and more could be, introduced within a much shorter timescale than urban road pricing. We recommend that the Department assess the extent to which physical measures could be used to restrain traffic in urban areas . . .'

In April 1995 the government decided to scrap the 14 lane proposals for the M25 and a number of other associated motorway schemes — not least because it was realised the proposal was deeply unpopular in many constituencies in Surrey which have traditionally voted Conservative. Further evidence of a shift away from traditional road policy came in the November 1995 budget. 5% of the road budget was cut, but significantly this related to projected schemes and no major new road starts were expected for 1996/97, save the continuingly controversial Newbury by-pass and a handful of other schemes. 77 motorway and trunk road schemes were withdrawn, while new privately financed road schemes were not expected to start until 1997/98. A total revision of roads policy seems likely, with more spending on public transport and integrated systems, but for the time being we must return to the relevant law.

Under s 10(5) of the 1980 Act, Sch 1, Parts I and III and Sch 2 apply to trunk road orders, and, under s 16(7), Sch 1, Parts II and III and Sch 2 apply to special road schemes. Where the Minister proposes to make a *trunk road order* he/she must prepare a draft and publish a notice in at least one local newspaper circulating in the affected area, and in the *London Gazette*. This must state the general effect of the proposal, name a place in the locality where a copy of the draft, and any maps or plans referred to in the draft, may be inspected, free of charge at reasonable hours, during a specified period of not less than six weeks from the date of publication, and must state the right of any person to object to the order. Additional publicity steps may be taken within the affected area. Environmental Assessment will already be under way on the preferred route for the road as shown in the draft; see above for the outline of procedure, and below for details of assessment. Not later than the day on which the notice is published the Minister must serve on certain persons a copy of the notice, a copy of the draft order and a copy of any map or plan referred to in the draft order relating to a matter which in the opinion of the Minister is likely to affect the persons served. The persons to be served are: (a) every council (including counties and districts) in whose area the highway or proposed highway is situated; and (b) where the order provides for bridges and tunnels or the diversion of navigable watercourses, relevant navigation authorities and the Environment Agency.

If any objection to the proposed order is received by the Minister from any person *statutorily* listed to receive a copy of the notice or from *any other person* appearing to the Minister to be affected, and that objection is not withdrawn, then he/she must hold a public inquiry. There is a discretion to dispense with this inquiry where it is considered unnecessary in the circumstances, *except* where the objection is made by a person statutorily required to be served with notice. A court will inquire only as to whether there is material on which the Minister could reasonably conclude an inquiry is unnecessary.[4] The Minister has no general discretion to dispense with an inquiry, nor may he do so on grounds of mere expediency. In *Binney v Secretary of State for the Environment*,[5] it was held that a Minister may not refuse to hold an inquiry simply because of a belief that enough about the matter in question is already known. The Minister must be satisfied that the objects to be attained by an inquiry, which include evaluating various conflicting public points of view and interests, and ensuring that those having rights to make representations have such representations considered, can be achieved without an inquiry. Where there are substantial groups holding conflicting views on a major road proposal a reasonable Minister should hold an inquiry, thus ensuring proper argument on and examination of the various points of view. Even where he/she decides an inquiry need not be held and that decision is proper in the circumstances, it may be he/she should at least allow both those supporting the proposal and those objecting to it to see each other's representations.

Where an inquiry is held the report of the person holding it must be considered. Thereafter the Minister may make the order with or without modifications as he/she thinks fit. Where any modifications proposed will, in the Minister's opinion, make a substantial change in the order, he/she must notify persons likely to be affected, give them an opportunity of making representations to him/her within a reasonable period, and must consider representations made (see below on the role of environmental assessment with regard to the decision making process).

Under s 257(3) of the 1980 Act proceedings under the power to acquire land compulsorily (part of the general land acquisition powers in connection with highway construction and improvement granted by Part XII of the Act) may be undertaken concurrently, in respect of trunk and special roads, with proceedings on relevant trunk road orders and special road schemes. The line order, side road orders (see s 14 of the 1980 Act) and compulsory purchase orders are not, in fact, generally taken together, because most public involvement in the road planning process will have been concentrated at the line order stage. When inquiries are held to hear objections to side road orders made in consequence of a major road proposal, the inspector holding the

4 *Shorman v Secretary of State for the Environment* [1977] JPL 98.
5 [1984] JPL 871.

inquiry may refuse to receive objections attempting to re-open the question of the line of the principal road already determined after an inquiry.[6]

Where the Minister proposes to make a *special road scheme* he/she must publish in local newspapers and in the *London Gazette* a notice which: states the general effect of the proposed scheme; names a place in the affected area where a copy of the draft scheme, and any map or plan referred to in it may be inspected by the public, free of charge at reasonable times, during a specified period of not less than six weeks from the date of the notice; and states the right of any person to object to the making of the scheme. Contemporaneously the Minister must serve a copy of the notice, together with a copy of the draft scheme and supporting maps, etc, on every council in whose area part of the route of the special road is situated, and, where bridges or tunnels are to be constructed over or under navigable waters, on relevant navigation authorities and the Environment Agency. Where objections are received from the specified authorities or from any other person appearing to the Minister to be affected, and these are not withdrawn, there is a general obligation to hold an inquiry similar to that imposed in respect of trunk road orders. After the inquiry is held, and the report thereof considered, the scheme may be confirmed with or without modifications. Modifications substantially altering a scheme must be notified to those likely to be affected and they must be given a chance to make representations, which must be considered.

Environmental assessment of roads

In order to implement Directive 85/337 on environmental assessment (see further chapter 5) s 105A of the 1980 Act as amended and SI 1988/1241 provide that in any case where the Secretary of State has under consideration the construction or improvement of a highway he/she shall initially determine whether it falls within Annex I or II of the Directive. Motorways are within Annex I while some trunk roads fall within Annex II. The Secretary of State must, under SI 1994/1002 determine whether the road will fall within Annex I, or whether it is within Annex II and is likely to have significant environmental effects, and the normal criteria for determination as announced in Department of Transport Standard HD 18/88 relate to: length (is the new road over 10 km long?); location (is the road in or within 100 m of a National Park, SSSI, conservation area, or nature reserve, or is it in an urban area where 1,500 or more dwellings lie within 100 m of its proposed centre line?), and quality (is it a motorway or trunk road improvement likely to have a significant effect on the environment?). These guidelines are now supplemented by s 105A (2A) of the Highways Act 1980 (inserted by the New Roads and Street Works Act 1991) making it clear that *any* project for the *construction or improvement of a special* road, even though it falls within Annex II of the Directive, *must* be treated as having such characteristics that it should be made subject to EA. The Secretary of State will also consider the criteria of DoE 15/88.

Where EA is required the Secretary of State must publish, *not later* than the date of publication of the details of the road project, ie the draft orders concerning the preferred route, a statement containing the information

6 *Mayes v Minister of Transport* [1982] LS Gaz Rep 448.

referred to in Annex III of the Directive to the extent he considers it relevant to the project and environmental features likely to be affected by it, but certainly including a description of the project and its site, design and size, statements of measures to avoid, reduce or remedy adverse effects, the data required to identify and assess the main environmental impacts and a summary of all this in non-technical terms. Thus information on: the physical characteristics of the project and its land use requirements; the quality and quantity of materials to be used in construction; expected emissions and residues likely to result from the proposed road's operation; alternative proposals considered and reasons for making the choice made (taking into account environmental effects); features of the environment likely to be significantly affected by the project and a description of likely significant effects may be given. However, the statement *must* identify, describe and assess in an appropriate manner, in the light of each individual case, the direct and indirect effects of the project.

Where an environmental statement is published the public must be given the opportunity to comment *before the project is initiated*, and certain 'environmental bodies' have rights to express an opinion in cases where a projected road would lie within 100 m of certain land, eg National Parks and SSSIs. The Secretary of State is required to consider the environmental statement and opinions received from the public and 'environmental bodies', such as the Countryside Commission or English Nature, etc. When the decision on whether or not to proceed is published it must state that the Secretary of State has considered the environmental statement, and the opinions expressed on it.

Much of the litigation over roads has arisen out of issues relating to the line inquiry stage. Procedure here is governed by the Highways (Inquiries Procedure) Rules SI 1994/3263. Certain general requirements relate to all types of highway inquiry. These rules, replacing earlier ones from 1976, are designed to establish a clear timetable for the procedural steps connected with an inquiry, and now specifically provide, inter alia, for the submission of written proofs of evidence in advance from those proposing to give, or call others to give, evidence, all with the object of streamlining inquiry procedure.

Where the Secretary of State proposes to hold an inquiry he/she must give notice within four weeks of the period within which objections to the road scheme should have been made. This must be given to each 'statutory objector', ie a person who has made and maintained an objection, *and* who is an owner, lessee or occupier of any land likely to be required for highway works, *or* is a person likely to be able to claim compensation in respect of the use of the highway works, *or* is a person likely to be able to claim compensation in respect of the use of the highway works, *or* one of the persons/bodies falling within Sch 1 of the 1980 Act. The Secretary of State's outline statement of case must be further served on these persons within a further eight weeks.

Particular provision is made with regard to pre-inquiry meetings — which have become so much a feature of major inquiry procedure over recent years. Such a meeting may be held if the Secretary of State considers it 'desirable', and he/she must then give notice of the meeting in local newspapers within three weeks of the notice of intention to hold a meeting — the inquiry inspector also has power to call such a meeting. Outline statements of other parties' cases must be served, if the Secretary of State so decides, within eight weeks of the local newspaper notice, and the actual meeting itself held within

16 weeks. The pre-inquiry meeting will be conducted in accordance with the inspector's total discretion, and he/she will determine the order and agenda and may eject and exclude disruptive persons — even to the extent, it appears, of forbidding them to attend the subsequent inquiry itself. More than one such meeting may be held at the inspector's discretion.

Not less than six weeks after notice of intention to hold an inquiry (or within four weeks following a pre-inquiry meeting) the Secretary of State must serve his/her statement of case on statutory objectors, and other persons may be required to serve notice of their case on the Secretary of State. Anyone who has submitted a statement of case may be required by either the inspector or the Secretary of State to amplify it.

Where a pre-inquiry meeting is held the inquiry thereafter *must* be timetabled by the inspector, and normally the inquiry must begin within 22 weeks of notice of intention to hold it and not less than eight weeks of the end of any pre-inquiry meeting.

All statutory objectors are entitled to appear at the inquiry, and other persons may be allowed to appear — such permission is not to be unreasonably withheld. Where government witnesses are called — and the Secretary of State *must* provide a representative to elucidate the official statement of case — they may be cross examined in just the same way as other persons, but they may *not* be required to answer any question which, in the opinion of the inspector, is 'directed at the merits of government policy' (see further below).

The regulations also make provision for summarised reading of proofs of evidence at inquiries, and for inquiry procedure — including giving powers to inspectors to exclude material they consider is irrelevant or repetitious.

One other feature worthy of note in the new regulations which is a departure from past practice is the ability for the Secretary of State to appoint an assessor to advise the inquiry inspector. Where that assessor makes a report to the inspector, the report must be considered by the inspector in making the inquiry report. It would appear that, as was the position under the previous rules, at the inquiry, the Inspector has no power to *require* the Department of Transport to carry out surveys on the soil and topography of alternative routes so that it may be put before the inquiry. All an inspector *can* do is *invite* the Department so to act, and even then he acts at discretion.[7]

The rules of natural justice generally apply, though these may not apply to a disruptive objector, and, of course, the 1994 rules specifically provide for the exclusion of disruptive persons.[8] However, objectors should normally be given an adequate opportunity to present their views, particularly as the inquiry may be the only opportunity they have to state a formal view in public.[9] Site inspections may be made. After the inquiry is over the inspector makes the report, including conclusions and recommendations, which *must* be considered, and the Secretary of State makes and notifies the decision. The Secretary of State may not take into account new evidence or facts, nor differ from the inspector on a finding of fact, so as to be disposed to disagree with the inquiry recommendations, and so come to a decision at variance with

---

7 *R v Vincent, ex p Turner* [1987] JPL 511.
8 *Lovelock v Secretary of State for Transport* [1979] RTR 250.
9 *R v Secretary of State for Transport, ex p Gwent County Council* [1987] 1 All ER 161.

them, without notifying the statutory objectors, and allowing them to make representations or ask for the inquiry to be re-opened. The Secretary of State may, however, consult his departmental staff on the issue. Where major new evidence comes to light from an outside source after an inquiry radically changing the whole basis for a proposed road, or where a major issue has not been taken into account at the inquiry, the rules of natural justice *may* require it to be re-opened.[10] The test *appears* to be whether the new evidence is of such importance that reopening the matter may lead to the whole issue being determined in an altered way. If that is so then the court appears to have no choice but to quash the decision and require the inquiry to be reopened. However, apart from situations such as this the courts are generally unwilling to interfere with decisions taken in consequence of inquiries. Their task is to see that the procedures are operated fairly and reasonably, not to try to attempt to answer questions to which there can be no objectively 'right' answer.[11] Indeed the courts have had little sympathy with cases brought by objectors with little merit, pointing to the disbenefits caused by delays to schemes that have been accepted as necessary.[12]

Under Sch 2 to the Act as soon as may be after a scheme or order has been made by the Minister, he/she must publish notice of that fact in the *London Gazette*, and take such other steps as he/she thinks best to inform affected persons of the notice. He/she must state that the order has been made, and name a place where a copy of it may be inspected, free of charge at reasonable hours. Persons aggrieved by a scheme or order who wish to question its validity on the grounds that it is not within the powers granted by the 1980 Act, or that there has been an irregularity in the procedures required by law, have six weeks from publication of notice to apply to the High Court. The High Court may suspend orders and schemes until final determination of issues, and, if satisfied that the scheme or order goes beyond the powers conferred by the Act, *or* that the interests of an applicant have been *substantially prejudiced* by a procedural irregularity, may quash the scheme or order either generally, or insofar as it applies to the applicant's property. Otherwise schemes and orders may not be questioned in legal proceedings, and become operative on the date on which notice of making is published, or on such later date as is specified in the scheme or order. The provisions of Sch 2 are a preclusive system of appeal. Challenge by way of judicial review *once an order or scheme has been made* is not possible, nor is any challenge out of time possible, even where an applicant has acted under misapprehension as to the effect of a scheme or order.[13] (The procedures highway authorities *other* than the Secretary of State for Transport must follow in respect of their highway proposals are similar to those above, see *Encyclopaedia of Highway Law and Practice*.)

Criticisms of highway procedure

Many criticisms of highway procedures have been made. Large numbers of people are opposed for a variety of environmental reasons to particular road

10 *Rea v Minister of Transport* [1984] JPL 876.
11 *Lewin v Secretary of State for the Environment* [1989] 1 LMELR 30.
12 *Burton v Secretary of State for Transport* [1988] 2 EGLR 35; and *R v Tickell, ex p London Borough of Greenwich* [1988] JPL 280 (summary).
13 *R v Secretary of State for the Environment, ex p Ostler* [1977] QB 122, [1976] 3 All ER 90.

schemes, or roads policy in general. There are those who wish to use inquiries as a forum in which to debate roads policy. There is also feeling that the odds at an inquiry are 'stacked' against objectors who face the might of a government department often thought of *not* as a department of overall co-ordinated transport policy, *rather* as a department of road building. But at an inquiry many competing voices will be heard. The Department will promote its proposals, and will be supported by organisations representing road users. There will be those seeking to argue a case for an alternative route; others will seek to argue a case for particular route changes. There will be those who oppose the road totally. Many objectors feel frustration because the inquiry is into a small scale scheme which they know is truly part of a much longer project yet they will be unable to question the wider scheme.

It is the frustration felt by many with road policy coupled with growing environmental consciousness that has led to a growth of direct confrontation between road builders and protesters, particularly, for example, at Twyford Down over the building of the M3. This has led the Department of Transport to seek a number of ways of preventing protest and otherwise stopping direct action against road building. Thus in *Department of Transport v Williams*[14] the Court of Appeal concluded that there is a tort of wrongful interference with business — a wrong which extends to unlawfully preventing the Department of Transport going about its lawful business of authorised road building. Those who wilfully obstruct road building may also commit an offence under s 303 of the 1980 Act, and commission of this offence is also enough to constitute an unlawful interference with the Department's 'business' *which can be restrained by injunction*. Similarly in *DPP v Todd*[15] the Divisional Court concluded that s 241 of the Trade Union and Labour Relations (Consolidation) Act 1992, which relates to those who wrongfully and without lawful authority hinder persons in their work with a view to compelling them to abstain from work, applies not just to trade disputes but is wide enough to allow prosecution of those who prevent road constructors from going about their work by non-violent protests such as positioning themselves in cranes.

Public inquiries do not stop roads being built, though they may result in particular re-routeings, simply because their function is to inform the Minister of the issues, not to debate or formulate policy. The decision on the road is for the Minister. Following *Bushell v Secretary of State for the Environment*,[16] and *Lovelock v Secretary of State for Transport*,[17] objectors to a road must be given a fair chance to put forward their arguments, and supporting factors. Equally they must be given sufficient information about the Department's case for the proposal. Nevertheless an inquiry is called to consider the *line (ie the choice of route) of a proposed road*, and may not be used to debate overall road policy. Neither may it be used to debate techniques used to decide whether there is a need for a road within the context of national policy. However, in view of the changes in roads policy outlined above, this latter point may now be less fixed than was once thought. It certainly appears possible to argue the need for a *particular* local link in the road system, on the basis that existing roads can

14 [1994] 6 ELM 12.
15 [1995] 7 ELM 127.
16 [1981] AC 75, [1980] 2 All ER 608.
17 [1979] JPL 456.

adequately take traffic. It may also be possible to attack the methods used in scheme assessment by the Department of Transport in relation to *special* local factors or conditions which raise doubts as to the applicability of normal assessment techniques, though such local issues are normally considered by the project assessment system.

Compulsory purchase powers

Part XII of the 1980 Act confers powers to acquire land, by agreement or compulsion, on highway authorities. Land may be acquired for road construction, or improvement, and for ancillary purposes such as the provision of service areas and public conveniences, under ss 239 and 240 of the Act. Land may also be acquired for mitigating any adverse effect on surrounding areas arising from the existence of a road constructed or improved, or proposed for construction or improvement, by a highway authority, see s 246. Under s 248 land may generally be acquired for highway purposes notwithstanding that it is not immediately required. So far as compulsory purchases are concerned this is not a '*carte blanche*' power. Where there is power to acquire land for an 'initial stage', adjacent land for a 'subsequent stage' may also be acquired compulsorily, even though not immediately required, *provided* the stages are linked as laid down in Sch 17, *and* it is intended to incorporate the 'subsequent stage' land forthwith upon acquisition within the boundaries of the highway or proposed highway, *and/or* the proposed use of the 'initial stage' land involves working on, under or over 'subsequent stage' land, *and/or* plans for use of the 'subsequent stage' land have been made by the Minister. Thus, for example, under s 239(1) the 'initial stage' may be concerned with acquiring land for the construction of a highway, the 'subsequent stage' for which, the above conditions being fulfilled, land could be acquired in advance of requirements is the improvement of that highway.

Compulsory purchase power is subject to limits on distance from the highway under s 249 of and Sch 18 to the 1980 Act. For example the power to acquire land under s 289(1) (land for road construction) is limited to 220 yards from the middle of the highway or proposed highway. Section 253 empowers the making of agreements with persons interested in land adjoining or in the vicinity of the highway for regulating the use of the land, permanently or temporarily, for the purpose of mitigating any adverse effect which the construction, improvement or existence or use of the highway has on its surroundings. As already stated, s 257 allows proceedings in respect of compulsory acquisitions to be concurrent, so far as is practicable, with making other related schemes and orders under highway powers. Compulsory purchase orders made in the exercise of powers to acquire land for specified highway purposes may come into operation on the same day as related schemes or orders, see s 257(3) and Sch 20. Section 258 lays down that where proceedings are required to be taken in respect of a compulsory purchase order made in the exercise of highway powers *after* the making of an order or scheme, the Minister may disregard in compulsory purchase proceedings any objection which, in his opinion, amounts in substance to an objection taken in earlier proceedings in the order or scheme.

Under s 247 of the 1980 Act the procedure applicable to the compulsory acquisition of land for highway purposes is, in general, that provided by the

Acquisition of Land Act 1981. In *R v Secretary of State for Transport, ex p de Rothschild*[18] a compulsory purchase order was made under the 1981 Act on land for a by-pass, and at the public inquiry into the order the appellants put forward four alternative routes over land they owned and were prepared to sell. The inspector found the advantages of these routes would be outweighed by extra cost and delays, and in due course the Secretary of State confirmed the order. The appellants sought to contend that confirmation of the CPO was wrong because such an order can only be confirmed if it can be shown to be in the public interest. The court rejected such a contention, but pointed out that because a CPO is a draconian measure it may be more vulnerable to challenge for failure to comply with the '*Wednesbury*' rules unless sufficient grounds can be adduced to justify it on its own merits. It is up to the Secretary of State to consider all relevant factors before confirming an order, including landscape issues, matters of feasibility, potential delays and costs. Provided he/she does that the courts are unwilling to intervene.

With regard to development on trunk roads and general highway considerations regarding development Department of Transport Circular 4/88 gave guidance clarifying the policies followed by the Department in the exercise of powers to give directions to restrict development on trunk roads and motorways. PPG 13 (reissued in 1994) gives general guidance on transport considerations in development control decisions.

PPG 13 — further changes in roads policy?

The PPG is, of course, concerned with development of land, not transport policy, but the two issues are so interlinked that guidance on one is bound to have implications for the other.

The keynote of PPG 13 is *planning of land use so there is less need to travel*, particularly by car. Applications of this are found in policy guidance favouring promoting alternatives to car use, and reducing local traffic on trunk and through roads. Thus under s 54A of the Town and Country Planning Act 1990 plans should co-ordinate land use and transport strategies so as to influence the location of development to ensure less travel, and to favour developments where use is made of walking, cycling and public transport as modes of travel. Thus major traffic generating developments should be sited in areas already well served by public transport, and local centres where journeys can be made without cars should be developed to meet public needs. At the same time parking provision should be reduced so as to discourage reliance on cars. Particular guidance on the application of 'planning for less travel' is given with regard to housing, employment, freight movement, retail trading, leisure, tourism, recreation, education and public facilities, eg housing should be located in urban areas already well served by public transport and away from small settlements dependent on private car use. Indeed there should be 'accessibility profiles' for public transport on particular sites to check whether they meet the criteria for development of the PPG. Policy is also clearly opposed to new employment centres not served by public transport being

18 [1989] 1 All ER 933.

created, and the PPG is clearly influenced by the Department of Transport's 1994 report 'Reducing Transport Emissions through Planning'.

PPG 13 is also of interest with regard to the planning of local roads. These should be planned within the framework laid down by structure plans and the need for such roads, together with their environmental implications, should be examined as structure plans are prepared with 'the possibility for discussion of need at an examination in public of . . . structure plan proposals'.

One omission from the PPG, however, somewhat odd in the light of its consideration of the impact of private car use, is guidance on how to measure the environmental impact of the private car.

C AERODROMES

'Look what hovers there above us, hanging on gigantic wing, O, eternal gods that love us, save us from this dreadful thing!' (Wimperis, Talbot & Monckton, 'The Arcadians', Act I)

Under the Civil Aviation Act 1982, s 105(1), an aerodrome is an area of land or water designed, equipped, set apart, or commonly used for aircraft to land and depart, including facilities for helicopters and vertical take off and landing fixed-wing aeroplanes. Aerodromes may be provided by various bodies including the Secretary of State, local authorities, the Civil Aviation Authority and private persons and companies.

In the management and administration of his aerodromes the Secretary of State must undertake adequate consultation with local authorities in the vicinity and other organisations representing the interests of those concerned with the locality, see s 26. The Civil Aviation Authority has a duty under s 5 of the 1982 Act to consider environmental factors in relation to licensing of any aerodrome which may be designated by the Secretary of State, *other than* those regulated in respect of noise and vibration from aircraft under s 78, ie Heathrow, Gatwick and Stansted airports.

The functions of the Secretary of State with regard to all civil aviation matters were entrusted to the Department of Transport by SI 1983/1127. Development by the Secretaries of State for Transport and Defence requires no planning permission, otherwise the construction of aerodromes and ancillary buildings and works does generally require permission.

Note, however, that Part 18 of Sch 2 of the General Permitted Development Order 1995 allows airport operators of sites falling within s 57 of the Airports Act 1986, to carry out on their operational land developments including erecting or altering operational buildings in connection with the provision of services and facilities, but *excluding* the building/extending of runways, terminal construction of over 500 m^2 and similar major terminal extensions, and in any case development is permitted subject to a condition requiring consultation with the local planning authority before commencement. Further permitted development rights are given to operators in respect of the provision at or near (ie within 8 km) airports of air traffic control services, and similar rights are given to the Civil Aviation Authority in respect of air traffic control services, air navigation and monitoring services. Note further that 'airport' as the popular term is used in the 1986 Act in preference to aerodrome, and is defined therein, s 82(1), as the aggregate of land, building and works in an aerodrome.

Guidance on permitted development rights initially found in DoE Circular 22/88 pointed to the restrictions on terminal development, see para 70, and stressed the need for consultation even before permitted development is carried out. (This guidance will be replaced to take account of the 1995 re-ordering of permitted development rights, see chapter 5.) With regard to non-permitted development Environmental Assessment (see chapter 5) is mandatory under Sch 1 of SI 1988/1199 in respect of aerodromes with basic runway lengths of 2,100 m or more, and so will also be subject to publicity and public consultation requirements. On EA and permitted development see SI 1995/417. In exceptional cases authorities or the Secretary of State may revoke permitted development rights under art 4 of the 1995 Order. Because of permitted development rights which were more extensive than is now the case, examination of proposals to develop a third London airport largely took place on a non-statutory basis. In respect of the 1980 proposals to develop Stansted airport the then British Airports Authority included some non-operational land in their planning application and opted to have the whole area treated as a single entity subject to planning control.

The airports for London controversy

Principal controversy concerning development by airport authorities has arisen in relation to airports for London; especially the Stansted site, a heated debate that continued for over 30 years. Readers wishing to pursue the factual history of the issue are referred to Hall *Great Planning Disasters* chapter 2, and Eyre *The Airport Inquiries 1981–1983* part II (inspector's report).

'Airports Policy' (Cmnd 9542) declared the intention of government to allow development of Stansted on grounds that Heathrow, Gatwick and regional airports could not meet projected traffic demands for the 1990s. The development of a second runaway at Gatwick was considered to be environ-mentally unacceptable, and there is also an agreement under planning legislation between the British Airports Authority and West Sussex County Council dating from 1979 whereby a second runway at Gatwick would not be built until 2019, see The Times letters, 5 June 1985. The proposal formed part of a 'package' dealing, inter alia, with further growth at Luton, encouragement for the use of Manchester for international services, and measures to increase use of regional airports, and to postpone a fifth terminal at Heathrow.

New powers to control numbers of aircraft, particularly those using Stansted were given under Part III of the Airports Act 1986. Section 31 of this Act gives the Secretary of State power to make traffic distribution rules providing for apportionment of traffic between two or more airports serving the *same area* in the UK, and note in this context the Traffic Distribution Rules 1986 which relate to the airports serving the London area, in particular Heathrow and Gatwick. Section 32 further empowers the Secretary of State to impose, by order, limits, overall or partial, on aircraft movements at particular airports where he considers the existing runway capacity of the airport is *not* fully utilised for a substantial proportion of the time when the runway(s) is/are available for take off or landing; such orders may not limit movements to numbers lower than the highest level of any corresponding movements at the airport occurring at equivalent periods within the three years before the order, or the level permitted under a previous order. Section 33 allows the Secretary of State, where a s 32 order is in force in relation to an airport, *or* where he/she considers that demand for an airport's use exceeds or will exceed in the near future its operational capacity, to direct the CAA to make a scheme to restrict access to the airport. Such schemes can prevent certain aircraft from using relevant airports, and can provide for charges in respect of take off and landing times or 'slots'. Use of this power has been avoided but may prove necessary if congestion builds up at individual airports, see further Shawcross & Beaumont *Air Law* paras 15.1–15.6.

The London STOLPORT

Along with the development of Stansted, a short take off and landing (STOL) airport to be known as London City Airport, was given ministerial approval on 23 May 1985. This is in the old London docklands and was built by private developers, with most flights being provided by a private airline. The Secretary of State for the Environment approved a single runway with associated terminal and hotel buildings, subject to conditions banning helicopters, club and recreational flying, limiting the number of flights and the times of operation of the airport, limiting the types of aircraft permitted to use the facility and the length of runway to be built, and requiring that noise barriers be provided. The Secretary of State's decision was challenged, inter alia on grounds of fairness, in *R v Secretary of State for the Environment, ex p Greater London Council*.[19] At the inquiry into the 'Stolport' application the inspector recommended that permission be granted subject to certain conditions as to numbers of aircraft movements and types of aircraft permitted to use the airport. The Secretary of State sought advice from the Department of Transport on the technical drafting of these conditions, though he gave the objectors a real opportunity to comment on the technical advice received. It was held that on the evidence no need to reopen the inquiry had arisen and that the Secretary of State had acted reasonably and fairly.

Continuing airport controversy

The debate on London's airports has continued for over 30 years: the official belief remains that a policy combining minimum environmental damage with the ability to protect jobs, attract foreign earnings, and so encourage economic growth, has been developed. Even in 1986, following the Stansted decision, the air transport industry began to call for further airport expansion such as a further runway at a south eastern airport.

In May 1992 BAA proposed a fifth terminal, though no new runway, for Heathrow, doubling its capacity to 80 million passengers pa, the new terminal itself to have a capacity of 600,000 passengers per week. The justification for the new development was the need to deal with a forecasted 3.25 million passengers per week by 2016 as opposed to 1.2 million per week in 1993, with the usual argument that Heathrow's expansion is vital to ensure the UK does not 'miss out' in the growth of air traffic. There was no argument for a further

19 [1986] JPL 32.

runway because the theory was that larger aircraft coming on stream would be able to deal with demand for flights.

However, by 1993 the Department of Transport's 'Runway Capacity to Serve the South East', basing its findings on total passenger demand up to 2025, with up to 170 million passengers a year then expected, with 195 million at the main London airports by 2015, recommended the provision of further runways at Heathrow or Gatwick by 2010, or at Stansted by 2015. It was, however, accepted that this could not happen without great environmental cost, either by affecting open landscape or, at Heathrow, entailing the demolition of 3,300 homes. It was further expected that there would be an aircraft noise problem (see chapter 11, below), though the report believed that with improved technology the numbers of those affected by noise in 2025 would not be greater than in 1993. Opposition to the proposals from affected local authorities and residents' groups was immediate and considerable, and BAA dropped its support for a further runway at Heathrow, preferring to rely on the proposed fifth terminal. In February 1995 the government rejected the proposals for new runways at Heathrow and Gatwick, arguing that more work needed to be done on the environmental impact of the proposals before any decision could be taken. In the meantime investigations are to take place in securing even greater use of existing runway capacity at Heathrow and Gatwick, including the fifth terminal (T5) at Heathrow.

BAA's formal planning application for T5 having been received, the matter went to a public inquiry which began in May 1995, and which was predicted to become the longest and most expensive on record, eclipsing even the Sizewell Inquiry (see below). The report on this matter will not be delivered until 1997 and the final decision by the Secretaries of the Environment and Transport will certainly be delayed until after the next general election.

The argument over airports may be expected to follow its traditional pattern with environmental protection arguments being set against the contention that more airport capacity is needed if the nation's air industry and London are to retain their pre-eminence in entry by air into Europe.

Compulsory purchase powers

The Secretary of State has power to acquire land and rights over land by agreement or compulsorily for civil aviation purposes, see the Civil Aviation Act 1982, ss 41 and 44. Where *land* is acquired the procedure is that under the Acquisition of Land Act 1981. This provides the standard procedure for land acquisition whereby land is taken under a compulsory purchase order made in draft departmentally, in the case of a ministerial acquisition, then advertised in local newspapers, and notified to owners, lessees and occupiers. The information required for this purpose is a description of relevant land, a statement of why it is required, a statement of the place where the draft order can be inspected, and a time period, at least 21 days from the date of first publication, within which objections can be made. Owners and lessees, etc, must also be informed of the effect of the order. Where objections are made and not withdrawn a public local inquiry or other hearing must be held. Thereafter, following consideration of the inquiry report, the order may be made, and due notice of this fact published, and notified to owners, lessees, etc. There is a limited right of challenge for 'persons aggrieved' on a point of law in the High

Court for a period of six weeks from first publication of notice of the making of the order.

The power to acquire *rights over land* is exercisable where the Secretary of State considers it expedient to secure the safety and efficiency of navigation of civil aircraft, the safe and efficient use of land vested in a 'relevant authority', or proposed for acquisition by them, or to provide services required in relation to such land. 'Relevant authorities' include the Secretary of State and the Civil Aviation Authority. The rights acquired or created by the Secretary of State's order may include easements, rights to enter, subject generally to giving notice to the occupier, to carry out and maintain works, and to install structures and apparatus, etc, see s 44 of the 1982 Act. Under s 43 where rights (to enter land, or to install and maintain apparatus, or to do works, or to restrict the use of the land) are granted to the Secretary of State or to the Civil Aviation Authority the grantor's successors in title are also bound by the grant. Schedule 7 to the 1982 Act contains the procedure for making orders obtaining *rights over land*, and for other connected civil aviation purposes.

Section 48 of the 1982 Act confers power on the Secretary of State, where satisfied such action is necessary for the safe and efficient use for civil aviation of any land vested in him/her or the Civil Aviation Authority, or proposed for acquisition by him or them, to authorise by order the stopping up or diversion of highways. Consequential action may also be taken, for example to secure the provision or improvement of highways so far as the Secretary of State thinks necessary or desirable in consequence of a diversion or stopping up. Section 49 empowers the Secretary of State to acquire land compulsorily to provide or improve highways under s 48.

Where, under s 52 of the 1982 Act, land has been acquired for aviation purposes and the use of the land by the person who acquired it, or executing the direction, will involve the displacement of residential occupiers, *and* there is no other residential accommodation available on reasonable terms to those persons, suitable to their reasonable requirements, a duty to provide such accommodation arises. This will generally fall to be discharged by either the Secretary of State or the Civil Aviation Authority as the case may be. Home loss, farm loss and disturbance payments may also be payable in such circumstances, see the Land Compensation Act 1973, ss 29–38 as amended. Section 9 of that Act also makes compensation payable for depreciation in the value of land caused by alterations at an aerodrome where these take the form of new runway construction, runway re-alignment, extension or strengthening of existing runways, or increased provision of taxiways or aprons in order to accommodate more aircraft. Merely to *intensify* the use of an existing runway, without more, gives rise to no claim for compensation.

The Civil Aviation Authority has power to acquire land compulsorily, subject to ministerial consent, in connection with the performance of its functions. The procedure is that under the Acquisition of Land Act 1981, see s 42 of the 1982 Act.

D ELECTRICITY UNDERTAKINGS

Certain works connected with electricity undertakings are given automatic planning permission under the General Permitted Development Order 1995:

(i) installation of electric lines on, over or under land, and the construction of ancillary shafts and tunnels; (ii) installing an electric line feeder or service pillars, transforming and switching stations not exceeding 29 cubic metres in capacity, (iii) installing telecommunications lines connecting electrical lines to plant or buildings; (iv) extending or altering buildings on operational land, subject to height and size limits; (v) temporary borehole sinking; (vi) erecting buildings on operational land, solely for protection of plant or machinery, subject to limits on height; and (vii) carrying out other development on, in or under operational land *except*: (a) erections or reconstructions materially affecting the design or external appearance of buildings; or (b) installing or erecting, by way of addition or replacement, plant or machinery, etc, exceeding 15m in height, or the height of the plant or machinery so replaced, whichever is greater. Carrying out works for inspecting, repairing or renewing cables and other apparatus does not constitute 'development', see the Town and Country Planning Act 1990, s 55(2)(c). However, if a tree preservation order is made under s 198 of the 1990 Act preventing the wilful destruction of trees save with the consent of the local authority, and in the course of laying underground cables an electricity undertaking severs the roots of trees and so reduces their life expectancy, the undertaking may be liable, provided injury is so radical that a competent forester would decide in the circumstances, and considering safety issues, that the tree ought to be felled.[20]

The construction of power stations and installation of power lines

Under s 36(1) of the Electricity Act 1989 a 'generating station' (which in the case of one driven wholly or mainly by water includes all the ancillary works and structures for holding or channelling water, see s 64) cannot be *constructed*, extended or operated save in accordance with consents granted by the Secretary of State, though this prohibition does *not* extend to stations not exceeding a capacity of 50 megawatts or less, or in the case of a station to be constructed or extended which will not exceed that capacity once constructed or extended. The 50 megawatt figure may be varied by the Secretary of State, and he/she may by order further direct that the restrictions on construction, etc, are not to apply to stations of particular classes or descriptions. Consents given under s 36 may include such conditions as the Secretary of State thinks fit, including conditions as to ownership and operation, and consents may be subject to time limitations. It is an offence to contravene the s 36 prohibition. The provisions outlined above, however, do *not* replace the need to obtain planning permission, though it appears clear that planning consent and generating stations consent procedures will be channelled together through a common public inquiry. Where the application is to build a nuclear station or a conventional one of 300 megawatts or more capacity EA will be mandatory, and may be required for other stations where there will be 'significant environmental effects'.

The procedure for obtaining consent is laid down in Sch 8 of the 1989 Act.

Applications must be in writing and must refer to maps showing the land on which the station is to be built, extended, etc, and must be supplemented by

---

20 *Barnet London Borough Council v Eastern Electricity Board* [1973] 2 All ER 319, [1973] 1 WLR 430.

such other information as is ministerially directed. Fees may be charged in connection with applications. A copy of the application must be served on relevant local planning authorities, and where such an authority objects and so informs the Secretary of State he/she must hold a public inquiry and must consider objections and the inquiry report before reaching a decision. Time limits for the making of objections may be laid down. Regulations may further be made for securing that consent applications are publicised in prescribed fashion and that copies are served on prescribed persons. Such publicity must state a time and manner for persons *other* than local planning authorities to make objections. Where third party objections only are received there is no obligation to hold a public inquiry, instead the Secretary of State must consider the objections along with all other material considerations to determine whether in any case an inquiry should be held. The clear assumption in case law is, however, that in such circumstances an inquiry should be held unless the minister is properly satisfied he/she can weigh the conflicting issues without an inquiry and that the objectors' representations will be in any case properly taken into account.[1]

Where a public inquiry is held the Secretary of State must inform the applicant and the applicant must then in two successive weeks: publicise in the local press the application and its purpose and describe the relevant land; state a local place where a copy of the application and supporting maps can be inspected; and announce the date and time of the public inquiry. The Secretary of State may direct the applicant to undertake further publicity measures. The public inquiry may subsume any inquiries for consents needed because multiple permissions are a prerequisite for a particular activity, eg compulsory acquisition of land by relevant generators — which may be authorised under Sch 3 of the 1989 Act, see also s 61.

On the grant of s 36 consent in respect of any matter amounting to 'development' the Secretary of State *may* direct that planning permission for the development and any ancillary matters is deemed granted, subject to such conditions as he may impose. Likewise where a s 36 consent relates to operations or changes of use involving the need for a hazardous substances consent (see further below) the Secretary of State may direct such consent deemed granted, but only after consultation with the Health and Safety Commission.

Overhead power lines may not be installed or kept installed save with the consent of the Secretary of State, see s 37 of the Electricity Act 1989. However, this prohibition does not apply to lines having a normal voltage of not more than 20 KV *and* used by a single consumer nor in relation to that portion of a line as is within premises occupied or controlled by the person responsible for installation. Other exemptions may be made. Consent may be given subject to conditions and may be varied or revoked by the Secretary of State at any time after the end of a specified period, and may in any case be made subject to time limits. It is an offence to contravene this provision though, just as with contraventions of s 36, proceedings for infraction can only be brought by or on behalf of the Secretary of State. EA may be requisite in the case of proposals to transmit electricity by overhead cables where there will be significant environmental effects.

1 *Binney v Secretary of State for the Environment* [1984] JPL 871.

Sch 8 once again provides the procedure for obtaining consent. This replicates that for generating station consents with appropriate modifications, eg the necessary map must show the land across which the line is to be installed and applications must state whether all necessary wayleaves have been agreed with the owners of relevant land. However, where an application states that the necessary wayleaves have *not* been agreed the Secretary of State may give notice to the applicant that he does not intend to proceed until satisfied that in relation to all affected land an application has been made under Sch 4, para 6. This latter provision applies where attempts to negotiate wayleaves have foundered (or where a land owner is attempting to bring an existing wayleave to an end). In such cases an application to the Secretary of State can be made and he may grant the necessary wayleave subject to such conditions as he thinks fit. However, a wayleave application cannot be entertained in respect of land covered by dwellings, and before granting wayleaves he must give occupiers and owners of the land in question the right to be heard. Compensation is payable in respect of wayleaves granted, and further compensation in respect of any damage caused by the exercise of the wayleave right. Where an overhead line is thus 'held up' pending resolution of wayleaves the Secretary of State *may*, however, give consent to the line on the condition that the work of installation may not be begun without his permission. Obtaining a wayleave for a line carries with it the power to support it on pylons, and the affected landowner may not specify the form of such pylons.[2]

The foregoing provisions are subject to the requirements of Sch 9 of the 1989 Act which provides that in formulating proposals, eg for generating stations, relevant persons must have regard to the desirability of: preserving natural beauty, conserving flora, fauna and geological or physiographical features of special interest and of protecting sites and buildings, etc, of historic architectural or archeological interest. They must further do what they reasonably can to mitigate the effects of their proposals on the countryside, flora, fauna, etc. Such considerations are also to be taken into account by the Secretary of State in considering applications for consents. These requirements apply to proposals to construct/extend generating stations of not less than 10 megawatts capacity, to install lines above *or below* ground or for the exemption of other electricity supply or transmission works. Regular statements are required from operators as to how they intend to comply with the foregoing requirements. Such statements must be published and must be based on consultations with the Countryside Commission and relevant nature conservatory and historic buildings bodies.

Relevant electricity operators (ie those licensed to supply electricity) have further important ancillary powers under Sch 4 of the 1989 Act. Where a tree is in close proximity to an electric line or plant so that it obstructs or interferes with the installation, maintenance or working of the line or plant, or otherwise constitutes an unacceptable source of danger, notice may be given to the occupier of the land on which the tree is growing requiring him/her to fell or lop the tree or cut back its roots so as to abate the problem. If such a request is not complied with within 21 days the operator may cause the work to be done provided he acts in accordance with good arboricultural practice, doing

2 *Central Electricity Generating Board v Jennaway* [1959] 3 All ER 409, [1959] 1 WLR 937.

as little damage as possible to trees, and making good damage to the land. Should any dispute arise as to the necessity for the work the matter is to be referred to the Secretary of State who, after giving the parties an opportunity to be heard may make such order as he thinks fit.

Should power lines be buried?

There are many who argue for the burial of many, if not all, overhead power lines. In 1994 the Countryside Commission argued that burial should take place, or lines should be at least screened, where they affect the beauty of the countryside. Planners, on the other hand are concerned they have no guidance on development in the vicinity of overhead power lines which *some* — but only some — studies link with the creation of cancers induced by electro magnetic fields (EMF). Many who live near power lines claim to suffer from general ill health, including headaches and nausea, as well as other more serious afflictions. It was a desire to prevent the erection of an overhead line which led to the *Duddridge* case (see chapter 1, above).

Operators may also authorise in writing the entry on land at reasonable times for the purpose of a survey to ascertain whether the land could be suitable for operational purposes. Fourteen days' notice of intention to enter must be given to occupiers of relevant land, and the power does not apply to land covered by a building including yards, gardens and outbuildings. The survey power extends to power to search and bore to ascertain the nature of the subsoil. It is an offence to obstruct the exercise of the above power.[3]

Special provisions for nuclear installations

The consent provisions are additional to nuclear site licensing in the case of nuclear powered generating stations. The Nuclear Installations Act 1965, s 1, requires a nuclear site licence for a nuclear powered generating station, and before such a licence is granted there must be consultation with the Environment Agency, see s 3(1A) inserted in 1995. Licences are issued by the Health and Safety Executive (HSE) operating via the Nuclear Installations Inspectorate (NII). The HSE must, under ss 3(6A) and 4(3A), consult the Environment Agency before such a licence is granted or varied, or is made subject to a condition relating to the creation, accumulation or disposal of radioactive waste, see further chapter 9. Licences are granted subject to safety conditions, which may be varied in the future or during construction. A licence is only granted after the NII has conducted exhaustive assessments, a process that can run parallel to other public inquiry procedures. Licences may only be granted to bodies corporate, and cannot be transferred, see s 3 of the 1965 Act. Before a licence can be granted applicants may be directed to inform (by serving notice on them containing specified *particulars*) local authorities of licence applications, giving them specified information and informing them of their right (within three months of the date of service) to make representations to the HSE, though this requirement is lifted where the application is in respect of a site where a s 36 consent application is being made, for otherwise

3 *R v Chief Constable of Devon and Cornwall, ex p Central Electricity Generating Board* [1982] QB 458, [1981] 3 All ER 826.

there would be duplication of effort. The conditions attached will vary from site to site and may cover matters as diverse as the provision of design information for the NII, quality approvals, the inspection of components, the authorisation of workers, protective measures in respect of radiation, storage of waste fuel and other wastes. Conditions under s 4 of the 1965 Act (which may only be imposed, varied or resolved following consultation with the Agency, see s 4(3A)) will also regulate the working life of a commissioned plant, requiring detailed regular inspections and other safety checks. Conditions may relate to: the efficiency of radiation emission monitoring devices; the design, siting, construction, installation, operation, modification and maintenance of plant; dealing with accidents and emergencies, and discharges; handling, treating and disposing of nuclear material. To ensure safety, plants should be shut down once in two years, and may not then recommence operation until the NII consents. An emergency plan will also be required by the licence conditions to deal with incidents involving escaping radioactive matter. Further conditions will relate to recording radioactivity, design, siting, construction and maintenance of plant. Conditions may be added at any time in respect of the handling, treatment and disposal of nuclear material, and conditions may be varied or revoked at any time. Site licences may be revoked by the HSE (following consultation with the Environment Agency) at any time (see s 5 of the 1965 Act) or surrendered by the licensee, though such revocation or surrender does not free the licensee of responsibility for the site, for licensees have a 'period of responsibility' from the date of grant of their licences until they are informed by the HSE that there has ceased to be any danger from ionising radiations from anything on site, *or* until a new licence supervenes the old one. During this period the original licensee remains subject to the HSE's supervision powers. The duty of licensees is, under s 7, to see that 'no' prohibited occurrence involving nuclear matter causes injury to any person or damage to any property where that injury arises from radioactive properties of matter, or these in combination with toxic, explosive or other hazardous properties of the matter, *and* that no ionising radiations emitted in the 'period of responsibility' from anything caused or allowed by the licensee to be on site even though not nuclear matter, or from any waste discharged from the site cause personal or property damage. Where there is an occurrence it must be reported under s 22 to the HSE, and an inspector's report may be required and published, or even a court of inquiry. The prohibited occurrences are: on site occurrences involving nuclear matter and certain off site occurrences involving material in carriage. The duty is not, however, *absolute*, despite s 7's use of the word 'no', for there can be no guarantee that a nuclear site will be free from natural but unforeseen events, or improbable failures of equipment, nor proof against human error (as seems to have been the case at Chernobyl) or acts of malice.[4]

A 'culture of safety' should, however, be the dominant feature of the operation of nuclear power stations so that there should be no hesitation on the part of staff in shutting down a power plant should even a minor incident occur. Operators of such plant may expect to incur hefty fines should they breach site licensing conditions and other health and safety provisions.[5]

4 *Re Friends of the Earth* [1988] JPL 93.
5 *Health and Safety Executive v Nuclear Electric* [1995] 7 ELM 203.

Central planning policy is generally averse to other developments in the neighbourhood of a nuclear powered generator. A planning authority may also be involved where there is an application for development involving nuclear installations *other* than generating stations. Planning permission is needed, but the issue is likely to be 'called in' by the Secretary of State, and may be made subject to special development procedure, as with the Sellafield (Windscale) plant, see Ian Breach *Windscale Fall-out*; chapters 2 (above) and 9 (below).

The most controversial inquiry so far held in relation to the building of an electricity power station was into the proposal to erect a pressurised water nuclear reactor (PWR) at Sizewell in Suffolk. This was an inquiry of monumental complexity and questions arose whether the inquiry could be full, fair and thorough because of the complexity of the issues involved; the tension between the interests of local people and national policy on nuclear power (see chapter 3 above), and the disparity in resources between the various parties, those objecting to the proposal being largely dependent on fund raising efforts of local and national pressure groups. It is, however, debatable how far the concepts of 'fairness' and 'thoroughness' are compatible. The more 'thorough' an inquiry, the greater the weight of evidence and the more daunting its bulk to objectors. However, an inquiry has to be as fair as possible to all parties because of the need to ensure that its recommendations are reached in a way acceptable to all.

The inquiry saw unusual combinations of allies, such as the National Coal Board, the National Union of Miners, the South of Scotland Electricity Board, the Town and Country Planning Association and the Council for the Protection of Rural England, to mention a few. The deceptively simple single issue of whether permission should be given for the erection of the first British PWR on a site next door to an already functioning nuclear power station, expanded as the inquiry progressed into consideration of disposal of nuclear waste, and decommissioning or 'entombing' nuclear stations whose economic life has ended. The inquiry could not concentrate on the safety issue, a major part of the inquiry in view of the incident involving a pressurised water reactor at Three Mile Island in the USA. It had also to consider and investigate the means whereby the Central Electricity Generating Board (CEGB) and the Department of Energy estimated national energy needs, bearing in mind prices of alternative fuels, variations in fuel supply and demand.

The inquiry had additionally to consider the views of objectors alleging, variously, that: demand forecasts had overestimated national generating capacity needs; better electricity generating options existed in the form of combined heat and power schemes; massive investment in nuclear capacity could starve other projects of much needed capital, for example, the development of solar, wind and wave power; the CEGB was wrong to believe a PWR could be quickly and cheaply built; preference could be given to another British type of reactor, the Advanced Gas Cooled system; on safety grounds the PWR was unacceptable, and that fuel from the reactor would form the basis for nuclear weapons. The inquiry thus became a complex multi-faceted entity in which the issue of nuclear energy policy, indeed energy policy overall, was never far from anyone's mind as the various issues were discussed.

Even though overall policy on nuclear power could not, as such, be questioned by the inquiry, it examined policy closely. To examine the issues the 'inquiry team' consisted of the person appointed to hear the inquiry, Sir Frank Layfield, with assisting technical experts in mechanical and nuclear engineering, economics and radio biology. Before the inquiry appeared a variety of legally qualified and lay advocates. Additionally Sir Frank Layfield appointed, following representations from the Town and Country Planning Association, a full time 'counsel to the inquiry'. His task was to help inexperienced objectors and to pursue lines of inquiry they were unable to.

The inquiry had to direct itself to key issues including: the *'need'* for the particular generator; its *economics*, and its *safety*. Each of these was a highly technical issue involving argument on many matters.

1 Likely future demand for generating capacity, which in turn depended on forecasts of economic activity, consideration of energy saving measures, provision for sudden demands for electricity, predictions of the future useful life of existing generating plant, and considerations of energy source diversification.

2 Cost savings alleged to flow from building a PWR constituted an issue involving complex economic modelling, argument over likely commissioning dates for the new reactor, and the likely future cost of alternative fuel sources; higher fossil fuel costs might justify the large initial capital cost of a PWR.

3 Safety issues involved consideration of highly technical matters such as fracture mechanics, 'probabilistic risk assessments' and other issues of 'engineering judgment'. Of course, the larger the number of safety restrictions placed on such a PWR the more its initial and operating costs become. British nuclear reactors have a long history of safe operation, but the near-disaster at Three Mile Island in the USA in 1979 involved a PWR. Issues of the safety of the proposal were raised and considered at the inquiry, though responsibility for approving the design of the proposed reactor lay with the NII (see above).

4 A final issue was whether the American PWR should be preferred to the British Advanced Gas Cooled Reactor. This was an issue less than appropriate for a 'planning type' inquiry as it involved questions of sustainable capacity in the *international* reactor construction industry.

NB The issue of the *cost of decommissioning* the PWR at the end of its working life was not a central topic, and was dealt with in much less detail in official evidence than was the matter of safe operation. Indeed it has only been in recent years that much official attention has been given to this problematic subject.

It is impossible for the law to supply a 'right' answer in such circumstances. The law's task is to provide a framework within which matters can be fairly and fully discussed so that *the most informed recommendations* can be made. The Sizewell inquiry was undoubtedly fair in the way it allowed the presentation of issues and afforded those interested a chance to present their case. In this respect it represented an important development in the handling of major public inquiries. The Sizewell inquiry lasted over two years with 340 days of hearings and in its conduct moved away from the traditional concept of an inquiry being a fact finding, administrative mechanism, albeit one conducted in adversarial fashion. This concept had been less than effective in explaining the nature of major inquiries for some time; it could not disguise ministerial involvement in promoting the very projects over which inquiries were being held, supposedly the 'better to inform' those same ministers. Nor could it account for the 'salami' technique whereby a major project could be authorised after a *series* of inquiries each separated from the others, nor yet the inability of the inquiry system to inquire into the statistical and other techniques underlying policy formulation. A further weakness in the traditional conception of a 'public' inquiry is the vast discrepancy in resources between promoting agencies and objectors making it hard for the latter to present their arguments fully. To meet the last objection the Sizewell inquiry introduced the major innovation of 'counsel to the inquiry', and this led to the inquiry adopting a much more inquisitorial role with the inspector, the assessors and counsel to the inquiry taking over functions from objectors. Though fair and thorough examination of the issues involved may dictate a more inquisitorial style of inquiry, it could result in objectors being marginalised, their lack of resources being even more emphasised by those of the inquiry mechanism itself.

National projects to implement policies, themselves the subject of fierce debate and concern are not, however, easily fairly investigated by public inquiries. The well rehearsed argument remains that such proceedings can never be truly legitimate. Projects may be too closely identified with their ultimate ministerial arbiters, who may be, without total justification, *assumed* to represent 'public interest', and the resources of proponents and opponents continue to be greatly unequal. Inquiries are thought by some to be merely cosmetic, giving a semblance of legitimacy to conclusions already reached. Controversy over trunk road proposals, the Vale of Belvoir Coalfield, the siting of, and need for, a third London airport, and the nuclear fuel reprocessing plant at Windscale led to major public inquiries becoming longer and more expensive as attempts to ensure fairness for all concerned. The Sizewell inquiry did not resolve any of these issues, even though it marked a major development in inquiry *procedure*. At the end of the day the inquiry still had to rely on expert evidence given, not always in a coherent fashion, by various bodies and agencies identified in the public mind as part of the structure of government. To that extent the inquiry could not bring about legitimation of the proposed PWR, even less legitimation of nuclear policy overall, policy formulation techniques, or public inquiry procedures in general.

The following fundamental flaws in major inquiry procedures must always be borne in mind:

1   An inquiry is not a means of formulating policy nor yet a means of policy critique.
2   Any inquiry must accept official policy and much of the techniques used to assess the factual basis of policy, even when they are not put forward in the most coherent style, and even where they alter during the course of events.
3   The resources of the various participants remain uneven, major 'players' may be able to afford the very considerable fees charged by leading counsel and their juniors, but many voluntary organisations have to depend solely on their own staff, and private citizens must look to their own resources, perhaps having to launch fighting funds to meet costs for not only are lawyers' fees considerable, there is also the high cost of expert witnesses.
4   Inquiries still consume much time, and ways of shortening them (by excluding *all* consideration of policy issues, by empowering inspectors

specifically to exclude evidence or questions on grounds of repetition or irrelevance, by more vigorously awarding costs against the long winded and by concentrating more on the pre-inquiry preparation stage) may further reinforce the argument that inquiry procedure cannot be fair.

E REFORM OF INQUIRY PROCEDURE

The form of future inquiries continues to be a matter of debate. There seems to be little consensus on a number of major issues.

1 Should inquiry procedure be so very adversarial, as traditional, with probing examination and cross-examination, or much more investigatory and inquisitorial, with the inquiry itself opening up questions and identifying issues it wishes to have studied and researched? Indeed, should inquiries be given powers to question the need for projects and policies in the broadest economic, social and environmental terms, with the ability to examine alternatives? This could raise constitutional issues over the conventional responsibility of ministers to Parliament for the formulation of policy. Such inquiries could become *non-elected* forums for debate.

2 Should inquiries be held by single inspectors who, no matter how eminent, and no matter how well assisted by assessors, cannot possibly be expert in all relevant fields of knowledge? It is questionable whether lawyers are the best equipped people to hold inquiries. Lawyers are 'at home' with very formal inquiry procedures, but many objectors find these inhibiting. Lawyers also use adversarial cross-examination techniques, but some descriptive and evaluative evidence, for example, the social consequences of similar projects elsewhere, is not susceptible of such examination. Lawyers are, by training, well equipped to identify *what the issue for debate* is, and to present arguments for and against a particular point of view; they are not, traditionally, trained to see how the *issue for decision* relates to its social, political, economic and environmental setting, though is any profession able to claim that its members could comprehend all these complex matters? Other critics direct their attention to the argument that there is insufficient public scrutiny of the process of appointing inspectors for major inquiries.

3 Do inspectors have sufficient powers to order the disclosure of all relevant documentation before an inquiry so that parties may know well in advance the various arguments? Indeed, is it even possible to know the arguments when policy is unclear?

4 Do objectors to a proposal have a fair chance to state their case? Legal aid is not available. The technical and financial resources of those proposing a project are greatly out of proposition to those of objectors, even considered collectively.

Furthermore would it be 'fairer' to hold major inquiries only in the evening so that those at work may be able to attend more easily, and also should child minding facilities be provided at inquiries to enable those with small children to participate more?

5 Assuming that 'pressure groups' opposed to a project can muster sufficient resources to enable them to present their cases, is more help needed for individuals to enable them to join in the debate effectively?

6 Are inquiries becoming too long, and expensive so that much needed projects are being delayed for unacceptable periods?
7 Would it be preferable for major projects to be subject, so far as policy issues are concerned, solely to Parliamentary debate? 'Site specific' inquiries would be limited then solely to local planning considerations, and to 'yes' and 'no' recommendations on such matters, with no wider debate; assuming it is possible to devise rules to prevent objectors raising policy issues under the guise of local considerations. Site specific inquiries raising no possibility of debating, albeit in limited ways, policy might be politically acceptable if they took place against a background of consensus on policies already well debated in Parliament, though such policies generally are rare. Such site specific inquiries might be appropriate in the context of *planning* law because planning control is a 'one-off' system designed to decide at a particular point whether a particular land use or operation should be allowed for the future. However, where continuing economic, social and environmental issues as well as pure land use considerations are present, as is the case with regard to road building, airport development and nuclear installation construction, where a development will have a continuing impact, certainly regional and probably national, it is debatable whether the *traditional* public inquiry is an apt mechanism for examining proposals.

There could be more public involvement. The Outer Circle Policy Unit as long ago as 1979 argued for 'Project Inquiries' comprised of Commissioners combining a wide degree of expertise with impartiality. Such inquiries would be able to examine the 'need' for proposed projects. They would have two stages, the investigation and the argument. The first stage would be inquisitorial, determining issues to be researched, and ensuring all relevant information is made readily available to inquiry participants. The second stage would concern itself with argument as to correct inferences to be drawn from determined facts. Thereafter the Commission would make its report which could contain recommendations, or clearly defined options for decision. The report stage could be followed by debate in Parliament and in the press, etc.

The foregoing concerns resurfaced at the commencement of the appeal inquiry into the 1994 refusal by Cumbria County Council for the construction of an underground laboratory at Gosforth near Sellafield, a facility which many people see as a step on the way to the building of a major underground repository for plutonium contaminated radioactive waste. One early exchange at the inquiry concerned an allegation that the government had limited the terms of reference of the inquiry to enable the project's promoters to press ahead. This was rejected by the inquiry inspector who stated only the judiciary would impose limits on the scope of the inquiry. That was an indication that, despite the 'official' line that the inquiry, as a planning matter, should be limited to local planning and amenity issues, the inspector believed that safety and site selection issues were also relevant. It is clear that the scope and effectiveness of individual inquiries thus depends to a considerable extent on the practice of the inspectors holding them: whether that should be so must be a cause for debate.

These matters raise the fundamental issue of what form of government is acceptably legitimate. In an increasingly articulate and informed society decisions on projects having major environmental implications will not be left simply to ministers, civil servants and public authorities. Many people want to participate in decisions that will shape their lives, and are no longer prepared to leave matters to their Parliamentary representatives. Many seriously question how it is that a whole mass of planning and conservation legislation can be seemingly set aside in the name of roads policy — and the easy legal answer that no Act of Parliament has a special sanctity which makes it immune from the operation of other Acts is not an acceptable response. There is clear evidence that at least some people will reject the framework of society if confronted by decisions to which they strongly and bitterly object, taken by procedures which seem to give them no effective means of debating the issues or of influencing the final outcome. Not all of those who protest can be dismissed as simply 'drop outs' and extremists. While it is, however, not possible to debate the issue more fully here it is clear that a policy and decision making framework more generally responsive to environmental concerns is needed.

Responses to concern over inquiry procedure

Governmental responses to the foregoing concerns have been muted. In 1988, in DoE Circular 10/88, the Code of Practice for major inquiries under the *Planning Acts*, was issued with the purpose of ensuring more smoothly running and better structured inquiries. The code applies to inquiries where major public interest is aroused because of national or regional implications, or where extensive and complex environmental, safety, technical or scientific issues are involved, and where there are numbers of third parties involved. However, it is for the DoE to decide whether or not in any given case the Code will apply. It is considered that only a few inquiries will have the Code applied to them, generally speaking those falling within the scope of rule 5 of SI 1992/2038 (the inquiry procedure rules), ie where pre-inquiry meetings have to be held.

Once the Code is applied to an inquiry copies of it will be sent to the applicant and the planning authority together with an indication of the matters the Secretary of State considers relevant to the issue under consideration. The authority will also be sent a form for use by those who wish to register as inquiry participants. This will indicate, inter alia, whether participants have affected land, whether they will be formally represented, and whether they wish to play a major role by calling witnesses, etc. All those having the *right* to appear will also be notified by the DoE to the authority. The application of the code has to be publicised in the local press and registration forms will further give the address of the Secretariat which will be set up in the DoE to handle the inquiry and liaise with the authority.

The next task is the creation of a register of participants. Part I will be 'major participants' who will be allowed to speak irrespective of the strict legalities. Part 2 will be those indicating a desire to give oral evidence only; they will normally be allowed to appear provided what they have to say is relevant and not repetitious. Part 3 will consist of those making written representations only, they may be allowed to appear at the inspector's discretion. This register will be circulated to the parties and the major participants, copies will also be publicly available. Major participants will thereafter be expected to comply with the Code, eg as to exchange of documents.

There follows the announcement of the name of the inspector, the assessors (if any) arrangements for pre-inquiry meetings and a target inquiry commencement date. This will be publicised locally by the authority. Not later than eight weeks after notification that an inquiry is to be held the applicant and the authority will be asked to provide outline statements of case and arguments. Others may be asked to provide statements within four weeks of receipt of a request. The statement should indicate the likely time presentation of the case will take and information about witnesses, special studies undertaken, etc. This information will normally be circulated to major participants and made publicly available. These statements will outline lines of argument thus enabling issues for the inquiry to be identified, and allowing the inspector to structure the inquiry, perhaps enabling the inspector to invite some participants to submit joint arguments, and showing whether any issues have been missed so that the deficiency may be remedied. Statements may also enable agreed *facts* to be identified thus enabling such matters to be settled before the inquiry commences.

At the following pre-inquiry meeting(s) chaired by the inspector clarification of issues is to be sought, eg on agreed facts, timetabling of any further pre-inquiry issues, identifying relevant issues, the role of the assessors. Procedural issues will also be considered, eg times and places of sitting, programming, the facilities needed by the inquiry, opening and closing procedures, document exchange systems. The conclusions of the meeting will be circulated to parties and major participants by the secretariat, and the date, time and place of the inquiry will be circulated to all relevant persons and bodies. Further meetings may be held to establish statements of agreed facts, and these will be reported and circulated. The parties and the major participants may then be required to write a statement giving full particulars of their proposed submissions and listing documents intended to be placed in evidence. These statements, where required, will have to be made within four weeks of the final pre-inquiry meeting. Statements of evidence to be read at the inquiry must under the statutory rules be given beforehand to the inspector, and summaries of such evidence may be required under the Code. Where a participant who gives oral evidence at an inquiry wishes to introduce an argument outside his pre-inquiry statement, an adjournment *may* be allowed for others to consider the issues raised. Unreasonable conduct leading to such an adjournment may result in an order for costs being made against the guilty person.

Annex 3 of Circular 10/88 tabulates the timetabling structure of pre-inquiry stages, while Annex 6 lays down good inquiry practice, reminding inspectors that they must combine openness, fairness and impartiality with efficiency. Thus while those who appear must feel they have had a chance to state their cases fully and that their cases have been understood, repetitious and unnecessary argument is not to be allowed.

However, Cm 43 issued in 1987 indicated that the government was averse to making certain other changes in the inquiry system that had been variously suggested, eg granting third parties rights to have some planning applications 'called in', likewise giving such parties financial assistance in connection with major inquiries and adoption of a two stage inquiry process with regard to major development proposals. It thus appears that the procedure available under s 101 and Sch 8 of the TCPA 1990 whereby a 'planning commission inquiry' may be set up to conduct such a two stage inquiry into both general and site specific issues will remain the 'dead letter' it has been since its introduction in 1968. Note, however, the extension of the Code of Practice's concepts to the vexed issue of highway construction via the recent Highways Inquiry Procedure rules, SI 1994/3263, see above.

Conclusion

The root of the problem lies not with inquiry procedure, but with antecedent policy formulation. No inquiry can legitimate what is opposed en masse by those who reject the entire policy concerned.

F THE TRANSPORT AND WORKS ACT 1992

Disquiet over inquiry procedure is a long standing issue, a matter of rather more recent controversy was the use of private/hybrid bill procedure in Parliament to give particular powers to persons/companies to proceed with major projects, eg the Channel Tunnel Bill 1986. (For a further examination of this issue see the second edition of this work at pp 226–227.)

To calm this anxious opposition the Transport and Works Act 1992 has now been passed whereunder an improved procedure is introduced to deal with such matters. Concerned with transport projects — railways, tramways and inland waterways — and ensuring that they can be constructed with their promoters being given appropriate planning consents and compulsory acquisition powers and freedom from liability in nuisance arising from their operation (such projects inevitably interfere with private rights), the Act nevertheless also addresses relevant environmental concerns.

Thus under s 1 of the 1992 Act the Secretary of State may make orders as to railways and tramways (and under s 3 with regard to inland waterways) where, under s 6, an application is made to him/her in due form: authorising their construction, alteration, repair, maintenance, etc; creating or extinguishing rights over land, etc; s 5 and Sch 1 of the 1992 Act. In particular approval may be given for: the compulsory acquisition of land; planning consent under s 90(2A) of the Town and County Planning Act 1990, and hazardous substances consent under s 12(2A) of the Planning (Hazardous Substances) Act 1990. Where, however, an application relates to matters considered by the Secretary of State to be of national significance, an order may *not* be made without the prior approval of both Houses of Parliament. Where an application for an order authorising the construction/operation of a railway, tramway, or canal, etc, provision is made under s 1 of the Act for holding a public local inquiry, and the procedure follows the 'normal' pattern for such events, see SI 1992/2817.

Rules made under s 6 of the 1992 Act ensure that EA of projects falling within the terms of the Act takes place, see SI 1992/2902 relating to the submission and consideration of environmental statements, while SI 1995/1541 requires that, where an environmental statement has been submitted, the Secretary of State must confirm he took it into consideration and the opinions expressed relating to that statement, before making or refusing an order authorising that project.

G PIPELINES: UNCONTROVERSIAL LAWS?

Pipelines, that is systems for transporting materials, other than air, water, steam or water vapour from one locality to another, not being drains or sewers, may not be constructed across country without ministerial authorisation, see the Pipe-lines Act 1962, ss 1 and 65. Procedure for deciding applications for pipeline authorisation is laid down in Sch 1, Part I, of the 1962 Act, as amended. Applications must, inter alia, specify the points between which a proposed pipeline is to run, and what is proposed for conveyance in the pipeline. The Minister (the Secretary of State) has discretion whether or not to grant authorisation. Where he/she proposes to grant authorisation he/she must inform the applicant, who must take specified steps to inform persons inhabiting land in the vicinity of the proposed route of the proposal, stating the time for making objections. Relevant local planning authorities must also be served with notice of the proposal. Where objections are received, objectors must be given a hearing. This *must* take the form of a public inquiry where the objection is made by a local planning authority. After considering the report of the person who heard objectors, the Minister makes his decision. If he refuses the application he must give the applicant a written statement of his reasons. Under s 5 of the 1962 Act upon granting authorisation the Minister may direct that planning permission is deemed to be granted for any work of development involved, subject to such conditions as he may lawfully impose. The procedure for inquiries is contained in the Pipe-lines (Inquiries Procedure) Rules SI 1995/1239 and follows the by now familiar modern pattern enabling the holding of pre-inquiry meetings, the timetabling of the inquiry service of witness statements, proofs of evidence, appointment of assessors, appearances and procedures at the inquiry, etc.

The statutory scheme only applies to 'cross country' pipelines, that is, *generally* under s 66(1) of the 1962 Act, a pipeline whose intended length will exceed ten miles. Other pipelines, being *generally* designated 'local', fall within development control powers of local planning authorities. In formulating pipeline proposals and in ministerial consideration of such proposals, regard must be had to the effect they will have on natural beauty, flora, fauna, geological and physiographical features of special interest and historic buildings and objects. The Minister must also consider the need to protect water against pollution from pipelines. A person executing pipeline works in agricultural land is under an obligation to secure, so far as practicable, that, on completion of the works, the land is restored so as to be fit for that use to which it was put immediately before the works began, see ss 43, 44 and 45 of the 1962 Act. The 1962 Act also does not apply to pipes and associated works for waste collection purposes, see s 45 of the Environmental Protection Act 1990.

Compulsory purchase powers in connection with pipeline construction are conferred by s 11 of the 1962 Act, alternatively compulsory acquisition of rights over land for construction purposes is allowed by s 12. These powers are subject to ministerial authorisation. Under s 13 the Minister may impose conditions on a compulsory rights *order*, and compensation in respect of such orders may be payable under s 14. Even though there is now a network of oil and gas pipelines nationwide this legislation seems to have been generally uncontroversial in practice, despite the fact that pipelines run through many scenic areas.

H HAZARDOUS LAND USES AND CONNECTED ISSUES

The UK has a number of provisions implementing the requirements of the EU law referred to earlier in this chapter, together with other relevant national provisions.

Directive 67/548 and its amendments, etc have been implemented by various regulations and the provisions of the Health and Safety at Work etc Act 1974, which is not, of course, generally an environmental protection measure. Nevertheless s 6 of the 1974 Act, as amended, imposes a duty on any person who manufactures, imports or supplies *any* substance to ensure that: so far as is reasonably practicable the substance will be safe and not a health risk at all times when being used, handled, stored or transported *by* a person at work; such testing and examination is carried out as necessary to comply with the foregoing duty; adequate information is given to those supplied with substances about inherent health and safety problems, together with information (updated as necessary) concerning any relevant tests and about conditions necessary for safe handling, etc, and disposal of substances. Further duties are imposed on manufacturers of substances to carry out research to discover health and safety risks and to eliminate or minimise them so far as reasonably practicable. These provisions are supplemented by the Notification of New Substances (NONS) Regulations SI 1993/3050 which impose duties on those who make and/or manufacture new chemicals or compounds of chemicals in either a natural or product state to inform the 'competent authority', ie the Secretary of State and the Health and Safety Executive (HSE) before one tonne or more of the relevant material is supplied, and likewise to inform the HSE of any changes in relevant material. The regulations apply to those substances not listed in the European Inventory of Existing Commercial Chemical Substances (EINECS) which dealt with substances on the market before 18/9/1981, and classified as 'dangerous' by reference to their being: explosive; oxidising; extremely flammable; highly inflammable; flammable; very toxic; toxic harmful; corrosive; irritant; sensitising (ie making a person hypersensitive to particular substances); dangerous to the environment on an immediate or delayed basis; carcinogenic; mutagenic (ie if inhaled or ingested capable of inducing heritable genetic defects).

In relation to such material technical dossiers must be given to the competent authority before a relevant supply is made. As standard notification arrangements the supplier must provide the competent authority with inter alia: a technical dossier supplying information necessary for evaluating foreseeable risks, immediate or delayed, which the substance may create for human health or the environment, including the certified results of tests specified in the regulations; a declaration concerning any unfavourable effects of the substance in terms of its foreseeable uses; if the substance is 'dangerous' proposals for its classification and labelling under the CHIPS regulations (see below).

Note that the purpose of these regulations is basically informatory as to new substances, to provide a flow of information via the HSE to the Commission. They are not primarily designed to control marketing; however, no notified substance may be placed on the market until 60 days have elapsed from the date of receipt by the HSE of due notification *and* there has been no objection by the HSE during that period (see further Burnett-Hall, *Environmental Law* paras 12–061 to 12–088). A system of control over existing substances (ie those listed in EINECS) exists under EU Regulation 793/93 to require their risk assessment according to a scheme of priorities established by the Commission, the first part of which appeared in May 1994. Once such assessments have been made proposals may be put forward by the Commission for risk limitation. Those seeking further detail are referred to Burnett-Hall, op cit, paras 12–034 to 12–056.

Further requirements as to the classification, packaging and labelling of 'dangerous substances' are contained in the Chemicals (Hazard Information and Packaging) Regulations (CHIP) SI 1994/3247 which implement Directive 92/32. These regulations are supplemented by an *Approved Guide to the Classification and Labelling of Substances and Preparations Dangerous for Supply*, 2nd edn (the Approved Labelling Guide), and *Information Approved for the Classification and Labelling of Substances and Preparations Dangerous for Supply*, 2nd edn (the Approved Supply List).

The basis of the CHIP regulations is a classification of 'substances' and 'preparations' into a number of risk categories. 'Substances' are chemical elements/compounds in a natural or produced state, while 'preparations' are mixtures or solutions of two or more substances. (Supply is defined to refer to supply of relevant material by sale, by supply of a commercial sample, by transfer from a warehouse, etc by a person acting as a principal or an agent.) Certain material is excluded from the ambit of the regulations because it is elsewhere controlled, eg radioactive material, while the HSE is also able to grant exemptions from the requirements of all/any of the regulations subject to such conditions as may be imposed.

The scheme of the regulations is to prohibit the supply of material 'dangerous for supply' unless it has been duly classified. What is 'dangerous for supply' may be determined by reference to the Approved Supply List and Sch 1 of the regulations. There are a number of 'categories of danger' into which material may fall: these are effectively those already encountered under the NONS Regulations, ie 'explosive', 'flammable', 'toxic', etc. Each category has a 'symbol letter' and under Sch 2 of the Regulations, usually, a symbol giving some indication of its dangerous propensities, such as a skull, which indicates toxicity. In the case of preparations there are particular rules under Sch 3 to determine classification based on the properties of their component substances: special provision is made under Sch 4 for the classification of pesticides.

If material is classified as 'dangerous for supply' it may only be supplied provided: it has been so classified; that in any advertisements for the material its hazards are mentioned; it is suitably packaged and labelled to indicate its reasons for being 'dangerous for supply' according to the requirements of the regulations, which are highly specific, for example in relation to flammable material. The regulations also impose requirements as to the keeping of records and information about the supply of relevant material by suppliers, and the provision by them of safety data sheets which enable the recipients of relevant material to take necessary steps to protect human health and the environment.

The enforcement of the CHIP regulations is by the HSE, and where a breach of the regulations is alleged it is a defence to show that all reasonable precautions were taken and all due diligence exercised to avoid the commission of an offence.

Carrying dangerous goods

The 'package' of regulations relating to the carriage of dangerous goods by road and rail is based on internationally agreed standards. As with the CHIP regulations the system of control is based on a set of statutory regulations, the Carriage of Dangerous Goods by Road and Rail (Classification, Packaging and Labelling) Regulations SI 1994/669 supplemented by the Carriage of Dangerous Goods by Rail Regulations SI 1994/670 and a number of other documents dealing with approved methods of transport and specific aspects of carriage by road and rail, etc.

The new system of regulation deals with the issues of Classification, Packaging and Labelling (CPL) of hazardous materials, subject to explosives and radioactive material being, in effect, separately regulated. Some substances are specifically listed in the supplementary documents to the regulations as hazardous while other material is caught by virtue of its possessing listed, hazardous properties, eg it is toxic, infectious or corrosive, etc. Such material cannot be consigned for carriage unless certain conditions are met, ie that: their classification and particulars have been ascertained in accordance with the regulations; where consigned in packages those packages are suitable for their purpose; no misleading marks are shown on packages; specified particulars are shown on packages according to particular methods of marking or labelling.

Again the enforcement of these regulations is a matter for the HSE, and it is a defence in cases of alleged breach to show that all reasonable precautions were taken and all due diligence exercised to avoid commission of an offence.

Marketing and use restrictions

Directive 76/769 and its 'train' have been variously implemented in the UK. Section 100 of the Control of Pollution Act 1974 empowered the Secretary of State to regulate by prohibition or restriction of the import, trade, use or supply of specified substances in order to protect humans or the environment.

The Secretary of State currently has enhanced powers under s 140(1) of the Environmental Protection Act 1990 by regulation to prohibit or restrict importation into, or landing and unloading in, the UK, use, supply or storage of any specified substance or articles to prevent pollution of the environment, harm to human, animal or plant health. Regulations may be general or area, time or person specific, and may provide for prohibited material to be treated as controlled waste and disposed of appropriately. Contraventions of regulations will be offences and may lead to relevant material being disposed of, treated or removed from the UK. Provision is made by s 140(4) for prohibitions, etc, existing under EU obligations or other enactments to be treated as made under s 140(1). Before regulations are made consultation will have to take place with a specifically established advisory committee; any regulations proposed will have to be publicised and made subject to a procedure whereunder the public may inspect the proposals and make representations which will have to be taken into account. These publicity requirements may be dispensed with in cases of imminent risk of serious pollution of the environment. Regulations when made may apply to articles and substances, the latter being natural or artificial substances, whether in solid, liquid gaseous or vapour form, and including mixtures.

The Environmental Protection (Controls on Injurious Substances) Regulations SI 1992/31, supplemented by SI 1992/1583, SI 1993/1, SI 1993/1643, provide for controls over the supply and use of various specified injurious substances in particular contexts, contravention of which is a criminal offence, eg lead carbonate and sulphate in paint; mercury compounds in heavy duty textiles; mercury, arsenic and certain compounds intended for use in the treatment of industrial waters; while use of cadmium as a pigment agent, or as an element in certain paints, or as a stabilising or plating agent is particularly restricted. In some cases the marketing or use of substances is totally banned other than for research and development and analysis purposes, eg pentachlorophenol. Other regulations made under earlier legislation continue to control other material capable of presenting a major health hazard, eg polychlorinated biphenyls and terphenyls (PCBs and PCTs) under SI 1986/902 and vinyl chloride monomer (VCM) as a propellant under SI 1980/136. It should further be noted that 'pincer like' control exists in relation to certain material in that not only is it specifically restricted under the regulations currently under consideration but the premises at which it is used will further be subject to regulation under Integrated Pollution Control (see chapter 10), for example pentachlorophenol. Note further SI 1994/234 imposing controls over batteries and accumulators containing certain levels of mercury, cadmium or lead.

Consumer protection

Directives 76/769 and 89/677 impose restrictions on the supply of certain ornamental objects, tricks, jokes and games which contain specified dangerous substances and preparations. These are implemented in the UK under the Consumer Protection Act 1987, see SI 1994/2844.

Special protection for workers

Framework Directive 80/1107, 82/605 (lead exposure) and 83/447 (asbestos exposure) which are concerned with worker protection are generally implemented under the Health and Safety at Work etc Act, see particularly the Control of Lead at Work Regulations SI 1980/1248 and SIs 1987/2115, 1988/712, 1992/3067 and 1992/3068 which are concerned with asbestos. Further worker protection is given under the Control of Substances Hazardous to Health Regulations (COSHH) SI 1994/3246 which impose duties on employers in respect of their employees (and others foreseeably affected).

The regulations impose a general requirement on employers to ensure that the exposure of employees to substances hazardous to health is either prevented, or is otherwise adequately controlled. The substances (and preparations) in question are, in general those regulated under the CHIP regulations (see above), specified substances under the COSHH regulations for which an assigned maximum exposure limit is laid down, biological agents, dust and other like hazard creating substances. The COSHH regulations further go on to prohibit the use of particular substances hazardous to health for specified purposes, for example the use of white phosphorus in the making of matches.

The COSHH regulations 'flesh out' the duty under s 2 of the Health and Safety at Work etc Act 1974 to provide safe and healthy work places. The details of the COSHH system are beyond the scope of this work being clearly matters of occupational health, but the *general* scheme is that worker exposure to relevant substances is controlled by maximum exposure limits or occupational exposure standards, complying with formal and regularly reviewed risk assessment of all health risks to workforces to be carried out by employers so that budgeting for appropriate control measures can be undertaken. Monitoring of exposure to substances hazardous to health has to be undertaken as does regular checking and surveillance of the health of workers together with maintenance, examination and testing of control measures.

With regard to controls over asbestos outside the specific context of occupational health, the reader seeking further information is referred to Richard Burnett-Hall, *Environmental Law*, paras 12–187 to 12–204. Chapter 12 of this work is an exhaustive treatment of the law on hazardous substances, to which indebtedness is acknowledged.

Controls over hazardous developments and installations on land, and major industrial hazard sites, etc

With regard to developments on land involving hazardous substances special regimes are needed. Planning law exists to control development on land, but not necessarily specific activities taking place after development. Nor is planning law an obviously appropriate medium for dealing with health and safety issues, for it has to deal with other matters such as social and economic factors such as the need to attract or preserve jobs, as well as safety matters in relation to a proposed development. Accordingly a dual system of control over hazardous developments has grown up with planning law running in parallel with, and sometimes connected to, various health and safety and other environmental controls.

Installations handling hazardous substances

The Notification of Installations Handling Hazardous Substances Regulations SI 1982/1357 (NIHHS) apply where a notifiable quantity of a dangerous substance is involved in an activity proposed for a site or pipeline. The materials in question *include*: liquefied petroleum gas at a pressure greater than 1.4 bar absolute (25 tonnes–50 tonnes where the pressure is 1.4 bar absolute or less); phosgene (2 tonnes); chlorine (10 tonnes); hydrogen cyanide (20 tonnes); ammonia (100 tonnes), propylene oxide (5 tonnes); sodium chlorate (25 tonnes) and liquid oxygen (500 tonnes). The substances and quantities are differently tabulated in relation to pipelines, and *include*: gases or mixtures thereof flammable in air (15 tonnes) and liquefied gases flammable in air having a boiling point of less than 0 degrees Celsius and normally held under refrigeration or cooling at a pressure of 1.4 bar absolute or less (50 tonnes).

Where relevant activity is proposed at least three months' written notice must be given to the HSE identifying the applicant, the site, describing the activity proposed and its proposed commencement date, the minimum and maximum quantities of relevant substances, and the name and address of the planning authority. These are the requirements for *sites*, those for pipelines are similar.

The administrative arrangements then are, according to DoE Circular 11/92, that the planning authority and the HSE are to liaise, though it is not for the former to duplicate the functions of the latter by way of inappropriate planning conditions. Where there is an application for permission for development involving hazardous installations, the local planning authority must consult the HSE. The Executive may not direct that planning permission should be refused.

Their advice will be based on the following principles: is the risk residual in the light of compliance with health and safety requirements, what is the likely risk of an incident, and what could its consequences be; what is the nature of the proposed development and will it lead to an 'exposed' population being vulnerable; if an incident occurred what would be the likely level of casualties? Where the HSE advise against granting permission authorities are strongly urged not to grant permission, and should an authority wish to grant permission contrary to advice, the Executive could ask the Secretary of State to use his 'call in' powers. The Executive could also advise a conditional grant of permission. The HSE undertakes to inform local planning authorities about notifications made to them under relevant statutory provisions, and to specify a 'consultation zone' within which planning authorities are advised to consult on applications for certain types of development, eg any development likely to result in significant increase in the number of people near the hazard. Planning authorities are also advised to consult the Executive with regard to other developments having hazardous characteristics, for example pipelines and licensed explosives sites.

The NIHHS Regulations are supplemented by the Dangerous Substances (Notification and Marking of Sites) Regulations SI 1990/304 which apply where there is on a site a quantity (in total) of 25 tonnes (or more) of substances falling within the definition of 'dangerous goods' under the Carriage of Dangerous Goods by Road and Rail Regulations, SI 1994/669 (see above). Persons controlling sites must ensure that the specified threshold is not passed without prior notification to the HSE *and the local fire authority*, of the notifier's identify, the address of the site, a general description of business on site, a list of classifications of the substances in question, the date when the threshold will be passed. Changes on site must further be notified. However, certain material is excluded from control, eg radioactive material, certain explosives and substances buried or deposited as waste. Certain *sites* are also excluded, eg those notified under NIHSS Regulations, those falling within CIMAH Regulations (see below), waste disposal sites appropriately licensed and nuclear sites. Where the regulations do apply, however, in addition to notifications appropriate marking must take place so as, for example, to warn fire authorities entering a site in an emergency. The signs are specified in BS5378: 1980/82.

Major accident hazard sites (the basic scheme of regulation)

Further safety and environmental protection measures exist under the CIMAH provisions. The Control of Industrial Major Accident Hazards (CIMAH) Regulations SI 1984/1902 as amended are designed to prevent and/or limit the effects of accidents arising out of industrial activity using dangerous substances. The Regulations apply to operations in industrial installations specified in Sch 4. This relates to plants producing or processing organic or inorganic chemicals and chemical substances, petroleum refineries, incineration plants, energy gas production plants, coal or lignite dry distillation plants, certain metal production plants, involving 'dangerous substances' as specified in Schs 1, 2 and 3 of the Regulations. The 'dangerous substances' include very toxic materials, flammable and explosive substances and specific chemicals in specified quantities. The regulations do not apply to industrial activities carried on at nuclear installations, as defined under the Health and Safety at Work etc Act 1974, s 44(8) and including nuclear reactors, ancillary nuclear plants, nuclear fuel or radioactive matter disposal plants. Also excluded are certain defence installations, premises licensed under the Explosives Act 1875, mines and quarries within the Mines and Quarries Act 1954, s 180. It has been contended that these restrictions on the scope of CIMAH, contained in reg 3, undermine their efficiency. Installations excluded by reg 3 are, of course, regulated by other legislation, but these various statutes were not drawn up with the same overall purpose. The outcome is that, for an ordnance factory, nuclear site, or quarry with a large LPT inventory, all of which present major accident hazards, no-one is responsible for co-ordinating off-site emergency planning (contrast CIMAH reg 11), no statutory framework exists for informing the public (contrast reg 12); while any local government agency taking the initiative in emergency planning for such sites cannot be sure who will pay the bill (contrast CIMAH reg 15). This anomaly could be remedied by bringing such installations within the scope of the relevant provisions of CIMAH. The situation is yet a further example of our ill-co-ordinated and unstructured system of environmental regulation. Note, however, that waste disposal sites previously excluded from CIMAH regulation were brought within control in 1994.

Those who control relevant activities must show they have identified major accident hazards and have taken sufficient steps to prevent incidents and limit their consequences, and have given those on site adequate training and equipment to ensure their safety. Any major accident, that is an uncontrolled occurrence leading to *serious danger to persons or the environment,* and involving dangerous substances must be reported to the HSE who are required to inform the Commission of the EU.

Regulations 7 to 12 apply to those having control over activities involving specific quantities or specified dangerous chemicals. Relevant manufacturers must not undertake their industrial activities without preparing a written report containing information as specified in Sch 6 to the Regulations, which deals with the dangerous substances involved in the activity; information about the installation in question, and about the system of management for controlling the activity and relating to potential major accidents. A copy of this report must be sent to the HSE, and this must be done, in relation to new activities, at least three months before the activity is commenced. Reports made must be kept up to date, and the HSE may require manufacturers to provide further specified information in relation to activities. Relevant manufacturers are further required to prepare and keep up to date adequate on site emergency plans detailing how major accidents will be dealt with on site.

Local authorities, generally county councils, are required to prepare and keep up to date adequate off site emergency plans detailing how major accidents at relevant sites will be dealt with, and in preparing such plans authorities must consult involved manufacturers, the HSE and other appropriate persons. Restrictions are imposed on the disclosure of information given under the Regulations. Enforcement is generally in the hands of the HSE.

The development of the CIMAH system

In 1987, the EC issued the first amendment of the 'Seveso' Directive and the CIMAH Regulations were modified to take account of this. The amendments were significant in that the thresholds for some toxic substances were lowered in order to bring a number of sites holding the substances within control. The changes were considered necessary in the light of the Bhopal disaster. However, in 1986 a major accident, following a large fire at a chemical warehouse in Basle, led to a perceived need for further revision of the basic Directive. Directive 88/610 was issued particularly with a view to extending control over the storage of certain dangerous substances. This Directive extended the 'Seveso' Directive's Annex II requirements to 28 named dangerous substances, as opposed to nine formerly, and six categories of dangerous substances and preparations — two formerly. Additionally, cover was extended to process associated storage as opposed to isolated storage as previously. Furthermore the public information requirements of the Directive were enhanced, so that a basic minimum content for information to be provided was laid down, and the items of information to be given are laid out specifically. Additionally, information required has to be made publicly available and repeated and updated on a regular basis, with the public having the right to obtain further relevant information.

The changes made by the 1988 Directive were designed to bring a number of further chemical stores within controls appropriate to sites with 'top tier' hazards. In October 1989, it was estimated that some 250 installations would be added to 550 existing 'top tier' activities then falling within CIMAH Regulations, with some 180 of these being either process associated or isolated chemical stores — the other 70 consisting of bulk storage installations of various sorts.

Schedule 2 of the Regulations as amended is divided into 2 parts: Part 1 lists 28 substances and groups of substances with threshold quantities the presence of which triggers regulation under the CIMAH system. The substances range from acetylene through, inter alia, ammonia, chlorine, formaldehyde, hydrogen cyanide, fluoride or sulphide, oxygen, phosgene, sodium chlorate, dioxide and trioxide to toluene di-isocyanate. Part II relates to four categories of substances and preparations not specifically named in Part I with associated thresholds, for example substances and preparations classified as 'very toxic' or 'explosive' or gaseous substances classified as 'highly flammable' or substances classified as 'highly or extremely flammable'. Part I covers primarily the bulk storage of individual substances, and Part II largely applies to warehouse and similar premises where a range of chemicals is packaged or stored. The general rule is that all storage at or above threshold level will trigger regulation, regardless of whether the storage is or is not process associated. In the past, Sch 2 of the CIMAH Regulations applied to isolated storage only. However, in one respect, this extension of regulation is more apparently extensive than it actually is. The extension of regulation does not apply to any storage which is both process associated according to Sch 4 *and* concerns a substance listed in

Sch 3 of the 1984 Regulations. These substances remain of course controlled by Schs 1 and 3. The effect is that, though 28 substances are specifically named in Part 1 of Schedule 2 for storage regulation, the extension of regulation to process associated storage applies only to such storage of diphenyl methane di-isocyanate, toluene di-isocyanate and non-liquid oxygen. Nevertheless, the extension of regulation to a wider range of storage than before marks a tightening up of control. Furthermore, control extends to situations where there are seasonal variations in storage of the specified materials so that, at times, the amount stored is below the threshold level of control . It is provided that 'the quantities to be considered are the maximum quantities which are, or are liable to be, in storage at any time.'

Summarising these requirements, the first major change in the original CIMAH requirements is to extend control to an increased range of storage activities, both isolated and process associated, though in the case of the latter group CIMAH requirements may already apply because they involve specifically named substances. Where CIMAH requirements apply they will do so despite seasonal variations in the amount stored; they will 'bite' if at any time the maximum amount stored is at or exceeds the quantity listed in the Regulations.

Under the revised reg 12 since 1990 it is the duty of the manufacturer who has control of a relevant industrial activity (ie in general one involving a listed quantity of a specified substance) to ensure that persons likely to be affected by a major accident are given, irrespective of any request on their part, particular information, and to make that information publicly available.

Thus, the statutory duty to be proactive in giving information lies clearly on the manufacturers, and there is an inescapable minimum amount of information to be given. This information is required by Annex VII of Directive 88/619 and relates to matters such as:

1 The name of company and address of site.
2 An identification by the position held of the person giving the information.
3 An explanation in simple terms of the on site activity.
4 The common names of substances and preparations on site which could give rise to a major accident, and an indication of their principal characteristics.
5 General information on the nature of the major accident hazards and their potential effects on the population and the environment.
6 Adequate information on how the population will be warned of relevant events;
7 Information on how to react in the event of an accident.
8 Confirmation that the manufacturer is required to make adequate on site arrangements to deal with accidents and minimise their effects.
9 A reference to an off site emergency plan.
10 Details of where further relevant information can be obtained.

The duty to inform the public, it would seem, is one to make the relevant information accessible to anyone who wishes to see it, and perhaps, via the agency of local authorities, may extend to placing it in public buildings, such as libraries. In preparing relevant information, the manufacturer will have consultations with the local authority in whose area the industrial activity is situated, together with any other appropriate persons, and the original duty under the former reg 12 to reach an agreement with the relevant local authority on dissemination of information is also retained. Information given in pursuance of the various duties outlined above must be updated and supplied again at appropriate intervals and made publicly available. No set period for the reinformation process exists; this may be determined on a case by case basis taking into account:

1 Population changes in the area, eg considering any influxes.
2 The need to remind those already informed.
3 Any changes in substances, processes, hazard planning procedures, etc.

Manufacturers should liaise with local authorities as to what are appropriate reinformation periods. The duty to give the necessary information in general arises before the relevant activity commences.

In May 1990, the DoE issued a consultation document on the operation up till then of the CIMAH system. Changes were needed to close a gap in the system of statutory safety reports which have to be made under the CIMAH Regulations. The regulations require relevant manufacturers to produce a safety case identifying major accident hazards and entailing preventative measures. What seemed to have escaped manufacturers' attention was the definition of 'major accident', which *includes* an occurrence or activity leading to serious danger *to the environment*. Likewise, there is an obligation to take safety measures to prevent accidents and limit their consequences vis-à-vis *the environment*.

Revised guidance was issued on 2 August 1991. Manufacturers should assess the environmental risks of their activities, and an appropriate environmental dimension should be incorporated in safety reports and off site emergency plans. Secondly, a 'major accident' is defined in terms of long term or permanent damage to particular, rare or unique aspects of the natural or built environment, or otherwise widespread loss or damage to the environment generally. Other *examples* of 'major accidents' are:

1 Permanent/long term damage to the special scientific interest of more than 10% of a SSSI.
2 Affectation of a freshwater or estuary so that it is reduced in quality to a specified extent.

Meeting these new requirements will considerably enhance the complexity of producing safety cases. The following steps are requisite:

1 Identification of events capable of leading to releases of dangerous substances.
2 Qualitative assessment of the likelihood of such events.
3 Estimation of the likely amounts of releases, dispersal patterns and likely consequences.

A consequence of measuring such risks against the criteria for defining a major accident to the environment could lead to the likelihood of a major accident being considered unacceptable, in which case suitable preventative action would have to be taken. In addition to the cost of any such preventive measures, industry's costs must inevitably be increased in line with the need to collect and collate a wider range of information on environmental effects than has heretofore been gathered.

Major revision of the 'Seveso' Directive is expected. The object of the revision, which has been long delayed, is to simplify the structure of the law, and to make it more coherent and integrated with land use controls. Thus only 29 substances will be mentioned as expressly 'hazardous', other substances will be 'caught' if they possess certain listed characteristics including 'dangerous for the environment'; the remaining distinction between process and storage will be abandoned for the new Directive will apply to all sites where there are likely to be relevant materials in prescribed amounts; the exemptions for explosives and non-nuclear material at nuclear sites will be withdrawn; planning controls are to ensure that vulnerable activities, etc are kept out of close proximity to hazardous installations.

Protection against ionising radiation in the work place

Turning to the particular issue of protection against radiation, the Ionising Radiation Regulations SI 1985/1333 (as amended) implement Euratom obligations. These apply to any *work*, which includes instruction, involving production, processing, handling, using, holding, storing, moving, transporting or disposing of any radioactive substance, or involving a radiation generator, or which exposes a person to atmospheres containing the short-lived daughters of Radon 222 at specified concentrations. Employers are under duties to protect employees *and others* against ionising radiation arising at such work with such radiation, and are further to inform the HSE of an intention to carry out first time work with such radiation. Dose limitation per calendar year lies at the heart of the Regulations, and all necessary steps are to be taken, so far as reasonably practicable, to restrict the exposure of employees, etc, to radiation by design, etc, features of relevant equipment. Where there is an area in which persons are likely to receive more than the specified annual dose it must be controlled and entry to it restricted. Further controls relate to the control of radioactive substances themselves. Such substances where used as radiation sources should be sealed wherever reasonably practicable, and relevant equipment must be suitably designed, made, maintained and tested. Employers must keep records of radioactive material used in ionising radiation work, and must observe requirements as to its storage and transport. There are particular controls with regard to monitoring radiation, and in respect of assessments of hazards likely to arise at work in the event of a reasonably foreseeable incident, which in particular cases must be forwarded to the HSE, while contingency plans for responding to incidents may be required. Overexposure by employees must be investigated and reported to the HSE, who must further be informed where specified quantities of radioactive material are released, lost or stolen. Note also the code of practice 'The Protection of Persons against Ionising Radiation arising from Work Activity' issued by the Health and Safety Commission. Note also SI 1993/2379 on protection for 'outside' workers who come onto sites operated by bodies other than their employers.

Planning and hazardous substance controls

With the implementation of the Planning (Hazardous Substances) Act 1990 (PHSA 1990) a further link in the chain of hazardous activity controls was forged. The powers exist to meet a deficiency in planning control, namely that a hazardous use can commence on land and not necessarily constitute development so that no planning permission is required.

The Act commences by defining 'hazardous substances authorities' (HSA) see ss 1 and 3. These are: in Greater London, London borough councils; elsewhere, district councils, save that in shire counties the county council is the HSA in respect of land subject to mineral working or waste deposition. Certain other bodies may have HSA functions, eg the Broads Authority, Urban Development Corporations and Housing Action Trusts.

Section 4 of the PHSA 1990 lays down the basic requirement that the presence of a hazardous substance on, over or under land requires the consent of the HSA. Regulations under s 5 of the Act specify what are 'hazardous substances'. The Planning (Hazardous Substances) Regulations SI 1992/656 lay down the material, and the 'controlled' quantities of such material, subject to control. Basically the list is derived from the NIHHS regulations with some additions from CIMAH to ensure effective co-ordination with controls under that system of regulation; but in effect the material is that which is toxic, reactive and explosive, and flammable substances, *generally* in bulk quantities of from 1 to 500 tonnes. Note, however, that controlled waste and radioactive waste and some specified explosives are excluded from regulation as they are separately controlled. See also DoE Circular 11/92 'Planning Controls for Hazardous Substances' which gives guidance on the way in which the legislation is to be operated alongside other relevant controls. Essentially the law's object is to ensure that relevant material is placed only in appropriate places, that proximate placing to vulnerable sites is avoided, and that materials are stored in safety. Exemptions from the need for consent apply where the aggregate amount of the substance on relevant land is below a specified threshold, where a substance is temporarily present by virtue of transportation, or in other cases as specified by the Secretary of State.

A hazardous substance consent (HSCo) may be *granted* on an application, or *deemed to exist* under ss 11 and 12 (see below), but in any case enures for the benefit of the land in question, see s 6. Section 7 of PHSA 1990 lays down a framework for applications for HSCos, and regulations (SI 1992/656) make provision for the way in which applications are to be made, information is to be supplied and publicity undertaken, and time limits for consideration of applications. 21 days' local press notice and site notice publicity for applications must be given. Provision is made for consultation to take place on applications and these are with the Health and Safety Executive (see Sch 13 of the Environmental Protection Act 1990) and other prescribed persons such as other relevant environmental regulation agencies etc. Under s 8 regulations may provide that applications for HSCos must be accompanied by certificates in prescribed form stating that the applicant is the owner of the land in question, *or* has given requisite notice to those who are the owners, *or* that he has attempted to give requisite notice but has been unable to do so, though in this latter case newspaper publicity for the application may be required. (Similar certification may be required in respect of appeals against refused applications or conditions of consents.)

Section 9 of PHSA 1990 empowers HSAs to decide consent applications conditionally or unconditionally or to refuse them. In coming to a decision a HSA must take into account only material considerations, especially: current and contemplated uses of the land in question; the way in which land in the vicinity is, or is likely to be, used; planning permissions granted for land in the vicinity; development plans, advice given by the HSE, etc, in consultations. It can thus be seen that the legislation is intended to be the 'mirror' of the NIHHS information provisions considered earlier and consultation arrangements existing between local authorities and the HSE in relation thereto. The procedure is also clearly derived from planning law, and thus decisions have, normally, to be made within eight weeks of applications, and where refused, rights of appeal exist, see below, while reasons must be given for refusals or any conditions imposed.

Where an application relates to more than one hazardous substance, s 9(3) allows different determinations to be made in relation to each, while s 9(4) requires that where consent is given it must contain a description of the land in question, the hazardous substance(s) and a maximum quantity to be on site in respect of each substance.

There are no specific requirements that an applicant should be a 'fit and proper person' (see chapter 9) but an applicant's history of abuse of hazardous substances would presumably justify a refusal, for the PHSA 1990 though a 'planning statute' is concerned with uses of land in a sense apparently wider than land use matters under the TCPA 1990. HSE statements on consultation would be relevant here also. What could be a little more problematic is whether an applicant has *sufficient experience* to handle a particular substance, and it may be asked whether HSAs will have the technical expertise to decide such issues. It is, however, worthy of note that s 29 of the Act provides that *nothing* in any HSCo is to require or allow anything to be done in contravention of 'relevant statutory provisions', ie the Health and Safety at Work etc Act 1974 and health and safety regulations.

Conditional consent

Consents may be granted subject to conditions, and this power is supplemented by s 10 of PHSA 1990 which allows grants to be conditional on the commencement or partial or complete execution of development on the land in question under a grant of planning permission. Further conditions may relate to: how and where relevant hazardous substances are to be kept or used; the times at which substances may be present; the permanent removal of substances at the end of specified periods; but in these cases such conditions can only be imposed on the advice of the HSE.

Reference has been made to deemed consents for hazardous substances; ss 11 and 12 relate to such consents. A HSCo is, under s 11, a matter of right where a hazardous substance was present on, over or under land at any time within the 12 months preceding the 'relevant date', ie 1 June 1992. If a valid claim to such a consent is made, it is deemed to be granted, and the relevant HSA need only take action in cases where they consider the claim is not validly made. Such consents are subject, however, to conditions restricting the quantities of hazardous substances to 'the established quantity.' This latter figure is: where before commencement there was a notification under the NIHHS regime, the quantity notified or last notified before commencement, *or* a quantity equal to twice the quantity so notified or last notified before the start of the period of 12 months before commencement, whichever is the greater. Where no such notification was required the established quantity is that which exceeds by 50% the maximum quantity which was present on, over or under the land at any one time within the period of 12 months before commencement. Further conditions are prescribed by the regulations, and these relate to issues of storage temperatures and pressures. Claims for deemed consent had to be made within the period of six months following commencement.

Further deemed consents may exist under s 12 of the PHSA 1990. Where the authorisation of a government department is required under a statute in respect of development to be carried out by a local authority or a statutory undertaker and that development would involve the presence of a hazardous substance in such a way as to necessitate a consent, on the grant of authorisation consent may also be directed to be deemed granted, though conditions may be imposed, and prior consultation must take place with the Health and Safety Commission (HSC). A similar provision, s 12(2), applies to consents given under s 36 of the Electricity Act 1989.

Variation and revocation of consents

Conditions imposed on consents may be, in effect, lifted or varied under s 13 in whole or part, or by the substitution of other conditions. Alternatively the initial conditions may be allowed to stand. This is brought about by means of an application for consent without the initial condition(s) which the HSA must then consider. Normally it will be the consent holder who applies, but it appears that a third party may make the application. Section 14(1) grants to authorities a *general* power by order to revoke or modify a HSCo where, on consideration of material circumstances, they consider it expedient so to act. In *particular* under s 14(2) they may revoke or modify consents where there has been a material change of use of the relevant land, or where planning permission has been granted for development involving such a material change and implementation of the permission has begun, or where the HSCo relates only to one substance and that substance has not for at least five years been present in controlled quantities on, over or under the land, or, in the case of a consent for many substances, none of them has been present for five years. Any order made, however, must specify the grounds on which it is made. However, orders under s 14 do not, under s 15, take effect unless ministerially confirmed, and the Secretary of State has a wide discretion in relation to such matters. Thus to revoke a consent the HSA must submit their order to the Secretary of State and must serve notice of the order on owners of the relevant land, persons having control over relevant land and any other persons likely to be affected by the order, and such persons must be given notice of their right to be heard by a ministerially appointed person. After confirmation of the order copies of it must be served on owners and controllers of relevant land and other affected persons. Compensation will then be payable under s 16 in respect of orders made under s 14(1), ie the *general* power of revocation, etc. *Any* person who has suffered damage in consequence of the order by virtue of depreciation of the value of his interest in the land, or by disturbance of his enjoyment of the land is entitled to compensation which is calculated according to the principles of ss 117 and 118 of the TCPA 1990.

Revocation, appeals and enforcement

Section 17 of the PHSA 1990 provides for the automatic revocation of consents where there is a change of the person in control of *part* of relevant land, save where a previous application for continuation of the consent is made. Note the revocation only occurs on a *partial* change of control, though the revocation will extend to the *whole* consent. The provision, it appears, is directed towards preventing the piecemeal disposal of sites having HSCos. Where in such a case of partial disposition a continuation application is made, the HSA may under s 18 modify the consent as they consider appropriate or may revoke it, and in coming to a decision they must consider all relevant factors, but in particular they shall consider the current and contemplated use of the land, the use of neighbouring land, any planning permissions granted on neighbouring land, the provisions of the development plan and any advice received on consultation with the HSE or HSC consequent on regulations made under s 17(2). A fixed period is prescribed within which continuation applications must be determined, otherwise the general rule is that they are deemed granted. Section 19 further provides that where on a s 17 continuation application, modification or revocation of the HSCo takes place compensation will be payable to the person in control of all the land before the application was made.

The Secretary of State has 'call in' powers with regard to consent or continuation applications, see s 20, though DoE Circular 11/92 indicates rare use of this power. Under s 21 there are powers to hear appeals against refusals of consents or continuation applications, and similarly in respect of non-determined applications and conditions imposed on consents. There is a wide discretion in relation to such matters, though the parties must be given an opportunity of being heard. The procedure on appeal is contained in the Schedule to the PHSA 1990, and in regulations made under s 21(3), so, for example, a public local inquiry may, and normally will, take the place of a hearing. Where a person is aggrieved by a decision of the Secretary of State under ss 20 and 21, a further appeal on a point of law only may be made within six weeks of the decision in question being made, otherwise the validity of such decisions cannot be questioned, see s 22.

The normal procedure is for the Secretary of State to make the decision on appeal having received advice from the inspector who heard the appeal. The appeal will be conducted in accordance with the spirit of the Inquiries Procedure Rules (see chapter 5).

Contravention of hazardous substances control by virtue of the presence of a quantity of a hazardous substance when there is no consent or above consent limits, or as a consequence of a breach of consent conditions is an offence on the part of 'the appropriate person'. Such a person can be a person who *knowingly* causes a substance to be on (etc) the land, or one who *allows* it to be present, or the person in control of the land, see s 23. It is provided by s 23(5) that it is a defence to prove one took all reasonable precautions and exercised all due diligence to avoid committing the offence, *or* that the offence could be avoided only by taking action amounting to a breach of statutory duty. Other defences effectively amounting to showing 'no knowledge' are also available. In determining fine levels for offences committed under s 23(4A), financial benefits accruing to the accused in consequence of the offence are to be taken into account.

Section 24 of PHSA 1990 empowers HSAs who consider there is or has been a contravention of hazardous substance control to issue notices specifying the alleged contravention and requiring specified remedial action. Copies of such 'hazardous substance contravention notices' must be served on the owner of relevant land, on the person in control of the land, and on such other persons as may be prescribed. Such a notice must also specify a date, at least 28 days after date of service, on which it will take effect and the time periods for the taking of requisite steps. One requisite step may be the removal of the hazardous substance in question, and in such a case a direction may also be given that any HSCo for the substance in question shall, at the end of a specified period, cease to have effect. The terms of such contravention notices may be waived or relaxed under s 24A. Note that such enforcement action may not take place: where the Secretary of State has issued a temporary exemption direction under s 27; in respect of Crown Land, s 31; where contravention of control can only be avoided by acting in breach of statutory duty, s 24(3), and nothing in a contravention notice may allow or require anything in contravention of health and safety requirements under the Act of 1974, s 29.

There are a number of miscellaneous provisions of interest. Section 26A, inserted by the Environmental Protection Act 1990, provides for regulations to be made concerning the charging of fees for consent applications, while s 26AA allows HSAs to seek injunctive relief to restrain actual or apprehended breaches of control, irrespective of the use of other powers of enforcement. Section 27 empowers the Secretary of State on a temporary basis (*generally* three months at a time) to exempt specified contraventions from criminal liability where he considers either that the community is, or is likely to be, deprived of an essential service or commodity, *or* that there is or is likely to be a shortage of such a service or commodity affecting the community, *and* that the presence of a specified hazardous substance is necessary for the effective provision of the service or commodity.

Section 28 of the PHSA 1990 imposes obligations on HSAs to maintain public registers containing prescribed information on applications, consents, deemed consents, revocations, modifications, and directions issued under s 27. Section 29 as already stated provides that no HSCo is to require or allow anything to be done in contravention of the Health and Safety at Work etc Act 1974, and avoids any consent which offends this prohibition, thus securing the primacy of that legislation and the leading role of the health and safety authorities. Section 30 applies the provisions of the Act generally to any consents needed by HSAs themselves while s 31 applies the Act to land where there is *a* Crown interest but *only* in relation to other interests in that land held otherwise than by or on behalf of the Crown. The Crown itself is not subject to control under the Act, though s 32 empowers the Crown to apply for HSCos so as to allow its land to have the benefit of consent for disposal purposes.

Finally, s 36–36B of the Act should be noted. Section 36 allows any person authorised in writing by the Secretary of State or a HSA to enter any land at any reasonable time to survey it (including power to search and bore to check subsoil) in connection with any application for a HSCo, or any proposal to issue a contravention notice. Furthermore such duly authorised person may enter any land at reasonable hours to ascertain whether any offence under the Act has been committed. Where a contravention notice has been issued similar rights of entry exist with regard to checking whether there has been compliance. Section 36A empowers justices to issue warrants to allow any person duly authorised in writing by a HSA to enter land for s 36 purposes, while it is an offence under s 36B to obstruct such a right of entry.

I GENETICALLY MODIFIED ORGANISMS (GMOS)

The mention of GMOs may conjure up motion film images of 'bug eyed monsters' though such are fantasy — far removed from actuality. Nevertheless the topic of genetic engineering has given rise to concern, a concern examined by the Royal Commission on Environmental Pollution in Cm 720 'The Release of Genetically Engineered Organisms into the Environment' 1989, which itself followed on earlier reports, see Cmnd 5880, Cmnd 6054 and Cmnd 6600, and controls introduced under the Health and Safety at Work etc Act 1974. Concern is most acutely felt in those cases where 'new' genes are incorporated into existing genetic material, as opposed to well established practices such as selective breeding. The EU has also issued Directives to which earlier reference has been made. The history of the development of the current law may be traced in greater detail in Tromans, *The Environmental Protection Act 1990*, and Burnett-Hall, *Environmental Law*, chapter 14: suffice it here to say that Part VI of that Act now provides a legal framework for the regulation of GMOs.

The basic structure of regulation

The legislation has the object of preventing or minimising damage to the environment which may arise from the escape or release from human control of GMOs, ie an acellular, unicellular or multicellular entity in any form (other than a human being or human embryo) where any of the genes or genetic material has been modified by means of a prescribed artificial technique (eg by recombining, inserting or deleting material), or where the genes, etc, have been inherited or derived from material which itself has been so modified, see s 106 of the EPA 1990. The techniques have been further defined, for example SI 1992/3217 states: 'the altering of the genetic material of [an] organism by a way that does not occur naturally by mating or natural recombination or both.' Section 107 supplements s 106 by defining 'damage to the environment' as the presence in the environment (either in itself or in another organism) of a GMO which has escaped from a person's control and is capable of causing, either individually or in combination or by their descendants, harm to the living organisms supported by the environment, by damaging the health of humans or other living organisms or interfering with the ecological systems of which they form part, or by causing offence to human senses or damage to human property. 'Escape from control' is defined in terms of escape into the environment from any system of physical, chemical or biological barriers used to ensure that organisms do not enter the environment or to ensure that those that do enter are harmless. A release from control occurs where a person causes or permits a GMO to cease to be under control and to enter the environment, see s 107(9) and (10).

Particular control over GMOs depends on whether the intention is for their 'contained use' or 'deliberate release' — a distinction which reflects EU obligations outlined above. 'Contained use' covers operations in which organisms are genetically modified, or in which GMOs are cultured, stored, used, transported, destroyed or disposed of, and in which barriers of a physical, chemical, biological or combined nature are in use to limit contact between the material and the general public and the environment. 'Deliberate release' covers situations where material is deliberately caused or permitted to move *from* control *into* the environment. It should further be noted that in some cases a distinction exists between a GMO and a genetically modified micro-organism (GMMO). Though the word 'organism' is apt to encompass plants and animals (excluding humans and human embryos) other multicellular organisms *and* micro-organisms, under the regulations relating to contained use, human *and* environmental risks associated with GMMOs are subject to control, while for GMOs it is only human health risks which are so controlled.

Section 108 of the EPA 1990 obligates all those importing, acquiring, keeping, releasing or marketing GMOs to assess risks to the environment as consequences of such actions before so acting, and in prescribed cases to give notice to the Secretary of State together with any prescribed information. An assessment is carried out by reference to the nature of the organism and the manner of its being kept after import or acquisition, or the intended manner of release or marketing as the case may be. Similar periodic assessments are required for those who keep GMOs; see s 108(3). The Secretary of State has extensive powers to require further information, or to exempt persons from control under s 108, or to impose requirements that a specific consent must be obtained before a person undertakes one of the specified acts, in which case the matter will fall to be dealt with under s 111, see below. Section 109 then imposes further duties on those importing, acquiring, keeping or releasing GMOs. Those who propose to import or acquire must take reasonable steps by reference to the nature of the GMO and the intended manner of keeping to identify risks of damage to the environment consequent on the import, etc, and must not import, etc, if it appears that despite any precautions that can be taken there is a consequential risk of damage. Those keeping GMOs must again investigate risks arising from such keeping, and must keep themselves informed of damage caused by their activities, and must cease (in a safe and quick fashion) to keep GMOs if it appears that despite any *additional* precautions that can be taken there is a consequential risk of damage. Such persons must also use the best available techniques not entailing excessive cost (BATNEEC) for keeping organisms under their control and to prevent environmental damage. Those proposing to release GMOs must identify damage risks arising from release and must not proceed to release if a consequential risk of damage arises, and must, if a GMO is released, use BATNEEC to prevent such damage.

Specific controls over contained use

The Genetically Modified Organisms (Contained Use) Regulations SI 1992/321, as amended by SI 1993/15, first classifies GMOs as GMMOs Group 1, GMMOs Group 2, and GMOs other than GMMOs, according to certain listed characteristics. The principal distinction between Group 1 and Group 2 is based on safety: the material in Group 1 which is to receive inserts is generally non-pathogenic, eg it has an established safe record of laboratory use, or is a non-virulent strain of a pathogenic virus so deficient in relevant genetic material that determines virulence as to ensure no reversion to pathogenicity. Likewise the insert or vector material is, eg, free from known harmful sequences. Group 2 material does not satisfy these criteria. GMOs, ie in this case organisms *other than* micro organisms, are those which are as safe in containment facilities as any recipient or parent organism. The regulations secondly distinguish Type A and Type B activities. The former are activities involving GMMOs for the purposes of teaching, research, development, non-industrial or non-commercial purposes on a scale at which the practices and conditions of the activities (relative to the culture, volume and numbers of organisms involved) is such that (a) the containment system for the organisms reflects good microbiological practice and good occupational safety and hygiene; and (b) standard laboratory decontamination techniques can render the organisms inactive. Type B activities are all others. Thus the degree and style of control depends upon the combination of the class of the material and the type of the activity.

It is a general rule that no operation in which organisms are genetically modified, cultured, stored, used, transported, destroyed or disposed of may take place unless it is 'contained' in accordance with the regulations. Further-more no one may use any premises for activities involving genetic modification for the first time *or* undertake any activity involving genetic modification unless a suitable and sufficient risk assessment in relation to human health and the environment has been made. Notification of an intention to use premises for the first time for activities involving genetic modification has to be given 90 days in advance to the HSE, while in addition it is a general rule that no one may undertake any individual activity involving genetic modification unless 60 days' notice has been given to the HSE, together with relevant details of the activity — the particulars will vary according to the class of the material and the type of the activity. In the case of a Type B operation involving Group II material the activity may only be commenced with the HSE's consent which may be given conditionally, and may be revoked or varied at any time. The HSE may only grant, revoke or vary consent with the agreement of the Secretary of State.

It is a further general requirement that those who undertake genetic modification work must also establish advisory genetic modification safety committees. Part III of SI 1992/3217 lays down further specific rules for the conduct of genetic modification activities, including standards of occupational and environmental safety and containment; rules as to the creation of emergency plans to deal with reasonably foreseeable accidents affecting the health and safety of persons outside premises where relevant activities are being carried on, or where there is a risk of damage to the environment; and also rules as to the notification of the HSE of accidents arising from relevant activities. Particular provision is made by Part IV for public registers to be kept of those notifications of relevant activities for which the HSE's consent is required, for fees to be paid in respect of notifications, and for the disclosure of information supplied by those making notifications; that information will not, in general, be treated as confidential.

SI 1993/15 supplements SI 1992/3217 by providing, inter alia, that where a risk assessment has to be made it should be kept for a period of 10 years.

Controls over importation, acquisition, marketing and release

Section 110 of the EPA 1990 empowers the Secretary of State to serve 'prohibition notices' on those he/she has reason to believe are proposing to import, acquire, release or market GMOs or who are keeping GMOs where he/she believes that such activities would involve a risk of damage to the environment. Where such a prohibition applies to a person keeping GMOs those organisms must be disposed of as quickly and safely as practicable.

Section 111 provides that no person may import, acquire, release or market a GMO in prescribed circumstances, or where a s 108 direction has been given by the Secretary of State requiring the obtaining of consent for an activity, save in accordance with ministerial consent. Similar requirements may be applied to those who have imported or acquired GMOs and who are keeping them. Consent applications have to be in prescribed form and must follow prescribed publicity requirements, and notice may be required to be given by applicants to specified persons. Consents may be given conditionally and are subject to ministerial powers of revocation and variation. Though consents may be subject to such conditions and limitations as the Secretary of State thinks fit, s 112 provides that they may not be imposed solely for health and safety at work purposes. Apart from this consent conditions may, inter alia, prohibit or restrict activities with regard to GMOs. Certain conditions are implied under s 112(3), namely that with regard to importation or acquisition consent holders shall take reasonable steps to keep themselves informed of risks of damage to the environment arising from the importation or acquisition of relevant GMOs, and to notify the Secretary of State if these risks become more serious than was apparent when consent was granted. Similar conditions are implied with regard to consents to keep GMOs and to consents to release or market them save that in these cases consent holders must also utilise BATNEEC to prevent any damage to the environment being caused as a result of the keeping, releasing or marketing of GMOs. A further implied condition in consents for keeping, releasing or marketing is that consent holders must take all reasonable steps to be informed of developments in techniques becoming available to prevent damage to the environment in relation to the consented act, and to notify the Secretary of State where better techniques than those required by any conditions *specifically* applied become available. The implied conditions are subject to any express conditions, see s 112(6).

The Genetically Modified Organisms (Deliberate Release) Regulations SI 1992/3280, amended by SI 1993/152 and SI 1995/304, provide for obtaining consent for the release into the environment of GMOs. Applications must be made in writing to the Secretary of State, and may relate to one or more releases of one or more descriptions of GMOs on one site for the same purpose for a limited period, *or* one or more releases of one description of GMO on *one or more* sites for the same purpose for a limited period. Specified information including a risk assessment must normally accompany the application, and the application must be publicly advertised by local newspaper notices. It must further be the subject of notification to, inter alia, the owners of the site of the release, the local authority, the relevant Conservancy Council, the Countryside Commission, the Forestry Commission, the Environment Agency, and the local water undertaker. Similar provisions apply to marketing of GMOs.

The Secretary of State must forward to the EU Commission summaries of applications for consents to release and to market. The Commission then inform competent authorities of other member states who have 60 days in which to object. The Secretary of State must additionally examine and evaluate the risk posed by the proposed release, carry out any necessary tests and inspections, take account of any comments received from any 'competent authorities' in other member states, and record his/her decision in writing. In the event of an objection from another EU member state the matter has to be referred to the Commission, but if no objection is received consent may be granted and the Commission and other 'competent authorities' will be accordingly advised. Where a consent to release relates to the protection of human health it may not be granted, revoked or varied by the Secretary of State without the agreement of the HSE. Provision is made for decision to be communicated to the applicant, and conditions may be imposed relating, inter alia, to site preparation, release methods, the amount of the release, worker protection, etc.

Enforcement

To enforce the requirements of the 1990 Act, s 114 authorises the appointment of inspectors, and such persons have, under s 115, extensive powers of entry and inspection in relation to premises on which an inspector has reason to believe a person is keeping or has kept GMOs or from which GMOs are believed to have been released or to have escaped, or on which it is believed there may be harmful GMOs or evidence of damage to the environment caused by GMOs, though premises used wholly or mainly for domestic purposes are excluded. The powers *include* ability to: enter premises with or without necessary equipment where entry is reasonably believed to be necessary at any reasonable time, or at any time where there is reason to believe there is an immediate risk of damage to the environment; carry out tests and inspections; take samples; cause relevant containers of GMOs which have caused, or are likely to cause, damage to the environment to be dismantled and tested; seize relevant material, eg a GMO or material including GMOs for examination purposes; require information from relevant persons or from records, including those on computer. Inspectors have powers under s 117 to deal with causes of imminent danger of damage to the environment with regard to GMOs or materials including GMOs found on premises they have power to enter. Such material may be seized and rendered harmless, if necessary by its destruction, though where practicable a sample of the material must be taken and part given to a responsible person at the premises in question, and after the action a written report of the circumstances must likewise be given to a responsible person and the owner. Section 116 further empowers the Secretary of State to obtain relevant information following service of notice in writing on those who are, have been, or who are about to be, involved in importing, acquiring, keeping, releasing or marketing GMOs. The information required may relate to the Secretary of State's functions under the 1990 Act with regard to GMOs or such functions under EU or international law.

Section 118 of the EPA 1990 creates various offences; in relation to some (identified hereafter by 'ARP') the defence of taking 'all reasonable precautions' and exercising 'all due diligence to avoid the commission of the offence' is available. The offences *include*: contravening s 108(1) (ARP) (importing acquiring, releasing or marketing GMOs without risk assessment); contravening s 108(3) (ARP) (keeping GMOs without risk assessment); acting in

contravention of s 111(1) and (2) (ARP) (consents required in certain circumstances); failure to comply with requirements under s 109(2), (3)(a), (b), (c) or
(4) (ARP) (self information requirements with regard to GMOs); contravening
requirements of prohibition notices (ARP); failing to assist inspectors or
obstructing them; making false or misleading statements in relation to the
giving of required information or obtaining consents; making intentionally false
entries in required records under ss 108 or 111. Note that with regard to
proceedings arising out of alleged failures to meet BATNEEC requirements the
burden can be on the defendant to prove that there was no better technique,
etc, than that in fact used: see s 119. Note also that in certain cases the court
may, in addition to fines and imprisonment, order a convicted person to
remedy the cause of the offence, see s 120, while s 121 further empowers the
Secretary of State to take remedial action with regard to the commission of
certain offences and to recover costs from convicted defendants.

Public registers of specified information must be kept by the Secretary of
State under s 122 relating to s 108 directions, prohibition notices, consent
applications, consents, relevant convictions. But such registers may not, by
virtue of s 123, include information whose inclusion would be contrary to
national security interests, or where such inclusion might result in damage to
the environment, or where an individual claims commercial confidentiality,
though this claim may not extend to, inter alia, a description of GMOs, their
location, the reasons for their import, acquisition, etc, risk assessment results.
In any case a successful claim for exclusion will only enure for four years after
which a fresh exclusion application has to be made. Particular provisions for
keeping registers are contained in the various regulations.

To advise the Secretary of State on the exercise of powers under ss 111, 112
and 113, on the making of regulations and on such other matters as he/she
directs, s 124 requires the creation of an advisory committee. This committee
continues the pre-existing body — the Advisory Committee on Releases to the
Environment (ACRE). Further advice may come from the Royal Commission
on Environmental Pollution who in their 14th Report, 'Genhaz: system for the
critical appraisal of proposals to release genetically modified organisms into
the environment', Cm 1557, considered the development of a systematic
inquiry into potential hazards from the release of GMOs. Developing the
Hazard and Operability Study (HAZOP) used in chemical plants, they arrived
at GENHAZ which is a team product, the result of interdisciplinary scientific
collaboration, led by staff trained in the evaluatory technique which is based
on a questionnaire the answers to which describe how a GMO is to be created,
its subsequent mode of release and possible environmental impacts. The
object is to produce a body of information identifying, inter alia, hazards and
ways of dealing with them, together with clear identification of who is to do
what. The Royal Commission's recommendation was that the GENHAZ
system should be a required part of the risk assessment procedure which is
obligatory as outlined earlier in a number of cases.

However, this recommendation was rejected, and to avoid over regulation in
1993 the DoE and ACRE jointly issued *guidelines* requiring a basic minimum
of hazard identification, risk estimation and evaluation to be used in those
cases where, under the statute and the regulations, a risk assessment in relation
to the release of a GMO is required. Following the *approach* to risk assessment
recommended by the guidelines seven steps will be taken: (a) identification of

hazards considering, inter alia, the capacity of the material to survive, establish and disseminate, its pathogenicity to other organisms and potential to affect the environment and human health; (b) identification of how each hazard could be realised in each receiving medium; (c) estimation of the magnitude of the harm which could be caused by each hazard; (d) estimation of how likely it is each hazard will be realised, and how often; (e) estimation for each hazard of the risk of harm being caused by the release/marketing proposal in the light of (c) and (d) supra; (f) modification of the proposal in the light of (e) to achieve the lowest possible level of risk; and (g) evaluation of the steps in assessment in terms of risks to the environment and human health. The assessment when complete must be given not only to the Secretary of State but also to the persons/bodies identified above under the regulations. (For further details see Burnett-Hall, *Environmental Law*, chapter 14, to which indebtedness is acknowledged.)

Finally note that s 125 empowers the Secretary of State to delegate his enforcement functions (see ss 110, 114(1), (4), 116, 118(10) and 121) to a 'public authority' which is the Health and Safety Executive, while under s 126 certain functions concerning agriculture fisheries and food will be jointly exercised by the Secretary of State and the Minister of Agriculture.

Further reading

EU LAW

Haigh, N, *EEC Environmental Policy and Britain* (1992) Cartermill Publishing, section 7.

ROADS

Bryant, B, *Twyford Down: Roads, Campaigning & Environmental Law* (1996) E & F N Spon.
Hall, P, *Great Planning Disasters* (1980) Penguin, chapter 3.
Joseph, S, 'Traffic Growth: The Problems and the Solutions' in Churchill, Gibson and Warren, *Law, Policy and the Environment* (1991) Blackwell.
McAuslan, P, *Land Law and Planning* (1975) Wiedenfeld and Nicolson, chapter 2.
Plowden, S, *Towns against Traffic* (1972) Andre Deutsch.

AIRPORTS

Eyre, G, *The Airport Inquiries 1981–1983* (1984) DOE.
Hall, P, *Great Planning Disasters* (1980) Penguin, chapter 2.

POWER STATIONS

Breach, I, *Windscale Fallout* (1978) Penguin.
Cameron, P, Hancher, L, and Kuhn, W, *Nuclear Energy Law After Chernobyl* (1988) Graham and Trotman.
Ince, M, *Sizewell Report* (1984) Pluto Press.
O'Riordan, T, Kemp, R, and Purdue, HM, *Sizewell B, An Anatomy of an Enquiry* (1988) MacMillan.

ARTICLES

Price, A, 'Pipelines and the Public' (1989) 40 Mineral Planning 8.
Purdue, M, and Kemp, R, 'A Case for Funding Objectors at Public Inquiries?' [1985] JPL 675.
Purdue, M, Kemp, R, and O'Riordan, T, 'The Layfield Report on the Sizewell B Inquiry' [1987] Public Law 162.
Tromans, S, 'Roads to Prosperity or Roads to Ruin' (1991) 3 Journal of Environmental Law 1.

OFFICIAL REPORTS

'Policy for Roads in England': 1987 Cm 125, HMSO.
'The Cost of Decommissioning Nuclear Facilities' (1993) National Audit Office HMSO.
'Runway Capacity to Serve the South East' (1993) Department of Transport.
Department of Transport: 'Environmental Factors in Road Planning and Design' (1994) National Audit Office, HMSO.
Royal Commission on Environmental Pollution, 18th Report: 'Transport and the Environment' (1994) Cm 2674, HMSO.
Standing Advisory Committee on Trunk Road Assessment: 'Trunk Roads and The Generation of Traffic' (1994) HMSO.
House of Commons Transport Committee, 3rd Report, Session 1994/95: 'Urban Road Pricing' (1995) HMSO.
'Guide to Risk Assessment and Risk Management for Environmental Protection' (1995) HMSO.

Chapter 8

Mineral extraction[1]

'Don't go down in the mine, Dad' (old music hall song, c 1910)

Society has a voracious appetite for minerals of all sorts, from energy minerals such as coal, oil and gas, to construction and industrial minerals such as sand, gravel, limestone, clays, slate, 'road-stone' and gypsum. Yet the effects of mineral exploitation are severe. Not only are vast quantities of waste produced (for example, nine tonnes of waste for every tonne of china clay) but mineral extraction destroys the very landscape from which it takes place. At best, a satisfactory or even positively beneficial after-use can be achieved, at worst the end product is land so damaged as to be incapable of after-use without substantial, and expensive, remedial treatment. As extraction technology has advanced, so has the demand for land for extraction and with it the potential for environmental dereliction. As Moss' *Britain's Wasting Acres* shows, in the mid-1970s large areas of land were taken for mineral extraction (up to 12,595 acres pa) with little being restored after use, whilst in 1988, 106,900 ha of land is recorded as having planning permission for mineral working. Furthermore, the period between 1974 and 1982 saw a 6% rise in the area of derelict land in the United Kingdom. That figure has since fallen: between 1988 and 1993 the area of derelict land in the UK fell from 40,500 ha to 39,600 ha, of which, 15,700 ha was directly related to mineral extraction.

A EXTRACTION AND THE ENVIRONMENT

As Mineral Planning Guidance Note 1 (MPG 1) reiterates, workable mineral deposits often encroach upon areas of great beauty or environmental worth, and whilst dereliction is largely avoidable, the use of such land for extraction is not. It is not possible to employ alternative sites as minerals can only be worked where they are found. Economic demands may also lead to a concentration of ancillary operations, including processing and manufacturing, in mineral producing areas, as witness the brickmaking plants of Marston Vale in central Bedfordshire. The expense of extraction in terms of plant and machinery, in relation to the low value by volume of extracted material is another reason for operations being locally extensive. Production of minerals

---

1 This chapter has been written by Tim Jewell. With thanks also to Leon Sartin for his valuable research assistance.

and the consequent use of land also varies over time: some minerals, such as iron ore and now offshore petroleum, are in decline whilst others have remained stable or increased. There has, for example, been a substantial growth in consumption of primary aggregates over the past 30 years, a trend exacerbated by projections of demand which anticipate that by 2011 annual demand for primary aggregates could be between 410 and 490 million tonnes: an increase of between 40 and 60% on 1989 consumption levels. Energy minerals (considered below) add to these figures, although the demand for bulk minerals ensures that aggregates account for the majority of mineral extraction permissions granted each year.

Problems consequent upon extraction are not amenable to easy solutions. The public wants minerals for construction but does not want extraction on its doorstep. The cause of this contention is the nature of mineral workings themselves: they are visually intrusive; working can go on for many years — up to 70 depending upon the mineral in question; noise and vibration from blasting can cause damage and distress; as can dust emissions and the use of land for post extraction waste disposal. Different types of mine have different environmental implications, from opencast coal, through sand and gravel pits to deep-mined coal sites, whilst marine extraction presents its own problem. What all mines share, however, is the ability to affect all environmental media, and both local interests and national ones (such as world heritage sites as in *Coal Contractors Ltd v Secretary of State for the Environment and Northumberland County Council*,[2] where an application was refused because of the possible effects on the setting of Hadrian's Wall).

But there is a broader environmental policy context too. The protection of the landscape for its own sake is increasingly advocated as, for example, PPG 7, 'The Countryside and the Rural Economy', testifies. This is now complemented by an apparently deepening policy commitment on the part of central government to the notion of 'sustainable development', both generally and in its particular application to minerals, a good example of a non-renewable resource. In a follow-up report to the Rio 'earth summit' of 1992, 'Sustainable Development: the United Kingdom Strategy' (Cm 2426, 1994), the key issues for sustainability and minerals are set out. These include: the need to encourage prudent stewardship of mineral resources while maintaining necessary supplies; and the reduction of environmental impacts of minerals provision both during extraction and when restoration has been achieved. However, against this background must be set the rights of landowners to develop and exploit land consistent with the presumption in favour of development in accordance with the development plan; the national need for minerals; and the economic benefits, locally and nationally, of allowing development. The most marked step towards these general objectives, in the case of aggregates at least, can be found in the new MPG 6 published in 1994, which heralds increasing reliance on secondary rather than primary sources, and on moderating traditional policy which has been driven more by commercially defined demand for aggregates than environmentally acceptable supply.

2 [1995] JPL 421.

B BASIC STRUCTURES OF CONTROL

No single legal code embraces extraction and infilling: controls exist under planning, public health, transport and environmental protection legislation. Detailed control is principally the responsibility of county and district local authorities, although a number of central departments, including the DTI and the DoE are also involved. Other public authorities and related organisations, eg the Coal Authority, National Power and PowerGen, also have specific responsibilities.

Control over mineral extraction as a use of land is exercised within the general planning system. Those general controls have been adapted, both in law and through practice, for specialist application to minerals. This is despite the principal recommendation of the landmark DoE report, 'Planning Control Over Mineral Working' (the 'Stevens Report') in 1976 that a 'special regime' should apply. Direct regulation through planning licensing is therefore the predominant method of regulating the environmental harm deriving from mineral extraction, although hybrid controls have been developed in relation to onshore energy minerals, including oil and gas. This places the responsibility on planners to impose appropriate environmental standards, although there remains some overlap in the case of, eg, discharges to water from extraction sites. Whilst the law thus provides a basic (and disparate) structure, the peculiarities of minerals and their incidence are such that both central and local authorities must exercise very flexible control.

Central supervision of minerals policy is unevenly divided between the Department of Trade and Industry (over industrial minerals, coal, oil and natural gas) and the Department of the Environment and the Ministry of Agriculture, Fisheries and Food (concerned with land use issues). In terms of regulatory planning the DoE has central responsibility, although subject to wide consultation. Government policy favours market forces as the main determinants of extraction programmes. This is anathema to environmental interests which advocate the principal importance of, eg, National Parks and other areas of great natural beauty or interest, whether statutorily designated or not. Guidance on minerals (now contained in a series of Mineral Planning Guidance Notes (MPGs) which have replaced the 1960 *Memorandum on the Control of Mineral Working* — the 'Green Book') emphasises this conflict between economics and the environment. MPG 1 recognises that the long term national need for minerals must compete with growing demands for environmental protection, yet reiterates that the many unique characteristics of mineral development inevitably result in environmental harm. For example, minerals can only be worked where they are found, often beneath high grade agricultural land or land of conservation or scientific importance; authorities should make a contribution to meeting local, regional and national demand for minerals; investment in mineral exploitation also has positive local and national economic effects. Authorities should therefore have a predisposition to grant permission unless there are very strong environmental objections or there is no real economic need (eg, *Mid-Essex Gravel Pits v Secretary of State for the Environment and Essex Country Council*[3]). In practice this is a difficult balance to achieve, as was recognised by both the Stevens Report and the report of the Verney Committee, 'Aggregates: The Way Ahead' (1976), in stressing the importance of long term planning. This is now also subject to the emergence of sustainable development as a central strand of planning policy.

Mineral planning authorities

Under s 1(4) of the Town and Country Planning Act 1990, authorities responsible for mineral development control and plan making are county councils, London borough councils and, where they exist, metropolitan district councils — known as mineral planning authorities (MPAs). With the reorganisation of local government under the Local Government Act 1992, the identity of these authorities is likely to change in some cases, although mineral planning will remain a strategic planning matter. This is already the case in Wales, where the new counties and county boroughs are designated as MPAs (s 1(4B) of the Town and Country Planning Act 1990, inserted by s 18 of the Local Government (Wales) Act 1994). This change is controversial. Under Sch 1 of the 1990 Act, the following, inter alia, fall within MPAs' jurisdiction: winning and working minerals and erecting any building or plant ancillary thereto, for the purpose, eg, of treatment, disposal or processing; using land or erecting buildings or plant for mineral processing, or manufacturing mineral products where the site in question adjoins or is part of a mineral-working area, or where the mineral is transported to the land by conveyor, pipeline or via a private road, rail or waterway; mineral exploration (but see further below); disposal of mineral waste; use of land in connection with the rail or water transportation of aggregates (ie, sand, gravel, crushed rock or similar manufactured or reclaimed material) or the erection of buildings or plant intended to be used in connection with aggregates; erection of buildings or plant for road-stone coating, or artificial aggregate or concrete production or processing, on land on or adjoining a mineral working area; development of land used or previously used for winning or working minerals where such development would prejudice restoration; and the development of land relating to the deposit of refuse or waste. Applications for planning permission for mineral development are to be made, under Sch 1 of the 1990 Act (as amended by s 19 of the 1991 Act), direct to the MPA.

As the Stevens Report heavily stressed, control over mineral extraction is dependent upon adequate numbers of well-trained staff. They must be able to advise on the feasibility of proposals and carry out continuing supervision of individual sites to ensure compliance with the terms of planning permissions. The recommendations of the Stevens Committee were that, in the absence of sufficient resources at county level, regional teams should be formed, or staff-sharing arrangements entered into. Although considered in the Stevens Report to be the mainstay of effective continuing control over mineral development, the availability of staff is still a problem. Indeed, in many counties it has precluded beginning the review of mineral working sites which until the Environment Act 1995 was not required within a specified timetable (see below). Hence the reorganisation of local government referred to above may have profound effects. The role of local residents in supplementing the responsibilities of MPA staff as 'quasi-enforcement officers' should, however, not be discounted: their detailed local knowledge and interest in local development can be a very effective method of overseeing extraction operations. Some development plans even provide for the formation of local 'liaison committees' to maximise this contribution. As a means of communication and negotiation between developers, authorities and local communities, both before and after the granting of planning permission, they provide perhaps the best existing example of *true* public participation.

Policy preparation and content

The policy context for determining applications for mineral extraction is provided by structure plans (or unitary development plans) and specialised minerals local plans, the preparation of which is the responsibility of MPAs. Mineral development is a 'key topic' under PPG 12, and strategic plans must contain authorities' 'general polices' for extraction. Minerals local plans must include a written statement setting out an authority's detailed policies in respect of development consisting of the winning and working of minerals or involving the depositing of mineral waste, and translate strategic policies to identifiable areas of land. MPAs should consider the interactions between minerals proposals and other matters. In formulating local plans authorities must take many views into account, including: central guidance (from MPGs and specific consultation with individual departments); the findings of Regional Aggregates Working Parties (RAWPs), as representative bodies of industry and central and local government concerned with matters of supply and demand; structure plan policies; those of other affected authorities, including the relevant district councils and, eg, the Agency on such things as hydrology and flood plain implications; as well as opinions expressed by the general public. Detailed provisions concerning consultation and comment on proposals for structure plan amendments and for local plan proposals are set out in ss 33 and 40 of the 1990 Act and the Town and Country Planning (Development Plan) Regulations 1991 (SI 1991/2794). Public involvement in plan making is of great importance in view of the controversy of many mineral development proposals, and the effect of s 54A of the 1990 Act (see chapter 5, above). Effective participation at an early stage may even make the question of individual applications, decided from the basis of plans, less contentious. In addition to making written representations, members of the public may appear at local inquiries held into plans.

MPG 1, 'General Considerations and the Development Plan System', sets out the aims of planning control in relation to mineral development. These aims are: to ensure that the needs of society for minerals are satisfied with proper regard to the protection of the environment; to ensure that any environmental damage or loss of amenity caused by mineral operations and ancillary activities is minimised as far as possible; to ensure that land taken for mineral operations is reclaimed at the earliest opportunity and is capable of an acceptable use after working has come to an end; and to prevent the unnecessary sterilisation of mineral resources. With this in mind, plans should contain policies on: an authority's proposed provision for mineral working consistent with the maintenance of local, regional and national supply; provision for a sufficient stock of non-energy mineral-bearing land with planning permission (a 'land-bank') to ensure continuity of production, taking into account the amount of capital investment and long lead-in times necessary to make a site operational; any potential for the re-use of waste materials in place of new extraction; safeguarding deposits which are, or may become, of economic importance from unnecessary sterilisation by surface development; and the identification of areas where there will normally be a presumption for or against mineral working. The appropriateness of defining such 'preferred areas', where there is a presumption in favour of development, will be dependent upon factors which include: the authority's knowledge of the extent of viable mineral resources; the precision of demand forecasts; the urgency with which consents to meet demand will be needed (itself dependent upon the existence of a satisfactory land-bank); the nature of the mineral; and pressure from competing land uses. Other policies relating to specific factors to be taken into account in deciding individual applications should also be included. These might incorporate: consideration of the impact of extraction, processing or distribution on, eg, the landscape, the local economy (including employment) and residential areas by way of visual intrusion or noise; the quality and extent of the deposit; traffic volume and consequent environmental disturbance; impact on agriculture, forestry or environmentally important areas; and any reclamation requirements (detailed further in MPG 7).

Plans may contain specific policies on individual minerals or groups of minerals such as: sand, gravel, crushed rock, high specification aggregates for road construction, pulverised fuel ash ('PFA') and other similar waste materials ('aggregates'); non-aggregate minerals such as industrial limestone (a major constituent of the flue gas desulphurisation process intended to reduce atmospheric emission of sulphur dioxide), gypsum (used in plaster manufacture), silica sand, slate, and china and ball-clay (of which the UK is a leading world producer and exporter); and energy minerals such as coal (including opencast coal), oil and natural gas. Each type may have appropriate constraint policies depending upon, eg, its availability or the extreme difficulties which its extraction causes (as in the case of opencast coal). Unless specific statutory controls exist in relation to certain types of minerals, the impact of legal constraints on the extraction of this range of minerals will therefore be determined not by different legal rules but by variations in policy. Policies on environmental safeguards might include: maintaining buffer zones between workings and residential or environmentally sensitive areas; minimising subsidence which might result in surface damage; protecting water supplies; controlling noise, blasting and dust; the provision of screens of vegetation; the location and design of stockpiles and soil storage, perhaps for the provision of protective 'bunds'; regulating the construction and location of ancillary development; maximising the use of less disruptive forms of transportation, such as canals or railways; requiring phased working and restoration; and guidance on suitable or preferred after-uses.

Plans must allow for flexibility in the application of their policies; real discussion of the merits of a case must not be pre-empted. Presumptions and pre-dispositions are permissible in plans, pre-determinations are not. For example, where a plan is too precise in restricting future extraction to certain areas, making it clear that applications outside those areas will be opposed, its legality is questionable: see *Buckinghamshire County Council v Hall Aggregates and Sand and Gravel Association*.[4] Similarly, whilst s 54A of the 1990 Act, which requires that planning decisions be made in accordance with the development plan unless material considerations indicate otherwise, has apparently introduced a period of plan-led planning, as indicated in chapter 5, this is not absolute. Plans cannot be prescriptive, central policy provides local authorities with considerable latitude in the formulation and interpretation of plans, whilst their wide content suggests considerable potential for conflict in their application. Given this intrinsic flexibility, local influences on local decision-making are, in practice, very important. Equally, other relevant factors not to be found in plans may include: sudden unforseen demand; advances in extractive and processing technology making previously uneconomic development feasible; and the discovery of previously unknown mineral resources or finding lower actual reserves than expected. Changes in attitude towards some policies may also necessitate reconsideration, as witness the increasing weight given to environmental factors. In evaluating the extent to which a plan will be relied upon, its age is therefore of crucial importance: a plan is always a consideration, the question for the authority in determining an application is the weight that it should be given.

Minerals applications, appeals and 'call-in' applications are always particularly contentious in areas of high scenic, environmental or amenity value — 'sensitive areas'. National Parks and Areas of Outstanding Natural Beauty currently amount to some 23% of the land area of England and Wales. Government policy in such areas is more restrictive than outside, hence policy dictates that proposals for mineral development in sensitive areas should, by virtue of the very serious effects which mineral development can have on them, be subject to 'the most rigorous examination'. With respect to National Parks the assessment should be made by reference to four criteria: the economic need for the development; the availability of alternative sources of supply; any detrimental environmental effects and the extent to which those effects could be moderated; and thus whether the proposal would be justified in the public interest. In March 1991 the National Park Review Panel recommended further restriction on development in National Parks in the light of their finding that the importance of protecting sensitive areas is not always given sufficient weight in deciding applications (see also chapter 6, above, on the duties of National Park Authorities). In the absence of clearer national guidance, applications will still be bitterly fought by applicants, authorities and objectors, and at great cost.

C 'MINING' AND 'MINERALS'

'Mining operations in, on, under or over land' constitute an act of development under s 55 of the 1990 Act. Whilst not otherwise defined, this includes: the removal of material of any description from a mineral working deposit; from a deposit of PFA or clinker; or from a deposit of iron, steel or other metallic slag; and the extraction of minerals from a disused railway embankment. Section 336(1) further provides that a 'mineral working deposit'

---

4 [1985] JPL 634.

is any deposit of material remaining after minerals have been extracted from land, or otherwise deriving from development for the winning and working of minerals. In relation to mining, every shovelful is a separate act of development, a conclusion also significant for enforcement purposes when limitation periods on enforcement action run from the alleged breach of planning control, including the act of unauthorised development: *Thomas David (Porthcawl) Ltd v Penybont Rural District Council*.[5] However, sample boring which is of short duration, unlikely to have a permanent effect and undertaken as preparatory to investigatory drilling is not development: *Bedfordshire County Council v Central Electricity Generating Board*.[6] Investigatory drilling of deep boreholes for the purpose, eg, of oil or gas exploration, *is* development requiring permission. Further definitions of mines, quarries and boreholes can be found in ss 180 and 182 of the Mines and Quarries Act 1954 (as amended).

'Minerals' are defined by s 336(1) of the 1990 Act to include 'all substances of a kind ordinarily worked for removal by underground or surface working, except that it does not include peat cut for purposes other than sale'. Section 315 provides a power to modify the effect of various provisions of the Act in relation to development consisting of the winning and working of minerals or involving the depositing of mineral waste. By virtue of sub-s (4), regulations so made shall not apply to development consisting of the winning and working of minerals: on land held or occupied with land used for agriculture, of any minerals reasonably required for that purpose; Coal Authority minerals; or gold or silver, which are vested in the Crown. Under this power, regulations have provided further relevant definitions and development rights. The Town and Country Planning (General Permitted Development) Order 1995 (SI 1995/418) grants certain rights (see below) and, with the Town and Country Planning (Minerals) Regulations 1995 (SI 1995/2863), further defines 'mining operations' as 'the winning and working of minerals in, on or under land, whether by surface or underground working'. This extensive definition of 'mining' has been necessary historically and has emerged by a process of evolution. The most notable amendments were made by the Town and Country Planning (Minerals) Act 1981, enacted to implement some of the recommendations of the Stevens Committee.

Development must normally commence within five years of consent (s 91 of the 1990 Act), and whilst in the case of mineral development this period was previously 10 years (Town and Country Planning (Minerals) Regulations 1971, SI 1971/756, reg 6) these regulations were repealed by the 1995 Regulations (SI 1995/2863, reg 4). Authorities have discretion to relax this constraint and have been urged, by, inter alia, the Stevens Report to do so where justified by a *developer's* real needs. Under s 91 of the 1990 Act it is further provided that the time limit does not apply to any permission for development by the winning and working of minerals or involving the depositing of mineral waste which is granted (or deemed to be granted) subject to a condition that the development to which it relates must begin within a specified period from the completion of other mineral development being carried out by that applicant, or after the cessation of the depositing of

5 [1972] 3 All ER 1092, CA.
6 [1985] JPL 43.

mineral waste already being carried out by that applicant. Although necessarily of longer duration than most developments, the permitted life of an extraction site is not unlimited. Schedule 5 of the 1990 Act provides that every permission granted after 22 February 1982 is subject to a condition restricting its life to 60 years from the date of the consent, although this may be extended or reduced by the planning authority. The same schedule also imposes a condition on permissions granted before February 1982 that they must cease after 60 years, ie 22 February 2042. Applicants may appeal to the Secretary of State against the imposition of a time limit. As well as accommodating the particular physical demand of mineral development, these time limit provisions (particularly the power to modify time limits) enable a mineral planning authority to limit the environmental effects of extraction in time. They have now been complemented by new powers introduced by s 96 and Schs 13 and 14 of the Environment Act 1995 which set out authorities' powers and duties in respect of reviewing *existing* minerals permissions. The relatively crude method of limiting the duration of extraction is therefore refined by this new review (considered in detail below).

Permitted development and development procedure

Whilst planning permission is generally required for all mining development, the consolidated general development orders made in 1995 (the Town and Country Planning (General Permitted Development) Order 1995, the 'GPDO', and the Town and Country Planning (General Development Procedure) Order 1995, the 'GDPO' (SIs 1995/418 and 419), provide for extensive permitted development rights and other modifications of general planning rules in respect of minerals. Classes of development permitted by the GPDO include: development ancillary to mining operations (Part 19); coal mining development by the Coal Authority and licensed operators (Part 20); waste tipping at a mine (Part 21); mineral exploration (Part 22); removal of material from a mineral working deposit (Part 23); and mineral working for agricultural purposes (Part 6, Class C).

Permitted development rights in respect of development ancillary to mining operations are granted by the order. In the case of underground workings, these are restricted to 'approved sites', ie, the site with planning permission for the winning and working of minerals or land immediately adjoining an active access to an underground mine which is used as such (the particular permitted development rights of the Coal Authority and licensed operators are examined below). Under Part 19, Class A, the carrying out of operations for, inter alia, the erection, rearrangement or other alteration of any plant, machinery, buildings, private railways or pipes, cables, etc, on land used as a mine is permitted. These rights do not apply where: the principal purpose of the development would be other than a purpose connected with the mineral development or the treatment, storage or removal of site-derived minerals or waste; the external appearance of the mine would be materially affected; if works carried out would exceed a height of 15 m from the level of the excavation, the level of any immediately adjacent unexcavated land or the height of the replaced, etc, building, plant or works (whichever is the greater) — if on the floor of the excavation; if works carried out would exceed a height of 15 m from ground level or the height of the replaced, etc, buildings, plant or work (whichever is the greater) — if not in the excavation; if a building erected would have floor space exceeding 1000 sq m; or if the cubic content of the alteration would exceed that of the original building by 25%, or the floor space by 1000 sq m. Development permitted under this Part is conditional upon the removal of such buildings, plant or works and satisfactory restoration of the site within 24 months (extendable by the MPA) of the permanent cessation of mining operations. Where the prior consent of the MPA has been given, the carrying out, on land used as a mine or ancillary mining land, of operations for, inter alia, the erection, rearrangement or other alteration of any plant, machinery, buildings, structures or erections is also permitted by Part 19, Class B. Such development is not subject to the height restrictions of Class A but must still be for a principal purpose: in connection with the operation of the mine; the treatment or utilisation, etc, of site-derived minerals; or the storage or removal from the mine of site-derived minerals or waste. The MPA may only refuse consent if it is satisfied that the proposed development would injure the amenity of the neighbourhood, and such injury cannot be avoided by the imposition of conditions, or the development ought, and could reasonably, be sited elsewhere. The restoration conditions applicable to Class A also cover Class B. Class C of Part 19 grants permission for works to repair or make safe a mine or land at or adjacent to a mine, subject to the authority's prior consent. Similar conditions to those restricting Class A permitted development apply.

The GPDO also gives certain permitted development rights in respect of mineral exploration. Thus, development of land for a period not exceeding 28 days consisting of drilling boreholes, carrying out seismic surveys or other excavations for the purpose of mineral exploration, and the construction of connected structures does not require consent (Part 22). However, such operations may not: be for petroleum exploration; be within 50 m of a school, hospital or occupied residential building; be within a National Park, an Area of Outstanding Natural Beauty or a site of archaeological or special scientific interest and result in more than 10 excavations in any 1 ha of land in the course of 24 months; use explosive charges of greater than 1 kg; exceed 10 m in depth or 12 sq m in surface area; exceed 12 m in height (or 3 m if within 3 km of an aerodrome). There are also requirements regarding hours of working, the protection of trees and soil, and post-operative remedial treatment. If the MPA has been informed and not, within 28 days, issued an order restricting or revoking permitted development rights at the proposed site, such operations can continue under Part 22, Class B for up to four months — subject to similar environmental protection conditions as apply to Class A permitted development.

Removal of material from a mineral-working deposit also requires planning permission unless it falls within Part 23. Two situations are covered: removal of material from a stockpile (Class A); and removal of material from a deposit other than a stockpile (Class B) where notification has been given to the MPA of the developer's intention to remove the material, and the deposit is smaller than 2 ha (unless it was deposited more than five years previously), and the deposit is not derived from permitted development rights allowing operations reasonably connected with agriculture (under Part 6). Interestingly, quite sophisticated conditions can now be placed on the exercise of Class B rights requiring not only compliance with a scheme of working submitted to the

MPA but also, if the authority requires, submission of a scheme providing for the restoration and aftercare of the site. In this way the authority can bring up-to-date environmental protection conditions to bear on existing areas of minerals-related dereliction without reliance on either an existing consent or a new application.

The final generally applicable mineral related development under the GPDO is the tipping of waste connected with the extraction, treatment, processing, etc, of minerals, on land used as a mine or on ancillary mining land, where that waste is a product of working at that site. Such development is permitted under Part 21, Class A provided that excavations are not filled higher than adjoining land, nor the size or height of sites existing on 21 October 1988 are enlarged by more than 10%, unless the terms of an approved waste management scheme so allow. In any case, a waste management scheme must be submitted to, and approved by, the MPA if that authority requires it, and all tipping must be in conformity with it.

Publicity requirements relating to applications for planning permission for mineral development are set out in the GDPO. With s 65 of the 1990 Act, art 8 of the order defines development involving the winning and working of minerals or the use of land for mineral working deposits as 'major development'. This must be publicised either by display of a site notice for 21 days on or near the land to which the application relates, or by serving notice on any adjoining owner or occupier, and by local advertisement. This is a change from the pre-1991 provisions which required display of a site notice in every case. Applications not conforming with the s 65 requirements 'shall not be entertained' (s 65(5)). This is supplemented by art 6 of the order which requires separate notification to be given to the owner or tenant of the land to which the application relates by individual notice, by local advertisement or by site notice left in place for at least seven days in the 21 immediately preceding the date of the application. Further, under art 16, where notice has been given to a MPA by the Coal Authority (in respect of coal), the Secretary of State for Trade and Industry (in respect of gas or oil), or the Crown Estates Commissioners (in respect of silver or gold), an authority shall not determine applications for mineral development in the area to which that notice relates without first informing the body giving notice.

Permitted development rights are extensive, and allow for a high degree of sophistication in controlling the environmental and other impacts of development associated with mineral extraction. Clearly, however, it may not be appropriate for such rights to be exercised in all cases. Article 4 of the GPDO therefore expressly enables MPAs to restrict permitted development rights. Article 7 further provides that rights under Part 22, Class B (mineral exploration for up to four months) or Part 23, Class C (removal of material from a stockpile) may be restricted where an authority considers that a planning application ought to be submitted because: the site is within a National Park, an Area of Outstanding Natural Beauty, a site of archaeological or special scientific interest, or the Broads; it would cause serious detriment to amenity or adversely affect the setting of a Grade I listed building; it would constitute a serious nuisance to the inhabitants of a 'nearby' residential building, hospital or school; or the development would endanger aircraft. Finally, it seems to be accepted that permitted development rights can be removed by a planning condition (eg, *Dunoon Developments v Secretary of State for the Environment and Poole Borough Council[7]*), although this should be limited to exceptional circumstances, and where that is a real and specific threat to an interest of acknowledged importance.

Continuing control I: conditions and obligations

The many unique characteristics of mineral development have been considered, their full implications have not. The potential duration of extraction is one feature of significance, as is the fact that, unlike other development, mineral extraction is not a 'one-off' operation: the development itself is the aim and not merely, eg, conversion of land to another purpose. Planning law, which has as its root the notion of 'once-and-for-all' permission, has been historically weak in extending control beyond the initial grant of permission. Little thought has been given to restoration and 'aftercare' — the establishment and maintenance of a specified standard in the condition of land. Current mineral planning practice is very different, with comprehensive control by the imposition of numerous conditions, under s 70 of the 1990 Act, now being the norm. Those conditions can be usefully compared with the sorts of conditions imposed on other environmental licences in that they may provide not only for detailed regulation of the process of mineral extraction, but also the ultimate impact of the development on the environment (see MPG 2, 'Applications, Permissions and Conditions'). Thus, matters commonly provided for in conditions include: methods of working, including the progressive working of a site with a rolling programme of restoration; hours of working and other limitations on noise emissions from extraction sites (sometimes including specific quantitative limits, see MPG 11, 'The Control of Noise at Surface Mineral Workings'); soil movement, storage (including screening), treatment and replacement; transport access and regulation (although conditions cannot normally be used to control off-site routes to be taken by works traffic); nuisance abatement; and the provision of vegetation to mitigate visual intrusion. As MPAs have become more conscious of the full environmental implications of mineral extraction, so conditions have become more sophisticated, both in scope and drafting. And so conditions have emerged in practice in relation to such matters as hydrogeological surveys of proposed sites, safeguarding groundwater resources, and the exploration and protection of archaeological interests revealed in the course of extraction.

The drafting of conditions can now also be very complex, sometimes including detailed provision for the protection of water courses and other environmental media (often at the suggestion of other environmental agencies), the separate treatment of different soil types, for notice to be given to the MPA in advance of environmentally sensitive operations to facilitate supervision, and for extensive record-keeping. Many of these details, and in particular the details of steps to be taken to restore a site for post-extraction use (see MPG 7, 'The Reclamation of Mineral Workings'), may be reserved for definition of 'schemes' of working or restoration. These will be subject to post-planning permission approval, frequently by local authority officers under delegated powers. The legality of these sorts of 'permissions within permissions' has been recognised by the Court of Appeal in *Cadogan v Secretary of State for the Environment*,[8] although it makes it more difficult for third parties to discover the detailed implications of planning controls in any given case. The incorporation of details in consents by reference to documents other than the consent itself (eg, correspondence in connection with an application) whilst also lawful, has been described as a 'very unfortunate practice' because of the relative inaccessibility of those documents: Wilmer J in *Wilson v West Sussex County Council*.[9]

Planning obligations under s 106 of the 1990 Act are a common supplement to conditions as a means of reducing the environmental impact of mining operations. They are used to control, eg, off-site screening, vehicle routing, and less frequently, to provide for the establishment of liaison committees of representatives of planning authorities, developers and local residents to enable on-going consultation and monitoring of long-term workings. DoE Circular 16/91, 'Planning Obligations', also recommends the use of obligations to offset the loss of, or impact on, any amenity or resources present on a site prior to development.

Continuing control II: aftercare

The environmental effects of extraction are not confined to the period of extraction itself, but extend to the risk of post-extraction dereliction and, eg, continuing pollution from materials deposited in extracted sites. To ensure that controls imposed on an active site, including restoration, are of lasting effect MPAs have unusual powers in relation to mineral development to extend their supervision of a site beyond the end of extraction operations and restoration. Following the recommendations of the Stevens Committee, s 72(5) and Sch 5 of the 1990 Act (originally to be found in the Town and Country Planning (Minerals) Act 1981) now provide that where permission for development involving the winning and working of minerals is granted subject to a 'restoration condition' (one involving reclamation with subsoil, topsoil or soil-making material) it may also be made subject to an 'aftercare condition'. Since 1991 this power may also be exercised over development involving the depositing of refuse or waste materials. This may require such steps as necessary to be taken to bring the land to the required standard for use in: agriculture (when its physical characteristics have been restored to as they were when the land was last used for agriculture as specified by MAFF or, if the land has not previously been used for agriculture, when it is reasonably fit for that use); forestry (reasonably fit for growing a utilisable crop of timber) or amenity (reasonably fit for sustaining trees, shrubs or other plants). The aftercare condition may either specify the required steps or provide that steps be taken in accordance with an 'aftercare scheme' approved by the MPA. Compulsory steps may include planting, cultivating, fertilising, watering, draining, or otherwise treating land. However, measures may only be required during the 'aftercare period': five years (or such other period as may be prescribed) from compliance with the restoration condition for the whole, or part, of the site.

8 [1993] JPL 664.
9 [1963] 2 QB 764 at 777.

Before imposing an aftercare condition, MPAs are required to carry out certain consultations. Where the proposed after-use is agriculture or forestry, MAFF and the Forestry Commission respectively must be consulted as to: whether the proposed use is appropriate; if so, whether control should involve an aftercare scheme; and the terms of any proposed scheme. Further consultation regarding the implementation of aftercare should be undertaken from time to time. On completion of aftercare to the satisfaction of the MPA, it shall issue a certificate to that effect on the application of any person with an interest in the land in question.

An aftercare condition may be the subject of an appeal to the Secretary of State under s 78 of the 1990 Act; judicial review would also be available to question its validity. Both of these possibilities are reduced by the modern practice of negotiating site management over a long period *prior* to the submission of the application. Detailed and time consuming discussions often take place between developers, authorities and affected third parties with a view to minimising a proposal's short and long term environmental effects. The concerns of local people and authorities can be assuaged by the establishment of a positive and continuing relationship with a potential developer, similarly, a developer who is willing to conduct such discussions can often reduce the potential for time wasting conflict. There is no requirement to conduct pre-application negotiation which, for large projects, can take as long as three years. Nor are local authorities empowered to levy charges for those negotiations (*McCarthy & Stone (Developments) Ltd v Richmond-upon-Thames London Borough Council*[10]), although the Secretary of State has an enabling power under s 150 of the Local Government and Housing Act 1989. If consultations are carried out after submission of an application, they could very easily force an application 'out of time' according to the eight week period for decision given by art 20 of the GDPO. Frustrated applicants always have the final resort of submitting their application and than appealing, after eight weeks, under s 78 of the 1990 Act against deemed refusal.

Continuing control III: review of planning permissions

The most controversial aspect of continuing control over mineral planning permissions — in fact an approach applying uniquely to them — is the compulsory review and modification of existing consents. Given that in the case of mineral extraction it is the development itself which is sought and not the conversion to some other or renewed purpose, the planning system is in fact licensing a continuing use of land which may last for many years. Given also the environmental effects of extraction, it is no wonder that a consent granted at the beginning of mineral extraction might soon lag behind emerging environmental standards. As has been explained, through the use of planning conditions and obligations and the availability after 1981 of aftercare, the planning system has adapted to accommodate the special needs of minerals. However, since 1991 more dramatic changes have been introduced which for the first time in any planning context allow for the widespread

10 [1992] 2 AC 48, [1992] JPL 467, HL.

review and modernisation of existing planning consents, often without compensation liability falling on planning authorities.

Old mining permissions

Before the introduction of the modern planning system and the uniform requirement for planning control under the 1947 Act, development could still be regulated by way of 'planning schemes'. These could be adopted by local authorities with a view to securing proper sanitary and amenity standards, and the convenient lay out and use of land. Schemes were voluntary unless an area had a population, after 1919, of 20,000 or more; they only became mandatory in 1943, under the Town and Country Planning (Interim Development) Act of that year. From 1932, their scope was extended to the general object of controlling the development of land and the preservation of buildings and objects of architectural, historic or artistic interest. The significance of planning schemes resulted originally from compensation. Whilst no restriction was placed upon the right to develop, once a scheme came into operation (sometime after an authority's resolution to prepare one) the authority had the right to remove, pull down or alter buildings or works not in conformity with it. Where a developer had begun works between the authority's resolution to adopt a scheme and its actual adoption — the 'interim development period' — and was injuriously affected by the coming into operation of the scheme, compensation was only payable where permission to build had been secured. Such permission was granted under the terms of an 'interim development order' (IDO) issued by central government.

IDO permissions were different from planning permissions in significant respects: they were not recorded in planning registers; they were subject to few, if any, planning conditions and those conditions which are imposed were, by modern standards, inadequate; and they were rarely of limited duration. These characteristics led to the recent significance of IDO permissions, as until 1991 it was still possible to develop under their terms. A survey by the Chief Planning Officers' Society in November 1990 found 980 largely unworked, 'ideal sites' with IDO permission for mineral extraction, whilst a survey of county councils also revealed more than 300 valuable wildlife habitats similarly affected, including 19 sites of special scientific interest. The fact that restrictive and expensive restoration and aftercare conditions are imposed on new permissions led to significant concern that these old and largely unrestrained (hence, cheap to work) sites would be 'resurrected' — the uncertainty of their existence and the potential for large-scale and unexpected mineral development in previously unspoilt rural areas led to the introduction of controversial provisions in the Planning and Compensation Act 1991 to eliminate them. Those provisions have now provided the basis for an extensive review of all minerals consents granted before 22 February 1982 under the terms of s 96 and Schs 13 and 14 of the Environment Act 1995 (which have effect as insertions into Part III of the 1990 Act).

Under s 22 and Sch 2 of the Planning and Compensation Act 1991 (inserted into Part III of the 1990 Act) all IDO permissions not worked 'to any substantial extent' in the two years before 1 May 1991 ceased to have effect on 1 March 1992 unless an application for their registration was made and approved by the relevant MPA. That application was required to include details of what the developer claimed to be an IDO permission's terms, including the land it covers and any conditions to which it is subject. If satisfied that the developer's interpretation was correct, the MPA must have registered the IDO permission. Having been registered and placed on the planning register kept under the 1990 Act, IDO permissions are now being made subject to modern conditions. These may include any conditions which may be imposed on a permission for the winning and working of minerals under the 1990 Act and must include one that all developments cease not later than 21 February 2042. Again, developers have had the onus of proposing the conditions to which permissions may become subject, although the MPA can substitute its own. Most IDO permissions will now have been registered, although the 1991 Act provides for the extension of the 12 month period for determination of new conditions. Having been registered and made subject to modern conditions, IDO permissions become the same in all respects as any other mineral permission (see also MPGs 8 and 9).

Other minerals permissions

The very complex provisions of the 1995 Act adapt the specific IDO provisions for a review of all minerals consents granted between 1948 and 1982. They also make some concessions to the existing powers available to all planning authorities to revoke, modify and discontinue existing planning consents in that compensation *may* still be available to operators for the effects of modifications required under the review. The distinctive feature is the fact of a mandatory review, which supersedes the review previously 'required' under s 105 of the 1990 Act. That review, although ostensibly mandatory, was not set within any prescribed time frame, nor did it provide for significant alterations to the compensation regime which had in practice proved to be a total bar on effective use of planning authorities' review powers. Section 105 has been repealed.

Section 96 and Schs 13 and 14 of the 1995 Act comprise four principal elements: an initial review of sites where the predominant minerals permission was granted before 22 February 1982; two reviews of active mineral sites in successive three year periods for the purposes of updating old conditions, the first relating to 'Phase I' sites where the permissions in question were granted after 30 June 1948 but before 1 April 1969, and 'Phase II' sites relating to permissions granted after 31 March 1969 and before 22 February 1982; and thereafter periodic reviews of all consents at 15 year intervals. Older consents are therefore to be reviewed first under Phase I, although this category will also include sites which are wholly or partly within National Parks, Areas of Outstanding Natural Beauty or Sites of Special Scientific Interest. With the exception of the 15 year periodic reviews, these provisions do not apply to remaining IDO permissions already subject to review under the 1991 Act. The potential effects of this review are severe. The lists of active and dormant sites to be prepared under the review will become exhaustive lists of those sites with planning permission for mineral extraction; permissions not included on those lists 'will cease to have effect' except insofar as they impose restoration or aftercare requirements (Sch 13, para 12).

By 31 January 1996 MPAs are required to prepare a list of all dormant or active sites in their area, to be known as 'the first list'. That list must distinguish between dormant sites, active Phase I sites and active Phase II sites. Following the example of the IDO provisions, the first list must specify for *active Phase I* sites a date by which an application for approval of conditions must be submitted to the MPA. If sites are omitted from those lists, a land or relevant mineral owner has the right to apply to the MPA within three months for its inclusion. There is a further right of appeal to the Secretary of State against the MPA's determination of that application. A site is 'dormant' if no minerals development has been carried out to any substantial extent in, on or under the site at any time in the period beginning 22 February 1982 and ending with 6 June 1995. In such cases, it is not lawful to carry out development until full modern planning conditions have been approved for that site by the MPA. There is no right of appeal against an MPA's decision to classify a site as dormant. By 31 October 1998, MPAs are under a further obligation to draw up a 'second list' of *active Phase II* sites, which must specify in respect of each site a date by which it too must be the subject of an application for the determination of new conditions. The second list is therefore an update of the first list in respect of Phase II sites, and will enable MPAs to concentrate their attention for the first three years of the review on the oldest sites and those in the most environmentally sensitive areas. Although the time limits for the preparation of the lists and the submission of applications for the determination of new conditions are set out in the Act (and, in the latter case, generally allow a year for the submission of revised conditions), there is provision for the review to be postponed in individual cases. Land or mineral owners can seek a postponement on the grounds that the existing conditions on the permission are satisfactory, and that a review would therefore be unnecessary. A postponement may be sought for a period of up to 15 years. Notice of an MPA's determination of an application for a postponement must be given within three months, failing which it is deemed to be approved.

The central feature of the review is the determination of new conditions for existing minerals consents. Conditions imposed in response to land or mineral owners' applications may include any conditions which may be imposed on the grant of planning permission for minerals development and may be in addition to, or in substitution for, any existing conditions. An MPA need not apply the conditions proposed for a site, but may alter them or substitute its own. The provisions in general serve to highlight the significance of changing policy for the scope and detail of conditions imposed on minerals consents, rather than any change in the law. The legal framework for controlling mineral-related environmental harm is not substantively changed by the new Act, rather, it allows the existing once-and-for-all system to be applied again.

But the power to apply new conditions is not unlimited: mineral operators with existing consents have been operating under what are effectively statutory licences to develop, and their curtailment has traditionally given rise to liability to pay compensation. However, compensation will only be payable when the effect of restrictions on workings imposed by an MPA would be such as to prejudice adversely to an unreasonable degree either the economic viability of the site or the asset value of the site. Paragraph 1(6) of Sch 13 provides that working rights are restricted or reduced if specified characteristics of the site are modified. These include: the size of the area which may be used for development; the depth to which operations may extend; the height of any deposit of mineral waste; the rate of extraction; the expiry date of the development previously permitted; or the total quantity of minerals to be extracted form a site or mineral waste to be deposited there. If an MPA does impose new limitations on any of these characteristics, it must then consider whether the operator is prejudiced adversely by it. If this is the case, then Parts IV and IX of the 1990 Act in relation to modification orders will have effect (see below). The effect of these limitations on the review (without compensation) is that a distinction is applied between conditions that deal with the environmental and amenity aspects of the working of a site, which should not affect asset value, and conditions that would fundamentally affect the economic structure of an operation. No compensation will be payable for any new environmental, amenity or restoration conditions imposed. A new MPG elaborating on these provisions has now been issued: MPG 14, 'Environment Act 1995: Review of Mineral Planning Permissions' (1995).

D REVOCATION AND MODIFICATION

Notwithstanding the 1995 powers of review and modification of existing consents, MPAs retain their existing powers to make orders revoking, modifying, discontinuing, prohibiting or suspending development involving the winning and working of minerals or the disposal of mineral waste. By an order under s 97 of the 1990 Act, and where it appears expedient, a local planning authority may revoke or modify a planning permission. In doing so it must have regard to all material considerations, and may affect only so much of a permission for operational development as has yet to be carried out, or a use which has yet to be materially changed. Such an order must be submitted for the approval of the Secretary of State (unless agreed) and, if subject to the opposition of people who may be affected and who have been notified as required by ss 98 and 99, may be the subject of an appeal inquiry. Alternatively, the Secretary of State himself may, having consulted with the local planning authority, issue a revocation order. Orders under s 97 in relation to mineral extraction may only include an aftercare condition if a restoration condition is either already attached to the permission or if one has been imposed by the order itself: Part II of Sch 5. The inability of this provision to affect operations already carried out, coupled with the compensation liability normally incurred by its use, restricts its application in terms of mineral permissions.

Where a permission is modified or revoked by an order under s 97, any person interested in the affected land or minerals who can show either that expenditure incurred in carrying works has been rendered abortive by the order, or that they have otherwise suffered loss or damage directly attributable to the order, can claim compensation under s 107. However, in respect of development consisting of the winning and working of minerals or depositing mineral waste, that compensation may be varied. Section 116 and Sch 11 of the 1990 Act previously set out the circumstances in which compensation for modification of planning permission might be varied in the case of mineral extraction. However, that Schedule was repealed by the 1991 Act and a new s 116 instead provides the Secretary of State with a power to make regulations to modify the basis for such compensation. Although no new regulations have yet been made, existing 1985 regulations, the Town and Country Planning (Compensation for Restrictions on Mineral Workings) Regulations 1985 (SI 1985/698, as amended by SIs 1988/726, 1990/803 and 1994/2576) continue in force in the meantime. These are complemented by the Town and Country Planning (Minerals) Regulations 1995 (SI 1995/2863) which make minor modifications to the Act in the case of compensation in respect of buildings, plant or machinery. Further to the powers introduced by the Environment Act 1995, the Secretary of State has announced his intention to review those regulations. The payment of reduced compensation by virtue of those regulations is only possible where the 'mineral compensation requirements' are satisfied, that is, if: the order does not impose any restrictions on winning and working minerals or replace pre-existing restrictions on such development; the MPA carried out special consultations about the making and terms of the order; and either the affected grant is at least five years old or the order merely applies an aftercare condition to a permission which was granted before 22 February 1982. If a revocation or modification order has previously been made concerning the affected site, the mineral compensation requirements may only be met if the previous order was made at least five years previously. The effect is that compensation will generally be payable at a reduced level only where 'fundamental planning issues' over the general acceptability of the site and its economic working are not interfered with. This reflects the opinion of the Stevens Committee that mineral developers ought not to bear the full cost of bringing old mineral permissions up to modern standards, and is mirrored in the provisions of the 1995 Act. Thus, where conditions governing the commencement of the development, the size of the working area, the depth of working, the rate or period of extraction, the duration of the permission or any other condition restricting the total quantity of minerals to be extracted are altered by a s 97 order, full compensation will be payable.

Where it appears to an MPA expedient in the interests of proper planning, and subject to the payment of compensation, they may, under s 102 and para 1 of Sch 9 of the 1990 Act, require the discontinuance of a *use* of land. For the purposes of this provision, 'use' includes development consisting of the winning and working of minerals and the depositing of refuse or waste materials. Discontinuance is not the only option; the authority may alternatively impose conditions upon the continuance of the use of land for mineral development or the depositing of waste, or require the alteration or removal of buildings, plant or machinery on land so used. Conditions imposed may relate to restoration and aftercare and must include, under Sch 1 of the 1991 Act, a condition restricting the duration of the development. Orders under this provision must be approved by the Secretary of State (who may modify them) and advertised in accordance with s 103. They may also grant planning permission for buildings or works constructed or carried out, or a use instituted, before the order was submitted for approval. The power under s 97 to revoke or modify permissions applies to any permission given under Sch 9. Schedule 9, para 1 may be used in relation to the discontinuance of development permitted under the GPDO (to which s 97 does not apply as no application need be made for permitted development — a requirement of the use of s 97); although it is also appropriate where an authority wishes to impose restoration and aftercare conditions on exhausted portions of a site upon other parts of which extraction is still continuing.

Discontinuance, suspension and compensation

Supplementing MPAs' powers to revoke, modify or discontinue mineral development is para 3 of Sch 9 which empowers them to prohibit the resumption of mineral development where it appears to them that such working has permanently ceased. Such an assumption may be made where no development has been carried out to any substantial extent anywhere on the site for two years, and it appears to the authority at the time it makes the order that resumption of working is unlikely. Subject to ministerial approval, an authority may require: the alteration or removal of any buildings used for, or ancillary to, the winning and working of minerals at the site; specified steps to be taken within a specified time to remove or alleviate damage to amenity resulting from the mineral development (except subsidence caused by underground working); compliance with any conditions to which the original permission was subject; and restoration and aftercare. Conversely, where working has only *temporarily* ceased, the powers provided by para 5 of Sch 9 to make a suspension order may be employed. Where it appears to an authority that no development has been carried out to any substantial extent anywhere on a site for 12 months and resumption appears unlikely, they may require steps to be taken for the protection of the environment. These are steps required during the period of the suspension for the purpose of preserving the amenity of the area in which the site is situated, protecting the area from damage or preventing a deterioration in the condition of the land. At any time after making a suspension order an authority may alter its terms by virtue of a supplementary suspension order (under Sch 9, para 6). Under paras 7 and 8, both types of order are subject to the approval of the Secretary of State and are registrable as local land charges. Paragraph 9 provides that MPAs are under a duty to review suspension and supplementary suspension orders, and whether they should make additional orders, at intervals of no more than five years. Whilst suspension orders do not prevent the resumption of development, under para 10 notice of the intended date of recommencement must first be given to the authority. Where development recommences to a substantial extent, an authority must revoke a suspension order; where there is a dispute as to whether development has actually recommenced, an appeal lies to the Secretary of State. If the Secretary of State is satisfied of recommencement, he must revoke the order himself.

As with revocation orders under s 97, action under paras 1, 3 or 5 and 6 of Sch 9 will result in the payment of compensation to land and mineral owners. For the level of compensation to be reduced, the mineral compensation requirements in Sch 11, which are different for each type of order, must be met. Discontinuance orders (para 1) must merely impose conditions on the continuance of mineral development or require alteration or removal of works, buildings, plant or machinery rather than completely discontinuing working. Also: (i) the development in question must have begun at least five years previously; (ii) the order must not impose a restriction on the winning or working of minerals (as defined by para 10 — see above) or modify such restrictions as already apply; and (iii) special consultations must have been undertaken with regard to the making, and terms, of the order. Finally, no similar order must have been made in respect of the site in the preceding five years. Orders under para 3 prohibiting the resumption of working must meet conditions (i) and (iii) above, and, similarly, no such order must have been made in the preceding five years. Suspension and supplementary suspension orders under para 5 and 6 need only meet condition (iii) above. The reduction in compensation consequent upon meeting the mineral compensation requirements is calculated from the appropriate sections (ie, 107 and 115) as modified by the 1985 compensation regulations. For modification orders made under s 97 and discontinuance orders made under Sch 9, para 1, the modified basis for compensation is: the total unmodified compensation, reduced by whichever is greater of *either* £3,200 *or* 10% of an amount calculated by multiplying the annual value of the right to work the site by a specified multiplier. For prohibition and suspension orders, £6,400 is deducted from the total unmodified compensation. These provisions do not apply to orders made in respect of mineral development carried out by the Coal Authority or licensees.

Section 189 provides that it is an offence to cause or permit the breach of any orders issued under s 102. It is a defence to prove that all reasonable measures were taken and all due diligence exercised to avoid the commission of an offence. In the event of non-compliance with any order under s 102, the MPA can enter upon land, take the steps required in the order and recover from the owner of the land expenses reasonably incurred in so doing. Revocation and modification orders under s 97 remain to be enforced under normal planning procedures. The modification and compensation regime is therefore complex and, for any authorities proposing its widespread use, expensive.

E EXTRACTION OF MARINE AGGREGATES

As the environmental pressures of onshore extraction have increased, and local communities have become more sensitive to proposals for land-based mineral extraction, so the consideration of alternative sources of supply has developed. Those alternatives include not just the use of extraction related wastes, such as china clay, sand, colliery minestone, slate wastes and recycled materials such as demolition arisings and asphalt road planings, but alternative sources of supply. One obvious source is marine resources, which provide a small but important supplement to land-won material. In 1991 marine aggregates accounted for 14% of national consumption, some 86 million tonnes, and a further 6 million tonnes was exported or directly used for coast protection works. Their percentage contribution is even greater in the south east of England and London, where 21% and 40% respectively of aggregates are from marine sources. That extraction is centred on six main areas: the east and south coasts, Thames Estuary, Bristol Channel, Humber and Liverpool Bay. Whilst central guidance is sparse, MPG 6, 'Guidelines for Aggregates Provision in England and Wales' (1994) recognises the importance of marine supplies whilst also noting the need to have full regard to the impact of extraction on the marine environment, sea fisheries and the potential effects on the coastline.

The benefits of marine extraction include a reduction in gross production costs through the relative proximity of wharfage to areas of high use; removal of the inevitable environmental disruption associated with onshore sites; and the ability to supply the demands of the south east of England with building materials. Whilst therefore preferable in many respects to onshore extraction, the exploitation of marine reserves does create a whole different range of environmental consequences. These include possible fisheries and habitat destruction, coastal erosion problems, deleterious water quality effects and the more mundane hazard to marine navigation and questions over the siting of wharfage and onshore processing facilities. It is unfortunate that the increasing significance of marine extraction in terms of volume is not balanced by a full understanding of these long term environmental consequences.

The control of marine extraction is radically different from land based controls exercised by MPAs. The seabed is vested in the Crown (Crown Estate Act 1961) as are rights exercisable beyond UK territorial waters in respect of the seabed and subsoil (Continental Shelf Act 1964). Marine dredging is therefore not subject to planning control. Potential extractors must instead obtain a licence from the Crown Estate Commissioners (CEC) who manage the foreshore and the seabed on behalf of the Crown. CEC licences take two forms: 'prospecting' and 'production' ('extraction') — the former being necessary before the latter. These licences are entirely non-statutory. The process of their issuance, their content, the grounds on which decisions are made, as well as monitoring and enforcement are determined not by law but by the adopted practice of the CEC. They are therefore a form of civil licensing quite unlike normal planning permissions, indeed, they are more analogous to private contracts to exploit natural resources vested in private landowners.

That having been said, the CEC and certain government departments have developed 'formalised' procedures for the consideration of applications to extract marine aggregates. In the case of prospecting licences those procedures are quite limited. As no formal consultation is undertaken (although the Department of the Environment and the Ministry of Agriculture, Fisheries and Food (MAFF) are informed in confidence) there is little external influence or scrutiny. Prospecting licences have a maximum (renewable) duration of four years with a ceiling tonnage on the material which may be extracted. Production licences, on the other hand, are subject to a complex process of consultation which was adopted in March 1989. Whereas with land-based proposals pre-application consultation is merely encouraged, with sea-based applications it is a prerequisite. Outline proposals must be submitted to the CEC and are then passed on for consultation. Bodies invited to comment include: local coastal protection authorities; other statutory bodies concerned with sea defence and flood protection (such as the Agency); local fisheries interests and the appropriate Sea Fisheries Committee; local offshore operators; the Department of Transport; the Hydrographic Department of the Ministry of Defence; the Nature Conservancy Council (regarding possible effects on marine nature reserves); and the relevant MPA. Trinity House will be consulted with regard to any marine navigation implications, as will authorities and companies with responsibility for the maintenance of under-water cables or pipelines — the existence of which effectively sterilises 3,600 km of seabed from dredging. Consultants are also notified to examine a proposal's possible coastal erosion consequences.

The CEC then consider any representations received and carry out negotiations and discussions as appropriate. If there is an unavoidable risk of coastal erosion, an application will be automatically rejected. A report of the consultations summarising the advantages and disadvantages of a proposal is then prepared — including any alterations which might be made to reduce environmental or maritime risks. If the CEC feel that a proposal's environmental effects are likely to be 'significant' in terms of its nature, size or location, then environmental assessment under the Town and Country Planning (Assessment of Environmental Effects) Regulations 1988 (SI 1988/1199, as amended) would be warranted. The criteria against which a proposal's significance will be judged include whether the proposal area: is within 1 km of a marine nature reserve; includes any important fish spawning grounds or nursery areas; would encroach upon a known important commercial fishery; the water is less than 18 m deep; the site is within 500 m of an historic wreck designated under the Protection of Wrecks Act 1973.

Following pre-application consultation (which should take no more than six months) a formal application for a production licence can be made. This should include a response to the pre-application consultation report, including any measures proposed to remove or alleviate any objections. The application is then subjected to the 'government view procedure' where the 'co-ordinating department', generally the Department of the Environment, initiates wide ranging inter-departmental discussion. This process avoids the confusion and embarrassment of government departments openly disagreeing — as happened before its 1989 initiation. If agreement that a proposal is in the public interest can be reached, then a favourable 'government view' is given (which may be conditional). If, however, any department has an overriding objection, an unfavourable view would result. On average, 50% of applications receive a favourable response, 25% do so when initial objections have been overcome, whilst 25% are rejected outright. Either way, the CEC aim to receive the government view within two months of submission.

In addition to the licence of the CEC, a potential extractor will have to seek consent from the Department of Transport where marine navigation is likely to be obstructed or endangered (Coast Protection Act 1949, as amended). A local coastal protection authority may have been granted a Coast Protection Order allowing them to control the extraction of material in water less than 15.2 m deep extending from the seashore in their area (under the Coast Protection Act 1949, s 18). In such a case a potential extractor would need that authority's consent in addition to a CEC licence. The power to control such extraction is, however, only exercisable where there is a reasonable apprehension of erosion or encroachment by the sea: *British Dredging (Services) Ltd v Secretary of State for Wales and Monmouthshire*[11] — in which case, if new extraction were proposed, a licence would not be forthcoming from the CEC in any event.

This non-statutory process has been the subject of considerable criticism. Most recently, the House of Commons Select Committee on the Environment, in its Report 'Coastal Zone Protection and Planning' (1992), expressed wide-ranging concerns. These included: the potential conflict between the

11 [1975] 1 WLR 687.

CEC's role as landowner and 'quasi-planning' authority; insufficient attention to the environmental effects of dredging; the fact that the licensing procedure is not sufficiently public; the lack of appeal or right of challenge to decisions on applications for licences; and the unreasonable length of time the process takes (which can be very unfavourably compared to time limits on land-based applications). To these criticisms can be added the absence of public inquiries or hearings, and the limitation of even the existing system solely to land owned by the Crown. From any view, the licensing system stands in stark contrast to the sophisticated system developed through planning for onshore applications. However, in a consultation exercise provoked by these criticisms and intended to consider the reform of the system, some of the positive aspects of the present system have been set out. These include: the use of independent consultants to assess the possible impacts of extraction on the coastline and fisheries; the existence of indicative criteria for requiring an environmental assessment; and the fact that the CEC include in its licences any conditions emerging from the government view procedure. Notwithstanding this, however, even the CEC are recorded as viewing the present system as unsatisfactory. Hence the present system is under review, particularly in respect of the CEC's dissatisfaction with it, its lack of transparency, the delays its creates for business and its inadequate assessment of environmental issues. Solutions have yet to be proposed in detail, although the options include retention of a revised non-statutory approach or introduction of a system based on the planning model with a statutory basis. Extension of the existing land-based system is felt to be inappropriate, partly because of the need for specialist expertise in marine extraction, but also because of the more than merely local implications of marine extraction.

F COAL

Few areas of industrial, and by extension minerals, policy have been as controversial in the last five years as coal mining. Not only has a growing reliance on opencast coal production increased awareness of the environmental implications of energy use, but major structural changes in the coal industry have increased the number of operators likely to be involved in extraction. Before 31 October 1994 the British Coal Corporation had exclusive rights to search for, bore for, work and get coal in Great Britain. However, the Corporation's interests have now been vested in the Coal Authority established by s 1 and Sch 1 of the Coal Industry Act 1994 (SIs 1994/2189, 2552 and 3063), and much of the Coal Industry Nationalisation Act 1946 has been repealed (see s 67(8) of the 1994 Act). Whereas the Corporation was previously responsible for the largest part of coal extracted in the UK (97%, or 95.4 million tonnes, in 1989), that responsibility, having passed to the Coal Authority, is now progressively falling to private contractors and licensees. Controls over coal extraction are therefore becoming subsumed by the general framework of planning controls over mineral extraction.

Notwithstanding this general position there remain certain variations in law, but more particularly policy, that alter the effect of general planning controls in the case of coal. For example, the British Coal Corporation had extensive permitted development rights in addition to those available to extractors of other minerals. Consistent with the general trend towards privatisation those rights were significantly reduced by the Town and Country Planning General Development (Amendment) Order 1992 (SI 1992/2450), but certain rights in connection with coal mining development by the Coal Authority and licensed operators remain under the GPDO 1995. Part 20, Classes A and B of the GPDO permit the winning and working underground by a licensee of the Coal Authority of coal or coal-related minerals in a mine started before 1 July 1948. Classes C and D permit development required for the purposes of a mine to be carried out on an authorised site at that mine by a licensed operator in connection with coal mining operations. 'Authorised sites' are either those sites identified in planning consents as being subject to Part 20 or land immediately adjoining an access which, on 5 December 1988, was in use for the purposes of that mine in connection with coal mining operations. Land used for the permanent deposit of waste or on which there is a conveyor, railway, pipeline, etc, not surrounded by other land used for that purpose is excluded. Class C covers less intrusive development than Class D, which needs the prior approval of the MPA. That approval may only be refused if injury to amenity could not be removed by the imposition of conditions or if the development ought, and could reasonably, be sited elsewhere. Class C development is subject to conditions restricting, eg, its height, volume and external appearance, whilst the creation of a new surface access to underground working is not permitted. Neither is such an access permitted by Class D, but the same conditions are not imposed upon Class D development in terms of height, appearance and volume. Both classes of development are subject to conditions requiring its removal, and the restoration of the site, within 24 months of working finally concluding (unless the MPA agrees otherwise). Rights in connection with prospecting for opencast deposits were revoked in 1992. Finally, Class E allows development for the purposes of maintaining or making safe mines or land adjacent to mines, whether active or disused. The prior approval of the MPA must be obtained (which may only be refused on the same grounds as under Class D), and any development is subject to, eg, height and volume restrictions. As with other permitted development rights, the above may be removed by the MPA by an art 4 direction.

Coal mining and planning policy

The policy differences between coal and other minerals are of two broad types. First, the role of coal as an energy mineral and the national interest in its production that results have historically been reflected in extensive exploration and then consultation in connection with both individual applications to extract coal, and regional or national planning for future production. Before applications are submitted, extensive investigations will include: examining potential prospects, ie, areas where coal is believed to lie; preliminary exploration of areas where coal is known to lie but where its boundaries are indeterminate; intensive exploration of areas where boundaries are known, and where tests are justified to discover the coal's physical characteristics; and the feasibility of a site, including issues of access, production levels and the economics of extraction. The broad environmental impact of proposals will also be considered. Only then, as a matter of practice, will the formal planning application be prepared and submitted.

Other interests will also be involved in the process of preparing the formal application, including National Power, PowerGen and other coal users, affected trades unions, and local residents and environmental groups. This is consistent with advice on pre-application consultation and liaison in MPG 3, 'Coal Mining and Colliery Spoil Disposal' (1994). Local and national interests may be in conflict, and decisions of MPAs may be subject to appeal, or pre-empted by the Secretary of State's call-in powers. The report of the Commission on Energy and the Environment, 'Coal and the Environment' (1981) made numerous recommendations designed to reconcile the inevitable conflicting interests. Amongst these were that central government should release more information on energy policy and options and likely future needs, this to be coupled with parliamentary debates on White Papers containing specific policies, thus helping public inquiries to take place against a clear policy background. Finally, although formal environmental assessment was not called for in the report, it may be required under the 1988 Regulations.

The second policy difference between coal and other minerals lies in the distinctive approach taken to determining the appropriate level of coal development. The new MPG 3 is strongly-phrased in this respect:

'It is not for the planning system to seek to set national limits or targets for any particular source or level of energy supply; nor to predetermine the appropriate levels of coal to be produced by underground or opencast mining. It is for the operators to determine the level of output they wish to aim for in the light of market conditions.' (para 6)

The implications of this policy are most pronounced in the case of opencast mining, which in the last 25 years has provided an increasing share of total coal production. For example, in 1989 opencast coal constituted 19% of all coal production, compared with 10.7% in 1979 and 4.2% in 1969. In the five years to 1991, production rose from 14 to 19 million tonnes pa, and in 1994 stood at 17 million tonnes. At the same time, deep mined coal production is in decline. In the five years to March 1992, production fell from 82.4 million tonnes to 71 million tonnes pa, whilst the number of working collieries fell from 94 to 50.

Since 1986, opencast coal mining has been controlled within the planning system, the special regime applying under the Opencast Coal Act 1958 having been repealed in that year. Opencasting has a number of advantages over deep mining: opencast coal is considerably cheaper to produce than deep mined coal, in 1987 costing £1.02 per gigajoule as opposed to deep mined coal's £1.57 per gigajoule; many millions of tonnes of high quality coal reserves lie at depths unsuitable for deep mining; modern opencast extraction techniques enable economic extraction of some reserves previously ignored; coal reserves from areas of industrial dereliction can be reclaimed as part of an opencasting scheme, providing a nett environmental improvement in the long term; valuable deposits which would otherwise be sterilised by, eg, housing and industrial development, can be exploited by opencast means; the chemical composition of shallow deposits can be such that, by a process of blending, it can make deep mined coal acceptable for sensitive industrial uses when it would otherwise not find a market; similarly, the quality of opencast coal in itself makes it a valuable resource; finally, opencasting, as with any mineral development, can make a valuable contribution to employment and the economy. However, much controversy is caused by the essentially environmentally destructive nature of opencasting. MPG 3 recognises the conflict between environmental protection and opencast coal extraction but stresses the national presumption in favour of development in accordance with the development plan and opencasting's other benefits. Proposals in National Parks and other sensitive areas, such as Sites of Special Scientific Interest, must be subject to the most rigorous examination. Similarly, opencast coal extraction need not be incompatible with green belt objectives, provided that high environmental standards are maintained and that restoration is comprehensive. Decisions on individual applications should be made on the basis that the greater the benefits of an opencast site, the stronger the environmental objections would need to be to deny permission, and in particular it is notable that cross-subsidisation of more expensive deep mined coal may provide justification for cheaper opencast working: *Northumberland County Council v Secretary of State for the Environment*.[12]

The ability of MPAs to deal adequately with any mineral application has been questioned in the past (most notably by the Report of the Stevens Committee, 'Planning Control over Mineral Working'), the question of opencasting is even more contentious. The lack of policy governing need, both of energy minerals and energy itself, and the environmental effects of both extraction and the use of fossil fuels, complicate an authority's decision. Coal operators may define their own need, but MPAs are not in a position to question it: even if they were, to do so would contradict government policy. In light of the growing contribution of opencast coal as a proportion of national production, controversy can only increase.

G ONSHORE OIL AND GAS

Onshore oil was first commercially discovered in 1895 in East Sussex, but real interest in onshore fields is a feature of the last 15 years. Between 1986 and 1990 onshore crude oil production increased by some 237% (to 1,752 thousand tonnes in 1990) and gas by 220% (to 48 billion cubic metres). Since then, oil production has declined, but gas production has increased to 52 billion cubic metres a year. Despite their relative insignificance in terms of total production (oil accounted for 2% of 1990 home-based supply), onshore reserves are a valuable resource. Many potential onshore sites, possibly with recoverable reserves similar to North Sea midrange fields, lie in the South and East of England, where strong and articulate middle class opposition to environmentally intrusive works can be expected. DoE Circular 2/85, 'Planning Control over Oil and Gas Operations', acknowledges potential conflict between environmental protection and development of onshore oil and gas. Factors in support of the case for exploitation include: the relative security of home-based reserves compared with imports; government policy (re-stated in MPG 1) to ensure maximum economic exploitation over time to boost tax revenue (whilst not jeopardising an operation's economic viability), to aid the national and local economy and create employment; onshore

12 [1989] JPL 700.

resources are ten times cheaper to exploit than North Sea reserves; free competition in the overall energy market is healthy, onshore oil and gas have their part to play and should be allowed to do so, although as oilfield development is costly and a long term issue, commercial companies must be allowed time to explore and appraise sites. However, exploitation must be consistent with the protection of the environment; in some cases environmental considerations will preclude development. Special policies will apply in National Parks, Areas of Outstanding Natural Beauty, Sites of Special Scientific Interest, National Nature Reserves, etc, with rigorous examination of any proposed working, and a burden of proof on the developer to show that need for development outweighs environmental objections (MPG 1). Similarly, the Countryside Commission has stated that conservation and exploitation are not necessarily in conflict provided that exploiters are prepared to 'pay the price' in terms of, eg, restoration costs. The feasibility of restoration must be considered before development begins. Water supplies must also be safeguarded.

Central control over oil and gas exploitation has been by exploration and production licences under the Petroleum (Production) Act 1934, as amended. The licensing process is now provided for by the Petroleum (Production) (Landward Areas) Regulations 1995, the Petroleum (Production) (Seaward Areas) Regulations 1995 and the Hydrocarbons Licensing Directive Regulations 1995 (SIs 1995/1436, 1435 and 1434 respectively), which introduce a single exploration and development licence which confers exclusive right in relation to a particular area in place of the separate exploration, appraisal and development licences available under the previous Regulations (SI 1991/981). The 1995 Regulations, and the model clauses for licences which they introduce, apply to all applications made after 30 June 1995; the 1991 Regulations continue to apply to applications made before that date. Applications for the new exploration and development licences must relate to specified geographical blocks identified by the Secretary of State and published in the Official Journal of the European Communities (in accordance with the requirements of Council Directive 94/22 on the conditions for granting and using authorisations for the prospecting, exploration and production of hydrocarbons). That publication must include the latest date by which applications are to be made, and the period within which licences are to be granted. As well as technical information in respect of an area's geology and its petroleum prospects and a work programme for evaluating the potential petroleum production from the area which the applicant would be prepared to undertake, applicants are required to provide evidence that they have sufficient resources available to them to undertake the work programme. This is intended, in part, to minimise the risk of activities commencing and than stopping prematurely through financial default, with only incomplete site remediation.

The Hydrocarbons Licensing Directive Regulations restrict the criteria which the Secretary of State may take into account when considering an application for a licence made under the principal regulations. Regulation 4 dictates that no licence shall be granted upon terms or conditions other than those justified exclusively for the purpose of: ensuring the proper performance of the activities permitted by the licence; providing for the payment of fees; or any of a limited number of considerations relating to health and safety, environmental or resources issues. These include national security, public safety, protection of the environment, protection of biological resources and of national treasures possessing artistic or archaeological significance, and planned management of hydrocarbon resources, including the rate at which hydrocarbons are depleted and the optimisation of their recovery. This is a more extensive list of relevant criteria than under the previous system and expressly introduces longer term, 'sustainable development' type consider-ations into individual decisions. Exploration and development licences have an initial term of six years (corresponding to the term of old-style exploration licences) which may be continued for a further five years (as with old-style appraisal licences) and then extended for a further 20 years (as with old-style development licences).

The licensing of exploration and development by the Secretary of State is in addition to, rather than in substitution for, planning controls. Local control over onshore oil and gas development remains the function of MPAs, although the Secretary of State may exercise 'call-in' powers in exceptional cases. Authorities should have adequate policies in structure and local plans to provide a policy background against which proposals can be assessed. Policies should deal with issues of exploration, appraisal and development. Some authorities have already taken a 'strong line' in having presumptions against oil and gas development on open down land, heaths and heritage coasts, though such policies, discouraged as they are by central guidance, might not prevail at a public inquiry or a planning appeal. Part 22 of the GPDO specifically excludes the drilling of boreholes for petroleum exploration from permitted mineral exploration development rights.

As with all planning consents, conditions may be attached to grants of permission for hydrocarbon exploitation. While these should not duplicate *specific* pollution controls under other legislation, conditions may be used to secure the environmental acceptability of a project. There may therefore be something of an uneasy relationship between planning controls and pollution controls, as well as the limitations on exploration and development licences themselves, although this may in practice be mitigated in the negotiations encouraged by policy guidance and typically pursued as good industrial practice. Conditions might relate to siting, screening, landscaping and design of works and plant, timing and method of gas flaring, noise minimisation, and transporting petroleum products. Details of such matters will be included in development programmes submitted to the Secretary of State (DTI) under licensing procedures, and may be referred to in planning applications. Aftercare requirements may also be imposed, and should be settled at the time permission is granted for exploration and development licences.

Further reading

Algar, P, 'Do we need onshore oil?' (1985/86) 4 Oil and Gas Law Taxation Review 219.

Cope, DR, Hills, P, and James, P, (eds) *Energy Policy and Land Use Planning* (1984) Pergamon Press.

Department of the Environment, 'Environmental Effects of Surface Mineral Working' (1992) HMSO.

Department of the Environment, 'Mineral Policies in Development Plans' (1991) HMSO.

Department of the Environment, 'Planning Control over Mineral Working' (1969), Report of the Committee under the Chairmanship of Sir Roger Stevens GCMG, HMSO.

Department of the Environment, 'Review of Licensing Arrangements for Minerals Dredging in England and Wales', Consultation Paper, 1994, HMSO.

Eggert, RG, (ed) *Mining and the Environment: International Perspectives on Public Policy* (1994) Resources for the Future.

Everton, ARE, 'The Lion and the Lamb — Developers and Objectors in Mineral Planning Control' (1994) 6 Environmental Law and Management 69.

Hammersley, R, 'Minerals planning and sustainability' (1993) 63 Town Planning Review xiii.

House of Commons Select Committee on the Environment, 2nd Report, Session 1991-1992, 'Coastal Zone Protection and Planning', HC Paper 17, 1992, HMSO.

Jewell, T, 'Paying for Environmental Improvement: The Potential Example of Minerals' (1992) 4 Land Management and Environmental Law Report 81.

Jewell, T, 'Planning Regulation and Environmental Consciousness: Some Lessons from Minerals?' [1995] Journal of Planning and Environment Law 482.

Rutherford, L, 'The Environmental Costs of Opencast Coal Mining: Issues of Liability' (1990) 2 Journal of Environmental Law 161.

Chapter 9

Waste, contamination and litter

'Tread under foot our ghostly foe, that no pollution we may know'
(from 'Te Lucis Ante Terminum', the evening hymn of the church)

A WASTE: THE BACKGROUND

Disposal of waste to land is one of the cheapest forms of disposal. Waste takes many forms but nearly all are capable of causing harm if not handled correctly. There is moreover a legacy of old waste sites now abandoned which continue to pollute, for example by leachate escaping from them as a result of water percolation. Such leachate can contaminate both land and water. Legal responsibility for such old sites may be hard to attribute as many were operational long before any form of legal regulation applied.

Public disquiet over waste, particularly the fear that the nation could become one of the world's 'toxic dustbins', increased for many years during the 1970s and 1980s, and cannot, as yet, be said to be allayed. In 1989/90 34,272 tonnes of 'special' waste entered Britain mostly destined for landfill, in 1990/91 the figure increased to nearly 44,000 tonnes, one third of which came from Switzerland. Of the landfill material the overwhelming majority was intended for direct deposition. Some highly toxic waste, such as poly-chlorinated biphenyls (PCBs), it was revealed in 1988, were entering the country by aircraft under licences granted by the CAA under s 65 of the Civil Aviation Act 1982, see The Times, 27 September 1988.

The old law and practice of waste disposal under the Control of Pollution Act 1974 was subject to stringent criticism in the 2nd Report of the House of Commons Environment Committee for the Session 1988/89 (the 'Rossi' Report). This concluded, inter alia, that:

1 Existing legislation was inadequate.
2 Waste control functions were not being taken sufficiently seriously, and existing structures of control promoted conflicts of interest for relevant authorities as both waste regulators and waste disposers.
3 There was a lack (centrally and locally) of sufficiently qualified and esteemed supervisory staff.
4 Many licensed waste disposers chose the path of the 'cheapest tolerable option' in their disposal methods.
5 There was a lack of waste minimisation and recycling strategies.

The government responded, somewhat sharply, to these allegations (Cm 679), but nevertheless considerable changes were made to the law of waste disposal by the Environmental Protection Act 1990. The government further committed itself in Cm 1200 to strategies on waste minimisation (arguing that the IPC provisions of the 1990 Act would do much to bring this about) to enhanced controls over waste disposal and litter (see also the 1990 Act), and to recycling measures, in particular a target of recycling 50% of *recyclable* household waste (ie some 25% of such waste) by the end of the century.

Certainly waste and its disposal is a major industry. In 1991 the value of the industry was estimated at between £2bn and £4bn. It was, even in the early 1990s, an industry increasingly concentrated, with under 12 companies controlling some 25% of the market — a trend which has continued as increasing legislative controls have driven out smaller operators and the less reputable companies. Landfill remains the principal means of waste disposal and it is central policy that the UK should have self-sufficiency in disposal facilities both nationally and, wherever possible, regionally and locally. Incineration will, however, play an increasing role in disposal, particularly from the point of view of energy generation, for the energy value of landfilled waste was some years ago estimated to be £1m per day (Environment Now, April/May 1988, p 26). Recycling must, under the terms of sustainable development policy, also increase, though there is still much room for improvement here.

However, the UK was for some years arguably poorly equipped to have a national recycling strategy, especially following the abolition of the Waste Management Advisory Council in 1981. Even so there has remained some controversy as to the best way of dealing with the waste that is produced, and currently that is some 24 million tonnes of controlled waste and 190 million tonnes of non-controlled waste pa, ie enough waste to fill Windermere every nine months.

Incineration of waste, for example to produce energy, has advocates amongst those who point to the inherent prodigality and dangers (leachate, rodents and production of methane) of simply landfilling waste which is where some 90% of the material still goes. However, the process is not cheap because consistently high temperatures have to be maintained in order to ensure that pollutants are destroyed. Energy recovery from municipal waste (ie domestic waste and similar material from commerce and trade) was commended by the Royal Commission on Environmental Pollution in their 17th Report, 'Incineration of Waste,' Cm 2181, 1993, with a financial incentive to continue to be available to encourage electricity production from waste (under the non-fossil fuel obligation (see chapter 3 above). However, they further argued that the standards for atmospheric emissions from combustion processes using waste as fuel should be brought more closely in line with newer standards for all incineration processes. They were further concerned about a proliferation of small waste incinerator plants and argued that a municipal waste incineration plant should not have a capacity of less than 200,000 tonnes pa. Most incinerators are regulated by either the Agency or local authorities under the IPC and LAAPC provisions of the Environmental Protection Act (see further chapter 10).

Proponents of recycling point to strict German laws which set recycling targets of 60% of household glass, 40% of tinplate and 30% of aluminium coupled with very stringent requirements on packaging (see later). Those less convinced argue that recycling costs often exceed the value of reclaimed material by many times, so that, even in Germany where landfill costs are 15 times higher than in the UK, recycling is unprofitable. Furthermore the transport of waste for recycling itself has environmental disbenefits. The economics of recycling are problematical. At times there can be a high demand for a particular substance, eg newsprint; at other times demand may almost disappear and this has made some waste collection and disposal authorities wary of committing themselves to recycling in general. Others are prepared only to encourage recycling of particular types of waste.

The new national waste policy

Official policy on waste has, however, been developing quite rapidly in recent years. In response to the Royal Commission report on incineration the government undertook to issue a non-statutory waste strategy. This was issued in consultative form in January 1995. A little earlier the House of Commons Environment Select Committee for the session 1993/94 examined the issue of waste recycling and the government responded to that with a White Paper, 'Recycling', Cm 2696 in November 1994. Most recently the various strands of policy have been brought together in 'Making Waste Work' Cm 3040 which develops ideas contained originally in the sustainable development strategy. This document contains non-statutory guidance on waste disposal. A statutory national waste strategy to be drawn up by the Secretary of State, is, however, required under s 44A of the 1990 Act. This will be drawn up following advice from the Agency and the conclusions of the national survey of waste facilities and arisings which the Agency is to conduct. There must also be extensive public consultation, and so the statutory strategy is unlikely to be published before 1997 at the earliest. Until then, and even after, the principles laid down in 'Making Waste Work' will be at the heart of disposal policy.

The objectives which the statutory policy must achieve are contained in Sch 2A of the 1990 Act (inserted in 1995). They are:

1 To ensure that waste is recovered or disposed of without endangering human health and without the use of environmentally deleterious processes or methods, in particular avoiding risks to water, air, soil, plants or animals, avoiding noise or odour nuisances and without adverse effect on the countryside or places of special interest.

2 To establish an integrated and adequate network of waste disposal installations taking account of the BATNEEC principle.

3 To ensure that this network enables both the EU and its member states to move towards self sufficiency in waste disposal, and that waste is disposed of in one of the nearest appropriate installations by the most appropriate methods and technology so as to ensure a high standard of health and environmental protection.

4 To encourage prevention of waste and reduction of waste production and its harmfulness by developing technologies that are more sparing in their use of natural resources by developing products which are designed (in

their various stages of manufacture, use and disposal) to make no, or very little, contribution to waste and its harmfulness, by encouraging appropriate techniques for final disposal of dangerous substances in waste.

5   To encourage recycling, reclamation and reuse and energy extraction.

The bedrock policies of the non-statutory policy are *reduction of waste, making the best use of waste*, and *choosing management practices to minimise both present and future environmental pollution and harm to human health*. Building on this is a 'waste hierarchy' of reduction — reuse — recovery (recycling, composting, use for energy) and disposal, and the government's objective is to find the best practicable environmental objective (BPEO) for any given type of waste within the hierarchy. In determining the BPEO environmental and economic costs and benefits have to be considered. The targets of the overall policy are (a) to reduce the proportion of controlled waste going to landfill to 69% by 2005; (b) to recover 40% of municipal waste by 2005; and (c) to set a target for overall waste reduction by 1998. This last target involves not just a reduction of absolute quantities of waste, but also a reduction in the 'hazardousness' of waste.

Clearly such policies cannot be simply imposed by legal action, and implementation will to a considerable extent depend upon the voluntary commitment of both producers and consumers of goods to reuse materials.

Thus recycling will be encouraged wherever it is economically and environmentally beneficial, and while currently only some 5% of household waste is recycled, there are targets to recycle or compost 25% of household waste by 2000, and to have an easily accessible recycling facility for 89% of households by that time. 40% of domestic properties with gardens will be encouraged to carry out home composting by 2000, with a target figure of 1 million tonnes of organic household waste composted. Energy recovery from waste will also be encouraged. Even so it is accepted that landfill will continue to be a necessary part of waste disposal; that said, however, the object of policy is to promote more sustainable landfill techniques (eg to provide greater control over and reuse of landfill gas) and to make the best use of the suitable disposal space.

Economic instruments and waste

In connection with landfill one most important recent development in 1994 occurred when the Chancellor of the Exchequer proposed a landfill tax. The initial impulse for this was economic rather than environmental; the transfer of tax burdens onto waste in order to fund reductions in employers' national insurance contributions. Even so the environmental benefits of the levy were lauded both in official policy and by environmental groups, especially as the levy will highlight that the production of waste leads to an environmental price that has to be paid by producers and consumers. The waste industry was less enthusiastic pointing to the fact the levy, as proposed, would be a 'blanket' measure and would fall equally on both well managed and poorly managed landfill sites. By 1995, however, policy had developed so that it was proposed to set up 'environmental trusts' to clean up old landfill sites and promote sustainable waste management practices funded largely by a rebate from the proposed landfill tax, with top-up contributions from the waste industry; ie to fund the trusts — which would be private sector bodies independent of government — the state would forgo landfill tax income by making rebates of tax available to landfill operators who make payments to such trusts for specified environmental purposes. However, the rebate would never be more than 90% of any payment made and then only up to a maximum of 20% of any contributor's landfill tax liability, while 10% of trust funds would be expected from further industrial contributions.

The formal go-ahead for landfill trusts was given by the 1995 Budget, and leading waste management companies have been invited to participate and provide a share of their financing — up to £100m it is officially predicted. The legal base exists under the Finance Act 1996. The features of the new trusts will be:

1 They will be separate legal entities independent of both government and the waste industry which will not be able to obtain commercial advantages for individual companies from trust operations.
2 A regulatory body approved by Customs and Excise will register them and audit their expenditure, and provision will be made for clawback of tax rebates if the trusts are abused by companies.
3 They will be able to undertake research into, and development of, more sustainable waste management practices and the provision of education and collection and dissemination of information, together with the remediation, restoration and amenity improvement of sites unable to support economic or social use due to past waste management *or* other industrial activities, and the creation of environmental, amenity and recreational facilities near landfill sites.

The landfill tax itself was initially to be charged on the value of the waste tipped (*ad valorem*), but this met with considerable opposition from industry and regulators alike. It is now to be weight based at a rate of £7 per tonne on general waste and £2 per tonne on inert waste such as construction waste. The tax is likely to raise £500m pa.

Under ss 39–70 and Sch 5 of the Finance Act 1996, the tax will be payable on a 'taxable disposal', ie a disposal to landfill at a landfill site after 1 October 1996. A disposal will depend on an intention to discard, and any usefulness the material could have is irrelevant. Disposal will take place where there is a deposit on land, on a structure set in land, or into land. Land will be part of a landfill site at any time where a waste management licence is in force in relation to it (see below). Tax will fall to be paid by the site operator, and where the operator is a company tax can be recovered from both the company *and* its directors on a 'joint and several basis'.

Waste imports and exports

In addition to the government's national waste strategy there is also a Management Plan on Imports and Exports of waste, initially released for public consultation in 1995. The basis of the plan is to aim for self sufficiency in waste disposal at both the national and EU levels.

1 Exports of waste from the UK for disposal are to be banned.
2 Exports for recovery will be allowed to OECD countries, but exports of hazardous waste to non-OECD countries for recovery will be generally banned.
3 Most imports for disposal will be banned save for hazardous waste from developing countries which cannot reasonably be expected to deal with waste themselves, and for small quantities of such waste from developed countries where the provision of special facilities would be uneconomic.
4 Imports for genuine recovery will be allowed. [For the Basle Convention and EU background to this plan see below.]

B WASTE DISPOSAL: THE INTERNATIONAL AND EU LEGAL REQUIREMENTS

International law and EU law lay down particular requirements as to waste disposal. In 1972 the Stockholm Declaration on the Human Environment stated that toxic substances should not be discharged so that ecosystems could be protected against harm. The United Nations Environment Programme (UNEP) has subsequently built on that formulation with regard to waste, while the Organisation for Economic Co-operation and Development (OECD) figures indicate that its member states produced in 1989 some 1.3 billion tonnes of industrial waste, 300 million tonnes of which were hazardous, 88% of this originating in the USA. International waters used to be a 'favoured' dumping ground for some of this waste (see further chapter 12 below) but international agreement has ended this means of disposal of certain wastes, and restricted the dumping of others. Likewise the dumping of high level radioactive material has been ended by international agreement, and a moratorium on the dumping at sea of *all* radioactive waste has been effective since 1983. However, restricting the use of the oceans as dumping grounds places enhanced burdens on landward disposal methods, especially as waste minimisation strategies will take some years to 'bite'. This in turn has led to some international trade in waste, especially as waste producers have sought worldwide to find places offering lower disposal costs than those in their own localities. Some of this waste has been sent by industrial nations to 'Third World' countries, but the evidence has tended to suggest that transfrontier shipments generally occur between industrialised (principally northern hemisphere) nations.

International law on interstate transfers of waste has been developing for some years, for example the OECD laid certain obligations on its member states between 1984 and 1988, and UNEP undertook to proceed towards a global convention on hazardous waste transfers in 1987 which superseded and subsumed the OECD's work. This led to the Basle Convention on the Control of Transboundary Movement of Hazardous Wastes and their Disposal of 1989. This is a framework treaty which makes provision for additional agreements to deal with waste issues bilaterally, or multilaterally, and to cover matters such as liability and funding.

The Basle Convention has at its heart the following principles:

1 International trade in hazardous waste is to be cut to a minimum.

2   Information is to pass between states on their decisions limiting/banning export/ import of hazardous wastes.
3   Hazardous wastes must be managed in an environmentally sound fashion and should be disposed of as close as possible to their place of origin, thus interstate transfer is exceptional.
4   Such exceptional transfer may take place in the interests of environmental protection and human health *from* a nation without appropriate storage/ treatment facilities *to* one with the necessary technology, see further below, etc.
5   Any such transfers must be subject to stringent control.
6   Nations must co-operate to ensure application of these principles, and it is a feature of the Convention that an international secretariat is established to further this end, also that developing nations should receive assistance to enable them to manage waste safely. The Convention entered into force on 5 May 1992, and by 1993 82 parties were adherent to it. The conference of the parties which it also set up decided in 1994 to phase out hazardous waste trading between OECD and non-OECD nations.

Certain other features of the Basle Convention are, however, worthy of note, for example its attempt to ensure that states adhering to the treaty export and import waste only to/from other adherent states. The Basle Convention notably further lays down that states from which an export of relevant waste is to take place must prohibit that export if the state for which the material is destined does not consent in writing to the import — this is the notion of prior information and consent — and adequate notification and information to importing states must be given. State sovereignty is also recognised in that any state adhering to the treaty retains the right to prohibit in general the import of hazardous waste for disposal, though such prohibitions are to be notified to other contracting states via the Convention Secretariat. States further have an implied power under the Convention to prohibit a specific import of waste. Even where a state does not impose a general ban on waste imports it still, of course, remains true that prior informed consent must be given to waste shipments. Indeed it is the general tenor of the Basle Convention that inter state transfers of waste are to be exceptional and that there is no global free movement of waste. This is to be allowed only where the exporting state does not have the appropriate means (ie technical capacity, facilities and sites) to ensure environmentally sound and efficient disposal of the waste, or where the material is required for recycling by appropriate industries in the importing states, or where the transfer satisfies criteria determined by the contracting states provided these do not conflict with the Convention objectives. The Convention further reinforces this by imposing quite extensive documentation requirements on those who transfer waste, eg as to receipt of consignments of waste, and its subsequent due disposal.

The Basle Convention is a major step forward in the international regulation of waste, and in particular, it should provide the less developed nations with internationally agreed powers to prohibit waste imports. There was a major role played by the then European Community in the formulation of the Basle Convention. Subsequently the EU has banned export of waste to some 69 countries in the Caribbean, Africa and the Pacific, while reg 259/93 implements the EU's commitments to the Basle principles.

Turning to EU legal regulation of waste it will be found that it parallels only in some ways the requirements of the Basle Convention.

Action on waste can be traced back to the 1973 first action programme which was concerned with eliminating toxic, or non bio-degradable or bulky wastes which needed cross national boundary solutions, and the first framework Directive on waste (75/442) was issued in 1975. In 1976 the Commission created a Consultative Committee on Waste Management to advise on the development and implementation of waste policy. Subsequent action programmes have laid down further principles:

1 Wastes arising are to be prevented where possible or otherwise reduced.
2 Where possible waste is to be recycled or recovered and reused.
3 Where non-recoverable waste arises it is to be properly managed and disposed of harmlessly. Polluting incidents such as that at Seveso have prompted further practical development of EU waste policies since 1984, and alongside these must be set EU financial aid for 'clean technologies' which minimise waste arising under reg 1872/84 ('ACE'). The Court has also assisted in this development and the landmark decision in *EC Commission v Denmark*[1] where it was held that *certain* national requirements that drinks containers be reused fell within the scope of the EU's commitment to environmental protection and this could justify a restriction on the free movement of goods principle.

The development of the law

The body of EU law on waste is founded on 75/442, a 'framework' Directive, which nevertheless obligated member states to so dispose of waste that human health and the environment are safeguarded and nuisances avoided. To this end certain basic principles were laid down:

1 There must be 'competent authorities' with responsibilities for organising, authorising and supervising waste disposal.
2 Waste disposal plans are required dealing with types and quantities of waste, technical requirements, site details, etc.
3 Waste is to be disposed of according to a permit system, and permits may impose restrictions or conditions on types/quantities of waste to be disposed of, technical issues, precautionary measures, information to be given by licensees.
4 The polluter pays principle is to apply.
5 Recycling is to be encouraged.
6 Regular three yearly reports are to be made by member states to the Commission on their waste disposal situation.
7 Certain wastes are excluded from the Directive's scope, eg radioactive and mining waste, and agricultural and animal carcases.

The 'Community Strategy for Waste Management' (1989) subsequently laid down that waste is to be primarily prevented, re-used if prevention is not possible, and only disposed of as a last resort — and then safely. Furthermore waste is to be disposed of in the nearest possible suitable place to its arising —

1 [1988] ECR 4607, [1989] 1 CMLR 619.

the proximity principle. In 1991 Directive 91/156 amended and virtually replaced 75/442. This stressed (art 3) the development of clean technologies as a means of preventing or minimising waste arisings, and reducing initial resource demands, and also the development of enhanced final disposal techniques for dangerous substances in waste destined for recovery. Further stress was laid on recycling in general and the use of waste in energy production, while repeating and developing the established principles relating to protection of the environment, particularly water, soil, air, flora and fauna, and human health, prevention of nuisances and countryside and 'places of special interest' protection. Member states are further directed, subject to the BATNEEC principle, to establish a network of disposal sites to make the EU self sufficient with regard to waste disposal, while moving member states individually closer to that goal. Enhanced planning for the disposal of particular wastes was required, while states are further enjoined to see that waste is only permitted to be dealt with by qualified persons, while such persons require licences from competent authorities. Collectors and carriers of waste were also required to be registered and inspected. Waste disposal costs must be borne by the person having it collected/disposed of, while records of and documentation relating to disposals must be maintained.

Waste was redefined to mean any one of a list of materials which the holder (ie the producer or processor or possessor) discards or intends or is required to discard. The listed materials *include* consumption and production residues, time expired products, spoiled or soiled materials, unusable parts, substances no longer performing satisfactorily, industrial residues, pollution abatement residues, finishing residues, raw materials extraction residues, adulterated matter, materials whose use is banned by law, material contaminated by remedial action taken re land, and any other materials, substances or products not otherwise specifically categorised. However, specifically *excluded* are gaseous atmospheric effluent emissions, and (where already covered by other legislation) radioactive waste, mineral prospecting, extraction, treatment and storage waste, animal carcases, agricultural faecal waste, waste waters (but *not* liquid waste) and decommissioned explosives. 'Disposal' includes tipping, landward treatment of biodegradable liquid wastes, deep injection, surface impoundment, engineered landfills (eg in concrete implacements), releases of solid waste into rivers, lakes, etc, release of any waste into seas, biological treatments, physiochemical treatments, incineration, permanent storage, blending, repackaging, temporary storage. All the foregoing must be carried out without environmental harm, eg harm to water, air, soil, plants, animals, risks of odour nuisances and affectation of the countryside and places of special interest. Member states must also take steps to prohibit the abandonment, dumping and uncontrolled disposal of waste.

The 1991 Directive lays, as stated, more stress on recycling and recovery, this *includes* reclamation and regeneration, re-refining, spreading material on land for agricultural or ecological improvement (saving, of course, material not counting as waste). However, such acts must as with disposal activities be carried out without environmental harm, see further above. Further provisions relate to: competent authorities being designated; the need for waste management plans; holders of waste being required to have it appropriately dealt with by a public or private waste collector; the need for disposal/recovery permits; registration of waste transporters and brokers; the keeping of records by relevant persons, and the application of 'the polluter pays' principle. Further provision on particular categories of waste may be laid down by daughter Directives, and provision is made to adapt the Directive to technical progress. Additionally Decision 94/741 lists, on a reviewable basis, wastes and categorises them according to Directive requirements. This is the 'European Waste Catalogue'.

Specific attention to toxic wastes was promised by the 1973 and 1977 action programmes and Directive 78/319 dealt with that issue, by laying down stricter controls than those contained in 75/442 with regard to precise lists of 'toxic and dangerous' waste, or material contaminated by such substances. Proposals for replacement of this Directive by a 'hazardous waste' Directive to draw on the work of the OECD (see also above in relation to the development of the Basle Convention) and which would reflect the growth in the amount of such waste since 1978 — and better management techniques that have emerged — were under discussion from 1988.

Directive 91/689 (amended by 94/31) which had binding effect from 27 June 1995 replaced Directive 78/319, and lays down stricter requirements for controlling hazardous wastes within the overall framework initially created by Directive 75/442 of competent authorities, plans and authorisations, etc. Domestic waste is excluded from the Directive's provisions, while other types of hazardous waste are generically stipulated, together with the constituents and properties of wastes rendering them hazardous. The Commission has the task of specifically identifying and listing hazardous wastes — a task not made easier by the contention that some waste is only hazardous in particular circumstances, and the chosen way out of this problem is to list wastes considered as hazardous beyond specified threshold concentrations.

The Directive lays down particular requirements for: hazardous waste producers and transporters to keep detailed records which have to be retained (for at least three and one years respectively); documentary evidence of waste management operations to be supplied to competent authorities or previous waste holders on request; waste to be recorded and identified on every hazardous waste tipping site; relevant waste to be packaged and labelled according to international and EU requirements while being collected, transported and stored; consignment documentation to accompany transfers; creation by member states of publicly available hazardous waste management plans; reports from member states to the Commission on implementation, and information to be sent on establishments undertaking disposal/recovery of hazardous waste primarily for third parties and likely to be part of a proposed network of disposal facilities throughout the EU, including information as to types and quantities of waste to be treated and treatment methods; triennial reports from the Commission to the Parliament and Council.

Shipments of waste

Following the 'Seveso incident' a number of barrels of dangerous material from the site went missing. Such was the consequent public disquiet that the European Parliament set up its own commission of enquiry into toxic and dangerous waste. A number of findings were made, including the importance of waste treatment as an economic activity and the extent of inter state transfers of waste. The findings were presented to the Council and

Commission in 1984, though the Commission had begun to proceed to legislation on interstate waste transfers in 1983. In 1984 Directive 84/631 was issued to create a system for controlling and regulating safely interstate waste transfers, from the point of collection to disposal, both as between member states and non-member states.

Replacing earlier Directive measures on waste shipments, and, as stated already, bringing the EU into line with Basle Convention requirements, reg 259/93 came into force on 9 February 1993. Though not applying to all wastes, for example radioactive waste is not covered, the regulation adopts the definition of waste in Directive 75/442. The system of controls is complex and varies according to: country of despatch, of destination, of transit; the intention behind the shipment (ie for disposal/recovery) and the type of waste in question. The various types of waste are listed by colour 'green', 'amber' and 'red', the latter being subject to the most restrictions, while some waste imports/exports are prohibited subject to specific exceptions. This results in there being numerous waste shipment regulatory regimes: 1A waste shipments between member states in the EU for disposal; 1B waste shipments between member states in the EU for recovery (with particular requirements according to whether the waste is 'green', 'amber' or 'red'); 1C shipments for disposal and recovery with transit of a third (ie non-member) state; 2 shipments within member states; 3A shipments from the EU for disposal; 3B shipments from the EU for recovery; 4A imports of waste into the EU for disposal; 4B imports into the EU for recovery; 5A transit from outside and through the EU for disposal/recovery outside it; 5B transit from outside (etc) the EU for recovery from and to a country falling within certain terms decided by the OECD. However, the basic scheme for all the regimes is that any person intending to ship waste across a member state's frontiers (the notifier) must notify nominated competent authorities in other affected states (ie the authority of destination and those of transit) with a consignment note. The authority of destination must acknowledge this within three days and send copies to other affected competent authorities. This allows the competent authorities in affected states a period of time (20 days where only EU states are concerned, 60 days in other cases) to seek further information or make an objection, impose conditions, etc. Once this period for objections is over, the destination authority has ten days to make a decision. Where approval is given, other relevant competent authorities are informed. The notifier is also required to complete the consignment note and send copies of it to relevant authorities three days before the waste is shipped. Receipt of the waste must be notified within three days and recovery/disposal within 180 days.

Where, however, an authorised shipment cannot be completed the competent authority of *despatch* must ensure the notifier returns the waste to the state of despatch unless satisfied the waste can be dealt with in an environmentally sound fashion. Non-compliant waste traffic is to be prohibited by appropriate legal measures within member states, while *all* shipments are required to have bonding or other financial systems to cover shipment, disposal/recovery costs. Where there is a regular trade in one type of waste to one consignee an annual notification may cover several consignments, but where any waste is subject to its own notification it cannot be mixed during shipment with other waste.

Consignment notes (which should conform to the type laid down in Commission Decision 94/774) are required to give the details of: waste's source, its composition and quantity; the identities of producer and consignee; the route of the shipment and its insurance; safe transport measures and recovery information. Consignments themselves must also comply with the provisions of relevant international transport conventions, while member states are to submit annual waste reports, in accordance with the Basle Convention requirements, for the Commission and the Convention's Secretariat.

The most obvious special feature of the foregoing regulatory regime is the allowance of prohibitions on imports of waste from other member states, even to the extent of a systematic objection to all such imports — a clear derogation from the normal free movement of goods philosophy of the EU.

As the regime exists in the form of a regulation it is directly applicable and hence requires no UK legislative action to implement it save with regard to certain matters such as the competent authority for preparing a waste management plan.

The current UK regulations are the Transfrontier Shipment of Waste Regulations SI 1994/1137, see also DoE Circular 13/94. In practice the UK does not export waste for final *disposal* in other nations. Export of waste for *recovery* is not generally prohibited, but is now only exceptionally allowed where the receiving nation is a non-OECD state (eg a developing nation) because of fears that such states are unable to handle and treat wastes in environmentally sound ways. Waste *imports* to the UK are similarly dealt with: waste in general is not to be imported for final disposal, either by landfill (historically never done anyway) or incineration (a one time legitimate trade), save where there is a genuine recovery operation intended, which, however, includes energy recovery. This is subject to certain transitional allowances in respect of imports for particular specialist disposal processes from nations as yet *unable* (as opposed to *unwilling*) to provide their own specialist facilities. It appears therefore that imports of waste for incineration (save for energy recovery) will be phased out by 1997. [For further detail see Haigh's *Manual of Environmental Policy: the EC and Britain* and Mumma's *Environmental Law: Meeting UK and EC Requirements*, to both of which sources indebtedness is acknowledged.]

A number of Directives have made specific provision with regard to particular types of waste. Directive 76/403 relates to polychlorinated biphenyls (PCBs) and polychlorinated terphenyls (PCTs). The Directive requires member states to prohibit discharge, dumping or tipping of PCBs in an uncontrolled fashion, to make the disposal by collection and (or destruction) of PCBs mandatory, to ensure disposal, etc, is carried out without harm to human health or the environment, and to promote regeneration of waste PCBs. Note also that a new Directive on this issue was proposed in 1988. The third North Sea Conference of 1990 agreed the phasing out and environmentally safe destruction of all identified PCBs and PCTs, with a final target date of 1999. The UK's National Waste Action Plan deals with the response to this resolution.

Directive 75/439 (as amended by 87/101) is concerned with waste oil disposal, by laying a *general* duty on member states to ensure that waste *or* used oil collection and disposal causes no avoidable damage to humans or the environment, coupled with specific duties to prohibit: waste, etc, oil discharge into water and drains; deposits/discharges of oil harmful to soil; uncontrolled process residue discharging; processing of waste oils causing air pollution exceeding levels prescribed by other provisions.

Wherever possible the collection and disposal of waste oil is to take place by recycling or regeneration or combustion for a purpose other than destruction. Undertakings are to be designated to be responsible for oil collection and disposal having been permitted by a 'competent authority' after due initial and periodical inspection of relevant installations, etc, though such bodies may be granted indemnities, financed by levies on waste oils, in return for the obligations they undertake. Those persons or bodies who hold waste oils and who cannot meet requirements imposed under the Directive must place the waste at the disposal of a disposal undertaking. Also note that the Directive requires any establishment producing, collecting or keeping more than 500 litres of waste oil pa, to keep records relating to quantity, quality, location, etc, of the material.

The spreading of sewage sludge on agricultural land has been a recognised problem in the EU since 1973. Even in 1976 it appeared that some 29% of the sewage produced in the community was used by agriculture. The material is rich in organic matter, but can pose a health hazard because of the presence of concentrations of heavy metals. Directive 86/278 accordingly provides that sludge use must be prohibited where heavy metal concentrations in the receiving soil already exceed limit values laid down by the Directive (for cadmium, copper, nickel, lead, zinc, mercury, and chromium). Sludge use must also be so otherwise regulated that the limit values are not transgressed; this may be achieved either by placing a limit on the amount of sludge applied per unit per year while observing the various limit values provided for by the Directive, or limits may be placed on metal introduction per unit per year according to the Directive's figures. Sludge must be generally treated before use and may not be used on soil for fruit and vegetable growth, subject to certain time limits. Records of sludge use are to be kept, its quantity and treatment.

Note also Directive 91/157 which applies to batteries and accumulators with mercury, cadmium or lead content above certain specifications, even prohibiting the marketing of some. Member states between September 1992 and January 1994 were to draw up programmes of battery heavy metal reduction and to provide for the separate collection and disposal of certain batteries. [For the relevant UK law see SI 1994/232.]

Directive 78/176 required member states to develop programmes for the reduction, and ultimate elimination, of pollution by titanium dioxide (TiO_2) waste from relevant plants. Directive 92/112 further required member states to put measures in place by June 1993 for the prohibition or control of TiO_2 waste discharges.

The EU and packaging

The over packaging commonly encountered with so many modern goods and commodities has been a frequent target for environmentalist complaints. Not only are valuable resources used in the manufacture of packaging, in one 'after life' form as litter it is also an environmental eyesore, while as waste it gives rise to disposal problems. The level of public and governmental concern over packaging has, however, varied from state to state within the EU. Germany, for example, has had very strict packaging and packaging waste targets since 1991 which basically pin liabilities for the recovery, re-use and recycling of packaging, on manufacturers, distributors and retailers. France since 1993 has required manufacturers and importers either to provide for, or make a contribution to, packaging waste disposal. Even earlier in the mid-1980s Denmark had attempted to require a mandatory scheme for the return and re-use of plastic beverage containers, which had led to a limited Directive, 85/339, on that specific issue.

Directive 94/62 which will, inter alia, replace 85/339 on 6 June 1996, now aims to (a) reduce packaging's environmental impact; (b) harmonise national packaging measures to eliminate distortions to the internal market; and (c) ensure free movement of packaged goods. So far as (a) supra is concerned, the objective will be to limit disposal of packaging and promotion of re-use and recovery, by (i) establishment of systems for return, collection and recovery of packaging; (ii) setting national recovery and recycling targets; and (iii) guaranteeing free circulation in the EU of certain specifically qualifying types of packaging.

The Directive applies to *all* products, irrespective of material, used to contain, protect, handle, deliver and present goods, under three main heads: *sales or primary packaging* (normally acquired by the purchaser), *grouping or secondary packaging* (generally removed by the distributor or retailer near the point of sale) and *tertiary packaging* (designed to help bulk handling or transport).

Member states are required, as from June 1996, to introduce a system of return, collection and recovery so that the 'return and/or collection of used packaging and/or packaging waste from the consumer, final user or from the waste stream in order to channel it to the most appropriate waste management alternatives' is achieved. While there is a further obligation to secure the 're-use or recovery including recycling of the packaging/packaging waste so collected.' There must be no discrimination against imported goods, and barriers to trade or competition must be avoided. Member states are, however, to include specific chapters on packaging waste in their waste management plans under Directive 75/442. To promote recovery and re-use target dates are set for recovery and re-use (including recycling, regeneration and use as fuel) of between 50 and 65% of packaging waste, with a minimum recycling target of 15% by weight for each packaging material. While some member states (Greece, Portugal and Ireland) are given some exemption from these requirements, other states are allowed to set more stringent requirements provided these do not distort trade. Systems of marking and identifying packaging will be introduced by 1997 to assist in the collection, etc, of packaging waste, while the marketing of packaging which does not comply with requirements as to 'composition and the reusable and recoverable nature of packaging' will be prohibited. Packaging which meets Directive requirements must be guaranteed free circulation within the EU from 1998.

National databases on packaging wastes are also required to give information on the 'magnitude characteristics and evolution of the packaging and packaging waste flows . . .'

The UK response

The UK's response to the Directive was initially to be a *voluntary* scheme developed in partnership with industry, and the Producer Responsibility Group (PRG) put forward a plan to recover a specified proportion of UK packaging waste by 2000 via an organisation to be known as VALPAK. However, the PRG also called for legislation to make participation in the scheme mandatory, and enabling provisions have been placed in the Environment Act 1995.

Thus under s 93 of the 1995 Act the Secretary of State is empowered to make regulations to impose 'producer responsibility obligations' on specified persons in respect of specified products or materials for the purpose of promoting or securing the re-use, recovery or recycling of products or materials. Such regulations will be in the form of a statutory instrument subject to Parliament's affirmative resolution, and can only be made after consultation with those bodies or persons who are likely to be substantially affected by the proposals. Furthermore, save where regulations have to be made to meet EU or international legal obligations, the Secretary of State must be satisfied before making regulations that they will:

1 Result in an increase in the re-use, recovery or recycling of relevant products/materials.
2 Produce environmental or economic benefits.
3 Result in such environmental, etc, benefits as are significant as against the costs to be incurred in consequence of the imposition of a producer responsibility obligation.
4 Impose only the minimum burden necessary to achieve the foregoing benefits.
5 Impose burdens on the persons most able to make contributions to achieving relevant targets having regard to the desirability of acting fairly between those who manufacture, process, distribute or supply products/ materials and taking account of the need to ensure the proposed producer responsibility obligation is effective to achieve its purposes. Particular obligations may, however, be imposed on particular classes or descriptions of persons, though, to meet EU requirements, the regulations must not, save to the extent required to produce the desired environmental, etc, benefits, restrict, distort or prevent competition.

Section 94 details the particular matters on which regulations may be made, eg the targets which are to be achieved for re-use, etc, with respect to proportion of material, by weight, volume or otherwise. Industry will, however, be encouraged still to set up its own voluntary recovery schemes, and those who are members of an approved voluntary scheme (an 'exemption scheme') will be exempt from controls under the regulations. Such schemes must not, however, restrict, distort or prevent competition and schemes will be registered and monitored by the Agency who will also monitor compliance with the statutory scheme by those who are not members of an exempt scheme. Non-compliance will be a criminal offence, while officers and managers of companies may be made responsible for crimes committed by companies with their consent or connivance or in consequence of their neglect. Draft regulations were announced on 7 May 1996.

The EU and the means of waste disposal

Turning to *means* of waste disposal Directives 89/369 on preventing air pollution from *new* municipal waste plants and 89/429 on reducing it from existing ones should be noted. 89/369 applied to plants authorised to operate post 1 December 1990 for incinerating domestic, commercial, trade and similar wastes, but *not* sewage sludge, chemical or clinical waste, or other toxic and dangerous wastes as these fall within Directive 84/360 concerning industrial air pollution. Member states are required to impose authorisation conditions relating, inter alia, to emission limits for heavy metals, specified acids and sulphur dioxide, temperature maintenance requirements, carbon monoxide concentrations, prevention of ground level pollution by design equipment and operational features, etc. Directive 89/429 applies similar requirements in respect of plants authorised pre 1 December 1990, the new regime to be applied to them over a phased period according to incinerator capacity down to 2000.

Proposals for a Directive leading to strict civil liability for damage caused by waste were put forward in 1989. Excluding nuclear waste and oil pollution damage, the initial proposal was that any producer of waste (ie one whose *occupational* activities produce waste, together with preprocessors, mixers or other operators changing the nature of waste) should be *strictly* liable (irrespective of any permits) for damage (ie death/physical injury or property damage) *or* damage to the environment (ie significant and persistent inter- ference caused by modification of physical, chemical or biological conditions of water, soil and air insofar as not otherwise property damage). Injured plaintiffs would be able to pursue preventative, compensatory and restorative actions with regard to *damage*, while 'public authorities' would have similar rights in respect of injury to the environment. Contracting out of these provisions would not be possible, though the defences of force majeure and contributory negligence would be available. A 30 year limitation period for bringing actions was proposed, as was some form of compulsory cover to meet liabilities, such as insurance.

The proposal was subject to comment from the European Parliament who wished, inter alia, to restrict the ambit of the proposal to hazardous waste only, but also to extend it to industrial activities, and who also proposed a wide definition of environment to extend to all biotic and abiotic natural resources so that impairment of the environment by waste would comprehend any significant physical, chemical or biological degradation of the environment. The Parliament further secured, however, that 'duly authorised' conservation groups should have rights to apply for prohibition of damaging activities, while it also successfully pressed for compulsory contingent liability funds for waste producers, somewhat along the lines of 'Superfunds' operating in the USA to meet environmental liabilities. These proposals were not, however, accepted by the Council of Ministers. Indeed the postponement of action led by late 1991 to the possibility of the issue being subsumed into a wider proposal for integrated civil liability for environmental damage with levies imposed on polluters to pay for remedial action not otherwise fundable under the proposed strict liability system, and a wider system of public access to the courts to pursue environmental claims.

The 'wider proposal' referred to above appeared as a consultative proposal in 1993, with a preferred option of imposing strict liability in respect of remedying *any* environmental damage, and the possibility of extending liability to areas where current principles may not apply, eg where there is damage as a result of chronic, past or authorised polluting activities. The UK government is officially opposed to the development of a union-wide system of such civil liability and the better view of matters is that any EU directive on this issue will not appear for some years at least.

Further EU measures on landfills

A further major system of controls over landfills has been under development since 1991 and is possibly to reach fulfilment shortly, the Council having reached a 'common position' on it in June 1994 (see chapter 4 above on 'common position').

The draft landfill directive has been subject to a long process of public consultation and amendment, and began life as a harmonisation measure based on art 100A. The scheme as proposed is that all landfills will require a permit from a competent authority, but landfills may be 'banded' into: 'hazardous waste'; 'municipal waste' (domestic trade and similar commercial wastes) *and* 'non-hazardous waste', and 'inert waste' (fulfilling particular physical and chemical criteria) sites. Under the proposal any site may be given a multiple classification, *but* the particular types of waste received will have to be disposed of in discrete areas on site. Provision is also made for mono landfills, ie sites where only one type of waste is received for deposit.

It is further provided that certain wastes shall not be landfilled, eg liquid wastes unless otherwise compatible with the type of waste otherwise acceptable for any given landfill site; explosive, oxidising, highly flammable or flammable wastes; and veterinary or medical waste. Monitoring of closed landfills and their after care will be required, with operators having to retain control after closure for at least ten years, while monitoring of leachate and groundwater from sites will be required for a minimum period of 30 years after closure. Landfill operators will be required to establish contingent liability funding or some other financial guarantee to cover the costs of closure and after care operations, with further *funds* being required to cover post closure after care costs, *and* costs of works to prevent damage produced by the disposal of waste where this is not otherwise provided for.

It is now appropriate to consider UK laws and practice in relation to these issues. Environmental protection and planning legislation lay down the UK legal framework for waste disposal, with some types of material being subject to special controls.

C UK WASTE DISPOSAL LAW

Control under planning law

In England waste disposal is a 'county matter' in nearly all cases. Thus while any development involving waste, however peripheral, is not automatically a county matter, where (in terms of the functions to be carried on and by considering which of those functions is predominant) there is a clear relationship with county responsibilities, the county is the appropriate planning authority.[2] Structure plans may contain appropriate policies. Under s 38 of the Town and Country Planning Act 1990, as substituted by Sch 4 of the Planning and Compensation Act 1991, authorities, ie primarily counties, are also to prepare, subject to the Secretary of State's directions as to timing, waste local plans for their areas, or include their waste policies in their minerals local plan. Waste planning is thus mandatory, though in formulating waste policies authorities are to have regard to such information *and other considerations as the Secretary of State prescribes or in particular directs*. Such plans must be in conformity with relevant structure plans, must contain illustrative maps together with diagrams, illustrations and other explanatory material as is prescribed or is otherwise thought appropriate. These plans are also generally subject to the provision of the 1990 Act (as amended in 1991) with regard to the alteration and replacement of local plans and public participation in their creation, etc, see further chapter 5. The plans must also *not* be confused with any plans required under environmental protection legislation. [See above on the national waste strategy and related documents which replace local environmental protection waste plans.]

Waste local plans should take account of the advice in PPG 23 (Parts 2 and 5 and Annex 6) in order to achieve certain obligations and yet avoid duplication of controls. It is still somewhat unclear what the relationship of control under the planning and environmental protection legislation is.

Planning authorities, however, have certain EU obligations with regard to waste, and those are contained in SI 1994/1056, Sch 4 Part I. Thus in drawing up waste disposal plans and in taking planning decisions, they are subject to obligations with regard to dealing with particular types of waste and finding suitable disposal sites or installations — a particularly 'pro-active' duty. In carrying out these duties, planning authorities must have regard to 'relevant objectives' under EU requirements, eg that waste is in general to be recovered/disposed of without endangering human health and without the use of environmentally harmful processes that could cause risks to water, air, soil, plants or animals, or cause odour or noise nuisance, or adversely affect the countryside or places of special interest. More particularly, there is a requirement to establish an integrated and adequate network of waste disposal installations, taking a BATNEEC approach to achieving this, and to ensure that waste is disposed of in one of the nearest appropriate installations, by the best appropriate means and techniques to ensure a high level of environmental protection.

Planning then clearly has a very important role in identifying suitable waste disposal sites and this extends way beyond mere response to any proposal to deposit waste at a particular site. There is a positive duty to identify and encourage the safe development of all appropriate sites for particular facilities.

The same pro-active duty extends to considering actual applications for waste disposal facilities. 'Relevant considerations' will include: site suitability, impact on adjoining land, prejudice to future long term proposals for land in the area, need to minimise transport of waste, site geology and hydrogeology, mode of transport, access, landforms, landscaping, timescales, hours of operation. It is entirely proper to impose conditions on a grant of planning

2 *R v Berkshire County Council, ex p Wokingham District Council* [1995] EGCS 57.

permission relating to: area of fill, timescales of operations, transport and access issues, hours of operation, noise levels, minimising nuisance from birds, vermin and litter, physical value of waste accepted *insofar* as this affects local amenity and neighbouring land uses, removal and preservation of top soil, standards for minimum depths of soil materials on restoration, specification of final contours and aftercare arrangements for closed sites.

Particular considerations and conditions may apply with regard to waste incinerators, eg visual impact, noise, storage facilities and traffic issues. Emissions should *only* be taken into account vis-à-vis their land use implications, but such consideration is unlikely as stringent controls over emissions will be imposed under environmental protection legislation.

However, a further PPG specifically dealing with waste planning aspects of various types of disposal, ie incineration, composting, landfill and land raise is proposed. It will take account of the proximity principle whereunder waste should be disposed of as closely as possible to its point of arising. Planning authorities will also need to take into account national strategies and plans drawn up under s 44A and Sch 2A of the EPA 1990 in drawing up their local plans and the various plans should be mutually reinforcing. The waste local plan will be, of course, part of the development plan along with structure (and unitary plans where appropriate) for the purposes of s 54A of the Town and Country Planning Act 1990 (see chapter 5 above).[3]

So far as development control is concerned the Town and Country Planning Act 1990, s 53(3)(b) specifically declares the deposit of refuse or waste materials on land is a material change of use, *notwithstanding the land comprises a site already used for that purpose* (and so requires planning permission), *if* the superficial area of the deposit is thereby extended *or* its height is thereby raised *and* exceeds the level of adjoining land. This must be read subject to the General Permitted Development Order. Part 20 Class C grants licensed coal operators rights to carry on any development at an authorised mine site in connection with coal-mining operations, save that this does *not* extend to any deposit of minerals or waste which would exceed a height of 15m. Furthermore, even where tipping is permitted there is a condition that the deposit must be cleared, within 24 months, or such longer period as the mineral planning authority allows, after mining has ended and the land restored to agreed condition. Part 21 grants to *all* mineral operators permission to deposit waste operationally derived from the site on premises used as a mine, or on ancillary mining land already so used. But this is subject to restrictions in that waste must not be deposited in an excavation where it would be deposited at a height exceeding adjoining land levels unless that is provided for in a waste management scheme approved by the mineral planning authority, or, in any other case, where the superficial area or height of the deposit (measured on 21 October 1988) would be increased by more than 10% again unless this is provided for by a scheme. Where development is permitted it is subject to requirements for waste management schemes to be submitted, approved and adhered to. Part 21 further permits the deposit on land comprised in a site used for the deposit of waste or refuse on 1 July 1948 of waste resulting from coal-mining operations, but this is subject to a requirement that there should

3 *Cory Environmental Ltd v Secretary of State* (1995) 15 Waste Planning 26.

be a scheme approved by the mineral planning authority before 5 December 1988, in connection with the tipping.

So far as return to the earth of *mineral and quarry* waste is concerned, controls also exist under the Mines and Quarries (Tips) Act 1969. The purpose of this Act is to prevent disused tips constituting a danger to the public, and to provide for security of tips associated with mines and quarries. Under Part I of the 1969 Act 'tips', ie above ground accumulations or deposits of waste, whether in a solid state, in solution, or suspension, and associated with mines or quarries, must be made and kept secure, see ss 1 and 2. Notification of the beginning and end of tipping operations must, under s 4, be given to the appropriate inspectors appointed by the Health and Safety Executive under the Health and Safety at Work Act etc 1974 for implementing mines and quarries legislation. Under s 5 regulations may be made to require formulation of rules, by mining managers and quarry owners, with respect to 'tipping operations', ie depositing refuse from a mine or quarry, and the nature of refuse to be deposited on relevant tips, see SI 1971/1377. Regulations may also, under s 6, require owners and managers to keep plans and sections of tips, see SI 1971/1378. Part II of the Act confers functions on local authorities, ie county councils and London borough councils, see s 11, to ensure that *disused* tips do not, by reason of instability, constitute public dangers. Section 12 confers powers on authorities to acquire information regarding stability of disused tips. Section 13 gives rights of entry to carry out exploratory tests on appropriate land. Instability constituting a public danger may be the subject of action under s 14. A local authority may require the owner of a disused tip to carry out specified remedial work, subject to rights of appeal to the court, ss 15 and 28, and to the authority's powers to carry out remedial and reinstatement works under ss 17 and 23. Central grants may be available for authorities carrying out such work under s 25.

Returning to planning law, creation of *new* tips requires planning permission, an important issue as so much waste in this country is tipped as landfill. Disposal of waste to land in any form is generally treated as a change of use.[4] Even where land has been used previously as a quarry and quarry waste has been dumped there, its use, after completion of excavation, as a tip for household refuse constitutes a material change of use.[5] There may be cases where deposit is ancillary to building or engineering projects.[6] Each case must be considered on its facts.

Development control functions with regard to waste disposal are *generally* exercised by county councils in England outside London. They consult relevant districts in discharging their functions and the Agency. (In Wales waste functions are *generally* exercised by the unitary authorities under the Local Government (Wales) Act 1994, and in the metropolitan areas the districts are the responsible authorities.) County functions extend to control over disposal of mineral waste, the use of land, or carrying out operations in or on land, for depositing refuse or waste materials, and erecting buildings, plant

---

4 *Alexandra Transport Co v Secretary of State for Scotland* (1973) 27 P & CR 352; *R v Derbyshire County Council, ex p North East Derbyshire District Council* (1979) 77 LGR 389.
5 See also *Roberts v Vale Royal District Council* (1977) 78 LGR 368, 39 P & CR 514; and *Bilboe v Secretary of State for the Environment* (1980) 39 P & CR 495.
6 *Northavon District Council v Secretary of State for the Environment* (1980) 40 P & CR 332.

or machinery designated for use wholly or mainly for treating, storing or disposing of refuse or waste.

Using land for waste and refuse disposal, or as a scrap yard or as sewage works or for sewage disposal, or for disposal of trade waste or sludge are developments which will be subject to the usual publicity requirements. Planning permission should be refused for waste disposal or tipping on unsuitable sites. The matters which may be taken into account in determining an application to create a waste disposal facility include whether the site will emit malodorous smells, its effects on local residents, whether the need for the facility outweighs environmental concerns, and risk assessments of the potential frequency and likely magnitude of incidents on site.[7] Refusal of permission for other operations, etc, can serve to isolate some disposal sites, though there are no statutory or administrative requirements to this effect.

Where a new landfill site is proposed care has to be taken with regard to existing buildings and the possible effects of gas arising from decomposition of waste migrating from the site, and the planning authority will thus need information on types and quantities of waste proposed to be infilled. Environmental assessment may also be required (see chapter 5). Conditions may be imposed in respect of gas from a landfill for example with regard to its management. Planning obligations under s 106 of the 1990 Act are also officially recommended as means of control over new landfills. Particular care is required where landfilled sites are proposed for redevelopment. Migrating landfill gas will be a relevant consideration here, and its presence may justify conditions being imposed to ensure, for example, its safe venting, or the gas may even justify a refusal of permission for permission should not be granted unless migrating gas dangers can be overcome. This may involve removal of gas generating matter or steps to prevent gas migration. See further below on contaminated land.

Planning controls must particularly ensure permission is not inadvertently given to deposits of unsuitable materials.[8] Thus where permission has been given to extract fire clay from a site subject to an infill condition requiring 'such quantity of fill as may be necessary to make good former levels', and, fill material was specified there is virtual consent to tipping.

Control under environmental protection legislation

Reference has already been made to the mounting criticism of the law of waste disposal throughout the 1980s. That law existed under the Control of Pollution Act (COPA) 1974. As that is now replaced by the provisions of the Environmental Protection Act (EPA) 1990, it is appropriate here only to give a skeletal outline of the old law, those requiring further detail may consult, for example, the first edition of this work pp 263–269.

The former law under the 1974 Act

Waste disposal authorities (generally counties in England) were under a duty to make plans for the disposal of waste within their areas. They were also the

7 *Envirocor Waste Holdings v Secretary of State for the Environment* [1995] EGCS 60, 16 Waste Planning 56.
8 *R v Derbyshire County Council, ex p North East Derbyshire District Council* (1979) 77 LGR 389.

licensing authorities for waste disposal, and that system depended on the prior obtaining of a grant of planning permission to deposit waste followed by the *licensing of the site*, it being an offence to deposit waste at an unlicensed site. Conditions would be imposed in site licences for example as to the duration of tipping and the kinds and quantities of waste to be tipped, etc, though it was not possible to impose a blanket 'no nuisance' condition in a licence.[9] Licence conditions could be varied and licences themselves revoked in particular circumstances, while it was the duty of authorities to oversee waste disposal and to enforce the law.

The transition from control under the 1974 Act to that under the 1990 Act was provided for by s 77 of the 1990 Act. Effectively licences granted under the 1974 Act became licences falling within Part II of the 1990 Act and are subject to its powers of variation, revocation, transfer, surrender, etc, see further below.

It was principally under the 1974 legislation that the UK sought to meet its EU obligations. So, for example, Directive 75/439 on Waste Oils was implemented under the 1974 Act. This was likewise the position with regard to Directive 78/319 on Toxic and Dangerous Wastes. The 1990 Act has, it is to be hoped, enabled a greater degree of compliance with EU obligations, but before turning to consider that legislation it is necessary to consider the Control of Pollution (Amendment) Act 1989, as amended by EPA 1990.

Control over unregistered transporters of waste

The 1989 Act is particularly directed to the control of 'fly tipping' — the unauthorised deposit of waste at unauthorised sites. The 'scheme' of control is to require registration of waste carriers. Thus under s 2 of the 1989 Act the Secretary of State is empowered to make regulations to provide that persons who carry controlled waste must be registered with a 'regulation authority', ie the Agency. The regulations may in particular provide for how an application for registration is to be made and determined, and provision may also be made for the registers to be open to the public. The regulations (the Controlled Waste (Registration of Carriers and Seizure of Vehicles) Regulations SI 1991/1624) are, however, subject to s 3 which provides distinct criteria for the grant or revocation of registration. Thus registration may be refused where there has been a contravention of regulations in relation to making a registration application — eg as to a request for information — or where the applicant or another 'relevant person' (eg directors, managers, secretaries, etc, of a body corporate where it is the company which is making the application) has been convicted of a prescribed offence (eg previous fly tipping) and the authority conclude it is undesirable that the applicant should be authorised to carry controlled waste (which has the meaning assigned under Part II of the Environmental Protection Act 1990, see below). Similar provisions relate to the revocation of registration, though periodic re-registration of carriers may in any case be required. Section 4 makes provision for appeals against refusal, non-determination or revocation of registration to the Secretary of State. Section 1 then makes it generally an offence for an unregistered person to carry controlled waste *in the course of his business or otherwise with a view to*

9 *A-G's Reference (No 2 of 1988)* [1990] 1 QB 77.

profit, though certain persons may be exempted from this restriction by regulations made by the Secretary of State. The 1991 regulations exempt local authorities, charities, voluntary groups, the railways, and waste producers carrying their own waste other than demolition or construction waste. As defences to charges under s 1 the accused may show *either* that the waste was transported in an emergency (ie the need to move waste in order to remove or reduce serious danger to the public or serious risk to the environment) *and* that the relevant authority was given notice of this emergency as soon as practicable after its occurrence; *or* that he/she neither knew nor had reasonable grounds to suspect that he/she was transporting controlled waste; *and* took reasonable steps to ascertain the nature of what he/she was carrying; *or* was acting under an employer's instructions.

Section 5 of the 1989 Act empowers uniformed constables on the road or anywhere and duly authorised officers of the Agency off the road, who are of the opinion that controlled waste is being transported contrary to s 1, to stop persons engaged in the transport and require their authority for the transport and to search vehicles and take away and test samples of material found. It is an offence to fail to comply with such a request or to obstruct the execution of the power.

Section 6 contains important enforcement powers, ie power for justices to issue warrants to the Agency for the seizure of vehicles where satisfied relevant contraventions of the 1974 and 1990 Acts (ie unlawful treatment, disposal or deposition) have been committed *and* where the vehicle in question was used in the commission of the offence, provided proceedings for the offence have not yet been brought against any person and that the relevant authority has failed after taking prescribed steps to ascertain the name and address of anyone able to provide them with prescribed Information about who was using the vehicle at the time of the offence. Once a warrant is issued to the Agency in respect of any vehicle, any authorised Agency officer may only seize property if accompanied by a constable. The power is one of seizure not confiscation, but regulations may authorise the Agency to sell or destroy property seized after such notice and taking such other steps as may be prescribed to inform persons entitled to the property it has been seized and may be claimed and either the condition of the property requires its disposal without delay or a prescribed period of time has expired and no obligation under the regulations has arisen requiring the return of the property, see reg 23 of the 1991 regulations.

Section 7 contains supplementary enforcement provisions including powers of entry by reference to s 71 of the Environmental Protection Act 1990. Note further that under SI 1991/1624 reg 3 provides for the establishment of public registers of carriers, while regs 4–14 detail: application for registration procedures, fees payable, and refusals, eg where an applicant has been convicted of a prescribed offence and it is considered undesirable for the carrier to be authorised; the information which must be recorded and its subsequent amendment, the duration of registrations (generally three years); revocation, eg for conviction of a prescribed offence, leading the Agency to conclude continued registration is undesirable. A registration may be renewed where it expires, though the carrier may at any time surrender it. Regulations 15–18 are concerned with appeals against registration, etc; these lie to the Secretary of State and must generally be made within 28 days of the act/refusal complained of. Regulations 19–25 deal with seizure of vehicles, etc, laying down the procedure for obtaining a seizure warrant, the power to remove seized vehicles and their subsequent disposal after due notice has been given, with proceeds being used to defray the seizing authority's expenses in connection with the 1989 Act. Further detailed guidance is given in DoE Circular 11/91.

The law under EPA 1990 as amended in 1995

The object of Part II of the EPA 1990 was to provide for the repeal and replacement of ss 1–21 and 27–30 of the Control of Pollution Act 1974, providing for new and stronger controls over waste. But the new law did not meet all the criticisms made of the 1974 provisions. One particular problem was the definition of 'waste', and further amendment was necessary in 1995; this was also needed to bring UK law into line with EU obligations (see Directives 75/442, 91/156 and 91/692).

The new definition of waste

Section 75, as amended, and Sch 2B of the 1990 Act define 'waste', 'household', 'commercial', 'industrial' and 'special' waste. The definition reflects that which is contained in regs 1(3), 24(8) and Sch 4 para 9 of the Waste Management Licensing Regulations SI 1994/1056, as amended.

'Waste'

This is *any* substance or object in the categories contained in Sch 2B which the holder (ie the producer whose activities create waste, or any person who carries out pre-processing, mixing or other operations resulting in a change in the nature or composition of this waste) *or* the possessor of the waste either *discards*, or *intends or is required to discard*.

The concept of discard — a legislatively undefined term

It is clear that the concept of 'discard' is central to the definition of waste. It was well established under the previous law that the fact that material was capable of being recycled did not prevent it from being waste.[10] However, the core meaning of discard as elucidated by DoE Circular 11/94 is to ask whether the substance or object in question has dropped out of the normal cycle or chain of utility. On this basis a bottle subject to a returnable deposit is *not* waste while it is in the hands of its buyer who intends to consume its contents, nor when that person returns it to the point of sale; neither is it waste in the hands of the shopkeeper who takes it back, or in those of the supplier of the bottle who retrieves it from the shop. However, the bottle is waste if placed in a bottle bank for recycling. This is in line with the EU concept of waste under Directive 91/156 which is that it is material which (a) poses a threat to human health or the environment, *and* (b) consists of substances or objects which have fallen from the commercial cycle or chain of utility — this material is

---

10 *Kent County Council v Rackham* [1989] 1 LMELR 172, *R v Rotherham, ex p Rankin* (1989) Times, 6 November.

'directive waste' (the term used in much of the relevant subordinate legislation) and it is such material which is subject to waste control policies (subject to exceptions, see below).

Thus it is not the possibility of further economic use of the material which determines the issue (eg by recycling). Substances intended for recycling or specialised recovery processes are waste, provided they have dropped out of the normal chain or pattern of use appropriate to their current forms. Accordingly dirty solvents may be re-used but they will be waste once their owner decides they can no longer be used as solvents at all because of contamination. This is in line with EU law,[11] and see also below.

Circular 11/94 further argues that a substance or object which is worn but functioning as originally intended or usable after repair for its original purpose is not generally waste, as neither is material which can be put to immediate use other than via *specialist* waste recoverers. On the other hand material which has degenerated and can only be put to use by waste recoverers is waste even if it has value or is transferred for value. Where, however, there is material which is simply unwanted, eg old furniture, and for whose removal a charge has to be paid, much will depend on the facts of individual cases. If the recipient of the material can use it without special processes (as, for example would be the case of a secondhand furniture dealer) the material would not normally be waste.

In addition to the general outline concept of material capable of being waste given above, both Sch 2B of the 1990 Act and Sch 4 of the 1994 Waste Management Licensing Regulations prescribe 16 specific categories of material. These include: production and consumption residues; sub-specification products; life expired products; spilled, lost or intentionally or unintentionally contaminated or soiled materials; unusable parts (eg expired batteries); substances no longer performing satisfactorily; industrial residues; residues of pollution abatement processes (eg a spent filter); machining or finishing residues; residues of extraction processes; adulterated materials; materials, etc, whose use is banned by law; products for which the holder has no further use (such as shop discards); contaminated material arising from remedial action taken to clean up land, and *any* materials substances or products not contained in the foregoing classes. But whether any such material *is* waste depends upon whether in addition it is subject to actual or intended discard by its holder; which also *may* depend upon whether the material has dropped out of its normal chain of utility or pattern of use, but may also depend on the intention of the holder.

Nearly all commentators on the law and those working as regulators and producers, holders, etc, of waste agree that though the foregoing concept may be reasonably easily applied in most instances, there will be cases where conflicts of interpretation can arise. For example Part IV of Sch 4 of the Waste Management Licensing Regulations 1994 lists certain 'waste recovery operations' which include: reclaiming or regenerating solvents; reclaiming or regenerating organic substances; recycling, etc, metals, metal compounds, or other inorganic materials; regenerating acids; recovery of components used for pollution abatement or of components from catalysts; re-refining or re-using oil which is waste; using waste as a fuel; spreading waste on land to benefit

---

11 *Vessoso and Zanetti (joined cases C-206/88 and C-207/88)* [1990] 2 LMELR 133; and see *Gotech Industrial Services and Pitcairn v Friel* [1995] SCCR 22 on how an intention to break up material in the course of demolition makes the breaker a waste producer.

agriculture or for ecological improvement including composting. Will the consignment of material to such an operation automatically make it 'discarded' and so waste?

According to Circular 11/94 the answer is 'no'. The test suggested is to ask whether the material can be used in its present form (albeit after repair) *or* in the same way as any other raw material *without* being subjected to *specialised recovery operations, and* is it likely to be so used? Where the answer is 'yes' it is suggested the material has not been discarded and so is not waste. Where, however, the answer is 'no' *or* where material can *only* be used after subjection to specialised recovery operations, the material is normally to be regarded as discarded and hence is waste.

However, this 'quasi legislative' test raises its own problems, for what is to be regarded as a 'specialised recovery operation' — a term defined nowhere in law. Such an operation is *not* one falling within the ordinary commercial cycle, etc. So, for example to spread manure produced on a farm on the land of that farm as a fertiliser is within the normal chain of utility, while to operate a process which derives its entire justification from the recovery of waste, for example to process bottles from bottle banks or to reclaim contaminated solvents, is to carry on a specialised recovery process.

The core concept which must always be applied is that of discard. It matters really quite little what the material is in itself; what is important is to ask whether as the material currently stands it has dropped out of the normal commercial pattern of use or chain of utility. Thus where the operator of stables also owns a market garden and spreads the manure from the former on the latter for its benefit, *or* where the manure is sold to customers for use on their land the activity is entirely within the normal commercial pattern of use or chain of utility. However, should the spreading of manure *exceed* what is needed for the benefit of the land then that manure has dropped out of the normal pattern of use. This is because the landowner is spreading the manure *wholly or mainly to avoid the burden of otherwise disposing of it and* if the manure in question were to cease to be available *no substitute material would be sought.* Similarly where material is consigned to a business or operator whose entire object is to specialise in waste recovery *as the only way of dealing with it,* it is waste; likewise where material is consigned specifically to a *disposal* operator (see Part III of Sch 4 of the 1994 regulations), or where a waste holder pays a person to provide the service of collecting and taking away objects which the holder wishes to get rid of, or where material is abandoned or dumped, or is in any other way discarded and dealt with *as if* it is waste.

Can waste cease to be waste?

There is no guidance in EU law here, but, applying a purposive interpretation, Circular 11/94 concludes that the purpose of the waste Directives would be defeated if the transfer of waste for collection, transport, storage, specialised recovery, disposal or a decision to subject it to specialised recovery operations were to result in a conclusion that the material in question is not waste. On this basis a substance or object which meets the criteria for being defined as 'waste' at its point of original production remains waste until it is recovered or disposed of. Recovery occurs when waste processing produces 'a material of sufficient beneficial use to eliminate or sufficiently diminish the threat posed by the original production of the waste', which will normally be when 'the recovered material can be used as a raw material in the same way as raw materials of non-waste origin by . . . a person other than a specialised recovery establishment or undertaking.' In some cases, however, the amount of processing required to produce such 'safe' raw material will be very little. Thus inert material such as clean ballast, broken pottery and building site rubble that is to be processed and reused in building and similar works may well not be 'waste' for long or at all: it is almost ready to be used as a new raw material.[12] However, waste does not cease to be waste simply because its holder does not regard it as waste, nor because it is valuable to its holder as an item for sale. It is for the law to define what 'waste' is.[13]

Controlled waste

Though it is the overall definition of waste which is important, especially insofar as that waste is 'directive waste', other definitions are relevant in particular contexts. Controlled waste, under s 75 of the 1990 Act is 'household, industrial and commercial waste or any such waste'. 'Household waste' is waste from domestic property, ie buildings used for living accommodation, caravans, residential homes, premises forming parts of universities and schools and premises forming parts of hospitals and nursing homes. 'Industrial waste' is waste from factories, premises used in connection with provision of public transport facilities, premises used in connection with the public supply of gas, water, electricity or sewerage services, premises used in connection with the provision of postal and telecommunications services, and see the Controlled Waste Regulations SI 1992/588 which list certain wastes which are to be treated as industrial waste, eg laboratory waste, clinical waste and waste from animal breeding establishments. 'Commercial waste' is waste from premises used wholly or mainly for the purposes of a trade or business or for sporting, recreational or entertainment purposes. 'Any such waste' is waste which is cognate with the waste in the three defined categories: it is not a 'catch-all expression enabling relevant authorities to give an inflated meaning to the word "waste"'.[14] In any case the 1994 regulations provide that before waste can be treated as household, industrial or commercial waste it must *also* be directive waste, and thus the categorisation has lost much of its previous significance.

Exempted material

Certain material is excluded from the scope of the framework directive on waste, and the 1994 regulations, reg 1(3), transpose this into UK law. This excluded material cannot be 'directive waste' and hence is also *not* controlled waste. The material excluded under the directive is:

1   Gaseous effluents emitted into the atmosphere, ie gases emitted *incidentally* from non-waste processes, but *not* gas from disposal itself such as landfill gas.

12 *Kent County Council v Queenborough Rolling Mill Co Ltd* [1990] JE 257; *Cheshire County Council v Armstrong's Transport (Wigan) Ltd* [1995] Env LR 62.
13 *Meston Technical Services Ltd and Wright v Warwickshire County Council* [1995] Env LR D 36.
14 *Thanet District Council v Kent County Council* [1993] Env LR 391.

2   Five categories of waste covered by 'other legislation' which the DoE takes, in Circular 11/94, to mean both EU and UK legislation already in force on (or consolidated or amended after) 18 March 1991 and which provides as an effective means of pursuing Directive obligations.

3   Radioactive waste under the Radioactive Substances Act 1993.

4   Waste resulting from prospecting, extraction, treatment and storage of mineral resources and the working of quarries, ie actual mineral waste which is regulated under the Town and Country Planning Act 1990 and the Mines and Quarries (Tips) Act 1969, but *non*-mineral waste from a quarry, eg worn out machinery and waste oils, remains within the definition of 'directive waste' even though, by a quirk of drafting, such material cannot be controlled waste for s 75(7) of the EPA 1990 excludes from that category *all* waste from mines and quarries.

5   Animal carcases and faecal matter and other natural, non-dangerous substances used in farming (note control under the Animal Waste Directive 90/667 and the Animals By-Product Order SI 1992/3303). But note again that *all* waste coming from premises used for agriculture is excluded from the definition of controlled waste, while the DoE considers that non-natural farm waste such as old tyres is not within the exclusion and so remains 'directive waste'.

6   Waste waters (saving waste in liquid forms) (note control under the 1991 water legislation); also note that 'waste in liquid form' appears to include liquid waste used in landfill, while waste waters discharged into the sea or into any controlled waters (see chapter 12) are outside the scope of the directive and so are not 'directive waste'. Likewise excluded is waste water from residential settlements originating in either the human metabolism or household activities and waste water from trade or industrial premises which is discharged into sewers or controlled waters.

7   Decommissioned explosives (note control under the Explosives Act 1875, SI 1991/1531, and SI 1989/615).

Special waste

This is controlled waste in respect of which regulations are in force under s 62 of the EPA 1990 (see further below) and this *can* include radioactive waste, see SI 1996/972.

One of the major problems of the law before 1990 was the 'poacher cum gamekeeper' syndrome in that 'waste disposal authorities' (primarily counties) were responsible for both licensing the disposal of waste and disposing of it themselves. The 1990 Act partially remedied this by divided overall waste responsibilities between Waste Collection Authorities (WCAs) who are primarily District Councils and London Boroughs in England, Waste Disposal Authorities (WDAs) primarily in England the 'shire' counties and certain other specially created statutory bodies for London, Greater Manchester and Merseyside, and Waste Regulation Authorities, again the 'shire' counties and special authorities for London, Greater Manchester and Merseyside. Clearly this still resulted in some authorities wearing more than one hat — for example in the areas of some unitary metropolitan districts — a continuing issue with the emergence of more unitary authorities in England and Wales under the 1992 and 1994 local government legislation. However, there was at least a degree of separation between the waste regulation and waste disposal arms of authorities. The Environment Act 1995 now transfers all waste regulation powers to the Agency in England and Wales, thus creating a national authority which oversees waste management licensing, special waste regulation, the supervision of the duty of care regarding waste and enforcement of the law.

Waste collection functions

Under s 45 of the 1990 Act, WCAs are to collect all household waste in their areas, unless it is so isolated as to be unreasonably expensive to collect, *and* where other adequate disposal arrangements have been made. They are to collect commercial waste where requested by the occupier of the premises, and a reasonable charge for this service may be made. They may collect, if requested by the occupier, industrial waste from premises, subject, in England and Wales, to the consent of the relevant waste disposal authority, and again a reasonable charge may be made. They may clear privies and cesspools and may provide facilities for waste collection and may, under ss 46 and 47, make arrangements for the provision of waste receptacles for household, commercial or industrial waste. Any waste collected by the WCA belongs to that authority, not to its employees or agents. Under s 48 they are to deliver waste to such places as the WDA directs, subject, in the case of household or commercial waste, to where the WCA has recycling arrangements; though the WDA may override such recycling by the WCA where it has its own arrangements with regard to relevant waste with a waste disposal contractor to recycle all or part of the waste.

Section 49 of the 1990 Act was a major new departure in that it imposes a duty on WCAs to make plans in connection with household and commercial waste in respect of its recycling. Initially authorities are to investigate waste with a view to deciding what arrangements are appropriate for separating, baling or packaging it for recycling purposes, and then to decide on arrangements for those purposes. They must prepare a statement ('the plan') of proposed and actual arrangements showing how they and others will deal with waste. The plan must be kept under review, and must be made, and modified, in the light of considering the effects of the plan on the amenities of any locality and the likely costs/savings to the authority attributable to arrangements to be made/modified. The plan must state: the kinds and quantities of controlled waste the WCA expects to collect in the plan period; the kinds and quantities of such waste they expect to purchase in the period; the kinds and quantities of such waste to be prepared for recycling; arrangements to be made with waste disposal contractors for them to deal with waste; plant and equipment to be provided under s 48(6), and the estimated costs/savings attributable to operations under the plan.

Plans must be publicised in relevant areas, and copies sent to the relevant WDA and the Agency and the Secretary of State so that he/she may ensure that the plan contains the requisite provisions. Plans must also be available for public inspection, but there is little public involvement formally in their creation.

Section 55 confers powers on WCAs *and* WDAs to further the recycling of waste. Thus WCAs may buy or otherwise acquire waste with a view to its recycling and may use, sell or otherwise dispose of to others waste they own or anything produced from it. WDAs may also buy or acquire waste for recycling, they may also make arrangements with waste disposal contractors for them to recycle waste collected in their area by WCAs or over which they have an agreement with a third party to dispose of or treat. They may agree with a disposal contractor for waste to be used to produce heat/electricity or both, and may use, sell or otherwise dispose of waste collected in their areas by WCAs or anything produced from it.

In connection with recycling note the concept of 'waste recycling credits' introduced by s 52. Where under s 48 a WCA retains collected waste for recycling, the relevant WDA is to pay to the WCA such amount as it determines represents the WDA's net saving of expenditure on the disposal cost which would otherwise have been incurred. Likewise where a WDA so discharges its functions so that waste arising in its area does not fall to be collected by a WCA that authority shall pay to the WDA an amount representing its saved expenditure in respect of the waste. And where a person other than a WCA collects waste in a WDA's area for recycling the WDA may pay to that person a sum in respect of net saved expenditure, and a similar power is entrusted to WCAs. These provisions may be supplemented by regulations made by the Secretary of State, for example, to transmute powers into duties and to provide for determination of net savings of expenditure. See also the Environmental Protection (Waste Recycling Payments) Regulations, SI 1992/462 and DoE Circular 4/92.

Note also s 52(1) under which a WDA is entitled to receive from a WCA such sums as are needed to reimburse it for the costs of making arrangements under s 51 (see below) for disposing of commercial and industrial waste collected in the WDA's area.

Waste disposal functions

WDAs under s 51 are under a *duty* to dispose of all controlled waste collected in their area by WCAs and to provide deposition places for residents to place their household rubbish. These places are to be reasonably accessible to residents, free of charge and generally open, and such sites may accept household waste from persons other than residents, and a fee may then be charged.

However, the 'meat' of s 51 is that WDAs are to discharge their duties in respect of controlled waste disposal and residents' deposited household waste by means of 'arrangements' with waste disposal contractors (WDCs) but by no other means. These 'arrangements' are regulated by s 32 EPA 1990 and Sch 2. Part I of that Schedule and s 32 made provision for transitional arrangements from WDAs to waste disposal companies who may take on the WDC role. The Secretary of State was empowered to give directions to WDAs to form, or participate in forming waste disposal companies (LAWDCs) and to transfer their relevant undertakings thereto, save that no such direction was to be given to an authority where the Secretary of State was satisfied that the WDA had already formed a LAWDC, had ceased to carry on relevant disposal activities or was making the necessary arrangements to cease operations. However, the Secretary of State could still give a direction if not satisfied with the transfer, etc, arrangements a WDA had made or if there was a failure to implement them reasonably expeditiously. The Secretary of State's directions were given in May and June 1991, see also DoE Circular 8/91 Annex C. A LAWDC so formed by an authority, should for so long as it remains under the control of the WDA, only engage in waste collection, disposal, keeping and treatment and ancillary matters, and furthermore must be an 'arm's length' company within the meaning of Part V of the Local Government and Housing Act 1989, ie one in general subject to the same statutory rules and rules of conduct as apply to local authorities themselves, and subject to the Secretary of State's regulatory powers. Companies are under the 'control' of an authority if they are subsidiaries of the authority, or the authority controls a majority of votes at company general meetings, or has power to appoint or remove the majority of the company's directors, but will be 'arm's length' companies if additionally there is a resolution by the authority to that effect and certain other conditions are satisfied, for example as to undertakings by the company to use its best efforts to produce specified positive returns on assets and as to restrictions on authority members and officers being directors of the company.

Thus WDAs may fulfil their obligations under s 51 to make disposal arrangements with WDCs for example by *either* setting up their own LAWDC or by transferring disposal entirely to private sector companies. LAWDCs may be particularly appropriate to conurbations where authorities wish to operate together, and this is contemplated by the legislation (NB Scotland has a different disposal system, see ss 53, 54 and 56 of EPA 1990).

To assist in the waste disposal process WDAs are, under s 51(4), to give directions to WCAs as to the persons and places to whom and to which waste is to be delivered, and may arrange for the provision of places by WDCs at which waste may be treated or kept prior to disposal/treatment, and may assist WDCs with appropriate plant, equipment and land. Part II of Sch 2 then further regulates the contracts WDAs are to make with WDCs. Contracts are to be put out to public competitive tender by advertisement in publications circulating generally amongst WDCs, and wherever possible, at least four tenders for the work are to be invited. The simple fact that a WDA has a LAWDC does *not* guarantee that company will be given the contract. The terms of contracts are to be drawn up bearing in mind the need to include terms concerned with minimising pollution and maximising recycling. Detailed guidance on the new law and practice may be found in DoE Circular 8/91. Judicial guidance on waste disposal contract tendering has also been forthcoming. In *R v Avon County Council, ex p Adams*[15] a waste disposal company (TAL) and its owner sought judicial review of a decision by a WDA to award a contract to its LAWDC (AWM). The Court of Appeal pointed out that the 1990 Act imposes three duties on WDAs: to have regard to environmental considerations in the disposal of waste, to dispose of their own waste disposal undertakings, and to open up waste disposal to competitive tendering to market forces. These duties are not easily compatible, and the 1990 Act gives no indication as to their ranking. WDAs must take all relevant factors into account in deciding on tenders and must not behave unreasonably. Keeping the cost of waste disposal down is a relevant consideration, but so is the need to ensure disposal does not harm the environment. WDAs must ensure that there is a degree of *fair* competition in the tendering process and

15 [1994] 6 ELM 49.

no *undue* discrimination in favour of LAWDCs. To show this there should be evidence that in any given case a WDA has been able to gather information on comparative waste disposal costs so as to make an informed decision. They are *not* bound to choose the cheapest option and are entitled to consider their environmental preference, though securing environmental objectives is not an overriding consideration. In *R v Cardiff City Council, ex p Gooding Investments*,[16] Owen J also considered that a preferred disposal strategy is a matter a WDA is entitled to consider in deciding where to award a contract.

Waste regulation functions

The Agency as successor to the Waste Regulation Authorities is the principal 'control' body with regard to waste, see also s 30(1) of the 1990 Act as amended.

Waste planning

The duty of the former county WRAs to undertake waste management planning for waste disposal and treatment under s 50 of the 1990 Act has now been repealed and replaced by the obligation of the Secretary of State under s 44A and Sch 2A to create a national waste strategy for England and Wales. Reference has already been made to this and its non-statutory precursors. However, the outline features of the Secretary of State's duties are to prepare and keep under review, so that it may be modified from time to time, a national waste strategy. This must state the policies for achieving the objectives specified in Sch 2A (see above) and in particular there must be provision relating to the type, quantity and origin of waste to be recovered or disposed of, general technical requirements and special requirements for particular wastes. The strategy is to be drawn up in consultation with the Agency, who will, of course, have to implement it, and other representatives of local government and industry, etc, as the Secretary of State considers appropriate. To assist in preparing the strategy the Agency may be directed to carry out surveys into waste, and waste disposal facilities, etc, and before carrying out such a survey the Agency is to consult with relevant local planning authorities and representatives of industry, etc.

Guidance to the former WRAs on drawing up their waste management planning strategies was given in 'Waste Management Planning: Principles and Practice' (DoE, 1995). The techniques laid down there will also be used by the Agency. Surveys carried out by the Agency will thus be concerned with matters such as: studies of waste movements such as waste flows within and between areas; taking censuses of waste management facilities, especially considering their types, their treatment plant, those which rely on landfill, their composting and recycling facilities, and the numbers of waste transfer stations; estimates of 'key waste arisings', ie how much controlled waste there is disaggregated not just into 'household', or 'commercial', etc, but further under 26 headings such as litter, power station ash, tyres, clinical waste, scraps, etc. Surveys will be carried out, inter alia, by selecting appropriate business

16 [1995] 7 ELM 134.

concerns to give an overview of the industrial population of an area as a whole, some of these will be surveyed by personal visit, others by means of postal questionnaires.

Section 64 required the keeping of registers by WRAs of prescribed particulars of current waste management licences (WMLs) they granted, together with details of applications for WMLs, for modifications of WMLs, notices revoking or suspending WMLs or imposing requirements on WML holders, appeals against WRA decisions, any certificates of completion issued (see further below), convictions of licence holders for offences under Part II of EPA 1990, occasions on which the WRA took supervisory action over a licence (s 42, see below), directions given by the Secretary of State, any other prescribed matters. The foregoing duty now, of course, passes to the Agency, while the Secretary of State has a new power under s 64(2A) to direct the removal from any register of any specified information not *required* to be kept, or which is required to be excluded under ss 65 and 66 which are concerned with national security and commercial confidentiality. Subsidiary registers must be kept by WCAs containing those prescribed particulars in the principal Agency register which relate to the treatment, keeping or disposal of controlled waste within their areas. These various registers must be open to the public free of charge at reasonable hours, and facilities for taking copies at a reasonable cost must be provided. Particular provision for inspection or taking copies may be made at the Secretary of State's direction. However, no information can be included in such a register if, in the Secretary of State's opinion, its inclusion would be contrary to national security interests, see s 65. The Secretary of State may give directions to relevant authorities specifying information, or descriptions of information to be excluded, or otherwise referred to him for a determination on exclusion, though authorities must inform the Secretary of State of any information they exclude in pursuance of his directions.

Section 66 further excludes from registration any information relating to the affairs of an individual or business without prior consent provided the material is 'commercially confidential' — ie its inclusion on a register would unreasonably prejudice the commercial interests of the person in question. On an application for a WML or any other relevant similar transaction the applicant may apply to have information supplied treated as commercially confidential, but it is for the Agency to determine whether it is or not, and it has 14 days from the date of the application to decide the issue, otherwise it is deemed decided in the applicant's favour. Where, however, the determination is that the information should be registered before registration the applicant may appeal to the Secretary of State, and has 21 days from the determination to do this. In any case the Secretary of State may direct the Agency to register certain information notwithstanding that it is commercially confidential on the basis that the public interest requires registration. Information excluded on the basis of confidentiality ceases to be so treated four years from the relevant determination, but a further application to exclude on the same basis may be made. Section 64(2) further provides that where information is excluded on confidentiality grounds a statement indicating the existence of information must be entered in the register.

The Agency has a general duty under s 52 of the Environment Act 1995 to produce an annual report on its work and this, presumably, will include material on waste regulation.

To enable it to carry out its various waste regulatory and other pollution control and environmental protection functions the Agency must have staff, and they in turn must have powers of entry, search and seizure, etc. These now exist under ss 108 and 109 of the Environment Act 1995 (see further chapter 3 above). Section 71 empowers the Secretary of State and the Agency to require the furnishing of information. Failure to comply with requirements is an offence.

The waste management licensing system

Turning to the operation of the law, s 29 lays down definitions of relevant terms. The 'environment' thus consists of land, water and air, while its 'pollution' in the context of controlled waste means pollution *by* the escape or release into land, air or water *from* land on which controlled waste is treated or kept or deposited *or* from fixed or mobile plant for treating, keeping or disposing of controlled waste, *of* substances which are waste *or result from it* (eg landfill gas) and which are capable of causing harm to human kind or living organisms. 'Harm' in this context means harm to health, or to ecological systems, or offence to human senses or harm to property. 'Disposal' of waste *includes* landward deposit, while 'treatment' means subjecting waste to any process including making it reusable or reclaiming matter from waste, and 'recycle' is to be interpreted accordingly. 'Disposal' thus comprehends other methods of dealing with waste than simple deposit. At one point the law favoured the concept of deposit being the dumping in a site with 'no realistic prospect of further examination' see per Bingham LJ in *Leigh Land Reclamation Ltd v Walsall Metropolitan Borough Council*,[17] and that appeared to mean physical incorporation into the site and burial under later material. However, in *R v Metropolitan Stipendiary Magistrate, ex p London Waste Regulation Authority*, and *Berkshire County Council v Scott*[18] the *Leigh Land* decision was doubted, and, by adopting a purposive interpretation of the legislation, it was held that 'deposit' did not mean only 'final deposit', similarly 'disposal' means only to get rid of something, it does not mean finding a final resting place for it. Thus a temporary deposit, as at a waste transfer station, can be enough to attract the attention of the law. 'Substances' means artificial or natural substances whether in solid or liquid, gaseous or vapour form.

Section 33 prohibits persons from depositing controlled waste or knowingly causing or knowingly permitting its deposit in or under any land unless a Waste Management Licence (WML) is in force *and* the deposit is in accordance with the licence *or* from treating, keeping or disposing of controlled waste, or knowingly causing or permitting such activities, in or on any other land, or by means of any mobile plant, *or* from treating, keeping or disposing of controlled waste in such a manner likely to cause pollution of the environment or harm to human health. It should be noted that the offence of treating, keeping or disposing of controlled waste in a manner likely to cause pollution of the environment, etc, is a general residual offence. Even where an activity involving controlled waste is exempt from licensing requirements an offence can still be committed if the waste is disposed of, etc, in such a way as to cause

17 [1991] 3 JEL 281.
18 [1993] 3 All ER 113.

environmental pollutions. The provisions of s 33(1)(c) of the 1990 Act also cover fly tipping, etc. (On 'knowingly causing' or 'permitting' see *Ashcroft v Cambro Waste Products*[19] and chapter 12.)

Exemptions

The Secretary of State may exempt certain activities from these provisions by way of regulations, and in doing so he/she is to have particular regard to the need to exempt small or temporary deposits or means of treatment or disposal which are innocuous, or where other legislative means of control are adequate. Thus reg 16 of the Waste Management Licensing Regulations 1994 (as amended by SI 1995/288) generally excludes the deposit in or on land, recovery or disposal of waste under an authorisation granted under Part I of the EPA 1990 in respect of an IPC process (see chapter 10) *provided* the 'activity is or forms part of' that process. Unfortunately the phrase 'in or forms part of' is undefined. Does it extend to cover situations where waste material is treated or stored on the site of an incinerator which uses waste oil as fuel? Similarly excluded is the disposal of waste where this is or forms part of an authorised incineration process subject to LAAPC powers (again see chapter 10). But both these exemptions do *not* apply where the 'activity' in question involves the *final* disposal of waste by deposit in or on land. Also excluded is the disposal of liquid waste under a discharge consent under the Water Resources Act 1991 and certain dumping at sea activities.

Regulation 17 proceeds further to exempt a whole raft of minor activities otherwise lawfully carried out on land subject to certain restrictions on quantities of waste and the use of certain disposal and recovery methods. The exempted activities in general include: using waste glass in glass making and storage of such glass pending use; small scale iron and steel processes where scrap is smelted in a scrap metal furnace, and storage of scrap pending smelting; burning straw, polluting litter, wood, waste oil, waste derived solid fuel and tyres where this is part of an LAAPC regulated process, and storage associated with such a use; treating packaging or containers for re-use up to certain weight (per period of seven days) limits; burning waste as fuel in certain small appliances; burning waste oil as fuel in the engine of certain modes of transport, eg a railway locomotive and associated storage; spreading specified wastes such as blood and guts from abattoirs or septic tank contents on certain types of land, eg agricultural land, again subject to weight and time limits; storage and spreading of certain types of sewage and septic tank sludge; spreading of, inter alia, rock, ash or demolition waste in connection with reclamation or improvement of land; sludge and septic tank sludge recovery operations in sewage works; certain preliminary actions such as baling and sorting particular materials such as glass, steel cans, waste paper, etc, again subject to weight and cubic capacity limits; composting waste which is biogradable, manufacturing certain construction products from waste resulting from, inter alia, demolition or construction activities; making finished goods from waste material such as plastic, glass, etc; storage in secure

---

19 [1981] 3 All ER 699, and see also *Kent County Council v Beaney* [1991] 5 Env Law 89, suggesting that one's 'knowing permission' may be inferred where it is clear one must have known what was going on.

places of specified wastes to be used for particular defined purposes; storage on a site of that site's demolition, construction or tunnelling waste for use on that site; laundering and cleaning waste textiles with a view to their rescue or recovery; disposing, shredding, cutting or pulverising waste plant matter subject to weight and time limits; recovering silver from photographic and printing processes, subject to volume and time limits; crushing, grinding, etc, of waste bricks and tiles under an IPC authorisation and associated storage up to certain limits; deposit of dredging waste from inland waters; recovery or disposal of any waste at its place of production as an integral part of the production process; baling, etc, waste at its place of production; storing returned goods that are waste by their manufacture, subject to time limits; disposal of certain waste by its producer in an exempt incinerator; burning as waste on open land where it is produced of wood, bark or plant matter by its producer, eg a garden bonfire; discharge of railway lavatory waste to the trackbed; burial of waste from sanitary conveniences with removable receptacles on the same premises; keeping or deposit of materials excavated during peat working; keeping or depositing spent railway ballast on a railway's operational land; depositing excavated material from exploration bore holes on the land where it is produced; burial of dead pets at their former homes; storing waste samples for later testing; secure storage of medicines at a pharmacy pending disposal; temporary storage of certain solid waste, eg old rails on a railway's operational land; temporary storage of certain waste pending collection on its site of production.

It should be noted that scrap metal and waste motor vehicle recycling and recovery is *generally* subject to waste management licensing for scrap metal is 'directive waste'. However, as with the other exemptions listed above, the Directive (art (1)) permits certain kinds and amounts of waste to be exempted from regulation. Thus *certain* activities such as sorting, grading, crushing, etc, relating to certain kinds of ferrous and non-ferrous metal waste are exempt subject to weight and time limits (see further DoE Circular 6/95).

Registering exempt activities

It is an offence under reg 18 of the 1994 regulations for an establishment or undertaking to carry on an exempt activity without registering it with the 'appropriate' registration authority. Which the appropriate authority is varies from case to case, but in cases where no specific authority is provided for by the regulations it is the Agency. Registration, however, is quite a formality, requiring only the provision of the name and address of the establishment in question, and the exempt activity and its location. In some cases the appropriate authority is deemed to know of the activity so no further action is required by the operator. Registration may not be refused, and once an exempt activity is registered registration does not have to be renewed. Registers must, however, be open to public inspection.

Offences in connection with depositing controlled waste

It is an offence to contravene the prohibition in s 33, but there are defences to charges that: the accused took all reasonable precautions and exercised all due diligence to avoid the commission of an offence; the accused acted under an employer's instructions and did not know nor had reason to suppose the acts constituted a contravention of the prohibition; the acts were done in an emergency in order to avoid danger to the public, and that, as soon as reasonably practicable thereafter the Agency was informed, but all reasonably practicable steps must have been taken in addition to minimise pollution and harm to human health. Where an offence is proven with regard to controlled waste the guilty person may be, on summary trial, imprisoned for up to six months, or fined up to £20,000, or be subject to both penalties, while on indictment two years' imprisonment and/or an unlimited fine may be imposed. Where *special* waste is involved on indictment the term of imprisonment may be up to five years. Note, however, it is *also* an offence to contravene *any* condition of a WML. In relation to the various offences and defences considered above, it should be noted that the 'due diligence' defence requires a real degree of vigilance on the part of those who seek to rely on it, so that the contents of skips and containers filled by other persons should always be checked by a person wishing to use the defence.[20] Similarly where a person seeks to rely on the defence of acting in an emergency, the defendant must show there was an emergency, and what constitutes an emergency is a matter for the court to determine.[1]

Where controlled waste is deposited in contravention of the s 33 prohibition in the area of a WCA or anywhere subject to the powers of the Agency either authority may under s 59 require the occupier of the land by notice to remove the waste and/or to take specified steps to eliminate or reduce the consequences of the deposit. An appeal to the justices against such a requirement can be made, and the court must quash the requirement where satisfied the appellant neither deposited nor knowingly caused or permitted the deposit or where there is a material defect in the notice. Failure to comply with requirements is an offence, and where an occupier is in default an authority may take the action they have required and may recover from the occupier their reasonable expenditure in so acting. This is in addition to extensive powers granted to WCAs and the Agency under s 59(7) to remove waste dumped in contravention of s 33 so as to take immediate steps to remedy pollution of land, water or air or harm to human health, or where the land has no occupier or where the occupier is an innocent party. Furthermore s 60 makes it an offence for any person to sort over or disturb anything deposited at a place provided for such a purpose by a WCA or by a WDC, or anything deposited in a waste receptacle provided by a WCA or WDC, unless he/she has the consent of the relevant authority, etc. Note that under s 157 of the 1990 Act where an offence is committed by a corporate body and it is proved to have been committed with the contrivance, or because of the neglect of any director, manager or secretary, etc, of the company that person is criminally liable along with the corporation. Determining who are directors and secretaries of companies is not difficult as these are legal terms: determining who is a 'manager' is a question of fact in each case. The approach of the courts appears to be to ask whether any given individual was part of the 'controlling mind' of the organisation, someone with 'real authority' with 'power and responsibility to decide corporate policy and

---

20 *Durham County Council v Peter Connors Industrial Services Ltd* [1993] Env LR 197.
 1 *Waste Incineration Services Ltd v Dudley Metropolitan Borough Council* [1992] Env LR 29.

strategy'.[2] Where *employees* commit a wrongful act, of course, their employers *may* be liable.[3] However, in cases where a due diligence defence operates, as in the present instance (which must be contrasted with the position under the Water Resources Act 1991), not every act of every employee will be attributed to an employer who operates sound supervisory practices. Liability will be imposed, however, in respect of those who direct and exercise the powers of the company.[4]

The types of operations for which a WML is required

It is not only the *deposit* of controlled waste for which a WML is required. As stated earlier it is also the *disposal, treatment,* or *keeping* of such waste. 'Treating' waste includes, under s 29(6) of the 1990 Act, subjecting it to any process including making it re-usable or reclaiming it. Furthermore because of the need to meet EU obligations the operations which attract the law's control are those classified as 'directive disposal' and 'directive recovery' operations which are listed in Parts III and IV of Sch 4 of the 1994 regulations. Waste disposal then is: tipping waste above or underground; land treatment of waste, eg by biodegradation; deep injection of waste; surface impoundment, eg by putting waste into a lagoon; emplacement in a specially engineered landfill, eg by placing it in lined discrete cells; releasing solid waste into water except seas and oceans; releasing waste into seas and oceans including seabed insertion; biological treatment of waste; physico-chemical treatment of waste; incinerating waste on land; incineration at sea; permanent storage of waste; blending or mixing waste prior to other listed disposal; repackaging waste prior to other disposal; storing waste prior to other disposal operations.

Waste recovery is: reclaiming or regenerating solvents; recycling or reclaiming organic substances, or metals, or inorganic materials, regeneration of acids and bases; recovering components used for pollution abatement or from catalysts; refining oil; use of waste as fuel; spreading waste on land to benefit agriculture, using, exchanging or storing wastes.

Thus as a general rule any *deposit* of directive waste whether permanent or temporary needs a WML as do directive disposal and recovery operations, though some activities are excluded from the need for a licence.

Registration requirements apply to carriers of waste, as has already been considered, under the Control of Pollution (Amendment) Act 1989 and SI 1991/1624, which, incidentally, removed the previous exemption from the need for registration for the railways. Registration requirements also apply under reg 20 of the 1994 regulations to 'brokers of controlled waste', as is required under directive obligations. A broker (which includes a dealer) in waste is an establishment or undertaking which *arranges* for the disposal or recovery of waste on behalf of others. Such brokers must register with the Agency on pain of committing an offence. However, persons and bodies holding a WML or some other form of statutory consent such as a discharge

---

2 *R v Boal* [1992] 3 All ER 177; *Woodhouse v Walsall Metropolitan Borough Council* [1994] Env LR 30.
3 *NRA v Alfred McAlpine Homes South Ltd* [1994] Env LR 198, a case under the Water Resources Act 1991.
4 *Tesco Supermarkets Ltd v Nattrass* [1972] AC 153.

consent, together with those that are charitable or voluntary registered carriers of waste are exempt, as are bodies having statutory waste responsibilities such as WCAs and WDAs. A 'broker', according to DoE Circular 11/94 Annex 8 is a person outside the chain of those who handle waste (such as producers, carriers, and those who carry out recovery and disposal operations), who arranges for waste disposal or recovery *on behalf of another* who has produced, etc, that waste, eg an environmental consultant who contracts to arrange for disposal of controlled waste from a particular producer. The procedure for registration is contained in Sch 5 of the 1994 Regulations. This is not dissimilar to applying for a WML. Thus the application is made to the Agency; fees and charges have to be paid; registrations may be refused if and only if there has been a contravention of any of the requirements relating to making an application or the applicant has been convicted of a relevant offence and in the Agency's opinion it is undesirable for the applicant to be authorised to arrange as a broker for waste disposal on behalf of others. See for details Circular 11/94 Annex 8. The registers must be available for public inspection, and registration lasts for three years, though renewal is possible.

The duty of care

Section 34 of EPA 1990 introduced an important new concept, the 'duty of care' (DOC) as respects waste. Persons importing, producing, carrying, keeping, treating or disposing of controlled waste or acting as brokers having control over waste are to take all reasonable and applicable measures to: prevent contraventions of s 33 and escapes of waste; transfer waste only to authorised persons (eg WCAs and holders of appropriate licences) and to transfer the documentation necessary to ensure that the transferee may avoid contravention of requirements and comply with the DOC. Failure to comply with these requirements is an offence. The duties are supplemented by regulations made under s 34(5), see the Environmental Protection (Duty of Care) Regulations SI 1991/2839. To assist compliance with DOC the Secretary of State must issue, after consultation, and keep revised a Code of Practice (COP), under s 34(7), on ways of meeting DOC requirements. COP was issued in 1991 and revised in 1996, and may be admitted as evidence to assist in determining whether or not DOC was complied with.

The detailed requirements of DOC are that those subject to it must try to:

1 Prevent other persons committing offences of disposing, treating or storing controlled waste without a WML, or without breaking licence conditions, or by acting in a manner likely to cause pollution, etc.
2 Prevent the escape of waste, ie to contain it.
3 To ensure that transfers take place only to authorised persons as listed in the 1990 Act, ie WCAs, holders of WMLs, registered carriers of waste or some statutorily exempted person, *or* for authorised transport purposes, ie transport within the same premises, transport within Great Britain of certain waste imports, and sea or air transport of controlled waste from Great Britain.
4 Ensure on transfer of waste there is also a transfer of a written description of the waste sufficient to enable the recipient to avoid committing offences and to prevent escapes of waste. Householders disposing of their own household waste are exempt from DOC, otherwise all waste holders are

expected to take reasonable steps in the *circumstances*, and ones that are appropriate to his/her *capacity* to ensure fulfilment of the duty. *'Circumstances'* in this context include what the waste is, the handling and treatment dangers it presents, how it is dealt with and what a holder can reasonably be expected to know and foresee, while *'capacity'* is determined by the degree of control a holder has and his/her connection with the waste. Furthermore a holder is only responsible for waste which is at some time under his/her control, though once one is in the 'chain' relating to a particular consignment of waste one is subject to the DOC.

It should be further noted that, under amendments made in 1995, where waste is transferred from person to person, and an appropriate written note of the waste should be transferred also, any transfer in stages is regarded as taking place where the first stage takes place, but a series of transfers between the same parties of waste of the same description is to be treated as a single transfer taking place when the first transfer in the series takes place.

COP 'fleshes out' DOC by advising waste holders first of all always to establish what the waste is, for example what is its legal status, what are the particular problems it presents (such as does it need special containers), can it be mixed with other waste, what can it not be mixed with, can it be crushed, can it be incinerated, if so at what temperature and for how long, and can it be landfilled? COP further advises on how an appropriate description of waste should be drawn up. It then proceeds to counsel waste holders to ensure that waste must be kept so that they are on guard for corrosion or wear of containers, accidental spills and leaks, accidents or breakages or weather conditions allowing waste to escape or blow away while in transit. They must also guard against thieves, scavengers and vandals. Particular advice is also given on ensuring transfers out take place to 'the right person'. Thus a carrier's registration should always be checked save in cases of repeated transfers by the same concern. Similarly the qualification of the next holder of the waste to receive the waste should be checked, eg by checking the terms and restrictions of a WML. Those who *receive* waste should always check its source and that it is being handed over in containers suitable for subsequent handling, etc.

On particular issues COP draws attention to being wary of waste that is wrongly or inadequately described on delivery, waste being taken away with incorrect packaging so it may escape, failure of consignees/consignors to complete the required notes, or apparent falsehoods on notes, unsupported claims of exemption from registration, failure of waste to arrive at its consigned destination.

There is a considerable amount of self regulation under COP. Relevant persons can only protect their own interests by insisting on strict compliance by others, by refusing to co-operate with infractions of DOC and by being prepared to report any such infractions to the Agency.

Particular requirements apply to transfer notes under SI 1991/2839, a form of which can be found in COP. Notes must identify waste, and say how much there is, what its containment is, times and place of transfer, names and addresses of transferor and transferee. These records then have to be kept for two years from the date of transfer and may be demanded by the Agency. Where, however, multiple consignments of waste take place within a year one transfer note may cover all provided the description of the waste and the identity of relevant parties, etc, remains the same.

The revision of COP was undertaken both to update the original version and also to take account of the application of DOC to the scrap metal recycling industry as from October 1995; that industry was previously exempted. Particular additions made in 1996 include advice on considering whether waste will change its state during transport or storage, and on 'checking on the source of waste'. Normally recipients of waste do not need to see the previous holder's WML, or registration as a carrier. It *may* not be an offence to receive waste from an unregistered carrier, but the self interest of recipients indicates the need to have full details of material in order to discharge their own duties.

Obtaining a WML

Those wishing to operate relevant operations are required to obtain a Waste Management Licence from the Agency under s 35. Such licences are also required, of course, for keeping or treating waste, and apply either to specified land or specified mobile plant. Licences are granted to persons — a point of distinction from the 1974 Act system — and are granted to occupiers of land and operators of mobile plant. Licences are granted on such terms and conditions as the Agency thinks appropriate and these may relate to the licensed activity and precautions to be taken and work to be done in connection with that activity, and they may relate to times *before and after* the activity is being carried out. Conditions may require a licensee to carry out works or do things despite his/her being unentitled to do them, and *any person* whose consent would be required *shall* grant the licensee such rights *in relation to the land* as will enable compliance with licence requirements; thus third parties, it appears, can be compelled to assist in the process of obtaining and operating a WML, perhaps in relation to the disposal site, perhaps in relation to the site of the required works or activities. Compensation may be payable by the licence holder in such circumstances under regulations to be made under s 35A. For consultation arrangements in such cases see below. Conditions may further relate, where waste *other* than controlled waste is to be treated, kept or disposed of, to the treatment, etc, of that waste.

It will be observed that the power to impose conditions is quite wide, and, in view of the overall emphasis of the 1990 Act on protection of the environment against pollution and the need to protect human health, including protection of the senses, and to protect property, seems to envisage the imposition of conditions going further than under the 1974 Act's provisions where there was a limitation to public health and water pollution issues.[5] However, note the powers of the Secretary of State under s 35(6) to make regulations to make provision as to conditions which are/are not to be included in licences, and under s 34(7) to issue mandatory directions to the Agency in respect of a licence application as to its terms and conditions. The Agency is also under a general duty under s 35(8) to have regard to the Secretary of State's guidance with regard to licences. Licences once granted may only be surrendered in particular circumstances (see further below) and are not transferable save by

5 *A-G's Reference (No 2 of 1988)* [1990] 1 QB 77, [1989] 3 WLR 397.

the Agency. Once in force a licence continues until it is revoked by the Agency or is surrendered.

Under amendments made in 1995 in any case where an entry has to be made in any records as to the observance of licence conditions and the entry is not made, that fact is evidence of non-observance of the condition. Furthermore any person who intentionally makes a false entry in any required records, or who forges a licence or possesses a document so closely resembling a licence it is likely to deceive commits an offence, see s 35 (7A)–(7C).

Applying for a licence

Applications must be made, under s 36, to the Agency; application will be made to the appropriate regional office bearing in mind the location of land, or, for mobile plant, the operator's place of business. The application must be made on a form provided by the Agency and accompanied by such information as they require, and by the due fee under s 41 of the Environment Act 1995 which generally makes provision for a scheme of fees. Failure to supply required information entitles the Agency to refuse to proceed with the application, s 36(1A). For the detailed information see the Waste Management Licensing Regulations 1994. Some form of planning permission either in the form of a grant or established use rights, is needed before a licence can be issued. Before issuing a licence the Agency must also refer the issue to the appropriate planning authority and the HSE and consider any representations they make. Where the land in question, or any part of it, has been subject to a notification under s 28(1) of the Wildlife and Countryside Act 1981 (see chapter 6) the application must be further referred to the appropriate nature conservancy body, eg in England, English Nature, for their views. Subject to the foregoing the Agency may not reject a licence application unless satisfied the applicant is *not* a 'fit and proper person' to hold a licence, or where satisfied rejection is necessary to prevent pollution of the environment, harm to human health or, where planning permission is not in force, serious detriment to local amenity.

Thus an application *must* be refused where there is a lack of planning permission for the proposed use of land, and *may* be refused where the Agency concludes this is necessary to prevent pollution of the environment or harm to human health, or serious detriment to the amenities of the locality, though this last ground is not applicable where planning permission is in force in relation to the use to which the land will be put under the licence. Furthermore a licence *may* be refused if the applicant is not a 'fit and proper person' (see further below).

In the exercise of their discretion the Agency must, under the 1994 regulations, and to meet the requirements of the Groundwater Directive 80/68, only grant a licence if under licence conditions technical precautions can be taken to prevent discharges of List I substances under the Directive, and groundwater pollution by List II substances. They must also bear in mind overall waste management policy and a principle of proportionality declared in Circular 11/94, that the use of regulatory powers should be proportionate to the risks involved and benefits to be obtained, that it should always be aimed at achieving specific goals, that it is not an end in itself, should not be over prescriptive and should not impose unjustifiable burdens on those subject to regulation.

Where the Agency fails within four months from the date of application to grant or refuse a licence the application is deemed rejected (save in a case where the agency is entitled to refuse to proceed under s 36(1A)). Note that under s 44 it is an offence in an application for a licence (or its modification, surrender or transfer) to make any statement known to be false or recklessly made. The period allowed for consultations under s 36 is 28 days, though this may be extended. Section 36A, however, lays down particular consultation requirements in certain cases. Where an application is made and the Agency proposes to grant the licence subject to conditions under s 35 which might require its holder to carry out works or do other things which he/she might not be entitled to carry out or do, they must serve a notice on every person who is the owner, lessee or occupier of any land over which rights will have to be granted to enable compliance with conditions. The notice must set out the nature of the works, etc, needed under the condition in question, and grant a period in which the recipient of the notice may make representations to the Agency — that period must be of such length as is specified in regulations to be made by the Secretary of State. Representations received in relation to such a notice must be taken into account.

Fit and proper persons

In the granting of a WML much will depend on whether the applicant is a 'fit and proper person'. Section 74 amplifies the meaning of this expression. The determination of the matter is firmly placed by s 74(2) in the context of 'the carrying on by [the person] of the activities which are or are to be authorised by the licence and the fulfilment of [its] requirements'. However, a person is *not* 'fit and proper' if it appears to the Agency that he/she or another 'relevant person' has been convicted of a 'relevant offence'. The 'taint' of an offence, it will be noted, also arises where the 'relevant offence' was committed by some other 'relevant' person. Effectively such others *include*: employees who have committed the offence during the course of employment by the licensee or would-be licensee; business partners; companies where the offence in question was committed while the licensee, etc, was a director, manager, secretary, etc, of the company making the application who has already been convicted of a relevant offence, *or* those persons who have held such offices in another company at a time when a relevant offence was committed by that company and of which it has been convicted. 'Relevant offences' are specified in the 1994 regulations, reg 3, and *include* offences under the Control of Pollution Act 1974 waste provisions, under the Control of Pollution (Amendment) Act 1989, under ss 23(1), 33, 34(6), 44, 47(6), 57(5), 59(5), 63(2), 71(3), 80(4) of the Environmental Protection Act 1990, under ss 85, 202 or 206 of the Water Resources Act 1991 (see chapter 12) or s 33 of the Clean Air Act 1993 (see chapter 10). It should be noted that 'non-environment specific' offences such as those of dishonesty are not included, as neither are those under town and country planning legislation.

'Fit and proper' status is also refused to those who are unable to show that the management of authorised activities will be in the hands of a 'technically competent person' (TCP). This requirement is 'fleshed out' by regulations, and qualifications are those instituted by the Waste Management Industry Training and Advisory Board (WAMITAB). Under regs 4 and 5 and Table 1 of the 1994 Regulations the technical competence requirements are met by those holding relevant WAMITAB certificates. However, to meet the needs of those 'qualified by years of service', ie 'existing managers' as they are known, 'transitional' qualification is extended to those registered as applicants for certificates with WAMITAB before 10 August 1994 who in the 12 months before application were managers of relevant types of facility. However, the exemption only lasts until 10 August 1999 to allow time for WAMITAB qualifications to be gained. Similarly where a person was 55 or over on 10 August 1994 and in the ten years previously had at least five years experience as manager of a relevant type of facility, the requirement for WAMITAB certification does not apply until 10 August 2004. This is the so-called 'grandfather exception'. Finally 'fit and proper' status is to be refused to those licensees, or applicants, who have not made and either do not intend to, or are not able to, make *financial provision adequate to discharge the obligations arising from the licence,* including post-closure obligations, and provision adequate to meet planning requirements as to after care and restoration of sites.

Guidance issued centrally is here less clear than on other 'fit and proper' issues. Waste Management Paper (WMP) 4 argues that operators should obtain insurance or show they can be their own insurers. Financial provision issues are particularly relevant at the stages of site acquisition and preparation, site operation, site restoration and landscaping or after care, and in relation to post closure controls and monitoring. While specific financial provisions may appear in a licence in order to meet particular obligations, in general an applicant's financial provision is to be considered by reference to licence obligations. WMP 4 counsels the Agency to look at an applicant's business plan in relation to the life of facilities such as landfill sites — though the existence of such a plan is never a guarantee of business success.

Variation of licences

Variation of licences is allowed by s 37, either on the Agency's initiative, though only to the extent that variation is both desirable and unlikely to impose unreasonable expense on the licensee, and on the licensee's application to the extent requested, in which case a fee is payable. The Agency *must* also modify licence conditions to the extent they consider necessary to ensure that licensed activities do not cause pollution of the environment, harm to human health or serious detriment to local amenity, or to comply with any regulations issued under s 35(6), see above. The Secretary of State may also direct modifications of conditions. Modifications are effected by notice served on the licensee, but are generally subject to a consultation procedure similar to that for licence applications. A deemed refusal of a modification application takes place if the Agency fails either to grant or refuse an application within two months of its date of receipt. DoE Circular 20/90 suggested review of licence conditions where waste containing List I substances under Directive 80/68 (the Groundwater Directive) are landfilled to prevent pollution of groundwater.

Under s 37A where the Agency propose to modify a licence under their own initiative, or where this is required for the purpose of preventing pollution of the environment or harm to human health, or detriment to local amenities, *and* the licence as modified would be subject to a 'relevant new condition' (ie a condition requiring the carrying out of works or doing of things which the holder might be entitled to do and could not be required to do under the pre-existing conditions) they must serve notice on relevant landholders who may have to grant rights to that licensee to enable compliance with the new condition(s). The notice must give details of the nature of the works in question and state a period within which affected landholders may make representations which will have to be taken into account before the modification is made. Compensation may be payable in such cases to affected landholders by the licensee, see s 35A.

Revocation and suspension of licences

Where it appears to the Agency that the holder of a WML has ceased to be 'fit and proper' by reason of having been convicted of a 'relevant offence' *or* that continuation of the licensed activities would cause pollution of the environment, harm to human health or serious detriment to local amenities, *and* that this cannot be avoided by modifying licence conditions, they have a choice of powers under s 38(3) and (4). In addition where it appears the licensee has ceased to be 'fit and proper' by reason of licensed activities ceasing to be in the hands of a TCP the Agency may exercise its s 38(3) powers. Section 38(3) empowers revocation of a licence so far as it authorises the carrying on of activities specified in the licence *or* such of them as the Agency specifies in the revocation. Section 38(4), however, allows the revocation of a licence entirely. Where a licence is revoked under s 38(3) it ceases to have effect to authorise the activities specified in the licence, or, as the case may be, the activities specified by the Agency on revocation, but revocation does *not* affect any requirements imposed by the licence which the Agency on revocation specifies as continuing to bind the licensee.

Suspension may occur where it appears to the Agency that the licence holder has ceased to be 'fit and proper' by virtue of the lack of management of activities by a TCP, *or* that serious pollution of the environment, etc, has resulted from, or is about to result from, licensed activities, *or* the happening or threatened happening of an event affecting those activities, *and* that the continuation of those activities or any of them will continue to cause or may cause *serious* pollution of the environment or serious harm to human health. Suspension may take place of authorisation of activities specified in the licence or such of them as are specified in the suspension. The Secretary of State may give directions as to the exercise of these powers.

During a suspension the Agency may require the licence holder to take steps to deal with or avert the pollution, etc, and it is an offence to fail to comply with such requirements, with enhanced penalties applying where there is a failure to comply with any requirements relating to any special waste. Where criminal proceedings would be an inadequate remedy the Agency may take proceedings in the High Court for injunctive relief, etc, see s 38(10)–(13). Requirements imposed may require the licence holder to carry out works he/she is not entitled to do — a situation already encountered before with regard to waste issues. The 1990 Act as amended in 1995 here follows the usual pattern of requiring consultation with other affected landholders and the taking into account of any representations received from them, though s 38(9C) specifically allows the postponement of service of any notice or the consideration of any representations received where by reason of an emergency it is appropriate to do so. As before a compensation liability may arise for the licence holder.

Surrender

Licences may be surrendered under s 39 but only if the Agency accepts the surrender. In order to surrender the licensee must apply on a form provided by the Agency giving such information as is required and such other information as is reasonably required, and paying the appropriate fee. The Agency must proceed to inspect the land in question and may require the furnishing of further information and evidence. The Agency must then determine whether it is likely or unlikely that the condition of the land resulting from its use (even where not permitted by the licence) will cause pollution of the environment or harm to human health. Only if satisfied that harm is unlikely to be caused by the condition of the land may a surrender be accepted. In all other cases surrender must be refused. Where the Agency proposes to accept a surrender they must first refer the matter to the appropriate planning authority, eg a London borough council, a non-metropolitan county council, a National Parks Authority, a unitary authority, or in Wales the relevant county or county borough council as the case may be. They must consider any representations made, generally within a period of 28 days beginning with the day on which the proposed surrender is received by the Agency or such longer period as is agreed. On the accepted surrender the Agency must issue the applicant with a notice of its determination and a 'certificate of completion' stating its satisfaction as to the lack of likelihood of pollution, etc, and thereupon the licence ceases to have effect. A deemed refusal of an application takes place three months after receipt of the application if the Agency neither accepts nor rejects it. It may not be assumed that completing surrender arrangements will be easy, and initial attitudes amongst the former Waste Regulation Authorities suggested they would require a deal of proof before declaring themselves satisfied as to the lack of pollution in a closed site. However, as yet there is little evidence on which to base a firm opinion.

Transfers and appeals

Licences may be transferred under s 40, even where partly revoked or suspended. The procedure is that the licensee and proposed transferee must make a joint transfer application to the Agency. The usual requirements as to information and fees apply. The Agency, if satisfied the transferee is 'fit and proper' must effect the transfer. A transfer not effected within two months of the date of receipt of the request is deemed refused.

Appeals by disappointed applicants, transferors, etc, are made under s 43 to the Secretary of State who is empowered to make regulations to determine the manner and form of appeals.

Where an appeal is made if a party to it so requests, or if the Secretary of State so decides, the appeal shall take the form of a hearing, which may be held in private. Under s 114 of the Environment Act 1995 the Secretary of State has delegated the function of determining appeals to planning inspectors. In general under s 43(4) while an appeal is pending a modification or revocation of a licence has no effect, though the Agency may circumvent this by stating in the notice of modification, etc, that the action is necessary to prevent, or minimise if prevention is not practicable, pollution of the environment, etc, see s 43(6). A suspension, however, is not affected by an appeal, see s 43(5).

Where a decision under appeal is one to modify or revoke a licence the licence holder may apply to the Secretary of State for a determination that the Agency acted unreasonably in excluding the operation of s 43(4), and in the case of a suspension an application may be made for a determination that this was unreasonable. If the appeal is still pending when a decision is made that the exclusion of s 43(4) or the suspension, as the case may be, was unreasonable, then s 43(4) will apply *and* compensation may be payable to the licensee in respect of loss suffered.

Under the Waste Management Licensing Regulations 1994 appeals have to be brought within six months of the decision in question.

Note that no appeal can be made where a decision has been taken by direction of the Secretary of State, for example, as to the terms and conditions of a licence, or as to suspension, revocation or modification. In such a case seeking judicial review of the Secretary of State's action would be the appropriate remedy. This is also the situation where a third party wishes to challenge the grant or the terms of a WML.[6]

Supervisory powers

Section 42 imposes important supervisory functions on the agency concerning waste disposal. Their overriding task is to ensure that authorised activities do not pollute the environment, harm human health or become a detriment to local amenity, and to ensure licence conditions are complied with. In emergencies authorised officers of the Agency may carry out work on relevant land or plant to ensure performance of supervision, and may recover their expenditure in this connection from the licensee. The Agency may also require compliance with licence conditions. The power to require compliance arises where it appears to the Agency that a condition is either not being complied with or is likely not to be complied with. In such circumstances they may serve notice on the licence holder stating their opinion, specifying the matters constituting the non-compliance or anticipated non-compliance, and specifying remedial or preventive action and the time within which action is to be taken, see s 42(5), as amended. If the required steps are not taken the Agency may under s 42(6) revoke the licence in whole or in part, or suspend it, while if this would afford an ineffectual remedy they may under s 42(6A) seek injunctive relief in the High Court. In the exercise of the s 42 powers the Agency is subject to direction by the Secretary of State.

Special waste and its disposal

'Special waste' is that waste in respect of which regulations are in force under s 62 of the 1990 Act. This provides that where the Secretary of State considers that controlled waste of any kind is or may be so dangerous or difficult to treat, keep or dispose of that special provision is needed for dealing with it, he/she may by regulations make provision for its treatment, etc. These regulations

---

6 *R v Vale of Glamorgan Borough Council & Associated British Ports, ex p James* [1996] 8 ELM 12.

may, inter alia, include provision: for the Agency to give directions in connection with the treatment, keeping or disposal of such waste; to secure that pending treatment, etc, that special waste is kept only in specified quantities; in connection with requirements imposed on consignors or consignees of such waste where such requirements are not met, to impose further requirements on any carrier of the waste to redeliver it as directed; to require any occupier of premises where special waste is situated to give notice of that fact and other information as prescribed. Provision may also be made for records of special waste to be kept by the Agency and those who import, export, keep, treat or dispose of special waste or deliver it to others for treatment, etc. Regulations may also provide, inter alia, for the supervision by the Agency of activities authorised by regulations and of persons carrying on authorised activities, for the recovery from such persons of the costs of supervision, and for the recovery of costs in respect of treating, keeping, disposing or redelivering special waste incurred under the regulations. Regulations in respect of special waste were originally made under the Control of Pollution Act 1974 in order to discharge obligations under Directive 78/319. This Directive was replaced by 91/689 — the Directive on Hazardous Waste — under which a list of hazardous wastes was drawn up by 1994 and the current regulations are SI 1996/972.

Under the 1996 regulations 'special waste' includes:

1   Material listed by Council Decision 94/904, and specified in Part 1 of Sch 2 of the regulations, provided it has a six digit code number, eg certain acids and alkalis.
2   Certain other waste considered by the UK, under art 4 of Directive 91/689, to display certain hazardous properties, eg it is toxic, corrosive, irritant or carcinogenic. Also included are medicinal products, while household waste is excluded.

The regulations also establish a consignment note system in respect of special waste movements. Consignment notes are required to travel with special waste and copies must be sent to the Agency, which must also be informed in advance of special waste movements. Initially the special waste's producer must prepare a note in five parts (A-E) of which there must be six copies. Parts A and B must give a precise description of the waste, the size, type and numbers of its containers, its collection point and destination. These details are filled in by the producer. One copy is then sent to the Agency to arrive not more than one month nor less than 72 hours before removal of the waste. The carrier of the waste then fills in part C before removing it, and the consignor fills in part D stating the carrier has been told of appropriate precautions. Part E is then completed by the waste's consignee who certifies receipt and sends the completed note to the Agency immediately. Disposers must also keep records of the location of special waste deposits. To cover consignments between the same consignee and consignor of the same type of waste between the same places in a 12 month period, a modified consignment note procedure applies.

Those who consign special waste must keep a register of consignment notes at their sites for a minimum of three years, with similar obligations being imposed on waste carriers and consignees, while the Agency also keeps notes under s 64.

A failure to comply with regulation requirements is a criminal offence. These requirements are cumulative to those under DOC and COP.

The new special waste regulations were issued for consultation in March 1995. As stated, they now reflect the 1991 Hazardous Waste Directive, and the key details of the changes are:

1   There is the new definition of special waste to embrace both the EU list of hazardous waste (some 250 separate classes defined by origin or chemical character) and various other wastes which are 'special' according to characteristics — in such cases the waste will possess one of a number of specified hazardous characteristics, such as flammability or toxicity.
2   The pre-notification requirements are simplified, with wasteholders being able to pre-notify a series of repetitive movements, and carriers being able to pre-notify collection rounds, while the consignment note has been redesigned to help wasteholders provide descriptions of their waste and its associated hazards.
3   Fees are payable when movements are pre-notified in order to recover supervisory costs in line with the polluter pays principle.
4   Restrictions are introduced on mixing by carriers and consignees of different special wastes, and of special and non-special waste.

The new special waste regulations were made and laid before Parliament on 1 April 1996 to come into force on 1 September 1996.

Miscellaneous waste powers

The Secretary of State may, under s 57 of the 1990 Act, by notice direct the holder of any WML to accept and keep, or accept and treat or dispose of, controlled waste at specified places on specified terms. The Secretary of State may by notice in writing direct any person keeping controlled waste on any land to deliver the waste to a specified person on specified terms with a view to its being dealt with by that person. Directions may impose particular requirements in respect of specified kinds of waste, and may also relate to the payment of costs in respect of dealing with the waste. It is an offence to fail to comply with such a direction.

Section 59 applies where any controlled waste is deposited in or on any land in contravention of s 33(1). The Agency or the relevant WCA may by notice served on the occupier of that land require that person to remove the waste within a specified period of not less than 21 days, and/or to take within such a period specified steps with a view to eliminating or reducing the consequences of the waste's deposit. A person served with such a notice may appeal to the justices and they must quash the notice if satisfied that the appellant neither deposited nor knowingly caused nor knowingly permitted the deposit, or that there is a material defect in the notice. In any other case they may either modify the requirements or dismiss the appeal. Where an appeal is made the requirements of the notice are suspended pending the appeal's determination, but it is otherwise an offence to fail to comply with a requirement unless there is a reasonable excuse. Where a person fails to comply with a notice the authority which served the notice may do what that person was required to do and may recover their reasonable costs from that person.

Where it appears that waste has been deposited in contravention of s 33(1) and that it is necessary that the waste be forthwith removed or that other steps should be taken to reduce or eliminate the consequences of the deposit in order to remove or prevent pollution of land, water or air or harm to human life, *or* that the land in question has no occupier, *or* that the occupier neither made nor knowingly permitted the deposit, the Agency or the relevant WCA may undertake the necessary measures, and may recover their reasonable costs either from the land's occupier unless he/she can prove his/her innocence of the deposit, or, in any case, from the actual depositor.

Waste other than controlled waste

The Secretary of State may under s 63 of the 1990 Act make regulations providing that prescribed portions of waste provisions shall have effect in prescribed areas as if references in those provisions to controlled waste included references to waste from any mine or quarry and waste from agricultural premises of specified kinds, though with such modifications as may be specified.

In December 1995 it was proposed by the government to extend waste management controls to certain types of agricultural and mining and quarrying waste. Such controls were said to be likely to come into effect by the end of 1996.

Conclusion

How far does the current law meet the criticisms levelled against its predecessor? A *start* towards stressing the importance of recycling is made, and policy stresses the importance of waste reduction and re-use, but there is no general legal duty on producers or vendors of goods to minimise waste production in the first place. The 'cradle to grave' duty of care is to be welcomed, as is the element of licensing only fit and proper persons, though it was open to question whether the WRAs had enough trained staff to ensure proper policing of these requirements alongside all their other supervisory functions: this question will also affect the Agency. There remains the legacy of improperly supervised and unfenced sites, some of them crossed by public footpaths see HC Welsh Affairs Committee First Report Session 1989/90, 'Toxic Waste Disposal in Wales'. Indeed there has been inadequate data on how controlled waste has been currently landfilled with no national data base as to landfill sites, their locations, age, type, throughput, ownership and management, though the *estimates* in the early 1990s were that there were 2,500 private licensed sites and 600 local authority sites. It was then considered that enhanced controls under the 1990 Act could lead to up to 80% of private sites ceasing to exist in current form. See further HC Environment Committee Session 1990–91 'Report on the Draft Directive on the Landfill of Waste'. Certainly one consequence of the 1990 Act appears to have been a contraction in the number of waste disposal companies, and the concentration of the industry. One further issue to cause concern is whether *landfill* sites may prove inadequate to receive the nation's rubbish leading to its landward disposal by *land raise*.

Finally it should be noted that there are commentators who argue that current regulations remain too lax, and that the government's regulatory resolve weakens too often in the face of opposition from the waste disposal industry. On the other hand the industry's major operators are quick to point to their generally good record of operation, and it is true that the vast majority of waste offences are committed by small 'one man and a dog' operators who either do not know, or who do not care, about legal and professional standards of operation. Furthermore it is true to say that the prosecution policies of the former WRAs differed greatly, though that, of course, could have had much to do with the different amounts and types of waste arising in different parts of the country. In addition it is clear that on the whole the justices, before whom the majority of waste offences are tried, have not taken so serious a view of such offences as they have with regard to water pollution offences. Levels of fines have been generally quite low, while in some cases defendants have been able to avoid fines by some highly dubious mitigatory pleas, eg 'I needed to break the law a little in order to raise money to meet other clean up liabilities.'

It remains to be seen what the Agency will make of the law relating to waste.

Litter

Litter continues to be a depressingly obvious manifestation of the problem of waste in a society over-devoted to disposability, over-packaging and not sufficiently concerned with health and amenity. Legislation was placed on the statute book on the issue in 1958 and 1971, consolidated in 1983 as the Litter Act, but to little avail. In 1989 a consultation paper on litter was issued and Part IV of EPA 1990 accordingly addressed itself to the problem.

Section 86 designates principal litter authorities; in England and Wales these are, generally, counties, districts and London boroughs. It proceeds to define 'relevant land' of such authorities as that which is open to the air and is land (other than a highway) under the direct control of an authority to which the public are entitled or permitted to have access with or without payment. It seems authorities need not *own* the land, but they must superintend it.[7] Other land may be 'relevant land' of bodies such as the Crown, statutory undertakers, educational institutions, though sometimes ministerial designation is required. Likewise responsibility for litter on highways is initially placed in England and Wales on districts and London boroughs, though s 86(11) permits ministerial transfer of responsibility for cleaning functions to highway authorities, and see SI 1991/337 for such a transfer. For descriptions of 'relevant land' see SI 1991/476, SI 1991/561 and SI 1991/1043.

Under s 89 it is the duty of principal litter authorities as respects their relevant land, and other bodies as respects theirs, together with the occupiers of relevant land within a litter control area as designated (by principal litter authorities acting in accordance with regulations made under s 90 and see SI 1991/1325) to ensure that land is, so far as is practicable, kept clear of refuse and litter. Commensurate duties are placed on local authorities (districts, etc) and the Secretary of State in respect of highways, trunk roads and motorways, and their duty extends to keeping roads, so far as practicable, clean. In setting

---

7 *Johnston Fear & Kingham v Commonwealth* (1943) 67 CLR 314; *Pardoe v Pardoe* (1900) 82 LT 547.

a standard of freedom from litter and cleanliness regard is to be had to the character and use of the land as well as the practicality of measures, while litter and refuse may be defined by regulations and may extend to animal faeces (see SI 1991/961), while a Code of Practice may give guidance in relation to the discharge of the above duties. Such a Code was issued in January 1991 and this stresses the need for land to be kept clean, though it does not lay down minimum cleaning frequencies. It also stresses practicability pointing out that litter clearance from motorways, for example, may entail traffic restrictions and these may take time to plan, while bad weather may also hold up cleaning. Four standards of cleanliness are illustrated in the code, A-D — from no litter to heavily littered. A is the 'ideal' grade which 'a thorough conventional sweeping/litter picking should achieve in most circumstances — although . . . it may not last for very long.' The code further divides land into 11 broad categories of zones ranging from general (town centres, residential areas, etc) through beaches, roads, educational institutions, railway embankments to canal towpaths where the various grades of cleanliness should be achieved either at particular times or over particular periods, with 'A' always as the ideal standard, and 'trigger points' to indicate where cleaning to A grade should occur. Two further key principles are laid down, that habitually heavily trafficked areas should be cleaned more regularly than less used areas while larger accumulations should be cleared more quickly than smaller ones. Further non-statutory advice is given on appraisal and action strategies, anti-litter campaigning, education and training programmes.

Where a member of the public (which would certainly include a resident in the area or a regular visitor) is 'aggrieved' because the s 89 duties have been breached, complaint may be made to the justices (in England and Wales) under s 91 against the person who has the duty to keep the land clear or clean as the case may be, though before instituting proceedings the complainant must have given the person in breach a minimum of five days' written notice of intention to complain, specifying the matter complained of. If the justices are satisfied that the land, etc, in question is defaced by litter and that the defendant has not complied with his/her duties, they make a litter abatement order requiring remedial action; failure to comply with this constitutes an offence, and compensation may be payable by the defendant to the complainant. In coming to their decision the justices will consider the Code of Practice. Note, however, that though the Crown has duties with regard to litter, it may not be prosecuted for their breach, see s 159(2). Principal litter authorities may not take action under s 91 but under s 92 certain authorities (principally districts and London boroughs) are to be actors in respect of certain land, eg that of a statutory undertaker, or land within a litter control area, though highways are excluded from the ambit of this power. The procedure is similar to that under s 91 though authorities are also given default powers under s 92(9) in cases of non-compliance.

Section 93 empowers certain authorities (effectively districts and London boroughs) to issue 'street litter control notices' with a view to preventing accumulations of litter in and around streets or adjacent open land. Such notices impose obligations on occupiers of premises in relation to litter. Relevant premises are those which fall within descriptions of commercial or retail premises prescribed by the Secretary of State under s 94 (see SI 1991/1324) and which have a frontage to a street where there is recurrent defacement by litter or refuse of the street, etc, in the vicinity of the premises, or where the premises include open land in the vicinity of the frontage whose condition is, and is likely to continue to be, detrimental to amenity by the presence of litter, etc, or there is produced as a result of activities on the premises quantities of litter, etc, of such an amount and nature as likely to cause defacement of the street in the vicinity. Notices must identify the premises and the grounds on which they are served, and the requirements they may impose may relate to provision or emptying of litter receptacles, carrying out specified works or activities either once and for all or periodically. Before notice is serviced the person to be served must be informed and given 21 days in which to make representations which must be taken into account before the authority decide the issue. A person served may appeal to the justices and the court may uphold, vary, quash or add to the notice. Where there is failure to comply with such a notice the authority may apply to the court for an order requiring compliance, and it is an offence to fail to comply with such an order, see s 94(4)–(9). Relevant authorities are to keep public registers of street litter control notices, and also of litter control areas, see s 95.

Section 99 allows local authorities, in England and Wales effectively districts and London boroughs, to apply, after consultation with affected persons and due advertisement in the local press, the provisions of Sch 4 of EPA 1990. This applies to abandoned shopping or luggage trolleys and allows their seizure, removal, or retention subject to notice to their owners, disposal or return to their owners, subject to a power in authorities to charge in respect of the activities. Authorities may also agree schemes of collection with trolley owners. In this connection it may be asked why more supermarket owners do not follow the French example of charging a deposit on trolleys, coupled with a locking mechanism to ensure payment; Messrs Sainsburys have this feature at some of their stores.

Note that, under s 96, the Secretary of State may extend the application of Part II of EPA 1990 to litter collected, inter alia, in pursuance of the s 89 duty. Such an extension would allow, for example, recycling of the material on the same basis as controlled waste. It appears, however, that commercial rubbish deposited (some of it in sacks) on a highway, though it falls within waste controls as within the definition of s 5(7) of the 1990 Act, also constitutes litter within ss 87(1) and (5). Thus where such waste is deposited pending collection its depositor runs a risk of also being prosecuted for a litter offence.[8] It remains an offence under s 88 for any person to leave litter in public open places or on highways or land of statutory undertakers, and guilty parties may be tried before the magistrates or made subject by authorised officers of relevant authorities to fixed penalties, see SI 1991/111.

An assessment of the litter provisions

It is possible to take widely differing views on how the litter provisions are working. In 1994 ministers stated that the Advisory Group on Litter had concluded that the law had produced significant benefits in public cleanliness, but there was still room for improvement. Specific targets for improvement were stated to be:

---

8 *Westminster City Council v Riding* [1995] 7 ELM 208.

1   Publication of information to citizens about how local authorities propose to fulfil litter duties.
2   Improving procedures for local authorities to deal with litter on private land.
3   Improved powers for authorities to target business activities which result in litter on adjacent public areas.
4   Introducing a national offence of failure to clean up after one's dog has befouled a public area.
5   Enhancing the fixed penalty litter system and extending it to dog fouling offences.
6   Increasing fixed penalty fines from £10 to £25.

Action remains to be taken on these proposals. More recently (January 1996) the Tidy Britain Group published in 'The State of the Nation 1996' evidence of wide variation in local authority responses to litter problems. Survey evidence showed that only 10% of sites were litter free, 76% had scattered small items, 12% had 'accumulations' of litter while 3% were 'strewn' with litter. Meanwhile the 'Beachwatch '95' survey found *twice* as much litter on beaches in 1995 as in 1994.

D RADIOACTIVE WASTE

Much waste disposal is controversial, but rarely as controversial as proposals to dispose of radioactive material, which usually raise fierce opposition in any affected area, as witness proposals to deposit material at Billingham, defeated by local opposition in 1985, and the abandonment of proposals in 1987 to establish a low level nuclear waste dump and consequent tests at Bradwell, Fulbeck, Elstow and South Killingholme, after intense public campaigns against the plans. Seaward disposal, see generally chapter 12, took place from 1949 onwards, but became subject to a degree of international regulation following the 1972 London Dumping Convention's inception in 1975, and then ceased following industrial action by ships' crews in 1983.

Dumping at sea is also subject to the 1972 Oslo and 1974 Paris Conventions (OSPAR) which are due to be replaced by the Convention for the Protection of the Marine Environment of the North East Atlantic signed by the UK in 1992. This will ban the disposal at sea of *all* radioactive waste, and it is currently being voluntarily applied in UK waters. However, it remains UK government policy that disposal at sea of low level solid radioactive waste (see further below) is the BPEO for bulk waste arising from decommissioned nuclear plants and OSPAR grants both the UK and France the *option* to resume sea dumping after a period of 15–25 years. This option is now, however, subject to an indefinite ban (adopted by the consultative meeting of parties to the 1972 London Convention which is a global treaty) on the seaward dumping of low and intermediate level waste. This ban was accepted by the UK in 1994, and this country also adheres to the pre-existing London Convention ban on seaward dumping of high level waste. The consequence is that landward disposal of waste remains the only option.

International guidelines and regulations

Various bodies lay down standards for the management of radioactive waste. The International Commission on Radiological Protection (ICRP) in 1990 produced revised guidelines, while the International Atomic Energy Agency (IAEA) established by the UN in 1957 has created a Radioactive Waste Safety Standards Programme (RADWASS) and has recently issued 'The Principles of Radioactive Waste Management' and 'Establishing a National System for Radioactive Waste Management'. The IAEA's fundamental safety guidelines are:

1 Waste must be managed so as to secure an acceptable level of human health protection.
2 Waste must be managed so as to provide an acceptable level of environmental protection.
3 In managing waste its possible effects on human health and the environment beyond national borders must be taken into account.
4 Waste management must proceed on the basis that predicted impacts on the health of future generations will not be greater than relevant levels of impact acceptable today.
5 Waste management today must not place unacceptable burdens on future generations.
6 National legal frameworks must allocate clear responsibilities with an independent regulatory framework.
7 Generation of waste shall be minimised.
8 Interdependencies in waste generation and management must always be taken into account.
9 The safety of management facilities must be appropriately assured during their lifetime.

These principles were largely echoed at the Earth Summit in Rio, 1992, and were reflected in Agenda 21. The UK's policy response in 'Sustainable Development — The UK Strategy' (1994) Cm 2426 (see also Cm 2822) was that radioactive waste should be managed safely so that the present generation may meet its responsibilities to future generations.

The EU is also committed to the development of a radioactive waste management strategy, while under the Treaty of the European Atomic Energy Community (Euratom) Euratom Basic Safety Standards Directive which lays down guidance on protection of nuclear industry workers and the public is being revised to take account the ICRP guidance referred to above.

The types of radioactive waste

[For the formal definition of such waste see below, s 2 of the Radioactive Substances Act 1993.] Waste is of four sorts: 'low-level' (not exceeding 4 GB q/te alpha or 12 GB q/te beta gamma levels); 'intermediate level' (above low level radiation limits, but not requiring heating to be considered in designing storage or disposal facilities); 'high level' or 'heat generating' wastes (wastes in which temperatures may rise significantly in consequence of radioactivity so as to require consideration of this fact in designing storage and/or disposal facilities); 'very low level waste' with the very lowest levels of activity may be disposed of with household refuse, eg the single item with less than 40 kBq beta gamma activity. High level waste comes in the form of a concentrated liquid and contains over 95% of total radioactivity from nuclear industrial waste: by the late 1980s some 1,000 cubic metres of such waste had been created. Intermediate level waste comes in both solid and liquid forms from power stations, fuel reprocessing, used reactor parts, nuclear fuel cladding, effluent treatment sludge, etc. Low level waste can be solid, liquid or gaseous, and includes matter such as used clothing and laboratory equipment from the nuclear industry, research institutions and hospitals. By the late 1980s/early 1990s some 30 cubic metres of high level waste was being produced annually in the UK, 3,000 cubic metres of intermediate level waste and 45,000 cubic metres of low level waste. By 2030, it was predicted in 1988, there would be 0.25 million cubic metres of intermediate level waste and 1.5 million cubic metres of low level waste from civil sources, with defence sources adding to this figure by 20%. That amount would be *less* than 50% of the then current annual production of toxic chemical waste. In addition, facilities that have run on nuclear power have to be disposed of. Nuclear submarines may have to be stored on land for 50–100 years before their reactor compartments can be removed, even following fuel removal, for international agreement (London 1972) has placed a moratorium on their sinking in the deep ocean, along with other forms of nuclear waste. Redundant nuclear power stations after removal of fuel *may* be left in 'deferred safe store' for 30 years, subject to constant security and regular inspection; then they would be encased in structures for a further 100 years and mounded over.

Current practice on nuclear waste is that high level waste is currently *stored* and cooled, and from 1990 onwards is increasingly being vitrified at Sellafield by BNFL. This process reduces the waste's volume by two thirds, but it can still produce heat for 50 years, and so the current policy is that it should be kept in an above ground secure *store* for at least 90 years, but thereafter some final *disposal* decision will have to be made. Most of this high level waste is the 3% of unusable waste left after BNFL has reprocessed spent nuclear fuel, 96% of which can be used again, and 1% of which becomes plutonium. The process is carried out for British reactors, though BNFL reprocesses fuel from overseas; nowadays most contracts for this latter purpose have clauses requiring customers to take back reprocessing wastes arising. Intermediate level waste is also dealt with by BNFL and as from 1991 is sealed in a £249m encapsulation plant ('the Cell') at Sellafield into concrete filled steel drums which are then *stored*, but again a long term *disposal* route will have to be found. Low level waste has been landfilled at Drigg, near Sellafield, by BNFL but is now placed at their site into specially constructed concrete vaults. Liquid low level waste, mainly cooling pond water from fuel rod cooling processes is 'cleaned' in the Site Ion Exchange Effluent Plant (SIXEP) before discharge to the sea, the extracted waste being encapsulated, once again, in concrete. An Enhanced Actimide Removal plant was scheduled to commence operations in the 1990s to further 'clean' the water so that discharge levels are negligible (see generally chapter 12).

It is clear that a distinction has to be made between 'disposal' and 'storage'. The latter is an *interim* practice designed to hold waste (currently high and intermediate level) in a facility until long term action, ie disposal, with no intention to take further action save some monitoring, is undertaken. Currently only low level waste is disposed of, but, as stated, policy is to *dispose* of all waste, despite much expert opinion that the search for an acceptable disposal site for high and intermediate level waste is unnecessary and that the waste could be stored for a long period.

Disposal: the regulatory framework

Disposal sites have to be found. But how should they be selected and monitored, and is existing legal control over waste in general sufficient? A number of bodies and institutions have responsibilities here.

Responsibility for radioactive waste management is shared between the government (maker of overall policy), the regulators (who implement policy) and waste producers (who manage it in accordance with regulatory requirements, and who, in accordance with the polluter pays principle, must have adequate financial provision to meet present and future liabilities).

The Secretary of State for the Environment (along with the Secretaries for Scotland, Wales and Northern Ireland) is the prime policy maker though there are inputs from MAFF, the DTI and the Ministry of Defence (MoD) and the HSE (see chapter 3). The government is advised by: the Radioactive Waste Management Committee (RAWMAC) an independent body of experts established in 1977, consisting of persons with expertise from nuclear, academic and medical backgrounds as well as lay persons; the Advisory Committee on the Safety of Nuclear Installations (ACSNI) set up in 1977 to advise on major safety issues affecting installations, and appointed partly by the Health and Safety Commission (HSC) and partly by the Confederation of British Industry (CBI) and the Trades Union Congress (TUC); the Ionising Radiation Advisory Committee (IRAC) created in 1995 by the HSC to consider all matters relating to protection against exposure to ionising radiation, eg worker protection standards, and whose membership is drawn from the CBI, TUC, local authorities, government departments and relevant professional bodies; the National Radiological Protection Board (NRPB) set up in 1970 to give advice, conduct research and provide technical services in the area of protection against ionising and non-ionising radiation; the Committee on Medical Aspects of Radiation in the Environment (COMARE) created in 1985 to advise on the health effects of natural and human created radioactivity and appointed by the Chief Medical Officer of the Department of Health.

The regulatory body in England and Wales under the Radioactive Substances Act 1993, and s 2 of the Environment Act 1995, is the Agency, which inherits the powers to authorise disposal of radioactive waste from nuclear sites such as power stations previously jointly enjoyed by Her Majesty's Inspectorate of Pollution and MAFF/the Welsh Office, though these ministries will retain a statutory consultative role. The management of waste *on* a nuclear site remains subject to regulation by the Nuclear Installations Inspectorate (NII — part of the HSE), and statutory consultation arrangements are in place under the 1995 Act between the Agency and NII on applications to dispose of radioactive waste, just as the Agency is a statutory consultee of NII for nuclear site licences under the Nuclear Installations Act 1965. The HSE remains responsible for controlling exposure to ionising radiation at non-nuclear sites (such as hospitals) under the Health and Safety at Work Act 1974 and the Ionising Radiation Regulations 1985. BNFL is the *operating* body that currently disposes of most nuclear waste, though currently high level waste is primarily *stored*. The Nuclear Industry Radioactive Waste Executive (NIREX) set up in 1982 by BNFL, the former CEGB, UKAEA, and the former South of Scotland Electricity Board is a *managerial* body charged with responsibility for *disposing* of most solid *low* and *intermediate* level waste. It has a share structure with the shareholders being BNFL, Nuclear Electric and Scottish Nuclear Ltd (see chapter 3) the UKAEA and the President of the Board of Trade to ensure governmental oversight. NIREX is a commercial service-providing body that exists to ensure a common approach to nuclear waste disposed amongst nuclear operators, for *legal* responsibility for disposal still lies with them. However, NIREX's services extend to keeping comprehensive nuclear waste records, planning, transport and waste disposal facilities and modes of transportation, managing waste disposal, identifying potential disposal sites, conducting appropriate research and development.

Central policy on waste management was originally as declared in Cmnd 6820, in response to the 'Royal Commission on Environmental Pollution' 6th Report, and in Cmnd 8607. It has been policy: to ensure the minimum creation of nuclear waste and to deal with waste management issues before large nuclear programmes are begun; to pay regard to environmental considerations in handling waste; to dispose of waste in a programmed fashion; to undertake research into disposal methods; to dispose of waste only in appropriate ways; to ensure that waste management issues have been considered in the design of nuclear installations.

Prime responsibility for the National Strategy on Radioactive Waste Management, published in 1984, lay with the Department of the Environment. The DoE initially drew up an inventory of past authorised discharges to help define the scale of future disposal problems. Extensive monitoring of radioactivity in the environment is carried out. Government policy was further developed in this document so that: waste had to be stored safely for as long as necessary pending final disposal decisions; disposals had to provide at least a degree of safety equal to that of supervised storage; decisions on disposal had to made, case by case, on the basis of what represented the best practicable environmental option; new disposal facilities for low and intermediate level wastes were to be developed.

This strategy was based on the polluter pays principle, with waste management costs being met by relevant industries. The co-ordinating body was NIREX. This was part of a system of management, with central government ensuring, under the now repealed and replaced Radioactive Substances Act 1960 and the Nuclear Installations Act 1965, that high standards of waste management were applied, hazards being kept as low as reasonably achievable (ALARA). Co-ordinated implementation of waste strategy was left to NIREX, though it was expected to liaise with the private sector in its operations.

In all cases the objectives of the strategy were that:

1   Practices resulting in radioactive waste had to be justified by need.
2   Exposure of persons to radiation had to be kept to levels as low as reasonably achievable, taking into account economic and social factors, while radioactivity coming from a site should be as low as reasonably practicable.

3   The average effective dose equivalent from radiation sources for representative persons should not exceed 5m Sv (0.5 rem) pa.
4   Where waste is *stored*, storage facilities had to contain associated radioactivity, but the waste remain retrievable, while other waste generated by storage should be minimised. And
5   Storage could only be justified where there were specific technical and radiological reasons for it, as in the case of high level waste.

The current policy

While none of the foregoing safety policies was given up, there was an extensive review of policy, contained in the 'Review of Radioactive Waste Management Policy', Cm 2919, presented to Parliament in July 1995. This placed policy in the context of sustainable development, and thus imported considerations of decisions being based on the best possible scientific information, with a precautionary approach being taken in cases of uncertainty and potentially serious risks, together with consideration of any irreversible effects and the application of the polluter pays principle.

Thus, the 1995 White Paper declared, the aims of policy will be:

1   Prevention of the creation of unnecessary radioactive waste.
2   Safe and appropriate management and treatment of such waste as is created.
3   Safe disposal of waste at appropriate times and in appropriate ways.
4   To place all these principles in the context of protecting both existing and future generations and the wider environment in such a way as to command public confidence while taking due account of costs involved.

The White Paper laid much stress on *producer responsibility* so that those who create radioactive waste must ensure:

1   They do not create management problems which cannot be resolved using current techniques or those which can be developed from current techniques.
2   They characterise and segregate waste on the basis of its physical and chemical properties and store it in accordance with the principle of *passive safety*, ie that the waste is immobilised with minimal need for maintenance, monitoring or other human intervention.
3   They undertake the strategic planning of waste disposal programmes for disposal of waste at nuclear sites within an appropriate timescale, and for the decommissioning of redundant plants, subject to the approval of regulators.
4   They remain responsible for the costs of managing and disposing of waste, including regulatory costs, making appropriate financial provision to meet these costs, and keeping that provision under regular review.

Current policy furthermore accepts the following ICRP principles:

1   No practice involving exposure to radiation is to be adopted unless it produces a benefit to exposed persons or to society to offset detriment caused (the principle of *justification*).
2   In relation to any particular source of radiation, the magnitude of individual doses of radiation, the numbers of persons exposed, and the

likelihood of incurring exposures should be kept as low as reasonably achievable bearing in mind economic and social factors (the principle of *optimisation* of protection).

3   The exposure of individuals to radiation resulting from the combination of all relevant practices must be subject to dose limits (the principle of *limitation*).

Implementation of policy via law

The Radioactive Substances Act (RSA) 1993 (as amended in 1995) provides that no person may keep or use radioactive material on premises used by that person for carrying on an undertaking without a registration (see ss 6 and 7), unless exempted from registration, or the material is mobile radioactive apparatus otherwise registered or exempt. Exemptions are provided for by s 8 of the RSA 1993 and in general exist in relation to sites currently licensed under the Nuclear Installations Act 1965, eg power stations. The Secretary of State also has power to exempt premises or materials from control and has used this power in respect of luminous articles and other low activity substances. Mobile radioactive apparatus is generally registered under s 10 of the RSA 1993, but again exemptions may be given under s 11. It is a criminal offence under s 32, RSA 1993 to fail to be registered.

Radioactive substances are defined by s 1 of the Act to be anything which, not being waste, is a substance falling with Sch 1 of the Act, and/or a substance possessing radioactivity which is wholly/partly attributable to a process of nuclear fusion, or some other process of bombardment by neutrons or ionising radiation, not being a process occurring in nature or in consequence of the disposal of radioactive waste. Schedule 1 of the Act specifically refers to a number of elements which in their solid, liquid or gaseous form may be subject to control by virtue of reaching a specified limit of radioactivity, eg polonium, radium, thorium and uranium.

The Agency is the registration body under s 7, and registration applications must contain specified information as to premises and substances, and must be accompanied by an appropriate fee under a charging scheme made under s 41 of the Environment Act 1995. Applications may be refused, granted, or granted subject to conditions which may relate to premises, apparatus, operating practices, and (save in relation to conditions concerning the furnishing of information or the sale or supply of radioactive material) the Agency is only to have regard to the amount or character of radioactive waste likely to arise in consequence of the keeping or use of radioactive material on premises when imposing conditions. Registrations may be cancelled or varied, and conditions may be varied at any time, see s 12. In addition the Agency may take enforcement action under s 21 if it is of the opinion that there is an actual or potential failure to comply with any condition or limitation of a registration. Where the Agency considers that the continuation of an activity involves an imminent risk of pollution of the environment they may take prohibitive action under s 22 which may suspend a registration to the extent specified by the prohibition notice. Appeals against Agency decisions lie to the Secretary of State under s 26, see also SI 1990/2504 for appeal procedures. However, it should be noted that s 23 of the RSA 1993 empowers the Secretary of State to give directions to the Agency in relation to registration applications in relation to the refusal, grant, variation, cancellation or revocation of a registration, while s 24 enables the Secretary of State to require certain applications to be determined by him, and no appeal lies against such a direction or decision.

Authorisation of disposal and accumulation of radioactive waste

Radioactive waste may only be accumulated with a view to subsequent disposal or disposed of according to the terms of an *authorisation*, see ss 13 and 14 RSA 1993. The same prohibition applies to any person causing or knowingly permitting the accumulation/disposal of radioactive waste. Furthermore the prohibition on unauthorised disposal extends to the disposal of radioactive waste from premises which are situated on a nuclear site but which have ceased to used for the purposes of the licensee's undertaking.

'Radioactive waste' is defined by s 2 of the RSA 1993 to be waste which consists wholly or partly of a substance or article which, if it were not waste, would be radioactive material within the meaning of s 1 of the Act (see above) or a substance or article contaminated in the course of production, keeping or use of radioactive material, or by contact or proximity to radioactive waste, eg spent nuclear fuel rods, and see above for the categorisation of such waste.

Authorisations (for which an appropriate application fee must be paid) are granted by the Agency under s 16 of the 1993 Act, as amended, but before the grant consultation must take place with the Minister of Agriculture, the Health and Safety Executive, relevant local authorities, and other relevant water bodies and public authorities, see s 16(4A), (5), (11) of the RSA 1993 and Sch 22 para 205 of the Environment Act 1995. Authorisations may be granted, refused or granted subject to conditions or limitations, and may apply to radioactive waste generally, or to such descriptions of waste as are stated in the authorisation. Under s 17 of the 1995 Act authorisations may be revoked or varied though, again, consultation with the Minister of Agriculture is required beforehand. Section 18 of the RSA 1993 provides that where radioactive waste disposal is likely to require the need for special precautions to be taken by a local authority, a relevant water body (eg a sewage undertaker) or other public authority, the Agency must consult with that authority or body before granting the authorisation. Furthermore where special precautions are taken by such a body and these precautions are either in compliance with conditions subject to which the authorisation in question was granted, or they are taken with prior Agency approval, the body may charge in respect of taking precautions. Under s 20 of the 1993 Act obligations may be imposed on authorisees in relation to the retention and production of site or disposal records in relation to keeping or using radioactive material or accumulating or disposing of radioactive waste.

The powers relating to enforcement and prohibition action under ss 21 and 22 of the 1993 Act, and the powers of the Secretary of State under ss 23 and 24 to give directions and 'call in' applications referred to above in connection with registrations also apply with regard to authorisations, similarly the provisions of ss 26 and 27 with regard to appeals.

It should further be noted that under s 25 of the RSA 1993 the Secretary of State has power to direct the Agency that knowledge of any particular application for a registration *or* an authorisation, or of applications of any specified description, should be restricted. In such cases the Agency may not send a copy of the application or any subsequent registration or authorisation to public or local authorities. This power may only be exercised on grounds of national security, and does not affect the Agency's obligations to consult the Minister of Agriculture, see s 25 (3A) of the RSA 1993 and Sch 22 para 213 of the Environment Act 1995.

Further powers of the Secretary of State and offences

Section 29 of the RSA 1993 empowers the Secretary of State to arrange provision of facilities for the safe disposal or accumulation of radioactive waste if it appears to him/her that such facilities are not available, though prior consultation with the local authority of any area where such facilities are to be provided must take place, as must consultation with other appropriate public or local authorities. Similarly under s 30 of the 1993 Act, as amended, where the Agency is satisfied that there is radioactive waste on any premises, and that it ought to be disposed of, but that for any reason it is unlikely it will be lawfully disposed of unless they exercise their powers, they may dispose of it as they think fit and recover their reasonable expenses from the owner/occupier of the premises.

To enforce its various powers under the 1993 Act the Agency has general powers along with its authorised officers under ss 108–110 of the 1995 Act inter alia to: enter premises at any reasonable time or at any time in an emergency — in the latter case by force if need be; enter premises it is reasonably believed it is necessary to enter along with other authorised persons and equipment; examine and investigate the premises; take measurements and photographs and other recordings; take samples; take possession of and retain for so long as is necessary (for the purposes of examination or to ensure it is available as evidence) any substance or article found on the premises which appears to have caused or to be likely to cause pollution of the environment or harm to human health; require information and records to be produced (see s 108). Particular powers to deal with causes of imminent danger of serious pollution of the environment or serious harm to human health by way of seizure and rendering the cause harmless, whether by destruction or otherwise, are granted by s 109, while s 110 provides where obstruction of persons exercising the foregoing powers occurs, or there is a failure to comply with requirements made under s 108, an offence is committed.

It is an offence under s 32 of the RSA 1993 to contravene the provisions relating to prohibition of unauthorised use of radioactive material, or its accumulation or disposal, or to fail to comply with the terms of registrations/authorisations. A fine of up to £20,000 and/or a term of imprisonment for up to six months is capable of being imposed on summary trial, while on indictment an unlimited fine and/or imprisonment for up to five years may be imposed. Section 32(3), as added in 1995, allows the Agency to seek an injunction from the High Court to secure compliance where it is felt proceedings for an offence in respect of an enforcement notice or prohibition notice would not provide an effectual remedy. Section 34A (as inserted in 1995) creates the specific offences of making false or misleading statements so as to obtain a registration or authorisation, and of falsifying requisite records.

The application of the law in practice

There have been few major cases on the waste disposal provisions of the RSA 1993 and its predecessor. Most prosecutions have been at the level of the magistrates' court and have related to comparatively minor infractions of the law. This is not to say there have been no nuclear incidents: operators have been prosecuted in respect of breaches of site licences (which result in action under the Health and Safety at Work etc Act 1974), see *Health and Safety Executive v Nuclear Electric*[9] and for infraction of authorisations, see *HMIP v Nuclear Electric*.[10] However, there has been little guidance from the courts on how regulators are to use their discretion in granting authorisations and registrations, etc.

However, the major decision of Potts J in *R v Secretary of State for the Environment, ex p Greenpeace*[11] has to be noted. This case arose out of an authorisation granted to BNFL to allow the start up of the Thermal Oxide Reprocessing Plant (THORP) at Sellafield. During the course of judgment Potts J accepted that EU law requires that national law should be read consistently with EU provisions which may allow the reading of words into a UK statute, though not so as to distort its plain meaning. On this basis he construed the 1993 legislation in the light of arts 6A and 13 of the Euratom Basic Safety Standards Directive. Thus while the 1993 Act alone does not require *justification* to be shown before an authorisation can be granted, in the light of the Directive such an exercise is required. See above p 421 on the principle of justification, but effectively regulators must be convinced that the advantages of the nuclear activity in question justify exposures to ionising radiation.

As Cm 2919 points out, this means that in deciding an application for an authorisation regulators must consider maximum discharges and limits of exposure, together with justification and optimisation, ie that exposures shall be kept as low as reasonably achievable with all relevant economic and social factors being taken into account. Such applications may be submitted at the same time as an application for full planning permission for the development of a nuclear facility is made, though the two procedures will progress separately, see further Cm 2919 para 62.

Cm 2919 further declares the principles that will be applied with regard to radioactive waste disposal.

1   In relation to discharges of air borne and liquid waste the dose to members of the public from *all* man-made sources of radioactivity (other than medical exposures) should be limited to one millisievert a year (lm Sv/y — a sievert being the international unit for measuring doses of exposure). In determining applications for authorisations a maximum dose constraint of 0.3m Sv/y will be applied to new nuclear installations, while existing facilities should also be operated within this limit, and where this cannot be done the operator must demonstrate that doses resulting from the operation are as low as is reasonably achievable and within dose limits. Where there are a number of nuclear sources with contiguous boundaries

9 [1995] 7 ELM 203.
10 [1994] 6 ELM 83.
11 [1994] 6 ELM 82.

at a single location there will be an overall 'site constraint' of 0.5m Sv/y irrespective of whether different sources on the site are owned or operated by the same or different organisations. Where, however, exposures are below 0.02m Sv/y regulators should not seek further reductions in exposures to the public provided they are satisfied the best practicable means to limit releases are being used.

The current policy is the result of a long process of reduction of discharges of radioactive waste to water. The Black Committee's 'Investigation of the Possible Increased Incidence of Cancer in West Cumbria' (HMSO, 1984) criticised discharge authorisation procedures as ill co-ordinated and unfocused and lacking in 'health input'. Even before this there had been attempts to reduce dose levels to local residents, and these had declined from 1.95 m Sv/y to 0.49m Sv/y between 1980 and 1985, with authorised discharges to the sea of material being particularly reduced, for the details of which see the second edition of this work at p 388. It does not, however, appear possible to impose a zero limit on discharges and the relevant legislation will not be interpreted and applied so as to impose such a requirement.[12]

Unauthorised or 'accidental' discharges may also take place, with some 672 such incidents having occurred for instance between January 1979 and March 1986 according to BNFL figures, though none was 'dangerous' within the meaning of the Nuclear Installations (Dangerous Occurrences) Regulations SI 1965/1824. There are four grades of incident:

(A)   Those falling within the 1965 regulations in that radiation has been emitted likely to cause death or serious injury, or there has been a fire or explosion *likely* to affect the safe operation of an installation.

(B)   Those involving major leaks/escapes of radioactive material or a radiation dose uptake of twice the maximum permitted annual rate.

(C)   Minor ground leaks of material, radiation uptake greater than annual or quarterly limits, or fire/explosions which *may* affect an installation's safe condition.

(D)   Leakages of radioactivity leading to widespread contamination levels more than 10 times the specification for on-site working areas, or radiation uptake greater than a third of quarterly dose limits or minor fires or explosions unlikely to affect safety.

Category B was administratively created, while C exists as a term of site licences.

Where radioactive waste is to be discharged to the sea via a pipeline its construction will be an act of development for which planning permission is required.

2   With regard to solid waste disposal, estimates of risk have to be considered in determining the safety of a proposed disposal facility, and the official target is that there should be a risk target in relation to design of developing either a fatal cancer, *or* serious hereditary defect of one in a million pa. Other technical factors also have to be considered, such as whether a

facility has been designed according to principles of good engineering and good science. There should be no prescribed cut off of the period over which risk is to be assessed. In each instance a site specific safety case will have to be made out.

Much will depend on the nature of the waste to be disposed of.

High level waste which remains after the reprocessing of spent nuclear fuel (which is itself *stored* pending reprocessing) is now being converted into glass cylinders (vitrification). This vitrified waste is to be stored for at least 50 years to allow cooling and decay of short lived radionuclides, while the long term preferred policy option is landward disposal in suitable geological formations.

Operational wastes, ie those actually arising during the reprocessing of foreign spent fuel, will, as currently, be returned to their country of origin, with any high level waste being returned as soon as possible after vitrification. It is, however, possible that a principle of radioactive waste substitution may be adopted whereby, rather than returning to its home all types of operational waste, BNFL should be allowed the option of offering its overseas customers the substitution of additional amounts of high level waste in return for which their intermediate and low level waste could be kept in this country for disposal. This would actually reduce the number of global waste movements. Official policy is that waste substitution *may* be adopted but only on a basis of broad environmental neutrality for the UK, ie there must be radiological equivalence between the different waste categories, so that what is retained in the UK is balanced by what is returned. This adoption, however, is dependent upon the establishment of a suitable NIREX repository for intermediate level waste in the UK.

Intermediate level waste should, according to policy, ultimately be disposed of in a deep facility, though once again planning permission will have to be gained *and* a sound safety case made out. One initially identified potential site for this facility is near Sellafield. However planning permission for the construction of a 'Rock Characterisation Facility' at the site to test its geology and hydrogeology has been refused by Cumbria County Council and, at the time of writing, this is the subject of a public inquiry — see further chapter 7. Such a facility could not be ready to receive waste before 2010, however. Until then both intermediate and low level waste will remain in store, and where the demands of safety are overriding the waste will be treated as necessary to improve storage conditions. In addition where early treatment will produce worthwhile safety benefits or economic benefits, without prejudice to safety, the presumption which has operated since 1984 against any form of treatment action may be relaxed.

Some low level waste may continue to be subject to controlled burial — a route available to 'small users' such as hospitals, universities and non-nuclear industries, though it is official policy not to encourage this mode of disposal by the nuclear industry itself. The Agency will, however, give advice to such 'small users' of radioactive material on appropriate disposal routes, while authorisation for controlled burial will still have to be obtained. Small users will also need the consent of relevant site operators before using controlled burial techniques. The Agency will, of course, be responsible for the issue of authorisations and waste management licences and so will be well placed to identify appropriate sites for controlled burial. The Agency will in all cases assess the type and activity of the waste and the containment characteristics of the site to which it is proposed to be sent. Where an authorisation is granted there will be, as at present, monitoring of leachate from the site to check for radioactivity and these results will be made public.

Though the contaminated land provisions of the 1995 Act do not apply to radioactive contamination, regulations are to be introduced by October 1996 to apply generally the contaminated land regime to radioactive contaminated sites.

It is, finally, general policy that radioactive waste should be neither imported into nor exported from the UK save in specific situations:

1   For the prime purpose of recovering re-usable materials.
2   For treatment to make the subsequent storage and disposal of waste more manageable where *either* the relevant processes are at a development stage *or* the quantity of waste involved is too small for treatment processes to be practicable in its country of origin (in the foregoing cases there is, however, a presumption that the activities in question must not add materially to the amount of waste needing disposal in the UK).
3   Waste may be imported for treatment and disposal if it is in the form of a spent source which was manufactured in the UK.
4   Waste may be imported if it comes from small users such as hospitals in EU member states producing such small quantities of radioactive waste that provision of specialised facilities would be impractical, or from developing nations which cannot reasonably be expected to have their own facilities.

Transporting nuclear waste

In 1973 the International Atomic Energy Agency (IAEA) issued 'Regulations for the Safe Transport of Radioactive Materials'. These formed the basis for British regulations, whose philosophy was to ensure that all transported nuclear waste must be appropriately and safely packaged in a manner sufficient to withstand a severe accident. The legislative position is now governed by the Radioactive Material (Road Transport) Act 1991. The Secretary of State is empowered by s 2 of this Act to make regulations to prevent any injury to health or property damage or damage to the environment being caused by the transport of radioactive material, and to give effect to the IAEA's regulations as issued from time to time. Such regulations may in particular make provision as to packaging of material and the manufacture and maintenance of packaging components; preparing, labelling, consigning, handling, transporting, storing in transit and delivery of radioactive packages, placarding of delivery vehicles, and keeping of records. Regulations may also provide for requisite approvals to be obtained. Failure to comply with regulations is an offence, while the Act maintains in force, until they are replaced by regulations previously made under s 5 of the Radioactive Substances Act 1948, see SI 1974/1735 as amended by SI 1985/1729.

Section 3 gives ministerially appointed inspectors powers to prohibit the driving of vehicles in contravention of regulations, or where relevant vehicles or radioactive packages have been involved in accidents, or where such material has been lost or stolen. Likewise the transport of packages may be prohibited if they do not comply with regulations. Notices of prohibitions must be given to the person in charge of the vehicle, specifying the infraction in question and stating the effect of the prohibition. Prohibitions have immediate effect on notice being given. Extensive powers of entry are given to inspectors under s 5 in order to enforce the regulations, both to enter land and vehicles. Entry under warrant is provided for where admission to a vehicle or premises has been refused.

Under s 4 enforcement action may be taken against manufacturers or maintainers of packaging who are failing or who are likely to fail to meet the requirements of regulations.

Where offences under the regulations have been committed by corporations with the consent, connivance or through the neglect of directors, managers, secretaries, etc, the individual(s) in question are liable with the company, see s 6.

Rail transport is regulated by (the former) British Rail's Conditions of Acceptance of Dangerous Goods BR 22426. The Railway Conditions do not permit loaded flasks to be carried on the same train as explosive, inflammable or spontaneously combustible material.

See also the Transfrontier Shipment of Radioactive Substances Regulations SI 1993/3031 implementing Directive 92/3/Euratom on supervision and control of shipments of waste between member states and into and out of the EU.

E CONTAMINATED LAND

Problems of contaminated land are not new: so called 'primitive' people may well still exhaust a site's resources and leave it fouled by their wastes and then move on to somewhere else (as our early ancestors did). But such small scale contamination is usually easily dealt with by natural regenerative forces: in modern society we encounter the problem of long term persistent damage to sites and their soil.

The history of attempts to deal legally with the issue

Contaminated and derelict land has long been recognised as a planning issue. DoE Circular 21/87, for example, gave advice on the development of contaminated sites such as former sewage farms and industrial land, and see chapter 6 above on derelict land reclamation. Contamination is certainly a 'material' consideration to be taken into account in the planning process, but long term problems such as the presence of toxic materials in soil and the possibility of their leaching out into surrounding areas and water supplies, or giving rise to atmospheric emissions or on site dangers, cannot be dealt with by planning controls alone.

Indeed, as has been pointed out by Robert Lewis in 'Contaminated Land: the New Regime of the Environment Act 1995',[13] there are very particular legal problems affecting contaminated land involving questions such as:

13 [1995] JPL 1087.

1   Where present contamination arises from past pollution, how does one deal with the disappeared polluter?
2   Should past contamination lawful at the time it arose be capable of giving rise to present liability?
3   To what standard should decontamination work remediate land?
4   Who should bear the cost of remedial work where it may be that the contamination arose from sequential acts of pollution?
5   Is it possible to avoid the feeling that any legislative scheme is an attempt to impose retrospective liabilities, some of which will inevitably impose costs on innocent parties?
6   How does one strike a balance between the public and private purses in allocating clean up costs and responsibilities — particularly where one has a government committed to the reduction of public expenditure?
7   Even though much land is 'contaminated' in the sense of having present substances not laid down naturally, how does one distinguish between the majority of effectively harmless sites and those which carry genuine risks of harm?

Following the government's policy statement 'Contaminated Land', Cm 1161, s 143 of the Environmental Protection Act 1990 made provision for the public registration of land which may have been subject to *contaminative uses*, with a duty to be imposed on local authorities to compile and maintain such registers. The idea was that particular uses would be specified in regulations, and that land potentially contaminated would thus be more easily identified and investigated so that appropriate action could be taken by those interested in the development of such land.

Immediate problems were encountered with this provision. Would local authorities have the necessary resources of personnel and expertise to compile the registers, would land become blighted once it had been registered as subject to a *contaminative* use, even though it was not in fact *contaminated*, and what about the lack of any provision for the *removal* of land from registers? Most importantly s 143 made no provision for cleaning up sites found to be contaminated and attributing liabilities to particular persons, it being thought that the market would sort out who would be prepared to pay what for any required works. In March 1993 the government abandoned the policy behind s 143, and in 1994 published a consultative document on the issues involved, 'Paying for our Past', and later that year a series of proposals in 'Framework for Contaminated Land', which stated official commitment to a policy that *land should be fit for the purpose to which it is to be put*.

The current principal provisions on contaminated land are to be found in the Environment Act 1995 which inserts them (as Part IIA) into the Environmental Protection Act 1990 and repeals s 143.

What is 'contaminated' land?

It is important to distinguish 'derelict' from 'contaminated' or 'polluted' land. Derelict land is that which is 'derelict, neglected or unsightly', ie damaged by industrial or other development so as to be incapable of beneficial use without treatment. Such land falls within the terms of the Derelict Land Act 1982, see chapter 6 above, and may not necessarily be contaminated.

The 1995 definition of 'contaminated' land centres on the presence in land of substances in, on or under it which may be likely to cause, or are causing *significant* harm or the pollution of controlled waters (see chapter 12 below for 'controlled waters'). 'Harm' in this sense means 'harm to the health of living organisms or other interference with the ecological systems of which they form part' or 'harm to human property', while 'substance' means 'any natural or artificial substance whether in solid or liquid form or in the form of a gas or vapour,' see s 78A(2), (4), (9) of the Environmental Protection Act 1990. (Harm to human senses, eg by virtue of an offensive but not otherwise harmful smell, is not included.) This is a definition closer in concept to 'polluted' than to the previously accepted definition of 'contamination' which had simply centred on the presence in the environment of particular substances without any judgment as to their harmfulness. The Act is thus confined to land which is actually causing or which poses a threat of harm. The definition also does not, at first sight, sit *entirely* comfortably with the concept of land being 'fit for its purpose'. Some land may be heavily impregnated with toxic material, though so isolated or so developed in a particular ways as to be unlikely to cause harm, yet the material is still present. However, the two notions are intended to fit together: land is 'contaminated' if it is giving rise to, or is likely to cause, 'significant' harm, which means both the extent of any harm and the nature of what may be affected by it must be considered, and thus the actual or potential use of the land is relevant to whether it is capable of being considered 'contaminated'.

In the past the concept of 'suitable or fit for use' has been used to determine the standard to which remediation should take place, in which context it has been juxtaposed against arguments that clean up should be 'multi-functional' (the approach effectively adopted in the Netherlands, for example) whereby land is remediated to an absolute standard of fitness for any purpose. However, under the 1995 legislation 'fitness for purpose' becomes part of the definition of contaminated land, for land is contaminated if it is unsuitable for its *current* purpose, as is made clear by draft government guidance (see further below). Thus in any given case whether land is 'contaminated' is a question of subjective judgment, and land may be considered 'uncontaminated' according to its present use, while its classification can change if there is a proposal to put it to a use where material in it could give rise to dangers to human health. This further raises the *possibility* of variations in what is considered contaminated from one part of the country to another, or over time as expert opinion alters and develops.

It should also be noted that the questions of what harm is to be regarded as 'significant', whether the possibility of harm being caused is 'significant', and whether pollution of controlled waters is being or is likely to be caused, are to be determined *in accordance* with effectively binding guidance to be issued by the Secretary of State under s 78 YA (see s 78A(5)) which seems to give little room for departure from the guidance. This guidance may make provision for different degrees of importance to be assigned to different descriptions of living organisms or ecosystems, different descriptions of places under different descriptions of harm.

Draft consultative guidance was issued on 5 May 1995, and the current indications are that 'significant harm' is that which is: harm to human users or occupiers of relevant land as currently in use, *or* harm to the health of current users/occupiers of other land; harm to or interference with ecosystems protected by the Wildlife and Countryside Act 1981, Directives 79/409 (wild birds) or 92/43 (habitats); harm to property in relation to the present use of land or other land — property to include livestock and crops. Harm to human health is defined in terms of death, serious injury or clinical toxicity. Harm to ecosystems is defined by reference to significant changes in their functioning. Harm to property refers to continuing physical damage irremediable without substantial work, or disease or physical damage to crops/livestock which causes loss of value. Harm is to be disregarded where it is the legal and intended consequence of the addition of substances to land, eg the destruction of pests by pesticides. Furthermore the identification of harm is to follow risk assessment principles, so then the first step is to identify the 'target' or 'receptor' to be protected (eg human health), then to identify and make a first assessment of possible 'sources' of harm (eg substances), next establish whether there is a plausible sequence or 'pathway' of harm from the 'source' to the 'target' (so that where the 'source' is a pollutant in the soil, and the 'target' is, for example, the health of a child, the 'pathway' could be consumption of contaminated vegetables), then to confirm and make further assessments of the actual presence of substances and their harm causing potential, and finally to estimate 'risk' (ie the *probability* and *degree* of harm). Thus the apparently very wide terminology of the statute may very well be restricted in practice by the terms of ministerial guidance by virtue of the need for a 'pollution linkage' in the form of a 'source-pathway-receptor' relationship.

Identifying contaminated land

Local authorities (ie London boroughs, district and unitary authorities in England and Wales) are, under s 78B, to cause their areas to be inspected from time to time for the purpose of identifying contaminated land (ie land appearing to them to be contaminated according to the foregoing definition) and identifying possible 'special sites' (see below). As already stated in carrying out these tasks, authorities are to act in accordance with ministerial guidance. On identifying land they conclude is contaminated authorities must inform (a) the Agency; (b) the landowner; (c) any person appearing to be in whole/part occupation of the land; (d) each person who is an 'appropriate person', ie a person determined to bear responsibility for remediation (see further below). Service of notice on an 'appropriate person' does not prevent later service on others who subsequently appear 'appropriate'. Note, however, that the Part IIA provisions do not apply to land subject to a current waste management licence, save where the contamination in question arises for reasons other than licensed waste disposal activities, see s 78YB (2).

The duty to inspect is pro-active, but, in the absence of particular funding for the purpose, in practice some authorities may be tempted to make inspections only in response to complaints about particular pieces of land. Ministerial guidance will require however, an ordered approach, and thus local authorities will have to set about producing 'appropriate' local strategies for inspections to ensure best use of resources, concentrating on those areas where the 'chance of discovery of significant harm is greatest'. It is certain that authorities in 'old' industrial areas such as the West Midlands may thus face earlier and heavier costs than those which have always been predominantly rural.

No formal appeal mechanism is provided against a notice of identification, and though informal challenge may be available, either internally within the authority or via the offices of the Agency, formal challenge appears available only by way of judicial review or via the intervention of the Commission for Local Administration where maladministration causing justice could be shown, eg persistent delay by an authority in considering evidence that a site is not contaminated.

Section 78C allows for certain contaminated sites to be classified as 'special sites', in which case responsibility for enforcing the law will lie with the Agency. 'Special sites' land is that which falls within regulations made by the Secretary of State under s 78 C(8), though in making regulations the Secretary of State is to consider land whose condition is such by virtue of the presence of substances that it could cause *serious* harm or *serious* pollution of controlled waters, *or* whether the Agency is likely to have expertise in dealing with the kind of significant harm, etc, by reason of which land of the description in question is classed as 'contaminated'.

If it appears to an authority that land may require 'special site' designation, the Agency must just be asked for advice. If then the authority decides the designation is merited, notice must be given to the Agency, the owner, the occupier, etc, and the designation takes effect generally within 21 days, unless the Agency serves a reasoned counter notice disagreeing with the designation: disputes of this sort are to be referred to the Secretary of State, see s 78D(1). However, once again there is no formal method of appeal against designation. Section 78C(4) allows the Agency to initiate the special site designation procedure — again any disputes with the local authority are to be referred to the Secretary of State.

Note that closed landfill sites are not automatically classified as 'special sites' by the legislation. In practice, however, this is likely to be the case for many of them.

The remediation procedure

'Remediation' under s 78A(7) means doing anything for assessing the condition of relevant land, adjacent land, affected controlled waters, doing works or carrying out operations *or* taking steps in relation to such land or waters to prevent, minimise, remedy or mitigate the effects of any relevant significant harm or pollution of controlled waters, *or* restoring such land or waters to their previous state, *or* inspecting such land or water subsequently to keep their condition under review.

Where land is either a 'special site' or identified as contaminated land, the 'enforcing authority' (ie the Agency or the local authority as the case may be) shall, under s 78E, according to prescribed procedure, serve on each 'appropriate person' (see above) a 'remediation notice' specifying what that person has to do by way of remediation and the time within which it is to be done. Different requirements may be imposed on different persons under s 78E(2) and (3) where more than one is 'appropriate', but the notice in each case is to state the proportion of costs for which each is liable. Notices may also require different persons to bear differing responsibilities in respect of different substances in or under land.

However, under s 78E(4) the enforcing authority may only require *reasonable* remediation measures having regard to *the likely costs of measures* and the *seriousness of the harm*, etc, in question. The authority is also *to have regard* (ie take into account in this context) to the Secretary of State's guidance on what is to be required to be done by way of remediation, the standard to which remediation is to take place, and any other issues relevant to deciding what is a 'reasonable' requirement in any given case, see also s 78E(5).

The obligation on authorities in the present context is only 'to have regard to' central guidance, which makes it *advisory* with authorities being free to determine the weight they will accord it — provided, of course, they do not behave unreasonably in the *Wednesbury* sense. Robert Lewis in his article already referred to argues that: 'It is doubtful whether a court could hold as unreasonable a required level of remediation simply on the ground that the standard demanded went beyond that necessary to remove the land from the restricted definition of "contaminated" . . . [especially as] the Act in s 78A(7) includes in the definition of "remediation" the restoring of land to its former state'.

Before a remediation notice is served, however, s 78H(1)–(3) requires the enforcing authority to make reasonable endeavours to consult the proposed recipient of the notice, the landowner, the occupier of the land, any other prescribed person, with regulations laying down the details (which presumably will include time periods) of procedures, etc. Furthermore no remediation notice may in general be served on any person until the expiration of three months from the time at which the owner, the occupier and any other relevant person were notified that the land was contaminated or was designated as a special site, as the case may be. However, this restriction does not apply in cases of imminent danger of serious harm, or serious pollution of controlled waters, see s 78H(4).

Remediation notices are to be served on 'appropriate persons', who are, according to s 78F any person(s) who 'caused or knowingly permitted' all or some of the contamination. However, the UK law differs here from US practice under the so-called 'superfund legislation' whereby *anyone* who has contributed to contamination, no matter how little, is liable to bear the full cost of remediation, then having a right to seek a contribution from other contaminators. Thus in the UK each 'appropriate person' is only liable to undertake so much of the remediation as is referable to a substance(s) he/she caused or knowingly permitted to be on the land, though he/she is responsible for *all* remediation in respect of that substance(s), even if he/she was responsible for only some of it (them) being there, or even if remediation is needed because of interaction between the substance(s) and some other substance(s) otherwise present. It is therefore clear that there could be joint liability in respect of a single contaminating substance introduced by more than one person. So, for example, if two successive owners of a factory each caused 'X' industrial solvent to be present on the land, each, in general, is responsible for the whole remediation process in respect of 'X', but not 'Y' which was introduced by a successor in title, but see below on cases of multiple liability.

With regard to the words 'cause or knowingly permit' the cases on the equivalent wording in the Water Resources Act 1991 are relevant, see chapter 12 below.

Where, after reasonable enquiry, no person can be found who caused or knowingly permitted a substance to be present, the owner or occupier for the time being of the land is the 'appropriate person' to be served with a remediation notice. Thus an 'innocent' landowner may be made residually liable for remediation costs where the original polluter cannot be found, and, it should be noted, even if the polluter is subsequently discovered there is no right under the statute for the landowner to recover remediation costs, which appears a little unjust. However, a current landowner's residual liability will only arise where the polluter cannot be found. It appears there is no such liability where the polluter can be found but cannot pay for remediation. In any case even where the responsible person can be found he/she will only be liable in respect of that substance(s) he/she introduced: any contamination attributable to a substance for which no 'importer' of that substance can be found again falls to be the liability of the owner/occupier of the land, see s 78F(3)–(5). A number of issues may arise for determination in court under these provisions. Does the word 'found' mean 'identified' or does it mean identified *and* physically found? Furthermore, what is to happen where the 'person' is 'found' to be a company which has been dissolved?

A number of further subsidiary points must be noted. First the legislation refers to 'substances' and this includes natural as well as the more obvious human-made contaminative materials. Hence a person could be liable in respect of contamination arising from a natural substance he/she had caused or knowingly permitted to be brought onto or put into land. Secondly, 'owner' includes those who in their own right or as trustees are entitled to receive the rack rent (ie the best rent available) of land, or would be so entitled if it were let, but *not* a mortgagee not in possession.

Finally, there is no formal provision allowing a person who sells land to transfer liability for material he/she has caused or knowingly permitted to be on land to the new owner, etc. This does not, however, prevent a person who is selling contaminated land from negotiating an indemnity in respect of contingent liabilities as part of the contract of sale.

Cases of multiple liability

In cases where more than one person is, in theory, liable to carry out remediation action, eg where they introduced contaminants while acting as partners, the enforcing authority is to determine whether any such person is *not* to be treated as an 'appropriate person' *in accordance* with guidance from the Secretary of State. Thereafter those remaining 'appropriate' must have the cost of action apportioned between them by the authority, again *in accordance* with central guidance, see s 78F(6) and (7). There may be room for dispute here (according to the degree of freedom allowed by the guidance), should an authority determine to apportion liability on the basis the 'the *original* polluter pays' if that person sold the land on to a subsequent polluter on the basis that its value was lessened by the initial contamination. Furthermore, what of situations where two are liable but one has disappeared? One indication of how ministerial guidance *may* deal with contribution issues was given in the course of debate on the legislation where it was indicated 'the whole responsibility for remediation [may] rest on the person with the most recent involvement with the contamination'.

Remediation notices may, under s 78G require their recipients to do things they are not entitled to do. However, any person whose consent is needed before anything required by a remediation notice may be done is to grant such rights in relation to relevant land or waters as will enable an 'appropriate person' to comply with notice served. Such third parties must, however, be consulted by enforcing authorities before a remediation notice is served, though not in a case of imminent danger of serious harm or serious pollution of controlled waters. Compensation may be payable in respect of any rights granted to an 'appropriate person' according to a scheme to be laid down in regulations. However, it also appears possible for the person granted the rights to stipulate for compensation to be payable on his/her own terms in the document granting those rights, and for there to be a requirement that the compensation is guaranteed by some form of bond, etc. It also behoves those who propose to acquire sites to take such steps as they can to inquire not only into the condition of the land they are purchasing but also into that of adjoining or adjacent land whose condition may subsequently require the granting of rights. It must, however, be remembered that there is no legal requirement either to serve a copy of a remediation notice on the owners/ occupiers of land adjacent to that in question, nor to register the *initial* identification of land as contaminated (see further below on registers).

Restrictions on remediation notices

In addition to the constraints on the time of service under s 78H referred to above, s 78H(5) provides service may not take place where:

1 The enforcing authority is satisfied having carried out the 'cost-harm' test under s 78E(4) and (5) (see above) that there is nothing by way of remediation which could be specified in a notice to be served on a specific person.
2 Appropriate things are being or will be done by way of remediation without the service of a notice. [This enables remediation to take place by negotiation, provided it is compatible with central guidance.]
3 It appears to the authority that the 'appropriate person' for service is the authority itself.
4 The authority are satisfied that the powers conferred by s 78N to do what is appropriate by way of remediation (see below) are exercisable.

Where a remediation notice cannot specify particular remediation action because the 'cost-harm' test precludes it, then a 'remediation declaration' must be published which records the reasons why the authority *would have* specified the particular action *and* the grounds on which the authority are satisfied they are precluded from specifying that action. Where the authority are precluded from serving a remediation notice under grounds (2)–(4) above, then a 'remediation statement' must be published which is to record the things which are being, have been or are expected to be done by way of remediation, the name and address of the person who has done, is doing or is expected to do those things, and the period for taking action. This statement is to be published by the 'responsible person' who is in the case of ground (2) above the person who is to do the work, and in the other cases the enforcing authority.

There are other cases of restrictions on remediation activity. Thus under s 78X(3) certain 'persons' acting in an insolvency are not personally liable to bear the costs of remediation activity, save where the contamination is referable to substances on land as a result of any acts/omissions on those persons' part which it was unreasonable to do/make. The 'persons' in question include insolvency practitioners and persons acting as receivers or as receivers and managers. Likewise under s 78YB(3) where a case falls within s 59(1) or (7) of the EPA 1990 and land is, or becomes contaminated land by reason of the deposit of controlled waste, no remediation notice is to be served to the extent that the powers of the Agency under s 59 may be exercised to deal with the deposit. Furthermore under s 78YB(4) no remediation notice may require the doing of anything the effect of which would be to impede or prevent the making of a discharge in pursuance of a discharge consent given under the Water Resources Act 1991 (see chapter 12 below). Additionally, under s 78YC Part IIA of the 1990 Act is *not* to apply to contamination attributable to radiation except as provided for by regulations made by the Secretary of State.

Restrictions on liability relating to pollution of controlled waters

Under s 78J where land is 'contaminated' by virtue of s 78A(2)(b), ie because of its effect on controlled waters, then (irrespective of whether or not the land is also 'contaminated' by falling within s 78A(2)(a) — other cases of significant harm) the *owner/occupier* of the land cannot be required to carry out remediation on that or any other land or waters other than that justified under s 78A(2)(a). The practical effect of this is that in such cases Part IIA is to be read as if all references to pollution of controlled waters are omitted, see s 78J(2).

Liabilities in respect of escaping contaminating substances: the concept of 'knock-on' contamination

Under s 78K(1) a person who has caused or knowingly permitted any substance to be in, on or under land shall also be taken to have caused, etc, those substances to be in, on or under any other land to which they have escaped — such receiving land being known under Part II A as 'land A'. Thus where P (the polluter) has caused contamination of Blackacre and it *appears* to the enforcing agency that contamination has spread to Whiteacre ('land A'), P is liable to remediate both Blackacre and Whiteacre.

In such circumstances O, the innocent owner of 'land A' (Whiteacre), provided he/she has not caused or knowingly permitted the substance(s) in question to be on land A, may be made residually liable for remediation of land/water of which he/she is the owner/occupier, and *cannot* be required to remediate any other land or waters not owned/occupied to him/her but which are affected by the condition of land A, or to which contaminants have escaped from the initially contaminated site via land A, see s 78K(3) and (4). The consequence of these somewhat complex rules is that where 'knock-on' contamination occurs the original polluter is liable for *all* remediation liabilities, while the innocent owners of the 'knock-on' sites are liable only for the clean up costs of their own sites in situations where the original polluter cannot be found. P's successors in title to the initially contaminated site cannot be required to remediate land A in consequence of the apparent acts or omissions of P except to the extent that a successor caused or knowingly permitted the escape to land A.

The enforcing authority may, however enter land A and exercise its powers under s 78N to remediate the land, subject, however to particular restrictions on its powers to recover its costs.

Ineffective defences to liability

It should be noted that there is no defence against liability in the form of an argument that the contamination was the consequence of a licence or permit such as an IPC authorisation (though to this there is an exception in respect of waste management licences, see s 78YB). Neither is there any possibility of arguing that the contamination arose because 'state of the art' practices current in industry at the time were being followed. Neither is there the possibility under the Act of arguing that the contamination was unforeseeable.

Appeals

Section 78L provides a 21 day period to appeal against service of a remediation notice to the justices where the notice was served by the local authority, to the Secretary of State where served by the Agency, and regulations may be made to prescribe grounds of appeal and to deal with suspension of notices pending appeal, see s 78L(4) and (5). On appeal a notice *must* be quashed if there is a material defect in it, otherwise the appellate authority may confirm the notice, with or without modification, or may quash it, eg where the notice was not justified on the facts of the case. The existence of the statutory appeal procedure will limit the availability of judicial review to challenge remediation notices.

Offences

It is, under s 78M an offence to fail without reasonable excuse to comply with any of the requirements of a remediation notice. However, where the cost of remediation has been apportioned under s 78E(3) it is a defence for one apportionee to show that the sole reason why he/she has not complied with requirements is that one or more of the other apportionees has refused or is unable to comply. Failure to comply is a continuing offence. The usual penalty is a fine of level 5 on the standard scale and one tenth of a level 5 fine for each day of the continuing offence, but where the land is used for industrial, trade or business purposes the maximum level of fine is increased to £20,000 with £2,000 per day for the continuing offence.

An enforcing authority may take proceedings in the High Court, ie for an injunction, if they conclude criminal proceedings will be an ineffectual remedy.

Powers of enforcing authorities to carry out remediation

Section 78N provides that authorities can carry out certain remediation works *provided* they consider them reasonable bearing in mind their cost and the seriousness of the harm. In effect remediation action can be taken in the following circumstances.

1 Where there is an emergency and it is impracticable to wait for service of a remediation notice, the power is limited to doing what is necessary to avert imminent danger of serious harm, or serious pollution of controlled waters.

2 Where a remediation notice has been served and the person served fails to comply *or* agrees that the authority shall carry out remediation work at his/her expense. ˙

3 Where it is appropriate for the authority to carry out the work and no remediation notice can be served on another person because, eg, it is a case where it has not been possible to find an appropriate person following reasonable inquiry, *or* because it would cause hardship to the appropriate person to bear remediation costs. Sections 78H(5)(d), 78N(3)(e) and 78P(2) read together provide for hardship cases, and in deciding whether hardship would be caused by service of a remediation notice authorities must *have regard to* guidance issued by the Secretary of State, though in such a hardship case a remediation statement must be published. It appears that 'hardship' will be defined so as to relieve householders and small businesses who discover that their homes/premises have been built on land which is later identified as contaminated, and where the original polluter cannot be found.

Where an authority incurs reasonable remediation costs these may in some cases be recovered from the person who would have been liable for them had the authority not done the work, see s 78P. Costs may be apportioned in appropriate cases, but before deciding whether to recover costs, and how much, authorities are *to have regard to* any hardship recovery may cause and guidance issued by the Secretary of State. Of course where remediation work is undertaken by an authority with the agreement of the appropriate person costs will be recovered under and according to the agreement. The recovery of costs can be enforced by means of a 'charging order' under s 78P(3)–(13). Such a notice can only be served where the person who contaminated the land also owns it. Once served the costs of works, and interest at a reasonable rate, constitute a charge on relevant premises, and this is enforceable as if it was a mortgage. Provision may be made for costs to be paid by instalments for a period of up to 30 years. Where a 'charging order' is served there is a 21 day period to appeal to the county court which may confirm, modify or quash the notice.

Section 78Q permits the Agency to adopt a remediation notice where one has been served by a local authority in respect of contaminated land which then becomes a special site.

Registers

Section 78R requires all enforcing authorities to maintain registers containing, inter alia, prescribed particulars of remediation notices they have served, appeals against such notices, remediation statements/declarations prepared and published under s 78H, appeals against charging notices, notifications relating to the designation/ending of designation of land as a 'special site', convictions for offences under s 78M and such other matters as may be prescribed. It appears that regulations will require appropriate persons/owners or occupiers of relevant land as the case may be to notify the relevant enforcing authority of what has been done to remediate land included on registers. Such information will then be registered, but registration constitutes no representation that the work has been satisfactorily carried out, see s 78R(3).

These registers must be publicly available for free inspection at all reasonable hours, while photocopying facilities must be made available at reasonable cost. Registers maintained by the Agency must be copied to relevant local authorities who must then enter the details on their own registers, see s 78R(4)–(6).

Note that there is *no* provision for land to be de-registered once remediation activity has taken place.

Certain information may, however, be excluded from registers. Thus under s 78S information may be excluded if its inclusion would, in the opinion of the Secretary of State, be contrary to the interests of national security. In connection with this provision the Secretary of State may give directions to authorities specifying information to be excluded. It is thought this power may be used in respect of land formerly the site of government research stations. Under s 78T where information relates to the affairs of an individual or business it cannot be registered without that individual or business's consent provided it is commercially confidential. Information falls into this class if publication would prejudice to an unreasonable degree the individual or business's commercial interests, see s 78T(1); though information relating only to the ownership/occupation of relevant land or to its value is not confidential, see s 78T(11). The decision on whether or not information is confidential is for the enforcing authority, subject to an appeal to the Secretary of State. Where the authority consider information might be commercially confidential they must, before registration, give the affected person the opportunity to object to its inclusion. Once information is excluded it remains excluded for four years, after which a further application for its continued exclusion may be made. The Secretary of State may by direction override the confidentiality exception in relation to specific information or descriptions of information where it is considered publication is in the public interest.

Agency reports and guidance

Under s 78U the Agency is to prepare and publish reports on the state of contaminated land in England and Wales, and may obtain information from relevant local authorities for this purpose. The Agency may also, under s 78V issue guidance to local authorities with respect to the exercise of their powers in relation to *specific* contaminated sites, and authorities are to have regard to such guidance in exercising their functions, save where the guidance is inconsistent with any guidance issued by the Secretary of State, who may also, under s 78W, issue guidance to the Agency on its contaminated land powers, to which the Agency must have regard.

Supplementary issues

Under s 78X:

1 Where it appears to a local authority that two or more sites when considered together are in such a condition as a result of substances in, on or under them that significant harm is being caused or is likely, etc, the Part IIA powers apply *whether or not* the condition of the land at any one site

when considered alone appears to be such that significant harm is being caused, etc.

2 Where it appears to a local authority that any land outside but adjoining or adjacent to its area is contaminated so that significant harm is being caused within its area, or may be caused, etc, it may exercise its Part IIA powers in relation to that land, either alone, or in conjunction with the authority in whose area the contaminated land lies.

Under s 78YB to avoid overlap with other regulatory regimes:

1 A remediation notice is not to be served where it appears to the enforcing authority that the Agency has power to deal with the situation under s 27 of the EPA 1990 (breaches of IPC control).

2 The Part IIA provisions do not generally apply in relation to land regulated by a site licence granted under the 1990 Act for disposal or keeping of waste — effectively meaning that those who grant licensees, or who operate in accordance with them, or who lease land for waste disposal in accordance with a licence cannot be held to have 'caused or knowingly permitted' the presence of contaminative substances if they are authorised by the site licence.

3 Where land is contaminated by the unlawful tipping of waste a remediation notice may not be served where the situation falls within s 59 of the EPA 1990 (power to require removal of unlawfully deposited ('fly tipped') controlled waste).

4 A remediation notice may not require the doing of anything the effect of which would be to impede or prevent the making of discharges to controlled waters where a discharge consent has been given under the Water Resources Act 1991.

Note also that s 79(1A) of the 1990 Act (inserted in 1995) provides that no matter is to be a statutory nuisance to the extent that it consists of, or is caused by, land being 'contaminated' within the meaning of the Part IIA provisions. It is now thought these provisions will not be operational until 1997.

Contaminated land and planning controls

Planning controls are appropriate measures of regulation with regard to contaminated land in a number of contexts.

The development plan stage

Plans must include policies on the improvement of the physical environment, see ss 12(3A), 31(3) and 36(3) of the 1990 Act, while PPG 12 urges the inclusion of policies on the re-use of derelict or underused land in preference to greenfield sites. PPG 23 adopts a preventive approach (subject to strictures on duplication of controls, see below) by urging the inclusion in structure plans of policies on the location of industries with polluting potential, and site specific allocations for such industries in local plans. It furthermore urges the inclusion of criteria against which development proposals for derelict and contaminated sites can be judged. While authorities are urged to keep housing and current polluting industry apart, they are also urged to remember the effects of past pollution in the siting of housing developments, and the need to consider the effects of contamination on health and the environment, though policies on the reclamation and re-use of contaminated land may also be included in plans. It is not unknown, however, for authorities to be much more specific in their policies and to require in plans detailed site surveys of land *suspected* of being contaminated to be submitted by developers, together with remediation plans to minimise pollution risks from land found, or known, to be contaminated.

A number of problems may arise from the over zealous application of planning controls to contaminated land. First, authorities may find they are actually discouraging the use of 'brownfield' sites, which both PPG 23 and the DoE paper 'Paying for our Past' promoted. Secondly, they may find they are committing the vice of unnecessary duplication of controls which, again, is condemned by PPG 23. Planning controls should complement other forms of regulation to influence the location of development and to control operations so that adverse effects of land uses on the environment are minimised or avoided, and to ensure that after development land and water resources are restored to a condition capable of supporting agreed afteruses. In order to avoid duplication careful consultation at all stages of the planning process with the Agency is needed.

The planning application stage

Again there may be conflict between local practice and central advice. Requirements of an over detailed site inspection may render a development's economic viability uncertain, and Tom Graham argues in *Contaminated Land* at p 114 that the better course of action is for outline planning permission to be granted which enables a site value to be established to underpin the cost of investigation upon which approval of reserved matters may be made conditional. Central guidance for *non-landfill* sites is that site investigation should only be required before determination of an application where it is known or strongly suspected a site is contaminated to a degree which would adversely affect the proposed development or infringe statutory requirements, see PPG 23 Annex 10 para 9 and DoE Circular 11/95 paras 74–76.

In determining which 'side of the line' a site falls with regard to requiring a site investigation, use may be made of the guidance issued by the Interdepartmental Committee on the Redevelopment of Contaminated Land (ICRCL), *Guidance on the Assessment and Redevelopment of Contaminated Land* (2nd edn) which sets out 'trigger' concentrations of contaminants, with 'threshold' levels providing an indication of the need for remedial action.

So far as former landfill sites are concerned, particular care has to be had to the possible presence of flammable and explosive landfill gases and geotechnical conditions on site rendering land unsuitable for construction purposes. Such considerations may even affect land *around* a former site because of the possibility of gas migration, and the usual 'rule of thumb' is to be wary of developments with a minimum radius of 250m from a closed site; but this is no hard and fast rule — much will depend on local soil conditions. DoE Circular 17/89 counsels against developments on or near such sites unless reliable arrangements can be made to overcome the dangers of migrating gas, and careful consultation is required with the

Agency under the terms of the GDPO 1995. The ICRCL guidance on redevelopment of closed landfills is opposed to 'hard' development such as buildings unless there is prior remedial work to the site and is particularly opposed to housing development without most stringent safeguards being emplaced. Certainly it is unlikely that a planning application for such a site would be considered without an extensive prior site investigation — the equivalent, maybe, where not statutorily required, of an environmental assessment in depth and rigour.

Control via planning conditions

So far as a non-landfill site is concerned, PPG 23 make it clear that cases of suspected or slight contamination may be dealt with by conditions in grants of permission which require postponement of development until after site investigation and assessment have been carried out, and incorporation in the development of any necessary remedial measures. Conditions may also be required that a developer should bring to a planning authority's notice the presence of significant unsuspected contamination encountered during development — any such action could now, of course, have considerable implications for the developer under the contaminated land provisions.

DoE Circular 11/95 indicated it is proper to impose a condition that development may not begin until a scheme to deal with contamination has been approved by the local planning authority, including measures to investigate and assess the extent of affectation and the necessary remedial measures. However, once again much will depend on local circumstances and it might be considered excessive to impose by condition a restriction on the development of a whole site where only a small area is affected by contamination.

It must, however, be once more reiterated that planning controls should not be used to duplicate regulation under other statutory codes, and there is no doubt that the 1995 provisions will enable local authorities to dispense with the use of planning restrictions by requiring remediation of land. Even so it must be remembered that planning authorities retain power under s 215 of the Town and Country Planning Act 1990 to serve notice on the owner and occupier of any land in their area which is adversely affecting the *amenity* (ie 'pleasantness') of a part of their area or of an adjoining area, to require remedial steps to be taken within a specified period of not less than 28 days. This provision will certainly apply to odiferous or unsightly land. However, the recipient of such a notice may under s 217 appeal, inter alia, on the basis that the damage is attributable to and a result of the carrying on in the ordinary course of events of an operation or use of land which is no breach of planning control.

Graham, *Contaminated Land* at p 106, argues, however, that s 217 would not extend to defending the emission of unpleasant smells from a factory built with planning permission where the odours result from a substandard implementation of the planning permission.

Failure to comply with a s 215 notice is a criminal offence, which is a continuing one under s 216, while s 219 further empowers the local planning authority to execute any necessary steps and to recover their reasonable costs from the defaulting owner.

Further reading

WASTE AND INFILL

'Annual Report of the Radioactive Waste Management Advisory Committee', 1979 to date HMSO.

Atkinson, S, 'The Regulatory Lacuna: Waste Disposal and Clean Up of Contaminated Sites' [1991] 3 JEL 265.

Burholt, GD, and Martin, A, *The Regulatory Framework for Storage and Disposal of Radioactive Wastes in Member States of the European Community* (1988) Graham and Trotman.

Cheyne, I, and Purdue, M, 'Fitting Definition to Purpose: The Search for a Satisfactory Definition of Waste' [1995] 7 JEL 149.

Coopers & Lybrand, 'Landfill Costs and Prices: Correcting Possible Market Distortions' (1993) HMSO.

Cuckson, D, 'Waste Regulation and Recycling: Present Legal Requirements and Future Prospects for Resource Recovery' [1991] 3 LMELR 6.

Department of the Environment: 'Licensing of Waste Management Facilities', Waste Management Paper No 4 (1994) HMSO.

Department of the Environment: 'Licensing of Metal Recycling Sites', Waste Management Paper No 4A (1995) HMSO.

Department of the Environment: 'Polychlorinated Biphenyls', Waste Management Paper No 6 (1994) HMSO.

Department of the Environment: 'Landfill Completion', Waste Management Paper No 26A (1993) HMSO.

Department of the Environment: 'Landfill Design, Construction and Operational Practice', Waste Management Paper No 26B (1995) HMSO.

Department of the Environment: 'This Common Inheritance' Cm 1200 (1990) HMSO chs 14 and 15.

Department of the Environment: 'Waste Management Planning — Principles and Practice — a Guide on Best Practice for Waste Regulators' (1996) HMSO.

Department of the Environment: 'Environmental Protection Act 1990: Code of Practice on Litter and Refuse' (1991) HMSO.

Department of the Environment: 'Review of Radioactive Waste Management Policy: Final Conclusions', Cm 2919 (1995) HMSO.

Department of the Environment: 'Making Waste Work: Strategy for Sustainable Waste Management in England & Wales', Cm 3040 (1995) HMSO.

Her Majesty's Inspectorate of Pollution: 'Disposal Facilities on Land for Low and Intermediate Level Radioactive Wastes: Guidance on Requirements for Authorisation', (1994) HMIP.

House of Commons Select Committee on the Environment: 1st Report Session 1985–86 'Radioactive Waste' (1986) HMSO, and Response to the Report Cmnd 9852 (1986) HMSO.

House of Commons Select Committee on the Environment: 2nd Report Session 1988–89 'Hazardous Waste Disposal' (1989) HMSO and Response to the Report Cm 679 (1989) HMSO.

House of Lords Select Committee on the European Communities 25th Report Session 1989–90 'Paying for Pollution' (1990) HMSO.

House of Lords Select Committee on Science and Technology Session 1988–89 4th Report 'Hazardous Waste Disposal'.

Lipworth, S, 'Packaging Levy: Report on Point of Funding' (1994) Producer Responsibility Group.

Lomas, O, 'Waste Management: Re-Use and Recycling: Developments in Europe' [1990] 1 LMELR 160.

Openshaw, S, Carver, S, and Fernie, J, *Britain's Nuclear Waste: Safety and Siting* (1989) Belhaven.

Pocklington, DN, 'Waste Holder Liability' [1996] 8 ELM 101.

Rossi, H, 'Paying for Our Past — Will We?' [1995] 7 JEL 1.

Royal Commission on Environmental Pollution, 17th Report: 'Incineration of Waste', Cm 2181 (1993) HMSO.

Tromans, S, 'The difficulties of enforcing Waste Disposal Licence Conditions' [1991] 3 JEL 281.

Vaughan, D, (ed) *Environment and Planning Law* (1991) Butterworths (chapters 9 [Bryce], 10 [Farha], 11 [Hawkins], 12 [Bos], 13 [Freeman]).

Part III

Legal protection for the atmosphere and integrated controls over major polluting activities

Chapter 10

Atmospheric pollution and integrated pollution control

'Sad the lot of poplar trees, courted by a fickle breeze' (W S Gilbert, 'The Pirates of Penzance', Act II)

A THE OVERALL PROBLEM

Air is intangible, ignored and easily damaged by pollution. The issue was fearsomely highlighted by the Bhopal disaster in India in 1984 when toxic substances escaped into the atmosphere near a major population centre. Atmospheric emissions could upset earth's fundamental ecological basis. Scientific debate on the so-called 'greenhouse effect' is based on concern over increasing atmospheric levels of carbon dioxide resulting from combustion of fossil fuels and emissions of other 'greenhouse gases' such as methane from decomposing waste, chlorofluorocarbons (CFCs) and nitrous oxides (NOx). Between 1978 and 1982 the concentration of carbon dioxide in the atmosphere increased from 315 parts per million to 340 parts per million. The Intergovernmental Panel on Climate Change (IPCC) reported in 1990 that up to one third of world grain production would be lost, the homes and livelihoods of 300m people set at risk from rising sea levels, and widespread desertification could flow from such an ecological imbalance which would result from global warming consequent on the greenhouse gases trapping heat within earth's atmosphere. Weather patterns will also become more unpredictable. The IPCC recommended an *immediate* cut in greenhouse gas emissions of 60%, but effective international action is still awaited despite the pronouncements of the Rio 'Earth Summit' in 1992. If, however, 'business as usual' emissions continue, by 2030 mean global surface air temperatures are likely to be 1.4°C higher than currently, carbon dioxide concentrations will have further increased from 350 parts per million by volume to 450, and global mean sea levels could be 20 cm higher than today, with consequences for agriculture, coastal areas, animal species, and indeed all sectors of human existence and activity. A most worrying aspect of the problem is the climatic uncertainty consequent on global warming, and this has led many to call for the application of precautionary principles nationally and internationally in the formulation of laws and policies designed, inter alia, to: promote greater energy economy; drive down the use of fossil fuels; promote the use of natural gas and renewable energy sources such as solar energy, wind, biomass and wave power; develop better public transportation and reduce consumption of fossil fuels by private vehicles.

Though 'global warming' is the most serious atmospheric pollution problem, public concern also exists, inter alia, in relation to 'acid rain', depletion of the ozone layer, levels of ambient lead, the low level ozone problem, benzene, straw and stubble burning and volatile organic compounds (VOCs).

B PARTICULAR PROBLEMS AND SOME SOLUTIONS

Atmospheric pollution is no respecter of international boundaries. Nor is it the province of any one discipline: to reduce atmospheric pollutants requires action on a wide variety of fronts — technological, planning, social, economic, as well as legislative.

Good industrial management and improved technologies are important in reducing airborne pollution. See Coal and Energy Quarterly (1984) No 41, pp 24–29. Coal burning furnaces using 'fluidised bed' technology can reduce emissions of sulphur dioxide by over 90% by trapping the gas in beds of red hot limestone, and can be 80% thermally efficient, compared with 37% for conventional power station coal furnaces, see The Times, 28 April, 1989, p 26. Efficiently designed furnaces can easily prevent the discharge of smokey volatile material. Incinerators can be prevented from discharging smoke into the air by the provision of afterburners. Emissions of grit and dust are controllable by use of settling chambers, bag filters, water scrubbers and electrostatic precipitators. The wise location of industry, taking into account prevailing weather patterns, topography and the incidence of population can reduce the potential for harm of emissions. Technology is, however, not so efficient in relation to polluting emissions caused by accidental leaks and spillages, evaporation from stored chemicals, and escapes arising from accidents during the course of transport. Furthermore unintended mixture of pollutants in air may produce secondary compounds.

Particular problems

'Acid rain'

There are certain emissions which are particularly difficult to control without further undesirable consequences. Sulphur dioxide (SO_2) is a major pollutant produced by chemical plants, oil refineries and power stations, yet not effectively controlled under the Clean Air legislation largely because in the 1950s no practical means of reducing SO_2 emissions was known, short of reducing fuel consumption. The method of control over SO_2 emissions was to disperse gas by discharging it at high velocity through tall chimneys, ideally, at least, two-and-a-half times the height of the nearest physical features. Discharged gas rises to a height of about 2,000 ft, dispersing over a wide area. This disposal method produced a 40% reduction in SO_2 concentrations at ground level in urban areas between 1956 and 1973, despite a 17% increase in gross energy consumption. Dispersal of SO_2 was widely accepted as the best means of control, see Scorer 'Technical Aspects of Air Pollution' chapter 3 of *Environmental Pollution Control* pp 54–56 and 58–61.

The growing body of evidence of the ill effects of SO_2 combined with water and other chemical agents to produce acid deposition, however, refocused

ACIDIFICATION (A SIMPLIFIED MODEL)

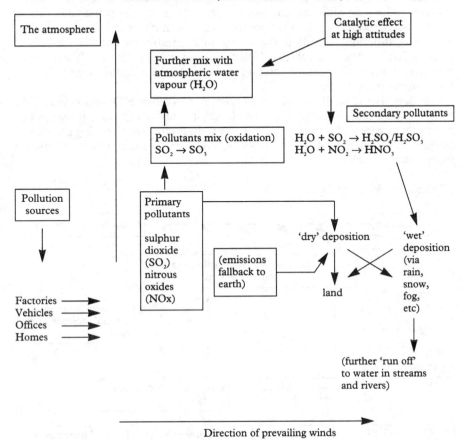

Direction of prevailing winds

In North Western Europe the direction of prevailing winds is South West to North East, hence the most affected areas of this part of the globe are Norway, Sweden and Finland, though 'fluxes' from the UK and France also affect Germany and Poland. France is affected by 'fluxes' from Spain and Portugal.

attention on this issue. Voices were raised internationally arguing that the UK's disposal methods have resulted in British SO_2 polluting much of the rest of Europe. The 10th Report of the Royal Commission on Environmental Pollution accepted that emissions of sulphur and nitrogen oxides cause damage to fresh water and terrestrial ecosystems, but also considered the economic cost of reducing such emissions. The Royal Commission recommended, inter alia, that the electricity supply industry should investigate in the short term the various methods to abate SO_2 emissions, so that the industry would be ready and able to introduce remedial action should this prove necessary in the face of international pressure, note also the findings of the House of Commons Environment Committee in 'Acid Rain' (4th Report, Session 1983–84). 'Acid Rain' Cmnd 9397 doubted whether ozone concentration (produced by sunlight acting on hydrocarbons and NOx) now thought to be a possible contributor to forest damage, was principally due to transnational pollution. It also pointed out the high cost of reducing SO_2 emissions, though declaring policy to be: further reductions of SO_2 by 30% of 1980 levels by the end of the 1990s; similar reductions in NOx; stricter emission standards for motor cars; further research into atmospheric pollution and control technologies.

Caution also officially prevailed in relation to British NOx emissions, 45% of which were then produced by the electricity supply industry. It was policy not to set targets and timetables controlling emissions from existing plants and setting limits for new plant. Policy was, however, to reduce NOx emissions from motor vehicles.

Depletion of the ozone layer

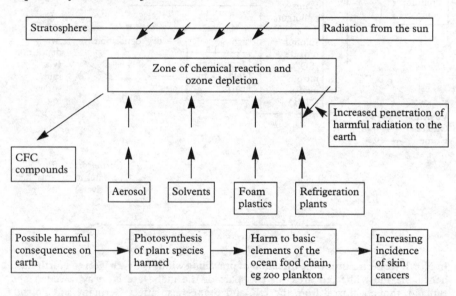

The chief cause of ozone depletion is a chemical reaction between various chlorofluorocarbon (CFC) gases and ozone. As a result of a complex process by which CFC compounds rise into the atmosphere reaching the stratosphere, they become 'dissociated' as a result of solar radiation and yield chlorine atoms, which destroy the ozone layer, which acts as a shield to filter out much harmful radiation from the sun.

1   CFCs are not the only 'culprits', but they are the main ones. Other 'depleters' include supersonic aircraft emissions, NOx emissions resulting from the application of nitrogen-based fertilisers, or from atmospheric nuclear weapon tests (now banned by international law) — but all of these are minor compared to the impact of CFCs.
2   CFCs are only slowly removed from the atmosphere by natural processes, and in 65–90 years' time virtually all CFCs ever produced will still be 'resident' in the atmosphere if released.

3   But remember CFCs have been seen in the past as very beneficial: easily made, cheap, non-toxic, non-flammable. To replace them is not easy. A range of substances can be used, the most popular were originally the HCFCs and HFCs. However, even these have various damaging effects and so they too have had to be brought under control. (See below.)

4   Similarly now subject to control are carbon tetrachloride (the 'classic' cleaning solvent) 1.1.1 trichloroethane, methyl bromide, hydrobromo-fluorocarbons (HBFC), and hydrochlorofluorocarbons (HCFC) as HCFCs are powerful greenhouse gases. This is 'the problem of technical bind', ie the solution to one problem creates another.

5   The hydrofluorocarbons (HFCs) are potent 'greenhouse' gases, and since January 1996 *voluntary* agreements between the UK government and the aerosol, air conditioning, refrigeration, fire protection and foam industries provide that where HFCs are used emissions will be minimised, and that they will not be used where emissions are unavoidable *and* safe, practical and more environmentally acceptable alternatives exist. However, the air conditioning and refrigeration 'agreement' is only a declaration of intent, as this industry is highly dispersed, and those who signed the document could not make a commitment on the part of those they did not represent.

The greenhouse effect

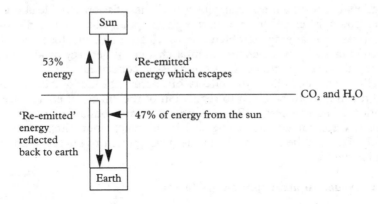

The earth receives its heat from the sun in the form of radiated energy. The atmosphere prevents most of this energy reaching the earth's surface, *only* 47% 'gets through' and that would not be enough for the planet to be habitable; its surface temperature would be some 20°C to 40°C. What keeps the planet habitable is *a* greenhouse effect — carbon dioxide (CO_2) and water (H_2O) in the atmosphere reflect back to the earth energy which is given off from the earth's surface after it has been received from the sun — this maintains an average surface temperature of 14°C. But a change of only 2°–3°C in temperature range would have a very marked effect on the earth's climate.

What is now called *the* greenhouse effect is that certain gases, principally CO_2, if emitted from earth so that they accumulate in the atmosphere, will reflect back to the earth's surface more of the 're-emitted' energy, thus raising its surface temperature.

1   The principal 'greenhouse' gas is CO_2 emitted consequent on the use of 'fossil fuels' such as coal and oil.
2   Other gases, though present in smaller quantities, are more potent as 'greenhouse' gases, eg methane — 'marsh gas' or 'fire damp', etc.
3   CO_2 can be locked inside natural 'safes' such as trees as they breathe in CO_2 and breathe out oxygen. Thus the destruction of such natural 'sinks' exacerbates the problem.
4   Much scientific uncertainty still surrounds the greenhouse effect — indeed many still deny that it is a phenomenon that *can* occur — and its consequences.
5   Life could exist with higher earth surface temperatures — it did 4,500–8,000 years ago — but it appears the result would be wetter conditions in most of Europe, Africa, Southern Asia, Southern North America and South America, and drier conditions in most of the USA and Russia — the world's principal wheat growing areas. Thus crop yields could change dramatically.
6   Other effects of the 'greenhouse' could be (a) melting of the polar ice caps leading to massive flooding of low lying areas of the earth; (b) loss of plant/animal and fish species intolerant to higher temperatures; (c) increased global weather uncertainty with more storms.

It is, however, impossible to end using fossil fuels 'overnight', nationally or internationally, nor is a mass changeover to nuclear fission a viable alternative. Nuclear power is 'clean' from an atmospheric point of view, but disposal of nuclear waste is a great problem. It is clear, however, that the closest connection exists between environmental change and energy production and use. The current generation of laws on the issue concentrate — where they do so at all — on controlling the effects of energy production. In the future attention will have to be given to regulation of the effects of energy use. The promotion of more energy efficient appliances and buildings, coupled with positive rewards for energy saving will be of much more importance than currently. This will be in addition to the development of energy sources of a renewable nature.

Further issues in atmospheric pollution

Consideration of 'global' atmospheric issues such as ozone depletion and the greenhouse effect should not detract attention from other problems which, though their incidence may be localised, are nevertheless capable of causing loss, injury and death. Environmental groups have argued that 10 million Britons are at risk from polluted air, and point to an alarming rate in the incidence of asthma, with 10% of children and 4–6% of adults affected, and which causes some 2,000 deaths in the UK each year (a doubling in 25 years), seven million lost working days, £400m losses to industry and commerce and £520m in costs to the national health and benefits budget with 200,000 people disabled by the disease. Particular pollutants causing concern include carbon monoxide, NOx and ozone, which is particularly implicated in the onset of asthma and bronchitis.

In addition fine particles in vehicle emissions, each less than 10 micrometers across and known as PM10, can be drawn into the lungs by respiration, carrying chemicals, some of them acidic. This further puts at risk the old, and those already suffering from chronic lung or heart diseases: some 2,000 to 10,000 deaths pa may be ultimately attributable to PM10. Diesel powered vehicles, heating systems and industrial systems are particularly implicated in the emission of solid particulate material, which now exceeds a realistic level of 50 micrograms per cubic metre of air on about 36 days pa in Britain, and which can reach 200 micrograms. Action on PM10 in the UK is likely to be initiated under the air quality strategy provisions of the Environment Act 1995, under new vehicle emission limits and EU measures.

Ozone, so essential at stratospheric levels, is, at ground or tropospheric levels, a highly corrosive pollutant which is formed by a complex chemical process based on reaction between sunlight, NOx and volatile organic compounds (VOCs). VOCs occur naturally, but 95% of those found in the atmosphere result from human activity. Some are highly toxic and can cause cancer, others are implicated in the formation of photochemical smog. VOCs are emitted in vehicle exhaust gases, and evaporation from petrol, paint and glue, and solvents. VOCs are gaseous pollutants containing carbon, and include hydrocarbons, and their oxygenated and chlorinated derivatives. Their common characteristic is the propensity to evaporate at normal outdoor (ie 'ambient') temperatures. A vast number of organic chemicals can be classed as VOCs, but examples include iso-octane, benzene, toluene, ethene and butane.

A regular summer problem in many cities is photochemical smog. Unlike the old 'pea souper' fogs of the 1950s (which were caused by large particles of soot and SO_2 emitted from coal burning power stations and which were common in winter when cold, dirty air can be trapped at ground level by warmer air above it) modern smog is made up of micro particles of VOCs and NOx. In summer, when anticyclonic weather over Britain induces an easterly air stream, bringing in polluted air from industrial areas on the continental mainland, the strong sunlight reacts with the 'chemical cocktail' to create ozone. To combat the problem international action, and certainly action on a world regional level, is needed. The UK's favoured approach is to press for action within the framework of the United Nations Economic Commission for Europe (UNECE). The current UNECE VOC protocol ratified by the UK in 1994, requires nations to achieve VOC reductions by 30% on 1988 levels by 1999. The UK aims to meet this target by applying the BATNEEC requirements of Part I of the Environmental Protection Act 1990 to solvent using industries and enhanced car emission controls. Action will also be taken under the UK's national air quality strategy (see below) and will include giving public warning of high ozone risks and pleas to motorists to limit vehicle use on days when such risks would occur because of atmospheric conditions.

These problems have, however, to be kept in perspective. Atmospheric pollution risks today are less than they were 40 years ago. We are right to be concerned about the incidence of asthma; we need more research into the problems associated with PM10 and benzene; we may well have to curb the use of petrol and diesel powered vehicles which are the source of many pollutants, but the harmful effects of pollution are still much less marked or clearly observable than those of smoking.

Once again, however, we face a problem caused by a degree of uncertainty in the scientific evidence. The official Committee on the Medical Effects of Air Pollutants in October 1995 concluded that atmospheric pollution may certainly *aggravate* asthma, but it appears not to be a major *cause* of it. The problem is one of an unexplained increase in allergies, and the presence of 'biological pollutants' such as pollen and fungal spores, and styles of living (ie cramped living space and poor ventilation, deficient diets, mothers who smoke while pregnant and use of foam bedding mattresses). On the other hand traffic fumes may be much more implicated in the incidence of bronchitis and heart attacks. The lack of certain medical conclusions renders it more difficult to argue for stringent preventive controls over polluting emissions.

C THE LEGAL RESPONSE

There are a number of international treaties relating to atmospheric pollution ranging from the Geneva Agreement of 1958, various portions of which relate to emissions from vehicle engines, through the 1979 Geneva Convention on long range transboundary pollution, and the Vienna and Montreal Conventions of 1985 and 1987 on the protection of the ozone layer, to the 1992 framework Convention on Climate Change, part of the 'Rio package'.

International law is, however, increasingly concerned with the issues of transboundary pollution, of which the 'acid rain' issue is the classic instance, and general protection for the medium of the atmosphere, as witness agreements on protecting the ozone layer and moves towards attempts to limit emissions of 'greenhouse gases'.

Customary international law (see further chapter 4) has also some role to play in this connection. The customary recognition of the territorial sovereignty principle carries with it the notion that states may use their resources for their own benefit — for example the burning of fossil fuels. Against this it is generally argued that states should not allow transboundary pollution from activities carried out on their territory to affect other states, and the United Nations Charter of Economic Rights adds that sovereign rights are only to be used 'without causing damage to the legitimate interests of others'. See also dicta in *The Corfu Channel Case (UK v Albania)*[1] that a state is under an obligation 'not to allow its territory to be used for acts contrary to the rights of other states': *The Trail Smelter Arbitration*[2] and *The Nuclear Tests Case (Australia v France)*[3]. The concept was also recognised by Principle 21 of the (non-legally binding) 1972 Stockholm Declaration on the Environment. Whether all this amounts to a firmly settled rule of international law, however, is still a matter for some debate. (See, for example, Sands, *Chernobyl: Law and Communication* p 13 et seq.) Assuming, however, that there is a rule of customary international law relating to transboundary atmospheric pollution, how is it to be expressed? The Montreal Rules (ILA Draft Rules on Transboundary Pollution) formulate a requirement that states must prevent transfrontier air pollution to the extent that no substantial injury is caused to other states' territory, and that states 'shall refrain from causing transfrontier pollution by discharging into the environment substances generally considered as being highly dangerous to human health'. Problems arise, however, with

1 (1948) ICJ Reps 15 at 22.
2 [1941] AJIL 684.
3 (1974) ICJ Reps 253.

regard to defining what constitutes 'substantial injury', as to what the requisite standard of care is, and to which injuries it applies.

Furthermore if the formulation of the customary rule in *The Trail Smelter* arbitration is followed 'clear and convincing evidence' of the injury in question must be brought forward. In that instance, however, the pollutants in question travelled only ten miles, and liability was admitted. Not all cases of transboundary pollution are so clear, and it has been a major weakness of international law that it has experienced difficulty — indeed often impossibility — in attributing responsibility for particular incidents of pollution damage in one state to particular polluting emissions from another — especially where several states emit emissions of the same type, as is the case with, for example, SO_2. It is, however, becoming easier to produce 'balance sheets' of pollution 'imports and exports' using enhanced monitoring techniques and more sophisticated mathematical models, and it is is thus becoming more feasible to produce evidence that a given nation is receiving, for example, specified proportions of acidifying agents from another state, see the 1984 EMEP Report (see below) as abstracted in the Report of the 1986 62nd Conference of the International Law Association. However, it remains to be generally accepted that these new techniques enable the attribution of particular incidents of pollution damage to emissions from particular states.

Atmospheric treaties

As a consequence of the less than satisfactory condition of customary law increasing emphasis comes to be laid on treaties, both those dealing with individual issues and concerning only two, or a very few, states and, more especially, those which lay down generally applicable rules on a multi-state basis. The modern treaty based international law on atmospheric pollution dates from the Stockholm Conference of June 1972 on the Human Environment. Various non-legally binding principles were declared at the Conference. Principle 21, already referred to, provided that: 'states have . . . the sovereign right to exploit their own resources and the responsibility to ensure that activities within their jurisdiction . . . do not cause damage to the environment of other states . . .'. Principle 22 further provided for international collaboration to develop laws concerning compensation for the victims of transboundary pollution. Following the Stockholm Conference the Organisation for Economic Co-operation and Development (OECD) undertook a study of transboundary sulphur pollution. This led to further work by the Co-operative Programme for Monitoring and Evaluation of Long Range Transmission of Air Pollutants in Europe (EMEP), the United Nations Economic Commission for Europe (ECE), and the United Nations Environment Programme (UNEP). Following this came the 1979 Geneva Convention on Long Range Transboundary Air Pollution which came into force on 16 March 1983 and which was ratified by 30 nations between 1980 and 1985, as well as by the European Community. A protocol was added to the Convention in 1984 providing for long term financial support for air pollution monitoring programmes. The 1979 Convention is a general law making framework under which signatory states commit themselves to develop strategies and policies to reduce, and eliminate where possible, atmospheric pollution, including transboundary pollution, and undertake to adopt the best available technology that is economically feasible to achieve such an end (see further below on the BATNEEC principle in the UK). The Helsinki Protocol added to the Convention in 1985 requires those states who sign it to achieve a 30% reduction from 1980 levels in the national emissions, or cross boundary flow, of sulphur by 2003 — the so called '30% Club'. Twenty one states have signed that Protocol, some promising more significant reductions than 30% by particular dates. The UK did *not* originally sign the Helsinki Protocol arguing that it had reduced its SO_2 emissions by 42% compared with 1970 levels by the mid 1980s and that it would achieve a further 30% reduction on 1980 levels by the late 1990s. However, on 14 June 1994 in Oslo the UK agreed to reduce SO_2 emissions to one fifth of 1980 levels by 2010; this follows the voluntary 37% reduction since 1980 and a projected 70% reduction by 2005. The reductions will benefit the UK as well as other nations for by the early 1990s up to 50% of our land area was receiving greater acidification than it could cope with: by 2010 there will only be 5% of land so affected. The reduction is possible because of the phasing out of coal fired power stations and their replacement by gas fired plant. It is likely that a few (currently there are two) modern coal fired power stations will be fitted with flue gas desulphurisation (FGD) equipment; but at some £0.5 bn per station this is an expensive option. FGD fitted stations will continue to burn coal at a rate of about 15m tonnes pa. (See further below on UK compliance with EU requirements on SO_2 emissions.)

The 1979 Convention also established machinery to review its own implementation and development and it imposes quite strict requirements on signatory states to carry out research into, and exchange information on, emission problems, with co-operative monitoring and evaluation programmes. Where a dispute arises between signatory states under the Convention the primary means of mediation is to be negotiation rather than punitive or compensatory sanctions.

Turning from acidification to the problems of ozone depletion and global warming, it is once more treaty based provisions of international law that are encountered. The Vienna Convention and Montreal Protocol (1985 and 1987) represent excellent examples of a 'framework' treaty and a subsequent 'fleshing out' protocol. The Vienna Convention furthered the use of a technique now common in international treaties, namely the 'conference of the parties' to keep the treaty under continuous review and a permanent secretariat.

The Montreal Protocol was subsequently amended to provide for the total elimination of use of CFCs and other ozone depleting chemicals. In Helsinki in 1989 the participating states declared the need for, inter alia, propagation of essential information between states, with all nations being committed to a concerted plan of action to counter the issue. Three conditions were identified as essential prerequisites to this: speedy development of alternative chemical substitutes for CFCs, transfer of appropriate technology to developing nations to enable them to eliminate the use and production of CFCs and an international funding mechanism to assist in meeting the costs of the developing nations in making the necessary technological changes.

Such a global environmental fund was created following the London amendments to the Montreal Protocol Convention in 1990, when a fund of $160–240m came into being so that developing nations can be assisted to adopt the use of CFC substitutes. This 'Ozone Fund' represents 'new money' set aside by the developed nations over and above their existing overseas aid budgets.

Principal features of the Montreal Protocol

A key clause is Article 6. This provides that the parties to the Protocol, beginning in 1990 and *at least* every four years thereafter, must assess, in the light of expert scientific evidence, the actual control measures which are found in Article 2. The parties can then decide whether further adjustments and reductions of production or consumption of the controlled substances from 1986 levels should be undertaken. The timing, scope and amount of any such changes are to be agreed by consensus; however, as a last resort, decisions can be adopted by a two-thirds majority vote of parties present and voting provided they represent at least 50% of the parties' total consumption of the substances in question.

Article 4 complements the undertakings in Article 2 by imposing trade restrictions between parties and states not party to the Protocol. Initially there was an import ban of controlled substances from any non-party state, and from 1 January 1993, developing country parties were not to export such substances to any non-party state. Article 5 is titled 'special situation of developing countries'. In essence, this gives any such country a 'limited grace' period of freedom from the operation of the control measures in Article 2, provided consumption of the controlled substances is less than 0.3 kilograms per capita on the date the Protocol enters into force or any time ten years thereafter. Parties also undertake to facilitate access to environmentally safe alternative substances and technologies for developing country parties and also to facilitate provision of financial assistance for this purpose.

Article 8 deals with 'non-compliance'. The parties, at their first meeting, were required to consider and approve procedures and institutional mechanisms for determining non-compliance with Protocol provisions and for treatment of parties found to be in non-compliance.

Following the Montreal Protocol came the Helsinki declaration on protection of the ozone layer, the London meeting of the parties in 1990, and the Copenhagen meeting of 1992. Meetings have been held more frequently than the minimum provided for.

The general pattern of adjustments, etc, has been to bring forward dates for phasing out production and use *in response to* scientific evidence of ozone thinning, not just over the Antarctic but in the Northern hemisphere. The USA has been a major force for pushing for the phase out, while the international process has been aided by the nations of the EU who have allowed the EU to act as an internationally recognised body whose politics supersede those of its constituents; hence Western Europe has effectively been one 'block' on this issue. By itself the UK might well have dragged its feet as the government was for a while much influenced by ICI, the major UK CFC maker. The current position for the EU is found in Regulation 3093/94 (see further below).

In 1995 further deleterious affectation of Antartic ozone was noted, with the yearly 'hole' in the ozone layer, which has been noted for the past ten years, covering an area the size of Europe. The 'thinning' process which leads to the 'hole' had by mid-1995 reached its most rapidly recorded rate, 1% per day, and the 1995 'hole' was at this time twice the size it was at the corresponding period in 1993 and 1994. Ministers of participating states met in Vienna in December 1995, and agreed to bring about an even faster phasing out of ozone depleting substances. Methyl bromide use in developed countries will be cut in 2001 and 2005 and phased out in 2010, apart from certain agricultural uses. HCFC consumption is to be reduced and phased out by 2020, with some exemptions. Developing countries agreed to freeze methyl bromide production and consumption in 2002, HCFC consumption in 2016, and HCFCs are to be phased out by 2040. Acceleration of these targets will be considered before 2000.

However, further evidence of the weakness of international regulation appeared in The Independent, 19 September 1995. It must be remembered that no nation can be forced to agree to a particular international treaty. Russia did not agree to key portions of the Montreal Protocol, and has publicly declared it was not able to honour its earlier commitments to phase out CFC production by the beginning of 1996, pleading poverty as the reason for being unable to meet the cost of replacing CFCs — some hundreds of millions of pounds. CFC *production* in the EU was banned as from 1 January 1995, but not *use* nor, in certain cases, *export* and it appears that users of CFCs may be smuggling in supplies from Russia. The evidence is that CFC prices in general have not risen — yet one would expect such a rise as users seek to purchase the dwindling stocks of a product no longer made. CFCs may be legally imported into the UK from Russia for recycling (and re-export) or destruction, up to a limit of 500 tonnes, yet trade statistics show six monthly imports in 1995 of 3,800 tonnes — these are almost certainly unlicensed, ie effectively smuggled imports. Yet, and here there is a weakness in UK law, we lack regulations to impose penalties on unlicensed offenders, for while the EU regulation is directly applicable and requires no further action on the part of the UK government, penalties for failure to comply with EU rules are left to member states and the relevant UK regulations (SI 1994/199) were deficient on this issue. As from 29 March 1996 SI 1996/506 supplements EU law by prohibiting and restricting import, landing and unloading of relevant substances. Customs officers may detain material imported, etc, in contravention of the regulations and provision is made for offences and penalties. Unlawfully imported substances are to be harmlessly disposed of.

With respect to global warming, suggestions were made at the Toronto Conference of 1988 for reductions of 20% in CO_2 emissions by 2005, and 50% reductions in other 'greenhouse' emissions by 2020. Thirty nations subsequently attended the UN World Climate Conference at Geneva in 1990 which agreed to develop an International Convention on global warming by 1992. The UK then undertook to reduce emissions to 1990 levels by 2005, and there was an overall EU commitment to reduce them to 1990 levels by 2000 'in general' with some nations meeting the target before then. However the International Panel on Climate Change (IPCC) argued that to *stabilise* 'greenhouse gas' emissions at 1990 levels would require immediate reductions globally of over 60%.

The United Nations framework Convention on Climate Change, which technically pre-dated the 1992 Rio 'Earth Summit', entred into force in 1994. It begins with acknowledgements that:

1 'Change in the earth's climate and its adverse effects are a common concern of mankind'.
2 'The global nature of climate change calls for the widest possible co-operation by all countries and their participation in an effective and appropriate international response . . .'
3 'States should enact effective environmental legislation, that environmental standards, management objectives and priorities should reflect the environmental and developmental context to which they apply . . .'

It also recognises the principle of state sovereignty but also enshrines recognition of differentiated responsibility for global emissions of greenhouse gases, and the need for developed nations 'to take immediate action in a flexible manner on the basis of clear priorities'. The convention further recognises the need of developing nations to have access to that advanced technology which they will need consequently on the energy growth they will experience as part of their development.

The Convention then lays down a number of important definitions, including:

1 'Climate change' — 'a change of climate which is attributed directly or indirectly to human activity that alters the composition of the global atmosphere and which is in addition to natural climate variability observed over comparable time periods'.
2 'Adverse effects of climate change' — 'changes in the physical environment or biota resulting in climate change which have significant deleterious effects on the composition, resilience or productivity of natural and managed ecosystems or on the operation of socio-economic systems or on human health and welfare'.
3 'Greenhouse gases' — 'those gaseous constituents of the atmosphere, both natural and anthropogenic, that absorb and re-emit infrared radiation'.
4 'Sink' — 'any process, activity or mechanism which removes a greenhouse gas, an aerosol or a precursor of a greenhouse gas from the atmosphere'.

The objectives and principles of the Convention follow in Articles 2 and 3.
   The objective is:

'. . . to achieve . . . stabilisation of greenhouse gas concentrations in the atmosphere at a level that would prevent dangerous anthropogenic interference with the climate system. Such a level should be achieved within a time-frame sufficient to allow ecosystems to adapt naturally to climate change, to ensure that food production is not threatened and to enable economic development to proceed in a sustainable manner'.

While the guiding principles to achieve this objective are to:

1 Protect the climate system for 'benefit of present and future generations of humankind, on a basis of equity and in accordance with their common but differentiated responsibilities and capabilities'.
2 Adopt 'precautionary measures to anticipate, prevent or minimise the causes of climate change and mitigate its adverse effects'. Where the threat is of serious or irreversible damage, lack of full scientific certainty 'should not be used as reason for postponing such measures, taking into account that . . . (such) measures . . . should be cost effective so as to ensure global benefits at the lowest possible cost'.
3 Promote sustainable development.

Article 4 proceeds to impose a variety of commitments on all participating parties to:

1   Make available to the Conference of the Parties (COP) national inventories of anthropogenic emissions by sources and removals by sinks of all greenhouse gases not controlled by the Montreal Protocol, using comparable methodologies to be agreed by the COP.
2   Formulate and implement national or regional programmes to mitigate climate change.
3   Promote and co-operate in the development and transfer of technologies, practices and processes that control, reduce or prevent anthropogenic emissions of greenhouse gases in all relevant sectors including energy, agriculture, forestry and waste management.
4   Promote sustainable development including co-operation in the conservation and enhancement of sinks and reservoirs for greenhouse gases including biomass, forests and oceans.
5   Co-operate in preparing for adaptation to the impacts of climate change.
6   Take climate change considerations into account to the extent feasible in their relevant social, economic and environmental policies.
7   Promote and co-operate in research related to the climate system and all facets of climate change; and to exchange relevant information related thereto.

There are additional obligations placed on 36 listed developed nations, largely those of Europe and North America together with Japan, Australia and New Zealand to:

1   Adopt national (or regional) policies and take corresponding measures on the mitigation of change by limiting anthropogenic emissions of greenhouse gases and protecting and enhancing greenhouse gas sinks and reservoirs.
2   Communicate regularly detailed information on the above policies and measures with the aim of returning individually or jointly to 1990 levels emissions of carbon dioxide and other greenhouse gases.

Twenty five developed nations further undertook to provide financial resources and to transfer technology needed by developing countries to meet the cost of implementing the treaty obligations and to promote and facilitate environmentally sound technology transfer. These were those listed before minus the former Communist states of Eastern Europe.

The Climate Change Convention in practice

Since 1992 evidence has continued to mount that global warming is taking place. However, even on the basis that a degree of warming will occur, there is still considerable room for disagreement about the level of increase and the rate of its occurrence. The rate could be as slow as 0.15°C per decade, but 0.2°C per decade seems more likely, though 0.3°C per decade is possible if acidifying emissions (see above) are curbed world-wide, because one of their by-effects is the creation of 'sulphate aerosol' which reflects sunlight into space before it can reach and warm the earth. An increase in temperature combined with rainfall changes would be swift enough to disrupt agriculture, forests and eco-systems.

It was against that background that the first review of the Convention took place in Berlin in 1995. Three years on from their Rio commitments, most signatory developed nations had compiled inventories of greenhouse gases and have programmes and policies to limit them. Officially the view was that good progress had been made in making the framework Convention on Climate Change operational, but it was also accepted that the existing commitments were inadequate to meet the long term objective of avoiding human induced climate change. In particular no objectives were set for controlling greenhouse emissions beyond 2000. Hence the purpose of the first review by the COP at Berlin was to 'set in hand negotiations' on such further commitments.

The framework Convention requires developed signatory states to submit information on:

1 National emissions of human induced greenhouse gases by sources, and removal of these gases by sinks.
2 A description of policies and measures to meet commitments to take steps aimed at returning emissions to 1990 levels by 2000.
3 Estimates as to the effects such policies will have on emissions.

By 1994 18 states had submitted programmes, including most of the Western and Central European states, Australia, New Zealand and the USA. Fifteen of these reports were synthesised by the UN Secretariat to the Convention; those from the nations accounting for 41% of global emissions of CO_2 from fossil fuel sources. Six nations anticipated meeting their target; others undertook to introduce other measures if it appears they will not meet targets. In terms of measures to be introduced the most common were legal regulations, economic instruments, voluntary agreements, education and information. These are to operate alongside and through greater competition in energy supply leading to improved efficiency and fuel switching, improved fuel consumption by industrial plants and processes, improved automobile efficiency and encouraging the use of public transport, greater energy efficiency in buildings, reduced animal emissions and reduced use of nitrogen fertilisers, preservation of forest biomass with new planting, minimising waste and emissions from landfills of methane. This last named very potent greenhouse gas is 39% accounted for by emissions from landfills and, if no action were to be taken, emissions in the UK alone would be 25% above 1990 levels by 2000. This has led nationally to an emphasis on recycling and energy recovery, and the tax on landfill introduced in the 1994 Budget.

The UK by 1995 was on course to meet Rio commitments: by 2000 emissions of CO_2 should be below 1990 levels. That is largely because of greater use of low carbon fuels in the economy, eg in power stations (see further below).

Berlin — the outcome

Considerable pressure was placed on the USA to agree to make definite and specific commitments to reducing greenhouse emissions while it was conceded by the oil producing countries that they would not block the proceedings by insisting that all decisions should be taken by consensus. The COP made some progress. It noted the inadequacy of existing commitments and reiterated the obligations of the developed nations to take the lead in reducing greenhouse emissions, while allowing developing nations to increase their emissions. Participating states also agreed to promote 'carbon sinks' such as forests and wetlands. The most important result was that the principle of actual cuts in emissions beyond 2000 was agreed. All signatories will be committed to set quantified limitation and reduction objectives within specific time frames before the next review in 1997. The 'time frames' in question are 2005, 2010 and 2020.

Since the Berlin gathering further research by the UN International Panel on Climate Change (IPCC) indicates the present reality of climate change, and this was publicly released in Madrid in November 1995, though not without some scientific dissent. The findings clearly implicate emissions, from human and industrial activity, of CO_2, methane and NOx, in global temperature rises, and point to the possibilities of a 100 year drought in southern Africa, increases in weather extremes such as hurricanes and massive downpours, the spread of tropical diseases, eg dengue and yellow fevers and malaria, reduced crop yields, while the UK and Western Europe could experience *drops* in temperature consequent on a southwards shift in the Gulf Stream. If the temperature rose by 3.5°C by 2100 sea levels could also rise by then between 15 and 95 cms.

EU and UK policy responses to the 'greenhouse' issue

It is convenient to consider these matters here, not least because by doing so it is possible to show how international law is reflected in regional and national policies and legislative programmes. The proposal from the Commission for a Carbon/Energy Tax (COM (92) 226 final, 03 No C 196/1) to drive down the use of fossil fuels has so far come to nought, and will not be adopted without the unanimous agreement of all member states. However, Directive 93/389 established a programme for the monitoring of greenhouse emissions and required member states to draw up and implement their own national programmes to meet international legal obligations, while CO_2 emissions are further combated by the SAVE programme on energy efficiency which exists under Directive 93/76 which requires, inter alia, thermal insulation for new buildings, regular boiler inspection, energy use auditing, and billing for space and water heating and air conditioning to reflect actual energy consumption. The alternative energy programme to promote, inter alia, renewable energy sources was also set up under Council Decision 93/500.

The UK's specific response, 'Climate Change — the UK's Programme' (1994), combines policy and practical measures along with legal regulation. Domestic energy consumption is to be reduced both by the imposition of VAT on energy use, by the work of an energy saving trust, the work of local energy advice centres and general publicity on the efficient use of energy, by use of eco labelling which states the energy use level of products, by setting consumption standards for domestic appliances, and by revising the building regulations to provide for enhanced energy efficiency. Industrial and commercial consumption is to be tackled by, inter alia, seeking corporate commitment to energy efficiency, use of 'best practice' techniques, giving advice to small concerns under the energy management assistance scheme and the energy design advice scheme. Specific target reductions in energy use are to be required of public sector bodies, while energy use in transport is to be driven down by fiscal measures such as increases in fuel duty over and above the rate of inflation. Renewable energy sources are also to be promoted.

There is, however, a problem with schemes of CO_2 emission reduction, and that is long term uncertainty over energy demands. At the end of 1995 DoE calculations as to the reductions needed to meet treaty obligations (to reduce CO_2 emissions by 10 mtc [million tonnes of carbon] to reach 1990 levels) indicated that the target would be overshot because of improved electricity output from nuclear plant, and switches to gas fired generation. In response to this target savings were reduced, with the likely consequence that fuel prices will not rise as sharply as was once considered necessary. Some energy analysts, however, warned that such a reduction in targets could be unwise, because energy demand increases after 2000 could lead to considerable increases in CO_2 emissions at a time when the scaled down reduction programme is unable to cope with them.

European Union law: 'non-greenhouse' issues

EU Law on atmospheric pollution was something of a 'late developer' growing rapidly only from the 1980s when a number of member states, Germany in particular, began to suffer from acidification. A number of techniques of regulation are used: air quality standards, sometimes known as Air Quality Limit Values (AQLVs) (either limit values for particular types of industrial plant, or limits for individual substances), vehicle emission standards, fuel composition standards and 'bubble' standards with upper limits on total emissions from all sources.

AQLVs prescribe legal maxima for the presence of pollutants in ambient air for particular time periods. A number of parameters can be used in specifying such a standard: absolute concentrations integrated over a chosen period of time, or average or percentile values. Furthermore an evaluative or subjective element enters into the creation of standards for once the physical, chemical and toxic properties of pollutants are determined, estimates of likely lethal or damaging levels of exposure have to be made, and these must then be divided by a safety factor to set a lower 'limit value' for exposure. The safety factor is determined subjectively taking into account issues such as varieties of sensitivity to exposure, the range of human pathological conditions, the possible consequences of pollutant recombinations and the quality of the data relied on. Indeed other factors of an ethical, economic, political, social and philosophical nature may well play a part in standard setting alongside purely physio-chemical, biological and mathematical issues.

The EU's reliance on AQLVs has caused difficulties for member states who have traditionally utilised emission standards to control individual stationary polluting sources. The EU also relies on the 'standstill' principle to ensure that significant deterioration in air quality set by relevant standards does not take place. AQLVs exist for SO_2 and airborne particulates and for NO_2. In respect of the former, Directive 80/779 set limits for their *ground level* presence, these to be met, where possible, by 1 April 1983, and a mandatory compliance date of 1 April 1993, together with a general duty to implement more stringent limits contained in 80/779 Annex II. The limit values are 80 microgrammes per cubic metre (pcm) for smoke over a year, with a winter limit of 130 and a year peak limit of 250. SO_2 limits vary according to the measure of smoke:

where smoke is low SO$_2$ may increase. 85/203 sets NO$_2$ standards for ambient air, with a compliance date of 1 July 1987, and a general limit of 200 microgrammes pcm, though member states remain free to set stricter limits. The implementation of AQLVs has met with resistance from member states and both France and Germany have been threatened with legal proceedings under Art 169; difficulties with monitoring compliance have also been experienced.

The EU introduced vehicle emission standards in 1970 which specified limits for carbon monoxide, hydrocarbons and NOx, though also allowing block or 'type approval' for vehicle models conforming to specified design and construction standards. Where competent authorities give block approval for a model on the basis that it complies with standards, manufacturers may commence to produce in series and no member state may thereafter refuse national type approval to vehicles of that type.

Emission limits have gradually become more stringent for vehicles, particularly since 1985 as the EU has moved towards 'cleaner cars', and Directives 88/76 and 89/458 set stricter limits to reduce emissions for cars of 2,000cc or more. Directive 91/441 extended the small car emission limit of 89/458 to new models from 1 July 1992 and to new registrations from 1 December 1992. These changes resulted in further emission reductions in carbon monoxide, hydrocarbons and NOx. Yet further reductions were introduced by Directive 94/12. Other Directives have applied increasingly stricter limits to diesel engined and commercial vehicles.

Directive 75/716 introduced fuel composition standards for 'gas oil' (ie fuel used primarily for domestic heating) with a view to reduce SO$_2$ emissions. Stricter standards as from 1 January 1989 were introduced by 87/219. Further restrictions were introduced by 93/12 which introduced a limit of 0.2% by weight of sulphur, with a limit of 0.05% for diesel fuel as from 1 October 1996.

Directive 84/360 was a general framework Directive enabling the EU to draw up a system of limit values for a whole range of emissions, and also requiring member states to ensure that, as from 30 June 1987, certain industrial plants, including, for example, combustion plants of more than 50 MW heat output and oil power stations, should only be constructed after prior authorisation including: requirements as to appropriate preventive measures concerning pollution; use of the *best available technology not entailing excessive costs*; no exceeding of emission limits, taking into account AQLVs and on the basis that significant air pollution may not be caused by emissions, especially SO$_2$ and NOx. Substantial alterations of existing plants are regarded under the Directive as new plant needing authorisation, and provision is also made for existing plant over time to be adapted to the best available technology, etc, principle. The daughter Directive 88/609 on large combustion plants (LCP) was introduced to further the above programme by reducing SO$_2$ and NOx emissions. SO$_2$ emissions from existing plant are to be reduced from 1980 levels in three stages, 25% by 1993, 43% by 1998 and 60% by 2003. NOx emissions from relevant plant are to be reduced by 20% by 1993 and 36% by 1998, and for new plant emission standards are reduced by 80% (SO$_2$) and 50% (NOx) compared with emissions from existing plant. The implementation of this programme is allowed to vary from state to state as some have coal supplies disproportionately rich in sulphur; some states will have met target reductions faster than others. However, the overall aim is to reduce SO_2 emissions from power and refinery plant by 6m tonnes pa by 1998 and halving them, compared to 1980, by 2003.

As part of its response to the LCP Directive the UK drew up in 1990 a large combustion plant national plan which sets reduction targets for SO_2 (60% by 2003 on 1980 levels) and NOx (30% by 1998) emissions from existing plants. This plan is kept under regular review by the Secretary of State, who consults on revision with relevant industries and official environmental regulation and countryside conservation bodies. The plan effectively allows various power station operators, principally PowerGen and National Power, gradually reducing emissions quotas per annum, while similar quotas are set for refineries and other relevant industries. Each relevant site has, for example, an annual SO_2 quota fixed by the relevant environmental agency. The national plan is, of course, reinforced legally by the IPC system, under the Environmental Protection Act 1990 (see further below) and formally exists under s 3(5) of that Act.

Directive 94/63 applies to volatile organic compounds (VOCs) arising from the storage and distribution of petrol, and is one of a number of VOC proposals to enable the EU to meet international obligations under protocols to the 1979 Geneva Convention on Long Range Transboundary Air Pollution (see above). Various dates between 31 December 1995 and 31 December 2004 are laid down for compliance by new plant with VOC emission limits. Further Directives on VOCs are to follow, though the UK government is anxious that EU action should compliment national initiatives reached within the context of the UNECE framework (see above). Even within the context of EU provisions, member states have freedom to meet targets in the most practicable and effective way, but the UK government wishes to ensure that the principle is not eroded.

A further framework Directive on Air Quality was agreed in June 1995 (COM (94) 109, COM (95) 312). This will set mandatory limit values for 13 particular pollutants which member states have to attain within specified time periods, and also sets 'alert thresholds' at levels where short term exposure to pollutant levels could pose health threats. In addition guidelines for minimum levels of pollution monitoring are laid down. This framework Directive will be followed by 'daughters' on 13 individual pollutants and these will set numerical goals for the standards set by the framework Directive. By the end of 1996 the first 'daughter' on SO_2, NO_2, fine particles, suspended particle materials and lead will be produced. (See further below on the UK's national air quality strategy.)

As part of this scheme the government has undertaken to introduce a 'sulphur permit trade' whereby operators more able to meet reduction targets at some sites would be able to transfer their SO_2 quotas to other sites less able to comply. It is, however, thought unlikely that such a scheme could be introduced before 1997, and English Nature has expressed concern lest the trade permits higher emission limits to be transferred to sites where they are likely to have an increased impact on sensitive habitats.

A miscellany of further EU measures

Directives 89/369 and 89/429 lay down emission limit values for both new and existing 'municipal waste incineration plants', ie plants handling only domestic, commercial or trade waste; sewage sludge, chemical, toxic/ dangerous waste and hospital waste incinerators are *not* covered. So far as new plants are concerned, their authorisations, eg as required under Directive 84/360, must contain emission limit values, operating and monitoring requirements in respect of specific matter (dust, heavy metals, acidic gases) according to capacity categories. For existing plants there is a timetable for compliance with the limits for new plants, again according to capacity category, with various dates applying between 1 December 1995 and 1 December 2000. Hazardous waste incineration is further regulated by Directive 94/67. Once again the authorisation for such an incinerator must impose emission limits, operating and monitoring requirements. Relevant incinerators are those burning solid/liquid hazardous waste as defined by Directive 91/689 excluding certain combustible liquid wastes, offshore oil and gas industry hazardous waste, non-hazardous sewage sludge, while animal carcass and non-hazardous clinical waste incinerators are further excluded, while not only are hazardous waste treatment incinerators generally included, but also those co-incinerators which use waste as a fuel component.

So far as ozone depletion is concerned, the EU has acted on behalf of its members and Regulation 3093/94 places controls on the production, import, export, supply, use and recovery of a number of listed substances, ie CFCs 11, 12, 113, 114, 115, 1.1.1 trichloroethene, methyl bromide, HBFCs and fully halogenated CFCs. Halon manufacture was banned from 1 January 1994, CFC and carbon tetrachloride from 1 January 1995, 1.1.1 trichloroethene and HBFCs from 1 January 1996, with methyl bromide production to be cut back to 1991 levels from 1 January 1995 and further reduced by 25% by 1 January 1998. HCFC supply is frozen at a set level from January 1995 with a progressive phase out until 2015, though HCFC use is allowable in certain inescapable situations. The regulations lay down requirements for the recovery, reclamation or recycling of relevant material in commercial and industrial refrigeration, air conditioning and fire fighting equipment, and for the prevention of leaks from such systems. Provision is further made for the supply of information to the Commission from producers, importers and exporters of relevant material and to/from national 'competent authorities'. This information relates to the recycling and destruction, etc, of material. Note, however, Regulation 2047/93 which permits trading in relevant substances with certain states who have not adhered to the Montreal Protocol. [For further exhaustive information on EU atmospheric policy see chapter 6 of Haigh's *Manual of Environmental Policy* to which indebtedness is acknowledged.]

For the future, attention may be drawn to the proposal for an Integrated Pollution Prevention and Control (IPPC) Directive. The proposal takes the UK's integrated pollution control system (see below) and translates it into pan-Union terms so that new installations shall not operate unpermitted, nor shall existing ones do so after 30 June 2005. These permits will be based on the concept of integrated environmental protection of air, land and water, with emission limits which do not breach either EU environmental quality standards, or those of the World Health Organisation where applicable. Permits will be subject to at least decennial review, and must adopt the best available techniques for pollution abatement. The 'best available' techniques are those representing the 'most effective and advanced stage in the development of activities' to meet emission limit values, or where that is not practicable, to reduce emissions and their impact on the environment as a whole. In addition to be 'available' a technique must be developed on a scale allowing viable implementation in the industrial sector in question from an economic and technical point of view, taking into account the costs and advantages of such techniques, which need not, however, be used or produced within any given member state, provided they are reasonably accessible to operators. It should further be noted that permits will take into account the geographical location of installations, and local environmental conclusions, while where there is an applicable environmental quality standard which requires stricter conditions that those achievable by the use of the best available techniques, additional measures *must* be required to meet the quality standard.

Domestic law

UK domestic law has attempted to combat atmospheric pollution for centuries. The pattern that has emerged is one of divided responsibility between central and local authorities. Planning law has a very limited role to play in this context, but the common law may have a contribution to make.

Atmospheric pollution may amount to an actionable nuisance (see chapter 2), though its existence may be difficult to establish. The creation of stenches, *Walter v Selfe*;[4] causing smoke or noxious fumes to pass over the plaintiff's land, *Crump v Lambert*;[5] raising clouds of coal dust, *Pwllbach Colliery Co Ltd v Woodman*;[6] and the emission of large black smuts, *Halsey v Esso Petroleum Co Ltd*,[7] have all been held actionable. Where the nuisance causes *only* personal discomfort the nature of locality has to be considered to see if an action should lie, *Sturges v Bridgman*,[8] but generally a landowner is entitled to have air untainted and unpolluted by the acts of his neighbours. By this is meant, at least, air not incompatible with physical comfortable human existence, though such air may not be as pure and fresh as when the plaintiff's home was built. Atmospheric pollution which is a substantial interference with the use and enjoyment of land, as with stench from a sewage farm in *Bainbridge v Chertsey Urban Council*,[9] or which actually causes physical damage to the land, as with noxious fumes in *St Helens Smelting Co v Tipping*,[10] and *Manchester Corpn v Farnworth*,[11] can be remedied in nuisance. An action in public nuisance may also be available. Note also ss 161 and 161A of the Highways Act 1980 (as amended) which create criminal liability in respect of the lighting of fires on or over highways, or off a highway, with the consequence that users of the highway are injured, interrupted or endangered.

4 (1851) 4 De G & Sm 315.
5 (1867) LR 3 Eq 409.
6 [1915] AC 634.
7 [1961] 2 All ER 145, [1961] 1 WLR 683.
8 (1879) 11 Ch D 852.
9 (1914) 84 LJ Ch 626.
10 (1865) 11 HL Cas 642.
11 [1930] AC 171.

D STATUTORY CONTROL OF SMOKE AND OTHER ATMOSPHERIC POLLUTANTS, INCLUDING THE IPC AND LAAPC SYSTEMS

'We know the complicated laws a parliamentary draughtsman draws cannot be briefly stated' (W S Gilbert, 'The Grand Duke', Act I)

The old law

The historic principal legislation was the Alkali, etc, Works Regulation Act 1906, as amended by the Health and Safety at Work etc Act 1974 and the Control of Pollution Act 1974. The 1906 Act was largely replaced by orders made under the Act of 1974.

It was principally the duty of a central inspectorate to enforce the law. Their powers historically extended to a number of industrial processes including alkali works, or treating copper ores by common salt or other chlorides whereby any sulphate is formed, in which hydrochloric acid gas is evolved, see ss 1 and 27(1) of the 1906 Act. Other works originally controlled under ss 6 and 7 of and Sch 1 to the 1906 Act, which respectively covered sulphuric and hydrochloric ('muriatic') acid and over 60 other processes, were subsequently covered by the Health and Safety (Emissions into the Atmosphere) Regulations 1983, SI 1983/943, made under the Health and Safety at Work etc Act 1974.

The obligations of operators of such processes varied at law. Every alkali work had to be carried on in such manner as to secure the condensation of the hydrochloric gas evolved to the extent of 95%. Additionally the 'best practicable means' had to be used for preventing escape of noxious or offensive gases from exit flues of apparatus used in the processes of such works, and for rendering such gases where discharged harmless and inoffensive.

Guidelines on the requirements of best practicable means were prepared by the central inspectorate following consultation with relevant industries. They could lay down a *non-statutory* standard of emission which, if exceeded, indicated a prima facie breach of the best practicable means standard. These standards provided a basis for negotiation between industry and the inspectorate. In practice inspectors specified locally what the best practicable means for individual works would entail.

'Best practicable means' was applied less than absolutely, taking into account the means of those subject to control and the economic consequences to the wider community of control, as well as the current state of knowledge and local conditions. Merely to comply with normal trade precautions might not be enough, see *Scholefield v Schunck*.[12] What was required was a genuine attempt to use the best means available to secure the objectives of control, see *Manchester Corpn v Farnworth*.[13] The technological limitations of older equipment were considered, particularly where no real complaint about emissions was substantiated. A burden of taking precautions disproportionately heavy to the degree of risk involved was not imposed, see *West Bromwich Building Society v Townsend*.[14] Historically only the most flagrant and

12 (1855) 19 JP 84.
13 [1930] AC 171.
14 [1983] ICR 257.

persistent breaches of the law were prosecuted. The inspectorate preferred to rely on co-operation rather than coercion, working with a particular industry to achieve an improvement in manufacturing processes over a period of years so as to reduce atmospheric emissions.

The current law

Since 1990 the previous legislation has largely been replaced by the provisions of the Environmental Protection Act at various dates, though the sections relating to Integrated Pollution Control (IPC) and Local Authority Air Pollution Control (LAAPC) principally came into force on 1 January 1991.

The prime issue to note about the Environmental Protection Act 1990 is that for the most complex processes the scheme of regulation is Integrated Pollution Control whereby the Environment Agency (the Agency) has supervision of emissions to *all* environmental media (land, air and water). Consequently what is said below about these processes though it is written in the context of atmospheric pollution generally applies with equal force to discharges to land and water. Less complex processes on the other hand are regulated by local authorities (London borough and district councils) who have jurisdiction under the new law with regard to *atmospheric pollution only*.

The 1990 Act is not, however, the only recent legislation relevant to atmospheric pollution, though it is the principal enactment under which the UK meets its international and EU legal obligations (see further above). Under s 2(2) of the European Communities Act 1972 the Air Quality Standards Regulations SI 1989/317 were made to implement Directives 80/779 and 85/203 on SO_2 and smoke and NOx respectively, setting AQLVs and requiring air quality monitoring, and to ensure that the specified pollutants are reduced below the specified levels.

The 1990 Act applies *generally* throughout England, Wales and Scotland, though there are detailed distinctions 'north and south of the border': in particular, of course, Scotland has its own Scottish Environment Protection Agency (SEPA). It also confers extensive powers on the Secretary of State to make regulations to enable the UK to meet obligations under EU and international law, see s 156. Part I of the Act is concerned with IPC and LAAPC. Section 3 empowers the Secretary of State to make regulations to establish 'standards, objectives or requirements in relation to particular prescribed processes or particular substances'. In particular these regulations may prescribe standard limits for the concentration or amount, generally or in a particular time period, of a substance released from a prescribed process into any environmental medium (air, land, water). The characteristics of releases of substances, measuring and analysis techniques, standards and requirements of prescribed processes may also be set by regulations. Further regulations may establish quality objectives or standards for environmental media in relation to any substances which may be released, mediately or immediately, from any process. Section 3(5) further empowers the Secretary of State to make and keep under review plans for establishing limits on any substances which may be released into the environment in the UK, to bring about progressive reduction of environmental pollution by limiting releases of substances from prescribed processes, and to improve progressively quality objectives and standards. See, for example, the National Plan on Implementing the Large Combustion Plants Directive to reduce SO_2 and NOx emissions between 1990 and 2003 from power stations, refineries and 'other' industries.

Section 4, as amended, proceeds to determine the allocation of functions under Part I of the 1990 Act. As already stated the principal distinction is between more and less complex processes which are divided between the Agency and local authorities, though all are enjoined to exercise their powers to minimise pollution, in the case of local authorities this being further limited to pollution of the atmosphere. The Secretary of State may, under s 4(4) and (5), direct that an atmospheric pollution regulation function under Part I normally exercisable by a local authority shall be transferred to the Agency. Section 2 further empowers the Secretary of State, to prescribe *processes* for the purpose of regulation, and to identify them as being subject to control either by the Agency or local authorities, see s 2(4). Under s 2(5) the Secretary of State may also prescribe *substances* whose release into the environment may be regulated, again providing for either central or local control. These substances are prescribed by SI 1991/472 Schs 4–6, as amended by SI 1991/836, 1992/614, 1993/1749, 1993/2405, 1994/1271, 1994/1329, and 1995/3247. Schedule 4 relates to substances whose release to air is subject to control and *includes* SO_2 and NOx *and* the oxides of carbon, as well as asbestos, halogens and smoke. Schedule 5 (based on the 'Red List' see chapter 12) relates to substances released to water and *includes* mercury, cadmium, isomers of DDT, aldrin, dieldrin, polychlorinated biphenyls (PCB), and atrazine (see further chapter 11). Schedule 6 relating to landward releases *includes* organic solvents, halogens, oxidising agents, phosphorous, and chemical pesticides. Some such *substances* may be released, of course, from a prescribed *process*, but where particular provision is made for a substance it must be complied with.

The 'A' and 'B' lists

Central to understanding the system is realisation that there are two lists, 'A' and 'B', of prescribed matters. The 'A' list is subject to IPC and is within the jurisdiction of the Agency, while the 'B' list is subject to local authority regulation with regard to atmospheric pollution only. (Pollutants entering, for example, water from 'B' list processes would still therefore fall within the powers of the Agency under water legislation, see chapter 12 below.) The 'A' and 'B' (which fall into six groups) lists have now been prescribed by Sch 1 of the Environmental Protection (Prescribed Processes and Substances) Regulations SI 1991/472 as amended. 'A' processes are:

1   Fuel production and combustion, eg gasification and associated processes, eg refining natural gas or producing gas from coal; carbonisation and associated processes, eg pyrolysis or distillation of coal or lignite; combustion processes carried on primarily for energy production, eg burning any fuel in a boiler or furnace with a net rated thermal input of 50 MW or more, or in gas turbine or compression ignition engines of like capacity; petroleum processes, eg physical, chemical or the thermal treatment of crude oil.

2   Metal production and processing, eg iron and steel production such as making, melting or refining iron, steel or ferro alloys, or desulphurising

iron or steel, heating iron or steel so as to remove grease, oil or other contaminants, eg burning plastic off scrap cable, where this is related to other Part A iron and steel processes; non-ferrous metal processes such as zinc or tin mining where cadmium may be released into water, refining non-ferrous metals, or processes for producing, melting or recovering by chemical means any lead or lead alloy which may result in lead tainted smoke being released.

3   Mineral industries, eg cement and lime manufacture such as blending cement or heating calcium carbonate so as to make lime; asbestos processes such as producing raw asbestos or making asbestos products or stripping asbestos from scrap railway vehicles; mineral fibre processes such as glass fibre making; glass manufacture and production such as making glass frit; ceramic production such as firing heavy clay goods.

4   Chemical industries, eg petrochemical processes such as production of unsaturated hydrocarbons; manufacture and use of organic chemicals such as manufacture of styrene or vinyl chloride or of acetylene or any aldehyde, amine, isocyanate, or organic sulphur compounds where the process may result in the release of such substances into air; acid processes, eg making sulphuric acid or oxides of sulphur or nitric or phosphoric acid; processes involving halogens such as making hydrogen fluoride/chloride/bromide/iodide or any of their acids; inorganic chemical processes such as making hydrogen cyanide or processes involving its release to the air or the production of compounds containing, inter alia, arsenic, gallium, indium, lead, tellurium, thallium; chemical fertiliser production; pesticide production likely to release into water, inter alia, mercury, cadmium, isomers of DDT, aldrin, dieldrin, PCBs, atrazine; pharmaceutical production, again where it is likely to result in the release to water of any of the immediately foregoing substances which are more particularly listed in Sch 5 of the regulations.

5   Waste disposal and recycling, eg incineration processes, eg of waste chemicals or certain compounds listed substances, or of animal remains; processes for recovery by distillation of, inter alia, oil or organic solvents; fuel production from waste by utilising heat to make a solid fuel from waste.

6   'Other industries', eg paper making processes above certain specified production levels; processes for making di-isocyanates; tar and bitumen processes; certain coating and printing processes; manufacture of dyestuffs if the process involves use of hexachlorobenzene; timber processes such as chemical treatment of timber using any 'Schedule 5' substance; treatment and processing of animal or vegetable matter, eg storing or drying dead animals or plants or plant products where a 'Schedule 5' substance may be released into water.

'B' processes are: combustion processes such as burning any fuel in a boiler or furnace for energy production where the plant has a net rated thermal input of not less than 20 MW but less than 50 MW; iron and steel processes such as small scale smelting, eg in an electric arc furnace with a designed holding capacity of less than seven tonnes; non-ferrous metal processes, again such as small scale production in furnaces with designed holding capacities of less than five tonnes; cement processes such as blending cement in bulk other than at a construction site, or batching ready mixed concrete; asbestos processes such as minor finishing of certain asbestos products; certain other mineral processes such as crushing or grinding designated minerals such as clay, sand, gypsum, boiler or furnace ash, etc; most glass manufacture and production processes, including those involving the use of lead, or where glass is polished or etched by hydrofluoric acid; certain types of ceramic production; some incineration processes such as crematoria; certain small scale di-isocyanate processes; certain medium scale coating and printing processes and likewise certain medium scale dyestuff, printing ink or coating material manufacturers; timber processes involving manufacture of wood products by, inter alia, sawing, drilling or sanding, where certain specified amounts of timber are used each year; processes involving rubber such as mixing, milling, or bleaching of natural rubber if carbon black is used; certain animal or vegetable matter processes such as maggot breeding.

It will be noted that the range and complexity of 'A' processes is greater than that of 'B', however, the *numbers* of places subject to local authority regulation are much greater than those within the jurisdiction of the Agency.

The timetable for the introduction of the new system of regulation was, in essence, that new processes, large combustion plants and substantial variations or changes in existing processes were subject to control from 1 April 1991 while existing processes were phased into control over a five year period down to 1996.

The amendments to SI 1991/472 provided, however, that certain processes initially prescribed ceased to be, while some initially prescribed as 'A' switched to 'B' and vice-versa.

Because of the existence of complex processes made up of many component parts not always immediately recognisable as either 'A' or 'B', and because of the existence of complex sites with more than one process 'in situ', the amended regulations, in general terms, provide:

1   Where *in one location* there are numbers of processes all *operated by the same person* and those processes fall into the same class under Sch 1 of the regulations only one authorisation is needed.
2   Where a part A process overlaps with a part B process as one of a number of processes in operation, only one authorisation will be required and that will *centrally* issued.
3   Where there are many processes each within a separate Sch 1 category separate authorisations will be required.
4   Processes not fitting neatly into a Sch 1 definition are to be treated as falling within that definition which is most apt.

Note that control is primarily exercised over *processes*, and that most releases of *substances* will be regulated consequentially as part of the process author-isation, but where a substance is prescribed the operators of certain prescribed processes have to deal in particular ways with the substance in question. Note also that certain processes are given exempt status so no authorisation is required for their operation. Broadly the 'exempt' group comprises processes where there are no emissions to air of Sch 4 substances, no discharges to water of Sch 5 substances and no release to land of Sch 6 substances. In addition there are exemptions for working museums, school displays, motive power sources for aircraft, hovercraft, road vehicles, locomotives and ships, and processes carried on purely domestically in connection with a private dwelling. Those claiming the benefit of an exemption must prove their case.[15]

As already stated IPC is implemented with regard to 'A' processes by the Agency in England and Wales, see ss 1 and 2 of the Environment Act 1995. Local authorities operate the LAAPC system as 'local enforcing authorities'. The various enforcing bodies have extensive powers under ss 37, and 108–110 of the Environment Act 1995.

General powers of entry, etc

NB. These apply to all the Agency's functions, not just those relating to IPC. The Agency has power to do anything calculated to facilitate the carrying out of its functions, including instituting criminal proceedings, under s 37 of the 1995 Act, while at both the local and central levels the enforcing bodies have considerable powers of entry and search, etc, see ss 108 and 109 of that Act.

Thus an enforcing body may in writing authorise a 'suitable person' to exercise certain powers: to determine whether pollution control enactments are being complied with, to exercise pollution control powers, or to determine whether and how such a function should be exercised. The various powers are:

1 To enter any premises it is reasonably believed it is necessary to enter at any reasonable time, or at any time in an emergency.
2 To enter premises accompanied by other persons or equipment or, where there is reasonable cause to believe obstruction will take place, a constable.
3 To carry out investigations and examinations.
4 To direct that premises which may be entered are to be left undisturbed.
5 To take measurements, photographs, and samples — the latter not just from the premises but also of land, water or air in, on, or in the vicinity of, the premises.
6 To test or dismantle any article found on premises where there is cause to believe it has caused, or is likely to cause, pollution or harm to human health, and to take possession of such material for the purpose of further examination.
7 To require persons to answer questions.
8 To require information to be given, including extracts from records.
9 To require assistance and facilities from any person with respect to matters in that person's control.
10 To undertake test borings on a site or to install equipment to determine issues of compliance with pollution regulation.

It appears that the power to take samples is not limited to *either* soil *or* water, where a soil sample is taken that includes water in it. The bringing of an appeal against the refusal of a licence or authorisation, etc, also does not prevent the taking of samples from the site which is the subject of the appeal.[16]

Except in emergencies, seven days' notice of intention to enter has to be given, and then entry may only take place under the authority of a warrant or with the consent of a person in occupation of the relevant premises. Similarly,

---

15 *Tandridge District Council v P & S Civil Engineering Ltd* [1995] Env LR 67.
16 *Polymeric Treatments v Walsall Metropolitan Borough Council* [1993] Env LR 427.

except in emergencies, where it is proposed to enter premises and the use of force appears on reasonable grounds to be likely to be called for, entry shall normally be by warrant.

Where in relation to any article or substance found on any premises there is power to enter and an authorised person has reasonable cause to believe that the article, etc, is a cause of imminent danger of serious pollution of the environment or of serious harm to human health, that person may seize, and if necessary render harmless, the article.

It is an offence under s 110 of the 1995 Act intentionally to obstruct authorised persons in the performance of their powers and duties. However, before any of the foregoing powers are used the Agency needs to have a reasonable belief that they should be.[17]

Following the progressive introduction of control over both 'A' and 'B' processes, under s 6 of the 1990 Act no person is able to carry on a relevant process without an authorisation from the appropriate authority. Those needing such authorisations will have to apply, paying, under s 8 of the 1990 Act in the case of LAAPC, and s 41 of the 1995 Act in the case of IPC, a prescribed fee. A long term goal is that charging for IPC authorisations should vary according to the toxicity of emissions and associated hazards. That was the goal set by HMIP and it is set to continue for the Agency, though this may not come about until after 2000. As steps towards the goal the object is to introduce an operator performance and risk appraisal scheme (OPRA) which has already gone through initial consultation. OPRA as first proposed had seven 'key indicators' by which operators' processes would be appraised, including compliance with limits, adequacy of records, frequency of incidents, justified complaints and auditable management systems. In addition there were seven pollution hazard appraisal indicators, including presence of hazardous substances, prevention, minimisation and abatement techniques, scale of process, location and frequency of operation. Each indicator was to be given a rating which would have been multiplied by a factor weighted according to an assessment system to produce of total sum for a process, with charges worked out accordingly. Such a system allows for comparisons to be made between processes of hazard and operator performance.

It currently appears that changes will be made to OPRA before it is introduced, but one possibility is that scales of charges will reflect directly the environmental harm caused by particular processes — irrespective of the amount of regulatory activity needed to control emissions, a matter of some controversy. Furthermore, it is open to doubt whether such a scale of charges would act as a real pollution levy to force down pollution levels as they could not impose a high enough cost on operators.

Schedule 1 of the 1990 Act lays down the authorisation process, providing for applications to be made in prescribed form, for their advertisement (see SI 1991/507), for consultations with specified persons, for representations to be received from others, eg in consequence of advertisements, for directions to be given to enforcing authorities by the Secretary of State, and for the Secretary of State to have 'call in' powers in respect of applications or classes thereof. SI 1991/507 provides, inter alia, for the following particulars to be required: the

---

17 *JB and M Motor Haulage Ltd v LWRA* [1993] Env LR 243.

address of relevant premises and a map of their location, a description of relevant processes and substances, of techniques to be used to reduce or mitigate releases, details of proposed releases and an assessment of environmental consequences, proposals for monitoring releases, and indications of how the BATNEEC obligation (see further below) will be achieved. Consultation is also required by the regulations with the Health and Safety Executive in all cases, MAFF in respect of 'A' processes, sewerage undertakers in respect of 'A' processes where releases to sewers will take place, the relevant conservancy council where releases will affect SSSIs. The Schedule also makes provision for a determination period, in general four months, and non-determination may be deemed refusal, see also SI 1991/513 which varies the determination period in particular instances. Enforcing authorities have, under s 6(3), power either to refuse applications, or grant them subject to conditions, though they may not grant an authorisation unless they consider the applicant will be able to carry on the process in accordance with conditions, and, in any case, the Secretary of State may, under s 6(5) direct any authority as to whether or not to grant a particular authorisation. Authorisations once granted must be periodically reviewed at least once every four years, though the Secretary of State may substitute some other period, see ss 6(6) and (7).

Under s 20 of the 1990 Act each enforcing authority must maintain a register of applications and authorisations (together with details of relevant variations, revocations, convictions, directions, information, appeals, and other prescribed matters). Local authority registers must also contain prescribed particulars of processes situated in their areas but subject to the powers of the Agency, and the Agency must supply relevant particulars. Such registers must be freely available for public inspection at reasonable times, and copies must be available at reasonable charges, and for this purpose the Secretary of State may prescribe places where these facilities are to be made publicly available. Registers may be kept in any form, so a computerised register is possible, but they must contain the prescribed information, see further SI 1991/507 regs 15 and 16 as amended by SI 1996/667.

Certain information may be excluded from registers under ss 21 and 22, for example information whose registration would be, in the opinion of the Secretary of State, contrary to national security, and no information relating to the affairs of an individual or business may be included without permission where it is commercially confidential, though the Secretary of State is empowered under s 22(7) to give directions whereunder certain information has to be registered irrespective of confidentiality. A mere claim of confidentiality is, moreover, not of itself enough to secure exclusion; it is for enforcing authorities to determine the issue, subject to a right of appeal to the Secretary of State, see ss 22(2) and (5) as amended, and also SI 1991/507 reg 7. Information is, moreover, only commercially confidential if its registration would prejudice commercial interests to an unreasonable degree, and generally loses that status after a period of four years, see s 22(8) and (11). Where such information is, however, excluded, a statement to that effect must appear on the register, see s 20(5).

The issue of 'confidentiality' was tested in 1992 by appeals to the Secretary of State by PowerGen and National Power in respect of requirements that those companies should register information about future fuel consumption in the case of National Power and future emissions in the case of PowerGen. The Secretary of State allowed the former appeal on the basis that information about future power supplies was not 'directly relevant' to the application made, but rejected the latter. This points to a distinction being made, at least in the case of power generators, between registration of information as to what *enters* a place where a prescribed process takes place and what *leaves* it in the form of emissions. It would be unwise, however, to extrapolate too much from these instances; overall there have been very few appeals under s 22.

At the heart of the new system of regulation is s 7, which obligates the inclusion in authorisations of such conditions as are specified by the Secretary of State, such other conditions as appear appropriate to the relevant authority, together with an implied condition that the authorisee will use the *best available techniques not entailing excessive cost* (BATNEEC) to prevent, in the case of 'A' processes, the release of substances prescribed for any environmental medium into that medium, or where such is not practicable to reduce such releases to a minimum and for rendering them harmless, and also to render harmless any other substance which might cause harm if released into an environmental medium.) (In the case of 'B' processes the references to release relate only to those to the air.) This implied BATNEEC condition may be supplemented, and superseded, by specific conditions requiring BATNEEC. Specific conditions are also required to ensure compliance: with any direction issued by the Secretary of State in order to ensure implementation of international or EU legal obligations; with any limits or requirements and the achievement of quality standards or objectives prescribed by the Secretary of State under any other 'relevant enactments' such as the European Communities Act 1972 and plan requirements arising under s 3 of the 1990 Act itself. The Secretary of State is entrusted with a general discretion to give directions on specific conditions to be/not to be included in authorisations, and conditions may further impose limits on the amount or composition of any substance produced or utilised in any process in any period, and requiring advance notification of any proposed changes in processes. However, *no* condition may be attached so as to regulate the *final* deposit in or on land of controlled waste (see chapter 9; this will be generally a matter for the Agency using its waste regulation powers) and furthermore where any process is regulated both under the 1990 Act and the Radioactive Substances Act 1993 and different obligations are imposed, those under the 1993 Act are to prevail.

In respect of 'A' processes likely to involve the release of substances into more than one environmental medium, eg both water and air, specific requirements are to be included in authorisations to secure the objective of ensuring that BATNEEC is used so as to minimise pollution to the environment taken as a whole having regard to the best practicable environmental option (BPEO) available *as respects substances which may be released.*

BATNEEC entails use not just of the best technologies, but is also determined by reference to the number, qualifications, training and supervision of relevant employees and the design, construction, lay-out and maintenance of relevant buildings. Furthermore the Secretary of State may issue guidance on techniques and this must held in regard by enforcing authorities in the discharge of their functions.

BATNEEC in practice

The implementation of the BATNEEC requirement has reflected attempts to pursue UK environment policy which is based, avowedly, on the principles of stewardship and sustainable development. Accordingly, the IPC system is operated on the basis that a process should be looked at in the round, with the need to protect the environment acknowledged and balanced against the cost of doing so, which should lead to a search for the best solution for the environment as a whole. This search requires adopting a holistic approach, ie one should search for releases of material to be to that medium where they will have the least impact, a philosophy that prevention is better than cure, and an approach that requires unavoidable emissions to be minimised and rendered harmless. In practice this may lead not simply to the regulation of processes but their entire replacement as is visible from the switch in electricity production from coal to gas fired power stations because the cost of cleaning up emissions from coal fired stations is punitive (£250m at Ratcliffe on Soar, £600m at Drax) and imposes an energy disbenefit in that the clean up equipment consumes 1½% of the energy output of the power station in question.

The UK approach to the implementation of BATNEEC is that though operators conceive, design, build and operate their plants so as to meet legal requirements, these are not all legally pre-set. There is, however, a dialogue with operators as to how best the object of environmental protection can be achieved — preferably with operators finding more economical ways to operate in the process. This results in a concentration of effort on individual processes and a consideration of each processes's effect on the environment as a whole, which further entails identification and qualification of releases from the plant in question, a determination of which are significant and what are the environmentally acceptable outcomes. This is clearly a very evaluative process which demands the active co-operation of processors if it is to succeed. It is against this background that official guidance on the meaning of BATNEEC has to be set.

The 1993 practical guide to IPC broke the phase down as follows, taking BAT and NEEC separately. 'BAT':

Best   what is most effective in preventing, minimising or rendering emissions harmless, but there may be more than one 'best' technique.

Available   procurable by the operator, even if not in general use, though a technique must always be operable with business confidence if it is to be considered 'available'.

Techniques both the plant in question and how the process is operated, including the numbers and qualifications of staff, working methods, training supervision, site design, construction, layout and maintenance, see s 7(1) of the 1990 Act.

'NEEC'. Various meanings attach:

New   Fixing the BAT requires environmental harm to be weighed
processes   against the cost of techniques; the more the damage, the more that can be demanded by way of costs.

            Where serious harm would still result even after BATNEEC requirements have been met, the application must be refused; the cost element is not to be affected by a particular operator's lack of profitability.

Existing
processes

Appropriate conditions in authorisations should be imposed on the basis of (a) developments as regards BAT; (b) the general environmental situation; (c) the desirability of avoiding excessive costs for any given plant having regard to the economic circumstances of the industrial sector concerned; particular account should be taken of the technical characteristics of plant, its rate of utilisation and length of remaining life, the nature and volume of its emissions, and the desirability of avoiding excessive costs having regard to the economic situation of undertakings in the category in question.

An individual BATNEEC will be expressed as a performance standard, ie a technique which produces release levels of 'X' or better. This does not constrain an operator from upgrading standards should this possibility eventuate. Furthermore though BATNEEC is individually determined in relation to each application and is reflected in individual authorisation conditions, a degree of overall consistency will be obtained by, inter alia, the use of IPC guidance notes for individual processes which will be subject to regular review and consultation, and whose legal status is that of material considerations to be taken into account in every case. Any departures from the guidance notes have to be justified. Such guidance has been issued in relation to LAAPC in the form of process guidance notes and general guidance notes, supplemented by non-statutory guidance on air quality. In relation to IPC, guidance has been issued so far in a non-statutory form using the reference 'IPR'; supplemented by technical guidance notes on issues such as stack heights, monitoring pollution, abatement equipment in respect of solvent vapour emissions, etc.

As stated above, the active co-operation of operators is required if the BATNEEC and BPEO concepts are to operate most effectively, yet as was pointed out in 'Integrated Pollution Control — the First Three Years' by the Environmental News Data Service, there was initially no clear guidance on how operators would assist by assessing the environmental impact of their operations. Subsequently 'Environmental, Economic and BPEO Assessment Principles for IPC' was issued on a consultative basis in 1994.

This more than technical document has been most usefully summarised by Dr Mumma in *Environmental Law: Meeting UK and EC Requirements* to which indebtedness is acknowledged. It is proposed that each applicant for an IPC authorisation will be asked to predict the environmental concentration of pollutants to be released using the range of available process options or abatement techniques. This prediction will give a figure known as PEC which is

1   In excess of a particular benchmark such as a relevant Environmental Quality Standard (EQS) or a non-statutory interim Regulatory Assessment Level (RAL).

2   Below a benchmark known as the Action Level, which is $\frac{RAL}{10}$, a level not requiring any abatement action.

3   Between RAL and $\frac{RAL}{10}$.

In case (1) no authorisation is to be issued and it will be for the applicant to propose alternative processes/techniques which will reduce PEC acceptably below RAL. In case (2) the process will be authorised and BATNEEC requirements will be met. In case (3) which, one may surmise, will apply to most situations, there will have to be an assessment of which of the options/techniques represents BATNEEC. It will be whatever reduces PEC as closely as possible to $\frac{RAL}{10}$ without being unduly costly. This does not mean that the lowest PEC *has* to be chosen, but if it is not it is for the applicant to justify the choice on grounds of excessive costs, etc. The point here is that it has always been understood that it is unacceptable to require a massive increase in operating costs merely to achieve a marginal reduction in emissions.

Because, however, in the case of IPC BPEO requirements also apply, each applicant will further have to express PEC as a proportion of EQS or RAL so that there is a 'tolerability quotient' (TQ) for the environmental media of earth, water and land. These TQs will be used to create a 'BPEO index', or series of indices for a number of processes and abatement techniques, and that option/technique with the lowest index rating is the BPEO. If this is not the applicant's preferred choice, that which is will have to be justified on cost, etc, grounds. [See now 'Best Practicable Environmental Option Assessments for IPC' (31 March 1996) HMIP.]

Transfers and variations

Once an authorisation has been given, s 9 of the 1990 Act allows its transfer to a person who is to carry on the original authorisee's undertaking, but the *transferee* must inform the enforcing authority within 21 days of the transfer. The legislation allows both the Agency and the relevant operator to begin variation procedures when a process change is contemplated. The procedure differs, however, according to whether the change is 'substantial' or 'relevant'. Section 10 empowers *authorities* to serve 'variation notices' specifying changes to be made in authorisations and their operative dates. Such notices require authorisees to inform the authority of action to be taken to meet the varied requirements. Schedule 1 Part II of the 1990 Act applies where a variation has taken place and the authorisee's action in response proposes a 'substantial change' in the manner of carrying on the process, ie a substantial change in substances released or the amount or characteristics of releases. A process of advertisement and consultation is required similar to that for an initial application for authorisation. These provisions enable authorisation requirements to be kept up to date, as the Agency is under a duty to do, while periodic review of authorisations is a further requirement of the 1990 Act.

Applications for variation *by authorisees* may, under s 11, generally be made at any time. An initial procedure is for the authorisee to inform the relevant enforcing authority, according to the form specified in regulations, of the proposed change requesting them to make a determination as to whether:

1   The proposal would involve any breach of authorisation conditions.
2   If not, whether they would be likely to vary authorisation conditions in consequence of the change.
3   If it would, whether they would consider altering conditions so that the change may be made.

4   Whether the proposal would lead to 'substantial change' (see above) in the manner of carrying on the process.

Where *no* 'substantial change' would be involved, but where some '*relevant*' change under either 2 or 3 above would be needed the authority must notify the authorisee of likely changes and he may then proceed to apply for variation. Where 'substantial change' is involved that would necessitate variation of conditions then the authorisee must be informed of likely changes and he may then proceed to apply, but, of course, the advertisement and consultation procedure outlined above will apply. A 'relevant change' is a change in the manner of carrying on the process which is capable of altering emissions or their characteristics/amounts, see s 11(11). Effectively nearly all changes if *not* 'substantial' will be 'relevant' and so will require variation procedures to be followed.

In any case, however, where an application for variation is made, the relevant enforcing authority must decide whether the requirements of Sch 1 Part II apply, and comply with them if they do. They have in all cases, however, discretion to refuse variation or allow it, in which case they must serve a variation notice on the authorisee.

It should be noted that to avoid the need for over-many variation applications and their attendant costs and delays, a system has been devised of 'envelope authorisations' which lay down outer parameters within which changes may be made without further action. This is particularly relevant to certain chemical industries where production quantities and qualities are subject to fairly regular change.

Revocation and enforcement

Section 12 empowers authorities to revoke authorisations at any time, and in particular where a relevant process has not been carried on, or not for a period of 12 months. They may further, under s 13, serve 'enforcement notices' on authorisees likely to contravene, or actually contravening, authorisation conditions. This notice must state the authority's opinion on the issue, and must specify, first, matters constituting the actual or apprehended breach, and the steps necessary to remedy or avoid it, and the time for taking action. Amendments made in 1995 allow enforcing authorities to withdraw enforcement notices. Where an imminent risk of serious pollution is a consequence of carrying on an authorised process, either generally or in a particular manner, an authority may serve a 'prohibition notice' under s 14 again specifying the issues and remedial measures *and* directing that the authorisation, wholly or completely, shall have no effect to authorise carrying on the process in question. In relation to ss 12, 13 and 14 the Secretary of State has wide powers to issue directions as to the exercise of their powers by relevant authorities.

It remains to be seen how the Agency will utilise its enforcement, etc powers. The pattern of use of the powers by the predecessor body (HMIP) was cautious, and followed a proportionality principle, ie that the level of enforcement action should be proportionate to the nature of the offence. Action would range from a mere letter of admonishment, through enforcement or prohibition action to a prosecution or revocation according to the seriousness of the incident concerned. The HMIP policy furthermore provided that *all* incidents should be dealt with at appropriate level within both

HMIP itself and the management of the operator in question. Prosecutions were brought in relation to incidents classified as 'serious'. In the classification of incidents a number of factors were relevant: the environmental consequences of the incident, eg whether any damage was negligible, slight, short or long term in effect, serious or dangerous; the culpability of the operator — consideration of which clearly imports a moral element into the classification of issues and which considers whether the operator had been given a previous warning; was merely forgetful, negligent, grossly negligent, wilful or even deliberately criminal in intent; the action necessary to secure remediation and to prevent recurrence of the incident.

Following the inception of the IPC regime, HMIP's *prosecution* rate per annum remained remarkably consistent at about 14, though some of these cases were brought under other legislation such as the Radioactive Substances Act 1993. However, the figures released by HMIP further indicated that the level of *enforcement* action from 1993 onwards was rising, though that, of course, also reflected the growing number of processes coming within IPC regulation.

The Agency's Enforcement Code of Practice, 14 May 1996, confirmed that the principles of enforcement will be: *proportionality*, ie action taken will be proportionate to environmental risks and the seriousness of breaches of the law; *consistency* as to advice given, the use of powers, prosecution decisions and responses to polluting incidents; *targeting*, to ensure that enforcement concentrates on those whose activities cause the most damage, or where hazards are least well controlled; and *transparency* so that those subject to action understand what is expected of them, and what they may expect from the Agency. See also further below.

Appeals

Section 15 provides rights for appeal, for those refused authorisations, or aggrieved by conditions imposed, or refused variations requested, or whose authorisations have been revoked, from the enforcing authority to the Secretary of State, as also is the case for those served with variation, enforcement or prohibition notices. It will be noted that the structure of this part of the legislation closely mirrors that of the relevant portions of planning legislation. The Secretary of State may determine appeals himself, or refer an appeal to a person appointed by him, or refer any matter involved in an appeal to such a person, in either case with/without payment. Before determining an appeal the Secretary has a discretion to cause the appeal to take, or to continue in, the form of a hearing, which may, at the discretion of the person holding the hearing, then be held in full or part in private. Alternatively the Secretary of State may cause a public local inquiry be held. The Secretary must hold an inquiry or require a hearing, if either party to the appeal requests to be heard.

The Secretary of State has on appeal various powers:

1 To affirm the original decision.
2 To grant refused authorisations.
3 To grant a varied authorisation.
4 To quash all/any conditions in an authorisation (save of course those required by law).
5 To quash a revocation.

6   To quash/affirm (with/without modifications) variation, enforcement and prohibition notices.

Detailed rules on appeals are contained in SI 1991/507, particularly as to procedures and time limits to be observed. Inter alia the regulations provide that where an appeal is to be held in the form of a hearing and it is decided that it shall be wholly or partly in public, notices of the hearing are to be published in the locality of the process, and that all those who have particular interest in the subject matter of the appeal are informed, as well as those who have rights of consultation under the regulations. At the appeal the appellant and the enforcing authority have the right to be heard together with the statutory consultees, others are heard at the discretion of the person holding the hearing, such a privilege not to be unreasonably withheld. After the appeal is heard the person holding it makes a report on conclusions and recommendations to the Secretary of State who then makes his decision and informs the parties.

Various issues have now been thrown up by the appeals system — largely in connection with LAAPC. It appears that the Secretary of State is unwilling to see authorisations *refused* simply on the basis of an operator's past environmental record. The official 'line' is that the 1990 Act grants enforcing authorities ample powers to ensure that past incompetence or poor management is remedied, and in this context the question is not whether an operator is *likely* to comply, but is *able* to. It appears to be policy not to close down operators for want of authorisation and to 'give them a chance' under the new regime, even if there is evidence that conditions on site will result in the creation of a statutory nuisance, prosecution of which may prove difficult because of the availability of the 'best practicable means' defence (see chapter 1, above). It also further appears that the Secretary of State is unwilling to require a particular technique to be pursued as the 'BAT' until it can be so pronounced following appropriate tests, see (1995) 244 ENDS Report 7 and (1995) 247 ENDS Report 22. It further remains a moot point whether an appeal against an authorisation condition suspends that condition until the appeal is determined, see (1993) 225 ENDS Report 12.

How is the IPC/LAAPC system working?

Much, inevitably, depends on the attitude of the enforcing authorities. Dr D Slater, the former Chief Inspector of HMIP, indicated at an early stage that he intended to take a vigorous line in enforcing the law — but queries arose as to whether he had enough staff while other commentators pointed out that HMIP's past prosecution record had been modest — only nine companies were prosecuted between 1987 and 1991. In addition, The Observer (23 August 1992) and The Independent (24 August 1992) revealed that HMIP intended to use a high degree of self regulation in operating IPC — responsibility for monitoring discharges would be primarily placed on dischargers. HMIP undertook to carry out regular sampling, however, to ensure that monitoring of discharges was taking place — but again the issue arose as to whether there were enough staff to carry out these 'spot checks'. Use has subsequently been made of contract monitoring staff.

There is evidence, however, both that the enforcing bodies have been prosecuting offenders with some degree of regularity while other enforcement action has also been increasingly undertaken. Even so a 1992 survey from the National Society for Clean Air and the Association of Metropolitan Authorities, 'Implementation of the EPA 1990, Part I' indicated that many processors had not applied for the authorisations they should have, while some authorities were finding they had insufficient resources to meet their obligations under the 1990 Act. Some processors were threatening to close down rather than pay authorisation fees. Some trade associations had apparently advised members to wait to be discovered before applying for authorisations. Ignorance on the part of processors of the law could also be a major reason for their poor rate of application. Such other investigation as there was of the system when first introduced suggested a limited pattern of effectiveness.

Jordan, 'Integrated Pollution Control and the Evolving Style and Structure of Environmental Regulation in the UK' (1993) II Environmental Politics No 3 pp 405–427, discovered that IPC had had a considerable impact because of its newness, and that there were particular problems concerned with increased costs, confidentiality and standard setting — all of which gave rise to tensions between regulators and regulated. Industry argued many small businesses would be made subject to costs quite incommensurate with any observable benefits.

However, as the system settled down, HMIP's own quarterly reports suggested a slowly improving rate of authorisation applications, while a backlog of applications which had built up was reduced. More inspectors were appointed, and the target was to have 451 in post by 1 April 1994.

Of considerable interest, however was *IPC in Practice — a Review* published by Environmental Data Services (January 1994) which revealed:

1 Application preparation is time consuming and costly, taking 100–500 man hours and costing £29,000–£150,000, though some application costs far exceed these figures.
2 Overall there have been few applications for exclusion from registration on the basis of commercial confidentiality — though claims have been made by the combustion, organic chemicals and minerals industries.
3 Operators in 1993 still remained ignorant of some of the basic requirements of IPC, and failed to comply with clear official guidance — unfortunately in many cases HMIP also failed to force operators to meet their obligations by appropriate enforcement action.
4 It was on upgrading of equipment/plant that improvement in practices was most likely to take place.
5 There appeared to be evidence that the variation procedure was not being properly applied, with some variations being granted 'off the record' without written justification or entry on registers, while some 'substantial' alterations had been nodded through without being subjected to the appropriate statutory procedure.
6 The number of appeals was increasing, and more appeals related to fundamental issues such as setting annual mass emission limits.
7 Industry's compliance costs had increased to some extent — IPC was then likely to double environmental expenditure on prescribed processes.
8 Public registers were not as effective as they should have been because a number of decisions had been made in an 'off the record' fashion.

9 It is not then clear whether HMIP was meeting the BATNEEC goal.
10 Many companies were concerned only to use technology to stop emissions 'at the pipe's end' rather than to have efficient, waste free, processes in the first place.
11 Overall, however, the system had brought about some real improvement in investment in environmental protection but this was largely amongst companies who were environmentally committed before 1990.

Section 23 of the 1990 Act (as amended in 1995) provides for offences committed, inter alia, by those who: operate relevant processes without authorisation, or in contravention thereof; fail to comply with enforcement or prohibition notices; knowingly or recklessly make false or misleading statements, for example so as to obtain the grant or variation of an authorisation, or make false entries in any required records. Fines of up to £20,000 or terms of imprisonment for up to three months, or both, may in general be imposed on summary conviction for offences, and, on indictment, unlimited fines and/or up to two years' imprisonment can be imposed. Section 157 further provides that where an offence committed by a body corporate is proved to have been committed with the consent or connivance of, or is attributable to any neglect on the part of, any director, manager, secretary or similar officer of the company, etc, the individual shall be liable along with the company and may be proceeded against accordingly. This is a most useful provision 'tearing the corporate veil' and enabling authorities to tackle corporate crime by pursuing guilty individuals (see also chapter 1). In any proceedings concerning a failure to comply with the general BATNEEC obligation s 25(1) provides that it is for the accused to prove that there was no better available technique not entailing excessive cost than that which was used. In addition where there is a failure to comply with the requirements of authorisation, or failure to comply with enforcement or prohibition notices and a conviction follows, the court may under s 26, in addition to any penalties imposed, specifically order the offender to take remedial action. Additionally in such circumstances the Agency may in England and Wales take remedial action and may recover the consequential costs from the party convicted of the offence, provided the Secretary of State has given written approval, see s 27 (as amended). It should also be noted that where an enforcing authority conclude that prosecution for failure to comply with an enforcement or prohibition notice would be an ineffectual remedy they may, under s 24, take proceedings in the High Court to ensure compliance. This raises the possibility of injunctive relief.

Where an injunction is sought, however, the court will be wary of granting relief unless it can be shown that nothing short of an injunction will restrain the defendant's unlawful activity. Furthermore, the plaintiff must show that there is a serious case to answer *and* that on the basis of the 'balance of convenience' an injunction should be granted. The balance of convenience test is an exercise in balancing whether the plaintiff could gain an ultimately satisfactory remedy, even in the absence of an injunction, against the loss to the defendant if an injunction is granted but no other remedy because the plaintiff's case fails when it comes to trial. In the context of pollution, issues relevant to this exercise are the nature of the harm alleged to be emanating from the defendant's land and activities, the number of persons affected, the likely consequences (in economic and employment terms) of an injunction for the defendant, whether there is an alternative criminal remedy with an up-to-date level of fines, and whether powers exist elsewhere to require the defendant to remedy the situation.[18]

A note on the overall position of the Agency on pollution policy

The Agency's enforcement code takes account of the principles of the Deregulation and Contracting Out Act 1994. In relation to *enforcement* there will thus be an entitlement for operators to have their views heard before formal action is taken, and to be told of appeal rights in such circumstances. See generally chapter 3, above.

Control of smoke

Industry is often said to be a major air polluter, but much smoke in the atmosphere this century came from domestic coal burning. Attempts to control domestic smoke were made by the Public Health (Smoke Abatement) Act 1926. This proved ineffective. The consequences of the great London smog of 1952 showed effective legislation was needed. The Clean Air Act 1956 introduced the now familiar system of domestic smoke control. That Act, coupled with changing habits as to choice of domestic heating, reduced the emission of domestic smoke, in million tonnes, from almost 1.50 to about 0.50 between 1953 and 1974. The 1956 Act, as amended in 1968, was consolidated in the Clean Air Act 1993.

The legislation controls emission of smoke; also grit and dust. 'Smoke' is defined by s 64(1) of the 1993 Act as including soot, ash, grit and gritty particles emitted in smoke. Visible non-carbonaceous vapours, for example water vapour, may also be classified as 'smoke', but not, it seems, invisible material such as carbon monoxide or free sulphur dioxide, see Garner and Crow *Clean Air Law and Practice* (4th edn) p 21. Grit and dust are differentiated from smoke by particle size, but all emissions of solid particles fall within the statutory definition. Visible fumes will be a constituent of smoke. These are defined as 'any airborne solid matter smaller than dust'.

The Clean Air Act 1993

Enforcing authorities are local authorities, that is district councils and London borough councils, see ss 55 and 64(1) of the 1993 Act. They have various powers and obligations.

CONTROL OF DARK SMOKE

Section 1 of the 1993 Act prohibits the emission of 'dark smoke' from a chimney of 'any building'. This prohibition extends, with appropriate modifications as to the identity of persons liable for the commission of offences, to railway locomotives, s 43, vessels within specified coastal waters, s 44, and chimneys serving furnaces of boilers or industrial plants attached to or

---

18 *Thameside Metropolitan Borough Council v Smith Bros (Hyde) Ltd* (1995) 250 ENDS Report 42.

installed on land, s 1(2). 'Dark smoke' is defined by s 3(1) of the 1993 Act as 'as dark as or darker than shade 2' on a Ringelmann Chart, though it seems in practice environmental health officers of long-standing do not use the Ringelmann Chart mechanically, but rely rather on their own experience. 'Chimney' includes structures and openings of any kind from or through which smoke, grit, dust or fumes may be emitted, and flues, whether forming part of a building or structurally separate. The prohibition extends to emissions from trade/industrial premises, see further below. Where dark smoke is emitted the occupier of the building with the offending chimney is guilty of an offence. The guilty occupier will be that person in control of that portion of the building where the relevant fireplace is found. Liability under the Act seems to be absolute, though there are statutory defences that the contravention:

1   Was due solely to lighting up a cold furnace and that all practicable steps had been taken to prevent or minimise emissions.
2   Was due solely to some furnace or furnace apparatus failure that could not reasonably have been foreseen or otherwise reasonably provided against, and that it could not reasonably have been prevented by action taken after the failure occurred.
3   Was due solely to use of unsuitable fuel, suitable fuel being unobtainable, that the least unsuitable available fuel was used, and that all practicable steps had been taken to prevent or minimise emissions.
4   Was due to a combination of the foregoing circumstances, and that requisite preventive, remedial and mitigating steps were taken.

Section 64(1) of the Act defines 'practicable' as meaning reasonably practicable in the light of local conditions and circumstances, financial implications, and the current state of technical knowledge. Also, under s 1(3) emissions of smoke lasting for no longer than as specified by regulations are to be left out of account for the purposes of the section. See SI 1958/498 which provides that dark smoke emissions from chimneys for not longer than any aggregate of ten minutes in any eight hour period or, where soot blowing is carried out during such a period, for not longer than an aggregate of 14 minutes in that period, are to be left out of account. Suitable increases in the length of time of emission are made for chimneys serving more than one furnace. Nothing in the regulations authorises either the continuous emission of dark smoke, caused otherwise than by soot blowing, for a period exceeding four minutes, or the emission of *black smoke* (that is smoke as dark or darker than Ringelmann Shade 4) for more than two minutes in aggregate in any period of 30 minutes.

EMISSIONS FROM TRADE PREMISES

Emissions of dark smoke from industrial and trade premises other than via chimneys are generally controlled by the Clean Air Act 1993, s 2. 'Industrial or trade premises' are those used for industrial or trade purposes, or other premises on which matter is burnt in connection with such purposes and processes. In *Sheffield City Council v ADH Demolition Ltd*,[19] a bonfire was lit on

19 (1983) 82 LGR 177.

a demolition site to burn rubbish resulting from demolition and dark smoke was emitted. It was held that demolition was a trade process, so burning this material in connection with it did come within control under the Act. Not all 'clearing-up' bonfires would be caught by the law; a reasonably close connection between the operation releasing the smoke and the industrial or trade process undertaken on site seems necessary. In proceedings under the provision it is a defence to prove contravention was inadvertent, and that all practicable steps had been taken to prevent or minimise emissions. The Secretary of State may, by regulations, exempt certain emissions from control under this section. See SI 1969/1263 which, inter alia, exempts matters such as the burning of: certain waste resulting from demolition or site clearances; tar, pitch, asphalt, etc, in connection with surfacing; and carcasses of diseased animals, or certain contaminated containers. These exemptions exist subject to conditions on supervision and minimisation of emissions. See also s 2(3) of the 1993 Act extending liability to persons causing or permitting dark smoke to be emitted from industrial or trade premises where there is taken to have been an emission of such smoke because material is burned on relevant premises and the circumstances are such that the burning would be *likely* to give rise to such emissions. In such cases it is for the occupier, or the person causing or permitting the burning to show no dark smoke was emitted. The provision is aimed, inter alia, at the problem of night time burning. It should be noted that an emission of dark smoke can take place without smoke moving beyond the boundaries of the site where burning is taking place.[20]

CONTROLS OVER NEW FURNACES

Under s 4 of the 1993 Act new furnaces, save those used solely or mainly domestically and having a maximum heating capacity of less than 16–12 kilowatts, must be, so far as practicable, capable of continuous operation without emitting smoke when used with design fuel. A boiler may be used domestically even where no residence is involved.[1] The courts have held where the purpose for which water is being used is one for which, according to ordinary usage, people require water in their homes, it is a domestic purpose. Central heating of water in a commercial building can thus be 'domestic'. Those furnaces that are subject to control may not be installed unless notice of proposed installation has been given to the local authority. Any furnace installed in accordance with plans and specifications submitted to and approved by the local authority is deemed to comply with the section. Approval under the Building Regulations would not be sufficient, nor would an approval under s 4 constitute a defence to charges of emitting dark smoke under s 1. It seems resiting of an existing furnace counts as installation for the purposes of s 4. Failure to comply with a requirement of the section constitutes an offence. Section 5 of the 1993 Act gives power to the Secretary of State to make regulations prescribing limits for the rates of emission of quantities of grit and dust from chimneys of furnaces in which solid, liquid or gaseous material is burnt, *not* being furnaces designed solely or mainly for

---

20 *O'Fee v Copeland Borough Council* [1995] 7 ELM 129.
 1 *Smith v Müller* [1894] 1 QB 192; *Re an Arbitration between the Mayor, Aldermen and Burgesses of the Borough of Willesden and Municipal Mutual Insurance* [1944] 2 All ER 600.

domestic purposes and used for heating boilers with maximum heating capacities of less than 16.12 kilowatts. See SI 1971/162 for detailed regulations and specific limits, which, subject to the standard defence of 'best practicable means', it is an offence to contravene.

Section 6 of the 1993 Act requires new furnaces in buildings burning pulverised fuel or solid waste or fuel at a rate of 45.4 kilograms or more an hour to be fitted with grit and dust arresting plant approved by the local authority. These obligations are modified by s 7 of the 1993 Act.

Section 7 enables the Secretary of State to make regulations exempting classes of furnace from the operation of s 6, see SI 1969/1262. Furthermore under s 7(2) where, on the application of a building's owner, a local authority are satisfied that the emission of grit, etc from any chimney serving a furnace in the building will not be prejudicial to health or a nuisance where that furnace is used for a particular purpose without complying with s 6, they may grant exemption from control to that furnace while it is used for that purpose, and a failure to notify a contrary decision within a period of eight weeks of receiving the application results in the furnace being deemed exempt. Where, however, the authority decide not to grant exemption they must give reasons for their decision, and an appeal to the Secretary of State against their decision is open to the applicant.

Under s 8 *domestic* furnaces are not to be used in buildings to burn pulverised fuel or solid fuel or waste at a rate of 1.02 tonnes an hour unless grit or dust arresting plant has been provided in accordance with the local authority's approval — again there is a right of appeal to the Secretary of State under s 9.

Various powers exist to measure grit and dust emitted from furnaces. Under s 10, where a furnace in a building is used to burn pulverised fuel, or (at a rate of 45.4 kg per hour) any other solid matter, or (at a rate equivalent to 366.4 kilowatts) liquid or gases, the local authority may, by notice in writing served on the occupier of the building, direct that the occupier shall comply with ministerial requirements as to making and recording periodic measurements of grit, dust and fumes emitted from the furnace; see also SI 1971/161. Where a notice under s 10 is in force, s 11 allows, in the case of furnaces burning solid matter, other than pulverised fuel, at a rate of less than 1.02 tonnes an hour or burning liquids or gases at a rate of less than 8.21 megawatts, the occupier of the relevant building to request the local authority to make and record measurements of grit, dust and fumes. It then becomes the duty of the authority to make such recordings. Under s 12, to enable them to perform their functions more effectively, local authorities have powers to require occupiers of buildings to furnish reasonable details of furnaces in their buildings and the fuel or waste burned. Under s 13, ss 5–12 apply in relation to any outdoor fixed boilers or industrial plant as they apply in relation to furnaces in buildings.

CONTROL OF CHIMNEYS

Section 14 applies to any furnace served by a chimney. Furnaces must not be used by, or with the permission of, the occupier of a building where they burn pulverised fuel, or solid matter of a rate of 45.4 kg or more per hour or burn liquid or gaseous matter at a rate of 366.4 kilowatts or more unless the height of the ancillary chimney has been approved, and the conditions of any approval have been complied with. A similar prohibition lies on those who have possession of fixed boilers and industrial plant, save where these have been exempted by regulations made by the Secretary of State, see SI 1969/411. Applications for such approval have to be made to the local authority in accordance with s 15, and such approval cannot be granted unless the authority is satisfied that smoke, grit, dust, gases or fumes emitted are prevented by the height of the chimney from being prejudicial to health or a nuisance having regard to the chimney's purpose, the position of neighbouring buildings and levels of neighbouring ground and other relevant circumstances. Conditions may be imposed on approvals, eg as to the rate and/or quality of emissions. Approvals not given within four weeks of applications are deemed granted; but if a refusal is given it must be reasoned, including an indication of minimum permissible height, and there is a right of appeal to the Secretary of State.

Modern high chimneys are designed to *disperse* pollutants produced by combustion, and to carry them away from the area of production. Chimney heights must be set at levels sufficient to prevent any increase in pollution at ground level beyond acceptable limits, bearing in mind geographical factors such as hills and valleys, and whether the relevant area is already highly developed with severe existing pollution levels, see DoE Circular 25/81 'Memorandum on Chimney Heights', replacing the earlier edition of 1967. This, however, has been insufficient to prevent pollution, either nationally or internationally, hence the further controls introduced the 1990 Act, see above.

SMOKE CONTROL AREAS

Under s 18 any local authority may, by order, declare all or part of their district a 'smoke control area'. The procedure for making an order is contained in Sch 1 of the 1993 Act. Before making the order advertisements must be placed in the London Gazette and the local press stating the proposal, its effect, a place where the proposed order can be inspected and the right of affected persons to object. Copies of the proposal must also be posted up within the affected area. Any objections made must be considered, but thereafter authorities may bring orders into effect within six months of their being made, though this is subject to a power to postpone coming into operation. Orders may be revoked or varied by subsequent orders, and may further limit prohibitions on the emission of smoke to certain buildings only, or may exempt specified buildings or classes of buildings from control, subject to conditions. Section 19 of the 1993 Act empowers the Secretary of State to require authorities to create smoke control areas where it is considered expedient to abate smoke pollution in a particular area and it is further considered the relevant authorities have not made use of their powers under s 18.

Once an order is in force under s 20 the occupier of any building in the area commits an offence if smoke is emitted from a chimney of that building, and similarly if smoke is emitted from the chimney of a furnace, fixed boiler or industrial plant. However, there may be exemptions for particular buildings under s 18, or in respect of particular fireplaces under s 21, or under particular provisions in specific areas made by the Secretary of State under s 23. Furthermore it is a defence in any criminal proceedings to show that the commission of the offence was not brought to the occupier's attention by an authorised local authority officer as required by s 51. (A similar defence exists in relation to charges concerning the emission of dark smoke under ss 1 and 2.) It is furthermore a defence to prove that an alleged emission was not caused by the use of any fuel other than an authorised fuel as specified in regulations. Under s 23 the acquisition and use of unauthorised solid fuels in a smoke control area is itself an offence, subject to any exemptions, for example under s 22, and also to the defence that the accused may prove reasonable grounds for believing that the building for which the fuel was sold was an exempt building.

Once a smoke control order is in operation in an area the local authority has power under s 24 to require owners and occupiers of private dwellings to adapt their fire places so as to avoid contraventions of s 20. Grants are, however, payable under Sch 2 of the 1993 Act towards the cost of such work. These are mandatory in respect of dwellings erected before 15 August 1964 to the extent of 70% of relevant expenditure, with authorities having a discretion to pay the remaining 30%. There is also a discretion to make payments in respect of adaptations of fireplaces in churches, chapels and buildings used by charities, see s 26.

Special cases

The provisions of Parts I to II of the 1993 Act considered above do *not* apply to prescribed processes under the Environmental Protection Act 1990, see s 41 of the 1993 Act, but the s 1 prohibition on the emission of dark smoke applies to railway locomotives whose owners must therefore use *any* practicable means available for minimising the emission of smoke if they are to avoid committing an offence, see s 43. A similar prohibition applies in respect of vessels within specified waters such as ports, harbours, rivers, estuaries, docks and canals under s 4. Under s 42 the owners of mines or quarries from which coal has been, or is being, or is to be, obtained must employ *all* practicable means for preventing combustion of refuse deposited from their mines/quarries and for preventing or minimising the emission of smoke and fumes from such refuse, though Parts I to II of the 1993 Act, and Part III of the 1990 Act (statutory nuisances), otherwise do not apply to smoke, grit or dust from the combustion of refuse deposited on such tips.

The successes of clean air legislation are catalogued in 'The Royal Commission on Environmental Pollution' 10th Report Cmnd 9149. The average urban concentration of smoke index fell from 260 in 1960 to under 40 in 1980. Total industrial and domestic smoke emission from coal combustion declined from almost 2m tonnes in 1960 to less than 0.5m tonnes in 1980. This was not, however, entirely due to legislation, and was partly due to changes in fuel usage, technological advance, dispersion techniques, conservation measures and decline in certain industries.

Are the Clean Air Act's provisions needed?

It is arguable that the 1993 Act is partly redundant in view of the LAAPC and statutory nuisance powers, particularly with regard to powers concerned with new furnace approval, dust and grit emission rates approval and approval of chimney heights. The government accordingly proposed partial repeal of the legislation in 1993, and has power to do so under the Deregulation and Contracting Out Act 1994. The proposal has, however been resisted by local authorities who point to the *preventive* nature of the powers in question, while statutory nuisance controls are essentially reactive. Even so it has to be remembered that the clear air legislation essentially reflects concerns current some 30–40 years ago and that it takes scant account of the problems of traffic pollution, hence the next major development in the law.

E THE NATIONAL AIR QUALITY STRATEGY

This new initiative, founded on Part IV of the Environment Act 1995, is designed in particular to ensure cleaner air in towns and cities *with a view to protecting human health* and is a national strategic plan for maintaining and improving air quality. It follows on from the government's proposals 'Air Quality: Meeting the Challenge' (January 1995). The Secretary of State is under an obligation by virtue of the 1995 Act to prepare a national air quality strategy (NAQS) which will enable the UK to meet international and EU obligations. NAQS is to be periodically reviewed and modified throughout the life time of the current sustainable development policy. In particular NAQS will contain standards on air quality with reduction targets for all main pollutants; restrictions on the levels at which particular substances are present in the air; measures to be taken by local authorities and other bodies. (An air quality standard (AQS) for SO_2 was thus recommended in September 1995 of 100 parts per billion measured over a 15 minute period, a standard stricter than under current EU requirements. Guideline advice has also been published on two VOCs, benzene and 1, 3-butadiene, and it is the government's intentions to use as a principal measure the BATNEEC scheme under Part I of the 1990 Act to implement quality standards.) NAQS is drawn up and reviewed following wide consultation, including consultation with the Agency (which is required under s 81 to take NAQS into account in discharging its functions) and representatives of industry, and before it is finally promulgated it has to appear in a draft form for public comment which has to be taken into account in the final revision. In drawing up NAQS the government will be advised by the expert panel on air quality standards (EPAQS) set up in 1990.

Under NAQS it will be a central government duty to identify a target or *base standard* towards which air quality should move, and *alert thresholds* which will trigger remedial action (probably the creation of an air quality management area, see below) if they are exceeded by particular pollutants. The object is to achieve the base standard by 2005, and some standards have been set, and some targets and associated policies have already been reached in respect of benzene, 1, 3-butadiene, CO, SO_2, ozone and particles, with future standards to be set for NO_2, lead and polycyclic aromatic hydrocarbons (PAH). The government will also issue *guideline* standards which will contain long term goals for rendering pollutants innocuous.

A key role in implementing NAQS will be played by local authorities who have long argued they are best placed to protect local air quality and who, under s 82 of the 1995 Act are now under a duty to cause air quality reviews (AQR) of current and future air quality to be made in their areas, and to assess whether they are reaching or will reach air quality standards in their areas, with any parts of their areas where standards are not being/will not be achieved being identified.

This is the *appraisal* duty which all authorities must undertake. The appraisal is intended to follow the pattern of appraisal of development plans (see chapter 5, above) and should be regularly and systematically carried out.

Where the AQR shows standards are not being achieved, etc the area of failure in question must, under s 83, be designated as an air quality management or 'designated' area (AQMA). This is the *action* duty. To assist authorities on these tasks central funding will be available, as will the involvement of the Agency. AQMAs will be similar in concept to smoke control zones (see above).

Where a AQMA comes into operation, s 84 requires the relevant local authority (which will be either the unitary authority or the district council if it is not a unitary authority) to obtain information and to cause a detailed assessment to be made of current and future air quality in the AQMA with particular reference to failures to meet air quality standards and objectives. A report on the results of the assessment has to be drawn up within 12 months of the coming into operation of the AQMA, and an 'action plan' (an air quality plan) prepared to bring about the achievement of standards and objectives, with a statement of timescales within which proposed measures are to be implemented. In preparing the plan the authority will be required to consult with central government, other local authorities, industry and the public, and the plan and the assessment which precedes it must be kept under periodic review. Central government will assist this process by granting authorities improved access to air quality databases, the publication of guidelines and the promotion of research and good practice. Funding may also be available for assessing air quality.

In drawing up plans authorities will be required to appraise their development, transport and pollution control policies, and will have to ensure that the relative contributions of industry, transport and other sectors to achieving plan objectives are cost effective and proportionate. The philosophy of plans should be to seek improvements by the most cost effective route; to balance out controls over various emission sources, ie domestic, industrial and transport; to avoid unnecessary regulation and to seek clarity and consistency, and certainly to draw on public, private and voluntary effort. Day to day information on air quality in an AQMA will be given to relevant sections of the public, while authorities will also be under a duty to prepare contingency plans for dealing with high pollution incidents.

Where the Secretary of State has cause to believe a local authority is not undertaking its duties, reserve powers exist under s 85, while in any case the Secretary has power under s 85(5) to give directions to local authorities to take specified steps for achieving UK obligations under EU or international law. Authorities are under a duty under s 85(7) to comply with any directions given. Furthermore where air quality problems extend beyond individual authorities, regional offices of central government will promote appropriate joint arrangements. The Secretary of State has extensive powers under s 87 of the 1995 Act to make regulations for the purposes of Part IV, and, under s 88, to issue guidance to authorities which they have to take into account in carrying out any functions under the Act.

As stated above the principal authorities for the purpose of the law are (a) unitary authorities (that is councils of counties in which there are *no* district councils, councils of districts in an area for which there is no county council, the councils of London boroughs and of county boroughs in Wales); (b) district councils in so far as they are not unitary authorities. However, county councils for areas in which there are districts have some functions under s 86, in that they may make recommendations to their districts with regard to carrying out reviews and assessments and the preparation/revision of plans, and these have to be taken into account by districts. Where an action plan is being prepared by a district the county must submit its proposals for exercising its powers to help achieve air quality standards and objectives within the area in question. Counties are furthermore subject to default action and central powers of direction with regard to the foregoing functions under s 86(6)–(7) and (8)–(9) respectively. Counties are relevant because of their strategic road traffic and highway powers, see further below on the use of Road Traffic Regulation Act 1984 power.

One of the principal concerns of NAQS will be with transport where it is officially accepted progress is needed in order to reduce pollution and improve air quality. To this end the government has adopted five 'key themes' on transport and air quality.

1   Continued action to encourage improvements in vehicle standards, fuel and technology, which entails: full participation at both the EU and domestic levels in promoting progressive improvements in vehicle emission standards; enhanced research into fuel and remote sensing of vehicle emissions; examination of retro fitting particulate traps to certain diesel powered vehicles.
2   Development of land and transport planning policies to achieve air quality improvements — this entails increasing emphasis on air quality issues when setting objectives for local authority transport expenditure; development of best practice guides; undertaking further research into traffic management and its impact on air quality; consultation with London authorities on developing a common approach to transport plans and programmes across the metropolis; consideration of establishing air quality monitoring subsequent to road development.
3   Ensuring that passenger transport, road haulage and taxi services play a full part in bringing about air quality improvement, which entails: consultation with relevant undertakings on improving their environmental performance, with performance targets being set for, eg, London Transport; greater consideration by the Traffic Commissioners of emission performance when considering disciplinary and other action against transport operators; enhanced inspection of taxi exhausts by local authorities with a view to appropriate action; consideration of extending the statutory nuisance regime specifically to cover emissions from vehicle depots.
4   Tighter enforcement of vehicle emission standards — it is a small minority of offenders who emit the largest amount of pollution.
5   More effective guidance for industry, commerce and the public.

Implicit in the NAQS is recognition — grudging perhaps — that the consequences of what Baroness Thatcher called 'the great car economy' are, at very best, mixed. Motor vehicles contribute 36% of hydrocarbon pollution, 51% of NOx, 89% of CO, 70% of lead, 42% of black smoke and 19% of CO_2. With 24 million road vehicles already and a predicted 115% increase to 51 million by 2025 it is clear, both in the UK and throughout the EU generally, that merely to control vehicle emissions further will not be enough to prevent environmental degradation. It may well be that NAQS will have to contemplate what to many remains almost unthinkable: legal restrictions on the use of vehicular transport coupled with financial disincentives for car use and incentives to use revived and extended public transport systems. Air quality plans may: advocate setting up more pedestrian only areas; impose speed restrictions; encourage companies to restrict free parking and replace company cars with free public transport passes. As a 'last resort' measure plans could provide for vehicles to be banned from particular roads at particular times, see further below, though it appears that only the police will have the power, as they presently do, to stop vehicles and check emissions, and that power will not be given to local authorities.

Note that under the Ozone Monitoring and Information Regulations (SI 1994/440) implementing Directive 92/72, the Secretary of State is already required where appropriate to designate or establish measuring stations for ozone concentration and to take the necessary steps to inform the public in the event of particular ozone concentration thresholds being exceeded.

F PLANNING LAW AND ATMOSPHERIC POLLUTION

Planning law has had a somewhat limited role in controlling atmospheric pollution. Planning control is suited to preventing new forms of air pollution, rather than remedying existing pollution sources. Planners are not normally conversant with the technologies of pollution control and have to rely on advice from Environmental Health Departments and the Agency, which is willing to comment on proposals for potentially air polluting developments and the proposed siting of developments near existing works subject to that oversight. In 'Industrial Air Pollution' (1976) the Health and Safety Commission supported the Royal Commission on Environmental Pollution's call for mandatory consultation by local planning authorities with the inspectorate on such developments. Under NAQS, however, planning authorities will be expected to take heed of national air quality standards in formulating development plans and this will be reflected in revised planning policy guidance.

At various points planning law may help to control atmospheric pollution. First at the stage of plan making; some local authorities have included air quality objectives in local plans. There have been historic limits to the effectiveness of such policies. Attempts to include strict and rigorous air pollution standards in structure plans resulted in ministerial intervention to prevent *land use* regulatory powers being used to impose controls over other parts of the environment, see Miller and Wood *Planning and Pollution*, chapters 2 and 3. A small change in this policy was signalled by para 6.8 of PPG 12 in February 1992, but, of course, the changes consequent on implementing NAQS outlined above will go much further than this.

Second, planning control exists over proposals involving development of works utilising processes falling within the powers of the Agency under Part I of the Environmental Protection Act 1990. HMIP, the Agency's predecessor, the Department of the Environment and the Royal Commission on Environmental Pollution consistently argued against the restrictive use of planning powers, especially the imposition of planning conditions under the Town and Country Planning Act 1990; certainly where this would trespass on, or go beyond, the functions of the central authority. The Secretary of State will be disinclined to support a local planning authority in their use of planning powers to control atmospheric pollution where the Agency is happy that the development in question will satisfy the BATNEEC requirements under its statutory powers. However, some developments arouse such local hostility that the only course for the local planning authority themselves is to refuse planning permission, though they may be reversed on appeal. See further Miller and Wood *Planning and Pollution* p 27, and Blowers *Something in the Air* pp 309–11. The issue was examined in *Gateshead Metropolitan Borough Council v Secretary of State and Northumbrian Water*[2] where there was a proposal to build a clinical waste incinerator for which the local planning authority had refused permission on the basis that insufficient attention had been given to pollution control issues. They argued that once planning permission was given it was unlikely an IPC authorisation would be refused and that would entail imposition of BATNEEC requirements, which, they considered, would not ensure any local environmental damage. In the Court of Appeal it was accepted there is an overlap between planning and pollution control powers, and that it is perfectly proper to identify pollution issues and to take them into account in reaching a planning decision. Furthermore where it is clear at the planning application stage that pollution from a plant is such as would lead the Agency to refuse an authorisation, it is proper on that basis to refuse permission. Where, however, the issue is not so clear cut and demands the exercise of particular skills and judgment, the pollution control matters must be left to the Agency. Furthermore a grant of planning permission does not obligate the Agency to grant an authorisation, and an authorisation will not be granted if the BATNEEC scheme cannot achieve a sufficient standard of environmental protection — though it should be noted the former HMIP refused only one authorisation on that basis. Planning authorities will be generally mindful of planning's managerial role, needing to achieve the best interests of their inhabitants by weighing environmental against social and economic considerations. Furthermore members of an authority will represent a wide spectrum of views within a local community on the merits of a proposed development, so it cannot be *assumed* they will wish to restrict the development.

Over processes not falling within the ambit of the Agency's powers, planning controls may be effective alternatives to some other forms of regulation. Planning conditions and planning agreements (now 'obligations') have been used to secure atmospheric pollution control objectives, particularly with regard to what Miller and Wood (op cit, p 29) call: 'anticipatory controls over odour pollution'.

2 (1993) 67 P & CR 179; affd (1994) 71 P & CR 350, CA.

G MISCELLANEOUS POWERS

The Secretary of State has power under s 30 of the 1993 Act, for purposes of limiting or reducing air pollution, by regulation to impose requirements as to composition and content of any motor vehicle fuel, and, where such requirements are in force, to prevent or restrict production, treatment, distribution, import, sale or use of fuels intended for use in the UK and failing to comply. Before making regulations consultation must take place with representatives of motor vehicle manufacturers and users, motor vehicle fuel producers and air pollution experts. Regulations may apply standards and tests, etc, laid down in documents not forming part of the regulations, and may authorise the Secretary of State to grant exemptions. Regulations may also require that information as to composition and content of regulated fuel is displayed in prescribed ways. Enforcement of regulations is in the hands of weights and measures authorities, that is (in general) county and London borough councils, see the Local Government Act 1972, s 201. Under these provisions EU fuel composition standards are implemented in the UK. The current regulations are SI 1994/2295.

The 1994 regulations replace previous provisions on the lead content of motor fuel and the sulphur content of gas oil, and lay down requirements for the composition and content of motor fuel based on British Standards Specifications BS 4040: 1988, BS EN 228: 1993, BS 7800: 1992, and BS EN 590: 1993. They furthermore embrace the requirements of Directives 85/210 and 93/12. To distribute a non-complying motor fuel from a refinery or import terminal is an offence, as is the retail sale of such fuel at a retail filling station, subject to certain minor exemptions, for example with regard to experiments in connection with the composition or content of fuel.

Under s 31 of the 1993 Act regulations may be made, after appropriate consultations, to impose limits on fuel (that is any liquefied petroleum product of a refinery) used in furnaces or engines. Regulations may prescribe fuels, furnaces and engines to which they will apply, may apply standards and tests, etc, laid down in documents not forming part of the regulations, may allow the Secretary of State to confer exemptions, and may make different provisions for different areas. SI 1994/2249 has been made under this provision, also to implement Directive 93/12. It is an offence to market gas oil with a sulphur content of more than 0.2% by weight. But the prohibition does not apply to gas oil in the fuel tanks of vessels, gas intended for processing before combustion or aviation kerosene. Local authorities (districts and London boroughs) enforce these regulations.

Section 33 of the 1993 Act makes it an offence for a person to burn insulation from a cable with a view to metal recovery unless the burning is a process falling under Part I of the 1990 Act.

The 1993 Act also makes provision relating to research into and publicity concerning atmospheric pollution. Under s 34 local authorities may undertake, or contribute towards, costs of investigatory research into air pollution, and may arrange for publication of information on the problems. They must act in conformity with regulations made under s 38, see SI 1977/19. In particular they may obtain information about polluting emissions. First, they may issue notices under s 36 of the Act, allowing them to require occupiers of premises, other than private dwellings, to furnish specified returns concerning polluting emissions from the premises, subject to rights of appeal to the Secretary of State under s 37. Second, they may measure and record emissions under s 35(1)(b), for that purpose entering premises, other than private dwellings, whether by agreement, or under s 56 of the 1993 Act giving general powers of entry to duly authorised persons. The power of entry under s 35(1)(b) may only be exercised after notice in writing has been given to the occupier specifying the emissions in question, and 21 days must elapse from the date of the notice. They may not exercise powers under the notice where the occupier requests them to proceed under s 36. Third, they may enter into arrangements with occupiers of premises, other than private dwellings, under which they measure and record emissions on behalf of the local authority. While exercising these powers the authority must from time to time consult appropriate persons carrying on any trade or business within their area, their representative organisations, and such others as are conversant with problems of air pollution, or have interests in local amenity, about the way in which the authority exercise their powers, and the extent and manner of release of any collected information to the public. Consultations must take place at least twice in each financial year. Nothing in s 35 authorises an authority to investigate emissions from processes subject to Part I of the Environmental Protection Act 1990, otherwise than by issuing a notice under s 36, or by exercising their investigatory powers without entering the work. Under s 36, which gives authorities power to require occupiers to furnish information about polluting emissions from their premises, where a notice relates to a process subject to Part I of the 1990 Act the person on whom it is served is not obliged to supply any information which, as certified by an inspector, is not of a kind which is being supplied to the inspector for the purposes of that Act. Section 36 applies to premises used for Crown purposes, but in relation to such premises local authorities may not use powers of entry, inspection and to obtain information under ss 56 to 58. Premises may also be exempted from control under s 36(6), see SI 1977/18, principally relating to defence establishments, including, inter alia, the Atomic Weapons Research Establishment at Aldermaston.

Under s 39 of the 1993 Act the Secretary of State may, for the purposes of obtaining information about air pollution, direct a local authority to make specified arrangements for providing and operating air pollution recording apparatus and for transmitting information so obtained to him. Such directions may only be given after consultation with affected authorities, though it is their duty to comply with a direction once given.

Under s 40 of the 1993 Act controls under the legislation cover 'emissions' into the atmosphere. These are construed as applying to substances in a gaseous, liquid or solid state, or any combination of those states.

H CONTROL OF VEHICLE EMISSIONS

Apart from lead, exhaust emissions contain substances such as NOx, carbon monoxide and hydrocarbons which may, in sufficient concentrations, be damaging to health. Emissions can be controlled by regulating fuel composition, or by vehicle design and construction regulations. UK standards have followed the tortuous development of EU Directives, while, sadly, there has not always been agreement between the EU, the USA and Japan, the world's major vehicle producers, as to the style and content of emission standards and their test parameters. Emission requirements for carbon monoxide, hydro-carbons and NOx generally depend upon the year of a model's introduction to the road and the limits in force for that year, generally those fixed under EU Directives. The Road Vehicles (Construction and Use) Regulations SI 1986/1078 (as amended), continued in force under s 41 of the Road Traffic Act 1988, provide in tabular form the minimum standards, so that from 1 October 1982 the standards of Directive 78/665 applied to motor cars while from 1 April 1991 Directive 83/351 was the basic standard for new vehicles. Directive 88/76 was the standard for new vehicles from 1993–94 depending on engine size, while provision was made for compliance with Directive 89/458 for vehicles of less than 1,400 cc capacity from the end of 1992. Further provision was made by Directives 91/441 which came into force as from 1992, applying new limits from 1996, 94/12 (cars and light vans) setting out new limits for all registrations from 1997, and from 1996 for new models, 93/59 and 91/542 which apply to larger and heavier commercial vehicles. Similar provision is made by the regulations in respect of particulate emissions, and emissions from diesel engined vehicles. The UK operates a type approval scheme as provided for by EU Directives, see SI 1994/981. It is an offence under s 42 of the Road Traffic Act 1988 to fail to comply with relevant requirements of the Construction and Use Regulations.

The Road Traffic Regulation Act 1984 contains powers to regulate traffic in order to preserve the amenities of areas through which roads run: these are more generally considered in chapter 11, below. However, ss 1, 6 and 122 (1) of the 1984 Act were amended by the Environment Act 1995, Sch 22 to provide that relevant authorities (shire counties, unitary and metropolitan district authorities and London borough councils) may make an order to achieve the purposes of the national air quality strategy (see further above), and indeed such authorities are to take the strategy into account in exercising road traffic regulation functions.

The official view is that use of 1984 Act powers should not take place on a temporary or ad hoc basis, or on the basis of giving little or no notice of restrictions, lest more congestion and pollution is caused by drivers seeking ways round restricted areas.[3] Such temporary bans could in any case be difficult to enforce. However, the new powers could be used on environmental grounds to allow the creation of contingency orders which regulate traffic on a planned basis and which come into effect, with restriction signs unveiled, when pollution reaches particular levels. This follows the precedent of closing certain moorland roads in times of high fire risk, but it is something of a 'weapon of last resort'.

I STUBBLE BURNING

An issue that caused much controversy was stubble burning in fields after harvesting of crops. In the early 1980s some 14m tonnes of straw were

3 See also *R v Greenwich London Borough, ex p Jack Williams* (1995) 255 ENDS Report 49.

produced annually, half being burnt on site. In 1984 the Home Office produced model byelaws on straw and stubble burning for local authorities to adopt. These provisions were supplemented by the National Farmers Union Code which counselled that straw should be burnt against the wind, only when the wind speed was low, and only after neighbours had been informed. Though it was questionable whether police and fire authorities had resources sufficient to ensure compliance with byelaws, the summer of 1984 did see an abatement of the problem as byelaws and the NFU Code were generally observed. In 1985 the government introduced media advertisements urging precautions on farmers burning straw and stubble.

The problem did not, however, disappear and a growing body of opinion forced legislative action on the issue in the form of s 152 of the Environmental Protection Act 1990 which empowers ministers to make regulations banning farmers from stubble and crop residue burning, either generally or specifically. An interim scheme was introduced by SI 1991/1590 as from July 1991.

The Crop Residues (Burning) Regulations SI 1993/1366 now prohibit the burning on agricultural land of listed crop residues (cereal straw, cereal stubble, residues of oil seed rape, field beans and peas) subject to certain minor exemptions, such as for educational or research purposes. There are also restrictions and requirements imposed in relation to burning linseed residues, for example as to the timing and extent of burning. Burning residues in contravention of the regulations is an offence punishable on summary conviction with a fine up to level 5 on the standard scale.

Further reading

GENERAL WORKS

Aldous, T, *Battle for the Environment* (1972) Fontana, Parts II and V.

Arvil, R, *Man and Environment* (1967) Penguin, chapters 6 and 7.

Bennett, G, (ed) *Air Pollution Control in the European Community* (1991) Graham and Trotman.

Blowers, A, *Something in the Air* (1984) Harper and Row.

Churchill, R, Warren, L, and Gibson, J, *Law, Policy and the Environment* (1991) Blackwell.

Churchill, R, and Freestone, D, (eds) *International Law and Global Climate Change* (1991) Graham and Trotman.

Johnson, SP, *The Earth Summit: The United Nations Conference on Environment and Development (UNCED)* (1993) Graham and Trotman, chapter 5.

ENERGY

Central Electricity Generating Board, 'Acid Rain' (1985) CEGB.

Everest, D, 'The Greenhouse Effect' (1988) Policy Studies Institute.

Grubb, M, 'The Greenhouse Effect' (1990) Royal Institute of International Affairs.

UK Climate Change Impacts Review Group, 'The Potential Effects of Climate Change in the UK' (1991) DoE.

PLANNING CONTROL

Miller, C, and Wood, C, *Planning and Pollution* OUP, chapters 2, 3 and 4.

TRANSPORT

Hughes, P, 'Exhausting the Atmosphere' (1991) 60 Town and Country Planning 267.
Quality of Urban Air Review Group, 'Diesel Vehicle Emissions and Urban Air Quality' (1993) University of Birmingham.
Sharp, C, and Jennings, T, 'Transport and the Environment' (1976) Leicester University Press.
Watkins, LH, 'Air Pollution from Road Vehicles' (1991) HMSO.

ODOURS

Artis, D, 'Control of Odour Pollution' [1982] JPL 481.
Artis, D, and Silvester, S, 'Odour Nuisance: Legal Controls' [1986] JPL 565.

IPC

Allot, K, 'Integrated Pollution Control: The First Three Years' (1994) Environmental Data Services Ltd.
Haigh, N, and Irwin, F, 'Integrated Pollution Control in Europe and North America' (1990) The Conservation Foundation.
Harris, R, 'The Environmental Protection Act 1990 — Penalising the Polluter' [1992] JPL 515.
Harty, R, 'Integrated Pollution Control in Practice' [1992] JPL 611.
Kitson, T, and Harris, R, 'A burning issue: Planning Controls, Pollution Controls and Waste Incineration' [1994] JPL 3.
Purdue, M, 'Integrated Pollution Control in the Environmental Protection Act 1990: A Coming of Age of Environmental Law?' (1991) 54 MLR 534.
Waite, A, 'Legal Aspects of IPC' [1992] 4 LMELR 2.

OFFICIAL REPORTS

'Acid Rain' (1984 Cmnd 9397).
'Acid Rain' (House of Commons Environment Committee 4th Report Session 1983–84, 446–1).
'CFC's and Halons' (1990) HMSO.
'The Effects of Acid Deposition' (1989) HMSO.
'Energy Paper No 58' (1990) HMSO.
Royal Commission on Environmental Pollution, 5th Report (1976, Cmnd 6371), 9th Report (1983, Cmnd 8852), 10th Report (1984, Cmnd 9149), 15th Report (1991, Cm 1631), 18th Report (1994, Cm 2674).
'Climate Change: Our National Programme for CO_2 Emissions' (1992) DOE.
'Climate Change: the UK Programme' (1994, Cm 2427) HMSO.
'Volatile Organic Compounds' House of Commons Environment Committee Session 1994/95, 1st Report, HC 39-1 (1995) HMSO (and the government's response of 27 June 1995).

Chapter 11

Noise

'When you've got a beehive in your head,
and a sewing machine in each ear,
and you feel like you've eaten your bed,
and you've got a bad headache down here'
(W S Gilbert, 'The Grand Duke', Act 1)

Humankind's capacity to *create* noise increases dramatically. Noise surrounds us; the roar of traffic, the irritating buzz of personal stereos, the inane outpourings of young men in flashy cars anxious to demonstrate their car radios to one and all, the bustle of crowds, the passage of trains and aeroplanes, and the working of industry and public utilities. The home can also be invaded by noise. The Wilson Committee on the Problem of Noise (Cmnd 2056) found that surveys carried out in 1948 and 1961 showed that whereas only some 23% of those surveyed at the earlier date claimed to have been disturbed at home by external noises, by the later date the figure had risen to 50%. By 1994 the National Society for Clean Air and Environmental Protection could claim also one third of Britons alleging invasion of their homes by unacceptable noise: 30% by traffic noise, 22% by neighbour noise, 16% by aircraft noise and 4% by train noise. It is hard to find, even in rural areas, any place where the only sounds are those produced by nature. Noise is undoubtedly psychologically and physiologically harmful and an invisible but insidious form of pollution: once hearing has been damaged by noise it can scarcely ever be restored to wholeness. Noise can also cause loss of sleep, distraction from work or leisure activities, annoyance, nervous tension, and failures of communication. Arguably noise may be a causal factor in conditions such as heart disease, migraine and gastro-intestinal disorders. Complaints about noise also increase: from 42,000 received by local authorities in 1984 to 131,153 in 1993/94 — this was the seventh successive increase.

A WHAT IS NOISE? THE PROBLEM AND THE INTERNATIONAL RESPONSE

The Wilson Committee in its 1963 report 'Noise', Cmnd 2056, defined noise as 'sound which is undesired by the recipient'. This subjective definition is alien to a scientist's description of noise in terms of *frequency and intensity*. The law has failed to produce an objective definition of noise, coupled with measurement and assessment techniques. The law cannot take account of every unwanted noise, but legal regulation cannot be restricted only to those noises that are objectively 'loud' in terms of decibels, sones and phons — a continuous low pitched 'quiet' buzz may be as annoying as the occasional 'loud' bang. The law is pragmatic regarding noise as a fit subject for action only if, in its context, sound becomes excessive, unnecessary or unreasonable. Scientific methods are, of course, useful in determining situations where noise 'steps out from its background' and becomes actionable.[1] Of course the 'louder', in scientific terms, a noise is, the more likely it is that legal action will have to be taken to shield the public against it or bring about its cessation.

The following is a table of commonly occurring noise levels in decibels.

Peak sound level in dB(A) (decibels)	Environmental conditions
140	Threshold of pain
130	Jet aircraft on ground, pneumatic road breaker
125	Noise under supersonic flight path within 5 miles of take-off
120	Jet take-off at 100m, loud motor horn at 3ft
110–125	Pop group
115	Noise under jet flight path within 5 miles of take-off, riveting machine in sheet metal works
100	House near airport, inside an underground train
90–92	Train, inside a bus
88–92	Heavy lorry
81–91	Sports car
77–83	Cars
80	Average street corner noise
75	Major road with heavy traffic (peak level)
70	Conversational speech
65	Residential road with local traffic
60	Business office
50	Living room in a suburban area with distant traffic noise
40	Library
30	Quiet bedroom at night
25	Rustling leaves
20	Broadcasting studio
10	Threshold of hearing

(Derivation: Kerse *The Law Relating to Noise* p 10 and Sharp and Jennings *Transport and the Environment* pp 53–54. Subjectively, an increase in sound levels of 10dB(A) is approximately a *doubling* of loudness.) Readers wishing to study the law relating to noise *at work* are referred to chapter 9 of Penn *Noise Control: the Law and its Enforcement*, 2nd edn (1995). This chapter will concentrate on noise in the environment.

International and European Union law lay down certain norms in respect of noise. International law has been much concerned in particular with aircraft

1 *R v Fenny Stratford Justices, ex p Watney Mann (Midlands) Ltd* [1976] 2 All ER 888, [1976] 1 WLR 1101.

issues (see further below on UK implementation of treaty provisions), and the principal standards-setting body is the International Civil Aviation Organisation (ICAO) set up under the Chicago Convention of 1944, art 9 of which also acts as the international legal basis for regulation of aircraft noise. This has been supplemented a number of times, and the provisions are known collectively as Annex 16 of the Chicago Convention, which since 1981, has borne the title 'environmental protection', while a Committee on Aviation Environmental Protection (CAEP) was set up in 1983 with the object of keeping Annex 16 under regular review so that signatory states can consider amending its terms to take account, for example, of enhanced noise abatement technologies. See further Shawcross and Beaumont *Air Law*, 4th edn, Vol I, Division II, chapter 9.

The EU formally took action on noise for the first time in its Second Action Programme of 1977 though there had been some antecedent measures. The EU relied on noise standards set by other international bodies such as ICAO, and, historically, tended to follow the paths of harmonising national standards, so that measures were mixed, partly directed towards the free circulation of goods and partly towards the imposition of noise limits. In the future more European noise standards may be expected, together with action on ambient noise levels as well as noise standards for individual generators of noise. The 'polluter pays' principle is likely to be involved in support of measures to relate airport landing charges to levels of aircraft noise, and as an encouragement for developing less noisy products.

Currently the EU has noise standards on: the permissible sound levels and exhaust systems for motor vehicles;[2] motorcycles;[3] tractors;[4] construction plant;[5] aircraft;[6] lawnmowers[7] and household appliances.[8] Action has also been taken on workplace noise. The Directive on aircraft noise is particularly interesting as an example of vertical integration between various systems of law. Directive 80/51 makes it an obligation for member states to implement the ICAO's Annex 16 noise emission standards for subsonic aircraft which otherwise would not have legal force within the legal systems of all member states. General comment on the implementation of EU requirements by UK law will be made where appropriate below.

B NOISE AND THE COMMON LAW

Noise can be either a public or private nuisance. The assessment of whether noise constitutes an actionable nuisance will depend on considering factors such as the: nature of the locality; duration of the noise; nature and desirability of the defendant's actions; nature of the harm suffered by the plaintiff, and the defendant's state of mind, though not all of these will be equally relevant in any

2 (Directive 70/157, amended 73/350, 77/212, 81/334, 84/372, 84/424, 92/97).
3 (Directive 78/1015, amended 87/56, 89/235).
4 (Directive 74/151, amended 82/890, and 77/311).
5 (Directive 84/532, 79/113, amended 81/1051, 85/405, 84/533 to 84/537, 86/662, 89/392).
6 (Directive 80/51, amended 83/206, 89/629, 92/14).
7 (Directive 84/538, amended 87/252, 88/180, 88/181).
8 (Directive 86/594).

given case. The following have been held to be noise nuisances: operating very noisy machinery during the night so as to disturb the plaintiff's sleep;[9] use of a circular saw for 12 hours a day;[10] playing fairground organs for eight hours a day;[11] operating a dairy with much clanging of churns, coming and going, loading of carts and noisy machinery;[12] though *not* simply supplying milk, even in large quantities;[13] *deliberately* making loud noises and shrieks so as to disrupt a music teacher's lessons;[14] using a steam hammer so noisy that it disturbed public worship and prevented schools from functioning;[15] broadcasting radio programmes loudly in the defendant's factory;[16] noisy testing of aero engines;[17] noisy operation of fish and chip shops or all night cafes;[18] using land as a speedway track, or for 'go-karts';[19] keeping particularly noisy animals;[20] the ringing of church bells;[1] allowing the use by night of a children's playground on a council estate by noisy children.[2]

The courts are particularly concerned with the nature, quality and duration of noise, and the time of day of its occurrence; night time noise being more likely to be actionable. Each case turns on its own facts: a given outcome is not always easy to predict. This uncertainty, coupled with the complexity and expense of litigation, render a nuisance action an unpopular method of dealing with noise. Between neighbours nuisance is an unpopular type of proceeding: actions, even in the county court, are drawn out and time consuming, frequently productive of bitterness, costly, and generally need a deal of proof from plaintiffs, such as listing and describing the quality and duration of noise in diaries. Such deficiencies justify the existence of public law controls over noise. Furthermore, planned strategies to control and reduce noise can only be implemented by public bodies: where noise afflicts a whole area or section of the community it is wrong to expect remedial action to be taken solely by individuals. However, the existence of public law controls does not inhibit the power of the court to grant a remedy stricter than that available under statute.[3] Furthermore a grant of planning permission may so change the character of an area that noise that would have amounted to a noise before a development took place may no longer do so afterwards.[4]

9 *Rushmer v Polsue and Alfieri Ltd* [1906] 1 Ch 234, CA; affd [1907] AC 121, HL.
10 *Husey v Bailey* (1895) 11 TLR 221.
11 *Lambton v Mellish* [1894] 3 Ch 163.
12 *Tinkler v Aylesbury Dairy Co Ltd* (1888) 5 TLR 52.
13 *Fanshawe v London and Provincial Dairy Co* (1888) 4 TLR 694.
14 *Christie v Davey* [1893] 1 Ch 316.
15 *Roskell v Whitworth* (1871) 19 WR 804.
16 *Gilbert v Marks & Co* (1949) 150 Estates Gazette 81.
17 *Bosworth-Smith v Gwynnes Ltd* (1919) 89 LJ Ch 368.
18 *Caradog-Jones v Rose* (1961) Times, 14 March; and *Charlton v Old Manor Cars* (1960) Times, 12 October.
19 *Tarry v Chandler* (1934) 79 Sol Jo 11; and *Manners v Chester* (1963) Times, 12 February.
20 *Leeman v Montagu* [1936] 2 All ER 1677; and *Broder v Saillard* (1876) 2 Ch D 692.
1 *Soltau v De Held* (1851) 2 Sim NS 133.
2 *Dunton v Dover District Council* (1977) 76 LGR 87.
3 *Lloyds Bank v Guardian Assurance plc* (1986) 35 BLR 34.
4 *Gillingham Borough Council v Medway (Chatham) Dock Co Ltd* [1992] 3 All ER 923.

C PUBLIC LAW CONTROLS OVER NOISE

The development of the law

There was for many years reluctance to introduce statutory noise controls. Some local Acts dealt with noise nuisances, as did some byelaws, but it was generally left to private citizens to take nuisance actions in respect of noise. However, nuisance actions are effective only in cases involving single, stationary continuous sources of noise, as opposed to combinations of noise of short and intermittent duration. Additionally a common law action is punitive and compensatory rather than preventive. It is better to plan and design the location and practices of industry so as to prevent noise, rather than imposing expensive remedial steps by means of injunctions.

Accordingly the Noise Abatement Act 1960 was passed, the first general Act devoted to controlling noise. However, it merely declared noise to be a statutory nuisance, and did little more than centralising and codifying existing byelaws of local authorities. Following the report of the Scott Committee, 'Neighbourhood Noise,' in 1971 further controls on noise were included in the Control of Pollution Act 1974, Part III. Certain controls are now to be found in the Environmental Protection Act 1990, as amended, while other statutes control 'raves'. The common law is also relevant.

Common law powers

Noise can amount to a public nuisance provided a class of Her Majesty's subjects is affected,[5] and it is established that a perpetrator may be liable where he/she knew or ought to have known of the nuisance.

The current statute law

Noise nuisances

Local authorities, eg district, metropolitan district and London borough councils, are under a duty to inspect their areas from time to time to detect noise nuisances and must take reasonable steps to investigate complaints of noise nuisances, see s 79(1)(g) on noise emitted *from premises*, and s 79(1)(ga) on noise from vehicles, machinery or equipment (including musical instruments) in streets; excluding traffic and protest marches. Where, under s 80 of the 1990 Act, the local authority conclude that noise amounting to a nuisance exists or is likely to recur in their area, they *must* serve a notice on the person responsible for the noise (that is the person by whose act, default or sufferance the noise arises, see s 80 or, with regard to vehicles the registered owner *and* the driver, and, with regard to equipment, etc, its operator, see s 79(7)), or if he cannot be found, or if the nuisance is only anticipated, on the owner or occupier of the premises from which the noise is, or may be, emitted. The notice may be served *either* on the person, or by being left at the person's proper address, *or* sent by post thereto, see s 233(2) of the Local Government Act 1972.[6] The notice may require abatement of the nuisance or prohibit or

---

5 *R v Shorrock* [1993] 3 All ER 917.
6 *Lambeth London Borough Council v Mullings* [1990] RVR 259.

restrict its recurrence, and may require the execution of such works, and the taking of such other steps, as may be necessary or specified. The notice must specify the time or times within which compliance is required. Where a nuisance is likely to recur a permanent prohibition of recurrence may be imposed.[7] It is helpful, though not mandatory, for an authority seeking to prevent the occurrence of a nuisance to set a decibel level which shall not be exceeded. However, where a decibel level is set, the notice must also say where that level is to be measured. The notice should be practicable and easily understood and should not require unnecessary repetition of works simply to reduce noise to a stated decibel level.[8] However, a nuisance may still arise for reasons other than noise decibel levels being exceeded.[9] An authority may base its actions on the expert evidence of its own officers, and does not have to prove nuisance to a particular occupier, and may require cessation of nuisance to the occupier of any residential property, though the authority's notice should make it clear which requirements are imposed under what provisions.[10] It is not enough, however, simply to allege 'a noise nuisance', though in the context of noise there is no obligation to specify works to be done, or other steps to be taken.[11] The person served with the notice has, under s 80(3), 21 days to appeal to the magistrates. The grounds of appeal are contained in SI 1995/2644 which replaced the previous regulations, SI 1990/2276, and which takes account of the amendments made to the 1990 Act, particularly with regard to noise in streets. However, before considering the particular defences under the regulations, it should be noted that there are two general defences under s 80, namely that the defendant had a 'reasonable excuse', and, where the noise was caused in the course of trade or business, that the 'best practicable means' were used to prevent, or to counteract it, see further p 510, below. The court may quash or vary the notice or dismiss the appeal, and has a wide discretion as to whom to order to execute, or pay for, any necessary work. In *Johnsons News of London Ltd v Ealing London Borough Council*[12] it was held that justices should decide the appeal on the basis of the facts at the time of the hearing, thus allowing a person to take steps to adopt 'the best practicable means' *after* service of the statutory notice.

Particular provision is made for appeals against s 80 notices in the context of noise by the Statutory Nuisance (Appeals) Regulations SI 1995/2644. There are additions to the general grounds of appeal (ie the notice is not justified, or is subject to some informality, defect or error, or the authority have refused unreasonably to accept compliance with alternative requirements, or the notice's requirements are unreasonable or unnecessary, or the time specified for taking action is not reasonably sufficient, etc, see chapter 1 above). In the case of alleged nuisances under s 79(1)(g) or (ga) of the 1990 Act which relate to noise emitted from premises, it can be a ground of appeal that the

7 *R v Birmingham Justices, ex p Guppy* (1987) 152 JP 159.
8 *Network Housing Association v Westminster City Council* [1995] Env LR 176.
9 *East Northamptonshire District Council v Fossett* [1994] Env LR 388.
10 *Cooke v Adatia* (1988) 153 JP 129.
11 *Greenline Carriers (Tayside) Ltd v City of Dundee* 1991 SLT 673; and *Sterling Homes (Midlands) Ltd v Birmingham City Council* (New Law Fax, Property Communication 120, 5 July 1995).
12 (1989) 154 JP 33.

requirements of the notice are more serious than the requirements for the time being in force in relation to the noise in question of any notice served under ss 60 or 66 of the 1974 Act (control of construction site noise), or any consent given under ss 61 or 65 (consent for work or construction sites and for noise to exceed a registered level) or any determination made under s 67 (noise control for new buildings). In the case of a nuisance under s 79(1)(ga) where noise is emitted or is caused by vehicles, machinery or equipment, it is a ground of appeal that the requirements of the notice are more serious than the requirements for the time being in force in relation to the noise in question under any condition of a consent given under para 1 of the Sch 3 of the Noise and Statutory Nuisance Act 1993 which relates to loudspeakers in streets or roads.

Where an appeal is made and the nuisance is one arising under s 79(1)(g) or (ga) of the 1990 Act *and* the noise in question was necessarily caused in the performance of some duty imposed by law on the appellant, the notice is suspended until the appeal has been abandoned or decided *save* for cases where the nuisance is injurious to health or is of such limited duration that suspension of the notice would render the notice nugatory, and the notice includes a statement to that effect and which gives a statement of the basis for non-suspension on which the authority rely. In such cases suspension does not take place.

It should, of course, be remembered that all the other grounds of appeal are available, just as with other statutory nuisance allegations.

Authorities may also apply for an injunction to restrain a noise nuisance pending the outcome of an appeal.[13]

Section 80(4) provides that if a person served with a notice under the section contravenes, without reasonable excuse, a requirement of the notice he commits an offence. Noise nuisance allegations are criminal in nature and hence the criminal burden of proof applies. Thus in *Lewisham London Borough v Fenner*[14] (admittedly only a Crown Court decision) it was found that in relation to an alleged nuisance arising from the operation of equipment, the fact that noise emitted was below the recommended limit of BS 8233 pointed to the burden of proof not being discharged, and the case failed.

Street noise

Where noise from a highway penetrates or vibrates premises and makes them prejudicial to health or a nuisance, action may be taken by the local authority under s 79(1)(a).[15] Noise emitted *from premises* may, as outlined above, be a nuisance under s 79(1)(g). Though 'premises' includes land, it would not appear to cover street noise[16] hence the enactment of s 79(1)(ga). Section 80A further provides in relation to such street noise nuisance that where the nuisance has not yet occurred, *or* where it consists of noise from an unattended vehicle, which includes loud hailers and, presumably, even radios, machines or

---

13 *Hammersmith London Borough Council v Magnum Automated Forecourts Ltd* [1978] 1 WLR 50 and s 81(5).
14 (1995) 248 ENDS Report 44.
15 *Southwark London Borough Council v Ince* (1989) 153 JP 597.
16 *Tower Hamlets London Borough Council v Manzoni* (1983) 148 JP 123.

pieces of equipment, the abatement notice is to be served on the person responsible for the vehicle or equipment if that person can be found. If the person cannot be found, or where the authority determine to follow this procedure, they may affix the abatement notice to the vehicle or equipment, etc. Where affixation takes place *only* because of the authority's resolution and the person responsible can be found, a copy of the notice must also be served on that person within one hour of the affixation to the vehicle. The person served may appeal as under s 80.

Traffic noise, military noise or noise from a demonstration, eg a political march, is exempt from control, see s 79(6A).

Failure to comply with a street noise nuisance abatement notice entitles the local authority to take action under s 81(8) — as with any statutory nuisance — to enter the source of the noise and remove it to a safe place if that is what is requisite to abate the nuisance. Penn *Noise Control* points, at p 103, to an instance of vehicle alarms going off at night and being disarmed by the local authority's environmental health officers. However, in such cases care must be taken not to cause more damage than is necessary, see Sch 3, para 2A(4) of the 1990 Act, while a vehicle that has been entered to abate a nuisance should be resecured as effectively as possible. The local authority may recover their reasonable expenses under s 81(4), while ss 81A and 81B allow for such expenses to be charged on relevant premises and paid by instalments.

General defences to noise nuisance allegations

'Reasonable excuse' already mentioned above seems to mean an excuse that a reasonable person would think consistent with a reasonable standard of conduct: mere lack of finance would not amount to such an excuse.[17] In *A Lambert Flat Management Ltd v Lomas*[18] the court considered the defence of 'reasonable excuse' is designed to cover cases where there is some special difficulty in relation to complying with the notice, for example severe illness. Holding a birthday party is not a 'reasonable excuse' for noise, nor is reducing noise levels on request though this may be relevant as an issue in mitigation, or in deciding whether there was a noise nuisance in the first place.[19]

A further defence is use of the 'best practicable means' to prevent or counteract the nuisance, see s 80(8). Some guidance on 'best practicable means' is found in s 79(9) which defines 'practicable' as 'reasonably practicable having regard among other things to local conditions and circumstances ... the current state of technical knowledge and to the financial implications'. 'Means' is defined to include design, installation, maintenance, manner and periods of operation of plant and machinery and the design and construction of buildings and acoustic structures. The test is applied only in so far as compatible with legal duties, any exigencies of emergencies, and safe working conditions. It is, however, for the accused to establish the defence, and mere increased costs of operation do not automatically render a 'means' impracticable.[20] Regard may also be had to any relevant provision of a code of

---

17 *Saddleworth UDC v Aggregate & Sand* (1970) 69 LGR 103.
18 [1981] 2 All ER 280, [1981] 1 WLR 898.
19 *Wellingborough Borough Council v Gordon* (1990) 155 JP 494.
20 *Wivenhoe Port v Colchester Borough Council* [1985] JPL 175 and 396; and *Chapman v Gosberton Farm Produce Co Ltd* [1993] 5 ELM 38.

practice for minimising noise made under s 71 of the 1974 Act (see further below).

Where the local authority are of the opinion that a prosecution would not be an adequate remedy, they may under s 81(5) take proceedings in the High Court to secure the abatement, prohibition or restriction of the nuisance, irrespective of whether they have or have not suffered damage.[21] In *City of London Corpn v Bovis Construction Ltd*[22] a local authority sought an injunction under s 222 of the Local Government Act 1972 in respect of repeated contraventions of a notice issued under s 60 of the 1974 Act. The court considered injunctive relief was appropriate where necessary to prevent damage not preventable by proceedings before justices, or: where criminal sanctions are otherwise insufficient or technically deficient; where unlawful activity will continue unless restrained by an injunction. See also *London Borough of Camden v Alpenoak Ltd*[1] where an injunction was granted after repeated noise complaints, and then breached 22 times before contempt proceedings resulted in a £50,000 fine with £5,000 costs. Authories must be able to show, however, that the activity in question is a threat to the proper exercise of statutory responsibilities, for the court will act with discretion and caution, and not to restrain mere infractions of criminal law.

Where *any* person is aggrieved by noise amounting to a nuisance he/she may make a complaint to the magistrates under s 82 of the 1990 Act. If the magistrates are satisfied that the nuisance exists or, though abated, is likely to recur on the same premises they must make an order requiring the defendant either to abate the nuisance within a specified time, and to execute any works necessary for that purpose, or prohibiting recurrence and requiring the doing of necessary works. Alternatively *both* these requirements can be imposed. The procedure is available against the creator of the noise, or if that person cannot be found, the owner or occupier of the premises from which the noise emanates. Where the noise nuisance enamates from unattended vehicles or equipment, proceedings lie against the person responsible for the vehicle/equipment. Where more than one person is responsible for noise each person responsible can be proceeded against. Making the order has similar consequences as to offences and defences under s 80, but where a person is convicted of an offence under s 82(11), the magistrates may, after giving him an opportunity of being heard, direct the local authority to do anything the convicted person was required to do by the order. The local authority may recover their expenditure from the person in default under s 81 of the Act of 1990. See also s 81A on expenses being charged on relevant premises and s 81B on payment by instalments. Section 82 proceedings are available in respect of *existing* nuisances (or those likely to recur). Additionally the complainant must be a person whose enjoyment of property in his occupation has been materially affected by the noise. (See also chapter 1 above on the technicalities of action under s 82.)

---

21 *Hammermith London Borough Council v Magnum Automated Forecourts Ltd* [1978] 1 WLR 50.
22 (1988) 86 LGR 660.
 1 (1985) Surveyor, 5 December 17.

Notices served under previous legislation

Noise abatement notices served under the predecessor legislation to the 1990 Act, ie the Control of Pollution Act 1974, remain effective to control noise even after 1990.[2]

Construction site noise

Erecting, constructing, altering, repairing or maintaining buildings, structures or roads, or breaking up, opening or boring under any road or adjacent land in connection with construction, inspection, maintenance or removal works, or any demolition or dredging work, or other work of engineering construction falls within s 60 of the 1974 Act. Where the local authority conclude that such works are, or are going to be, carried out on any premises, they *may* serve notice imposing requirements as to the manner of doing the works. Notice has to be served on the person who appears to be carrying out, or going to carry out, the works, together with such others appearing to the authority to be responsible for, or having control over, the works. Requirements may include provision as to, inter alia: specifications of plant or machinery prescribed or proscribed; permitted hours of working; permitted noise levels generally, or in specified places or at specified times, and may provide for changes of circumstances. The authority must have regard to relevant provisions of any code of practice issued under Part III of the 1974 Act,[3] together with the need to ensure that the best practicable means are employed to minimise noise. Before specifying particular methods or plant they must consider alternatives similarly effective to minimise noise and more acceptable to the persons to be served with the notice. General regard must be had to protecting persons in the area against noise. The notice may specify requisite steps and periods for compliance. Following service there is a 21 day period in which to appeal to the magistrates, see SI 1975/2116, reg 5. It is an offence to contravene a notice without reasonable excuse. However, a notice may only apply to works actually in progress or in contemplation at the time of its issue.[4]

Noise from construction *plant* is further controlled under the Construction Plant and Equipment (Harmonisation of Noise Emission Standards) Regulations SI 1985/1968, as amended by SI 1989/1127. These, inter alia, implement Directives 84/532–84/537, 86/662, and 89/392. Plant, eg generators and concrete breakers, must conform to EU noise standards, and is subject to periodic examination to ensure conformity. See further SI 1989/361 and SI 1992/488.

Because the provision to control site noise is discretionary, practice varies widely. Local authorities tend to prefer informal arrangements and agreements with builders and other similar contractors to notices. Liaison between environmental health and planning departments can be useful in alerting relevant officers to sites where planning permission for relevant work is sought. Officers then decide whether or not to implement noise control powers; much depends on whether the authority has the resources to take action.

2 *Aitken v South Hams District Council* [1995] 1 AC 262, [1994] 3 All ER 400.
3 See SI 1984/1992 and SI 1987/1730.
4 *Walter Lily & Co Ltd v Westminster City Council* [1994] 6 ELM 44.

Section 61 of the 1974 Act allows a person intending to carry out works to which s 60 applies to apply to the local authority for consent. Where approval under building regulations is required in respect of the works, any application for consent must be made at the same time as, or later than, the request for building regulation approval. A s 61 application must contain particulars of the works in question, methods to be used in carrying them out and steps proposed to minimise noise. Where these satisfy the authority that they would not need to serve a s 60 notice, consent must be given. Before issuing consent they must have regard to any relevant code of guidance, need to ensure the use of the best practicable means to minimise noise, suitable alternative methods similarly able to minimise noise, and the need to protect persons in the locality against noise.

Consent may be given subject to conditions, particularly with regard to limiting consent following changes of circumstances and as to duration. It is an offence knowingly to infringe or to fail to comply with such a condition.

Decisions on applications must be given within 28 days from receipt. If the authority fail to give consent within that period, or if they do consent but attach conditions or limit or qualify the consent in any way, the applicant has 21 days in which to appeal to the magistrates, see SI 1975/2116, reg 6.

Where proceedings are brought for contravening a s 60 notice it is a defence to prove that the alleged contravention amounted to carrying out works in accordance with a s 61 consent. Such a consent constitutes, however, *no* defence of itself to proceedings under s 82 of the 1990 Act. Where consent has been given and the works themselves are carried out by a person other than the applicant, the applicant's duty is to take all reasonable steps to bring the consent to the notice of the person doing the works: to fail is to commit an offence.

Loudspeaker noise

Section 62 of the 1974 Act generally makes it criminal to operate a loud-speaker in a street between the hours of nine in the evening and eight the following morning *for any purpose*, and at any other time for the purpose of advertising *any entertainment, trade or business* though exceptions exist for vendors such as those of ice cream, see s 62(3). 'Street' means any highway or other road, footway, square or court for the time being open to the public. Exceptions exist where loudspeakers are used by, in connection with, or form part of, as the case may be:

1 The police, fire brigade, ambulance service, water undertakers in the discharge of their functions or a local authority within their area.
2 Persons communicating with others on a vessel for the purpose of directing the movement of that or other vessels.
3 A public telephone system.
4 Persons employed in connection with a transport undertaking used by the public, where the loudspeaker is operated otherwise than on the highway for the sole purpose of making announcements to passengers or employees of the undertaking.
5 Travelling salesmen on land used temporarily for a pleasure fair.
6 Emergencies (for example immediate risks to life and health). And
7 Where the loudspeaker is in or fixed to a vehicle, *and* is operated solely for the entertainment of, or for communicating with, the driver or passengers,

or forms part of traffic warning devices, *and* is reasonably operated so as not to give annoyance to persons in the vicinity.

The prohibition who does not apply to any loudspeaker operated under local authority consent under Sch 2 of the Noise and Statutory Nuisance Act 1993. Such consent may be conditional, and may not authorise use for election, trade, business or entertainment advertisement purposes. Schedule 2 applies where an authority resolves it shall apply in its area.

Noise abatement zones

Section 63 of the 1974 Act allows a local authority to designate all or any part of its area as a noise abatement zone, though all authorities are required by s 57 to inspect their areas with a view to declaring zones. Such an order must specify the classes of premises to which it applies. 'Premises' includes land under s 105(1) of the 1974 Act. The classes of premises suitable for control, include commercial industrial and agricultural premises, places of entertainment, transport and public utility installations. Once an order is in force the provisions of ss 64 (registers of noise levels), 65 (noise exceeding registered levels), 66 (reduction of noise levels) and 67 (powers to deal with new buildings) apply. Authorities should not designate noise abatement zones unless they have the resources to undertake functions under these provisions. See also Penn *Noise Control*, chapter 4. Designation of a noise abatement zone should be considered whenever a planning application for new industrial development is made, especially where this could lead to mixed industrial and residential uses. A noise abatement zone will apply to existing as well as proposed land uses, and will cover noisy developments which, as a result of statutory permissions and exemptions, would otherwise escape planning control.

Procedure for designating zones

This is laid down in Sch 1 to the Act (as substituted by the Local Government, Planning and Land Act 1980, s 1(2)). Before making the order the authority must serve notice on every owner, lessee and occupier (other than tenants for a month or less) of affected premises, and also publish the notice in the London Gazette and, for two successive weeks, in a local newspaper. The notice must state the intention to make the order and its general effect; a place where the order can be inspected (free of charge and at reasonable hours) during a period of not less than six weeks from the last date of publication, and must state the right of affected persons to object in writing to the authority. If objections are made they must be considered before the order is made. Objections can be ignored where the authority conclude consideration is unnecessary having regard either to the nature of the premises to which the order will relate or to the nature of the objectors' interests. The order once made generally comes into force *not less* than one month from the date of making. There is nothing in s 63 to *oblige* authorities to carry out inspections before making orders under that provision,[5] though such an inspection is desirable.

---

5 *Morganite Special Carbons v Secretary of State for the Environment* (1980) 256 Estates Gazette 1105.

Every local authority which has designated a noise abatement zone must, under s 64, measure and record in a public register ('the noise level register') the level of noise emanating from premises of any relevant class within the zone. Methods to be used in measuring noise levels and keeping records are laid down in the Control of Noise (Measurement and Registers) Regulations 1976, SI 1976/37. The regulations include a memorandum giving guidance on where and how to measure noise, how to determine measurement points and their heights, the time of measurements and how to take into account meteorological conditions, see Leeson *Environmental Law* pp 291–293, and Penn *Noise Control* 2nd edn, pp 123–130. The register must contain the noise level which has been ascertained, and the Regulations require that the methods of measurement or calculation employed, details of all relevant measurements and calculations, including locations and heights of each point at which computations were made, details of equipment used, dates and times of computations, and prevailing weather conditions must be included. Clear identification of affected premises must be made, relevant dates stated, and other appropriate details recorded. Detailed guidance is also given on when and where to take measurements, the number of measurement points, the times of measurements and compensations to be made for background noise.

A copy of the recorded measurement must be served on the owner and occupier of the premises in question, thereafter there is a 28 day right of appeal to the Secretary of State, otherwise the validity of the registered entry may not be questioned in any proceedings under Part III of the 1974 Act, and see SI 1975/2116, reg 9. The Secretary of State may allow or dismiss the appeal or reverse or vary any part of the record. He may also give to the local authority such directions as he thinks fit for giving effect to his determination.

By s 65 the level of noise recorded in the register in respect of any premises may not be exceeded except with the written consent of the local authority, which may be given subject to conditions as to permitted levels of excess noise, and the duration and timing of such excess. Details of any consent must be recorded in the noise level register. A decision on an application for consent for noise to exceed registered levels must *generally* be notified to the applicant within two months of date of receipt, otherwise consent is deemed to be refused. Disappointed applicants may appeal to the Secretary of State within three months, beginning with the date of notification, or, in the case of a deemed refusal, within three months of the expiry of the two month period following the lodging of the application. The Secretary of State has a wide discretion on appeal, see SI 1975/2116, reg 9, and the local authority must act in accordance with his decision on appeal. Under s 65(8) a consent must contain a statement that it does not of itself constitute any ground of defence against proceedings instituted by an aggrieved occupier under s 82 of the 1990 Act.

Offences

Where noise is emitted from any premises in contravention of either the registered recorded level, or a condition attached to a consent to exceed that level, the person responsible commits an offence under s 65(5). On convicting for such an offence magistrates may, if satisfied the offence is likely to continue or recur, make an order requiring the execution of necessary preventive works. Contravention of any requirement of such an order without reasonable excuse is itself an offence. The magistrates may, after giving the local authority an opportunity of being heard, direct them to do any works that would be required of the convicted person, either instead of, or in addition to, imposing requirements on that person. Where the local authority are ordered to execute works they may recover their expenses from the convicted person under s 69.

Where, under s 66, it appears to the local authority that the level of noise from any premises subject to a noise abatement order is unacceptable, having regard to the purposes for which the order was made, *and* that a reduction in that level is practicable at reasonable cost and would afford a public benefit, they may serve a noise reduction notice on the person responsible. The notice must require reduction of noise emitted to specified levels, to prevent any subsequent increase in the level of noise emitted, unless the local authority consent, and to take such steps as may be specified to achieve the purpose. The notice must give at least six months from the date of service for compliance, and its particulars must be recorded in the noise level register. The notice may make specific requirements as to noise reductions for particular dates and times, *and takes effect irrespective of any s 65 consent authorising a higher level of noise.*

A person served with such a notice has three months to appeal to the magistrates, see SI 1975/2116, reg 7. It is an offence to contravene a notice without reasonable excuse, though in any proceedings for an offence arising out of carrying on any trade or business it is a defence to prove that the best practicable means has been used for preventing or counteracting the noise.

Where it appears to a local authority that a building is going to be constructed to which a noise abatement order will apply once erected, or that any premises will, as a result of any works, become premises to which an order applies, they may, under s 67, on *either* the application of the owner or occupier (prospective or actual) of the building *or* on their own initiative, determine an acceptable level of noise for emission from that building. This level must then be registered. Notice of intention to make a determination must be given to the relevant person(s) who may appeal to the Secretary of State within three months, see SI 1975/2116, reg 9. Where an owner or occupier makes an application to the local authority in respect of a building falling within s 67, they have two months to notify him of their decision. Failure to do so is deemed to be notice that they have decided not to make a determination, and the applicant may then appeal to the Secretary of State. Where at any time after the coming into force of a noise abatement order, any premises become, as a result of building or other works, premises to which the order applies, and no noise level has been determined under s 67, the noise reduction provisions of s 66 generally apply.

Noise abatement zones — the practice

These noise abatement provisions were designed to enable authorities to introduce gradual reductions in noise in selected localities. In reality they are used to hold ambient noise levels steady if not actually to reduce them, see Penn *Noise Control* 2nd edn, p 122, and Adams & McManus *Noise and Noise*

Law p 175. A significant comment on the provisions was the conduct of the Darlington 'Quiet Town' experiment. Following the report of the Noise Advisory Commission 'Noise in the Next Ten Years', Darlington participated in an experiment between 1976 and 1978 aimed at reducing noise levels throughout the town. The results of that experiment were published in 'Darlington Quiet Town Experiment' in 1981. All sections of the local community were involved in the project, with a strong lead given by the local environmental health department. Use was made of the powers in Part III of the 1974 Act together with voluntary agreements, forms of encouragement and education (especially for children), traffic management schemes and vehicle noise testing. No systematic study was made, however, of the usefulness of the Part III powers. Only one noise abatement zone was designated, and that not until the end of the study period. The experiment was considered a success. Other local authorities have been urged to implement similar projects. Success in Darlington seems attributable to a broad approach of *co-operation, education* and *exhortation* as opposed to compulsion — a very British way of achieving results! Some authorities have introduced zones to abate noise on an area basis, for example on industrial estates; others have 'mini-zones' relating to single noisy industrial locations.

Noise from plant and machinery

Wide ranging powers exist under s 68 for the Secretary of State to make regulations for limiting noise levels caused by any relevant plant or machinery, or for requiring the use of noise suppression devices on such plant or machinery, and to provide that contravention of the regulations shall be offences. Before such regulations are made the Secretary of State has to hold consultations with representative producers and users of plant and machinery with a view to ensuring that no requirements are imposed which would be impracticable or would involve unreasonable expense. No regulations have yet been made, and there is no early intention to make any.

Supplemental provisions

Under s 69 of the 1974 Act the local authority *may*, in respect of noise reduction notices and s 65(6) notices respectively, execute works in respect of noise, and may be *directed* to under ss 82(11) of the 1990 Act and 65(7) of the 1974 Act as the case may be. In such cases they may recover their necessary expenses.

Persons guilty of the various offences existing under the noise provisions are liable inter alia, under s 74 of the 1974 Act as amended, on summary conviction, to fines.

To aid noise minimisation the Secretary of State has power, under s 71 of the 1974 Act, to prepare issue and approve codes of practice containing guidance, and a duty to approve a code of practice for the carrying out of construction works falling within s 60 of the 1974 Act. These codes may be relevant in determining whether the defence of 'best practicable means' should be available. For the purposes of s 60, the approved code is the British Standards Institution Code of Practice relating to noise control on construction and demolition sites, BS 5228, 31 May 1984, SI 1984/1992. Other codes include Codes of Practice on: Noise from Ice-Cream Van

Chimes;[6] Noise from Audible Intruder Alarms;[7] Noise from Model Aircraft;[8] Noise from Construction and Open Sites.[9]

A miscellany of codes

Codes of practice have been developed by the Noise Council in relation to noise arising from some motorcycling events, by the Midlands Joint Advisory Committee for Environmental Protection on clay pigeon shooting, and by the National Farmers Union on bird scaring devices. A draft code on concert noise has also been produced by the Noise Council. A further draft code to be issued under the 1974 Act has been drawn up in relation to powerboat racing and water-skiing. The s 71 statutory codes may be taken into account in relevant legal proceedings, and compliance with their terms is evidence that the 'best practicable means' have been used, where such a defence is relevant. A voluntary code *might* be given a similar status by a court but the point is undecided.

D OTHER SOURCES OF NOISE AND MODES OF NOISE CONTROL

'A fly's footfall would be distinctly heard' (W S Gilbert, 'The Pirates of Penzance', Act II)

Audible intruder alarms

The Code of Practice on audible intruder alarms suggests measures to reduce the possibility of misfiring alarms, and, more particularly, suggests that cut-out devices should be fitted to de-activate alarms after 20 minutes, while the police should be notified of the names and addresses of key holders who can obtain access to end an alarm signal. Intruder alarms do not fall within s 62(1) of the 1974 Act as loudspeakers in streets, but a continually sounding alarm could fall within s 81(3) and Sch 3 of the 1990 Act so an authority could take appropriate remedial action against it. In London special powers apply under s 23 of the London Local Authorities Act to enable deactivation of an alarm causing annoyance to local residents and workers where it has been ringing for more than an hour. Similar powers will exist on an adoptive basis in the rest of the country on the coming into force of s 9 and Sch 3 of the Noise and Statutory Nuisance Act 1993.

Motor sports

Though holy scripture records that 'the roar of David's triumph was heard throughout the land', today motor sport competitions on public roads are prohibited under s 13 of the Road Traffic Act 1988 unless carried out in accordance with the Motor Vehicles (Competitions and Trials) Regulations, SI

6 SI 1981/1828.
7 SI 1981/1829.
8 SI 1981/1830.
9 SI 1987/1730.

1969/414, which, in particular, limit the amount of night time driving. Off road racing is subject to voluntary controls operated on a contractual basis by the Royal Automobile Club Motor Sports Association over its members. Outside of these controls sanctions lie in the ordinary law of noise.[10]

'How sweetly he carols forth his melody to the unconscious moon' (W S Gilbert, 'HMS Pinafore', Act II)

Entertainment

A variety of controls exist over entertainment noise which, though defined by statute for certain purposes to include noise from boxing and similar contests, increasingly means musical noise. Such noise can be controlled if it is organised, inter alia, by way of an injunction and amounts to a nuisance.[11]

But as prevention is undoubtedly better than cure in this context a number of licensing provisions exist. Section 4 of the Licensing Act 1964 enables licensing justices to impose conditions on the grant of liquor on-licences in the public interest, and this could be used to control live music and other sources of noise in public houses, see further Cmnd 5154. Schedule 1 of the Local Government (Miscellaneous Provisions) Act 1982 enables local authorities outside London to exercise controls over public entertainments. (For 'music and dancing licences' in London see s 52 and Sch 12 of the London Government Act 1963.) An 'entertainments licence' from the district council is thus required for public music or dancing or similar entertainments and sporting events at any place. Music at religious events and pleasure fairs is exempted, but an all night dance party for 7,000 people organised on the fictitious basis they formed a club is caught.[12] Public musical entertainments in the open air on private land may also be similarly regulated should the local authority so resolve. Licences may contain provisions to prevent unreasonable disturbance of people in the neighbourhood by noise. Constables, fire officers and other duly authorised local authority officers have powers of entry to ensure that licence conditions are being complied with; penalties of up to a £20,000 fine and/or imprisonment for six months may be imposed in cases of non-compliance under the Entertainments (Increased Penalties) Act 1990, while confiscation of proceeds of unlicensed entertainments may occur under s 71 of the Criminal Justice Act 1988, see SI 1990/1570.

Authorities may also adopt the provisions of the Private Places of Entertainment (Licensing) Act 1967 where they already have other powers to licence public music and dancing. These powers enable control to be exercised over places which are not open to the general public but which operate for private gain, though bona fide clubs and other places where intoxicating liquor is sold and which are controlled under other legislation are excluded from the 1967 Act's operation. Where adopted, the powers apply a similar pattern of control to that under the 1982 Act. This enables authorities to control that range of events known popularly as 'warehouse', 'acid house', and 'dance' parties — also 'pay' parties where a number of people (usually up to 100) pay

---

10 *A-G v Southport Corpn* [1934] 1 KB 226.
11 *New Imperial and Windsor Hotel v Johnson* [1912] 1 IR 327.
12 *Lunn v Colston-Hayter* (1991) 155 JP 384.

to attend a gathering in a house/flat. Where a noisy party is held/is going to be held *otherwise* than for gain the means of control is under the normal noise nuisance powers.

Section 81(5) of the 1990 Act and s 222 of the Local Government Act 1972 enable authorities to seek injunctive relief, and this can be used to *prevent* noisy incidents such as major parties. In an emergency an injunction may be obtained very rapidly. The procedure, as pointed out by Penn in *Noise Control*, is expensive and technical and is available only in respect of unlicensed events, where the location is known, also the names of the landowner and/or the organisers. The authority also has to show a nuisance will occur unless the event is restrained. It is, however, possible to obtain an open ended injunction against named persons to prevent an event taking place anywhere in an authority's area at *any* time where it is clear there is a proposal to hold a series of events.[13]

It is also possible to prosecute for the crime of public nuisance a landowner who has allowed his land to be used for an 'acid house' party which has resulted in major noise disruption.[14]

The Criminal Justice and Public Order Act 1994 grants particular powers *to the police* in relation to 'raves' provided they are unlicensed. A 'rave' is a gathering on land open, or partly open, to the air of 100 or more people, whether or not trespassers, at which during the night amplified music is played, including sounds 'wholly or predominantly characterised by the emission of a succession of repetitive beats'.

Such 'music' must be such by reason of its loudness *and* duration *and* the time at which it is played as is likely to cause serious distress to local inhabitants. Such 'raves' had become a feature of a variety of gatherings during the 1980s. A police officer of the rank of Superintendent or above having reasonable belief that two or more persons are making preparations for a 'rave' on land, or that ten or more persons are waiting for a 'rave' to begin or are actually attending such a gathering which is in progress, may direct those persons, and any others preparing or waiting for or attending the gathering, to leave the site; see s 63 of the 1994 Act. Constables in uniform may, under s 65, prevent persons from proceeding in the direction of such an event, though only at places within five miles of the boundary of the site of the gathering. It is an offence to fail to comply with directions given under these provisions. Sections 64 and 66 contain powers to seize and forfeit relevant sound equipment.

Early reactions to this legislation indicated a patchy use of it by the police, and by September 1995 only 11 'ravers' had been arrested. Indeed by criminalising raves the law may drive them 'underground' and actually harder to regulate.

Some future developments

Following a review of the effectiveness of neighbour noise controls by the Neighbour Noise Working Party, the government issued in 1995 a consultation paper recommending:

---

13 *East Hampshire and Waverley District Councils v Scott and Bailie* [1993] 5 ELM 131; and
    Langbaurgh on Tees Borough Council v Jowsey and Munroe [1994] 6 ELM 44.
14 *R v Shorrock* [1993] 3 All ER 917.

1 Dissemination to authorities of good practice guidelines on noise.
2 That authorities should publicise their noise complaints services and should raise public awareness of noise issues, with, possibly, central initiatives to identify noise considered unacceptable.
3 That there should be consideration of general guidance indicating when noise constitutes a statutory nuisance.
4 That out of hours noise complaints services should be provided by authorities.
5 That local arrangements should be developed to streamline procedures to facilitate obtaining warrants to enter domestic premises to deal with noisy equipment and alarms.
6 Relevant policies and local government organisations should issue codes of good practice to encourage effective local liaison.
7 Specific powers should be introduced to provide for temporary confiscation of noise making equipment.
8 Authorities should be encouraged to seek permanent confiscation orders for noise making equipment after prosecution.
9 A specific offence to cover night time neighbour noise disputes should be considered. This offence would relate to noise emanating from private dwellings, where affected persons had complained to the local authority, and where one of their officers had concluded there was reasonable cause for allegation of serious disturbance — evidence for which would be a noise level of 35 dB(A), exceeding background noise levels by at least 10 dB(A).

Clearly 7 and 9 above would require primary legislation.

It was left to a private member, Harry Greenway MP, to introduce the necessary legislation, and at the time of writing the Noise Bill 1996 is on its way to enactment. This will give adoptive powers to local authorities in respect of new 'night noise' provisions. Once adopted, the provisions will require authorities to take reasonable steps to investigate complaints of excessive noise at night from domestic buildings, ie between 11.00pm and 7.00am. The Secretary of State will set a level which noise should not exceed. Provision is made for warning notices to be served on persons responsible for noise, and where these are ignored offences are committed, for which a fixed penalty of £40 may be imposed by the authority, or which may be prosecuted. Further powers are given to enter and seize noise making equipment, and, to avoid uncertainty, the power to abate nuisances under the 1990 Act is specifically declared to include forfeiture.

In addition, ministers are to encourage all local authorities to adopt 'best practice' with regard to noise so that there are not disparities between levels of service provided by neighbouring authorities with similar levels of problems. Authorities will be encouraged to adopt a graduated service standard and this will identify the type of noise service on offer. Local authorities and police forces are also to be encouraged to draw up a code of practice on effective liaison between the various agencies concerned with noise.

So far as the long term future of the law of noise is concerned, attention may be focused on the concept of the 'tranquil area' put forward in 1995 studies commissioned by the Council for the Protection of Rural England and the Countryside Commission. These areas of tranquillity are peaceful and unspoilt places, 1–3 km from roads, 4 km from power stations, beyond large settlements and noisy activity. Such areas are now much smaller and more fragmented than they were 30 years ago. The preservation of their peace and quiet is a matter for planning controls, but it may also require curbs on car ownership and use.

Byelaws

Local authorities (ie district and London borough councils) have power, subject to confirmation by the Secretary of State, to make byelaws, under the Local Government Act 1972, s 235, for the good rule and government of their areas; also for the prevention and suppression of nuisances. Byelaws have been made to cover diverse matters such as barking dogs, model aircraft, bird scaring devices, musical instruments played in streets, wirelesses, loudspeakers, gramophones and amplifiers. Breach of a byelaw is a criminal offence, though available defences include: that the byelaw was incorrectly made; that it exceeds the powers given by the statute under which it was made; that it is uncertain; that it is unreasonable in that it is partial and unequal in its operation as between citizens, or is manifestly unjust, or discloses bad faith, or constitutes such a gratuitous or oppressive interference with the rights of those subject to it that no reasonable person could accept that Parliament intended the power to make byelaws to be used in that way.[15] Byelaws must also be consistent with the common law and statute.

But byelaws must not be made if provision for that purpose in hand has already been made by, or is or may be made under any other enactment. Officially byelaws still have a part to play in controlling particular instances of noise, see 'The Code of Practice on Noise from Model Aircraft' (1982) which refers to the byelaw powers of local authorities in respect of municipally owned land and certain land subject to countryside legislation. See further Penn *Noise Control* pp 78–84 on model noise byelaws.

Planning controls

Noise may be a planning issue. General guidance was for many years given in DoE Circular No 10/73 'Planning and Noise'. This was concerned primarily with noise at the development control stage. However, noise can be an important consideration taken into account in drawing up statutory plans. Some authorities have, for example, included policies on noise in local plans, though practice seems to favour the control of noise at the planning application stage. Imposition of planning conditions on a grant of planning permission or coming to a 'planning obligation' under, for example, the Town and Country Planning Act 1990, s 106, may obviate the need for use of the stricter noise control powers in the Environmental Protection Act 1990. Furthermore planning powers can be used even when the actual noise level in question would not constitute a nuisance under this Act.

So far as development control is concerned close liaison between planning, highway and environmental health authorities, collation of information between them, sharing services of experts in noise reduction, and use of

15 *Kruse v Johnson* [1898] 2 QB 91.

objective standards of noise measurement in the discharge of functions is clearly desirable. Practice again, however, varies in this respect. Planning Policy Guidance Note (PPG) 24 currently gives central guidance on the use of planning powers with regard to noise.

General principles

These include: separating noise sensitive developments such as hospitals and schools from major noise sources such as roads; siting new noisy developments away from noise sensitive land uses; using planning conditions/obligations where such separation is not possible to minimise noise; considering where intensification or changes of use will result in intrusive noise; considering not just the level of noise but also its qualities, incidence and duration; accepting that people may expect reasonable peace in their homes and gardens in residential development areas; normally refusing permission for noise sensitive developments in areas which are, or will be, places with unacceptable noise levels, particularly at night; taking into account predicted noise levels from roads over a period of 15 years in respect of new developments; using design and layout features to minimise noise from roads and other noisy developments, eg the use of belts of trees or limiting hours of operation.

PPG 24 counsels that noise policies should be set down in development plans, with area specific policies where appropriate, and that regard may be had to safeguarding areas currently largely undisturbed by noise and which are accordingly valued for their recreational and amenity value. Particular guidance is given on a number of issues.

Noise exposure for residential developments

The guidance introduces the concept of Noise Exposure Categories (NECs) from A–D. Where a residential development proposal is received it should be 'banded' in an appropriate category. In A noise need not be considered as a determining factor; in B noise should be taken into account and appropriate noise protection conditions imposed; in C permission should normally be refused save where for example no alternative quieter site exists and then noise protection conditions should be imposed; in D permission should normally be refused. This approach is to be used where residential development is to be introduced into areas with existing noise sources, not when the reverse is true, in which case normal planning rules apply. Similarly the NEC levels are *not* to be used for assessing the impact of industrial noise on proposed new housing, though the contribution of industrial noise to other more dominant noise sources can be taken into consideration. The NEC concept thus relates to noise coming from road, rail and air traffic or from 'mixed sources', ie transport noise plus industrial noise, a categorisation only to be used where no individual noise source is dominant.

The NEC categories have been drawn up largely but *not* exclusively on the basis of research findings or existing regulatory norms, for example World Health Organisation standards. *Generally* to fall in category A the noise sources affecting land should generate outdoor noise levels of *less* than 55 dB(A) from 7.00 to 23.00, and less than 45 dB(A) from 23.00 to 7.00. The outer parameters for category B are less than 55–63 dB(A) daytime and less than 45–57 dB(A) night time noise, for category C the figures are 63–72 and

57–66 respectively, while figures over 72 dB(A)/66 dB(A) place the land in category D.

Noise from road and rail traffic

Where development is proposed near a major new or improved road the planning authority should ascertain forecast noise levels for the next 15 years with help from the Highways Authority who should be consulted so that the necessary predictions for using the Department of Transport's 1988 scheme of 'calculation of road traffic noise' can be used. Co-operation with Highway Authorities can be helpful so that they may use their powers of traffic management under the Road Traffic Regulation Act 1984. Similar consultation is needed with railway operators before development near railways is contemplated. Vibration may be more of a problem from rail than from road traffic and PPG 24 counsels use of British Standard 6472: 1992 on advising on acceptable vibration levels for new developments.

Industrial and commercial development noise

Again British Standards can be used to check on acceptable limits for noise from such developments, BS 4142: 1990 being the appropriate one. Where an increase in noise of 10 dB(A) or more over the existing background noise is likely as a result of a new development, complaints about noise may be expected. Particular provision may have to be made in respect of installations operating at night or over weekends. This is particularly relevant to commercial food outlets such as takeaways, and also to discos, night clubs and public houses.

Noise from construction sites

This is already specifically dealt with under the terms of the 1974 Act, but see also BS 5288: 1984.

Sporting and recreation noise

Recreation, etc, activities will normally be controlled under the licensing provisions discussed above, but in relation to some activities planning controls may be appropriate as they involve a material change of use of land and so require planning permission. Alternatively some activities may take place by virtue of permitted development rights (see chapter 5 above). Such 'pd' rights may, of course, be withdrawn.

Waste disposal site noise

Controls over disposal practices in waste management licences will have an indirect effect on noise, and conditions in the licence may be used to control noise in the interests of local amenity protection. In addition where a planning application for a new waste disposal facility is received specific noise controls can be imposed as conditions of the grant. Consultation here with the appropriate waste regulator is essential. Conditions may relate to hours of operation, the numbers and capacity of vehicles using the site, entrances and exits from the site and provision of screening to reduce noise.

Planning conditions clearly have a generally important part to play in noise control, but any conditions imposed should be necessary, relevant to planning in general and to the development proposed in particular, enforceable, reasonable and precise. Applications for minor development should not, according to PPG 24, be used as opportunities to impose conditions on activities already having permission. Where ambient noise levels are already high conditions can be used to mitigate the effects of that noise, eg to require layout of a site so that noise barriers are erected. Where it is desirable to allow a noisy development near a noise sensitive development, conditions may again be used to mitigate the effects of noise, eg to keep the noisiest activities as far as possible from neighbours. The sort of conditions considered generally acceptable include ones: requiring that work on a more sensitive development shall not begin until a noise protection scheme has been approved and the relevant parts have been completed; to require a building style which provides a stated level of sound attenuation against external noise; to restrict the total number of movements at an airport, or the times at which they occur, or to restrict the sort and weight of or the total number of movements by aircraft using an airport; or to restrict noise emitted from industrial or commercial buildings or sites, to require the creation of a noise minimisation scheme for a site, to limit certain activities to certain parts of the site, to require plant and machinery to be enclosed in sound insulating material, limiting specified machinery to operations only within specifications.

Where planning conditions are used they may either set an absolute limit of noise not to be exceeded over a specified time period, or a relative limit derived from permitted increases in noise levels with respect to background levels. The latter are *not* appropriate where a substantial — say 15 dB(A) or more — permitted increase in noise over background levels is allowed. Authorities must also remember to have fixed monitoring points from which to measure compliance with conditions. Such points must be carefully selected to ensure that the level of noise recorded is a reliable indicator of noise levels concerning particular noise sensitive premises.

E THE CONTROL OF AIRCRAFT NOISE

Most earlier enactments on aircraft noise were repealed and replaced by the Civil Aviation Act 1982, which contains important measures, some deriving from international law. Section 60 of the 1982 Act enables the Crown, by Order in Council, to give effect to the Chicago Convention on International Civil Aviation (Cmnd 8742) (6th edn 1980, International Civil Aviation Organisation, Doc 73006) with respect to the operation of aerodromes and the safety of aircraft. An 'Air Navigation Order' made under s 60 may, in particular, provide for the: licensing, inspection and regulation of aerodromes; conditions under which, and in particular the aerodromes to or from which, airdraft entering, leaving or flying within the UK may fly; securing the general safety, efficiency and regularity of air navigation; safety of aircraft, their passengers and contents, preventing aircraft endangering other persons and property; prohibiting aircraft from flying over specified areas of the UK, and for regulating or prohibiting the flight of aircraft over the UK at speeds in excess of Flight Mach 1.

These provisions, with other Acts and delegated legislation, provide a general framework for the public control of aircraft noise. This will be examined below. First it is necessary to consider tortious aspects of aircraft noise.

Civil liability for aircraft noise

Under s 76 of the 1982 Act no action lies in respect of trespass or nuisance by reason only of the flight of an aircraft over any property at a height above the ground which, having regard to wind, weather and all the circumstances, is *reasonable*, or the ordinary incidents of such flight, provided the aircraft is not being flown in a dangerous manner contrary to s 81 of the Act, and provided the provisions of any Air Navigation Order are complied with. *Unreasonable* flight over a particular property, eg frequent low level flights, appear *not* to be exempted.[16]

Furthermore s 77 of the 1982 Act states that an Air Navigation Order may provide for regulating the conditions under which noise and vibration may be caused by aircraft *on* aerodromes and may also prevent any action lying in respect of aircraft noise and vibration nuisances caused *on* aerodromes covered by the order provided the provisions of any such order are complied with. The Air Navigation Order SI 1989/2004, provides that the Secretary of State may prescribe conditions under which noise and vibration may be caused by aircraft (including military aircraft) at government aerodromes, aerodromes owned or managed by the Civil Aviation Authority, licensed aerodromes or aerodromes used in the course of the business of manufacturing or repairing aircraft. Such aerodromes are exempted from liability in nuisance for aircraft noise on the ground. Further detailed conditions are laid down in the Air Navigation (General) Regulations SI 1993/1622. Noise and vibration are permissible where aircraft are taking off or landing, or moving on the ground or on water, or where engines are being operated (while *in* aircraft) for the purpose of either ensuring satisfactory operation, or bringing them to a correct flight, or end of flight, temperature, or ensuring that instrumentation is in satisfactory condition. Noise *outside* statutory exceptions may be actionable;[17] where an injunction was granted to restrain certain work on the testing of aeroplane engines. A claim that s 76(1) violated arts 6, 8 and 13 of the European Convention on Human Rights was heard in *Powell and Rayner v United Kingdom*.[18] It was argued that the statute prevented the claimants from having a fair public hearing of what would otherwise be their nuisance claims, and that the noise permitted by the statute interfered with the claimants' homes and private lives contrary to the convention. The claim was rejected. Art 13 of the convention guarantees no right that signatory states will provide modes of challenge to the legality of their legislation. A right to sue exists where aircraft noise occurs *outside* the terms of the statute, and that satisfies art 6. There was no breach of art 8 as the UK government had struck a proper balance between individual and community interests in respect of airport operation.

16 *Roedean School Ltd v Cornwall Aviation Co Ltd* (1926) Times, 3 July.
17 *Bosworth-Smith v Gwynnes Ltd* (1919) 89 LJ Ch 368
18 Case no 3/1989/163/219, (1990) 12 EHRR 355.

Under s 76(2) of the 1982 Act where material loss is caused *to* any person or property on land or water *by*, or by a person in, or an article, animal or person falling from, an aircraft *while in flight, taking off or landing*, then, unless the loss was caused or contributed to by the negligence of the person suffering it, damages may be recovered *without proof of negligence or intention or other cause of action*, as if the loss had been caused by the wilful act, neglect or default of the owner of the aircraft. This *statutory* right of action could be used in respect of damage caused by sonic boom or reverberation caused by aircraft 'breaking' the sound barrier, or arising from the spraying of chemicals.[19] The provision only applies to 'material' damage, which seems probably to mean damage measurable in monetary terms, though it may mean only 'physical' damage, in which case other damage could only be recovered on proof of negligence and loss. The better view is that material damage is any damage capable of monetary measurement. Even so, certain forms of strain and anxiety, not leading to loss of income but arising from aircraft noise, are outside such a definition.

The future of the exemption from liability has been the subject of some controversy. The Noise Review Working Group's 1990 report concluded the exemption was 'no longer appropriate'. In particular they concluded the exemption should not apply to non-commercial aircraft, ie those of a certain weight who fly beyond airspace customarily used in the zone of an aerodrome. They also considered ground running, taxiing and other static aircraft source noise should no longer be exempt from control under COPA 1974. In its response, 'Control of Aircraft Noise,' 1991, the government rejected these contentions.

Public regulation of aircraft noise

Engine noise

In order to give effect to international agreements and EU requirements, see Directives 80/51, 83/206, and 89/629, the Air Navigation (Noise Certification) Order SI 1990/1514, has been made, applying to: all propeller driven aeroplanes having a maximum total weight authorised of 9,000 kg or less, supersonic civil aeroplanes first obtaining certificates of airworthiness on or after 26 November 1981, and conforming to prototypes, airworthiness certification of which was requested before 1 January 1975, or derivatives of such prototypes, microlight aeroplanes, helicopters, airworthiness certification for which has been requested after 1 August 1986, all other subsonic aircraft with certified take-off distances of more than 610 metres, and helicopters for which the order contains applicable standards.

The order prohibits an aeroplane to which it applies from landing or taking off in the UK unless it has a noise certificate issued by the Civil Aviation Authority, or by the competent authority of such countries as are considered by the Secretary of State to operate standards substantially equivalent to the CAA's, or issued in pursuance of the Chicago Convention of 1944. *Military aircraft and the naval, military and airforce authorities and members of any visiting forces and any international headquarters are exempted from control*, see art 15(2)

19 *Weedair (NZ) Ltd v Walker* [1961] NZLR 153.

and (3) of the Order. Likewise under art 16 the Civil Aviation Authority may, after consultation with the Secretary of State, exempt any aeroplane or person, or any class of aeroplanes or persons, from control either absolutely or subject to conditions. Subsonic aeroplanes registered in the UK after 1 November 1990 powered by turbo jets or turbo fans with either a maximum authorised weight of 34,000 kg or seats for more than 19 passengers may not take off or land in the UK or any EU member state unless certified as complying with specific noise standards in Sch I Part II of the 1990 Order.

The Civil Aviation Authority are under a duty to issue a noise certificate in respect of any aeroplane covered by the Order if they are satisfied that it complies with the relevant noise standards in the Order, see art 6 and Sch 1, Parts I to IX. For this purpose applicants for certificates must furnish such evidence and submit aeroplanes to such flying trials and other tests as the authority may require. The authority must issue noise certificates subject to conditions as to the maximum total take-off and landing weights, and may impose such other conditions as they think fit. An aeroplane may not take off or land in the UK unless it carries any noise certificate required under the law of its country of registration, and UK registered aeroplanes must when in flight, whether in the UK or elsewhere, carry the requisite noise certificate.

Under art 9 of the Order the authority may provisionally suspend a noise certificate pending investigations, and may, following them, revoke, suspend or vary a certificate. Breach of a condition in a noise certificate renders the certificate invalid during its continuance. It is an offence under art 10 for a person, with intent to deceive: to use any noise certificate which has been forged, altered, revoked or suspended or to which he is not entitled; to lend any such certificate to, or allow its use by, any other person; or to make false representations for the purpose of obtaining the issue, renewal or variation of a certificate. Contravention of the Order renders a person liable to penalties contained in art 14. Under art 11 if it appears to the authority that any aeroplane is intended or likely to be flown in such a way as to contravene noise certification requirements, they may direct the operator or commander not to permit the aeroplane to fly. They may take such steps as are necessary to detain the craft. They have rights of access to aeroplanes, aerodromes and other places to see that the order is being complied with and to enforce their duties.

As from 1 April 1995 further controls over aircraft noise have existed under the Aeroplane Noise (Limitation of Operation of Aeroplanes) Regulations SI 1993/1409 implementing Directive 92/14, itself reflecting international agreements of October 1990. Aircraft not meeting the standards of chapter 3 of volume 1, annex 16/5 of the Convention on International Civil Aviation, may not be operated, though there are exemptions for aircraft less than 25 years old meeting chapter 2 standards: these may operate until 1 April 2002.

Future developments

In 1993 in its 'Review of Aircraft Noise Legislation' the government undertook to consider introducing powers to designate selected aerodromes, including private and company owned landing sites, so that they would be subject to noise control provisions, with guidance being given on reasonable and feasible aircraft noise controls. The provisions would enable the preparation of noise amelioration schemes and would penalise non-compliant operators. These powers would also cover the operations of private helicopters which some consider have become an increasing source of noise nuisance since 1981.

Control of airport noise

Various bodies have powers to provide and/or operate and manage airports and aerodromes. (An aerodrome is any area of land or water designed, equipped, set apart or commonly used for the landing or departure of aircraft, including sites for the take-off and landing of vertical take-off craft, see the Civil Aviation Act 1982, s 105(1).) The Secretary of State may establish and maintain aerodromes under s 25 of the 1982 Act. The Civil Aviation Authority may not establish or acquire aerodromes (other than those vested in it under the Civil Aviation Act 1971, Sch 2) but may, with the Secretary of State's consent, undertake to *manage* any aerodrome (s 28). Local authorities may, subject to consent by the Secretary of State, establish and maintain aerodromes (s 30), though he also has power to direct authorities to transfer their airports to companies which they own, see s 13 of the Airports Act 1986. Powers to make airport byelaws are conferred by s 63 of the Airports Act 1986, including, inter alia, a power to control aircraft operation in, or directly above, airports in order to limit or mitigate noise, vibration and atmospheric pollution. The Secretary of State has a general duty under s 36 of the 1982 Act to prevent danger to public health from aircraft arriving at any aerodrome which is vested in or under his control, or at any UK aerodrome which is owned or managed by the Civil Aviation Authority. That authority has certain licensing functions in respect of aerodromes used for public transport or instruction in flying under the Air Navigation Order SI 1989/2004, art 78, and, under the Civil Aviation Act 1982, s 5, *specified* aerodromes subject to such licensing control may be made subject to further requirements that the Civil Aviation Authority must have regard to the need to minimise, so far as is reasonably practicable, any adverse effects on the environment and any disturbance to the public arising from noise, vibration, atmospheric pollution or other cause attributable to use of aircraft for civil aviation purposes. This power, which has in fact never been used, does *not* apply to aerodromes designated by the Secretary of State under s 78 of the 1982 Act (see below). Section 38 of the 1982 Act allows any aerodrome authority owning or managing a licensed aerodrome to encourage the use of quieter aircraft and the diminution of interference from aircraft noise by fixing airport use charges by reference to either the amount of noise caused by aircraft in question or the extent or nature of any inconvenience resulting from such noise. The same provision enables the Secretary of State to direct specified aerodrome authorities so to fix their charges. BAA plc aerodromes charge differential rates favouring quieter aircraft, and penalising noisy night time departures.

Certain major airports (Heathrow, Gatwick, Stansted, Prestwick, Edinburgh, Glasgow, Aberdeen and Southampton) are controlled by BAA plc under Part I of the Airports Act 1986. The Civil Aviation Act 1982, s 78, enables the Secretary of State to prescribe by notice that it shall be the duty of the *person who is the operator* of an aircraft which is to take off or land at a designated aerodrome to secure that it complies with the Secretary of State's requirements for limiting or mitigating the effect of noise and vibration arising from take-off or touch-down. He may, inter alia, prohibit aircraft of specified types from taking off or landing during specified periods, or specify a maximum number of take-offs and landings for specified types of aircraft during specified periods (see further below). An attempted contravention of take-off limitations may lead to the aircraft in question being detained. There is general power under s 78(2) to withhold aerodrome facilities at the designated site from operators whose aircraft do not comply with the Secretary of State's notices. Heathrow, Gatwick and Stansted Airports are 'designated' for the above purposes, see s 80 of the 1982 Act and SI 1981/651. See further Penn *Noise Control* pp 215–222 for technical details.

Control of noise by means of air transport licences

Air transport licences are generally required for air transport of passengers or cargo for reward by UK registered aircraft under the Civil Aviation Act 1982, s 64. Administration of the scheme is entrusted to the Civil Aviation Authority under s 65. The authority has a wide discretion, subject to holding hearings, as to granting, revocation, suspension, variation, duration and other terms of licences, though much of the 'meat' of the scheme is in regulations made by the Secretary of State. Note the Civil Aviation Authority Regulations SI 1991/1672 and the Air Navigation (Aeroplane and Aeroplane Engine Emissions of Unburned Hydrocarbons) Order SI 1988/1994. One general duty in administering the licensing system is, under s 68(3) of the 1982 Act, to have regard to the need to minimise, so far as reasonably practicable, any adverse effects on the environment and disturbance to the public from noise, vibration, atmospheric pollution or other cause attributable to the civil aviation use of aircraft.

This duty may not, however, conflict with the authority's duty to ensure that British airlines are able to compete effectively in aviation markets, and that they provide services to satisfy the substantial categories of public demand, see ss 4 and 68(1) of the 1982 Act.

A miscellany of other controls

In 1974 the Noise Advisory Council identified the concept of 'noise preferential routes' (NPR) which, on safety *and* amenity grounds, are designed to ensure that aircraft climb away safely from aerodromes over open ground and away from densely populated residential areas wherever possible. NPRs now exist for aerodromes next to developed residential areas, but they are not, and cannot be, mandatory for all wind and weather conditions and the need to maintain safety dictates departures from NPRs on occasions. Similar *operational* procedures exist to ensure that take-offs and landings take place over areas least likely to subject to noise affectations. At Heathrow, for example, take-off and landing is normally to/from the west to avoid the built up area of London to the east.

Night flying is a particularly contentious issue with regard to noise. Using powers under s 78 of the 1982 Act, ministers have introduced two schemes trying to establish quotas for night time flights with the loudest classes of aircraft being prohibited from flights into/from Heathrow, Gatwick and

Stansted. Both schemes were quashed in court.[20] The total number of night aircraft movements for an aggregate of periods, without any maximum number for each of those periods, has now been fixed.[1]

Planning controls may also be used to ameliorate aircraft noise problems. PPG 24 annex 3 points to the existence of Department of Transport measures known as 'noise exposure contours'. The general noise exposure categories considered above apply to new residential developments affected by aircraft noise, but any new major noise sensitive development, such as a school, should not normally be built where its exposure to noise would place it in NEC category B. In some cases new or replacement community facilities will be needed in areas subject to high aircraft noise. In such case consideration should be given to requiring noise insulation measures, and account taken in deciding siting of patterns of aircraft movement. Where land is, or is likely to become, subject to significant aircraft noise it should be determined within which NEC it is likely to fall, and authorities should accordingly develop clear and consistent constraint policies in development plans. See further PPG 24 annex 3, paras 10–12, on military aerodromes, paras 13 and 14, and, on helicopter noise, paras 15–18.

F THE CONTROL OF TRAFFIC NOISE

Control under traffic regulation powers

Traffic noise, identified by the 1990 Noise Review Working Party as 'the most serious of all transportation noise problems' is also virtually intractable. The nation has become excessively dependent on road transport for goods haulage, and what remains of the rail freight transport network is ill located in relation to commerce and industry to take much freight from the roads without a massive investment and redevelopment policy. Simply moving traffic away from settlements by building bypasses can encourage the growth of more traffic on the new roads which have their own inherent environmental disbenefits, such as land take. There is no short, easy, obvious answer to this problem, hence such legal responses as exist inevitably fall into the class of ameliorative 'controls' rather than full remedial measures.

Powers exist under the Road Traffic Regulation Act 1984 to regulate traffic, particularly for preserving or improving the amenities of areas through which regulated roads run: 'amenities' meaning the pleasantness and enjoyability of an area.[2] On trunk roads these powers are entrusted to the Secretary of State, and on other roads the appropriate authority is generally the county council, see s 1. Similar powers exist within the Greater London area under s 6. Under s 2 of the 1984 Act a traffic regulation order may provide for the prohibition, restriction or other regulation of vehicular traffic, either generally or specifically on a road. In exercising their functions under the 1984 Act, s 122 requires authorities generally to secure expeditious, convenient and safe movement of

---

20 *R v Secretary of State for Transport, ex p Richmond upon Thames London Borough* [1994] 1 WLR 74; (No 2) [1995] 7 ELM 52; (No 3) [1995] 7 ELM 127.
1 *R v Secretary of State for Transport, ex p Richmond upon Thames London Borough (No 4)* [1996] 8 ELM 77.
2 *Cartwright v Post Office* [1968] 2 All ER 646.

vehicles, having had regard to the need to secure reasonable access to premises, the effect on the amenities of affected localities, the need to facilitate passage by public service vehicles, etc. In *London Boroughs Transport Committee v Freight Transport Association Ltd*[3] the House of Lords held that the road traffic regulation powers could be used to *supplement* controls existing under national and EU legislation on vehicle construction on the basis that relevant EU legislation (Directives 70/157 and 71/320) was not, on full examination, totally exhaustive in relation to the issue in hand, the control of noise emitted from lorry braking systems. Furthermore, it was considered that *local* traffic regulation should be primarily the preserve of *local* authorities, for the EU only takes powers to itself when a particular objective can be obtained better at Community level that at any other — the 'subsidiarity' principle. The House of Lords concluded that the traffic regulation powers of local authorities may be exercised after environmental considerations have been taken into account, and that the powers may be used to regulate where *particular* vehicles may go at *particular* times, and to require the modification of such vehicles if they are to be allowed into particular places, *provided* restrictions do not amount to across the board prohibitions or restrictions on vehicles' use. The powers do not allow restrictions in respect of vehicle emissions.[4]

'The roaring traffic's boom'

Particular powers exist under s 2(4) for local authorities to make regulatory provision specifying through routes for heavy commercial vehicles or prohibiting or restricting heavy commercial vehicle use in specified areas or on specified roads, subject to any exemptions contained in the order. This is to be exercised to improve the amenities of localities. Heavy commercial vehicles are defined by s 138(1) of the 1984 Act. Under Sch 9, Part I of the Act the Secretary of State has a reserve power to give authorities directions, after due consultation with them, in respect of regulatory orders, either to make an order, or prohibit the making of an order. Schedule 9, Part III of the Act lays down the procedure for making a regulatory order. Initial consultation must take place with relevant chief officers of police. The Schedule makes provision for the Secretary of State to make regulations providing detailed procedures for the making of orders. In particular these regulations may provide for publicity for proposed orders, the reception and consideration of objections to proposals, the holding of inquiries into proposals, the submission of proposals for ministerial consent, and publication of notices about the making and effects of orders. Under Sch 9, Part VI, challenges in court to regulatory orders on the basis that they are substantively or procedurally ultra vires may be made by any person within six weeks of the making of an order.

Section 90G of the Highways Act 1980, as inserted in 1992, gives powers to highway authorities to 'calm' traffic by reducing vehicle speeds and hence traffic noise by creating particular features such as traffic islands or constrictions of the carriageway, see further SI 1993/1849. However, the introduction of traffic calming in some areas may simply have the effect of encouraging drivers to use other 'uncalmed' roads thus merely shifting the incidence of noise.

3 [1991] 1 WLR 828.
4 *R v London Borough of Greenwich* (1996) 255 ENDS Report 49.

Control of vehicle noise

Current standards are provided for under the Road Traffic Act 1988, and detailed rules are to be found in the Road Vehicles (Construction and Use) Regulations SI 1986/1078, as amended. It is an offence under the Road Traffic Act 1988, s 42, to contravene the regulations, though as CS Kerse pointed out in *The Law Relating to Noise*, comparatively few offences are detected and prosecuted, and fines are generally low. Under s 7 of the Road Traffic (Consequential Provisions) Act 1988 nothing in the Road Traffic Acts authorises a person to use on a road a vehicle so constructed or used as to cause a public or private nuisance, so preserving general common law liability.

Regulation 54 of the 1986 Regulations requires every vehicle propelled by an internal combustion engine to be fitted with silencing equipment through which engine exhaust gases must pass, and this silencer must not be altered or replaced in any way so that the noise of the exhaust is increased by the alteration or replacement and must be maintained in good and efficient order. The actual noise emission standards for vehicles are contained in reg 55 which introduces new standards of noise emission control pursuant to European obligations, designed to supersede the previous system of regulation from 1983. In effect vehicles may comply with the specific requirements of regulation 55 or they may comply with the noise regulation requirements for vehicles sold in the EU of the relevant Directive[5] in force at the time of their first use. Over a period of years Directives have reduced permissible vehicle noise considerably. In 1970 the permitted 'noise value' for cars was 82 dB(A), reducing to 80 in 1977, 77 in 1984 and 74 in 1992, the last limit applying to new vehicles sold within the EU from 1 October 1994. The European Parliament wishes to reduce the noise value for cars to 71 dB(A). Similar reductions in noise values have been brought about in respect of buses and goods vehicles. (For the details of the Regulations it is best to refer to *The Encyclopaedia of Road Traffic Law and Practice*, which contains the 1986 Regulations, as amended, together with the necessary references to the European Union legislation relating to noise emission controls.)

Provision exists under s 57 of the Road Traffic Act 1988 and the Motor Vehicles (Type Approval) Regulations SI 1980/11, and the Motor Vehicles (Type Approval) (Great Britain) Regulations SI 1984/981, as amended, for the issue of type approval certificates in respect of motor vehicles. See also SI 1982/1271 with regard to goods vehicles. 'Type approval' means that the vehicle in question is of a type conforming to specified requirements of design, construction and equipment, etc, including requirements on noise and silencers, see Sch 1 to the 1984 Regulations. It is an offence for any person to use, or cause or permit to be used, any vehicle subject to type approval requirements unless there is the necessary certification to show compliance with relevant type approval requirements; see generally ss 54–65 of the Road Traffic Act 1988, and especially s 63. The successive type approval requirements are those laid down in EU Directives.

It is noise emitted by heavy goods vehicles that disturbs most people. 'Lorries, People and the Environment', Cmnd 8439, pointed out that the

---

5 The Directives are 70/157, 73/350, 77/212/, 81/334, 84/372, 84/424, 92/97.

regulations coming into force in 1983 made reductions in permitted noise levels for these vehicles, though admitting that the reduction, which applies both to UK vehicles and foreign vehicles on UK roads, is insufficient. SI 1986/1078 and SI 1982/1271 with reference to type approved vehicles are relevant in this context. The numbers of lorries fell between 1967 and 1986, but their weights increased, and both numbers of vehicles and vehicle movements are likely to increase in the future, with more freight being carried by the heaviest vehicles, while 89% of freight was already moving by road in the UK in the mid 1980s. It is arguable that more of the social and environmental costs of road freight, such as noise, should be borne by the relevant operators having to pay enhanced vehicle taxes, however, regulation by construction and use standards remains the preferred means of control.

Regulation 97 of the 1986 Regulations states that no motor vehicle shall be used on a road in such a manner as to cause any excessive noise which could have been avoided by the reasonable care of the driver. Regulations 54–59 lay down noise emission limits for a wide variety of vehicles, including motor cars, goods and agricultural vehicles and motor cycles. The *basic* limits are those laid down from time to time by relevant EU Directives, see further *Encyclopaedia of Road Traffic Law and Practice*. Regulation 98 of the 1986 Regulations requires the drivers of motor vehicles to switch off machinery attached to or part of such vehicles when stationary, otherwise than when this is an enforced stoppage because of the necessities of traffic, or where the machinery has to be run as part of a necessary examination following some breakdown.

Motor cycle noise is also controlled under construction and use regulations, and, as from 1 January 1996, motor cycles first used on or after that day will be subject to enhanced silencer requirements by virtue of SI 1994/14. To assist in ensuring compliance with motor cycle noise requirements — a never easy task — power exists for the Secretary of State to appoint that it shall be an offence to supply in the course of business exhaust systems for motor cycles, silencers and other relevant parts not complying with prescribed requirements. Trading standards authorities will enforce their requirements at the point of sale. These powers exist under the Motor Cycle Noise Act 1987 which will be brought into force by SI 1995/2367 on 1 August 1996. Note also SI 1995/2370 which lays down requirements for silencers, etc, supplied in the course of carrying on a business.

G NOISE INSULATION SCHEMES

People can be protected against the worst effects of noise if they can afford the necessary insulation. Limited help in the form of grants is available for some adversely affected by certain aircraft and traffic noise.

Grants in respect of aircraft noise

Assistance in respect of insulation against aircraft noise has been uneven. In respect of certain local authority owned airports there *may* be provision for a scheme in local legislation. See CS Kerse *The Law Relating to Noise* pp 79–80. On a national basis certain grants have been payable since 1965. The current legislation is the Civil Aviation Act 1982, s 79. The Secretary of State has power, following consultations with affected managers, to make schemes to require such managers of designated aerodromes to make grants towards the cost of insulating such buildings or parts of buildings as he thinks fit, and which, being near to the aerodrome, appear to him to need protection against noise. The buildings must be within specified areas. Local authorities, other than county councils, may be authorised to act as agents for airport managers in the administration of the grant system. Schemes are now in place for five BAA plc airports including Heathrow, Gatwick and Stansted.

A number of airports are not covered by the scheme, nor are any military airbases. It is a frequent complaint that low flying military aircraft are a major noise nuisance, yet they are subject to hardly any legal regulation. The 5th Report of the Commons Defence Committee for the Session 1989–90 recommended that consideration should be given as to whether there ought to be advance warning of low flying, and publication of areas pilots are told to avoid, together with details of the extent to which overflying of towns is allowed, and further that areas such as National Parks should be avoided at peak usage times, as should hospitals. An overall reduction of low flying was recommended together with the establishment of a complaints 'hotline' at the Ministry of Defence, (MOD) and published guidelines on compensation for low flying damage.

See also Case C61/88 Selected Cases 1990 Vol 1, p 10, Parliamentary Commissioner for Administration, where it was disclosed that ex gratia payments are made where loss or damage is caused by Crown or visiting forces aircraft shown to have flown in the manner complained of. Likely causation of the damage in question must be shown, and that the damage was the likely consequence of low flying, other likely causes having been eliminated. Claims are handled by the RAF flying complaints department and the DoE.

In its response to the Defence Committee's Report on the issue, the government accepted the need to minimise the environmental effects of low flying, while retaining adequate defence training. Enhanced pilot instruction is now undertaken to ensure that particular sites are not subjected to over-much low flying. Furthermore MOD consults with English Nature, etc, about the adverse effects of low flying on sensitive sites. MOD undertakes, moreover, to handle compensation claims expeditiously, though stressing that delays occur where claims are not supported by appropriate evidence.

The government thus went some way towards meeting criticisms of low flying.

Grants in respect of traffic noise

Under the Land Compensation Act 1973, s 20, and the Noise Insulation Regulations 1975, SI 1975/1763 as amended by SI 1988/2000, grants are available towards insulating certain buildings against traffic noise where this has increased following alterations to, or construction of new roads, but *not* following the making of a traffic management scheme, including specification of lorry routes, or ordinary road repairs. Where a new highway or additional carriageway is opened to the public after 16 October 1972, and its use causes or is expected to cause noise not less than a specified level to a dwelling or other building used for residential purposes, the appropriate highway authority must carry out sound insulation works or make a grant in respect of carrying out such works. The specified level of noise is 68 dB(A) during an

18 hour normal working day from 6.00 to 24.00 hours, and the use of a highway is taken to cause noise at a level not less than this if, first, the relevant highway traffic noise level as measured 1m in front of the most exposed of any windows or doors in a building's facade, is greater by at least 1 dB(A) than the noise level before the road in question was built, and is not actually less than 68 dB(A), *and*, second, the noise caused by traffic using, or expected to use, the road in question makes an effective contribution to the relevant noise level of at least 1 dB(A). Certain buildings are ineligible for grant aid, for example buildings subject to compulsory purchase orders, clearance area procedures, demolition or closure orders, buildings *first* occupied after the date on which the highway or additional carriageway in question was first open to public traffic, any part of a building in respect of which a grant for insulation has been paid, or is payable, under other legislation, buildings *more* than 300m from the nearest point on the road in question. A grant will basically cover the *reasonable* cost of double glazing and associated ventilation work.

Powers to make insulation grants in respect of, for example, highways opened to the public after 16 October 1969 and before 17 October 1972, altered highways, and in respect of highway construction noise also exist under the 1975 Regulations. These are at the discretion of the local highway authority.

Section 20A of the Land Compensation Act 1973, as inserted by the Planning and Compensation Act 1991, empowers the Secretary of State to make regulations to provide for compensation to be paid in respect of dwellings which are not buildings and which are affected or likely to be affected by noise carried by the construction or use of public works. This will enable mobile home owners whose units are on permanent sites to receive compensation.

A noise insulation scheme in respect of railways and tramways was proposed in 1995 and came into force in March 1996, see SI 1996/428.

H MISCELLANEOUS FORMS OF COMPENSATION

Under the Land Compensation Act 1973, ss 1 and 2, compensation is payable to certain landowners, that is 'owners' (being either freeholders or tenants with at least three years to run of their leases) of dwelling houses, occupied as residences by such owners where their interest so qualifies them, or such owner occupiers of land other than dwelling houses, being land which is, or forms part of, an agricultural holding or other hereditament of a prescribed annual value. This compensation is payable where land is depreciated in value by certain physical factors such as noise, vibration, smell, fumes, smoke, artificial lighting, and discharges onto land, caused by the *use*, but *not construction*, of a new or altered highway, aerodrome or other public works. The physical factor causing depreciation must have its source on or in the relevant works. This includes aircraft arriving or departing from aerodromes. Furthermore if an action for nuisance is available, in other words if there is no statutory immunity, no claim will arise under these provisions, and a claim must be pursued in nuisance. This does *not* apply to depreciation caused by the use of a highway. The claim must be in respect of depreciation caused after

17 October 1969 by the opening of a new highway or the first use of other new public works. No compensation is payable in consequence of depreciation arising merely from intensification of use of existing works or highways. Furthermore, the claimant must have acquired his interest in the affected land before the new highway or public works came into use for the first time. Claims must generally be made within the period from one to three years of the first coming into use of the relevant new development, see s 3(2) of the 1973 Act.

Under s 28 of the 1973 Act where the enjoyment of a dwelling is affected by construction or improvement works on an adjacent highway or other public works, so that its continued occupation is not reasonably practicable, the relevant authority may pay the additional expenses of the occupier in providing himself with temporary alternative accommodation while the works are carried out.

Highway authorities have powers under the Highways Act 1980 to do works to mitigate the adverse effects of constructing or improving highways, including power to plant trees and shrubs, etc, see s 282 of the 1980 Act. Section 246(2A) of the Highways Act 1980 provides that where a highway authority proposes to carry out work on 'blighted land' to construct or improve a highway, they may acquire by agreement land whose enjoyment they consider will be seriously affected by those works *or* the use of the highway. 'Blighted land' is that which is immediately affected by the line of a proposed road, and effectively means land which is unsaleable in consequence of the proposal. Before the amendment of s 246 in 1991 the only power of acquisition related solely to properties already seriously affected by highway construction. The extent of this provision was tested in *R v Secretary of State for Transport, ex p Owen* (reported as *Owen v Secretary of State for Transport*).[6] The Secretary of State had issued guidelines as to how the statutory discretion should be used. These *included* criteria indicating purchase of a property should occur if it was considered to be likely to be affected by an unacceptable level of noise — 78 dB(A) averaged over a 12 hour period for six months, or where a property had proved incapable of sale save at a price substantially lower than what could have been sought but for the proposed road.

The section, however, requires a two stage approach, first to ask whether the land in question will be *seriously affected* by the proposed works, and secondly, if the answer is 'yes', whether acquisition should take place, ie whether a purchase by the public purse is warranted. In the subsequent case of *R v Minister for Roads and Traffic, ex parte McCreery* (CA, unreported) it was considered that *Owen* had established that in cases of proposed roads the acquiring authority must always, when considering the issue of whether the enjoyment of the land will be seriously affected, take into account any likely diminution in its value. It has since been established that it is legitimate for the Secretary of State to refuse to purchase where the applicant acquired the property with knowledge of proposed roadworks. The Secretary of State may take into account the prior foreseeability of the affectation of property values.[7] Under s 253, for the purpose of mitigating an adverse effect which the construction or improvement, existence or use of a highway has or will have on

6 [1995] 7 ELM 52.
7 *R v Secretary of State for Transport, ex p Owen (No 2)* [1996] ELM 9.

its surroundings, the authority may enter into agreements with persons interested in land adjoining, or in the vicinity of, the highway for restricting or regulating the use of such land. Agreements may make provision for the planting and maintenance of trees and shrubs as shelter belts.

Further reading

GENERAL

Bettle, J, 'Noise, The Problem of Overlapping Controls' [1988] JPL 79.
Hawke, N, and Himan, J, 'Noise Pollution Law Enforcement' [1988] JPL 84.
McKnight, A, Marstrand, PK, and Sinclair, PC (eds) *Environmental Pollution Control* (1974) George Allen and Unwin, chapters 10 and 11.
Macrory, R, 'Street Noise — The Problem of Control' [1984] JPL 388.
Penn, CN, *Noise Control* (2nd edn, 1995) Shaw and Sons.
UKELA, 'Report of The United Kingdom Environmental Law Association working group on noise on the statutory nuisance provisions of the Environmental Protection Bill' [1990] 2 LMELR 9.

OFFICIAL REPORTS

'Darlington Quiet Town Experiment' Noise Advisory Committee (1981) HMSO.
'Department of Transport: Regulation of Heavy Lorries', National Audit Office (1987) HMSO.
'Lorries, People and the Environment' Armitage Committee Report (1980) HMSO.
'Lorries, People and the Environment' White Paper (1981, Cmnd 8439) HMSO.
'Neighbourhood Noise' Scott Committee (1971) HMSO.
'Noise Final Report' Wilson Committee on the Problem of Noise (1963, Cmnd 2056) HMSO.
'Noise in the Next Ten Years' Richards Committee (1974) HMSO.
'Noise in Public Places' Archer Committee (1974) HMSO.
'Noise Review Working Group', DoE (1990) HMSO.
'Pop Festivals Report and Code of Practice' Advisory Committee on Pop Festivals (1973) HMSO.
'Control of Noisy Parties' (1992) Home Office and DoE.
'Neighbour Noise Working Party', (1995) DoE.

EC REQUIREMENTS

Haigh, N, *Manual of Environmental Policy: The EC and Britain* Longman, chapter 10.
Johnson, SP, and Corcelle, G, *The Environmental Policy of the European Communities* (1989) Graham and Trotman, chapter 7.

MOTOR VEHICLES

Plowden, W, *The Motor Car and Politics in Britain* (1973) Penguin Books.
Sharp, C, and Jennings, T, *Transport and the Environment* (1976) Leicester University Press.

AIRCRAFT

'Report of a Field Study of Aircraft Noise and Sleep Disturbance' (1992) DoT.

PLANNING POWERS

Miller, C, and Wood, C, *Planning and Pollution* (1983) Clarendon Press, chapter 9.

THE ECONOMICS OF NOISE

Flowerdew, ADJ, *The Statistician* (1972) vol 21, no 1, pp 31–46, reprinted in Porteous, A, Attenborough, K, and Pollitt, C, (eds) *Pollution: The Professionals and the Public* (1977) Open University Press, pp 167–83.

Part IV

Protection of the aqueous environment

Chapter 12

Water: pollution, protection and provision[1]

'We sail the ocean blue' (W S Gilbert, 'HMS Pinafore', Act I)

Rivers and seas are abused as repositories for unwanted, and often dangerous, matter. Such material can move from its place of deposition, causing damage, even on an international basis. Anti-pollution measures must be internationally agreed, co-ordinated and enforced to be effective. Both international and EU law have provisions relating to water, the former being largely concerned with protection of the world's oceans, while the latter, along with UK law, is concerned with protection of the water medium, and the provision of water for consumption and recreation.

The international law of the sea is an enormous body of principle and regulation which, for reasons of space, can only be briefly touched on here, those requiring more detail are referred to standard texts such as Birnie and Boyle's leading work, *International Environmental Law* and their more recent companion volume of relevant documents. Customary international law of the sea has developed for hundreds of years, but treaty based law, as usual, is now of more importance; for an illustration of customary law in this area, however, see the *Lake Lanoux Arbitration*.[2] The 1868 Mannheim Treaty was in part concerned with protecting water supplies, and that has been followed by many others, some of which serve to create a framework for the protection of the oceans' flora and fauna, a topic which cannot be gone into here, while others have been concerned with international marine pollution, particularly as a result of oil spillages. Of these Montego Bay 1982 — the United Nations Conference on the Law of the Sea (UNCLOS III) — is generally considered to be potentially the most important. UNCLOS is divided into a number of parts, Part XII being concerned with marine environmental protection and preservation, some 46 articles. The Treaty declares the general obligation of states to protect the marine environment, though it does not abrogate sovereign rights to exploit natural resources. More specific measures follow on pollution control, etc, while particular provision is made with regard to scientific and technical co-operation and assistance between states, and for monitoring pollution and publishing information. Special rules apply to deal with land based marine pollution, or that which arises from states' seabed

---

1 This chapter has been written by Neil Parpworth.
2 (1957) ILR 101.

activities, or from dumping. Particular provision is made for enforcement of treaty obligations, and for the responsibility of states to fulfil the same, for example by affording remedies under their laws against persons under their jurisdiction who damage the marine environment by pollution. Provision is also made to preserve state obligations under other conventions. The weakness of UNCLOS is that though many states initially signed the treaty, these did *not* include major nations such as the USA, the UK and Germany. Furthermore the convention did not come into force until 16 November 1994 when it was finally ratified by a sufficient number of states. While most nations of the EU have signed the treaty, it is worth noting that the initial ratifications were almost exclusively undertaken by developing nations (see further Birnie and Boyle's *Basic Documents on International Law and the Environment* chapter 3). See further below on the implementation of this convention in UK law.

As indicated above numerous treaties have been made to ensure various degrees of protection for the world's oceans and their beds. There is consensus that international action is required to protect the marine environment. Particular attention may be drawn to the 1972 London–Washington Convention of 29 December 1972 (in force 30 August 1975, and subsequently amended in 1978, 1980 and 1994) on the prevention of marine pollution by dumping of wastes and other matter, and which the UK ratified in 1975. This Convention binds its parties (art I): to 'individually and collectively promote the effective control of all sources of pollution of the marine environment', and 'to take all practicable steps to prevent the pollution of the sea by the dumping of waste and other matter that is likely to create hazards to human health, to harm living resources and marine life, to damage amenities or to interfere with other legitimate uses of the sea.' Art II further binds the parties, according to scientific, technical and economic capabilities, to prevent pollution by dumping and to harmonise their policies in this respect. The treaty provides that certain Annex I wastes are not to be dumped at sea at all, eg mercury and cadmium (see further (1972) 11 ILM 1310) radioactive wastes or other radioactive matter and industrial waste, while certain Annex II substances may only be dumped with a prior special permit ((1972) 11 ILM 1311) while all other waste dumping requires a general permit (see below for relevant UK law). Parties to the treaty further bind themselves (art VIII) to make regional agreements to counter marine pollution, to develop dispute resolution procedures (art X) and to promote measures to protect the marine environment against listed forms of pollution, eg hydrocarbons and radioactive pollutants (art XII).

Other treaties are particularly concerned with oil pollution of the sea and dumping. Those concerned with oil include the International Convention for the Prevention of Pollution of the Sea by Oil (London 1954, amended in 1962, 1969 and 1971); the International Convention relating to Intervention on the High Seas in cases of Oil Pollution Casualties (Brussels 1969, protocol added 1973); the International Convention on Civil Liability for Oil Pollution Damage (Brussels 1969, protocol added 1976, amended 1984); the International Convention for the Establishment of an International Fund for Compensation for Oil Pollution Damage (Brussels 1971, protocols 1976 and 1984), and the International Convention for the Prevention of Pollution from Ships (London 1973, protocol 1978, MARPOL). The implementation of these provisions by UK law will be principally considered below but it should be noted that MARPOL lays down detailed rules on discharges and tanker construction, see further Howarth, *Water Pollution Law* chapter 9, and Abecassis and Jarashow, *Oil Pollution from Ships* chapter 3. Note also SI 1990/2605 on dangerous goods and marine pollutants. Treaties concerned with dumping include: the Convention on the Prevention of Marine Pollution by the Dumping of Wastes and Other Matter (London 1972, see above); the Convention for the Prevention of Marine Pollution by Dumping (etc) (Oslo 1972, protocol 1983) and the Convention for the Prevention of Marine Pollution from Land Based Sources (Paris 1974, protocol 1986). This last named Convention is, of course, not simply concerned with dumping but is designed within the confines of the North Sea and North East Atlantic to counter pollution of the sea coming from the land via rivers, pipelines, and other man-made structures. States party to the Convention have agreed that their national pollution measures will be at least as strict as the treaty requirements, and that they will control and reduce pollution of water. Harmful substances are classified into various 'lists'. Those on the 'black list' are the most harmful, eg cadmium, mercury, oil, organohalogen compounds, and persistent synthetic materials; pollution by these is to be eradicated, though a staged approach is allowed. Those on the 'grey list' are less harmful and include arsenic, heavy metals, non-persistent oils, and organic compounds of phosphorus; pollution by these is to be limited, and discharge authorisation is required in respect of them. The third 'list' contains all other pollutants save radioactive substances which form the fourth 'list'. With regard to the third list states are exhorted to reduce pollution, while with regard to the fourth they undertake to forestall/eliminate pollution. The Paris and Oslo Conventions both feature a commission of representatives from relevant states which has powers of oversight over treaty implementation, and these commissions share a common secretariat. The EU is a contracting party to the Paris Convention, as are most member states, and has adopted programmes on discharges of mercury and cadmium. But where the EU is a party to Marine Conventions it shares powers with the member states and does not monitor treaty observance intensively. See further Howarth, op cit, chapter 8.

Note also the Merchant Shipping (Prevention of Pollution) (Law of the Sea Convention) Order 1996, SI 1996/282 which empowers the Secretary of State to make regulations to implement the 1982 Law of the Sea Convention for the purpose of protecting and preserving the marine environment from pollution from ships outside UK territorial waters. This order was made under powers conferred by s 129 of the Merchant Shipping Act 1995.

EU Water Directives

Mention of the EU prompts discussion of the 'European' aspect of water protection. The chosen vehicle, historically, for action has been the Directive (see also chapter 4), but there is evidence that both the Commission, through failure to monitor implementation, and the member states, through tardy action, have not 'pushed' the aquatic protection measures adequately, even though water protection is the oldest sector of EU environmental policies; see further Kramer *EC Treaty and Environmental Law* paras 1.11–1.19. The list of failures include: not applying the Surface Water for Abstraction of Drinking Water Directive (75/440) in full, likewise the

Drinking Water Quality Directive (80/778); not applying the Bathing Water Directive (76/160) to a sufficient number of beaches and not designating waters for the purposes of the Water Supporting Fish Life and Shellfish Waters Directives (78/659 and 79/923). The problem is compounded by differences of opinion as to the form of certain water protection standards, whether water quality objectives should be the chosen form as opposed to maximum limits for discharges.

'Stick close to your desks, and never go to sea' (W S Gilbert, 'HMS Pinafore', Act I)

The Water Directives are quite a 'complete' package, having the *general* aim of preventing polluting discharges into water and *specific* objectives of providing quality standards or objectives for particular types of water, though it may be that the distinction between quality objectives and fixed limit standards may disappear over time with attempts made to apply the best features of both systems, see further Howarth, *Water Pollution Law* chapter 10. There are certain features which the Directives tend, however, to share:

1   The use of 'I' (imperative) and 'G' (guide) lists whereby member states may not set water standards less strict than 'I' and should aim to observe 'G'.
2   There is sometimes discretion vested in states as to which waters shall be designated for the purposes of Directives — this is a weakness for it enables states to evade responsibilities.
3   Compliance with Directives is not to lead to any degradation in the quality of relevant waters, ie a 'standstill' rule applies, though derogations may exceptionally be allowed.
4   Competent authorities' in each state are required for the purposes of sampling, analysing and inspecting waters.
5   Provision is made to adapt Directives to technical progress (see further below).

The Dangerous Substances Directive

Directive 76/464 'The Dangerous Substances Directive', is a *framework* to bring about the *elimination* of certain types of pollution and the *reduction* of other types, with daughter Directives setting the standards for individual substances. It relates to virtually *all* the EU's aquatic environment. The Directive was designed to further, inter alia, the provisions of the 1974 Paris Convention on the prevention of marine pollution from land based sources (see above) and hence it has two 'lists' (I and II) of substances, those from which pollution is to be eliminated and those from which it is to be reduced; unfortunately the Directive's lists are not absolutely identical with those of the Convention.

List I (the 'black' list) is of individual substances which belong to certain families and groups of substances whose toxicity, persistence and bio-accumulation make it desirable that they should be eliminated; they are organohalogen, organophosphorus and organotin compounds, proved carcinogens, mercury and cadmium and their compounds, persistent mineral oils and hydrocarbons and persistent synthetic substances. The elimination of pollution by List I substances is to be brought about primarily by the setting of limit values by daughter Directives, but see further below. List II (the 'grey' list) contains families and groups of substances which have a deleterious effect on the aquatic environment, but which can be confined to a given area and which depend on the characterisation and location of the receiving water, such as metals, metalloids and their compounds, *including* zinc, chromium, lead, arsenic, antimony, beryllium, uranium, cobalt, thallium and tellurium, biocides not appearing in List I, substances having a deleterious effect on the taste/smell of products derived for human consumption from the aquatic environment, toxic/persistent organic compounds of silicon, inorganic compounds of phosphorous, non-persistent mineral oils, cyanides and fluorides and substances having an adverse effect on oxygen balance. Also included in List II are all List I substances for which limit values have not yet been set. It took some years for work to begin to produce such results in the setting of the specific standards for List I substances by daughter Directives, but note the following: 82/176 and 84/156 — mercury and its compounds; 83/513 — cadmium and its compounds; 84/49 — hexachlorocyclohexane, 86/280 — carbon tetrachloride, DDT and pentachlorophenol, 88/347 — aldrin, dieldrin, endrin, isodrin, hexachlorobenzene, hexachlorobutadiene and chloroform. Note also the further amendments by Directive 90/415 relating to 1,2 — dichloroethane, trichloroethylene, perchlorethylene and trichlorobenzene.

Discharges liable to contain List I substances require prior authorisation by a 'competent authority' within a state. Such an authorisation must be time limited and must generally lay down emission standards concerning quantities and concentrations of material. The individual standards, which are *minimum* Union wide limit values, are contained in daughter Directives and are set taking account of toxicity, persistence and bioaccumability, and the best technical means available to eliminate/reduce pollution. However, as a 'parallel' quality objectives may be set, and a member state may follow this latter system of regulation *provided* the Commission can be convinced by monitoring procedures the quality objectives are met and maintained. The UK prefers the quality objective approach, other member states prefer limit values.

List II substances also require prior authorisation before discharge, and are subject to programmes whereby member states reduce pollution according to timetables whereunder emission standards for List II substances will be applied based on *quality objectives* for relevant waters drawn up in accordance with national standards or, where appropriate, other existing relevant Directives.

The task of producing daughter Directives for the purpose of List I will be time consuming (though attempts have been made to expedite matters since 1986) for *families* of substances are identified in 76/464: these could amount to 1,500 actual substances, though 129 were targeted for study and action in 1982. Results achieved so far have been detailed above.

The Groundwater Directive

Paralleling the Dangerous Substances Directive is the Groundwater Directive, 80/68, which is designed to prevent, reduce or eliminate pollution of groundwater arising from 'families and groups of substances'. 'Groundwater' is defined as that below the ground surface in the saturation zone and in direct contact with the ground or subsoil. 'Pollution' of such water is defined in terms of the discharge into it directly or indirectly of substances resulting in dangers to human health, water supplies, or harm to living resources or aquatic ecosystems, or interferences with legitimate uses of water. The Directive's pattern is similar to that on dangerous substances, with List I (black) and List II (grey), but the lists are not identical as between the Directives, though they are very similar. For example cyanides are List I in the Groundwater Directive and List II in that on Dangerous Substances. The Directive exempts from cover discharges of domestic effluent from isolated dwellings, also those where relevant substances are in innocuous quantities and those with radioactive substances.

Black list substances are to be prohibited from 'direct' discharge into ground water, while 'indirect' discharge (ie by percolation) must be subject to investigation before authorisation. Grey list substances must also undergo prior investigation before either direct or indirect discharge can be authorised. Authorisations are to be granted for limited periods and must be subject to four yearly review, and must specify place and method of discharge, maximum permissible quantities, precautionary and monitoring measures. For the purposes of implementing Directive 80/68, reg 15 of the Waste Management Licensing Regulations SI 1994/1056 provides that the investigation process involves the consideration of a number of factors including an examination of the hydrogeological conditions of the relevant area, and, a determination of whether the discharge of List I or II Substances into groundwater is a satisfactory solution for the environment. The regulation further provides that authorities, ie the Agency are required to review all current waste management licences in the light of the Groundwater Directive and vary or revoke them where necessary.

On 20 February 1995, the Council of the European Union passed a resolution[3] expressing concern at the fact that ground-water resources in certain areas 'remain seriously endangered, both qualitatively and quantitatively'. An earlier resolution (25 February 1992) calling upon the Commission to submit a detailed action programme for groundwater protection and to draft a proposal for the revision of the Groundwater Directive has not been acted upon to date. Thus the more recent resolution requests that the Commission consider revising Directive 80/68, where it is felt necessary to do so, and that it expedites the production of the groundwater protection programme so that it may be submitted to the Council by the *middle of 1995* at the latest. In formulating the programme, the Council resolution suggests that emphasis should be placed on the following points:

1 Licensing systems and other instruments providing an appropriate national management of (ground) water.
2 Measures providing preventative, far-reaching groundwater protection, inter alia, in view of diffuse sources.
3 General provisions for the safety of installations handling substances harmful to water.

3   1995 OJ C/49 1.

4 General provision to promote agricultural practices consistent with groundwater protection.

Other EU Directives concern themselves with particular aquatic environmental issues, eg the quality of particular waters for stated purposes, and certain substances that find their way into water.

The Surface Water Directive

Directive 75/440 is concerned with the quality of surface water whence drinking water may be abstracted and is intended to ensure that standards are met and appropriate treatment given before the water in question is supplied to the public. The Directive, however, goes beyond simple public health requirements and is designed to secure the progressive improvement of relevant surface waters, see art 4. These waters are required to be classified (A1, A2, A3) by quality, which is determined according to the complexity and type of measures needed to produce drinking water from the surface water, and member states are bound to ensure that such relevant waters do not fall below the standards set in the Directive, some of which are mandatory ('I' values) while others — the 'G' values — are *guidelines* which *should* be respected. Further requirements on sampling surface water for drinking were laid down 79/869.

The Bathing Water Directive

Directive 76/160 is concerned also with public health and environmental quality in its application to bathing waters, ie those fresh or sea waters in 'which bathing is either explicitly authorised ... or is not prohibited and is traditionally practised by large numbers of bathers', and the object is to protect the quality of such waters by laying down micro-biological (particularly with regard to sewage) and physio-chemical characteristics to which they should conform. Member states are required to set standards for their bathing waters — the date for implementation was 1985 — and must send regular reports on such waters to the Commission. Again a set of 'I' and 'G' values is utilised by the Directive to lay down minimum requirements and desirable targets. Regular and frequent sampling is also required of bathing waters and they are generally deemed to satisfy requirements if samples meet test parameters for the quality of the water in 95% of samples ('I' values) and 90% of samples ('G' values).

In *EC Commission v United Kingdom*: C-56/90,[4] the European Commission brought an art 169 action against the UK for its failure to take all the necessary measures to ensure that the quality of bathing waters at Blackpool, Southport and Formby conformed with the limit values set out in Directive 76/160. On 31 December 1985, the date for implementation of the Directive, the UK had designated only 27 resorts as bathing waters within the meaning of the Directive. This figure, which did not include Blackpool, Southport or Formby, was later revised so that from 2 February 1987, 389 bathing waters were identified for the purposes of the Directive, this time including the three

4 [1993] Env LR 472.

resorts. In response to the Commission's application, the UK advanced a number of grounds in its defence, including the argument that the definition of bathing water in art 1(2)(a) of the Directive was too imprecise to identify adequately those bathing waters that fell within the scope of the Directive. The relevant article defined 'bathing water' to include waters in which 'bathing is not prohibited and is traditionally practised by a large number of bathers'. In what was claimed to be an attempt to clarify matters, the UK had decided to adopt additional criteria to help identify the relevant bathing waters. Such criteria took account of, inter alia, the number of bathers using the bathing waters. The UK's arguments, including that relating to the vague nature of the definition of 'bathing water' were ultimately rejected by the European Court of Justice. The court declared, inter alia, that it would frustrate the underlying objectives of the Directive if bathing waters could be excluded from the scope of the provision solely on the basis that the number of bathers was below a specified numerical threshold. Accordingly, the UK was held to have failed to fulfil its obligation under the EC Treaty by not taking all the necessary measures to implement the Bathing Waters Directive.

Further doubts have been cast on the UK's proper implementation of the Bathing Water Directive during the course of judicial review proceedings relating to a decision made by the NRA to grant a consent to Welsh Water for the discharge of sewage from the Tenby Headworks, see *R v National Rivers Authority, ex p Moreton*.[5] Whilst the application was ultimately dismissed, in relation to the submission that the UK government and the NRA had decided not to apply the 'I' standard in the Directive relating to entero-viruses because of their belief that there were scientific doubts as to its validity, Harrison J observed that: 'All I can say on the evidence before me is that it would appear that they [the government] are not implementing the mandatory virus standard as required by the Directive.' Moreover, although the available evidence was not sufficient to lead to the conclusion that the NRA had decided not to comply with the mandatory virus standard, Harrison J felt that such a possibility could not be discounted.

Directive 78/659 as last amended by Directive 91/692 lays down requirements for setting quality objectives in respect of designated portions of rivers and other fresh waters to support freshwater fish life. Member states are to designate waters to which the Directive applies, and waters may be designated either as 'salmonid' (suitable for salmon and trout) or 'cyprinid' (coarse fish). The Directive lays down both 'I' and 'G' values and member states are to create programmes of pollution reduction so that any designated water will comply with the values within a period of five years. At intervals of three years, member states are required to send the Commission a sectoral report informing the Commission of the record of the implementation of this Directive and of other pertinent Directives. Moreover, the Directive further lays down sampling requirements.

Directive 79/923 makes provision for quality of waters suitable for shellfish growth, ie bivalve and gastropod molluscs. Member states may designate coastal and brackish waters in need of protection or improvement so as to support shellfish. As with the foregoing Directive 'I' and 'G' values are

5 (1995) 250 ENDS Report 43–44.

specified, together with sampling techniques and frequencies. Programmes of pollution reduction must also be introduced in respect of designated waters.

The Drinking Water Directive

Directive 80/778 is the Drinking Water Directive (see also chapter 4 on possible 'direct effect' litigation in respect of this provision) laying down requirements for water to be drunk or used in cooking, with the exception of natural mineral waters, provision for which is made in Directive 80/777. Though a public health measure it is also concerned with environmental protection, for inexpensive water treatment predicates water sources free of contaminants. Extensive provision is made in Annexes II and III of the Directive as to water monitoring and analysis techniques, but it is Annex I which lists the water quality standards. As with many directives both mandatory and guide level standards are provided. In relation to matters subject only to guide level standards member states have discretion as to how to act, but in relation to the other standards, ie Maximum Admissible Concentration, and Minimum Required Concentration, member states must set their own drinking water standards, no less stringent than those of the Directive. Provision is, however, made for derogations by arts 9 and 10 of the Directive, and for delays by art 20. Art 9 allows for derogations in connection with exceptional meteorological conditions *or* the structure and nature of the ground whence the water supply comes, and in this latter case a long term derogation can apply. Art 10 allows for short term derogations in cases of emergency or where there is a constant need to use substandard water while it is not possible to treat it adequately. The Commission may under art 20 permit a delay to a member state experiencing compliance difficulties. The failure of the water extracted from the Sawston Mill bore hole to comply with the standards laid down in the Drinking Water Directive was the reason why litigation ensured in *Cambridge Water Co v Eastern Counties Leather* (see chapter 2 above).

In *EC Commission v United Kingdom*,[6] the European Court of Justice held that the UK had failed, inter alia, properly to implement the Drinking Water Directive within the prescribed time limit and to meet the Directive's maximum admissible concentrations for nitrates in 28 supply zones in England. In its defence, the UK had advanced various arguments of a procedural and a substantive nature, but with one exception, the fact that the Commission had failed to prove its case concerning excessive lead levels for 17 supply zones in Scotland, all such arguments were rejected by the court. Indeed, the outcome of the case was never really in doubt, particularly since the UK's belated introduction of the Directive implementing Water Supply (Water Quality) Regulations 1989 had occurred nearly two years after the first stage of the enforcement procedure required by art 169 of the EC Treaty — the letter of formal notice — had been completed.

The approach taken by the UK in relation to Directive 80/778 was further at issue in *R v Secretary of State for the Environment, ex p Friends of the Earth Ltd*,[7] where the applicants sought judicial review of a decision by the Secretary

---

6 [1993] Env LR 299.
7 [1996] 1 CMLR 117, CA.

of State to accept undertakings, in accordance with s 19(1)(b) of the Water Industry Act 1991, from Thames Water and Anglian Water that they would respectively take steps to ensure compliance with the Directive. Friends of the Earth advanced three main arguments. First, that the acceptance of the undertakings did not amount to a sufficient compliance with the primary obligations, to comply with the Directive, and the secondary obligations, to comply with the judgment of the European Court of Justice in *EC Commission v United Kingdom*.[8] Secondly, it was argued that the Secretary of State had not approached his duty under the Directive in the correct manner because instead of using his best endeavours to achieve compliance with Directive obligations by taking all practicable steps, he should have been aware that what his duty actually entailed was to achieve a particular result as soon as possible. Thirdly, it was contended that the undertakings were so vague and imprecise that they could not be effectively monitored to ensure compliance or to issue an enforcement notice under s 18 of the Water Industry Act 1991 in the event of a breach. These arguments were rejected both at first instance[9] and on appeal.

The Court of Appeal felt that it was clear that considerations of practicability formed part of the equation of what was possible, and there was no principle of either European or domestic law that required a court to ignore practicalities. The Secretary of State's acceptance of the undertakings constituted compliance with the secondary obligation (the ECJ ruling) to remedy the breach of the primary obligation (the failure to comply with the Directive) as soon as possible. Moreover, it was apparent in the opinion of the Court of Appeal that the Secretary of State's acceptance of the water companies undertakings by no means precluded a subsequent service of an enforcement notice under s 18 of the 1991 Act where it was felt appropriate to do so.

Detergents Directive

Directive 73/404 and its 'daughters' 73/405, 82/242, 82/243 and 86/94 are concerned, inter alia, with the composition of detergents so as to protect water against impairment of photosynthesis and oxygenation, and to prevent interferences with sewage treatment. To this end detergents must meet a specified standard of biodegradability in their principal constituents, the 'surfactants'.

The Titanium Dioxide Directive

Directives 78/176, 83/29 and 82/883 relate to titanium dioxide. T_1O_2 is used in paint making and waste by-products of its manufacture can pollute water if dumped — the 'red mud' phenomenon. Directive 78/176 (as amended by 83/29) provides for prior authorisation by a 'competent authority' to be required for acts of discharge, dumping storage or injection of T_1O_2 waste products; such authorisation only to be given if the material cannot be more appropriately dealt with, and only after it has been determined by assessment that there will be no deleterious consequences. Further authorisation is required for new T_1O_2 plants and then only after a survey of environmental

8 [1993] Env LR 299.
9 [1995] 7 Admin LR 26.

impact and undertakings being given that the least damaging environmental techniques and materials generally available will be employed. Programmes of reduction of T_1O_2 waste pollution are required and must be notified to the Commission by member states, and regular reports on these and on monitoring of waste pollution must be made. The monitoring requirements themselves are amplified by 82/883. It is a further requirement that the various national T_1O_2 waste reduction programmes should be harmonised and in 1989 the Commission adopted Directive 89/428. Inter alia this prohibited dumping into inland or marine waters of solid waste and certain strong acid waste, and waste from the treatment of such strong acid waste, etc, as from the end of 1989, together with landward discharges of such waste. The legal base chosen for the Directive by the Council, art 130S (see chapter 4 above) became the subject of proceedings before the European Court of Justice in *EC Commission v EC Council*: C-300/89,[10] where it was argued by the Commission that the Directive should have been based on art 100A. It was apparent that the purpose and content of the Directive demonstrated that it pursued the dual objectives of protection of the environment and the improvement of conditions of competition. Nevertheless since arts 130S and 100A required different legislative procedures to be followed, the Directive could not have a dual legal basis. Accordingly, the court held that the appropriate legal basis for Directive 89/428 was art 100A since the Directive was an environmental measure contributing to the establishment of the internal market. The practical consequence of this decision was the adoption of a reissued measure, Directive 92/112 which has art 100A as its legal base. Under this new harmonising Directive, the time limit for prohibiting dumping of the most polluting forms of waste arising from the manufacture of titanium dioxide has been extended to 15 June 1993.

The Urban Waste Water Treatment Directive

Directive 91/271 makes requirements in respect of treatment of urban waste water. Where agglomerations of population are high enough for waste water to be collected for treatment, collection systems must be generally in place, according to population size, between 2000 and 2005. The Directive also lays down treatment standards for such water, and these are strict for areas to be defined as 'sensitive' by member states, according to criteria in the Directive *including* freshwater estuaries or coastal waters in danger of eutrophication, and surface freshwaters intended for drinking water abstraction in danger of exceeding permitted nitrate levels under Directive 75/440 though they may be relaxed elsewhere. Treated waste water is to be reused wherever possible. Provision is also made for sludge disposal to be allowed only by permit and for sludge disposal to surface waters by pipeline or by dumping from ships to be phased out by the end of 1998. Within 'sensitive areas' locations with populations of over 10,000 must be subject to strict regulation by 1998. (This was also agreed by the Third North Sea Conference, see above.)

Note also the Resolution and Decisions to set up a programme of action to control and reduce hydrocarbon maritime discharge pollution (OJ C162

8/7/78) and the Decision to establish a system for the exchange of information on the quality of rivers and watercourses within the Community, 77/795 (OJ L334 24/12/77). See further Haigh, op cit, chapters 4.16 and 4.17. Further EU legislation has dealt with matters relating to vessels bound for or leaving community ports and carrying dangerous or polluting goods, Directive 93/75, and the transfrontier shipment of waste, Regulation 259/93. Directive 93/75 is intended to ensure that information about any dangerous or polluting goods aboard ships bound for or leaving their ports will be readily available to member states. For the domestic implementation of this provision, see the Merchant Shipping (Reporting Requirements for Ships Carrying Dangerous or Polluting Goods) Regulations SI 1995/2498. Marine pollution as such has yet to be tackled head on by the EU.

It should be noted that with regard to radioactive waste and the marine environment, the EU has very limited powers, derived from the weak provisions of Chapter III of the EURATOM Treaty 1957. Member states remain free to decide location of plants and radioactive emission limits. The EU has 'norms' of radiation protection, but these are not emission standards. However, the Commission has a consultative role with regard to liquid effluents which may result in transfrontier radiological effects, and opinions are given on, inter alia, discharge limits. Though opinions have no legally binding status and require no positive compliance from the state receiving them, they do have to be considered prior to any relevant authorisation being given, see *Saarland v Ministry of Industry*.[11]

It is now appropriate to consider how the UK implements its international and EU legal obligations.

A POLLUTION OF THE SEA IN UK LAW

Under SI 1983/1106, originally made under the Merchant Shipping Act 1979, s 20, giving effect to international obligations (The 1973 London 'MARPOL' Convention), and the Merchant Shipping (Prevention of Oil Pollution) Regulations 1983, SI 1983/1398 as amended, UK ships under reg 12 (including oil tankers where discharges are from *machinery space* bilges) anywhere and other ships, similarly defined, within UK territorial waters must not discharge oil (ie petroleum including crude oil, fuel oil, sludge, oil refuse and refined products) or oily mixtures into any part of the sea. Exceptions to this are where vessels proceed on voyages, *and* are not within 'special areas' for example, the Mediterranean, *and* the oil content of the discharge is less than 15 parts per million (ppm) of the mixtures, *and* the vessel has in operation oil discharge monitoring and control systems. No discharge may contain chemicals or other substances in concentrations likely to harm the marine environment. 'Ships' are vessels of any type operating in a marine environment, including submersible craft and fixed or floating structures but *not* hovercraft. UK tankers and other tankers in British territorial waters are further regulated by reg 13. They may not discharge oil, etc (other than reg 12

11   (1989) 54 CMLR 529.

discharges) into the sea unless they are: proceeding on a voyage; not within special areas; more than 50 miles from land; the rate of discharge does not exceed 30 litres per mile; the total quantity discharged does not exceed specified percentages of the cargo, and monitoring and control systems are operating. There are exceptions in respect of discharges: necessary for securing safety of ships or saving life at sea; resulting from damage to ships or equipment, provided all reasonable precautions were taken after the damage to prevent or minimise discharges, and provided that the owner or master acted without intention or recklessness with regard to probable damage; in connection with combating other specific pollution incidents.

Construction requirements relating to oil discharge monitoring and control systems are contained in reg 14. Regulation 15 requires appropriate means of cleaning oil cargo tanks to control discharges. Part 5 of the Regulations imposes constructional requirements to minimise pollution from tankers due to side and bottom damage. It is an offence under reg 34(1) to fail to comply with these requirements. If any ship fails to comply with regulations, the owner and the master shall each be guilty of an offence. High fines can constitute a real deterrent to polluting behaviour, and may cover costs of any 'clean-up' operations, but cases must not be so hurried that the accused are prevented from preparing cases properly, *R v Thames Magistrates Court, ex p Polemis*.[12] Prosecutions under the legislation have in any case been limited in number. UK oil tankers of 150 Gross Registered Tonnage (GRT) and above, and other UK ships of above 400 GRT are subject under reg 4(1) to five yearly surveys to ensure compliance with regulations, in addition to annual and intermediate surveys for vessels in respect of which an International Oil Pollution Prevention (IOPP) certificate has been issued. Defects in, or accidents to, UK ships affecting their integrity or the efficiency of their equipment must be reported to the appropriate UK authority in case surveys are necessary; similar requirements apply to non-UK vessels. After any survey of a UK ship under the Regulations no material change may be made in its structure, equipment or arrangements without the approval of the Secretary of State, see reg 8.

The Merchant Shipping Act 1995 makes provision for improvement and prohibition notices in connection with specified statutory provisions. Section 261 of the 1995 Act enables a ministerially appointed inspector who considers there has been a contravention of a relevant statutory provision to serve an 'improvement notice' on the person responsible specifying issues and remedial measures required. Section 262 enables an inspector, who is of the opinion that activities falling within the ambit of relevant statutory provisions are being, or are about to be, carried on ship by, or under the control of, any person in such a way as to involve risk of serious pollution of any navigable waters, to serve a notice prohibiting the activities. Contravention of notices constitutes an offence under s 266 of the Act.

SI 1983/1398, reg 10, requires an Oil Record Book which lists specified operations concerned with movements of oil and tank cleaning, etc. The Oil Record Book must be kept readily available for inspection and copying by appropriate authorities. Part 7 of the Regulations requires reports to appropriate bodies, for example the coastguard, of discharges or likely discharges of

12 [1974] 2 All ER 1219, [1974] 1 WLR 1371.

oil or oily mixtures as a result of damage or other emergency in connection with: all ships within 200 miles of the UK; all UK ships within 200 miles of land; all UK ships of 10,000 GRT and above. Regulation 31(4) and (6) requires masters within 200 miles of the UK and masters of UK ships more than 200 miles from the UK to make those reports and further reports without delay. Reports must include appropriate details of, inter alia: date and time of the incident; position and extent of pollution, approximate rate of continuing discharges; weather conditions; type of oil discharged; remedial action taken and assistance requested; likely forecasted movement and effect of pollution, and all relevant information regarding the vessel's condition. Note also the Merchant Shipping (Control of Pollution by Noxious Liquid Substances in Bulk) Regulations SI 1987/470 originally made under 1979 legislation to give effect to the 1973 London Convention to control discharging of tank washings into the sea, and to require certain construction matters for carriers of noxious liquid substances, eg UK chemical tankers, see also SI 1987/549, SI 1987/550, SI 1987/586, SI 1988/2252 and SI 1988/2292. These were also made under the Merchant Shipping Act 1979 to give effect to international conventions on control of marine pollution by matter, not just oil, from ships.

Under the Merchant Shipping Act 1995, s 136, if any oil (ie crude oil, fuel oil and lubricating oil and specified heavy diesel oils) or any mixture containing oil is discharged from a ship into a UK harbour or is found escaped there from a ship, the owner or master of the vessel must report to the relevant harbour authorities. Reception facilities at UK harbours and terminals may be provided by harbour authorities and operators (who may be directed to act by the Secretary of State), for residues, oil mixtures and noxious liquids, see SI 1984/862.

The provisions of the 1995 Act and the 1983 Regulations do not apply to warships of the Royal Navy or naval auxiliaries.

SI 1983/1398, reg 33(1), allows the Secretary of State to deny entry to a ship to UK ports or off-shore terminals where satisfied that, in consequence of non-compliance with regulations, the ship presents an unreasonable threat of harm to the marine environment. Regulation 33(2) allows detention of ships where contravention of regulations is suspected. Part 6 of the Regulations applies their requirements with appropriate modification to 'offshore installations' for example, oil drilling platforms.

Under s 3 of the Prevention of Oil Pollution Act 1971 if any oil or oily mixture is discharged into *any* part of the sea from a pipeline or (otherwise than from a ship) as a result of operations for exploration or exploitation of the sea bed, in a designated area (under the terms of the Continental Shelf Act 1964), the owner of the pipeline or the person carrying on the operation are guilty of an offence, unless the discharge was from a place in his occupation, and was due to the act of a person who, without his permission, was there. Under s 2(1)(c)–(e) of the 1971 Act within UK territorial waters' seaward limits and all other waters (including inland waters) within those limits and navigable by sea-going ships, if any oil or oily mixture is discharged from a place on land (including anything resting on the sea bed or shore) the occupier of that place commits an offence unless he can show the discharge was caused by a person there without his permission. Similar provisions apply to discharges in the exploration or exploitation of the sea bed. Section 131 of the Merchant Shipping Act 1995 provides generally that discharges of oil/oily mixtures from vessels into waters, including inland waters, which are landward of the baseline for measuring the breadth of UK territorial waters and are navigable by sea-going ships constitute offences. It is a defence to prosecution under s 131 to prove that neither the escape nor any delay in its discovery was due to want of reasonable care and that remedial steps were taken as soon as practicable after discovery. Where the charge is under s 2 of the Prevention of Oil Pollution Act 1971, it is a defence to prove the oil was in an effluent produced by oil refining operations, that it was not reasonably practicable to dispose of the effluent otherwise than by discharge into the water, and that all reasonably practicable steps had been taken for eliminating oil.

The Merchant Shipping Act 1995, s 137 applies where an accident *has* occurred to a ship, and the Secretary of State believes that use of his powers is urgently needed because oil from the ship will or may cause large scale *pollution* in the UK or its territorial waters. The Secretary of State may give directions to prevent or reduce pollution as respects ship or cargo to the ship-owner, its master, or any person or salvor in possession of the ship. Directions may, inter alia, be given that the ship shall/shall not be moved, or that oil or other cargo shall/shall not be removed, or specified salvage operations shall/shall not be taken. Where the Secretary of State concludes that these powers are inadequate he may, to prevent or reduce oil pollution, take any action with regard to ship or cargo, including sinking or destroying it or taking over control. It is an offence under s 139 of the 1995 Act not to comply with a s 137 direction. Under s 141 an order in council may provide that s 137, inter alia, may apply to ships not registered in the UK and which are for the time being outside UK territorial waters. See further the retained SI 1980/1093. See also the Dangerous Vessels Act 1985, ss 1 and 3, giving harbour masters power, subject to the directions of the Secretary of State, to give directions concerning dangerous vessels in respect of their harbour areas. No directions under s 137 can, however, apply to any Royal Navy vessel, s 141(4) of the 1995 Act. Where a harbour master has reason to believe that the owner/master of a ship has committed an offence by discharging from the ship oil or a mixture containing oil into the harbour waters contrary to s 131, he may detain the ship by virtue of s 144 of the 1995 Act.

The Merchant Shipping Act 1995 has brought together the Merchant Shipping (Oil Pollution) Act 1971 and the Merchant Shipping Act 1974 which implemented international agreements of 1969 and 1971 on the civil liability of shipowners. Importers of oil (ie crude oil and fuel oil as defined by s 173(9) of the 1995 Act) into the UK or persons receiving the oil are liable to pay contributions to the International Oil Pollution Compensation Fund in respect of oil carried by sea to ports or terminal installations in the UK. No liability to make contributions arises where the amount of oil imported or received in the year does not exceed 150,000 tonnes, s 173(5).

The fund, based on the 'polluter pays' principle so that those who derive benefits from potentially polluting activities must help bear costs of pollution, is to ensure that pollution victims may obtain compensation. The fund is therefore liable for pollution damage caused outside the ship in question by contamination resulting from escapes or discharges of oil and including the cost of measures taken after the occurrence to prevent or minimise damage. Ships covered are sea-going vessels and other seaborne craft provided they carry *oil in bulk as cargo*. Liability is dependent on the person suffering damage being unable to obtain full compensation under s 153 of the Merchant Shipping Act 1995 (see chapter 2 above) because one of the following applies.

1   The discharge or escape resulted from an exceptional, inevitable and irresistible phenomenon, or was due wholly to the malicious act or omission of a third party, or was due wholly to the negligence or fault of a government or navigation authority in relation to navigation aid duties, because liability is accordingly wholly displaced by s 155 of the 1995 Act.

2   The owner or guarantor liable for the damage cannot meet his obligations in full.

3   The damage exceeds the limit of liability under the 1995 Act.

The fund incurs no obligations: if it can prove the damage resulted from an act of war, or insurrection; or resulted from oil discharged by a warship or by a ship state-owned or operated and used at relevant times only on government non-commercial service, or where the claimant cannot prove that the damage resulted from an occurrence involving a ship identified by him. Section 178 lays down time limits in respect of claims against the fund. UK courts may not entertain claims unless action is commenced, or appropriate third party notice of an action to enforce a claim is given, within three years of the claim arising.

Dumping at sea

The Food and Environment Protection Act 1985, Part II, replacing the much criticised Dumping at Sea Act 1974 is now the governing provision. It was slightly amended by the Environmental Protection Act 1990. Under s 5 licences are required for depositing substances in UK waters from vehicles, vessels, aircraft, marine structures and other constructions for marine deposition. Licences are also required: for deposits *anywhere* from British vessels, etc; for scuttling vessels; for loading vessels in the UK or its waters, etc, with substances for deposition. See further Tromans, *The Environmental Protection Act 1990* pp 43–299 to 43–301. Under s 6 licences are required for incinerating substances on vessels or marine structures in UK waters, or anywhere at sea on a British vessel, and for loading vessels with material for incineration. Exemption from these requirements, subject or not to conditions, may be made by ministers in the form of a statutory instrument, see s 7 and SI 1985/1699.

Under s 8 licensing authorities, that is under s 24(1), ministers responsible for fisheries ie in England and Wales MAFF, in determining whether to issue licences must have regard, inter alia, to the need to protect the marine ecosystem (ie the marine environment itself and the living resources it supports), human health, and other legitimate uses of the sea. Conditions may be inserted in licences, generally those designed to protect the marine ecosystems, etc, but also including measures to give the licensing authority a degree of detailed oversight over operations, or to require provision of recording equipment. Licensees may under Sch 3 request a statement of the reasons for inclusion of any provision in a licence. In considering licence applications authorities are to have regard to the practical availability of alternative disposal methods. Reasonable fees may be charged for licences to cover administrative costs and the costs of the authorities' investigative and inspection activities in respect of applicants and operations. A licensing authority may require applicants for licences to supply information and undergo examinations for the purpose of deciding applications, and further fees may be charged in this connection by the authority. Licences may be refused, but reasons for refusal must be given, see Sch 3. Licences may be varied or revoked where there is a breach of licence provisions, or where such action is necessary because of changes in circumstances relating to the marine ecosystems or human health, or increases in scientific knowledge relating to such matters, or for any other relevant reason. Schedule 3 to the 1985 Act lays down rights of representation for *licensees and disappointed applicants* with regard to the terms of licences, refusals, revocations or variations of licences. Representations made must be considered by an expert committee, who must afford a hearing if requested, and report their findings and recommendations to the licensing authority who must reconsider the initial decision in the light of that report, and inform the representer of the result of the reconsideration.

It is an offence under s 9 to do anything for which a licence is required except in pursuance of a licence and in accordance with its terms, though it is a defence to prove that the acts were done to secure the safety of a vessel, etc, or to save life, *and* that ministers were given relevant details within a reasonable time. Under s 22 it is a defence to a charge to show the accused took all reasonable precautions and exercised due diligence to avoid the offence. In particular this may be done by showing that the accused acted under his employer's instructions or in reliance on information supplied by another, and in both cases took reasonable steps to ensure no offence was committed.

Section 10 of the 1985 Act allows ministers to carry out necessary operations to protect the marine ecosystem, human life or other legitimate uses of the sea in any case where operations requiring a licence have been done otherwise than in pursuance of a licence and/or licence conditions. Under s 14 licensing authorities must compile and keep available, for free public inspection, registers containing specified details of licences issued. The required details are contained in Sch 4 and include, inter alia, the nature of containers or packaging in which substances were intended to be deposited and the results of any toxicity tests carried out to determine whether or not a licence should be issued, or the terms on which it should be issued.

MAFF issued in 1989 a 'Report on the Disposal of Waste at Sea 1986 and 1987' on the implementation of the 1985 Act pointing out that its provisions enabled compliance with the 1972 Oslo and London Conventions on dumping. The report detailed how applications for licences are assessed according to issues such as chemistry and toxicity. Licences may be issued on an annual basis for specific dumping sites, and conditions are imposed to avoid creation of hazards, with maximum flow and load limits as appropriate. Public registers of licences and licensees are held, and fees are charged to cover the administrative costs of licensing. Enforcement has largely been concerned with ensuring that only licensed waste has been dumped. Infractions of a minor nature have resulted in formal warning letters; more serious matters, taking into account the nature and gravity of the offence and the persons involved, may result in revocation of licences and/or prosecution. Monitoring of waste disposal sites also takes place and this can lead to restrictions on dumping being imposed, eg in Liverpool Bay. The categories of waste dumped include liquid industrial waste, largely alkaline or acidic solutions, and applications for licences to dump are determined on the basis of the sea's ability to deal with the material, and so that no short or long term damage shall be caused by the waste and its constituents. The figures for such waste dumped in 1986/87 showed a reduction on previous years. Millions of tonnes of sewage sludge are also dumped, and steps are taken to ensure that chemically or heavy metal contaminated material is not dumped. Some solid industrial waste has been dumped in the form of colliery spoil or power station ash, as is dredged material, where, again, steps are taken to ensure no contaminated material is included in deposits. With regard to incineration at sea the MAFF report argued for its overall environmental acceptability and revealed that the system of control adopted by the UK covers all stages from the production of the waste to its final burning at sea, and only certain types of waste are licensed for incineration, eg organohalogens, and pesticides; 1987 saw an increase in this means of disposal over previous years.

The 1985 Act is the legislation under which the UK can meet the targets declared by the North Sea Conferences, see (1991) 201 ENDS Report 26. Note that the substituted s 14 of the 1985 Act makes provision for the keeping of public registers of licences similar to those to be kept under the Environmental Protection Act 1990, see chapter 10.

The question of the abandonment/decommissioning of the Brent Spar oil platform in the North Sea became something of a *cause célèbre* in the summer of 1995 when it was accepted by the government that the deep sea disposal of the 65,000 metric ton structure would satisfy UK international obligations as well as according with domestic legislation on dumping at sea.[13] Shell UK maintained that the dumping of the Spar in this manner represented the safest and the most environmentally satisfactory option, whilst in response, Greenpeace conducted a concerted campaign against Shell, including a consumer boycott of the company's products.

Ultimately it was announced that plans to sink the Spar would be abandoned and thus Greenpeace appeared to have won a considerable victory. However some of the gloss was taken off this victory when it subsequently emerged that a study undertaken by independent assessors revealed that the oil platform did not contain anything approaching the levels of toxic wastes which Greenpeace had earlier claimed. Greenpeace later admitted that there had been flaws in the way that it had sampled the Brent Spar's tanks during the course of its summer occupation of the platform which eventually came to an end, despite the fact that Shell were initially legally powerless to evict the protesters.

Shortly after the Brent Spar episode, the British Association for the Advancement of Science were informed that most industrial wastes, including radioactive materials from power stations and obsolete oil platforms, ought to be dumped at sea rather than disposed of on land, provided that a sufficiently deep site was chosen for any sea disposal.[14]

13 See for example, The Times, 20 June 1995, 6 September 1995, 12 September 1995, 19 October 1995, The Independent, 19 October 1995, and The Lawyer vol 9 issue 32.
14 The Times, 2 September 1995.

Other provisions controlling exploitation of the sea

Under the Petroleum and Submarine Pipe-lines Act 1975, s 20, no person may execute in, under, or over any 'controlled waters', (ie UK adjacent territorial sea and seas in any area designated under the Continental Shelf Act 1964) works for constructing pipes, or use pipelines in such controlled waters, unless authorised by the Secretary of State. 'Pipeline' is defined by s 33 of the Act as a pipe or system of pipes, excluding drains or sewers, for the conveyance of any thing, together with associated ancillary works and apparatus, and see also the Oil and Gas (Enterprise) Act 1982, s 25. Authorisation procedure is found in s 21 of and Sch 4 to the Act. Authorisation may only be granted to bodies corporate. The procedure allows the Secretary of State to further consider authorisation applications or to reject them, in each case after giving reasons for the decision to the applicant. Applications to be considered further must be advertised, and representations in connection with them may be made. During authorisation periods the Secretary of State may notify the applicant, and other persons likely to be affected, that the proposed route of the pipeline ought to be altered for the purposes of, inter alia, avoiding or reducing danger to marine flora or fauna or reducing interference with fishing or the exploitation of marine resources. An opportunity must be given to make representations in response. When consideration is concluded the Secretary of State may decide to issue an authorisation. This may contain such terms as the Secretary of State considers appropriate, for example as to routeing, design, capacity, steps to be taken to avoid or reduce interference with fishing, etc, material to be conveyed, meeting contingent liabilities for damage attributable to releases or escapes, mode of operation, etc. Under s 24 an authorisation may be terminated in accordance with its own terms, by agreement, or by the Secretary of State serving notice on its holder that, inter alia, a term of the authorisation has been contravened. Before terminating for breach, however, the Secretary of State must give the holder an opportunity of making written representations and must take them into account. A termination notice is not to be served where the Secretary of State considers, having regard to the nature and consequences of the contravention, that it would be unreasonable to terminate and that the holder has taken adequate preventative steps for the future.

Prior to its repeal by SI 1993/1823, s 26 of the 1975 Act enabled the Secretary of State to make regulations, after consultation with representatives of affected persons (s 32), to provide for proper construction and safe operation of pipelines. This power was exercised to make various regulations which continue in force despite the repeal of s 26, see SI 1982/1513 as amended by SI 1986/1985, SI 1989/1029 and SI 1991/680. These provide for the safe construction, operation and maintenance of pipelines, for periodical inspection schemes, and prior notification of substantial repairs to the Secretary of State (ie the DTI). Effective means of shutting pipelines down are required, and maximum allowable operating pressures are not generally to be exceeded. Emergency procedures are required. It is an offence to contravene the Act, see ss 28, 29 and 32. Civil liability exists in relation to personal injuries.

The Deep Sea Mining (Temporary Provisions) Act 1981

The Deep Sea Mining (Temporary Provisions) Act 1981, an interim measure, regulates exploration for and exploitation of the hard mineral resources of the deep sea bed (manganese, nickel, cobalt, copper, phosphorus and molyb-denum). Section 1 prohibits unlicensed exploration or exploitation of the bed of the high seas not subject to the sovereign rights of states, by citizens of, or bodies incorporated in, and who are residents of, the UK. Licences are granted under s 2, by the Secretary of State on payment of a prescribed fee, for such period as he thinks fit, and on such terms and conditions as he thinks fit. In determining licence applications all relevant factors must be considered, including the desirability of keeping areas free of mining operations to provide comparisons with areas exploited. Under s 5 in determining a licence application the Secretary of State must have regard to the need to protect, so far as reasonably practicable, marine flora, fauna and other organisms and their habitat from the harmful effects of authorised activities. He must consider any representations made to him concerning such effects. Conditions in a licence under ss 2 and 5 may relate to inter alia: processing minerals on board ships; disposal of waste resulting from processing and action to avoid or minimise harmful effects on the marine environment. Exploration licences can only be granted in respect of periods *after* 1 July 1981, and exploitation licences only after 1 January 1988. Licences may be revoked or varied where necessary, inter alia, to protect marine flora, fauna and their environment. The details of implementation are in regulations made under s 12, see SI 1982/58 concerning modes of application for licences, and the prescribed application fees; see also SI 1984/1230.

The Petroleum (Production) Act 1934

In respect of petroleum licensing, the Secretary of State has powers under the Petroleum (Production) Act 1934. Any person may apply in writing for such licences in respect of exploration or production. Applications may be invited or non-invited. Licences to search for and get petroleum generally contain prescribed model clauses. A production licence for a 'seaward' area, that is an area lying on the seaward side of a prescribed dividing line (generally low water line off the mainland coast), will set rules and standards for conducting operations, especially by making certain activities subject to ministerial consent, for example commencing the boring of oil wells. Licensees must conform to 'good oil field practice' (an undefined term) in confining petroleum to tanks, pipelines and receptacles. Apparatus, appliances and wells must be kept in good repair and condition. Petroleum must be prevented from escaping, and licensed areas must be conserved against waste. Gas from a licensed area must not be flared without ministerial consent. Operational mishaps must be reported to the Secretary of State. Where petroleum escapes into the sea the Chief Coastguard Inspectorate must be notified. Licensees must not interfere unjustifiably with fishing in licensed areas, nor with conservation of living resources. Licensees must also comply with reasonable ministerial instructions on making funds available to meet contingent liabilities in respect of release or escapes of petroleum, see the voluntary Offshore Pollution Liability Agreement 1974. (Exploratory drilling for oil was licensed in 1984 in certain major estuaries. Such drilling is dealt with according to the onshore licensing system, see further chapter 8 above, and DoE Circular 2/85.) See generally SI 1988/1213, SI 1990/1332, SI 1992/2378 and the Offshore Safety Act 1992 in respect of seaward licensing and SI 1984/1832 and SI 1991/981 in respect of landward licensing.

Sand and gravel are increasingly extracted from UK coastal waters, as is marl for fertiliser. This could have future ecological effects. Such dredging is licensed by the Crown Estates Commissioners. The Crown, prima facie, has perogative rights over arms of the sea, publicly navigable rivers, and the foreshores (land between high and low water marks). Foreshore management, etc, is generally vested in the Crown Estates Commissioners under the Crown Estate Act 1961, s 1. Under s 3 of that Act they may not sell, lease or otherwise dispose of any land of the Crown Estate, or any right or privilege over or in relation to such land, except for the best consideration reasonably obtainable. In practice, before the Commissioners licence sand and gravel dredging they consult appropriate bodies such as English Nature, the Department of the Environment and the Ministry of Agriculture to obtain a 'government view'. Removal of shingle and sand from the area between high and low water marks can only, as a general rule, take place under licence. See further chapter 8 above.

Planning permission is not generally required for removing sand and gravel from the seabed *below* low water mark in an area *outside* the jurisdiction of the local planning authority. Most current extraction sites are between seven to twenty miles offshore. *The Conservation and Development Programme for the UK* recommended, at pp 287 and 290, that planning control over new developments, and major extensions of existing activities, should be extended three miles out to sea, and that environmental impact assessments should be carried out in appropriate cases. Restrictions on rights to remove materials from the sea may, however, be imposed under the Coast Protection Act 1949. [For disposal of radioactive material at sea, see chapter 9 above.]

B CONTROLS OVER FRESH WATER

Common law controls over fresh water are almost exclusively concerned with individual rights. The reader is referred to chapter 2. Various statutory provisions have for many years governed the regulation of water. A major restructuring of the law was undertaken in the Water Act 1989 on the privatisation of the water industry (see also chapter 3) but this did not entirely replace all pre-existing legislation. Furthermore important changes were wrought by the Environmental Protection Act 1990 and it must be stressed that *for those processes and substances regulated by the IPC system the relevant law is now to be found in chapter 10.* The process of consolidation of the water legislation in 1991 has effected yet more change in at least the form of much of the law, whilst the Environment Act 1995 has introduced important substantive changes to this legislative framework.

The Environment Agency is the principal regulatory body with respect to the protection of water and exists under Chapter I of Part I of the Environment Act 1995, though the Director General of Water Services has general environmental and recreational duties with regard to water under the Water Industry Act 1991, s 3. The Agency has functions with regard to water pollution under Part III of the Water Resources Act 1991, and consideration of these will form the bulk of what is to follow. However the Agency also has functions concerning water resources, droughts, flood defence and land drainage, fisheries and navigation, and a brief mention of some of these is essential as all relate to protection of the aqueous environment.

Water resource management

Section 6 of the Environment Act 1995, which in part replicates the terms of s 19 of the Water Resources Act 1991 (WRA), imposes two general duties on the Environment Agency in respect of their water resource management functions. Under the first such duty, the Agency is required to promote: the conservation and enhancement of the natural beauty and amenity of inland and coastal waters; the conservation of flora and fauna which are dependent on an aquatic environment; and the use of such waters and land for recreational purposes, taking into account the needs of chronically sick or disabled persons. In addition, the Agency has a general duty to conserve, redistribute, augment and secure the proper use of water resources in England and Wales. It should be noted that any discharge of a water resource management function is subject to the principal aim and objectives of the Agency, see s 4 of the Environment Act 1995 and generally chapter 3 above.

Draft guidelines entitled 'Guidance to the Environment Agency under the Environment Bill on its objectives, including the contribution it is to make towards the achievement of sustainable development' were published by the government on 20 April 1995. With regard to the protection and enhancement of the water environment, the Agency is expected to exercise its many functions such as IPC and waste regulation in an integrated manner. Moreover, the guidance encourages the Agency to, inter alia, take a strategic approach to river management, integrate technical, economic and environmental factors in decision making, and assess the costs and benefits, including those to people and the environment, of its activities. This latter guidance reinforces the general duty under s 39 of the Environment Act 1995 requiring the Agency to have regard to costs and benefits in exercising its powers generally, see chapter 3 above. In terms of water resource control, the draft guidance highlights the government's belief that pressures on water resources will be a key issue in sustainable development. Accordingly, the Agency is expected to use its regulatory powers in such a manner as to ensure that there are adequate water supplies for domestic, agricultural, commercial and industrial purposes, while at the same time seeking to maintain and enhance the natural environment.

Under s 20 of the WRA 1991, the Agency has duties to make water resource management schemes with water undertakers for the purpose of conserving, redistributing, augmenting and securing the proper use of water resources in England and Wales. Section 21 further empowers the Agency to submit draft statements to the Secretary of State concerning the minimum acceptable flow of inland waters (ie rivers, streams and water courses both natural and artificial, lakes, ponds or docks, channels, creeks, bays, estuaries and arms of the sea) which are *not* discrete waters (ie lakes, ponds or reservoirs not discharging to other inland waters). Such statements can only follow a publicity exercise under Sch 5 and a consultation process with relevant water undertakers, drainage boards, harbour and conservancy authorities. The Agency in drawing up the statement must have regard to water flow, to its general environmental duties under the Environment Act 1995, and to any relevant water quality objectives. The minimum flow established must both safeguard public health and meet the requirements of existing lawful uses of the water in question for agriculture, industry, water supply or other purposes. Section 21(7) and Sch 5 empower the Secretary of State to approve statements while WRA 1991, s 22 empowers him to direct the Agency to consider the minimum acceptable flow of an inland water, and s 23 further empowers the Agency to consider the level or volume of inland waters in addition to or in substitution for the flow of inland waters in cases where they are taking action.

The procedure for dealing with minimum acceptable flow statements is found in Sch 5 of WRA 1991. Provision is made for publicity to be given to draft statements, and for relevant bodies and institutions to be served with copies, objections may then be made to the Secretary of State who may approve the draft or amend it as he thinks fit following which it comes into force. Calls for increased use of water conservation powers have become more urgent of late in the light of evidence of low — even no — flows in streams and rivers in some parts of the country — many famed for beauty or fishing. The problem has been compounded by low rainfall rates in some parts of England since 1988 — 20% below average in some cases. This has depleted aquifers. Rivers and bore holes for water have suffered from depleted resources. By the early years of the next century, despite new reservoirs and new wells, demand may outstrip supply, particularly in the south-east, though figures supplied by the old NRA indicate that, nationally, by 2011 supply will, narrowly, exceed demand. This has led bodies such as the Council for the Protection of Rural England, to call for 'demand management' with some form of metering, the introduction of which *could* lead to 10–15% decreases in demand. In addition some abstraction licences may have to be revoked to protect some rivers in danger of drying up.

Licences to abstract water

Chapter II of Part II of the WRA 1991 deals with licences to abstract water. Thus WRA 1991, s 24 generally prohibits the abstraction of water from any source of supply save in pursuance of a licence, though, under s 28, this prohibition does not extend to abstraction in the course of land drainage. Licence applications are made, advertised and dealt with according to regulations made under s 34 of the Act, and can only be made by qualifying persons, effectively those occupiers who are contiguous to the source of supply. Further provision as to publicity for licence applications are contained in WRA 1991, s 37 which requires newspaper advertisements and notifications to, inter alia, relevant drainage boards and water undertakers. It is the Agency which determines licence applications according to s 38; they must take into account any representations received as a result of the publicity process, and must also in exercising their wide discretionary powers consider both existing rights of other persons to abstract water, the need to maintain river flows, whether or not a minimum acceptable flow has been determined (see ss 39 and 40 of the WRA 1991) and the reasonable requirements of the applicant for water. A licence, if granted, may contain such provisions as the Agency thinks fit. Licence applications may also be called in by the Secretary of State for his determination, see ss 41 and 42, and appeals to him against Agency decisions may be made under ss 43–45. WRA 1991, ss 46 and 47 make provision as to the form and content of licences in particular specifying the person who has the licence to abstract, for such licences confer a *right* under s 48 to which rights of succession exist under ss 49 and 50, as amended. Licences may be modified or revoked, see ss 51 to 53. If the Agency proposes such action due notice must be given to the licensee who may object to the Secretary of State who must determine the matter under ss 54 and 55 taking into account representations made in writing by the Agency and licensee, and, if he so determines, after the holding of a local inquiry. Compensation may be payable by the Agency to a licensee under s 61 of the WRA 1991 where a licence is modified or revoked and, inter alia, this leads directly to the licensee suffering loss or damage. Decisions of the Secretary of State under the foregoing provisions may only be challenged on a point of law within six weeks of the decision in question being made, see WRA 1991, s 70. It should finally be noted that the Agency has powers under s 41 of the Environment Act 1995 to make a scheme providing for charges to be levied in respect of the abstraction of water under licence.

Droughts

Chapter III of Part II of WRA 1991 makes provision for dealing with droughts: s 73(1), as amended by para 139 of Sch 22 to the Environment Act 1995, empowers the Secretary of State to make 'ordinary drought orders' to meet the situation where satisfied that because of an exceptional shortage of rain, there either exists or is threatened a serious deficiency of supplies of water in any area, or, such a deficiency in the flow or level of inland waters that a serious threat is posed to the flora or fauna which are dependent on those waters. Section 73(2) empowers the making of 'emergency drought orders' where there is a serious deficiency of supply because of a shortage of rain and the economic or social well being of persons in the affected area is likely to be impaired in consequence. The Secretary of State can only act on the basis of requests made by the Agency or a water undertaker in situations other than when an ordinary drought order is being sought as a consequence of a serious threat to the flora and fauna of inland waters. Section 74 of the WRA 1991 provides that an ordinary drought order may authorise, inter alia, the taking of water, prohibitions on taking water or its use for any purpose and may modify restrictions or obligations concerning the taking or discharge of water. Emergency drought orders may contain all the foregoing and may further authorise the supply of water via stand pipes and water tanks.

A new system of drought permits is provided for in s 79A of the WRA 1991, as inserted by para 140 of Sch 22 to the Environment Act 1995. As with drought orders, a drought permit may be issued where a serious deficiency of water supplies either exists or is threatened due to an exceptional shortage of rain. However, unlike drought orders, whether or not a drought permit is issued is a decision for the Agency following an application made by a water undertaker which supplies water to premises in the area concerned. A drought permit may, inter alia, authorise the water undertaker to take water from any source specified in the permit and suspend or modify any restrictions or obligations to which the undertaker is subject as respects the taking of water from any source. The permit itself remains extant for a period of up to six months from the date on which it came into force, although the Agency may, by giving notice to the water undertaker, extend the life of the permit for a further specified period provided that the total life span of the permit is no longer than one year from the date on which it first came into force.

Drought orders are made as statutory instruments and the procedural requirements in connection with their making, eg as to publicity and the making, reception and consideration of objections, etc, are contained in Sch 8 to the WRA 1991. In the summer of 1995, these provisions were germane to the convening of a public inquiry to consider a request by Yorkshire Water to increase its daily abstraction of water from the River Wharfe by an extra three million gallons in order to cope with the greater demands imposed on the water supply as a consequence of a prolonged spell of dry weather.[15] At the inquiry, opposition to the request was voiced by environmental campaigners, watersportsmen and an assortment of local groups all of whom were incensed at earlier reports suggesting that Yorkshire Water was losing approximately one third of its output each day through leakages. The episode itself reflects a wider debate in the Yorkshire region about a privatised water utility which made substantial pre-tax profits and yet which is regarded by some as under-investing in the improvement of mains and the discovery of leaks.

In addition to Sch 8, s 79 and Sch 9 to the WRA 1991 provide for compensation to be made in respect of drought orders. By virtue of the new s 79A, these procedural and financial arrangements will also take effect in relation to any drought permits that are issued.

Control of pollution

Section 82 of the WRA 1991 enables the Secretary of State to lay down a scheme of classification of water quality for 'controlled waters' — ie under s 104:

1 Relevant territorial waters, those extending seaward for three miles from specified baselines for England and Wales.
2 Coastal waters, those extending landward from the specified baselines to high tide/freshwater limits.
3 Inland freshwaters, lakes and ponds (natural or artificial and above or below ground) which discharge into rivers and watercourses mediately or immediately together with such rivers and watercourses which are not public sewers nor drains or sewers into a public sewer.
4 Groundwaters, those in underground strata.

The quality criteria may be general requirements as to the purposes for which the waters in question are suitable for application, or may be specific as to substances to be present in/absent from the waters, their concentrations, etc, or as to other characteristics of the water. Section 83 further empowers the Secretary of State to maintain and improve water quality by serving notice on the Environment Agency specifying water quality objectives for waters, and thereafter keeping objectives under five yearly review. Notice of the setting of quality objectives must be given by serving notice on the Agency and giving

15 The Times, 10 August 1995.

such other publicity — not less than three months in duration — of the notice as the Secretary of State deems appropriate to ensure those likely to be affected are aware of the proposal. Any representations received in response to the publicity must be taken into account before objectives are fixed/varied as the case may be.

It is s 83 which provides 'teeth' for maintaining or improving the quality of waters while s 82 simply provides for their classification, hence the difference in administrative procedures. The powers given by s 82, coupled with the general power under s 102 of the WRA 1991 to make regulations to give effect to EU and international legal obligations, enable compliance with, inter alia, EU requirements as to the quality of surface water intended for drinking water abstraction, see Directive 75/440 above, and see the Surface Waters (Classification) Regulations SI 1989/1148 which classifies waters into three bands, DWI, DW2, DW3, according to the presence of specified quantities of named substances in accordance with mandatory Directive requirements. See also the Surface Waters (Dangerous Substances) (Classification) Regulations SI 1989/2286 and the Surface Waters (Dangerous Substances) (Classification) Regulations SI 1992/337 which supplement the foregoing 'bands' by three further classifications, DSI, DS2 and DS3 whereby inland and coastal waters are classified as not exceeding stated concentrations of specified substances.

The power to classify waters by way of regulation under s 82 has been further exercised to make the Surface Waters (River Ecosystem) (Classification) Regulations SI 1994/1057. These regulations classify waters into five bands RE1–RE5 on the basis of sampling results relating to the water's dissolved oxygen saturation, biochemical oxygen demand, ammonia concentration, un-ionised ammonia concentration, ph value, dissolved copper concentration and zinc concentration.

Section 84 of the WRA 1991 imposes a duty on the Secretary of State and the Agency to use their general water pollution powers so as to achieve water quality objectives set under s 83. The Agency is further required to monitor the extent of pollution in controlled waters and to consult as appropriate with river purification authorities in Scotland. Inevitably there will be those who will continue to make illegal or otherwise uncontrolled discharges, but the decrease in river quality in England and Wales of 4% between 1985 and 1990[16] appears to have been turned round. In 'The Quality of Rivers and Canals in England and Wales (1990–1992)' (Water Quality Series No 19), the NRA pointed out that the trend of deteriorating river quality in the 1980s was in part due to the preceding years of low rainfall which had a distorting effect on the overall assessment of river quality. In addition, the NRA indicated that the reversal in the trend could be attributed to, inter alia, the effectiveness of pollution control measures and the capital investment programmes of the water utilities and other industries.

The 'causing' and 'knowingly permit' offences

Section 85 of the WRA 1991 is a key provision in the context of the protection of the aqueous environment since it creates a number of offences of causing or

16 See The Sunday Times, 16 June 1991, The Times and The Independent, 12 December 1991, and The Guardian, 18 December 1991.

knowingly permitting various pollutants to enter waters of various types. Accordingly, it is an offence:

1 To cause or knowingly permit any poisonous, noxious or polluting matter or any solid waste to enter any controlled waters.
2 To cause or knowingly permit any matter, other than trade/sewage effluent, to enter controlled waters by discharge from a drain/sewer where a prohibition has been imposed under s 86 (see further below).
3 To cause or knowingly permit any trade/sewage effluent to be discharged into any controlled waters or from land in England and Wales through a pipe into the sea beyond the seaward limit of controlled waters.
4 To cause or knowingly permit any trade/sewage effluent in contravention of a s 86 prohibition from a building or fixed plant onto or into any land or into any waters of a lake or pond which are not 'inland' freshwaters.
5 To cause or knowingly permit *any* matter whatever to enter inland freshwaters so as to tend (either alone or in combination with any material) to impede the proper flow of waters so as to lead, or be likely to lead, to a substantial aggravation of pollution otherwise caused or its consequences.

In the event that one of the above offences has been committed or a person contravenes the conditions of any discharge consent which has been granted, a guilty party may, on summary conviction, be subject to a fine of up to £20,000 and/or three months' imprisonment. Where, however, the conviction is on indictment, the punishment may be an unlimited fine and/or two years' imprisonment.

In *R v Ettrick Trout Co Ltd and Baxter*,[17] the appellants had been charged with contravening the conditions of a trade effluent consent contrary to s 107(6) of the Water Act 1989 (now s 85, WRA 1991) where a discharge of fish farm effluent during a 24 hour period greatly exceeded a 10 million gallons condition imposed by the NRA. In their defence, the appellants argued before the Crown Court that the condition as to volume was invalid because it had not been imposed for the permitted purpose of pollution control, but rather, it had been imposed for another purpose, to limit the volume of water which the appellants were permitted to extract. In effect, the appellants were suggesting that since the condition imposed upon them was legally invalid, any breach of such a condition could not amount to an offence. However, in dismissing the appeal, the Court of Appeal held that such a collateral challenge represented an attempt to by-pass both judicial review procedures and the statutory appeal procedure, and as such it represented an abuse of the process. In part the appellants' case failed on the basis that the evidence which they sought to adduce in support of their arguments was deemed to be inadmissible by the court, but interestingly, the Court of Appeal felt itself 'unable to say that in no case could the validity of a condition be challenged by way of a defence to a criminal prosecution'. Accordingly, there may be circumstances where such a challenge is permissible, but this will depend very much upon the facts of each particular case.

Many of the words and phrases used in the statute have no statutory definition, and these have had to be supplied either by the practice of water

17 [1994] Env LR 165.

authorities or from litigation. Thus in the case of *R v Dovermoss Ltd*[18] where the defendant company had been convicted of causing polluting matter, namely slurry, to enter controlled waters contrary to s 85(1), the Court of Appeal were required to consider, inter alia, the meaning of words such as 'noxious' and 'pollute'. 'Noxious' evidently means 'harmful', whilst the Court of Appeal favoured the *Oxford English Dictionary* definition of 'pollute', ie 'to make physically impure, foul or filthy; to dirty, stain, taint, befoul'. Thus it would seem that in the light of *Dovermoss* and the decision of the Crown Court in *National Rivers Authority v Egger (UK) Ltd*,[19] 'polluting matter' denotes material that has the potential for causing harm to organisms rather than material that has actually caused harm. Other 'matter', however, could cover inert material such as cans or bottles whose ability to pollute is primarily visual. Whether or not the matter has in fact polluted controlled waters will of course be a question of fact and degree for the jury. Trade and sewage effluent are, however, defined by s 221 of the WRA 1991 to mean any effluent discharged from premises used for trade/industry (other than surface water and domestic sewage), and this includes premises wholly or mainly used for agriculture, fish farming or scientific research, while sewage effluent means effluent from the sewage disposal or sewerage works of a sewerage undertaker.

The fact that a phrase has been defined by the statute does not of course preclude judicial consideration of what is actually meant by the phrase. For example, in *Dovermoss*, it was necessary for the Court of Appeal to determine what was meant by 'controlled waters' and 'watercourse' despite the fact that they are defined by ss 104 and 221 respectively of the WRA 1991. It was argued on behalf of the appellant company that water is only controlled water while it is flowing in the watercourse; once it is diverted from its normal course as would be the case where it overflowed, it is no longer controlled water. The Court of Appeal rejected this submission. A watercourse such as a ditch does not cease to be a watercourse simply because it is dry at a particular time of the year. Moreover, where water overflowed from a river, stream or ditch, that water remains water of the watercourse. Furthermore, in *National Rivers Authority v Biffa Waste Services Ltd*,[20] the divisional court was required to consider whether a river bed was part of the controlled waters. The company had undertaken work on a river which involved the driving of tracked vehicles along the river bed. This operation stirred up mud and silt from the river bed and thus caused severe discolouration of the water. In the opinion of the divisional court, magistrates had been right to acquit the company where they had been charged with an offence contrary to s 85. It was clearly the case that the draftsman of the WRA 1991 had intended that a river bed was part of controlled waters, and thus the respondents had not caused anything to enter the watercourse that was not there already; their actions had merely stirred up matter that was already present. Whilst there appears to be much sense in the finding that a river bed is part of the controlled waters, it is a moot point whether the court would have reached the same conclusion had the river bed

18 (1995) 159 JP 448.
19 (1992) Water Law 169.
20 (1995) Times, 21 November.

contained foreign matter in addition to the natural mud and silt.[1] Moreover, it is not entirely clear why the defendant company was not charged with an offence contrary to s 90 of the WRA 1991 which provides for activities that, inter alia, disturb the bottom, channel or bed of an inland freshwater.

'Cause or knowingly permit' is a phrase that is by no means uncommon in environmental statutory provisions. It was found in the predecessors to s 85, such as s 2(1) of the Rivers (Prevention of Pollution) Act 1951, and currently it is to be found in, inter alia, s 4(1) of the Salmon and Freshwater Fisheries Act 1975 and s 33 of the Environmental Protection Act 1990, though admittedly the latter occurrence is modified by the inclusion of 'knowingly' prior to the word 'cause'. Accordingly, 'cause or knowingly permit' has been the subject of interpretation by the courts. In *McLeod v Buchanan*,[2] it was interpreted disjunctively so as to constitute two offences. In the context of the water pollution offences, the leading authority on what the law requires to 'cause' pollution is the House of Lords decision in *Alphacell Ltd v Woodward*.[3] Thus a defendant will only be guilty of having caused pollution where he has undertaken some active operation or chain of operations which resulted in the pollution of a watercourse. It is not necessary for the prosecution to establish that the defendant intended to cause pollution or that he was negligent as to the likely effect of his actions. The approach adopted in *Alphacell* has been followed in subsequent decisions such as *Wrothwell Ltd v Yorkshire Water Authority*,[4] *Southern Water Authority v Pegrum*[5] and, the Scottish case, *Lockhart v National Coal Board*.[6] However, some confusion in this area arose as a consequence of the decision of the divisional court in *Wychavon District Council v National Rivers Authority*.[7]

The Council held the sewage agency for the Severn Trent Water Authority, the statutory sewerage undertaker. The effect of this arrangement was that the Council undertook, on behalf of the undertaker, the operation, maintenance and repair of sewers, ie they had day-to-day responsibility for the sewage system. The Council were charged with an offence under s 107 of the Water Act 1989 (the predecessor of s 85, WRA 1991) where sewage effluent entered controlled waters as a consequence of an initially undetected blockage in a sewer pipe. At first instance, the Council had been convicted by magistrates of the offence and thus the issue for the divisional court was whether it could be said in law that Wychavon had 'caused' the pollution by their failure promptly to discover the source of the polluting discharge, and, when once the source had been discovered, by their failure to take action to clear the blockage as soon as possible. In purported compliance with the *Alphacell* approach, the divisional court found the Council not guilty of the causing offence on account

---

1 For instance, it is alleged that part of the river bed of the Fosse in Yorkshire contains different coloured layers that are the result of the production of a popular brand of chocolate confectionery. It would be a bold court which held that such a river bed was part of the controlled water.
2 [1940] 2 All ER 179.
3 [1972] AC 824, [1972] 2 All ER 475.
4 [1984] Crim LR 43.
5 [1989] Crim LR 442.
6 [1981] SCCR 9.
7 [1993] 2 All ER 440, [1993] 1 WLR 125.

of the passive nature of their actions. The delay in the detection of the pipe blockage may have been such as to amount to negligence,[8] but it did not constitute a positive act that could be said to have caused the pollution.

The decision in *Wychavon* thus reflects a rather restricted view of what constitutes 'causing' as indeed does the decision in *National Rivers Authority v Welsh Development Agency*[9] where the defendants were also held not to have caused pollution despite the fact that they had designed, constructed and maintained the drainage system which carried the effluent into a stream. It is open to doubt however whether these decisions will be relied upon in the future. In *National Rivers Authority v Yorkshire Water Services Ltd*,[10] the House of Lords in reversing the earlier decision of the divisional court[11] was invited to express support for the view that in *Wychavon*, 'the law had taken a wrong turning by insisting on a positive act by the accused as an essential prerequisite for a successful prosecution'. Whilst Lord Mackay who gave the judgment of the court declined the invitation, he did however observe that *Wychavon* was a case that turned on its own particular facts. Interestingly, the House of Lords were of the view that, but for a valid statutory defence under what is now s 87(2), WRA 1991, Yorkshire Water Services could have been guilty of the causing offence where effluent containing the chemical iso-octanol had been discharged from a sewer for which the water company was responsible.

Further clarification is to be found in the recent decision of the Court of Appeal in *A-G's Reference (No 1 of 1994)*.[12] In these proceedings, the Court of Appeal was faced with three points of law referred to it by the Attorney General by virtue of s 36 of the Criminal Justice Act 1972. Dealing with the first point, the court felt that the causing offence could be committed by a number of parties who performed different and separate acts, all of which either contributed to the polluting matter entering the waters, or without which the matter would not have entered the waters. With regard to the second question, their Lordships felt that a sewerage company's acceptance and disposal of polluting matter into a watercourse as a consequence of a defective pumping system did amount to a chain of operations and thus a positive act in compliance with the *Alphacell* approach. Thirdly and finally, the Court of Appeal held that a failure properly to maintain a sewerage system where a party had undertaken the day-to-day running and maintenance of that system was sufficient to entitle a jury to find a defendant guilty of the causing offence. In the light of these findings, especially the final point, it is clear that *Wychavon* is now a questionable decision which must be approached with caution. The restricted interpretation of 'causing' that it adopted would appear to have been superseded by the wider meaning given to the term by the Court of Appeal in *Attorney-General's Reference*, where less emphasis was placed on the need for a positive act.

In the light of the fact that causation is required under this limb of the offence, an intervening act of a third party may constitute a defence to the

8   [1993] 2 All ER 440 at 448.
9   [1993] Env LR 407.
10 [1995] 1 All ER 225.
11 [1994] 4 All ER 274.
12 [1995] 2 All ER 1007.

accused. This occurred, for example, in the case of *Impress (Worcester) Ltd v Rees*[13] where an unknown person entered the appellant's unguarded premises at night and opened the gate valve on a fuel oil storage tank with the result that oil escaped into a river. The appellant's conviction was quashed by the divisional court on the basis that the act of the unauthorised third party constituted an intervening act of so powerful a nature that the conduct of the appellants was not a cause at all, but rather merely part of the surrounding circumstances. Further instances of acts by third parties which have broken the necessary chain of causation are to be found in *Welsh Water Authority v Williams Motors (Cymdu) Ltd*[14] and *National Rivers Authority v Wright Engineering Co Ltd.*[15] In the latter case, the divisional court rejected the NRA's appeal against the decision of magistrates to dismiss an information against the defendant company on the basis that the defendants could not be said to have caused pollution where a sight gauge on a tank used for storing heating oil had been vandalised with the result that the oil polluted a nearby brook. The defendants thus avoided conviction despite the fact that vandalism had previously taken place at their engineering works, a fact which inevitably made them aware that their site was a potential target for vandalism.

It would seem that on the basis of the remarks of Lord Wilberforce in *Alphacell,*[16] there may be circumstances when the acts of a third party are insufficient to break the chain of causation, but in the *Wright Engineering* case, since the vandalism that resulted in the pollution was of a different type and on a larger scale than that which had occurred previously, it did break the chain of causation because it was not of a reasonably foreseeable nature. Whilst *Alphacell* remains authority for the proposition that foreseeability need not be proved in relation to the causing offence as a consequence of the strict nature of the offence, foreseeability is clearly a factor to be taken into account in determining the cause of pollution where vandals are involved. An issue which is related to the preceding discussion concerns the question whether a company may be vicariously liable for those acts or omissions of its employees which result in the pollution of a watercourse contrary to s 85. In *National Rivers Authority v Alfred McAlpine Homes East Ltd,*[17] the divisional court held that a company could be criminally liable in such circumstances. For such liability to arise, it is unnecessary for those in the company's head office to play a direct part in the events that gave rise to the polluting incident. It is enough that those with immediate responsibility on the site were employees of the company and that they were acting within the course and scope of their employment.

The second limb of the offence, 'knowingly permit', has rarely been considered by the courts for the simple reason that defendants are not often charged with the offence. The offence itself involves a failure to prevent pollution occurring together with actual knowledge of that failure.[18]

---

13 [1971] 2 All ER 357.
14 (1988) Times, 5 December.
15 [1994] 4 All ER 281.
16 [1972] 2 All ER 475 at 479.
17 [1994] 4 All ER 286.
18 See *Alphacell Ltd v Woodward* [1972] 2 All ER 475 at 479.

Accordingly, where a defendant stands by and allows effluent or some other polluting matter to pass over his land into a watercourse and he does nothing to prevent it, it would seem that he is guilty of the 'knowingly permit' offence.[19] However, convictions for this offence are not numerous, perhaps in part because the prosecuting authorities have sometimes charged a defendant with the causing offence when the 'knowingly permit' limb would have been the more appropriate charge. This view has been cautiously expressed by the judiciary on several occasions[20] and it serves to highlight the care that needs to be taken by prosecutors when framing the charge. Indeed in one reported decision, judicial surprise was expressed not at the offence that was charged, but rather at the identity of the party being prosecuted by the NRA.[1]

In the leading case on the 'knowingly permit' limb, *Schulmans Incorporated Ltd v National Rivers Authority*,[2] the divisional court directed that the appellants should be acquitted of both charges of 'knowingly permitting' contrary to s 107(1)(a) of the Water Act 1989 and s 4(1) of the Salmon and Freshwater Fisheries Act 1975. The acquittal was on the basis that there was no finding, and for that matter no evidence that the appellants could have prevented the escape of fuel oil from a tank on their premises into a nearby brook sooner than they did, or that there was an escape at any time that they could have prevented but failed to prevent. This latter point emphasises an important feature of the knowingly permit offence, that is that there is a defence to such a charge where it was not within the defendant's power to prevent polluting matter from entering controlled waters. It would seem that for the defendant to have been found guilty of either of the knowingly permit offences in the instant case, it would have been necessary for the prosecution to prove that the company knew that: a substantial spillage of fuel oil had occurred on their premises; fuel oil from the spillage had entered their drainage system; the drainage system discharged into the brook; and, unless the drainage system was attended to, fuel oil would soon enter the brook from the drain. Furthermore, for a successful conviction on a charge under s 4(1) of the Salmon and Freshwater Fisheries Act, it would also have been necessary to establish that the defendant knew the extent of the contamination that had taken place. A final point of interest to arise from the *Schulmans* case relates to the issue of constructive knowledge. Where a defendant refrains from giving evidence of the absence of knowledge, the decision in *Schulmans* confirms that a court is entitled to infer that they had the required knowledge.[3] It remains to be seen to what extent this principle will be applied in practice since, in theory at least, it may be sufficient for all or any of the elements of knowledge that the prosecution are required to establish as outlined above.

Much can depend upon whether a discharge of effluent, etc, has been prohibited. Section 86 of the WRA 1991 provides that discharge is prohibited if:

---

19 Ibid at 491.
20 See for example *Price v Cromack* [1975] 2 All ER 113 at 119; *Wychavon District Council v National Rivers Authority* [1993] 2 All ER 440 at 448.
 1 See *National Rivers Authority v Welsh Development Agency* [1993] Env LR 407 at 415.
 2 (1991) unreported.
 3 See *Westminster City Council v Croyalgrange Ltd* [1986] 2 All ER 353.

1   The Agency has given the discharger notice prohibiting the making or continuing of the discharge.
2   The Agency has given notice prohibiting the discharge save where specific conditions are observed and they are not.
3   The effluent, etc, discharged contains a prescribed substance or prescribed concentration of a substance.
4   The effluent, etc, derives from a prescribed process or from a process which uses prescribed substances, or such substances in prescribed amounts. Regulations may be made to 'flesh out' 'prescribed' substances and concentrations, etc.

In general terms three months' notice, at least, is required for a s 86 prohibition, save that it may be brought into force earlier where the Agency is satisfied there is an emergency justifying early commencement. General exemption from the prohibition provisions of s 86 is given to discharges from vessels.

Section 87 of the WRA 1991, as amended, provides that for the purposes of s 85 where any *sewage* effluent is discharged *into* any controlled waters, or into the sea via a pipe, or on to land, or into a lake, etc, which is not an inland freshwater *from* any sewer or works, the 'discharging sewer', vested in a sewerage undertaker, the 'discharging undertaker', *and* the undertaker did not cause or knowingly permit the discharge but was *bound* (conditionally or unconditionally) to receive into the sewer, etc, the matter in the discharge, the undertaker is *deemed* to have caused the discharge. But an undertaker is not guilty of an offence under s 85 by reason only of the fact that the discharge from 'his' sewer, etc, contravenes discharge consent conditions if the contravention is attributable to a discharge caused, etc, by another person into the sewer, etc, and the undertaker either was *not* bound to receive the discharge, or was so bound but subject to conditions which were broken, and the undertaker could not reasonably have been expected to prevent the discharge. In the event that the discharging undertaker has an agreement with a 'sending undertaker' under s 110A of the WIA 1991, and the sewage effluent was, before being discharged from the discharging sewer, discharged into that sewer by the sending undertaker, then it is the sending undertaker who is deemed to have caused the discharge, see s 87(1)(c). Furthermore a person cannot be guilty of a s 85 offence where he causes or permits a discharge into a sewer or works vested in an undertaker where the latter is bound to receive the discharge or to receive it unconditionally and all conditions are observed.

The scope of the defence afforded by what is now s 87(2) of the WRA 1991 was considered by the House of Lords in *National Rivers Authority v Yorkshire Water Services Ltd*,[4] referred to above. It was argued on behalf of the NRA that the defence only applied when it had been alleged by the prosecution that there had been a contravention of a consent relating to the relevant discharge. This argument had been accepted by the divisional court,[5] but in the opinion of their Lordships, the defence did not have such a restricted application. The words used in s 87(2) were such as to constitute a defence in respect of any

4   [1995] 1 All ER 225.
5   [1994] 4 All ER 274.

allegation of an offence under what is now s 85, WRA 1991. Accordingly, although Yorkshire Water Services could be said to have caused pollution where iso-octanol was discharged into a river, the fact that the initial discharge of the chemical into a sewer for which they were responsible was attributable to an unknown person, entitled the water company to rely on the statutory defence.

Sampling evidence

In order for a successful prosecution to be mounted, it is axiomatic that the Agency will be required to take a sample from, for example, an effluent channel, as evidence of the fact that the defendant's acts or omissions have polluted a watercourse. Under s 209 of the WRA 1991, the old NRA was obliged to comply with a tripartite sampling regime whereby any sample that was taken was 'there and then' divided into three parts with each part being placed in a separate container and marked accordingly. One part was then given to the occupier of the land or the owner or master of the vessel, one part was retained by the NRA, and, the other sample was submitted for analysis, see s 209(1)(c). This procedure inevitably became a matter for the consideration of the courts in several cases[6] since if the sampling procedure that was adopted contravened the terms of the statute, it followed that any resultant analyses became inadmissible and the prosecution case consequently became that much harder to prove. For the purposes of a private prosecution however, s 209 need not have been complied with for the tripartite procedure related only to the analysis of samples taken 'on behalf of the Authority'.

In *A-G's Reference (No 2 of 1994)*,[7] the Court of Appeal were concerned with two principal issues: first, whether the statutory requirement to notify the occupier of the land or the owner or master of the vessel of an intention to have a sample analysed should precede the tripartite division of the sample; and, secondly, the meaning of 'there and then' in s 148 of the Water Act 1989 (the predecessor of s 209). In relation to the first point, the Court of Appeal held that notification need not necessarily precede either the taking or the division of the sample. It was observed that if the draftsman of the Act had intended that the occupier should be notified prior to the taking of the sample in order to enable him to be present, a specific provision to this effect would have been included in the statute. On the second point, it was held that the words 'there and then' should be given a wider meaning than that which they literally implied, for to divide a sample into three parts at the exact time or immediately after it had been taken would in some instances be impracticable. Accordingly, 'then' meant on the occasion of taking the sample and 'there' meant at or proximate to the place where the sample was taken. Thus the statutory procedure had been complied with where an NRA officer had, immediately after taking a sample, carried the container to a car park some 300 yards away where the division into three parts then took place.

---

6 See for example *R v Rechem Industrial Ltd* (1993) unreported, where it was held that the tripartite procedure for sampling was not rendered invalid despite the fact that the deterioration of a sample made comparison impossible.
7 [1995] 2 All ER 1000, [1994] 1 WLR 1579.

Section 209 is to be almost entirely repealed as a consequence of s 111 of the Environment Act 1995. Thus the old tripartite rule discussed above will be abolished and along with it the expectation that Agency prosecutions will be based on evidence obtained by way of manual periodic sampling. In *R v CPC (UK) Ltd*,[8] the Court of Appeal were concerned with, inter alia, the admissibility of evidence in the form of an analysis of readings taken from a phOX systems mobile water unit, a permanent static testing device. Under this system, water was diverted from the flow in mid-stream by means of a pipe connected to the machine. The water was then pumped through the machine and analysed, and it was then returned to the river by way of a discharge pipe. In ruling that the Crown Court had been correct to admit in evidence the readings taken from the machine, the Court of Appeal did so on the basis that although the machine could be said to 'sample' the water in the colloquial sense of the word, it did not *take* a 'sample' of water within the meaning of s 209. The *Oxford English Dictionary* defined a 'sample' as 'small separated parts of something illustrating the quality of the mass it is taken from, specimen, pattern'. Accordingly, a sample was not created in the instant case since the water that was analysed by the machine was not physically separated and isolated from the whole body of water by being placed in a container.

With the advent of the almost complete repeal of s 209, it is therefore no longer necessary to speculate as to whether automatic monitoring and remote sensing fall within the terms of the Water Resources Act. Indeed, s 111 of the 1995 Act stipulates that information obtained by means of 'any apparatus' shall be admissible in evidence in any proceedings. For the purposes of the section, 'apparatus' is defined to include 'any meter or other device for measuring, assessing, determining, recording or enabling to be recorded, the volume, temperature, radioactivity, rate, nature, origin, composition or effect of any substance, flow, discharge, emission, deposit or abstraction'. Thus the various automatic sampling devices[9] that have been developed for the continuous monitoring of controlled waters will continue to be used and perhaps further refined by the new Agency as it seeks to reduce the number of polluting incidents that occur.

Defences to the foregoing offences are contained in ss 88 and 89 of the WRA 1991. Thus no s 85 offence occurs where the discharging entry occurs or the discharge is made under and in accordance with:

1 Consents given under the Water Resources Act 1991 and its predecessor the Water Act 1989; but note that where consent conditions are breached a separate offence occurs each time a discharge in breach occurs, see *Severn Trent Water Authority v Express Foods Group Ltd.*[10]
2 Authorisation given in connection with IPC under Part I of the Environmental Protection Act 1990 (see chapter 10).
3 Waste management/disposal licences.

---

8 (1994) Times, 4 August.
9 For a description of 'Merlin', 'Sherlock' and 'Cyclops', see Dr Albert Mumma's 'Use of compliance monitoring data in water prosecutions' (1993) 5 Journal of Environmental Law 19.
10 (1988) 153 JP 126.

4   Licences granted under the Food and Environment Protection Act 1985 (see above).
5   Section 163 of the WRA 1991 (discharges by the Agency itself in connection with works on reservoirs, wells, boreholes, etc).
6   Section 165 of the Water Industry Act 1991 (discharges by water undertakers in connection with works on reservoirs, etc).
7   Local statutory provisions.
8   Other prescribed enactments.

Likewise no offence is committed where the discharge is caused, etc, in an emergency in order to avoid danger to life or health, *and* all reasonably mitigating measures are taken, *and* the Agency is furnished with particulars as soon as reasonably practical. In order for the 'emergency' defence to be available, it would seem that the emergency itself must amount to circumstances which are beyond the defendant's control. Accordingly in one particular case where a factory explosion resulted in the escape of chemicals, the court was not prepared to accept that such circumstances fell within the ambit of the defence.[11] Specific exemptions from liability are given to those who cause or permit trade/sewage effluent to be discharged from a vessel, or those who merely permit water from abandoned mines to enter controlled waters, or who deposit solid mine/quarry waste on any land so that it falls into inland freshwaters provided the Agency has consented to the deposit, *and* no other reasonably practicable deposition site can be found, *and* all reasonably practicable steps are taken to prevent the ingress of the material, *and* provided the matter is *not* poisonous, noxious or polluting.

Abandoned mines

As a consequence of an amendment made to s 89 by s 60 of the Environment Act 1995, the defence in relation to an abandoned mine will no longer be available to the owner or operator of such a mine where the abandonment of the mine or part of the mine occurs after 31 December 1999. In the event that a mine or part of a mine has become abandoned on two or more occasions, and at least one falls on or before the relevant date and at least one falls after that date, the amended s 89 provides that the mine or part is to be regarded as becoming abandoned after that date.

Further changes to the law relating to abandoned mines are to be made by the Environment Act 1995. As a consequence of a number of recommendations made by the NRA in its report 'Abandoned Mines and the Water Environment' (Water Quality Series No 14), s 58 of the Environment Act will insert Chapter IIA into the WRA 1991 consisting of ss 91A and 91B. Accordingly, what the NRA considered to be the most unsatisfactory aspect of the law, the absence of a statutory definition of the concept of 'abandonment' in relation to a mine, is to be rectified by s 91A where it is stated that the abandonment of a mine includes:

---

11 *National Rivers Authority v ICI Chemicals and Polymers* (1992) 204 ENDS Report 37; 4 LMELR 131. See also *National Rivers Authority v North West Water* (1992) 208 ENDS Report 40; 4 LMELR 131.

1 The discontinuance of any or all of the operations for the removal of water from the mine.
2 The cessation of working of any relevant seam, vein or vein-system.
3 The cessation of use of any shaft or outlet of the mine.
4 In the case of a mine where activities other than mining activities are carried on, whether or not mining activities are also carried on, abandonment will occur where some or all of those other activities are discontinued and there is a substantial change in the operations for the removal of water from the mine.

The above definition of what 'abandonment' means in relation to a mine only has a limited application. It is for the purposes of the new Chapter IIA and the notification requirement for those intending to abandon a mine that the term is defined. Therefore, the definition does not apply in relation to the statutory defence under s 89(3), WRA 1991. The phrase 'activities other than mining' has been included in order to ensure that mines which are now used for educational and recreational purposes will fall within the scope of the provisions. In response to another NRA suggestion, where it is proposed to abandon a mine, s 91B imposes a duty on the operator of the mine to notify the Agency at least six months before the abandonment takes effect. A failure to give the required notice will be an offence for which a guilty party will be liable, on summary conviction, to a fine not exceeding the statutory maximum, and on conviction on indictment, to a fine. The notice itself shall contain such information as is prescribed for the purpose, and it may include information about the operator's opinion as to any consequences of the abandonment. In addition, prescribed particulars of or relating to the notice are required to be published in one or more local newspapers circulating in the locality where the mine is situated. Thus whilst a number of the NRA's recommendations have found their way onto the statute book, the new s 91B stops short of giving effect to one of the NRA's principal recommendations, the imposition of a statutory duty on a mine operator to prepare a complete mine abandonment programme.

Discharge consents

In relation to offences much depends upon whether a particular discharge is/is not consented. Sch 10 of the WRA 1991 as inserted by Sch 22 of the Environment Act 1995, provides for discharge applications and their handling, *but* nothing in a *disposal licence* can be treated for discharge offence purposes as authorising any discharge consisting of matter (other than trade/sewage effluent) entering controlled waters from a drain/sewer in contravention of a s 86 prohibition, *or* any discharge of trade/sewage effluent into any controlled waters or the sea, *or* any discharge on to land or into a lake, etc, which is not an inland freshwater, of trade or sewage effluent in contravention of a s 86 prohibition. Applications for discharge consents must be made on the form provided for the purpose and must be advertised by or on behalf of the applicant in such manner as may be required by regulations made by the Secretary of State, unless it appears to the Agency that it is appropriate to dispense with the advertising requirement. Furthermore, the Agency may give the applicant notice requiring him to provide it with such information as the Agency may require for the purposes of determining the application.

Where an application has been made for a discharge consent, the Agency is required to give notice of the application, together with a copy of the application, to all those persons prescribed or directed to be consulted in regulations or directions issued by the Secretary of State. Any representations received from consultees within six weeks of the date on which notice of the application was given must be considered by the Agency, as must any representations made by any other persons which also relate to the application. The Agency may decide to grant (conditionally or unconditionally) or refuse the application, and they have in general, four months from the day of the application to make the determination; otherwise it is deemed refused. There is a general discretion as to the imposition of conditions but in particular they may relate to:

1 Times and places of discharge and design of discharge outlets.
2 Nature, origin, composition, temperature, volume, rate, timing of discharges.
3 Steps to be taken to minimise polluting effects.
4 Sampling facilities.
5 Metering facilities.
6 Keeping of records and making returns, etc.

In consequence of representations made to him or of his own motion, the Secretary of State may 'call-in' the application. In such cases the Secretary of State may cause a local inquiry or hearing to be held to consider the issue and must do so if so requested by either the applicant or the Agency. Thereafter the power to determine the application and to impose conditions, etc, belongs to the Secretary of State.

In certain cases where unconsented discharges have taken place the Agency may, where future unconsented discharges are likely, serve notice on the discharger giving consent, subject to any conditions they specify. Such consents must, however, be publicised and any representations received in consequence considered.

The Agency is further under a duty to review consents and conditions, and thereafter they may, by notice, revoke or modify a consent. The Secretary of State may direct the Agency in the exercise of this power either to enable the UK to meet EU or international obligations, or to protect public health or flora and fauna dependent on the aquatic environment. In addition, the Secretary of State may at any time direct the Agency to conduct a general review of consents and conditions that have been granted. The Agency has a particular power to revoke a consent where it appears on review that no relevant discharge has been made at any time during the preceding 12 months. However, the variation and revocation powers are subject to restrictions in that there is, generally, a period of four years from the date of a consent/modification during which changes may not be imposed. It should also be noted that revocation or modification of a consent may involve the Agency in the payment of compensation. The holder of a consent may apply to the Agency, on a form provided for the purpose, for the variation of the consent. Furthermore, the new Sch 10 provides for the possibility of the transfer of a consent by a holder to a person who proposes to carry on the discharges in place of the holder, provided that the Agency is notified by the transferor within 21 days of the date of transfer. In the event of the death of a consent holder, the consent is regarded as part of the deceased's personal estate and is thus vested in his personal representatives.

Discharge consents are not free. Sections 41 and 42 of the 1995 Act enable the Agency to make, subject to publicity, consultation exercises and ministerial approval, schemes of charges. The old NRA had under the 1991 Act such a scheme in respect of both initial application fees and ongoing monitoring charges. Such schemes reflect the Agency's *administrative* costs and are based on costings which reflect the type of pollutants whose discharge is consented, the nature and location of the receiving water, etc. The charges do *not* represent a pollution tax as considered in chapter 1.

Under s 91 of the WRA 1991 Act where the Agency (otherwise than at the Secretary of State's direction) refuses, inter alia, a discharge consent application, or grants it subject to conditions, or revokes or modifies a consent, the disappointed applicant may appeal to the Secretary of State, who has power to make regulations concerning such appeals, see SI 1989/1151. The Secretary of State has a wide discretion on appeal to direct the NRA to give consents conditionally/unconditionally, and to modify and impose conditions.

Note in passing s 90 of the WRA 1991 which creates particular offences in connection with deposits and vegetation in rivers. It is an offence to remove from the bed or channel of an inland freshwater any deposit accumulated by a dam, weir or sluice by causing the deposit to be carried away in suspension by the waters. Likewise to cause or permit a substantial amount of vegetation to be cut or uprooted in inland waters or so near to them that it falls in followed by failure to remove the vegetation is also an offence. In both cases the Agency may consent to the acts, subject to conditions if they think fit. As a consequence of Sch 22 to the Environment Act 1995, new s 90A and 90B have been inserted into the WRA 1991. Section 90A makes provision for applications for consent for the purposes of the defence to a s 85 offence under s 89(4) and the s 90 offences. Accordingly, any such application must be made on a form provided by the Agency and must be advertised in such manner as the Secretary of State may prescribe in regulations. In order for the Agency to proceed with the application, it is necessary for the applicant to provide it with all such information as it reasonably requires, with all such information prescribed by the Secretary of State, and with any further information that the Agency may by notice require from the applicant. Where the Agency takes the view that a condition of a consent under ss 89(4) or 90(1) or (2) *or a discharge consent* is being contravened, s 90B provides that it may serve an enforcement notice on the holder of the consent. The enforcement notice will specify the matters constituting the contravention together with any remedial steps which need to be taken within a specified time limit. It is an offence to fail to comply with a requirement imposed by an enforcement notice for which a guilty party may, on summary conviction, be subject to a maximum of three months' imprisonment or to a fine not exceeding £20,000 or to both, or on conviction on indictment, to a maximum of two years' imprisonment or to a fine or both.

There are a number of important supplementary provisions concerning discharge consents. Under WRA 1991, s 99 the Secretary of State has power to make regulations modifying the pollution control provisions with regard to discharge consents required by the Agency itself, see SI 1989/1157. Pollution control information together with other information about its functions must be included in the Agency's annual report required under s 52 of the

Environment Act 1995, and s 51 further requires the Agency to supply the Secretary of State with such relevant information as he may reasonably require. More important are the pollution control registers required under s 190 of WRA 1991, as amended by para 169 of Sch 22 to the Environment Act 1995. These registers must be maintained in accordance with regulations made by the Secretary of State, see SI 1989/1160, and must contain prescribed particulars of:

1   Section 83 notices of water quality objectives.
2   Applications for consents.
3   Consents given and conditions imposed.
4   Samples, information derived therefrom, and any consequential steps taken.
5   Applications made to the Agency for the variation of discharge consents.
6   Enforcement notices served under s 90B.
7   Revocations of discharge consents under para 7 of Sch 10.
8   Appeals under s 91.
9   Directions given by the Secretary of State in relation to the Agency's functions under the water pollution provisions of the WRA 1991.
10   Convictions, for offences under Part III of the WRA 1991, of persons who have the benefit of discharge consents.
11   Information obtained/furnished in pursuance of conditions of discharge consents.
12   Works notices, appeals and convictions under ss 161A, 161C and 161D respectively (see below). And
13   Such other matters relating to the quality of water or the pollution of water as may be prescribed by the Secretary of State.

In addition to the considerable expansion in matters to be included in the pollution control register effected by the Environment Act 1995, that Act has inserted new ss 191A and 191B which make provision for the exclusion from registers of information affecting national security or information which is of a commercially confidential nature.

These registers must be kept publicly available at reasonable times and copies must be available at reasonable charges. The Agency is under a specific duty in WRA 1991, s 202 to furnish ministers with relevant advice and assistance in connection with their water pollution control functions and ministers and the Agency may serve notice on any person requiring specified information to be given in connection with water pollution control functions, it being an offence not to comply. The Agency and water undertakers are under mutual obligations by virtue of WRA 1991, s 203 to provide information on the quality of any controlled or other waters and concerning any incident in which poisonous, noxious or polluting matter or any solid matter has entered any such waters. However, there is a general restriction on the disclosure of information, under WRA 1991, s 204, obtained under any provision of the 1991 Act which relates to the affairs of any individual or business, though exceptions to this restriction exist, inter alia, in respect of the carrying on of their functions by relevant authorities, or in connection with criminal investigations and proceedings or in pursuance of EU obligations.

The Environment Agency has a general discretion to enforce the provisions of the WRA 1991 relating to water pollution, but note that, under s 217 of the

Act, where a body corporate is guilty of an offence and it can be proved it was committed with the consent or connivance of, or is attributable to the neglect of, any director, manager, secretary or other similar officer then that person is guilty of the offence along with the body corporate. Agency designated officers may be given extensive rights of entry to premises in connection with enforcement of pollution control functions and related matters under the general power of entry which the Agency possesses by virtue of s 108 of the Environment Act 1995 (see chapter 3 above), but note also residual powers under ss 169 and 172, WRA 1991.

Anti-pollution works and operations

Section 161 of the Act, as amended, gives the Agency a general power to carry out anti-pollution works and operations where it appears that noxious, poisonous or polluting matter or any solid material is likely to enter, or has been present in, any controlled waters. This power is obviously subject to the discharge consent provisions and, as a consequence of new s 161(1A) inserted by para 161 of Sch 22 to the Environment Act 1995, is only exercisable where the Agency considers it necessary to carry out any works or operations forthwith, and, where the Agency has not been able to find, after reasonable inquiry, a person on whom to serve a works notice under s 161A (see below). The costs of any works which the Agency does undertake may be recovered from the polluter, see s 161(3).

In *Bruton and National Rivers Authority v Clarke*,[12] the NRA initiated civil proceedings against a farmer in order to recover the costs involved in remedying or mitigating the polluting effects of the discharge of three million gallons of ammonia-saturated slurry into the River Sappiston. The NRA's claim involved the recovery of the costs of various surveys which were undertaken following the polluting incident, the scientific costs that had been incurred in terms of the investigation of the incident by scientists, and, the costs of restocking the river with mature fish and fry. In making an award of some £90,000 to the NRA, Mellor J demonstrated that any claim for costs under s 161(3) will be closely scrutinised by the courts so that only those costs which can properly be attributed to polluting incidents will be recoverable. The fact that not all the surveys which had been undertaken by the NRA were as a direct result of the polluting incident ensured that not all their costs could be recovered under this head of their claim.

The Environment Act 1995 has inserted four new sections into Part VII of the WRA 1991, all of which relate to notices requiring persons to carry out anti-pollution works and operations. Section 161A entitles the Agency to serve a works notice on any person who either caused/knowingly permitted any poisonous, noxious or polluting matter or any solid waste matter to be present at a place from which it is likely to enter controlled waters, or caused/knowingly permitted the matter in question to be present in any controlled waters. The 'works notice' may require the person on whom it is served to remove/dispose of the polluting matter, or remedy/mitigate any pollution caused by its presence in the waters, or, so far as is reasonably practicable, to

---

12 (1993) unreported, see [1995] Env Liability CS13–14.

restore the waters and such flora and fauna which is dependent on the aquatic environment of the waters to their state immediately before the polluting matter became present in the water. Prior to serving a notice on any person, the Agency is required reasonably to endeavour to consult that person concerning the relevant works or operations to be undertaken. Any works notice which is served must specify a time limit for achieving the requirements which it specifies. Continuing the special provision made in respect of an abandoned mine or an abandoned part of a mine which is a feature of the WRA 1991, no works notice is to be served on an owner or former operator who permitted water from such a source to enter controlled waters, provided that the mine or part of a mine became abandoned prior to 31 December 1999.

Section 161B provides that a works notice may require a person to carry out works or operations in respect of land despite the fact that he is not entitled to carry them out. In order to enable the person on whom the notice has been served to comply with it, any person whose consent is required before such works, etc, may be carried out shall grant those rights in relation to any land or waters and such a person shall be entitled on application to be compensated by the person carrying out the works, etc.

Section 161C confers a 21 day right of appeal against a works notice on the person to whom it has been served, and on appeal, the Secretary of State may confirm the notice, with or without modification, or quash it. The grounds on which appeals may be made and the procedure to be followed at such appeals are to be dealt with by regulations. It is an offence to fail to comply with the requirements of a works notice, see s 161D. In the event of non-compliance, the Agency may perform the works or operations which the notice required and may recover from the person on whom the notice was served any costs or expenses which it has reasonably incurred in so doing. This latter provision is thus similar to that which is found in s 161(3), WRA 1991 (see above). Extensive powers to protect water in waterworks from pollution or contamination, including powers to break up and open streets, sewers, drains and tunnels, are also granted to the Agency by s 162 of the WRA 1991. The Agency also has power under s 210 and Sch 25 of the Act to make byelaws in connection with its functions under the Act and these it may enforce under s 211.

What, however, can be said of the Agency's enforcement record and its policies in relation to this matter? The prosecution of Shell following pollution of the Mersey by massive oil leaks in 1989 and the imposition of a £1m fine was often cited as evidence of the NRA's determination to use its 'teeth', and indeed that body did carry out a number of quite well publicised prosecutions in the years between its inception and abolition, including prosecutions of water undertakers. Private prosecutions may also be brought: see *Wales v Thames Water Authority*[13] and *Greenpeace v Allbright and Wilson*.[14]

However, despite the fact that the various water pollution offences are of the 'strict liability' variety with no mens rea required, the Agency possesses 'institutional discretion' both as to the decision to prosecute in any given case and as to the standard of compliance with pollution control provisions which

13 (1987) unreported (Aylesbury JJ).
14 [1991] 3 LMELR 132, 170 and 202.

will be sought in the bringing of prosecutions, for it is quite clear that not all incidents of pollution result in prosecution: in 1994 there were 1,123 recorded Category 1 and 2 (see below) related pollution incidents but only 74 resulted in prosecutions. In 1989 the NRA issued a Guidance Note on Enforcement and Prosecution which clarified the position on when prosecutions would be brought and gave guidelines to enforcement officers on how to exercise the discretion to prosecute. Polluting incidents were 'banded'. Major incidents were classified as Category 1 and involved one or more of potential or actual persistent effect on the quality of water or aquatic life, closure of a source of potable water, 50 or more fish kill, major or frequent breach of consent conditions, extensive remedial action needed, major affectation of amenity value.

Category 1 incidents normally resulted in prosecution. Category 2 comprised 'significant' polluting incidents and covered situations where: notification to abstractors was needed, or where there was fish kill between one and 50, or some measurable effect on invertebrate life, or water became unfit for its stock or had a contaminated bed, or where amenity to owners, users or the public was reduced by odours or the appearance of the water, or a consent condition was breached. Here either a warning was issued or a prosecution undertaken. Category 3 comprised 'minor' incidents of suspected or probable pollution which were not substantiable or had no noticeable effect. These were normally dealt with by a warning.

The Agency's policy on prosecution was published on 14 May 1996. Prosecution will depend on the exercise of discretion where this is warranted, even without warning or recourse to alternative sanctions, such as enforcement action, where appropriate. Action will be taken where it will draw attention to the need for compliance with the law and maintenance of required standards, and where prosecution will deter others. It will also be taken where it is considered an incident has had potential for considerable environmental harm; similarly where an offence is grave and the general record and attitude of the offender warrant such action, eg where there has been an apparent reckless disregard of standards, or repeated breaches or persistently poor compliance with standards. However, the chances of a successful outcome will also be taken into account in deciding whether to prosecute. The two overriding issues in prosecution policy therefore appear to be, first, whether prosecution is in the public interest, and, secondly, whether the evidence suggests a likely conviction. There also appears to be a continuation of a moral element of 'culpability' clearly present in the former NRA policy now replaced.

The pragmatic approach to the question of whether or not to initiate proceedings against a polluter will thus be continued by the Environment Agency. It was certainly manifested in the most recent of the NRA's reports on 'Water Pollution Incidents in England and Wales' (Water Quality Series No 25). During 1994 some 35,291 pollution incidents were reported to the NRA of which 25,415 were later substantiated. In order to facilitate the reporting of such incidents as well as environmental incidents generally, 1994 marked the first full year of operation of the NRA's national freephone number which was manned 24 hours a day at its eight regional control rooms. The fact that some 30,000 calls were received during the year demonstrated the utility of this service. Despite the high number of substantiated incidents, only 229 were Category 1 incidents, a significant decrease from the previous year's total of 331. Of the 237 prosecutions brought by the NRA at the time of writing,

222 resulted in a conviction with the highest fine of £30,000 awarded against a polluter for an oil pollution incident in the Welsh region. Evidently in the discharge of its enforcement functions, the NRA recognised that it was operating not just within a legal 'world' but also an ethical one in which the moral perception of acts of pollution is important in deciding whether or not it is legitimate to take action in respect of any given incident.

Levels of fines have risen since the start of 1991 but still compare poorly with the total award of £284,000 damages in respect of five pollution claims brought in 1989 by anglers against a number of companies in respect of fish kill.[15] Furthermore it has been argued that there is little point in prosecuting some dischargers when others have 'permission to pollute' under consented discharges. Though dischargers usually reply, their consents are for maximum emissions not often reached in practice, and usually reflecting only history. The NRA was also subject to inconclusive judicial review proceedings alleging it failed on occasions to monitor discharge consents with a view to enforcement.[16] Certain powers of the Secretary of State to make regulations and give directions must be noted for they can have important repercussions for the law and practice of water regulation.

Ministerial regulations/directions

Under WRA 1991, s 92 the Secretary of State has power to make regulations which may prohibit a person from having custody or control of any noxious, poisonous or polluting matter unless prescribed steps are carried out to prevent or control the entry of such material into controlled waters, or for requiring persons having custody or control of such matter to take precautionary and other relevant steps. The detailed application of such regulations may be entrusted to the Agency. Under this power the Control of Pollution (Silage, Slurry and Agricultural Fuel) Regulations SI 1991/324 have been made. These require persons with custody or control over crops being made into silage, etc, or over certain fuel oils to ensure that controlled waters are not polluted, for example by taking certain steps as to storage and construction of relevant emplacements. The Agency is empowered to require action in certain circumstances, but an appeal against their decision can be made to the Secretary of State. The regulations also require compliance with certain British Standards, eg BS 5502 on buildings and structures for agriculture. Ministers may also, under WRA 1991, s 97 issue and approve codes of good agricultural practice on activities that may affect controlled waters and promote good practices to avoid or minimise pollution. Contravention of such a code is not a criminal offence in itself but the Agency must consider contraventions in relation to, inter alia, the issuing of prohibitions under s 86. See The Water (Prevention of Pollution) (Code of Practice) Order SI 1991/2285.

Ministers also have extensive powers to enable the Agency in the performance of its functions to acquire land compulsorily (s 154) or to carry out compulsory works (s 168). In cases of civil emergency, ie situations where in the opinion of the Secretary of State there is such disruption of water or sewerage services in an area, or such destruction of or damage to life or

15 See The Times, 12 July 1989.
16 See [1991] 3 LMELR 202.

property as to seriously and adversely affect the area's inhabitants, he may, under WRA 1991, s 207 give such directions to the Agency as he considers requisite to mitigate the effects of the emergency.

It is also, of course, for the Secretary of State to use his powers under WRA 1991, s 102 and s 2 of the European Communities Act 1972 to make regulations to give effect to EU Directives by way of regulations. Thus Directives 73/404, 73/405, 82/242 and 82/243 on the biodegradability and composition of detergents are implemented by the Detergents (Composition) Regulations SI 1978/564 (amended SI 1984/1369 and SI 1986/560). Directive 75/440 on surface waters has been, as already stated, implemented by SI 1989/1148 (for Scotland see SI 1990/121), the Trade Effluents (Prescribed Processes and Substances) Regulations SI 1989/1156 (Scotland: SI 1990/126) as amended by SI 1990/1629, and the Trade Effluents (Prescribed Substances and Processes) Regulations SI 1992/339 implement the Dangerous Substances Directive 76/464, etc, by listing (the 'Red List') certain prescribed substances (*including* mercury, cadmium, DDT, aldrin, dieldrin, atrazine) and certain prescribed processes whose discharge as trade effluent into sewers is subject to review and prohibition by the Secretary of State, see further below on the Water Industry Act 1991 Part IV. See also SI 1989/2286 further implementing Directive 76/464 by classifying surface waters according to the presence of the substances prescribed under the Directive and its daughters. Note further the Sludge (Use in Agriculture) Regulations SI 1989/1263 implementing the Sewage Sludge Directive 86/278 which are designed, inter alia, to protect the environment against the harmful effects of uncontrolled spreading of sewage sludge, for details see *Encyclopaedia of Environmental Law* vol 4, para D24–001 et seq.

The Bathing Waters (Classification) Regulations SI 1991/1597 (in Scotland see SI 1991/1609) are designed to fulfil the requirements of Directive 76/160 on the quality of bathing waters. Criteria are laid down for BW1 classification which reflect the mandatory requirements of the Directive with regard to designated bathing waters, though the Secretary of State is empowered to allow certain derogations as contemplated by the Directive. BW1 will be used for the setting of quality objectives for bathing waters under the terms of WRA 1991, s 83. However, there was some doubt between 1989 and 1991 as to whether the UK was fully complying with the requirements of the Directive, for example, in respect of the presences of viruses on certain beaches and in 1990 the EC Commission successfully commenced action against the UK in respect of 140 beaches which failed, it was claimed, to meet cleanliness standards.[17]

Directive 76/160 stipulates that in each member state, there shall be a 'competent authority' to sample and analyse bathing waters in accordance with the requirements of the Directive. The NRA in the past served as the competent authority for the purposes of the Directive in England and Wales, although this is yet another task which now falls to the Environment Agency. In the performance of these duties, the NRA conducted a series of bathing water surveys, the results of which were published in an annual report on Bathing Water Quality. The fifth such report published in July 1995 details the results of the 1994 survey and puts the number of identified bathing waters in England and Wales at 419. The 1994 figures show that there has been an

---

17 *EC Commission v United Kingdom*: C-56/90 [1993] Water Law 168.

increase in compliance with the mandatory coliform standards ('I' values) from the 1993 figure of 79.4% to the present figure of 82.5%. Furthermore, the percentage of bathing waters complying consistently over a three year period with the mandatory coliform standard has increased from 63% for the 1991–1993 period to 65% for the 1992–1994 period. During the same time periods, the percentage of bathing waters consistently failing the standard has fallen from 9% to 5%.

The Urban Waste Water Treatment (England and Wales) Regulations SI 1994/2841 have been made by the Secretary of State in order to give effect to Directive 91/271 on the treatment of urban waste water. These regulations are expressed in broadly similar terms to the Directive save for the fact that they prefer the term 'high natural dispersion areas' to the 'less sensitive areas' referred to in the Directive. Controversy surrounding the determination of estuarine limits for the purposes of art 2(12) of the Directive culminated in a ruling that the Secretary of State acted unlawfully by classifying the Humber and Severn estuaries as 'coastal waters'.

In *R v Secretary of State for the Environment, ex p Kingston upon Hull City Council* and *R v Secretary of State for the Environment, ex p Bristol City Council*,[18] the issue between the parties related to whether primary or a more thorough, and therefore more expensive, secondary treatment level of household and industrial sewage was necessary for the purposes of the legislation. The High Court held that whilst member states have a discretion in establishing outer estuarine limits under the Directive, by classifying the Humber and Severn estuaries as 'coastal waters' so as to avoid the need for more costly secondary treatment, the Secretary of State had taken account of an irrelevant consideration. In exercising his discretion, he ought to have had regard to the characteristics of the area of water in question since such water either was or was not an estuary regardless of the costs involved in treating waste water discharged into it.

The UK has also made considerable use of circulars and other forms of guidance on the implementation of EU obligations and other legislative requirements, see, for example, DoE Circulars 4/82, on the implementation of Directive 80/68 on the protection of groundwater where it was considered prior to its cancellation for England, by PPG 23 that it was not necessary to introduce any new legislation because existing legislative powers were adequate; 13/85 on public registers of discharges to the water environment; 18/85 on the implementation of Directive 76/464 and its daughters, as supplemented by 7/89 which gives specific guidance on mercury, cadmium, hexachlorcyclohexane, carbon tetrachloride, DDT, pentachlorophenol, the drins, HCB, HCBD, chloroform, and 20/90 which gives further guidance relating to the Protection of Groundwater Directive 80/68, in particular by requiring revision of waste disposal practices to ensure waste sites do not lead to prescribed substances and families of substances entering groundwater.

Section 98 of the WRA 1991 empowers the Secretary of State to make regulations to apply the Act's provisions to dealing with radioactive waste, otherwise the pollution control provisions of the 1991 Act do not apply to such waste within the meaning of the Radioactive Substances Act 1993, see SI

18 (1996) Times, 31 January.

1989/1158. These regulations subject radioactive waste to the provisions of the 1991 legislation relating to classification of waters, water quality objectives, pollution offences, pollution precautions, Agency consents, anti-pollution works, registers, information collection and exchange, but in such a way that no account is to be taken of the radioactive properties of such waste; this remains subject to the 1993 Act.

Water protection zones and nitrate sensitive and vulnerable areas

Section 93 of the WRA 1991 empowers the Secretary of State (after consultation with MAFF with regard to areas in England) to designate an area as a water protection zone (WPZ) where it is considered appropriate with a view to preventing or controlling the entry of any poisonous, noxious or polluting matter into controlled waters, or to prohibit or restrict activities within the area considered likely to result in such pollution. The result of designation is that specified activities within the area may be prohibited or restricted, though this is not to extend to the entry of nitrate into controlled waters as a result of agricultural use of land; for the control of this, special regimes may be set up — see further below. A WPZ designation may particularly empower the Agency inter alia, to determine the circumstances in which the carrying on of an activity is prohibited, and to determine the activities to which any prohibition or restriction applies. It is worth noting that to date, the Secretary of State has not made any water protection zone orders, though it had been proposed by the NRA that the River Ree catchment should receive a designation.

With regard to nitrates under WRA 1991, s 94 ministers may, for the purpose of preventing or controlling the entry of nitrate into controlled waters as a result of the agricultural use of land, designate land as a nitrate sensitive area (NSA). Orders made under this power may consequentially require, prohibit or restrict the carrying on of specified activities, and may provide for sums of money to be paid by ministers to designated persons in respect of obligations imposed. Contravention of requirements may amount to an offence. Where an area has been designated as such, WRA 1991, s 95 further empowers ministers to supplement orders by making agreements with relevant land owners, etc, whereby, in return for payments made by ministers, obligations are accepted with regard to the management of the land, eg with regard to nitrate application. Such agreements amount to restrictive covenants 'running with' the land.

By virtue of the Nitrate Sensitive Areas (Designation) Order 1990 SI 1990/1013, which is revoked with effect from 1 June 1996, 10 areas were originally designated as nitrate sensitive areas. The order provided for two types of agreement between the minister and a farmer. The first, the basic scheme agreement, imposed various restrictions on the use of inorganic nitrogen fertiliser on crops whereas the premium scheme agreement, with its higher rates of payment, demanded the cessation of arable production and the establishment and maintenance of grassland on the land to which the agreement related. Whilst the basic scheme proved to be quite popular with farmers, the lack of enthusiasm for the premium scheme became clear when in 1993, the government introduced an amendment order, SI 1993/3198, which increased the rates of payment for agricultural land in this particular scheme.

Further developments have occurred in this area with the introduction of the Nitrate Sensitive Areas Regulations 1994 SI 1994/1729. These regulations which, like their predecessors extend to England only, came into force on 26 July 1994 in order to comply with EU Regulation 2078/92, the so-called 'Agri-environmental Regulation'. They expanded the number of nitrate sensitive areas from the original 10 to 22. In addition, the regulations provided for three different types of scheme to apply in such areas: a basic scheme; a premium arable scheme; and a premium grass scheme. The undertakings given under each of the relevant schemes last for a period of five consecutive years, but, at the request of the farmer, the minister has the power to vary the terms of any undertakings given in accordance with the regulations.

The 1994 regulations have been the subject of amendment on two separate occasions during the course of 1995, see SI 1995/1708 and SI 1995/2095 respectively. As a consequence of these amending regulations, there are now some 32 designated nitrate sensitive areas all of which are shown on maps deposited at the offices of MAFF. In addition, the 1995 regulations have created two new options, an arable woodland scheme option and a set-aside option, which are available to a farmer who wishes to comply with the premium arable scheme in a nitrate sensitive area.

Section 96 of the WRA 1991 supplements the foregoing provisions by empowering the Secretary of State and Ministers to make regulations relating to, inter alia, applications for any consents requisite under any order, conditions which may be imposed, revocations and variations of consents, appeal and dispute resolution mechanisms, charging and registration schemes. By virtue of para 145 to Sch 22 of the Environment Act 1995, in performing the function of determining an appeal under s 96, the Secretary of State may delegate the task to an appointed person in accordance with s 114 of the 1995 Act. It is for the Agency to initiate the designation of WPZs and NSAs by applying to ministers for orders. Schs 11 and 12 of the WRA 1991 lay down the requirements as to publicity for proposals and the procedures for making, receiving and consideration of objections. It should be noted that Sch 12 further provides that the Agency shall not apply for an NSA designation unless it appears to them that pollution is likely to result from the entry of nitrate into controlled waters as a result of agricultural purposes carried out on particular land, *and* that the provisions otherwise in force in relation to that land and those waters are insufficient to prevent or control the ingress of nitrate. It appears that the legislation allows for the creation of NSAs where controls are voluntary — the result of management orders and grant aid, those where controls are mandatory, and those where they are mandatory but where compensation will be payable. It is these powers, that will be used to implement an EU Directive agreed in June 1991 designed to reduce nitrate pollution of drinking and other waters.

Directive 91/676, the Nitrate Directive, has two principal aims: to reduce the level of nitrate from agricultural sources in those areas where water is being polluted as defined by the Directive; and to prevent the new pollution of water from arising. Accordingly, member states are required to identify water catchment areas which have nitrate levels in surface or underground waters of more than 50 parts per million. Areas with high nitrate levels are required by the Directive to be designated as a 'nitrate vulnerable zone' (NVZ). In November 1995, the DoE published the latest in a line of consultation documents on the implementation of the Nitrate Directive. This consultation paper confirmed that ministers were considering a report of the Independent Review Panel which made proposals as to which areas should be designated as NVZs. Of the 217,000 farmers in England and Wales, it is estimated that some 8,000 would be affected by the designation of the zones. In addition, the paper sought comments on the measures which the government proposed to adopt in NVZs. SI 1996/888 now designates 68 NVZs, and measures farmers will have to take should be implemented by 1999.

Under the terms of the Directive, member states are required to establish an action programme detailing the measures which farmers in the NVZs should follow in order to reduce the levels of nitrate. Specific reference is made to the need to include rules concerning matters such as closed periods for the application of fertiliser, manure storage capacity and fertiliser application rates. For organic manures, the Directive states that the application rates should not exceed a nitrogen content of 170 kg per hectare assessed over the farm as a whole. However, for the first four years of the programme, a derogation of 210 kg per hectare is available to the farmer. The outline action programme which appeared in the consultation paper will become binding by regulations by December 1999. It states the basic requirements in NVZs which it is proposed to incorporate in the regulations. These include, inter alia, the requirement that inorganic and organic fertilisers should not be applied to fields during particular times of the year, nor should they be applied to steeply sloping fields or when the soil is waterlogged, flooded, frozen hard or snow covered. Moreover, any new, substantially reconstructed or substantially enlarged installations for the storage of slurry and silage are required to comply with the Control of Pollution (Silage, Slurry and Agricultural Fuel Oil) Regulations 1991, SI 1991/324.

Three further points which arise from the consultation paper are worth noting. First, the paper contains a compliance assessment which describes the financial implications of the Directive for those farmers within designated NVZs. For example, the total compliance costs in meeting the measure and the 170 kg per hectare nitrogen limit are estimated at £10 m. Secondly, the consultation paper points to the fact that whilst the Directive applies in all member states, in certain other states such as the Netherlands and Denmark, the Nitrate Directive is to apply throughout their territory. Therefore, the UK's policy of restricting the designation of NVZs to particular areas is seen to enhance its competitive position in relation to these, its major livestock competitors. Thirdly, it seems that in the light of the foregoing, the Code of Good Agricultural Practice for the Protection of Water, which was issued by MAFF in 1991, will continue to operate on a voluntary basis in non-NVZ areas.

The Water Industry Act 1991

The relevant provisions of the WRA 1991 were, prior to their repeal by the Environment Act 1995, concerned with the structure and functioning of the Environment Agency's predecessor, the NRA, but the privatisation of the water industry created other bodies with aquatic environmental responsibilities. The water, etc, undertakers have responsibilities with regard to sewers, drains, discharges and drinking water, as in certain cases, do local authorities.

These are now principally to be found in the Water Industry Act 1991 (WIA 1991). This deals with the Director General of Water Services, Ofwat and the appointment and regulation of water and sewerage undertakers. It is also concerned with the quality and provision of drinking water and the use and abuse of sewers.

It is important to appreciate both the distinctions and overlaps between the functions of the Agency and the water and sewerage undertakers. The old 'poacher cum gamekeeper' problem that troubled the former water authorities has largely disappeared as a consequence of the creation of the NRA and its successor, the Environment Agency. The Agency is the principal pollution regulatory body while the undertakers are primarily commercial organisations subject to supervision from both the Agency and the Director General and Ofwat. However, the undertakers do have regulatory powers of their own and these can result in a polluting activity being subject to prosecution by both NRA and an undertaker, see *National Rivers Authority v Appletise Bottling, Northumbrian Water v Appletise Bottling*[19] where an unconsented polluting emission damaged both controlled waters and storm drains resulting in a double prosecution. Undertakers have enjoyed something of a privilege in that though their discharges from sewage works were subject to the need for consent, the regime which governed the position before the Water Act 1989 (and now, of course, the Water Resources Act 1991), ie the Control of Pollution Act 1974, was somewhat lenient in that discharge consents usually required only a 95% compliance rate. Thus a treatment plant would not necessarily be in breach of its consent if on a few occasions it transgresses discharge limits. Thus it was possible for a sewerage undertaker to commit serious polluting incidents from time to time and to avoid legal liability. This loophole was closed as from September 1991 in order to comply with EU groundwater requirements.

An historic, and continuing, problem is under investment in the water industry. Polluted rivers will not be cleaned up without the devotion of resources — by the government to the Agency, and by the water companies in appropriate plant and technology. Despite increased charges for water, which it is claimed have risen by 13% since 1991–1992 — and enhanced profits for companies, insufficient resources have been devoted to pollution abatement, while finance has certainly been devoted to diversifying some companies' commercial operations, an issue to be subject to strict Ofwat supervision.

'Water, water everywhere?' (with apologies to both Coleridge and his Ancient Mariner)

Sewers and drains

Part IV of the WIA 1991 deals with sewerage services. Section 94 imposes a general duty on sewerage undertakers (effectively the privatised water companies) to provide a system of public sewers and to cleanse and maintain them, and to make provision for the emptying of sewers by means of sewage disposal works. In performing these duties undertakers must have regard to the needs to allow trade effluent to be discharged into public sewers and to dispose of such discharges.

19 [1991] 3 LMELR 132.

Section 111 of the WIA 1991 places a general prohibition on the throwing, emptying, turning or passing, whether actively or by permission or sufferance, of any matter into any public sewer (or drain or sewer communicating with such a sewer) where that matter is likely to injure the sewer/drain, *or* to interfere with the free flow of its contents, *or* prejudicially to affect the treatment and disposal of its contents. Similar prohibitions are placed on the discharge into sewers of chemical refuse or waste steam, or liquids with a temperature exceeding 110°F which are 'a prohibited substance'. Such substances are those which either alone, or in combination with the contents of the sewer/drain in question, or when heated, are dangerous, or the cause of nuisances, or are injurious, or likely to cause injury, to health. Similar prohibitions are further imposed on the discharge of petroleum spirit or carbide of calcium. 'Petroleum spirit' means crude petroleum, oil or petroleum products or mixtures containing petroleum which give off inflammable vapours at temperatures of less than 73°F. It is an offence to contravene the provisions of the section. In determining for the purposes of actions whether any discharge will prejudicially affect the treatment and disposal of the contents of an affected sewer/drain the issue will turn on the balance of the available scientific evidence, see *Liverpool Corpn v Coghill & Son Ltd.*[20]

Trade effluents

The foregoing provision is, however, expressly subject to Part III of the WIA 1991 which relates to trade effluents. Section 118 of the WIA 1991 allows the occupier of any trade premises in a sewerage undertaker's area to discharge trade effluent via drains or sewers into public sewers *subject to* the undertaker's consent — unconsented discharges constitute offences. Likewise s 106 permits, *as to right*, occupiers of premises to have their drains and sewers connect with an undertaker's sewers and to discharge *surface* (including storm) water and foul water (including domestic sewage) into those sewers. On the basis of a Scottish case concerned with a near equivalent of s 106, s 12 of the Sewerage (Scotland) Act 1968, it would seem that the fact that a public sewer is already overloaded will not necessarily entitle an undertaker to refuse a connection, see *Tayside Regional Council v Secretary of State for Scotland.*[21] Trade effluent is defined by WIA 1991, s 141 as liquids produced wholly or partly in the course of trade or industry at any premises, while trade premises are those used or intended to be used for carrying on any trade or industry, including those used for agricultural, horticultural, piscicultural, scientific research or experimental purposes. 'Trade' has been widely construed so that a launderette is 'trade premises', see *Thames Water Authority v Blue and White Launderettes Ltd.*[1]

Trade effluent consents

Section 119 of the WIA 1991 lays down the general procedure for obtaining the requisite consent. The relevant owner/occupier of trade premises must serve notice on the undertaker stating the nature and composition of the trade

---

20 [1918] 1 Ch 307.
21 (1995) Times, 28 January.
 1 [1980] 1 WLR 700.

effluent, the maximum quantity of daily discharge and the highest proposed rate of discharge. However, some effluents are categorised as 'special', and where an application to discharge any of these is received the undertaker must (unless they refuse consent) further refer the matter to the Environment Agency asking whether the discharge should be prohibited or whether special conditions should be imposed on any consent. The would-be discharger must be informed of the reference, see s 120. By virtue of the new s 120(9) inserted by the Environment Act 1995, an undertaker commits an offence if they fail to make a referral to the Agency within a period of two months from the date on which the notice containing the application was served on them. Where a consent to make discharges of special category effluent has been granted in contravention of sub-s (9), the Agency may exercise its powers of review under ss 127 and 131, WIA 1991, see new s 120(10).

This provision gives the Environment Agency considerable control over trade effluent discharges and enables a precautionary policy on water protection to be applied, and also implements the requirements of Directive 76/464 on dangerous substances, as defined by WIA 1991, s 138, the Trade Effluents (Prescribed Processes and Substances) Regulations SI 1989/1156 (as amended by SI 1990/1629 — the 'red list') and the Trade Effluents (Prescribed Processes and Substances) Regulations SI 1992/339. A principal objective underlying the creation of the Environment Agency was to reduce the instances of overlap of functions as between the various environmental agencies. Accordingly, the additional role which HMIP played in dealing with consents in respect of discharges of substances on the list will no longer be necessary, although for the time being, the relevant statutory consent and authorisation systems remain extant, no doubt awaiting attention at some later date. The Environment Act 1995 has made changes to s 28 of the Environmental Protection Act 1990 by, inter alia, repealing s 28(3) under which the former NRA had the power to veto the discharge of a red list substance under an IPC authorisation where that discharge would result in, or contribute to, failure to achieve quality objectives for the medium of water.

Section 139 of the WIA 1991 enables the Secretary of State by order to apply the powers over trade effluents to other effluents. It should also be noted that Sch 8 of the 1991 Act generally preserves discharge authorisation and agreements made before the coming into effect of the Water Act 1989 as deemed consents. However, such 'old' authorisations, etc, are subject to the 1991 Act's powers of cancellation, replacement and variation, with the necessary provision for appeals against such changes being made. See further on s 132, etc, of the WIA 1991 below.

Sewerage undertakers themselves have powers under WIA 1991, s 121 to impose discharge consent conditions relating to the sewers into which any discharge of any trade effluent may take place, the nature and composition of discharges, maximum quantities of discharges and discharge rates. With regard to discharges of trade effluent from trade premises further conditions may relate to the daily timing of discharges; exclusion of condensing water from discharges; elimination or diminution of specified constituents of effluents where the constituent, alone or in combination with other matter, would injure or obstruct sewers or make the treatment or disposal of sewage from such sewers specially difficult or expensive or, in relation to sewer outfalls into harbours or tidal waters, would cause injury to navigation, etc; temperature of discharges, their acidity/alkalinity; payment for discharges; provision and maintenance of inspection facilities and meters and sampling and monitoring equipment; keeping of records of discharges, and the making of returns. Payment conditions must, under s 121(4), reflect the nature, composition, volume and rate of discharges, the costs of undertakers in receiving discharges and any revenue they are likely to derive from effluents. Breach of discharge consent conditions constitutes an offence.

Persons aggrieved by refusals to give consents, or by failures to give them within due time (two months from the day after the date of service of notice of application to discharge) or by any discharge consent condition may appeal to the Director General of Water Services who has a wide discretion under s 122 of the WIA 1991 to grant consents, and impose or vary conditions. Under s 137 the Director General may refer any issue of law on appeal to the High Court, this also applies to s 126 proceedings, see below.

Section 124 of the WIA empowers sewerage undertakers to vary, annul or add discharge conditions by direction, though this is subject to a *general* restriction that such variations may not be made within two years of consent being given. Notice of proposed directions must be given to the owners/occupiers of relevant premises, and, under s 126, there is a right of appeal to the Director General of Water Services against the direction in relation to which again the Director possesses a wide discretion. The time restriction on variation restrictions does not, under WIA 1991, s 125, apply to proposed changes considered necessary by the undertaker in order to provide proper protection for persons likely to be affected by relevant discharges, but such a course of action normally involves the payment of compensation to the discharger unless it is necessary to make the change in consequence of changes of circumstances otherwise than other discharge consents given which have occurred within the period of two years from the date of consent and which could not reasonably have been foreseen at the time of consent. (Similar compensation requirements relate to the powers of the Environment Agency to review discharge consents in certain cases, see s 134, as amended.)

Note also the power in WIA 1991, s 128 to enable an undertaker to apply to the Director General for a postponement of a date specified for a discharge of trade effluent on the grounds that, inter alia, because of failure to complete works in connection with the reception and disposal of the discharge, a later date ought to be set.

The Director General, it is clear, has extensive powers under the provisions examined above. They are, however, subject to the powers of the Environment Agency in certain cases falling within s 123 of the Act. Effectively where a s 122 appeal is made and the case is one in which a 'special category of effluent' reference should have been made to the Agency, the Director General may not determine the appeal unless he first submits the matter to the Agency and has received notice of the Agency's determination on the issue. The Environment Agency also has extensive powers to review consents relating to 'special category' discharges under WIA 1991, s 127. Constraints exist on the exercise of this power in that the Agency may not review a consent unless one of the following applies.

1 The consent has not been previously reviewed and was given before 1 September 1989.

2   A period of more than two years has elapsed since the time when notice of the Environment Agency's determination on a reference relating to the consent was served.
3   There has been since the time of service of such a notice a contravention of any requirement of a consent.

These constraints do *not* apply where a review is carried out to enable the UK to comply with EU or international legal obligations or otherwise to protect public health or flora or fauna dependent on an aquatic environment.

Under WIA 1991, s 132 where any reference or review is made under ss 120, 123 or 127 (see above) or under ss 130 or 131 (see below) the Environment Agency must before making a determination allow relevant owners/occupiers of trade premises and the undertaker to make representations/objections to the Agency and must consider any such as are made. Once the determination is made the parties and the Director General must be informed by notice stating the conclusions and determinations of the Agency, and it is then the duty of the undertaker and the Director General under s 133 to give effect to the Agency's determination. An undertaker who fails to perform this duty is guilty of an offence, see new s 133(5) inserted by the Environment Act 1995. Moreover, in order to secure compliance with a s 132 notice, the Environment Agency is empowered by virtue of new s 133(6) to serve notice on the undertaker and owners/occupiers of trade premises that any consent to make discharges of special category effluent or any agreement under s 129 (see below) may be varied or revoked.

Section 129 of the WIA 1991 confers a general power on undertakers to make agreements for the reception and disposal of trade effluents with the owners/occupiers of any trade premises within their areas. Such an agreement may authorise discharges otherwise needing consent. However, such an agreement must be referred to the Environment Agency under s 130 where special category effluent is concerned for the Agency's determination as to whether the operations necessary under the agreement should be prohibited or whether any further requirements should be imposed. Once more, the Environment Act 1995 has made it an offence for an undertaker to fail to comply with a statutory duty. See new s 130(7). Where the Agency becomes aware of an agreement relating to special category effluent which has not been referred to it, the Agency may proceed as if the reference had been made, see new s 130(8). The Agency's power under s 131, WIA 1991 to review such agreements is subject to the same constraints as the power to review consents contained in s 127. However, both these powers of review may be exercised by the Agency notwithstanding these constraints where an undertaker has failed to comply with the duty to refer the consent or agreement to the Agency, see new s 130(9).

In order that it may discharge its functions under Chapter III of Part IV of the WIA 1991, new s 135A, inserted by para 113 of Sch 22 to the Environment Act 1995, confers a power on the Environment Agency to require of any person such information as the Agency reasonably considers it needs for this purpose. It is an offence to fail, without reasonable excuse, to comply with such a requirement or knowingly or recklessly to make a false or misleading statement when providing information. The penalty for a summary conviction is a fine not exceeding the statutory maximum, whilst a conviction on indictment may result in a fine or a term of imprisonment not exceeding two years, or both.

Section 196 imposes a duty on undertakers to maintain publicly available registers of discharge consents, any directions given and all agreements made. Section 202 imposes a duty on undertakers to furnish the Secretary of State with such relevant information as he may reasonably require, though s 206 imposes restrictions otherwise on the disclosure of information. These provisions are very similar to the corresponding measures under the WRA 1991, as is the s 208 power of the Secretary of State to give directions in the national security to undertakers, and the provision as to offences by bodies corporate, s 210.

Drinking water

Chapter III of Part III of the WIA 1991 is concerned with the quality and sufficiency of supplies of water. Section 67 of the WIA 1991 provides that the Secretary of State may make regulations as to whether water supplied to premises is/is not to be regarded as 'wholesome' by reference to prescribed requirements. 'Wholesome' so far as the courts are concerned appears to mean safe and pleasant to drink, see *McColl v Strathclyde Regional Council*.[2] The regulations may make both general and specific requirements as to the quality of water, substances present in it, and its characteristics. Sampling techniques may also be specified. The Secretary of State may also authorise departures from prescribed requirements, though these may be subject to conditions. The regulatory powers exist to fulfil obligations under Directive 80/778 on the quality of drinking water, earlier attempts by the UK to meet its obligations by administrative measures only, eg DoE Circular 20/82, having been of dubious legality. The current regulations are the Water Supply (Water Quality) Regulations SI 1989/1147 amended by SI 1989/1383 and SI 1991/1837. These provide mandatory standards for domestic drinking, washing and cooking water and water used for food production. The standards include the EU requirements together with further UK requirements. Monitoring and sampling requirements are also laid down, as are provisions as to information and registers to be made publicly available and annual reports. The regulations also make provision for certain relaxations of standards by the Secretary of State on an application by an undertaker, subject to a right for local authorities to make representations.

The Private Water Supplies Regulations SI 1991/2790, which impose quality requirements on waters from private sources or waters which are supplied by an unlicensed supplier, are substantially the same as the 1989 Regulations discussed above, save for the monitoring requirements which they lay down. These divide private water supplies into either Category 1 or Category 2 supplies depending on whether the water is supplied for domestic or food production purposes, and impose a duty on the local authority to take and analyse samples from each category in their area. Where the private supply is found to be unwholesome or insufficient, the local authority may serve a notice on the owner/occupiers of the premises which is either using the supply

2 [1984] JPL 351.

or is the place where the source is located or on any party which exercises powers of management and control in relation to the source, specifying the remedial action that is necessary, see further below.

Section 68 of the WIA 1991 imposes a duty on water undertakers (the privatised water companies) to ensure that water supplied to any premises for domestic or food production purposes is wholesome at the time of supply and, so far as is reasonably practicable, to ensure in relation to each source of supply of water, or combination thereof, from which such water is supplied that there is no deterioration in the quality of supply from time to time. In *R v Secretary of State for the Environment, ex p Friends of the Earth*,[3] which was discussed earlier in this chapter, the undertakings which the Secretary of State accepted from Thames and Anglian Water in accordance with s 19(1)(b), WIA 1991 were that the water companies would meet their obligations under Directive 80/778 and comply with the duty under s 68(1) to supply wholesome water. These duties may be enforced by the Secretary of State under WIA 1991, s 18.

It is an offence under s 70 of the 1991 Act for an undertaker to supply water unfit for human consumption, though defences include that the undertaker had no reasonable grounds for suspecting water supplied would be used for human consumption, or that all reasonable steps were taken and all due diligence exercised to secure that the water was fit at the point of leaving the undertaker's pipes, or, if not fit, was not consumed by humans. The Secretary of State and the DPP only may institute proceedings under this provision. Severn Trent Water has become the first water company to be convicted of charges brought under s 70 in respect of premises in the Worcester area which were found to have contaminated water present. In *Drinking Water Inspectorate and Secretary of State v Severn Trent Water*,[4] the Crown Court found that Severn Trent's failure to take sufficient steps to avert contamination resulted in their supplying to three premises, a bakery, a children's home and Lea & Perrins, water which was unfit for human consumption. Accordingly, they were fined £45,000 and ordered to pay £67,000 costs. The case is of particular interest in the context of the WIA 1991 since it draws a distinction between the 'fitness' and the 'wholesomeness' of water. It would appear that water may be 'unfit' for human consumption for the purposes of the Act despite the fact that it is 'wholesome' within the meaning of the drinking water standard regulations and does not pose a risk to public health. In a further case, *Secretary of State for Wales v DWR CYMRU*,[5] Welsh Water was found guilty of an offence contrary to regulation 28 of the Water Supply (Water Quality) Regulations 1989 where it failed to observe the conditions of approval for use of an epoxy resin material used for the internal relining of water mains. Despite the fact that no evidence was adduced to show that drinking water quality was affected once the main was returned to service, Welsh Water's failure to carry out the necessary checks in accordance with the conditions of approval ensured that the company could not be certain that consumers had not been exposed to any risk.

3 [1996] 1 CMLR 117.
4 (1995) Independent, 25 April, (1995) 243 ENDS Report 45.
5 (1995) 242 ENDS Report 45.

Outside the statutory framework, it appears that there may be residual liability in public nuisance for the supply of unwholesome water. This was the offence charged in *R v South West Water Authority*,[6] following the accidental and mistaken placing of aluminium sulphate into a tank of water intended for public supply in the Camelford area of Cornwall. A number of customers suffered various ill effects in consequence, and up to 5,000 people were affected in some way. The authority, which by then had ceased to exist due to the privatisation of water authorities under the Water Act 1989, was ultimately found guilty of committing a public nuisance in respect of its actions and accordingly fined £10,000 and ordered to pay £25,000 costs. The relatively low level of the fine despite the seriousness of the polluting incident was justified by the Crown Court on the basis that the authority's guilt was limited to their tardiness in tackling the pollution.

The Secretary of State has a further power under WIA 1991, s 69 to make regulations to ensure compliance with the s 68 duty to supply wholesome water. In particular regulations may impose obligations on undertakers, inter alia, to:

1 Monitor and record the wholesomeness of water supplies to premises.
2 Monitor and record the quality of water sources.
3 Ensure water sources are not used until prescribed requirements for establishing water quality have been complied with.
4 Comply with requirements as to water analysis.
5 Forbid the use of certain processes or substances, or to require them to conform to standards.
6 Publish information about water quality.
7 Act with regard to the use of specified processes and substances and products containing such substances as might affect water quality.

See, again, SI 1989/1147 and SI 1989/1384. Section 86 of the WIA 1991 enables the Secretary of State to appoint assessors (the Drinking Water Inspectorate) of water quality to assist him in his duties in this regard, see further (1991) 198 ENDS Report p 18.

Special provision is made by the WIA 1991 for combating the contamination or waste of water. Under s 71 it is an offence to cause or allow any underground water to run to waste from any well, borehole or other work, or to abstract from any such well, etc, water in excess of reasonable requirements. Section 76 further enables water undertakers if of opinion that there is, or is threatened, a serious water deficiency, to prohibit the use of hosepipes for watering gardens or washing cars, ie a 'hose pipe ban'. Such bans must be publicly advertised before coming into force, thereafter contravention of the ban constitutes an offence. Section 72 creates an offence of committing any act of neglect whereby the water in any waterworks likely to be used for human domestic purposes or food production is or is likely to be polluted. The offence does not extend to prohibit any method of land cultivation in accordance with the principles of good husbandry or the use by highway authorities of oil or tar on public highways. Section 73 further makes it an offence for any owner or occupier of premises to cause or permit (intentionally or negligently) any of his water fittings to be so out of repair or so misused as to lead to the contamination or waste of water, and s 74 supplements this by enabling the Secretary of State to make regulations concerning water fittings in order to prevent the waste or contamination of water, while s 75 confers emergency power on undertakers to prevent damage to persons or property or the contamination or waste of water.

Local authorities (districts and London boroughs) are under a duty by virtue of WIA 1991, to be informed about the wholesomeness and sufficiency of water supplies in their areas, and they have certain other powers and functions, in the exercise of which they are subject to the direction of the Secretary of State, see s 77(2). For this and other connected purposes the Secretary of State has power to make regulations under s 77(3) imposing duties and conferring powers on local authorities with respect to information gathering and regulating the performance of their functions. In this connection see Part VIII of SI 1989/1147, and note in particular that water undertakers are required to inform local and district health authorities of events threatening water supplies by giving rise to significant health risks. Authorities are furthermore required by WIA 1991, s 78 to notify undertakers of anything which appears to them to suggest that any supply of water is, or has been, or is likely to be unwholesome or insufficient for domestic purposes, that the unwholesomeness or insufficiency is likely to endanger life or health or otherwise to lead to the breach of the duty to supply wholesome water. If an authority then becomes dissatisfied as to remedial action on the part of the undertaker they must refer the matter to the Secretary of State because he is the enforcing body with respect to undertakers.

Local authorities, however, have remedial powers over private water supplies to premises within their areas. Under WIA 1991, s 80 where satisfied a private supply is not wholesome or is insufficient, they may serve notice on a 'relevant person', ie owners and occupiers of the premises and of the source of supply. This notice *must* give details of why it has been served and must specify necessary remedial works and the time within which representations and objections responding to the notice may be made. The notice *may*, inter alia, require the person served to take specified steps within specified periods, or it may designate certain action to be taken by the authority themselves. Requisite steps may include ensuring that an adequate supply of wholesome water to the premises is provided by an undertaker or some other person. Where such a 'private supply notice' is served and objections are received and not withdrawn the local authority, if they wish the notice to proceed, must submit the matter to the Secretary of State. He then has a wide discretion, under s 81, to confirm, quash or vary the notice, or to direct the local authority as to the issue of notices, and to this end he may cause a local inquiry to be held. Once a private supply notice is in force it 'runs with the land' and its subsequent enforcement and/or variation is a matter for the local authority, see WIA 1991, s 82. In connection with their functions under the 1991 Act authorities are also granted extensive powers of entry and to obtain information by ss 84 and 85.

Supplemental

Section 92 of the WIA 1991 enables the Secretary of State to make regulations modifying the Act to give effect to EU or international legal obligations; while the Crown is *generally* subject to the legislation under s 222 of the WRA and s 221 of the WIA. These Acts came into force on 1 December 1991.

The future

The creation of the new Environment Agency with its wide powers and its various duties and obligations in relation to the discharge of its many functions will of course have an effect upon the way in which the aqueous environment is protected. It is to be hoped that the establishment of such a body will go some considerable way to achieving the objective of a 'fully integrated, effective and multi-media approach to pollution control', but inevitably only time will tell whether the Agency performs the tasks of water resource management and water pollution control any more effectively than did its predecessor, the NRA.

The water companies have been the subject of heated political debate during recent times with the suggestion from the opposition parties that the government has failed to protect the consumer from a 40% rise in water prices since the industry was privatised some five years ago.[7] In response to such arguments, the government has contended that privatisation has resulted in an investment in the water industry to the tune of £15 billion. Whilst such debates seem likely to continue, it is interesting to remember a Private Member's Bill which was reported to have the backing of both the government and the NRA[8] and would have sought to limit abstractions from rivers as well as setting mandatory targets for the prevention and repair of leaks by water companies. In view of the criticism levelled primarily at Yorkshire Water during the course of the summer of 1995 for its failure to make adequate provision for dealing with leakages, such mandatory targets could well be a stimulus for action, provided that is that they are set at appropriately rigorous levels.

A final point to note in relation to the domestic scene is that the old NRA announced that it was to put into effect a pilot scheme in eight of its regions with the aim of setting legally binding water quality targets. In each of the relevant river catchments, the Agency would thus have the power under the WRA 1991 to firm up the terms of any discharge consents which have been granted in order to ensure that the quality objectives are met. It is reported however, that the targets would be set at levels which are considered to be reasonable to achieve.[9]

Further legislative initiatives from Europe to deal with the protection of the water environment appear to be on the agenda for the future. The EU Council has issued a proposed Directive which would replace Directive 76/160, the Bathing Water Directive. Foremost among the revised provisions is a new classification of bathing water as being of 'excellent quality' where 'guide' rather than imperative standards laid down in the Directive are satisfied. In addition, a member state will be required to display information at each bathing water site indicating, inter alia, whether the bathing water complied

7 See, for example, The Times, 31 January 1996.
8 The Times, 15 December 1995.
9 Environment Business, 31 January 1996.

with the Directive last bathing season and the quality of the bathing water during the current bathing season. In the event that pollution constitutes a threat to public health, the proposed Directive requires a member state to prohibit bathing at the bathing area in question. It is to be hoped that any new EU provision on bathing waters will not pose the same problems in terms of implementation which have arisen in relation to the current Bathing Water Directive. However, the fact that the Council's proposed measure retains the same 'I' standard for viruses as Directive 76/160 immediately raises questions in the light of *Ex p Moreton* discussed earlier in this chapter.

Finally, in this look ahead to the future, the European Commission has submitted a proposal for a Council Directive on the ecological quality of water to take effect from the end of 1997 at the latest [OJ 94/C 222/06]. The proposal concerns the adoption of measures by member states for the control of pollution of surface waters from point sources, sources of diffuse pollution and other anthropogenic factors having an effect on surface water quality. Unlike other EU Water Directives, the proposal affords member states the opportunity to work out the detailed content of the legislation at national or regional level. In relation to surface waters, the proposal requires member states to: set up a measuring and monitoring system to determine the ecological quality of surface waters; identify and conduct a qualitative and quantitative assessment of both point sources and diffuse pollution in such waters; notify the public of the findings of the monitoring and assessment process; define operational targets for good ecological water quality; adopt, publish and implement integrated programmes for the purpose of improving the quality of surface waters, making use of economic instruments where appropriate.

In addition, the proposed Directive requires member states to carry out checks on the implementation of the Directive and then report accordingly to the Commission on a triennial basis. Interestingly, since it is felt that the effect of this Directive will be to achieve a level of protection of surface waters at least equivalent to that provided by Directive 78/659 and Directive 79/923, it is proposed that these measures are to be repealed with effect from 1 January 1999.

C MARINE NATURE RESERVES

Under the Wildlife and Countryside Act 1981, ss 36 and 37, English Nature, etc, have power to make applications to the Secretary of State concerning land covered by tidal or sea waters in or adjacent to Great Britain or its territorial waters. If it appears expedient to the Secretary of State that such land should be managed by the appropriate Council so as to conserve marine flora, fauna, geological or physiological features of special interest, or to provide special opportunities for studying and researching such matters, he may, by order, designate the land and its waters as a marine nature reserve. Before making such an order he must under Sch 12 to the 1981 Act: consult with appropriate persons; prepare a draft order, giving notice that he proposes to make it and stating its general effect, naming a place in the relevant locality where it may be inspected, and specifying a period of at least 28 days during which representations or objections may be made.

The Secretary of State's proposal must be published in the London Gazette and in at least one local newspaper, and must be served on persons having interests in affected land, relevant authorities for the area and other prescribed or appropriate bodies including the Agency and relevant water and sewerage undertakers. His proposal must also be displayed locally. An unopposed order may be confirmed with or without modification. Opposed orders must be made subject to a hearing or local inquiry, at which representations heard must be considered before the order is made, with or without modification.

After making the order the Secretary of State must, as soon as practicable, give further notice describing its effect and stating its date of commencement, naming a place in the locality where the order can be inspected freely, and where copies may be obtained at reasonable cost. Notice must be served on those who were served with notice of the initial proposal, etc. Proceedings over the legality of orders must be commenced within 42 days of the date of publication of notice of the effect and commencement of the order.

English Nature may, under s 37, with the consent of the Secretary of State, make byelaws to protect marine nature reserves and their contents against entry, disturbance, destruction, molestation, removal or pollution by rubbish deposition. Applications by English Nature under s 36 must be accompanied by a copy of byelaws proposed for the reserve. An order made under s 36 authorises the making of the proposed byelaws without need for further central consent. Byelaws may provide for permits to enter reserves, but may not prohibit or restrict rights of passage of vessels other than pleasure boats, nor prohibit exercise of such rights by pleasure boats except with respect to particular parts of the reserve at particular times of the year. Nothing in the byelaws may make unlawful: anything done for securing vessel safety, or to prevent damage to any vessel or cargo, or to save life; discharging any substance from a vessel; or anything done more than 30m below the seabed. Under s 36(6) nothing under s 36 or byelaws made under s 37, is to interfere with the function of a relevant authority (which includes local authorities, water authorities, harbour authorities, etc), nor any functions conferred by an enactment or any right of any person. The marine nature reserve powers are seriously limited by these exceptions.

D PLANNING AND WATER POLLUTION

The legitimacy of using planning powers for purposes covered by water legislation is questionable. A restraint on development policy may be justifiable in order to preserve the existing high quality of water in a river or estuary, or to prevent further deterioration in an already polluted stretch of water. The Secretary of State for the Environment may be unwilling, however, to allow planning authorities to trespass on the preserves of the Environment Agency and water undertakers, though collaboration between them is another matter. An example of this was the consultation between Leicestershire County Council and the Severn Trent Water Authority in the preparation of the Leicestershire Minerals Subject Plan. Consultation began some time before the plan was made to satisfy the water authority that the county council was aware of the need to protect water resources, means of water supply and land drainage issues. In particular the authority declared itself in favour of planning policies normally leading to refusal of planning permission in respect of an extraction that could prejudice water resources. The authority also acknowledged that, despite the existence of other statutory controls, planning control is an essential feature of the protection of water courses and resources. This is especially true with regard to incorporating provision for pollution control in the after care requirements in a mineral planning permission, or, more appropriately, an obligation. DoE Circular 17/91 gives advice to planning authorities on developments involving water industry investment, including counselling 'sympathetic' consideration of proposals to enhance the treatment of sewage, and 'expedited' handling of applications in respect of water treatment works needed to meet legal obligations, eg under EU law.

In certain cases planning authorities are under an obligation to consult the Environment Agency before granting planning permission, see the Town and Country Planning (General Development Procedure) Order 1995, SI 1995/419, arts 10(1)(k), (p)–(t) and (y) which apply to: development involving or including mining operations; the carrying out of works or operations in the bed of or on the banks of a river or stream; development for the purpose of refining or storing mineral oils and their derivatives; using land for the deposit of refuse or waste; development relating to the retention, treatment or disposal of sewage, trade-waste, slurry or sludge; using land as a cemetery; and, development for the purposes of fish farming.

E LAND DRAINAGE

Drainage of rural land became an environmental issue in the 1980s, see Pye-Smith and Rose *Crisis and Conservation: Conflict in the British Countryside* pp 36–39. The powers are to be found in the Land Drainage Act 1991. Briefly, Part I of the Act states the various bodies involved in land drainage. The Environment Agency has general supervisory powers over drainage functions under s 7 of the Land Drainage Act 1991, and without Agency consent water may not be discharged into a main river except by way of maintenance of existing works. The 'on the ground' work is carried out by internal drainage boards who, under s 1 of the 1991 Act, supervise all drainage work within their districts, ie those areas as 'will derive benefit, or avoid danger, as a result of drainage operations'. Though such boards are initially ministerially appointed provision is made by Sch 1 of the Act for their subsequent partial election, though the franchise is very limited. Relevant ministers (the Secretary of State and the Minister of Agriculture), the Agency and internal drainage boards are, by virtue of s 61A of the Land Drainage Act 1991 (inserted by the Land Drainage Act 1994) under a general duty in relation to drainage board functions to further the conservation, and enhancement of natural beauty and of flora, fauna and geological and physiographical features of special interest; to protect and conserve historic and architecturally interesting buildings and to have regard to the effect any proposals would have on urban or rural habitats. There is also a duty to preserve and enhance recreational enjoyment. Internal drainage boards may also be subject to notification of the existence of an SSSI, see s 61C of the Land Drainage Act 1991 (inserted by the Land Drainage Act 1994), and thereafter may not carry out works likely to damage flora or fauna, etc, without consultation with the appropriate notifying authority, eg English Nature. A similar obligation applies to land in National Parks and The Broads.

Even allowing for the foregoing environmental duties, boards have extensive drainage powers to maintain, improve and construct new land drainage works. In relation to 'main rivers' (ie those shown on a 'main river map') such drainage functions belong to the Agency by virtue of s 107 of the WRA 1991. The drainage powers include that to dispose of spoil by deposition, see s 15 of the Land Drainage Act 1991, though compensation may be payable for any injury caused, see *Marriage v East Norfolk Rivers Catchment Board*.[10] Similar drainage powers are also conferred on local authorities, and the Agency has powers, as do local authorities, under s 18, to carry out small area drainage works where it would not be practicable to constitute an internal drainage board. Drainage boards have powers also to control the erection of mills, dams, weirs and culverts likely to affect the flow of watercourses, see ss 23 and 24, and to require works to be done to maintain a watercourse's flow, see ss 25 and 26. Part IV Chapter II of the Land Drainage Act 1991 authorises the levying of rates to finance drainage, while s 62 confers compulsory purchase powers on drainage boards, and s 64 grants them powers of entry. Section 66 enables boards to make byelaws in connection with their functions. Development by a drainage body consisting of works on, in or under a watercourse for its improvement, maintenance or repair have 'permitted development' status under Sch 2, Part 14 of the Town and Country Planning (General Permitted Development) Order 1995, while Part 15 confers similar rights on the Environment Agency.

F RESERVOIR CONSTRUCTION

Section 155 of the WIA 1991 confers compulsory purchase powers on water and sewerage undertakers, the procedure in such cases being, generally, that under the Acquisition of Land Act 1981. Though, however, water undertakers have certain development rights under Sch 2, Part 17, Class E of the Town and Country Planning (General Permitted Development) Order 1995, the construction of reservoirs on land acquired generally requires planning permission.

Use of these powers has been controversial. Some argue water authorities are allowed to create large new reservoirs too easily and wastefully, swallowing up great acreages of land and dramatically changing landscapes. See Pye-Smith and Rose in *Crisis and Conservation: Conflict in the British Countryside*, and note that purpose-built reservoirs occupy 22,500 hectares of land in the UK. The Kielder reservoir in Northumberland covers 1,086 hectares, holding 4.1 billion litres of water. Rutland Water is even larger at 1,500 hectares. Ann and Malcolm McEwan add in *National Parks: Conservation or Cosmetics?* that 29% of the land surface of the Peak National Park is given over to water catchment. In the Brecon Beacons there are 16 reservoirs supplying the water demands of South Wales. During the debates on the Water Bill in 1989, however, it was made clear in the House of Lords that a good case for compulsory acquisition would have to be made out by an undertaker, and that

10 [1950] 1 KB 284, [1949] 2 All ER 1021.

a public inquiry would examine any opposed acquisition. Water undertakers may prefer to acquire land by agreement in such circumstances.

Important safety provisions with regard to reservoirs are contained in the Reservoirs Act 1975, which applies to 'large raised reservoirs', that is those capable of holding 25,000 cubic metres of water or more _above_ the natural level of any land adjoining the reservoir. The Act also applies to reservoirs altered so as to increase capacity to above 25,000 cubic metres, and to artificial lakes, etc, provided they are of appropriate capacity, _but not_ mine or quarry lagoons within the meaning of the Mines and Quarries (Tips) Act 1969, or canals, etc. Under s 2 of the 1975 Act local authorities, generally county councils as enforcing bodies, must set up public registers of relevant reservoirs, and must obtain relevant information from reservoir undertakers. Undertakers are under a duty to give information under s 24 of the Act, and s 21 further requires them to furnish authorities with information about reservoirs constructed, altered, abandoned, or brought back into use.

Reservoir undertakers are under obligations to ensure safety in the construction, alteration, supervision and regular monitoring of relevant reservoirs by the employment of qualified civil engineers, and authorities have general and specific enforcement powers in relation to the appointment of appropriate engineers, inspection and supervision of reservoirs, discontinuance, abandonment and reuse of reservoirs, see ss 6, 8, 9, 10, 11, 12, 13, 14 and 19 of the Act. Where a reservoir owner is unknown and cannot be found, or where he has no funds to maintain the reservoir as required by the Act, authorities may carry out safety works under s 15, and s 16 grants powers to act in emergencies. Section 3 of the Act requires authorities to make reports on their functions to the Secretary of State.

For regulations concerning the implementation of the Act see SI 1985/177 on reports and records, as amended by SI 1985/548, 1984/1874, 1985/175, 1985/1086, and 1989/1186 on the appointment of civil engineers, SI 1986/468 on certificates, reports and prescribed information.

Further reading

BOOKS

Abecassis, DW, and Jarashow, RL, _Oil Pollution from Ships_ (1985) Stevens.

Bates, JH, _United Kingdom Marine Pollution Law_ (1985) Lloyd's of London Press Ltd.

Birnie, P, and Boyle, A, _Basic Documents on International Law and the Environment_ (1995) OUP.

Churchill, R, Warren, L, and Gibson, J, _Law, Policy and the Environment_ pp 95–109 (1991) Basil Blackwell.

Hawkins, K, _Environment and Enforcement_ (1984) OUP.

Howarth, W, _Water Pollution Law_ (1988 & 1990 Supplement) Shaw and Sons.

Krämer, L, _EC Treaty and Environmental Law_ (1995) Sweet & Maxwell.

Pye-Smith, C, and Rose, C, _Crisis and Conservation_ (1983) chapter 2 Penguin Books.

Richardson, G, Ogus, A, and Burrows, P, _Policing Pollution_ (1983) OUP.

Saetevik, S, _Environmental Co-operation Between The North Sea States_ (1988) Belhaven.

JOURNALS

Land Management and Environmental Law Report/Environmental Law and Management

Bates, I, 'Water Quality: The New Regime' [1990] 1 LMELR 156.

Forster, M, 'The Third International Conference on the North Sea: International Concerns and Domestic Solutions' [1990] 2 LMELR 12.

Forster, M, 'Nitrate Sensitive Areas — Too Voluntary a Settlement?' [1990] 2 LMELR 48.

Forster, M, 'Bathed in Confusion?' [1990] 2 LMELR 83.

Forster, M, 'Enforcing the Drinking Water Directive' [1991] 3 LMELR 56.

Hughes, D, 'The NRA Scheme of Charges in Respect of Discharges into Controlled Waters' [1991] 3 LMELR 115.

Jewell, T, 'Agricultural Water Pollution Issues and NRA Enforcement Policy' [1991] 3 LMELR 110.

Poustie, M, 'The demise of coal and causing water pollution' [1994] 6 ELM 95.

Warn, T, 'Discharge Consents: how they are set and enforced' [1994] 6 ELM 32.

Water Law

Ball, S, 'Protected Nature Conservation Sites and The Water Industry' [1990] 1 Water Law 74.

Collins, K, 'The directive on municipal waste water treatment' [1991] 2 Water Law 116.

Howarth, W, 'Reappraisal of the Bathing Water Directive' [1991] 2 Water Law 51.

Howarth, W, 'Fish farming in the UK' [1991] 2 Water Law 92.

Howarth, W, and Somsen, H, 'The EC Nitrates Directive' [1991] 2 Water Law 149.

Kodwo Bentil, J, 'Nature of obligations imposed by EEC Clean Water Directives' [1991] 2 Water Law 200.

McGillivray, D, 'Discharge Consents and the Unforeseen' [1995] 6 Water Law 72 and 101.

Somsen, H, 'EC Water Directives' [1990] 1 Water Law 93.

Wathern, P, 'Environmental Impact Assessment and the Water Industry' [1991] 2 Water Law 27.

Wilkinson, D, 'Causing and Knowingly Permitting Pollution Offences: A Review' [1993] 4 Water Law 25.

Journal of Environmental Law

Ball, S, 'Causing Water Pollution' [1993] 5 JEL 128.

Burchi, S, 'Current Developments and Trends in the Law and Administration of Water Resources: A Comparative State-of-the-Art Appraisal' [1991] 3 JEL 69.

Howarth, W, 'Water Pollution: Improving the Legal Controls' [1989] 1 JEL 25.

Lomas, O, 'The Prosecution of Marine Oil Pollution Offences and the Practice of Insuring against Fines' [1989] 1 JEL 48.

Utilities Law Review

Byatt, ICR, 'The Office of Water Services: Structure and Policy' [1990] 1 ULR 85.

Monthly reference should also be made to The ENDS Report published by Environmental Data Services.

OFFICIAL REPORTS

'Bathing Water Quality in England and Wales — 1994', NRA Water Quality Series No 22, HMSO 1995.

'Discharge Consents and Compliance: the NRA's Approach to Control of Discharges to Water', NRA Water Quality Series No 17, HMSO 1994.

'Implementation of the EC Freshwater Fish Directive', NRA Water Quality Series No 20, HMSO 1994.

'National Rivers Authority: River Pollution from Farms in England', National Audit Office, HMSO 1995.

'Nitrate in Water', House of Lords Select Committee on the European Communities 16th Report, Session 1988–89 HL Paper 73–1.

'Pesticides in Major Aquifers', NRA Research and Development Report No 17, HMSO 1995.

'Policy and Practice for the Protection of Groundwater', NRA, HMSO 1992.

'Safer Ships Cleaner Seas', Cm 2560 and the government's response, Cm 2766, HMSO.

'Third International Conference on the Protection of the North Sea, UK Guidance Note on the Ministerial Declaration', DoE 1990.

'This Common Inheritance', Cm 1200 chapter 12, HMSO 1990 and the subsequent annual environment White Papers to date.

'Water, Nature's Precious Resource, an Environmentally Sustainable Water Resources Development Strategy for England and Wales', NRA, HMSO 1994.

Index